Comparative Environmental Politics

American and Comparative Environmental Policy
Sheldon Kamieniecki and Michael E. Kraft, series editors

For a complete list of books in the series, please see the back of the book.

Comparative Environmental Politics

Theory, Practice, and Prospects

Edited by Paul F. Steinberg and Stacy D. VanDeveer

The MIT Press
Cambridge, Massachusetts
London, England

For information about special quantity discounts, please email special_sales@mitpress.mit.edu.

This book was set in Sabon by Toppan Best-set Premedia Limited, Hong Kong. Printed and bound in the United States of America.

Library of Congress Cataloging-in-Publication Data

Comparative environmental politics: theory, practice, and prospects / edited by Paul F. Steinberg and Stacy D. VanDeveer.
    p.   cm.—(American and comparative environmental policy)
Includes bibliographical references and index.
ISBN 978-0-262-19585-0 (hardcover : alk. paper)—ISBN 978-0-262-69368-4 (pbk. : alk. paper)
1. Environmental policy—United States. 2. Comparative politics—United States. 3. United States—Environmental conditions. 4. United States—Politics and government. I. Steinberg, Paul F. II. VanDeveer, Stacy D.
GE180.C655   2012
363.7—dc23
                                                                    2011024908

10   9   8   7   6   5   4   3   2   1

To Barbara Steinberg, for her worldly wisdom.—P. S.
To Dorothy Taylor, for decades of inspiration.—S. V.

Contents

Series Foreword

The study of comparative environmental politics and policy dates back at least to the 1970s, when scholars began to compare systematically the way different countries dealt with environmental problems of the time. As interest in the environment and environmental policy grew over the succeeding decades, comparative studies lagged to some extent. Certainly, we have had no shortage of analyses of individual nations and a large number of edited collections examine environmental politics and policy across both developed and developing nations. What has been relatively rare, however, are truly comparative studies—particularly those well grounded in theory—that build on the broader literature of comparative politics and that seek to answer fundamental questions about variation across nations in the way they react to problems of common pool resources, climate change risks, protection of biological diversity, regulation of toxic chemicals, and other environmental threats.

Some political systems, for example, are open and invite widespread participation that affects the kind of legislation and regulatory rules that are adopted. Others are far less amenable to outside influences of this kind. Some nations adopt a flexible and consensual process of policy making and implementation; others are far more rigid and adversarial, resulting in a stronger role for the courts to settle the inevitable disputes and lawsuits. Countries also tend to differ as to whether their environmental protection and natural resource conservation efforts are largely centralized in a national government or are basically pursued by lower levels of government. These are fascinating political questions that can be addressed through the comparative study of environmental politics and policy. Moreover, the answers can have both academic and practical value.

In this volume, Paul Steinberg and Stacy VanDeveer seek to advance just this kind of study. The two introductory chapters set out the purpose of such inquiry, comprehensively reviewing the pertinent literature and its limitations and laying the groundwork for the "systematic study and comparison of environmental politics in different countries around the globe." The rest of the book offers chapters by leading figures in the field of comparative environmental politics on a range of key topics, including the greening of the state; the role of nonstate actors such as businesses, political parties, and environmental organizations; the globalization of public concern for the environment; patterns of national governance and multilevel governance; institutional effectiveness; and future directions for the field. The authors do a masterful job of capturing the critical aspects of all these subjects and describing them in a way that should appeal to a broad readership.

In this way, these chapters collectively advance the study of comparative environmental politics by recognizing the complexity of political processes and the value of using theoretical tools to make sense of that complexity and thus to provide rich insights into why nations make the choices they do. The result should be of great interest not only to scholars of environmental politics and policy, but also to the many practitioners (including policy makers, natural resource managers, and activists) who seek a better understanding of why governments choose to adopt, implement, and alter environmental policy and what might influence them to change directions. Researchers who study comparative politics and policy more generally should find this volume informative and relevant to their inquiry as well.

The book illustrates well the goals of the MIT Press series in American and Comparative Environmental Policy. We encourage work that examines a broad range of environmental policy issues. We are particularly interested in volumes that incorporate interdisciplinary research and focus on the linkages between public policy and environmental problems and issues both within the United States and in cross-national settings. We welcome contributions that analyze the policy dimensions of relationships between humans and the environment from either a theoretical or empirical perspective. At a time when environmental policies are increasingly seen as controversial and new approaches are being implemented widely, we especially encourage studies that assess policy successes and failures, evaluate new institutional arrangements and policy tools, and clarify new directions for environmental politics and policy. The books in this series are written for a wide audience that includes academics, policy makers, environmental scientists and professionals, business and labor leaders, environmental activists, and students concerned with environmental issues. We hope these books contribute to public understanding of environmental problems, issues, and policies of concern today and also suggest promising actions for the future.

Sheldon Kamieniecki, University California, Santa Cruz
Michael E. Kraft, University of Wisconsin–Green Bay
American and Comparative Environmental Policy Series Editors

Acknowledgments

Given the highly collaborative nature of this project, and our goal of promoting a new field of research that amounts to more than the sum of its parts, it is fitting that from start to finish this book has benefited from the insights of scholars working in diverse areas of inquiry. Above all, we are grateful to the chapter authors for their energetic participation in three separate venues: the panels at the International Studies Association annual meetings in 2007 and 2008 and the Comparative Environmental Politics authors' workshop at the University of California Berkeley in March 2008. Their feedback on the project's framework and on each others' work proved invaluable and energizing.

At the Berkeley workshop, we benefited enormously from the thoughtful critiques and sage advice provided by Christopher Ansell and David Vogel. Miranda Schreurs participated in each of these events and lent the sort of broad perspective that can come only from someone with long-term empirical research agendas on three continents. Funding for the meetings was provided by the Center for Environmental Studies at Harvey Mudd College. The European Union's Jean Monnet program also supported Stacy D. VanDeveer's participation in the project, as did the University of New Hampshire's College of Liberal Arts. At the outset of the project, Kathryn Hochstetler helped to lay the conceptual foundations for the book by identifying priority areas of comparative politics to which bridges might be built from environmental studies. Along the way, our undergraduate and graduate students at the Claremont Colleges and the University of New Hampshire offered inspiration and valuable feedback. Others to whom we owe a debt of gratitude include Clay Morgan, Martin Heisler, Ron Mitchell, Mike Wood, Marcie Anderson, Rachel-Mikel Arce Jaeger, and Lydia Jahl.

Contributors

Arun Agrawal is Professor and Research Associate Dean in the School of Natural Resources and Environment, University of Michigan (USA).

Liliana B. Andonova is Associate Professor in Political Science and Deputy Director of the Center for International Environmental Studies, Graduate Institute of International and Development Studies (Geneva, Switzerland).

Riley E. Dunlap is Regents Professor of Sociology at Oklahoma State University (USA).

Deborah Rigling Gallagher is Assistant Professor of the Practice of Environmental Policy at Duke University (USA).

Kathryn Hochstetler is CIGI Chair of Governance in the Americas at the Balsillie School of International Affairs, University of Waterloo (Canada).

James Meadowcroft is Professor in the School of Public Policy and in the Department of Political Science (and Canada Research Chair in Governance for Sustainable Development), Carleton University (Canada).

Kate O'Neill is Associate Professor of Environmental Science, Policy and Management, University of California at Berkeley (USA).

Michael O'Neill is Reader in Politics and Jean Monnet Professor in EU Politics, Nottingham Trent University (United Kingdom).

Henrik Selin is Associate Professor of International Relations, Boston University (USA).

Jeannie Sowers is Assistant Professor of Political Science, University of New Hampshire (USA).

Paul F. Steinberg is Associate Professor of Political Science and Environmental Policy, Harvey Mudd College (USA).

Stacy D. VanDeveer is Associate Professor of Political Science, University of New Hampshire (USA).

Erika Weinthal is Associate Professor of Environmental Policy at the Nicholas School of the Environment, Duke University (USA).

Richard York is Associate Professor of Sociology, University of Oregon (USA).

I

Building Bridges: Comparative Politics and the Environment

1

Comparative Environmental Politics in a Global World

Paul F. Steinberg and Stacy D. VanDeveer

Questions Transcend Borders

At first glance, the Maine lobster industry and traditional forest users in western Uganda would appear to have little in common. Yet upon closer examination—and with the benefit of the right analytic tools—patterns emerge that suggest common elements of social organization and similar challenges. In each area, resource users have collectively devised rules to manage a shared resource—controlling access, defining property rights, and establishing a monitoring and enforcement regime. In Maine, coastal territory has traditionally been controlled by groups of fishers known as "harbor gangs" who operate under a strong conservation ethic and well-known norms of territoriality (Acheson 2003). In Uganda's Echuya forest reserve, forestry officials have partnered with the Abayanda pygmy community to help monitor illegal harvesting of forest products by residents living outside the reserve (Banana and Ssembajjwe 2000).

By adopting a common conceptual currency—in this example, insights from research on common-pool resource regimes—new lines of inquiry arise. What are the rules governing ownership and use of natural resources and how are they established, enforced, and changed? Who participates in rule making? What is the relationship between local rules-in-use and official government policy? How have these local institutions responded to changes driven by technology, shifting social norms, global trade, immigration, and new government regulations?

Turning to the regulation of industrial chemicals and food additives, we might reasonably expect that government assessments of chemical risks would be similar across the countries of Europe and North America. The physiological effects of carcinogens and other harmful chemicals are, after all, identical across borders. Moreover, these countries have strong scientific communities that share professional norms and standards of evidence and have access to the same body of scientific knowledge.

Yet marked differences exist in the assessment of chemical risks even between the United States and the United Kingdom, despite their common linguistic, cultural, and legal heritage. This variance is due in part to differences in the way that science is organized in distinct national settings. In Western Europe, groups of experts insulated from the public are called upon by policy makers to provide input on regulatory decisions. In contrast, American regulatory agencies have large technical staffs that conduct risk assessments subject to public scrutiny and judicial review. The openness of the US regulatory system is a direct consequence of that country's constitutional dispersal of power, augmented by legal provisions for citizen oversight that were included in major environmental statutes of the 1970s and 1980s. This has produced what Sheila Jasanoff terms "scientific pluralism" in the United States, with highly contested and often inconclusive debates over the scientific basis of government decisions. In response, US regulators have resorted to uniform, quantitative risk assessment methodologies that can withstand judicial challenges, whereas their European counterparts tend to rely on expert consensus (Jasanoff 1990).

These differences in the assessment of environment risks are compounded by distinct regulatory styles. Compared to the United States, the enforcement of laws governing industrial processes in Sweden, the United Kingdom, France, and Germany is more flexible and consensus-based, with greater adaptability to the circumstances surrounding specific chemicals and industries and more leeway afforded to regulatory bureaucracies (Kelman 1981; Brickman, Jasanoff, and Ilgen 1985; Vogel 2003). Cross-national differences in environmental regulation arise not only from government practices but also from the comparative strength and strategies of environmental movements and their relations to the state (Dryzek et al. 2003; Dalton 1994). Moreover, different values and concerns animate the various publics of Western industrialized countries. Genetically modified foods have encountered considerable public opposition in Canada and the European Union, where citizens are skeptical of their safety and benefits, yet these foods have become a mainstay of the American food supply with barely a nod from the public (Gaskell et al. 2006; Jasanoff 2005; Kurzer and Cooper 2007).

Operating alongside and countervailing the "pull" toward national distinctiveness are powerful pressures producing a "push" toward convergence. Harmonization of standards and approaches is promoted through international environmental treaties and their associated consensus-building processes, regional trading blocs with common environmental standards (most notably, the European Union), multinational corporations seeking uniform regulatory approaches, shared colonial legacies, and transnational networks among advocacy groups, scientists, and regulators promoting similar ideas in diverse countries (Busch and Jörgens 2005; Haas 1990; Selin and VanDeveer 2006; Garcia-Johnson 2000; Slaughter 1997; DeSombre 1995; Keck and Sikkink 1998; Jordan and Liefferink 2004). As a window into broader processes of globalization, the global spread of environmental concerns demonstrates that declining national insularity implies something infinitely more nuanced than homogeneity.

Beyond "Spaceship Earth": Engaging Complexity, Fostering Understanding

To better understand the political forces shaping social responses to industrial chemicals, forest management, and numerous other environmental problems surely counts among the most important intellectual challenges of our time. When we approach this subject by paying careful attention to domestic politics and institutions, and with an eye to cross-national comparison, we enter the realm of comparative environmental politics (CEP)—the systematic study and comparison of environmental politics in different countries around the globe. To get a handle on this vast subject requires two major analytic tasks: an appreciation for *complexity*— for the diverse and changing manner in which social actors and institutions interact to define and respond to environmental issues in far-flung corners of the globe—and the use of *theoretical tools* that enable us to make sense of this complexity. These two tasks are fundamental to the promise and challenge of comparative environmental politics, so let us begin by considering each in greater detail.

To appreciate the complexity of this subject matter requires that we revisit the seductive holism of the imagery of "spaceship Earth." Few images have exercised as powerful a force on contemporary political imagination as that of the earth seen from outer space, first transmitted in its entirety by the Apollo 17 spacecraft in 1972. The political connotation of this image as it has been interpreted in an outpouring of cultural literature—particularly the unity and common cause of humankind and the beautiful yet finite physical underpinnings of our civilization—has left an indelible mark on our understanding of ourselves (Jasanoff 2001), one further pronounced by renewed interest in globalization. That the common cause of humanity is both an unmet aspiration and a physical reality plain for all to see suggests the hope and irony of the image.

Yet as with all powerful symbols, the success of the imagery of planetary unity lies in highlighting certain features at the same time that it downplays others. If we change our analytic lens slightly, focusing on portions of the earth rather than on the whole, the images are far from uniform. Large-scale human-induced changes can be seen from space, including huge urban centers and plumes of smoke from forest fires that obscure entire countries across the Amazon basin and throughout Southeast Asia. But some areas are markedly more urbanized than others, and some places produce little in the way of air pollution. If we switch our analytic lens to a yet more powerful resolution, what snaps into focus is an exciting array of human actions of almost endless variety. In Tehran, we find artists organizing an exhibition to publicize the plight of children hospitalized as a result of poor air quality.[1] In

Hong Kong, lawmakers are struggling to protect the aesthetic and environmental qualities of Victoria Harbor in the face of an intransigent planning bureaucracy and uncertain political environment following the transition from British to Chinese rule (Husock 1998). In Ecuador, Amazonian indigenous peoples are demanding approaches to conservation that respect traditional land rights and are forging transnational linkages with indigenous groups throughout the world (Brysk 2000). In both Hanford (United States) and Mayak (Russia)—the sites of the largest nuclear weapons production facilities during the Cold War—the frustrated efforts of citizens living with a legacy of radioactive waste raise important questions about the relationship between national defense and democratic control (Dalton et al. 1999).

Confronted with this diverse array of domestic political experiences, we encounter a second analytic challenge, namely, that it is easy to become overwhelmed with the details. What could Iranian scholars and activists possibly learn from political outcomes in Hong Kong? Should a student interested in community water management in Bogotá read about experiences in Dakar? Clearly, one cannot become an expert in every country; gaining a sophisticated understanding of politics in even a single country (or, indeed, in a single region or city) is a formidable undertaking.[2] But does this mean that we are condemned to study in isolation the cases we know best?

This challenge is well known to the broader field of comparative politics. Reflecting on the demands of making meaningful comparisons across disparate societies, Gabriel Almond wrote in 1960, "The magnitude of the formal and empirical knowledge required of the political scientist of the future staggers the imagination and lames the will. We have been accustomed to working in a dim and fitful light" (64). The answer, then and now, resides in the use of theory—the shared vocabulary, concepts, analytic approaches, and methods that enable us to make sense of this complexity and to engage in a cumulative conversation across borders. Although a theoretical orientation is needed in every area of social science inquiry, it is especially important for comparative political studies because of the geographically dispersed nature of the field research. Too often the product of research goes unnoticed because it confines itself, in its inspiration and applications, to the geographical borders in which the study was conducted.

Theory is indispensable for understanding the world, learning from it, and changing the course of events. Although familiar terrain to scholars, many students and practitioners assume that to be theoretical in orientation is to willingly detach one's investigation from events in the real world. A theoretical approach by necessity entails abstraction from the details (see Sartori 1970; Collier and Mahoney 1993). But this is done for the purpose of greater understanding, to bring insights from a broader category of phenomena (social movements, democratization, and the like) to bear on particular cases of these phenomena—suggesting lines of inquiry, concepts, explanatory hypotheses, and measurement tools. In turn, theory allows the investigator to contribute insights from the case to this broader enterprise involving a larger research community (see Wapner 2003). To be theoretical in orientation therefore means two things: to draw on and contribute to an identifiable conversation in the research literature, and to attempt to project beyond the data at hand, crafting conclusions that can be tested in other settings. Thus theory requires the use of concepts and methods that travel well, offering a medium for the exchange of ideas among contributors with diverse geographic and topical interests. This approach allows us to ask, "What is this a case of?"

To resist the facile holism of spaceship Earth yet provide a medium for meaningful comparison of the complexities: this is the core challenge of comparative environmental politics. When we do so, we can speak to questions that are not only relevant for human-environment interactions but that also address the central and enduring concerns of social science. Why are social movements more successful in some countries than in others (Dryzek et al. 2003)? Why do many political leaders choose to squander their countries' natural wealth, seemingly against their own national interests (Ascher 1999; Ross 2001)? What processes govern the spread of policy ideas across borders (Busch and Jörgens 2005; Steinberg 2001)? Which types of policies achieve what goals—and under what conditions (Scruggs 2003; Harrington, Morgenstern, and Sterner 2004)? Will the decentralization of political power produce better social outcomes (Ribot 1999; Kingston 2001)? Can global governance objectives be achieved while respecting local autonomy (Brechin et al. 2003)? Under what circumstances are new political parties likely to have an influence (Kitschelt 1989)?

This book is born of a sense that comparative political inquiry has a great deal to offer our understanding of such questions, yet largely as a result of the inadequate attention paid to theory, it is difficult to know where to turn. Our goal is therefore to take stock of the developing field of CEP and to identify promising new avenues for exploration with the following audiences in mind. The first consists of faculty and students in the field of global environmental politics (GEP) who would like to complement the international relations focus of their courses and research with analytic frameworks for understanding the domestic forces shaping global environmental outcomes. Alternatively, those in the field of comparative politics who would like to focus on environmental issues, or those in environmental studies and public policy who would like to better understand what comparative politics has to offer, will find here a number of useful approaches and will hopefully emerge with a clear sense of the leading edges and current gaps in the field. Finally, although practitioners (policy makers, activists, resource managers, and others) will not find a "how to" approach in these pages, our hope is that they will come away with a new understanding of the broader phenomena of which their daily experiences are a part.

In what follows, we begin by describing some of the distinctive advantages of comparative research. We then argue that comparative political inquiry has much to offer the established field of global environmental politics and should occupy a more central position in the field, alongside and in close conversation with contributions from international relations. We conclude with an overview of the book chapters, each of which tackles a distinct set of social problems and exemplifies the diversity of intellectual approaches possible within this exciting field.

The Comparative Advantage

Why compare political systems across borders? There are many reasons for doing so, and the question is admittedly akin to asking why one might read a hundred books on a subject rather than just one. One answer comes from policy-oriented research: comparative inquiry expands the political imagination. If politics is the art of the possible, then comparative inquiry brings into view a wide array of political experiences, raising new possibilities that had previously not been considered. Portugal's advances in energy efficiency, Costa Rica's exemplary national park system, Singapore's successful anticorruption efforts—such efforts inspire, suggest models for study and emulation, and force a reexamination of our assumptions regarding political feasibility. How can it be "impossible" to achieve lower carbon emissions or habitat and species protection in one country, when these goals are being achieved through policy making and social change in other countries?

Another answer to the question "Why compare?" stems from the theoretical and explanatory aims of comparative politics. Systematic cross-national comparison helps us to understand the importance of *political context*. Nations and other geographical political units—cities, regions, states—are in many respects worlds onto themselves, representing unique combinations of actors and institutions. Notwithstanding the intensive exchange of ideas and resources across borders, these combine in distinctive ways in particular places. Political systems are "systems" in the sense that they develop system-wide norms, identities, rules, and axes of contention that affect the operation of the system components (executive-military relations, media practices, ethnic identities, social cleavages, legal traditions, policy-making styles, and so on). Path-dependent processes reinforce these self-referential tendencies of political units. Cultures "dig in," whether these are cultures of protest (student barricades in the streets of Paris, puppet theater in Javanese villages) or the norms guiding legislative debate in the British Parliament. Party systems emerge, legacies of democracy and authoritarianism shape institutional designs, and shared historical memories infuse events (such as the adoption of biotechnology) with different meanings in different places.

These forces produce unspoken assumptions about what is normal, feasible, and right. Socialization processes imbue the citizen and scholar alike with countless such assumptions, and these are suddenly called into question when we leave the place or case we know best and enter another such world. Like foreign travel generally, comparative inquiry opens our minds, challenges our assumptions, and creates a burning desire to make sense of it all. We discover anomalies that do not fit our most cherished theories and new patterns that call out for new explanations.

Comparative research, at its best, occupies this position between theoretical generalization and an appreciation for the importance of context. As Richard Rose argues, "The study of comparative politics rejects the extremes of universalism and particularism; it assumes what may be termed 'bounded variability.' Anyone who engages in comparative research immediately notices differences between countries. Yet anyone who persists in wide-ranging comparative analysis also recognizes boundaries to these differences" (1991, 447). Neither sweeping generalizations nor an endless stream of unique descriptive case studies will produce accurate or useful knowledge about environmental politics around the globe.

It is equally important to clarify what comparative research is not. It is not the "practice of comparison" in any general sense. Investigations of variance across two or more cases play a central role in every field of research, from epidemiology to history to a regression analysis of congressional voting behavior. Comparative politics lays no special claim to the method of comparing two or more outcomes in order to discern broader patterns. Rather, the hallmark of comparative politics research is that it relates particular empirical instances to broader theories by making systematic comparisons across political units. Thus a single-country study that thoroughly engages a broader comparative literature represents the best of the comparative tradition in a way that a three-country study with only a passing nod at theory does not. The litmus test in each case is whether the results speak directly to the interests of those studying other topics and places.

Nor is the essence of comparative research an approximation of controlled laboratory experiments through "the comparative method," commonly interpreted as the controlled comparison of cases. Some pioneers of the field, such as Lijphart (1971), hoped that comparative case approaches—notably John Stuart Mill's ([1843] 1967) method of difference and method of agreement[3]—would provide political scientists with an analog to statistical and experimental techniques of scientific inquiry. But the controlled comparison of cases is a blunt tool for drawing conclusions about cause-and-effect relationships, especially in complex settings governed by multiple and probabilistic causation (Lieberson 1991; Steinberg 2007; George and Bennett 2005, 163)—precisely the sorts of settings that confront students of environmental politics. The limitations of the "controlled" comparisons of cases (of which Mill was keenly aware) can be appreciated by considering a smoker and a nonsmoker, each of whom live to be a hundred years old. Inferring that smoking is therefore causally irrelevant to longevity would require the highly unrealistic assumption that to qualify as a cause, an antecedent must be sufficient to produce the outcome in every case. It is because of the probabilistic nature of causation—with antecedents *tending* to produce particular outcomes, in ways that are highly dependent on the broader context—that experimental control and analogous methods of control in statistical analysis require large-N research designs.

Mill's methods do often serve as a valuable first step in comparative research, raising interesting questions worthy of exploration. For example, the observation that Western industrialized nations with active environmental movements vary in their responses to climate change suggests that there are other causal forces at play, beyond wealth and social mobilization, that shape national responsiveness to global environmental problems. However, identifying and characterizing those causal forces requires an alternative to controlled comparison, such as historical process tracing and other forms of within-case analysis (Roberts 1996; George and Bennett 2005; Gerring 2007; Tetlock and Belkin 1996) as well as various quantitative approaches (Ragin 2008) and creative combinations of methodologies (Tashakkori and Teddlie 2003). As the contributions to this volume demonstrate, comparative research draws on a wide range of intellectual traditions and methodological approaches.

A Fresh Take on Global Environmental Politics

By far the most prolific source of political science research on the environment has been the field of international relations. Especially since the rise to prominence of new transboundary and global-scale environmental issues in the late 1980s—from the Chernobyl nuclear accident to climate change, stratospheric ozone depletion, concern over the plight of tropical rainforests, and the rise of the discourse of "sustainable development"—international relations has provided a fertile theoretical terrain for political scientists interested in understanding and responding to these issues. As is usefully summarized in a number of reviews (Dauvergne 2005; Mitchell 2002; Zürn 1998; Paterson 2005), the challenge of motivating international cooperation on the environment in the absence of any government authority at the global level has led researchers to study topics like international agenda setting (Young 1998; Lipschutz 1991), the impact and effectiveness of international treaties (Miles et al. 2002; Hovi, Sprinz, and Underdal 2003), the influence of science on multilateral decision processes (Parson 2003; Haas 1990), and the relative roles of sovereign states and nonstate actors in responding to global problems (Betsill and Corell 2001; Wapner 1996). The result is a vibrant field that sheds light on the ways in which actors, institutions, power, and ideas shape the prospects for cooperation and the distributive results among participants in international politics (see also O'Neill 2009; Mitchell 2010; and Axelrod, VanDeveer, and Downie 2011).

Dauvergne (2005) observes that as the field of global environmental politics has grown in confidence and independence, it has begun to expand beyond its traditional base in international relations, incorporating insights from disparate fields ranging from sociology to law, philosophy, geography, and economics. Therefore, the time is ripe to tap deeper into the comparative politics tradition and to bring its many insights to bear on environmental questions (see Kamieniecki and Sanasarian 1990; McBeath and Rosenberg 2006). Indeed, this task is long overdue. For too long, analyses of global environmental politics have been confined to international negotiations, paying lip service to the role of domestic politics and institutions without engaging in theoretically grounded empirical research on these topics. Comparative environmental politics will likely constitute one of the leading edges of the next generation of research on global environmental politics and environmental studies. It is essential, however, that this new field develop in close conversation with international relations research. At a time when the discipline of political science is witnessing increasing integration between international relations and comparative politics, we do not propose the creation of a new fiefdom. Rather, we hope that CEP rapidly matures into one major stream in the mainstream of global environmental politics. To appreciate the potential synergies, let us consider what comparative politics research can offer our understanding of collective action to protect the global environment.

Understanding Causal Processes

The success of international initiatives to protect the global environment depends on our ability to produce an accurate picture of the behaviors and social relations driving environmental problems. It also demands a sophisticated understanding of what is actually required to bring about change in a given social system (Young 1999; Steinberg 2007). This requirement presents a special challenge for analysts accustomed to focusing their attention exclusively on either the local, national, or international level because—in contrast to the traditional subjects of international diplomacy, such as military relations and trade—the success of international environmental policy typically requires reforms at multiple levels of social organization. Whereas trade and arms control regimes consist of agreements among governments to change government behavior, international environmental regimes consist of agreements among governments to change private behavior within their borders. The activities driving global environmental outcomes are so heterogeneous that we cannot possibly understand the prospects for international environmental governance merely by studying diplomatic negotiations. The success of accords forged in places like New York and Geneva ultimately depends on political dynamics in

Jakarta, Beijing, Sacramento, and São Paulo. Comparative politics is ideally suited to the task of analyzing domestic environmental governance, encouraging comparative inquiry into institutions, policy-making styles, modes of social mobilization, and the origins of public preferences.

The importance of studying causal processes becomes clear when we consider the causal aspirations of multilateral environmental institutions and nongovernmental advocacy campaigns. If one goal is to change the attitudes and behaviors of policy-making elites, what do we know about the origins of elite policy preferences (Putnam 1971; Grindle 2000; Peritore 1999)? If the goal is to build capacity for environmental management in participant countries (Haas, Keohane, and Levy 1993), what does the literature tell us about the dynamics of capacity building (Jänicke and Weidner 1997; VanDeveer and Dabelko 2001)? If the aim is to institutionalize norms of sustainability in domestic systems, what determines whether new mandates become merely a document on a shelf, a short-lived burst of activity within one administration, or a long-lasting program of reform (Thelen 2002; Sikkink 1991; Steinberg, chapter 10, this volume)?

Comparative investigations into causal processes can shed light on a question of central importance to global environmental politics, namely why countries support or shun international environmental cooperation (Bernauer et al. 2010; Bernhagen 2008; Bättig and Bernauer 2009; Raustiala 1997). If a country's support for a climate treaty is partly a function of national interests, as Sprinz and Vaahtoranta (1994) argue, we are left with the question of what determines those interests. Surely it is not material conditions alone. When the government of the Philippines is forming a position with respect to mandatory limits on carbon dioxide emissions, several conflicting interests are at play (Steinberg 2002, 14). The country is a vast archipelago vulnerable to rising sea levels produced by climate change, which would dictate support for strong emissions reductions. Yet strategic links to the Middle East, where many Filipino expatriates work, would suggest support for OPEC's go-slow approach to regulating fossil fuels. As a member of the G-77 coalition of developing countries, the Philippines would be wise to stand behind the positions favored by Brazil, India, and China, which dominate the G-77 and oppose mandatory limits on emissions for the developing world. Clearly, interest-based models of national support for international regimes would benefit from more systematic inquiry into domestic processes of interest aggregation, such as interagency competition, the relative roles of bureaucrats and politicians in policy formation, and interest group access to foreign policy making—all factors that have been intensively studied within the comparative politics tradition.

Comparative political analysis also has a great deal to offer constructivist and pluralist approaches to the question of national interests (see Katzenstein 1996; Moravcsik 1997). Haas (1990) makes a compelling argument that national support for environmental treaties is affected in part by the ability of networks of concerned technical experts to shape policy makers' conceptions of national interests. Yet this approach begs the question of the causal mechanisms through which experts influence the state and why this differs across nations. The same question applies to pluralist models emphasizing the pressures exerted by social groups. Only through the comparative study of political parties, think tanks, legislatures, electoral systems, bureaucracies, and social movement influence can we begin to come to terms with the domestic origins of national interests (see Putnam 1988).

The Enduring Relevance of Domestic Policy

International environmental policy making is an extremely difficult undertaking, and the need to achieve consensus among large numbers of states often hinders efforts at effective regulation. Bodansky observes, "Attempting to achieve consensus is time-consuming and difficult. Agreements tend to be inflexible, given the difficulties of gaining agreement on any changes. Moreover, agreements must either represent the least-common-denominator, and thus be weak, or must create different obligations for different states. In many cases, reaching agreement at all is impossible" (1999, 607).

Because the international system is not governed by an authoritative legal infrastructure, the most powerful nations may have the ability to torpedo agreements favored by a large majority of the world's nations (witness the US role in the Law of the Sea). Long-standing grievances in North–South relations further complicate matters, as developing countries eager to escape the legacy of colonial rule are wary of entering into agreements that would grant foreign powers a say in the management of their natural resources (Najam 2005). Both of these dynamics have visibly slowed global responses to problems like climate change. Moreover, the sheer number of international environmental commitments has produced "summit fatigue" (VanDeveer 2003) as decades of diplomatic initiatives and the burden of national reporting requirements under dozens of agreements have tempered enthusiasm for events like the 2012 UN Conference on Sustainable Development ("Rio+20"), which is a mere shadow of the international mobilization surrounding the Rio Earth Summit in 1992.

Given these challenges, it is not uncommon for students (and more than a few professors) to emerge from courses in global environmental politics with a sense of discouragement about the prospects for positive change. Yet there are other stories and other social arenas in which the possibilities for creative institutional reform are only beginning to be explored. While North and South often seem at loggerheads in multilateral diplomatic venues, far removed from the halls of the United Nations one finds environmental officials and nongovernmental organizations (NGOs) from developing countries engaged in a wide range of agreements with counterparts in the North—from the creation of innovative institutions for financing conservation to collaborations among air quality regulators. At the international level, the United States became the pariah of climate change policy in the years following the signing of the Kyoto Protocol and has a dismal record of ratifying and implementing the environmental treaties it signs (Schreurs, Selin, and VanDeveer 2009). Domestically, however, during this same period a grassroots movement for the reduction of greenhouse gases emerged at the level of American cities, college campuses, and states— many of which have adopted reduction targets more stringent than those required under the protocol (Rabe 2004; Selin and VanDeveer 2005, 2007, 2009).

The contrast between domestic initiative and international stalemate is equally apparent in the forestry sector. While the prospects for an international forestry treaty appear increasingly remote—due in no small measure to opposition from countries like Brazil that fear incursions on national sovereignty—at home, Brazil is experimenting with a system that distributes tax revenues to local governments on the basis of their success with biodiversity conservation. Demonstrating the perils of consensus-based international policy, the capstone legal instrument for protecting the earth's natural heritage—the Convention on Biological Diversity—is far too vague in its regulatory commitments to protect much of anything. Yet domestically, and with help from an array of international collaborators, numerous tropical countries are working to increase the size and effectiveness of their national parks (Brooks et al. 2004). In diplomatic venues, developing countries rightly bemoan the lack of overseas development assistance for sustainable development, yet billions of dollars in tourist revenues are pouring into nature-based tourism in these countries (Honey 2008). Many of these initiatives are experimental and suffer no fewer challenges than international regimes, though the hurdles are different. The point is that there is a world of social activity and institutional innovation beyond the corridors of international summitry.

GEP scholars have taken a growing interest in local environmental politics, particularly as it interacts with processes and discourses of globalization (Rodrigues 2000; Cooper and Vargas 2004). This interest in "rediscovering the local" (Jasanoff and Martello 2004) connects well with the goal of this book to promote greater use of the comparative politics tradition in environmental research. Yet to characterize the initiatives described earlier as principally "local" or even "nongovernmental" in nature would be inaccurate. In the conceptual repertoire of global environmentalism, the phrase "think globally, act locally" has created a habit of overlooking the level of social organization in which political authority to act on environmental problems is concentrated: the nation state. As Barry and Eckersley argue, "It would be a great pity if environmental activists and NGOs were to turn their backs on what still remains the primary and most pervasive form of political governance in the world today. Despite the changes wrought by globalization, democratic states still have more steering capacity and legitimacy to regulate the activities of corporations and other social agents along ecologically sustainable lines in more systematic ways than any nonstate alternative" (2005, xii).

For international relations scholars steeped in traditions of state-centric analysis, a focus on nongovernmental actors has provided a refreshing alternative line of inquiry (Lipschutz 1992; Wapner 1996). And to be sure, the growth of transnational activity by nonstate actors is one of the most exciting and important developments in global environmental politics in recent decades. In the rush to document and understand this new phenomenon, however, it would be a mistake to overlook the enduring relevance of national institutions and associated political processes. According to Ostrom (1990), supportive national policy is one of the few recurring ingredients necessary for the success of local, community-based environmental initiatives. Moreover, national policy has a profound influence on the strength and impact of civil society organizations. Tax breaks for nonprofit organizations, the protection of civil liberties including the right to organize and protest, citizen access to the courts, comanagement arrangements that allow NGOs to participate in the provision of public services—all of these speak to the enduring relevance of the nation-state and the need to move beyond zero-sum conceptions of state-society relations (Steinberg 2005; Krishna and Uphoff 2004). More than any other field, comparative politics has devoted enormous energy to understanding modern states and their characteristics, preferences, impacts, social origins, and evolution. Comparative political inquiry can infuse GEP with a greater understanding of this central player in global environmental politics and its many roles.[4]

From Nonstate Actors to Social Histories

Comparative research can also offer GEP a more complete, historically grounded account of the role of nonstate actors in global environmental politics. There is a tendency in GEP research to focus on categories of nonstate actors—scientists, NGOs, business interests, indigenous groups—disembodied from their social milieu and from the specific social histories that give rise to them and shape their strategies and demands. This analytic bias mirrors the quasi-corporatist organization of the United Nations negotiating forums and summits that are the subject of so much GEP research, where public participation is segmented into officially designated representatives of "youth," "NGOs," "the private sector," and the like. The disembodied nature of research on nonstate actors is abetted by a tendency to study only the transnational component of these groups' activities. The NGOs and indigenous groups appear on the empirical canvas only when they sit at the international negotiating table or launch a transnational advocacy campaign, and are viewed in isolation from their national cultures and histories. Nonstate participants in international politics are a small and unrepresentative subset of social actors in their home countries (Steinberg and Garcia-Johnson 2001). There they are deeply embedded in relations with diverse organizations, demands, and expectations stemming from unique configurations of politics and history (Hsiao et al. 1999; Hunold and Dryzek 2002). We need comparative research on the sociology of national scientific and business communities, on the formative political experiences of environmental activists, and on the ways in which environmental demands—such as concern about intellectual property rights under the Convention on Biological Diversity—are shaped by long-standing social concerns like sovereign control of resources (see Mortimer 1984). A more socially grounded understanding of nonstate actors inevitably involves comparative social history and the systematic study of historical materials (Lipschutz 2001). An historical turn in GEP research would be a welcome development in a field in which the divide between the contemporary environmental era and a murky prehistory is usually placed somewhere around 1972.

Studying social actors within their social histories is necessary if we are to make sense of one of the most important recent developments in global environmental politics: the rise of popular support and mobilization for environmental causes in a wide range of non-Western societies (Lee and So 1999; Baver and Lynch 2006; Christen et al. 1998). Researchers have begun to document and analyze these phenomena, but there have been few attempts to share results across regions, to take stock of the state of the art, and to identify promising directions for future collaborative research programs. Just as the rise of new nation-states after World War II prompted research on political development and postcolonial studies, the environmental movements that have arisen in the 1980s and 1990s in developing and postcommunist economies require that we revisit established orthodoxies, like the clearly mistaken notion that environmental concern is the province of wealthy people and wealthy nations (Dunlap and York, chapter 4, this volume; Steinberg 2001). By embedding comparative social history within the field of GEP, we are also in a position to appreciate the importance of transnational exchanges of resources and ideas in the development of domestic environmental movements and to explore how these interact with changing domestic opportunity structures shaped by national processes such as democratization, economic development, urbanization, decentralization, and state building.

An Overview of the Book

To take advantage of the enormous potential of comparative environmental politics research requires that we build bridges between the broader field of comparative politics and the traditional concerns of environmental studies. To this end, chapter 2 surveys the literatures in comparative politics and comparative environmental politics in order to identify actual and potential points of contact between the two.

To our knowledge, this is the first comprehensive review of the literature in comparative environmental politics.[5] We find a surprisingly large literature that explores domestic environmental politics around the world. We also discover, however, that it has developed in a fragmented manner and largely in isolation from comparative politics, with its enormous literature, diverse theoretical traditions, and status as one of the major fields within political science. Scholars of comparative politics, in turn, have been silent on environmental questions, foregoing the opportunity to explore the associated processes of social transformation and to engage in a theoretically informed discussion of one of the greatest challenges facing humanity today.

In the remaining chapters, the authors undertake this bridge-building task in a variety of ways, each exemplifying the "comparative advantage" of melding the general and the particular, using theoretical lenses to better understand concrete, real-world problems of politics and environmental management, and casting the results in terms that travel well across borders. Our aim is to offer readers a convenient way to sample the major intellectual currents of this new field within the covers of one volume. Given this goal, we deemed it counterproductive to impose a uniform analytic framework running throughout all of the chapters. Rather, each author was invited to contribute a self-contained overview of one dimension of the field—introducing readers to specific literatures within comparative politics and using these to shed light on environmental politics around the globe. Instructors of courses in comparative politics will find a fresh take on a number of standard topics, including democracy and authoritarianism (chapters 8 and 9), European Union enlargement (chapter 11), policy theory (chapter 10), social values (chapter 4), states and political development (chapter 3), federalism and decentralization (chapters 12 and 13), political parties (chapter 7), social movements (chapter 5), state-society relations (chapters 5 and 6), and institutional design (chapters 10 and 12). In terms of geographic diversity, the volume includes explicit treatment of industrialized countries on both sides of the Atlantic (chapters 3, 7, 11, and 13), as well as Central and Eastern Europe (chapters 8, 10, and 11) and a wide range of developing countries (chapters 5, 6, 8, 9, 10, and 12). Those interested in specific environmental issues will find coverage of forests (chapter 12), climate change (chapter 13), water (chapter 9), land use and pollution (chapter 8), and many other topics. There are many issues and regions worthy of stand-alone chapters that we could not include without producing an unwieldy text. By adopting an explicitly theoretical orientation and applying this to real-world problems, each chapter is designed to offer conclusions with relevance far beyond the particular cases and countries discussed.

The chapters in part II provide a broad perspective on the challenge of transforming states and societies to take greater account of environmental concerns. The "greening" of state structures and social relations is an ongoing, uneven, and highly contested process. In chapter 3, James Meadowcroft explores the history and prospects of incorporating environmental protection alongside the traditional concerns of modern states. Exemplifying the tradition of comparative macrosocial analysis (see Pierson 2003), Meadowcroft situates the relatively recent phenomenon of environmental regulation in the broader context of the evolution of the state as it has branched out from a focus on national security and economic growth to include the modern welfare state and now, perhaps, environmental sustainability. In chapter 4, Riley Dunlap and Richard York demonstrate the value of combining systematic empirical investigations—in this instance, cross-national surveys of environmental public opinion—with theoretical frameworks that facilitate cumulative learning and allow us to draw broader conclusions about the social dimensions of environmental problems. Based on an extensive review of the published research, they conclude that significant levels of environmental concern are in evidence in a wide range of countries and at every socioeconomic level within societies. These results not only require that we revisit theories positing that environmentalism is an elite concern, but also raise a host of practical questions as to why we see so much variance in institutional performance across countries whose citizens profess concern about environmental quality. Chapters 3 and 4 draw as heavily on sociological research as political science, demonstrating that comparative environmental politics, like comparative political research more broadly, need not confine itself to insights issuing from the discipline of political science.

The authors in part III look more closely at nonstate actors and social mobilization. In chapter 5, Kate O'Neill provides an overview of the stunning array of environmental movements that have arisen around the world and shows how social movement theory can help us understand their origins, aims, methods, and impacts at both domestic and transnational levels. Of course, the set of nonstate actors shaping environmental outcomes is by no means limited to environmental NGOs. A significant contribution of environmental politics research to our broader understanding of political life can be found in renewed attention to the behavior of firms and industry associations, the subject of analysis by Deborah Rigling Gallagher and Erika Weinthal in chapter 6. Traditionally, the social sciences have considered the political behavior of firms to be a relatively fixed (and therefore analytically uninteresting) function of the requirements of capital accumulation, viewed through a Marxist lens, or as regrettably influential, in the disproportionate impact of business in liberal democracies and in international economic relations (Lindblom 1982; Evans 1979). Gallagher and Weinthal find that in the environmental realm, the role of the private sector is often considerably more complex, as they demonstrate through an analysis of the movement for corporate social responsibility.

Political parties play a special role as moderators between social interests and policy outcomes, and research on their origins, strategies, and different roles cross-nationally is well represented within comparative politics (Mair 1990; Aldrich 1995; Kitschelt 1989). Michael O'Neill demonstrates in chapter 7 that parties have been viewed by environmental movements as an important venue for translating green social concerns into green state structures. He examines this process in Western Europe, where green parties have enjoyed the most success yet face trade-offs between the need to retain support from grassroots constituencies and to strike political bargains within governing coalitions in order to have an impact on public policy.

The origin and effectiveness of public policies in diverse political settings is the focus of part IV. In chapter 8, Kathryn Hochstetler compares the environmental performance of democracies and authoritarian regimes. She reviews contributions from political theorists regarding the possibility of sustainability within democracies and compares these theoretical expectations to the empirical record, examining quantitative and historical evidence on the environmental performance of different regime types within Latin America and Central and Eastern Europe. Jeannie Sowers takes a closer look at policy making under authoritarian regimes in chapter 9, asking why attempts to promote more participatory and decentralized approaches to water management in Egypt have failed despite strong support from international donors and domestic water experts. She argues that to understand the prospects for environmental policy change in the Middle East, we must disaggregate the concept of the authoritarian state, moving beyond assumptions of monolithic central bureaucracies with strong regulatory capacities and instead paying closer attention to the "local state" and the operation of political coalitions and networks across different scales. In a different take on the relationship between governing structures and environmental outcomes, in chapter 10 Paul Steinberg explores the prospects for environmental policy reform in developing and postcommunist countries, many of which are plagued by chronic political and economic instability. In industrialized democracies, system-wide "shocks" of this nature are commonly associated with opportunities for institutional innovation. Steinberg finds that in most of the world, however, where these same factors are present in excess, institution reform is inhibited unless there are mechanisms of continuity that allow for long-term "governance across governments."

Part V takes up the theme of multilevel governance. In chapter 11, Liliana Andonova and Stacy VanDeveer describe how Europeanization has shaped environmental politics and ecological outcomes in the postcommunist states of Central and Eastern Europe over their two decades of transition. They argue that international commitments, such as those found in treaties, and broader transnational socialization processes help to explain the rapid and profound influence of international institutions on domestic policy and politics in the region. However, the substantial policy convergence witnessed in the region is revealed to be something other than homogenization. Although many new member states have moved closer to

European Union standards, considerable divergence remains. In chapter 12, Arun Agrawal takes stock of what we have learned from the literature on local governance of common-pool resources, a topic that was the focus of the 2009 Nobel Prize in economics. As is the case with O'Neill's overview of environmental movements, the sheer volume and diversity of these local experiences speaks to the challenge outlined at the beginning of this chapter, namely, the need to convey an appreciation for complexity without become overwhelmed by it. Agrawal accomplishes this task by identifying recurrent themes that run across all studies of local commons and places these alongside a number of context-specific factors that warrant against hasty generalizations about the conditions under which local communities will manage resources sustainably.

The final chapter in part V, by Stacy VanDeveer and Henrik Selin, explores the ways in which federalism and multilevel governance help to explain divergence in the responses of the European Union and the United States to global climate change. GEP researchers are increasingly interested in how environmental governance plays out across multiple levels of authority, from local to national to global. Yet this research has not taken adequate advantage of the comparative politics literature on federalism and the ways in which federal institutions shape political mobilization and policy outcomes. VanDeveer and Selin argue that to explain the cross-Atlantic divergence in climate policy, we must pay attention to the federalist structure of government within the European Union and the United States. Comparative federalism can help us to understand why California's climate change and energy policies resemble those of the European Union more than those of the US federal government. Given the growing number of federalist and decentralized governance systems around the world, research on comparative environmental federalism has a rich future and further demonstrates the need to incorporate theories and concepts of comparative politics into the mainstream of GEP research.

In the concluding chapter, we return to the relationship between comparative environmental politics and the broader field of comparative politics, exploring more systematically the causes of the present disconnect between the two. Based in part on an empirical analysis of leading comparative politics journals, we conclude that the current schism is largely the result of a mutual distaste (if not disdain) between those concerned with practice (which includes many environmental politics researchers) and those interested in advancing theory (a central concern of scholarship in comparative politics). Echoing Theda Skocpol's (2003) call for "doubly engaged" social science that is both theoretically rigorous and socially relevant, we argue that the sort of bridge-building exercise advocated throughout this volume will benefit both fields. We describe a number of approaches for bridging the worlds of theory and practice, highlighting promising methodologies and research agendas that warrant further attention as the field develops.

Notes

1. National Public Radio, *All Things Considered*, "Artists Protesting Pollution in Tehran," Washington, D.C. (March 5, 2000).

2. Consider, for example, the empirical underpinnings of such classic works as Dahl's (1961) study of New Haven, Connecticut, or Putnam's (1993) analysis of regional differences within Italy.

3. Mill's method of difference posits that if conditions present in two cases are alike in all relevant respects but one, and their outcomes differ, then the antecedent condition that varied caused the variation in outcome. Under Mill's method of agreement, if two cases share a similar outcome but differ with respect to some antecedent, that antecedent is ruled out as a cause.

4. See, for example, Evans, Rueschemeyer, and Skocpol 1985; Krasner 1984; Pierson 1996; and Laitin 1992.

5. A pioneering analysis by Lundqvist (1978) was necessarily limited by the small number of publications available for review at the time; a subsequent overview by Kamieniecki and Sanasarian (1990) focuses on environmental policy rather than politics more broadly. Interestingly, both articles reached the same conclusion that we do regarding the need to take fuller advantage of insights from comparative political science.

References

Acheson, James M. 2003. *Capturing the Commons: Devising Institutions to Manage the Maine Lobster Industry*. Lebanon, N.H.: University Press of New England.

Aldrich, John. 1995. *Why Parties?* Chicago: University of Chicago Press.

Almond, Gabriel A. 1960. Introduction: A Functional Approach to Comparative Politics. In *The Politics of the Developing Areas*, ed. Gabriel A. Almond and James S. Coleman, 3–64. Princeton: Princeton University Press.

Ascher, William. 1999. *Why Governments Waste Natural Resources: Policy Failures in Developing Countries*. Baltimore: Johns Hopkins University Press.

Axelrod, Regina, Stacy D. VanDeveer, and David Downie, eds. 2011. *The Global Environment: Institutions, Law, and Policy*. Washington, D.C.: CQ Press.

Banana, Abwoli Y., and W. Gombya Ssembajjwe. 2000. Successful Forestry Management: The Importance of Security of Tenure and Rule Enforcement in Ugandan Forests. In *People and Forests: Communities, Institutions, and Governance*, ed. Clark Gibson, Margaret McKean, and Elinor Ostrom, 87–98. Cambridge, Mass.: MIT Press.

Barry, John, and Robin Eckersley, eds. 2005. *The State and the Global Ecological Crisis*. Cambridge, Mass.: MIT Press.

Bättig, Michèle B., and Thomas Bernauer. 2009. National Institutions and Global Public Goods: Are Democracies More Cooperative in Climate Change Policy? *International Organization* 63 (2): 281–308.

Baver, Sherrie L., and Barbara Deutsch Lynch, eds. 2006. *Beyond Sun and Sand: Caribbean Environmentalisms*. Piscataway, N.J.: Rutgers University Press.

Bernauer, Thomas, Anna Kalbhenn, Vally Koubi, and Gabriele Spilker. 2010. A Comparison of International and Domestic Sources of Global Governance Dynamics. *British Journal of Political Science* 40 (3): 509–538.

Bernhagen, Patrick. 2008. Business and International Environmental Agreements: Domestic Sources of Participation and Compliance by Advanced Industrialized Democracies. *Global Environmental Politics* 8 (1): 78–110.

Betsill, Michele M., and Elisabeth Corell. 2001. NGO Influence in International Environmental Negotiations: A Framework for Analysis. *Global Environmental Politics* 1 (4): 65–85.

Bodansky, Daniel. 1999. The Legitimacy of International Governance: A Coming Challenge for International Environmental Law? *American Journal of International Law* 93 (3): 596–624.

Brechin, Steven R., Peter R. Wilshusen, Crystal L. Fortwangler, and Patrick C. West, eds. 2003. *Contested Nature: Promoting International Biodiversity with Social Justice in the Twenty-First Century*. Albany: SUNY Press.

Brickman, Ronald, Sheila Jasanoff, and Thomas Ilgen. 1985. *Controlling Chemicals: The Politics of Regulation in Europe and the United States*. Ithaca: Cornell University Press.

Brooks, Thomas M., Mohamed I. Bakarr, Tim Boucher, Gustavo A. B. Da Fonseca, Craig Hilton-Taylor, Jonathan M. Hoekstra, Tom Moritz, et al. 2004. Coverage Provided by the Global Protected-Area System: Is It Enough? *Bioscience* 54 (12): 1081–1091.

Brysk, Alison. 2000. *From Tribal Village to Global Village: Indian Rights and International Relations in Latin America*. Palo Alto: Stanford University Press.

Busch, Per-Olof, and Helge Jörgens. 2005. The International Sources of Policy Convergence: Explaining the Spread of Environmental Policy Innovations. *Journal of European Public Policy* 12 (5): 860–884.

Christen, Catherine, Selene Herculano, Kathryn Hochstetler, Renae Prell, Marie Price, and J. Timmons Roberts. 1998. Latin American Environmentalism: Comparative Views. *Studies in Comparative International Development* 33 (2): 58–87.

Collier, David, and James Mahoney. 1993. Conceptual Stretching Revisited: Adapting Categories in Comparative Analysis. *American Political Science Review* 87 (4): 845–855.

Cooper, Phillip J., and Claudia Maria Vargas. 2004. *Implementing Sustainable Development: From Global Policy to Local Action*. Lanham, Md.: Rowman and Littlefield.

Dahl, Robert Alan. 1961. *Who Governs? Democracy and Power in an American City*. New Haven: Yale University Press.

Dalton, Russell J. 1994. *The Green Rainbow: Environmental Groups in Western Europe*. New Haven: Yale University Press.

Dalton, Russell J., Paula Garb, Nicholas P. Lovrich, John C. Pierce, and John M. Whiteley. 1999. *Critical Masses: Citizens, Nuclear Weapons Production, and Environmental Destruction in the United States and Russia*. Cambridge, Mass.: MIT Press.

Dauvergne, Peter. 2005. Research in Global Environmental Politics: History and Trends. In *Handbook of Global Environment Politics*, ed. Peter Dauvergne, 8–32. Northampton, Mass.: Edward Elgar.

DeSombre, Elizabeth R. 1995. Baptists and Bootleggers for the Environment: The Origins of United States Unilateral Sanctions. *Journal of Environment & Development* 4 (1): 53–75.

Dryzek, John S., David Downes, Christian Hunold, and David Schlosberg. 2003. *Green States and Social Movements: Environmentalism in the United States, United Kingdom, Germany, and Norway.* New York: Oxford University Press.

Evans, Peter B. 1979. *Dependent Development: The Alliance of Multinational, State and Local Capital in Brazil.* Princeton: Princeton University Press.

Evans, Peter B., Dietrich Rueschemeyer, and Theda Skocpol, eds. 1985. *Bringing the State Back In.* Cambridge, UK: Cambridge University Press.

Garcia-Johnson, Ronnie. 2000. *Exporting Environmentalism: US Multinational Chemical Corporations in Brazil and Mexico.* Cambridge, Mass.: MIT Press.

Gaskell, George, Agnes Allansdottir, Nick Allum, Cristina Corchero, Claude Fischler, Jürgen Hampel, Jonathan Jackson, et al. 2006. *Europeans and Biotechnology in 2005: Patterns and Trends. Final Report on Eurobarometer 64.3—A Report to the European Commission's Directorate General for Research.* London: Centre for the Study of Bioscience, Biomedicine, Biotechnology and Society, London School of Economics.

George, Alexander L., and Andrew Bennett. 2005. *Case Studies and Theory Development in the Social Sciences.* Cambridge, Mass.: MIT Press.

Gerring, John. 2007. *Case Study Research: Principles and Practices.* Cambridge, UK: Cambridge University Press.

Grindle, Merilee S. 2000. *Audacious Reforms: Institutional Invention and Democracy in Latin America.* Baltimore: Johns Hopkins University Press.

Haas, Peter M. 1990. Obtaining International Environmental Protection through Epistemic Consensus. *Millennium: Journal of International Studies* 19 (3): 347–363.

Haas, Peter M., Robert O. Keohane, and Marc A. Levy, eds. 1993. *Institutions for the Earth: Sources of Effective International Environmental Protection.* Cambridge, Mass.: MIT Press.

Harrington, Winston, Richard D. Morgenstern, and Thomas Sterner, eds. 2004. *Choosing Environmental Policy: Comparing Instruments and Outcomes in the United States and Europe.* London: RFF Press/Earthscan.

Honey, Martha. 2008. *Ecotourism and Sustainable Development: Who Owns Paradise?* 2nd ed. Washington, D.C.: Island Press.

Hovi, Jon, Detlef F. Sprinz, and Arild Underdal. 2003. The Oslo-Potsdam Solution to Measuring Regime Effectiveness: Critique, Response, and the Road Ahead. *Global Environmental Politics* 3 (3): 74–96.

Hsiao, Hsin-Huang Michael, On-Kwok Lai, Hwa-Jen Liu, Francisco Magno, Laura Edles, and Alvin Y. So. 1999. Culture and Asian Styles of Environmental Movements. In *Asia's Environmental Movements: Comparative Perspectives*, ed. Yok-shiu F. Lee and Alvin Y. So, 210–229. Armonk, N.Y.: M. E. Sharpe.

Hunold, Christian, and John S. Dryzek. 2002. Green Political Theory and the State: Context Is Everything. *Global Environmental Politics* 2 (3): 17–39.

Husock, Howard. 1998. *Executive-Led Government and Hong Kong's Legislative Council: Debating Harbor Protection.* Case Study 1431.0. Cambridge, Mass.: Kennedy School of Government, Harvard University.

Jänicke, Martin, and Helmut Weidner, eds. 1997. *National Environmental Policies: A Comparative Study of Capacity-Building.* Berlin: Springer.

Jasanoff, Sheila. 1990. *The Fifth Branch: Science Advisors and Policy Makers*. Cambridge, Mass.: Harvard University Press.

Jasanoff, Sheila. 2001. Image and Imagination: The Formation of Global Environmental Consciousness. In *Changing the Atmosphere: Expert Knowledge and Environmental Governance*, ed. Clark A. Miller and Paul N. Edwards, 309–338. Cambridge, Mass.: MIT Press.

Jasanoff, Sheila. 2005. *Designs on Nature: Science and Democracy in Europe and the United States*. Princeton: Princeton University Press.

Jasanoff, Sheila, and Marybeth Long Martello, eds. 2004. *Earthly Politics: Local and Global in Environmental Governance*. Cambridge, Mass.: MIT Press.

Jordan, Andrew, and Duncan Liefferink. 2004. *Environmental Policy in Europe: The Europeanization of National Environmental Policy*. New York: Routledge.

Kamieniecki, Sheldon, and Eliz Sanasarian. 1990. Conducting Comparative Research on Environmental Policy. *Natural Resources Journal* 30 (2): 321–339.

Katzenstein, Peter, ed. 1996. *The Culture of National Security: Norms and Identity in World Politics*. New York: Columbia University Press.

Keck, Margaret E., and Kathryn Sikkink. 1998. *Activists Beyond Borders: Advocacy Networks in International Politics*. Ithaca: Cornell University Press.

Kelman, Steven. 1981. *Regulating America, Regulating Sweden: A Comparative Study of Occupational Safety and Health Policy*. Cambridge, Mass.: MIT Press.

Kingston, Paul. 2001. Patrons, Clients and Civil Society: A Case Study of Environmental Politics in Postwar Lebanon. *Arab Studies Quarterly* 23 (1): 55–72.

Kitschelt, Herbert. 1989. *The Logics of Party Formation: Ecological Politics in Belgium and West Germany*. Ithaca: Cornell University Press.

Krasner, Stephen. 1984. Approaches to the State: Alternative Conceptions and Historical Dynamics. *Comparative Politics* 16 (2): 223–246.

Krishna, Anirudh, and Norman Uphoff. 2004. Civil Society and Public Sector Institutions: More than a Zero-Sum Relationship. *Public Administration and Development* 24:357–372.

Kurzer, Paulette, and Alice Cooper. 2007. What's for Dinner? European Farming and Food Traditions Confront American Biotechnology. *Comparative Political Studies* 40 (9): 1035–1058.

Laitin, David. 1992. *Language Repertoires and State Construction in Africa*. Cambridge, UK: Cambridge University Press.

Lee, Yok-shiu F., and Alvin Y. So, eds. 1999. *Asia's Environmental Movements: Comparative Perspectives*. Armonk: M. E. Sharpe.

Lieberson, Stanley. 1991. Small N's and Big Conclusions: An Examination of the Reasoning in Comparative Studies Based on a Small Number of Cases. *Social Forces* 70 (2): 307–320.

Lijphart, Arend. 1971. Comparative Politics and Comparative Method. *American Political Science Review* 65:682–693.

Lindblom, Charles E. 1982. The Market as Prison. *The Journal of Politics* 44 (2): 324–336.

Lipschutz, Ronnie D. 1991. Bargaining Among Nations: Culture, History, and Perceptions in Regime Formation. *Evaluation Review* 15 (1): 46–74.

Lipschutz, Ronnie D. 1992. Reconstructing World Politics: The Emergence of Global Civil Society. *Millennium: Journal of International Studies* 21 (3): 389–420.

Lipschutz, Ronnie D. 2001. Environmental History, Political Economy and Change: Frameworks and Tools for Research and Analysis. *Global Environmental Politics* 1 (3): 72–91.

Lundqvist, Lennart J. 1978. The Comparative Study of Environmental Politics: From Garbage to Gold? *International Journal of Environmental Studies* 12 (2): 89–97.

Mair, Peter, ed. 1990. *The West European Party System.* New York: Oxford University Press.

McBeath, Jerry, and Jonathan Rosenberg. 2006. *Comparative Environmental Politics.* New York: Springer.

Miles, Edward L., Arild Underdal, Steinar Andresen, Jørgen Wettestad, Jon Birger Skjaerseth, and Elaine M. Carlin. 2002. *Environmental Regime Effectiveness: Confronting Theory with Evidence.* Cambridge, Mass.: MIT Press.

Mill, John Stuart. [1843] 1967. *A System of Logic: Ratiocinative and Inductive.* Toronto: University of Toronto Press.

Mitchell, Ronald. 2002. International Environment. In *Handbook of International Relations,* ed. Thomas Risse, Beth Simmons, and Walter Carlsnaes, 500–516. Thousand Oaks, Calif.: Sage Publications.

Mitchell, Ron. 2010. *International Politics and the Environment.* Thousand Oaks, Calif.: Sage Publications.

Moravcsik, Andrew. 1997. Taking Preferences Seriously: A Liberal Theory of International Politics. *International Organization* 51:513–553.

Mortimer, Robert A. 1984. *The Third World Coalition in International Politics.* Boulder: Westview Press.

Najam, Adil. 2005. Developing Countries and Global Environmental Governance: From Contestation to Participation to Engagement. *International Environmental Agreement: Politics, Law and Economics* 5 (3): 303–321.

O'Neill, Kate. 2009. *The Environment and International Relations.* New York: Cambridge University Press.

Ostrom, Elinor. 1990. *Governing the Commons: The Evolution of Institutions for Collective Action.* New York: Cambridge University Press.

Parson, Edward. 2003. *Protecting the Ozone Layer: Science and Strategy.* New York: Oxford University Press.

Paterson, Matthew. 2005. Theoretical Perspectives in the Study of International Environmental Politics. In *Palgrave Advances in International Environmental Politics,* ed. Michele Betsill, Kathryn Hochstetler, and Dimitris Stevis, 54–81. New York: Palgrave Macmillan.

Peritore, N. Patrick. 1999. *Third World Environmentalism: Case Studies from the Global South.* Gainesville, Fla.: University Press of Florida.

Pierson, Christopher. 1996. *The Modern State.* London: Routledge.

Pierson, Paul. 2003. Big, Slow-Moving and . . . Invisible: Macrosocial Processes in the Study of Comparative Politics. In *Comparative Historical Analysis in the Social Sciences,* ed. James Mahoney and Dietrich Rueschemeyer, 177–207. New York: Cambridge University Press.

Putnam, Robert. 1971. Studying Elite Political Culture: The Case of "Ideology." *American Political Science Review* 65 (3): 651–681.

Putnam, Robert D. 1988. Diplomacy and Domestic Politics: The Logic of Two-Level Games. *International Organization* 42 (3): 427–460.

Putnam, Robert D. 1993. *Making Democracy Work: Civic Traditions in Modern Italy.* Princeton: Princeton University Press.

Rabe, Barry. 2004. *Statehouse and Greenhouse: The Emerging Politics of American Climate Change Policy.* Washington, D.C.: Brookings Institution Press.

Ragin, Charles C. 2008. *Redesigning Social Inquiry: Fuzzy Sets and Beyond.* Chicago: University of Chicago Press.

Raustiala, Kal. 1997. Domestic Institutions and International Regulatory Cooperation. *World Politics* 49 (4): 482–509.

Ribot, Jesse C. 1999. Decentralisation, Participation, and Accountability in Sahelian Forestry: Legal Instruments of Political-Administrative Control. *Africa* 69 (1): 23–65.

Roberts, Clayton. 1996. *The Logic of Historical Explanation.* University Park: Penn State University Press.

Rodrigues, Maria Guadalupe. 2000. Environmental Protection Issue Networks in Amazonia. *Latin American Research Review* 35 (3): 125–153.

Rose, Richard. 1991. Comparing Forms of Comparative Analysis. *Political Studies* 39 (3): 446–462.

Ross, Michael L. 2001. *Timber Booms and Institutional Breakdown in Southeast Asia.* New York: Cambridge University Press.

Sartori, Giovanni. 1970. Concept Misformation in Comparative Politics. *American Political Science Review* 64 (4): 1033–1053.

Schreurs, Miranda, Henrik Selin, and Stacy D. VanDeveer. 2009. *Transatlantic Environmental and Energy Politics.* Burlington, Vt.: Ashgate Press.

Scruggs, Lyle. 2003. *Sustaining Abundance: Environmental Performance in Industrial Democracies.* New York: Cambridge University Press.

Selin, Henrik and Stacy D. VanDeveer. 2005. Canadian-US Environmental Cooperation: Climate Change Networks and Regional Action. *American Review of Canadian Studies.* Special Issue on the State of Canadian-US Relations (Summer): 353–378.

Selin, Henrik, and Stacy D. VanDeveer. 2006. Raising Global Standards: Hazardous Substances and E-waste Management in the European Union. *Environment* 28 (10): 6–17.

Selin, Henrik, and Stacy VanDeveer. 2007. Political Science and Prediction: What's Next for US Climate Change Policy? *Review of Policy Research* 24 (1): 1–27.

Selin, Henrik, and Stacy D. VanDeveer. 2009. *Changing Climates in North American Politics.* Cambridge, Mass.: MIT Press.

Sikkink, Kathryn. 1991. *Ideas and Institutions: Developmentalism in Brazil and Argentina.* Ithaca: Cornell University Press.

Skocpol, Theda. 2003. Doubly Engaged Social Science: The Promise of Comparative Historical Analysis. In *Comparative Historical Analysis in the Social Sciences*, ed. James Mahoney and Dietrich Rueschemeyer, 407–428. New York: Cambridge University Press.

Slaughter, Anne-Marie. 1997. The Real New World Order. *Foreign Affairs* 76:183–197.

Sprinz, Detlef, and Tapani Vaahtoranta. 1994. The Interest-Based Explanation of International Environmental Policy. *International Organization* 48 (1): 77–105.

Steinberg, Paul F. 2001. *Environmental Leadership in Developing Countries: Transnational Relations and Biodiversity Policy in Costa Rica and Bolivia.* Cambridge, Mass.: MIT Press.

Steinberg, Paul F. 2002. Environmental Foreign Policy in Developing Countries: A Capacity-Building Approach. Paper presented at the International Studies Association Annual Convention, March 24–27, New Orleans.

Steinberg, Paul F. 2005. From Public Concern to Policy Effectiveness: Civic Conservation in Developing Countries. *Journal of International Wildlife Law and Policy* 8:341–365.

Steinberg, Paul F. 2007. Causal Assessment in Small-N Policy Studies. *Policy Studies Journal* 35 (2): 181–204.

Steinberg, Paul F., and Ronie Garcia-Johnson. 2001. Transnational Environmental Actors: Toward an Integrated Approach. Paper presented at the International Studies Association Annual Convention, February 20–24, Chicago.

Tashakkori, Abbas, and Charles Teddlie, eds. 2003. *Handbook of Mixed Methods in Social and Behavioral Research.* Thousand Oaks, Calif.: Sage Publications.

Tetlock, Philip E., and Aaron Belkin. 1996. *Counterfactual Thought Experiments in World Politics: Logical, Methodological, and Psychological Perspectives.* Princeton: Princeton University Press.

Thelen, Kathleen. 2002. How Institutions Evolve: Insights from Comparative-Historical Analysis. In *Comparative Historical Analysis in the Social Sciences*, ed. James Mahoney and Dietrich Rueschemeyer, 208–240. New York: Cambridge University Press.

VanDeveer, Stacy D. 2003. Green Fatigue. *Wilson Quarterly* 27 (4): 55–59.

VanDeveer, Stacy D., and Geoffrey D. Dabelko. 2001. It's Capacity, Stupid: International Assistance and National Implementation. *Global Environmental Politics* 1 (2): 18–29.

Vogel, David. 2003. The Hare and the Tortoise Revisited: The New Politics of Consumer and Environmental Regulation in Europe. *British Journal of Political Science* 33 (4): 557–580.

Wapner, Paul K. 1996. *Environmental Activism and World Civic Politics.* Albany: SUNY Press.

Wapner, Paul K. 2003. Ecological Thinking. In *Encountering Global Environmental Politics*, ed. Michael Maniates, 17–25. Lanham, Md.: Rowman & Littlefield.

Young, Oran R. 1998. *Creating Regimes: Arctic Accords and International Governance.* Ithaca: Cornell University Press.

Young, Oran R., ed. 1999. *The Effectiveness of International Environmental Regimes: Causal Connections and Behavioral Mechanisms.* Cambridge, Mass.: MIT Press.

Zürn, M. 1998. The Rise of International Environmental Politics: A Review of the Current Research. *World Politics* 50 (4): 617–649.

2

Bridging Archipelagos: Connecting Comparative Politics and Environmental Politics

Paul F. Steinberg and Stacy D. VanDeveer

Systematic comparisons of domestic environmental politics allow us to move beyond ill-defined exhortations to "save the planet" toward a greater understanding of the vast array of social responses to environmental problems in diverse countries around the globe. With the help of conceptual tools that enable meaningful comparisons across national borders, we can gain insights into the cause-and-effect relationships that lead states and social actors to practice or ignore environmental stewardship, at a level of resolution much different from that of research analyzing the positions of national delegations during international treaty negotiations.

To take advantage of the potential synergies between comparative environmental politics (CEP) and the broader field of comparative political science requires that we build bridges between two largely unconnected fields of study. The first step is to identify the broad contours of the research literature in each domain. To this end, we provide a succinct overview of some of the major clusters of scholarship in the comparative politics tradition, then take stock of the state of the art in research on comparative environmental politics. Whereas the first task requires considerable humility—comparative politics is, after all, a major subfield with political science and the subject of countless introductory volumes—the second brings discovery and surprise. The discovery comes in the course of searching far and wide in the literature and assembling what is, to our knowledge, the first comprehensive overview of comparative environmental politics research. Our surprise came in uncovering a remarkably large literature in this area—so large, in fact, that we faced a trade-off between comprehensiveness and readability, a dilemma that we have resolved by means of an online bibliography to supplement the literature reviewed in this chapter.[1]

It is tempting to deploy the metaphor of bridging two islands when thinking about how to build meaningful connections between these two bodies of research. But the challenge is of a different sort. Comparative politics and comparative environmental politics each represent diverse and disparate collections of literatures and scholarly communities. One is a self-identified subfield of political science, sustained across generations of researchers and with important connections to adjacent areas of comparative social science such as sociology, political economy, and history. The other has no such self-conception; its hundreds of investigators only occasionally cite one another's work. Given the diversity within each of these intellectual spheres, they are more accurately thought of as separate archipelagos. The challenge for a cumulative research program, then, is to selectively build bridges (with emphasis on the plural) connecting identifiable literatures in comparative politics with questions occupying the attention of environmental researchers. We leave that task to the chapters that constitute the rest of the book, as each exemplifies a causeway for productive collaboration among those concerned with the fate of the planet and its people and those engaged in the comparative study of political life. Before crossing those bridges, let us begin by exploring the terrain of these distinct collections of islands.

The Comparative Politics Tradition

Comparative political inquiry is a rich intellectual tradition encompassing diverse areas of research that share two distinctive features.[2] First, comparative politics research takes seriously the role of domestic politics. Second, comparative politics draws on and contributes to an understanding of political phenomena in more than one country. Together these two commitments allow the field to pay careful attention to national and subnational contexts while promoting a broader understanding of politics that transcends national boundaries. Let us consider each of these in turn.

Politics within Nations

To say that comparative research focuses on domestic politics does not mean that it downplays international phenomena. To the contrary, comparativists are keenly interested in the ways in which international processes—such as trade, war, colonialism, European Union formation, and transnational advocacy, to name a few—influence and are shaped by domestic politics. Dependency theory, which occupied an important position in the field in the 1960s and 1970s, was primarily concerned with how the international rules of the game constrain domestic economic growth in developing countries (Cardoso and Faletto 1979; Evans 1979). Likewise, research on democratization pays careful attention to the causal influence of international politics—from the Second Vatican Council's support for grassroots mobilization against authoritarian regimes to the impact of changes in the foreign policy strategies of the Soviet Union and United States during the Cold War (Huntington 1991, 45). The comparative literature on policy diffusion tracks the movement of policy ideas across borders (Knill 2005) and social movement scholars are increasingly interested in cross-national linkages among movements (McAdam and Rucht 1993;

Tarrow 2005). It is the inclusion of careful attention to domestic political life, rather than the exclusion of cross-border relations, that is the hallmark of comparative politics research.

Explanations beyond Individual Countries

The second defining feature of comparative politics is an emphasis on explanation beyond a single country. This emphasis does not reflect disdain for insights into the political processes shaping the course of individual nations. If one has "merely" contributed to our understanding of the consolidation of democratic reforms in South Africa, or even the operation of electoral institutions within Johannesburg, the results shed light on the lived experiences of millions of people. Moreover, for those who wish to use knowledge to change the world for the better, it is worth recalling that initiatives like human rights advocacy, administrative reform, economic restructuring, rural development, or wetlands conservation are achieved one country at a time, through painstaking processes that typically require commitments of advocacy and expertise over a period of decades. Far from downplaying the significance of outcomes within a single country, comparativists wish to bring insights from a wide array of national experiences to bear on our understanding of these outcomes.

Comparative inquiry is pursued in a number of ways. One might study an individual country with an explicit attempt to produce explanations relevant to a broad array of national settings. Robert Putnam's (1993) study of the relation between social capital and government performance in Italy is designed not only to account for differences within that country, but also to illuminate political phenomena worthy of exploration around the globe. The reader is treated to a rich discussion of Italian history and society, but the emphasis is on the exploration of questions with relevance to the world at large, enabling a cumulative conversation among researchers with diverse geographic and topical interests. Another example is Alfred Stepan's (1988) study of military politics in Brazil, which shows how a change in the reigning philosophy of Brazil's military academies facilitated a more active (and ultimately more destructive) role for the military in the state. By keeping the study in close conversation with the literature from a wide variety of countries, Stepan's results have influenced subsequent research on civil-military relations around the world (Feaver 1999). The potential value of single-country studies is an important consideration given that in-depth studies of any country require a considerable time commitment (see also Rueschemeyer 2003).

Alternatively, one can analyze larger numbers of countries through either small-N designs (using fewer than a dozen cases) or quantitative approaches. Illustrative of the former are Robert Bates's (1981) classic study of the political economy of agricultural development in tropical Africa, or Theda Skocpol's (1979) influential work on the origins of social revolution. Skocpol's analysis of revolutions in China, Russia, and France strikes a balance between in-depth case research and theory building "to develop explanations of revolutions that are at once historically grounded and generalizable beyond unique cases" (Skocpol 1979, 6). Bates asks, "Why should reasonable men adopt public policies that have harmful consequences for the societies they govern?"—a question he pursues with economic data and historical process tracing from a half-dozen countries, augmented with evidence from throughout the African continent. For both researchers, an attractive solution to the trade-off between historical depth (which is frequently necessary for reaching credible conclusions within cases) and geographic breadth (a prerequisite for generalizable theory) is to draw extensively on secondary sources (see Skocpol 1984, 382).

Quantitative approaches to comparative politics include Ronald Inglehart's (1990) research on shifting worldviews, which marshals public opinion data from dozens of countries, as well as comparative analyses of the stability of democratic and authoritarian regimes (Geddes 1999). A comparative research agenda does not insist that the national level is the only valid unit of analysis. Research comparing the roots of urban insurgency in Ireland, Pakistan, and Iraq (Staniland 2010), or comparing experiments in federalism across Europe and Latin America (Eaton 2008), invite us to situate local and regional politics in the context of a broader set of experiences around the globe.

The field of comparative politics draws on a wide variety of analytic approaches and does not derive its identity from any particular methodology. Over the last century, generally accepted methods, concepts, and assumptions in what is now seen as the comparative politics tradition have changed repeatedly. This evolution has occurred partly in response to important changes in the world, such as the rise of new social movements, the export of neoliberalism, or the "third wave" of democratization. Blyth (2006) argues that these shifts within the field are also a consequence of a collective inclination to view the complex subject matter of comparative politics as more predictable than it probably is, leading to the development of theories that are surprised by events on the ground. Comparativists have been at the forefront of recent efforts to develop new research methodologies capable of causal assessment in complex settings (Brady and Collier 2004; George and Bennett 2005; Gerring 2007; Hall 2003; Rogowski 1995; Bates et al. 1998; Mahoney 2007; Munck 1998).

Theoretical Approaches: Interests, Ideas, and Institutions
While the systematic comparison of domestic political forces distinguishes comparative politics from other fields, its vitality also derives from an eclecticism befitting a research endeavor that covers so much empirical and theoretical terrain. Comparative politics research draws on innumerable political and social theorists, claiming

a distinguished ancestry that includes Aristotle, Marx, Weber, Durkheim, and many others (Lichbach and Zuckerman 1997, 3–16). Virtually every major school of thought in the social sciences has an analog within comparative politics, and the field has evolved in close conjunction with areas like economic history, comparative sociology, cultural anthropology, and game theory. Notwithstanding the diversity of approaches represented within comparative politics, it shares in common with the parent discipline of political science three broad research traditions, which may be summarized in terms of interests, ideas, and institutions.

Interest-based explanations emphasize political actors' rational pursuit of goals, often construed as material self-interest calculated through cost-benefit analysis and typically modeled with the use of game theory (for an overview, see Munck 2001). This type of mathematical reasoning can be applied to a wide range of individual or collective behaviors, including voting, revolutionary action, breaking or abiding by the law, and preserving or destroying natural resources. Emphasizing the micro-foundations of strategic interaction among social actors, rational choice offers explanations based on theoretically plausible mechanisms of social choice, in contrast to approaches that infer causation from statistical correlations without specifying underlying behavioral models. Researchers in the rational choice tradition prize parsimonious and generalizable explanations and are willing to sacrifice empirical realism for the sake of a cumulative research program that can produce nonintuitive insights applicable to a wide range of subjects.

The study of ideas constitutes a second major tradition within comparative politics. Emphasizing the conceptual dimensions of political life, this tradition explores the values, concepts, identities, symbols, and interpretive frameworks that shape understandings about what is important, what is or is not a political problem, who should participate in politics, and by what means. How individuals and groups see themselves and how they are viewed by others influences how people engage in politics. In contrast to interest-based approaches, many researchers in this tradition downplay the criteria of parsimony and broad applicability, focusing instead on the ability to illuminate particular cases through interpretation and thick description. This is unsurprising given the centrality of social context in constructivist research. As Finnemore and Sikkink point out, "Constructivists need methods that can capture the intersubjective meanings at the core of their approach" (2001, 395). Yet Benedict Anderson's (1991) classic study of the origins of nationalism shows that research on the political impact of ideas can leverage insights of broad applicability. Still others study shared attitudes through the use of quantitative public opinion surveys on subjects such as the durability of political party affiliation (Lupu and Stokes 2010) or the effect of generational turnover on cultural norms (Inglehart 1990). Indeed, Rochon (1998) argues that because cultural discourse is expressed through language, changes in ideas are ideally suited to empirical analysis (see, e.g., Sabatier 1989).

The third major research tradition within comparative politics focuses on institutions, analyzing how socially constructed rules of the game shape individual and collective behaviors (Hall and Taylor 1996; March and Olsen 1966, 1989; Douglas 1986). Institutionalist research focuses on a wide range of social and political arrangements—from formal political institutions such as laws, political parties, constitutions, and the structure of governments to social class, gender roles, patronage networks, and other enduring social structures (Goodin and Tilly 2006; Thelen and Steinmo 1992; North 1981). Topics range from how institutions reflect and propagate social norms to the strategies used by states to regulate markets and the institutional mechanisms through which certain interests are privileged over others. Institutional analysis is so central to comparative politics research that, as Kopstein and Lichbach observe, "Many comparativists consider the study of politics to be synonymous with the study of institutions" (2005, 26).

The distinction among interests, ideas, and institutions is often portrayed in ways that may cause confusion, as the categories simultaneously refer to two distinct but partially overlapping phenomena. On the one hand, these are used as empirical categories, denoting tangible realities that shape and give meaning to political life, such as the economic interests of France, the idea of a unified Europe, or the institution of the European Commission. On the other hand, these terms are used as shorthand for distinct epistemological approaches to the study of politics, referring respectively to rational choice theory, constructivism (and its more radical postmodern variants), and historical institutionalism.[3] Lichbach and Zuckerman (1997) have these epistemological distinctions in mind when they portray the three categories as competing research traditions. When these terms signal ways of studying politics, there may indeed be inherent incompatibilities, insofar as a commitment to one requires deviation from the conceptual foundations and preferred methodological canons of the other. Each of these epistemological approaches can be applied to a wide range of empirical and theoretical problems, further suggesting their status as competing research traditions.

Yet when interests, ideas, and institutions are used to categorize empirical realities, tangible relationships among these phenomena are identifiable and can be studied from a variety of epistemological angles. Elements of each are often incorporated in combination in individual studies. This can be seen in the literature on the relation between ideas and institutions (Yeo 2010; Goldstein 1993; Sikkink 1991; Hall 1989), in rational choice approaches to the study of culture (Bednar and Page 2007; Laitin 1998; Axelrod 1997), and in the prominent pairing of interests and institutions in the rational choice variant of the "new institutionalism," which shows how individual choices are shaped by alternative configurations of social rules (Shepsle 1989; Dewan and Shepsle 2008). The reciprocal influence of ideas and the institutions that embed them is on display in research on political culture and political attitudes, which have been studied from the perspective of elite ideology (Putnam 1971; Higley and Burton 2006), mass attitudes toward democratic institutions (Almond and Verba 1963; Muller and Seligson 1994), and the ways that deeply held social beliefs are reflected and transmitted through history via institutions for collective action (Greif 1994).

Given the eclecticism of comparative politics research, we find it useful to retain both the epistemological and empirical usages of interests, ideas, and institutions while keeping the distinction clearly in mind. As alternative approaches to political understanding, these have been applied in creative ways to illuminate major topical themes in comparative politics. For example, the origin of nation-states and nationalities can be understood in terms of the administrative and regulatory strength of state institutions (Herbst 1990; Migdal 1988), the financial interests of ruling elites (Olson 2000), and the conceptual constructs that bind communities (Anderson 1991). The relation of the state to markets and economic growth—a central concern for environmental politics—has likewise been studied from each of these three perspectives. Chalmers Johnson's (1982) work on the developmental state in Japan emphasizes, among other influences, the world views that led Japanese policy-making elites to adopt their particular form of state-market collaboration. Further testimony to the payoff of drawing on diverse analytic approaches is provided by Douglass North's (1981) seminal work on the expansion of state institutions as a prerequisite for capitalist development and by rational choice analyses of state regulation of the economy (Bueno de Mesquita and Root 2000).

The ways in which interests are aggregated in diverse institutional and cultural settings—through voting, civic organizations, mass protest, political party formation, and constitutional divisions of power—have long been a major focus of comparative politics research (see Kitschelt 2000). Interest aggregation is also of keen interest to environmental studies, given the multiple scales at which environmental advocates work, from changing individual attitudes toward recycling to trying to catalyze grassroots mobilizations and shifts in local, national, and international policy. Yet those interested in the human dimensions of environmental problems have made little use of this research. Returning to our archipelago metaphor, it is as if the inhabitants of one chain of islands are struggling to invent the wheel, unaware that on the other a thriving civilization is teeming with modern roadways.

Interest aggregation is affected by the inclination and ability of citizens to engage in politics, which has been studied from the perspective of cross-national differences in mass participation and from the vantage point of the most politically active individuals (Norris, Walgrave, and Van Aelst 2005; LeDuc, Niemi, and Norris 1996; Powell 1986; Dahl 1961; Pierce et al. 1986). The construction and expression of social interests through mass social movements has been the focus of a substantial comparative literature (McAdam, McCarthy, and Zald 1996), as Kate O'Neill details (chapter 5, this volume). Interest aggregation also occurs at the ballot box, and voting behavior has been intensively studied by rational choice theorists, including assessments of voter priorities and of the ways in which electoral rules influence voter strategies and shape the organization of political parties (Duch and Stevensen 2006; Powell and Whitten 1993; Kedar 2005; Cox 1997). Macrolevel comparisons of state structures and their impact on the aggregation and mobilization of social interests include comparisons among regime types, such as corporatist states (Molina and Rhodes 2002; Collier and Collier 1979), presidential and parliamentary systems (Mainwaring 1997; Stepan and Skach 1993), and authoritarian regimes (Linz 2000; Stepan 1973). Given the impact of institutions on interest aggregation, it is not surprising that the electoral systems, constitutions, and other institutions mediating state-society relations are themselves the subject of contestation and change (Benoit 2004; Boix 1999; Skocpol 1979).

Toward a Distinctive Tradition in Comparative Environmental Politics

Unlike comparative politics and its component literatures, there is little in the way of a distinctive comparative environmental politics tradition. But a closer examination reveals two important caveats to this statement. First, there is a very substantial body of work in environmental politics that is, broadly speaking, comparative but has simply not coalesced into a self-identified field of research. A large literature exists on the environmental politics of many individual industrialized countries and, to a lesser extent, groups of such countries (e.g., Kelemen and Vogel 2010; Börzel 2002; Kelemen 2004; Jänicke and Jorgens 1998; Schreurs 2005; Aguilar 1993; Weale et al. 1996; Rose-Ackerman 1995; Scruggs 2001; Dryzek et al. 2003; Cashore, Auld, and Newsom 2004; Jordan 2005; Vig and Faure 2004).[4] The journal *Environmental Politics* has been a focal point for comparative research on the industrialized nations, serving as one of the few venues in which this otherwise disparate literature comes together. Research on environmental politics in the developing world can be found in diverse literatures drawing on traditions of rural sociology, anthropology, development studies, environmental history, rational choice theory, and policy analysis (examples include Watts 2005; Dove 2006; Agrawal and Ostrom 2001; Steinberg 2003; Grove 1993; White and Runge 1994; Christen et al. 1998; Garcia-Johnson 2000; Harris 2005; Ascher 1999; Carruthers 2001; Hochstetler and Keck 2007; Lee and So 1999; Auer 2001). Environmental politics has also been a lively area of research in the context of the profound political and economic transformations experienced in Central and Eastern Europe (Carmin and Fagan 2010; Carmin and VanDeveer 2005; Botcheva 1996; Andonova 2004; Auer 2005; Dawson 1996; Hicks 1996).

Although it is convenient to convey the scope of CEP research in terms of its geographic coverage, this book seeks to foster comparative learning and research beyond geographic limitations by tapping comparative politics for theoretical insights that travel well across political jurisdictions. This brings us to our second caveat regarding the absence of a CEP tradition. Though comparative politics and environmental politics remain largely distinct areas of inquiry, there is considerable overlap in the intellectual interests and research agendas of the two. Significantly, studies of environmental politics count among the best-known works in the three comparative politics traditions (interests, ideas, and institutions) discussed in the previous section, as can be seen in the canonical status of Ostrom's (1990) work within rational choice theory, the influence of Inglehart's (1990) research on post-materialism within cultural studies, and the fact that Kitschelt's (1989) work on green parties remains the gold standard for comparative research on political parties.

Notwithstanding their shared interests, researchers in these two fields have worked largely in isolation. Environmental scholars too often neglect theoretical insights from comparative politics, reinventing conceptual wheels, relabeling empirical phenomena, and overlooking entire categories of questions that have long been the focus of study within comparative politics. In the other direction, there is a wealth of literature on comparative environmental politics and its associated theoretical and empirical puzzles that demand attention from any group of scholars—in comparative politics, international relations, or other fields—who wish to keep social science research relevant to today's social problems.

Here we provide an overview of the CEP literature, organized into four categories that reflect the core interests of both comparative politics and environmental studies: (1) social mobilization and the roles of nonstate actors; (2) values, culture, and knowledge; (3) political institutions and governance; and (4) multilevel linkages (see table 2.1). As is fitting for a topic like ecology, which permeates and links together so many aspects of social organization, the challenge for practitioners and scholars of environmental politics is to appreciate the connections among these phenomena, such as the relations between state and society, between ideas and institutions, and among different levels of governance. Running across these categories are some foundational questions for this new field: who participates in environmental politics,

Table 2.1
Research clusters

Comparative politics	Comparative environmental politics
Interests	Social mobilization and nonstate actors
Ideas	Political institutions and governance
Institutions	Values, culture, and knowledge
	Multilevel linkages

how, and with what effects? How do institutions influence and reflect social and environmental conditions including the distribution of power and resources? What role do ideas play in the constitution of political demands and in the normative underpinnings of institutional arrangements? And how can we begin to understand the prospects for collective action to address planetary-scale environmental problems in a world that is so heterogeneous in its social parameters across political jurisdictions and among levels of governance? Moving across the columns in table 2.1, we expect that a conceptually rich and empirically sound research program can be designed by combining aspects of the comparative politics tradition with areas of comparative environmental politics research.

Social Mobilization and Nonstate Actors

Social mobilization is one of the defining characteristics of environmental politics. Many environmental problems can be shaped by local actions and are often highly localized in their impacts. As a result, the information bearing on environmental decision making—the polluting behavior of firms, changes in wildlife populations, and the quality of the air, water, and soil—is often more readily perceived by local residents than by distant regulatory bureaucracies. Ordinary citizens are often in a much more influential position to address these problems than is the case with issues such as trade policy, national defense, or public sector reform. Many of the ideas and approaches used by environmental regulatory agencies today first originated in civil society organizations, which also play a key role in implementing policy and undertake independent initiatives ranging from private land conservation to pollution monitoring (Steinberg 2005). Moreover, unlike health issues—for which many proactive measures like improved diet and exercise can be implemented on an individual basis—the prevalence of collective action problems (notably market failures) as causes of environmental deterioration makes coordinated social action necessary even when addressing small-scale environmental problems (Maniates 2002). Beyond the inherent logic of social mobilization for the environment, there are historical reasons for the linkage between mass participation and environmental politics. The modern environmental movement arose on the heels of new social movements in Western democracies the late 1960s, imbuing large segments of this multinational movement with a philosophy of protest, social action, and radical critique (Gottlieb 2005, 121–158).

As Kate O'Neill discusses (chapter 5, this volume), environmental movements have attracted the attention of social movement scholars in political science and sociology, who offer perspectives on the goals, tactics, and impacts of environmental movements around the world (Rucht 1995; Rootes 1999; Jimenez 1999). In a special issue devoted to this topic in the flagship journal *Mobilization*, della Porta and Rucht observe that over the past three decades, "Environmental activism has changed remarkably. By and large, conflicts are no longer marked by a relatively simple constellation of one challenger facing one target or opponent. Instead, we find a complex web of involved actors reaching from local to international levels" (2002, 1). The focus of environmental movements is affected by both the internal characteristics of their constituent organizations and by external influences from the societies in which they operate. With respect to internal drivers, Dalton (1994) finds that divergence in the tactics of political engagement used by environmental groups in Western Europe stems in large part from differences in these groups' core philosophies. The ideas that motivate an environmental organization shape its substantive focus and the goals and values that it seeks to embed in state institutions. Yet environmental movements do not exist in isolation from other social movements and the problems and discourses that animate domestic and transnational politics. Researchers have begun to explore the relationships of environmental movements and NGO activism with issues of gender, organized labor, nationalism, indigenous peoples, revolutionary and democratizing movements, and social justice (Carmin and Bast 2009; Kim 2000; Adeola 2000; Bennett, Davila-Poblete, and Rico 2005; Obach 2002; Dawson 1996; Carruthers 1996; Taylor 2000) and their roles in broader citizen coalitions responding to globalization (O'Neill and VanDeveer 2005; Fox and Brown 1998).

Social movements and NGOs are also strongly affected by state institutions, accounting for much of the observed cross-national variation in movement activity. Schreurs (2002) demonstrates that national laws and practices shape the character and size of domestic social movements, producing marked differences among countries that have similar levels of economic development and face essentially the same sets of environmental issues. Japan, for example, witnessed an explosion of local grassroots environmental activism in the 1960s and 1970s, but the movement was soon stifled by stringent state requirements governing nonprofit status and by the lack of independent philanthropic organizations. In *Green States and Social Movements*, Dryzek and colleagues (2003) argue that cross-national differences in the influence of environmental movements in the United Kingdom, Germany, Norway, and the United States can be explained by state practices of social inclusion and exclusion and by the extent to which movements have been able to tie their cause to core state imperatives of economic growth, internal stability, and legitimacy. Steinberg (2001) shows that state structures also influence patterns of transnational activism. Northern environmental NGOs shunned relations with Bolivia until its transition to democracy in the early 1980s, at which point they helped to fund and inspire the growth of the Bolivian environmental movement.

Environmental movements are shaped by the social contexts in which they operate, but they also aspire fundamentally to transform those contexts to take greater account of environmental quality. A considerable body of research evaluates the impact of environmental NGOs on national and international policies and practices, particularly as these organizations engage a growing list of transnational environmental issues (Betsill and Corell 2006; Raustiala 1997b; Clark, Friedman, and Hochstetler 1998; Keck and Sikkink 1998; Rodrigues 2004). Far from shunning the state, efforts to reform state institutions are a recurrent theme in NGO activities in every part of the world. In a survey of 248 environmental organizations in 59 countries, Dalton, Recchia, and Rohrschneider (2003) report that environmental groups routinely interact with government officials at national and local levels. Rochon and Mazmanian (1993) find that the policy impact of environmental groups in the United States is less a function of their influence on specific regulatory standards and more a consequence of institutionalizing their preferred regulatory processes, such as legal requirements for citizen oversight. Without denying the significance of policy reform, Wapner (1995, 320) argues that the impact of NGOs is "significant in world affairs not only because they influence states but also because they affect the behavior of larger collectivities throughout the world. They do so by manipulating governing structures of global civil society," engaging in "world civic politics" and "disseminating an ecological sensibility" (see also Lipschutz 1992; Dobson and Bell 2006). These forms of nonstate advocacy have gained increasing attention in evaluations of the effectiveness of environmental certification programs spearheaded by NGOs to motivate change in industrial practices in areas like forestry and food production (Cashore, Auld, and Newsom 2004). Interestingly, these nongovernmental certification schemes are found to be most effective when combined with the threat of state regulation (Carraro and Lévêque 1999).

Political Institutions and Governance

A second major area of CEP research analyzes the processes through which distinct types of political institutions aggregate domestic interests, respond to international environmental regimes, and shape social and environmental outcomes. The emergence of green parties and the impact of environmental movements on traditional party politics have proved to be a fruitful area of research (see Michael O'Neill, chapter 7, this volume). Research on green parties demonstrates one of the great advantages of environmental subjects for comparative political inquiry—the relatively recent appearance of a new set of political concerns and associated institutions in multiple countries, which presents opportunities for comparative analyses of how these new phenomena interact with long-standing domestic structures. Here scholars have documented how parties aggregate and articulate environmental views, how institutions such as voting rules affect the development of new parties and the salience of environmental ideas within traditional partisan politics, and how parties handle the competing demands of accountability to grassroots constituencies and the parliamentary requirements of bargaining, professionalization, and electoral success.

Beyond the study of political parties, macrolevel analyses have compared environmental regulatory styles as a function of political regime, including comparisons of policy processes under corporatist versus pluralist systems, in parliamentary versus presidential systems, and in democratic versus authoritarian regimes (see Aguilar 1993; Scruggs 2001; and Hochstetler, chapter 8, this volume). Studies of specific state agencies, such as Craig Thomas's (2003) analysis of the challenge of interagency coordination for biodiversity conservation in California, or Nancy Peluso's (1992) study of the legacy of colonial forestry practices in Java, illuminate the concrete ways in which political institutions structure the possibilities for environmental reform (see also Tang and Tang 2000; Gibson 1999).

Given the strong normative orientation of environmental studies, it comes as little surprise that institutional performance—the actual impact of political institutions on environmental and social outcomes—figures prominently in the CEP literature.[5] Scruggs's (2003) quantitative analysis of environmental performance in seventeen wealthy democracies assesses the relationship of environmental performance (such as pollution levels, waste management, and access to clean water) to factors including national wealth, economic structural changes, public environmental concern, the scale and scope of environmental NGO activities, and state models of interest aggregation. This and other cross-national comparisons of institutional performance (such as Verweij 2000; Crepaz 1995; Ascher 1999) are matched by a considerable body of work interrogating the causes and consequences of environmental degradation in particular countries and regions (Economy 2004; Díez 2006; Duffy 2000; Gibson 1999). Unlike Scruggs's work, most of this literature employs qualitative case studies connecting particular policies or institutions to environmental and social outcomes.

The literature on administrative capacity reviews the conditions under which national and local institutions are capable of fulfilling global mandates for sustainable development and environmental management (VanDeveer and Sagar 2005; Jänicke and Weidner 1997). There is a large literature within studies of common-pool resources documenting the heterogeneous and changing prerequisites for institutional effectiveness in managing shared local resources (see Agrawal, chapter 12, this volume). Other research has examined the role of local social capital and community pressure in efforts to provide environmental goods and services in diverse political settings (Tsai 2007; Press 1998; Rydin and Holman 2004).

In addition to assessing the environmental performance of political systems, researchers have evaluated the merits of specific environmental policy and management approaches, comparing national experiences with traditional environmental regulation to newer instruments such as tradable permits, environmental taxes, the polluter pays principle, right-to-know legislation, product certification, voluntary industry agreements, the precautionary principle, and participatory scientific assessments (Blackman 2008; Eckley and Selin 2004; Jordan, Wurzel, and Zito 2003; Cashore, Auld, and Newsom 2004; Harrington, Morgenstern, and Sterner 2004; Durant, Fiorino, and O'Leary 2004; de Bruijn and Norberg-Bohm 2005; Grant, Matthews, and Newell 2000). A small but growing literature on comparative sustainable development has also emerged in the wake of global interest and debate surrounding this concept (Balsiger 2007; Cooper and Vargas 2004).

Values, Culture, and Knowledge

Political responses to environmental problems do not arise in any deterministic sense in response to worsening physical conditions. Gamson and Modigliani (1989) point out that a serious nuclear accident in 1966 near Detroit went virtually unnoticed by the American public prior to the rise of mass environmentalism, whereas thirteen years later, an accident of comparable intensity at the Three Mile Island nuclear plant provoked a national outcry. Rochon observes, "With no organized critics of nuclear energy in 1966, and with no culturally accepted language for talking about nuclear energy other than as the energy of the future, the accident at Fermi was viewed as an anomaly, a temporary problem that the experts would take care of" (1998, 15). The study of values, culture, and knowledge plays a central role in CEP research precisely because social responses to environmental problems are shaped by predominant cultural understandings, modes of knowledge production and transmission, and the values and interpretive frameworks of the actors and institutions shaping environmental conditions. Moreover, from the inception of the modern environmental movement, advocates have sought to not merely reform institutions but to instill in the public new ways of thinking about and relating to the world around them.

There is a large body of research documenting public and elite environmental attitudes in different national settings (see Dunlap and York, chapter 4, this volume). A number of these studies have moved beyond basic comparisons of public survey responses, offering theoretically grounded efforts to identify clusters of attitudes, values, and interpretive frameworks, as well as their origins, their relation to actual behaviors, and how these viewpoints differ across social groups and national borders (Inglehart 1990; Oreg and Katz-Gerro 2006; Dunlap et al. 2000; Brechin 1999). Other work explores the relationship between changing public views and institutional reforms (Steinberg 2001)—indeed, some of the most influential theories of policy change have emerged from studies of the connection between ideas and institutions in environmental policy making (Baumgartner and Jones 2009; Weible, Sabatier, and McQueen 2009).

The role of environmental concern in the construction of national identity has been explored by authors such as Dawson (1996), who traces the influence of environmental ideas in the development of independence movements and articulations of national identity in former Soviet republics (see also Weinthal 2002). Nash (1967) argues that wilderness became an essential component of American identity, as articulated by urban elites in the nineteenth century in an effort to distinguish the new nation from the cultural achievements of its European progenitors. A number of studies have explored the ways in which predominant cultural norms, regulatory styles, and legitimizing discourses influence environmental movement tactics and state regulatory choices (O'Neill 2000; Hsiao et al. 1999). Research on ecological modernization traces the emergence of environmental regulation as part of what it means to be a legitimate sovereign state, a transformation driven in part by environmental movements and changes in broad understandings and expectations among significant parts of the citizenry (see Meadowcroft, chapter 3, this volume).

Properly assessing environmental conditions and crafting appropriate policy responses requires a great deal of technical information, raising important questions about how knowledge is generated and perceived by stakeholders and decision makers in democratic societies (Jasanoff 2005). Research combining aspects of science and technology studies with a focus on the environment has analyzed the role of scientific advisory panels within the US government (Jasanoff 1990), how developments in scientific understanding shaped Japanese environmental policy over time (Wilkening 2004), and the challenge of incorporating traditional or indigenous knowledge into environmental planning and assessment (Martello 2001; Jasanoff and Martello 2004; Agrawal 1995). Researchers associated with the Social Learning Group use comparative social histories to understand how different societies learn about and respond to global environmental risks such as climate change, ozone layer depletion, and acid rain (Social Learning Group 2001). Others have compared the influence of environmental science assessment processes on domestic and transnational organizations (Mitchell et al. 2006; Farrell, Jäger, and VanDeveer 2001; Farrell and Jäger 2006). In common with the Social Learning Group, these studies find that domestic institutions play pivotal roles in shaping how policy makers and the public interpret and respond to organized scientific and technical information. The information provided by environmental science assessments can at times change actors' understanding of the issues and of their material interests, especially when the information is perceived to be credible, salient to their concerns, and produced through legitimate means. Achieving all three criteria across various audiences (professionals versus citizens, national versus local stakeholders, and across countries and cultures) is an exceptionally difficult task. Haas (1990) argues that these problems can be overcome to some extent when expert communities sharing common normative and evaluative commitments work in their respective societies to foster cross-national convergence in normative concerns, standards of evaluation, and policy approaches. Indeed, environmental ideas have been the focus of much of the literature on policy convergence and on the cross-national diffusion of policy ideas and social movement demands (Busch and Jörgens 2005; McAdam and Rucht 1993).

Multilevel Linkages
One of the distinctive features of sustainability as a political problem is the mismatch between the geographic scope of environmental problems and the spatial jurisdiction of the institutions responsible for their management. Research on multilevel governance is motivated to a significant degree by a recognition that environmental problems require sustained institutional responses operating at multiple geographic scales (Ostrom 1998; Young 2002). The challenge of coordinating political activity across levels of governance has likewise animated political science since its founding. The salience of this issue is apparent in debates among eighteenth-century political theorists concerning representative versus direct democracy (Montesquieu [1777] 1989; Madison [1787] 2003), in the considerable attention devoted to interest aggregation in the literature on comparative political systems (Kitschelt 2000), in research on the reciprocal influence of domestic and international political structures (Gourevitch 1978; Putnam 1988), and in the pivotal role of scale and group size in theories of collective action (Olson 1968).

Looking across the domestic-international divide, a primary question in environmental politics research concerns the impact of international institutions on domestic interests, ideas, and institutions and how domestic political forces mediate these influences (O'Neill, Balsiger, and VanDeveer 2004; DeSombre 2006; Cass 2006; O'Neill 2000; Schreurs 2002). The same forces shape international institutions themselves, which may be "greened" over time by lead states and NGOs (Werksman 1996; Gutner 2002). This has been an especially active area of research in the European context, where states are increasingly integrated politically, socially, and economically and participate in comparatively high numbers of multilateral institutions. This literature examines the extent to which domestic environmental policy and politics are affected by European integration and the mechanisms underlying this "Europeanization" (described by Andanova and VanDeveer, chapter 11, this volume). Even without an explicit agenda of political integration, extensive economic integration still substantially shapes environmental politics and policies among integrated countries (Selin and VanDeveer 2006). Research on the interplay of domestic and international politics in regional environmental initiatives has also been carried out in North America (Selin and VanDeveer 2009; Le Prestre and Stoett 2006; Allison 1999), Asia (Lebel, Garden, and Imamura 2005; Takahashi 2000), Africa (Wolmer 2003), and Latin America (Mumme and Duncan 1997–1998).

Foreign policy making is another action arena where the interplay between domestic and international politics is clearly visible (Putnam 1988). Although foreign environmental policy making frequently receives coverage in research on environmental diplomacy, most of the work produced to date has only a passing engagement with the complexities of domestic politics. Important exceptions include Paul Harris's edited volumes (2000; 2005; 2007), which catalog an impressive array of national experiences as well as analytic approaches offered by authors such as Barkdull and Harris (2002), DeSombre (2000), and Raustiala (1997a).

The challenges of multilevel governance are at least as great in moving across levels of social organization within nations (see Selin and VanDeveer, chapter 13, this volume). In the United States, for example, cities and states have responded to national-level intransigence on climate policy by adopting numerous and diverse policies reflecting local contexts. The growing ambitiousness of these initiatives has, in turn, increased pressure on the US government to enact new policies (Selin and VanDeveer 2009). Research on "environmental federalism" of this sort examines the impact of federalist structures on environmental performance (Wälti 2004), the relationship between the locus of regulatory authority and the relative influence of environmental and industrial interests (Revesz 2001), cross-national comparisons of federalist institutions (Kelemen 2004; Gillroy 1999), and the influence of federalist structures on social movement strategy and organization (Dryzek et al. 2003; Pralle 2006).

A recurring question for those studying local environmental politics is how local outcomes are shaped by larger-scale political institutions and processes. Within the literature on common-pool resources, investigators have explored how the effectiveness of local governance of natural resources varies with group size (Agrawal 2000) and the impact of national and international forces on the viability of local institutions (Berkes 2002). The field of political ecology, which analyzes local environmental politics from the perspective of anthropology and rural sociology, has from the outset aspired to explain local outcomes in terms of multilevel governance— looking upward and backward, in Blaikie's (1985) terms, to assess how political and economic structures and historical influences (notably the legacy of colonialism) shape local patterns of conflict surrounding the use of natural resources (Gadgil and Guha 1985; Bryant 1992). In practice, however, political ecology research too often combines careful assessments of local politics with forgone conclusions about the nature of state institutions and the motivations of policy elites, which are allowed little variance from the scripted roles inherited from Marxist political economy. Closer collaboration between political ecology and comparative political science could imbue the former with more nuanced conceptions of policy processes and state behavior while prodding CEP researchers to pay close attention to local configurations of power politics, including patterns of social privilege and institutionalized forms of exclusion and control, thereby avoiding the temptation to reduce the study of environmental politics to an apolitical analysis of management options.

Studies of multilevel governance are rendered all the more timely, and all the more difficult, by the rapid and profound changes taking place in the distribution of power and resources among levels of political authority. Public concern over the effects of economic globalization on environmental and labor standards has fed a growing stream of research on the interactions between trade and environmental issues (Sampson 2005; Vogel 1995), including assessments of the environmental impact of free trade agreements (Ederington 2007; Audley 1997) and of the international neoliberal agenda more broadly (Liverman and Vilas 2006). While regulatory responsibilities are being redirecting "upward" by globalization, regional integration in Europe, and the proliferation of international environmental regimes, another major trend—decentralization—is dramatically changing the landscape of environmental politics, particularly in developing countries. According to Ribot (2002), in recent years, no fewer than sixty developing countries have undertaken efforts to decentralize control over important aspects of environmental policy and natural resource management, transferring unprecedented levels of authority to provinces, townships, and local user groups (see also Andersson, Gibson, and Lehoucq 2006; Kingston 2001; Thorburn 2002). These simultaneous shifts in the locus of authority for environmental decision making have required social actors to adopt strategies for multilevel advocacy, including cross-border collaboration among domestic NGOs (Hochstetler 2002; Keck and Sikkink 1998), bridging strategies by policy reformers immersed in both international and domestic processes (Steinberg 2003), and the mobilization of local social capital to influence decision processes at higher levels (Birner and Wittmer 2003).

The Challenge Ahead

As this preliminary survey makes clear, the literature on comparative environmental politics is vast. Why has such a large and important literature not taken shape as a self-identified field of research? How might this change? As argued in chapter 1, the answer lies in making greater use of theoretical approaches that facilitate systematic cross-national comparison, and comparative politics offers many promising possibilities for doing so. To illustrate the benefits of this strategy, the contributors to this book describe a number of distinct approaches for bridging islands of research across the archipelagos of comparative politics and comparative environmental politics. Each author has been charged with two tasks. First, authors were asked to provide a broad overview of an area of CEP research, drawing together and distilling lessons from the existing—if disparate—comparative work in a particular area of environmental politics and policy studies. Second, contributors were asked to demonstrate how our understanding of these issues can be enhanced by drawing on identifiable literatures in comparative politics. The result is a diverse collection of analytic approaches unified by the goal of advancing a cumulative research agenda in comparative environmental politics. In the concluding chapter, we offer a more systematic examination of why CEP research has developed in isolation from comparative politics, emphasizing the long-standing tension between theoretical and practice-oriented research. We argue that a reconciliation between theoretical rigor and social relevance not only is feasible, but also carries substantial benefits for theory and practice alike. The following chapters seek to demonstrate the advantages of this approach.

Notes

1. See http://www.hmc.edu/CEP.

2. For a more complete introduction to the field and the historical evolution of its many intellectual strands see Lichbach and Zuckerman 1997; Rogowski 1993; Chilcote 1981; and Bill and Hardgrave 1981.

3. This troika of approaches has been alternately described as rationality, culture, and structure (Lichbach and Zuckerman 1997), and interests, identities, and institutions (Kopstein and Lichbach 2005).

4. Many additional examples of the research discussed in this section can be found in the CEP bibliographic database at http://www.hmc.edu/CEP.

5. On the distinction between studies of political processes and outcomes, see Press (1998).

References

Adeola, Francis O. 2000. Cross-National Environmental Injustice and Human Rights Issues. *American Behavioral Scientist* 43 (4): 686–706.

Agrawal, Arun. 1995. Dismantling the Divide between Indigenous and Scientific Knowledge. *Development and Change* 26 (3): 413–439.

Agrawal, Arun. 2000. Small Is Beautiful, but Is Larger Better? Forest-Management Institutions in the Kumaon Himalaya, India. In *People and Forests: Communities, Institutions, and Governance*, ed. Clark C. Gibson, Margaret A. McKean, and Elinor Ostrom, 57–85. Cambridge, Mass.: MIT Press.

Agrawal, Arun, and Elinor Ostrom. 2001. Collective Action, Property Rights, and Decentralization in Resource Use in India and Nepal. *Politics & Society* 29 (4): 485–514.

Aguilar, Susana. 1993. Corporatist and Statist Designs in Environmental Policy: The Contrasting Roles of Germany and Spain in the European Community Scenario. *Environmental Politics* 2 (2): 223–247.

Allison, Juliann Emmons. 1999. Fortuitous Consequence: The Domestic Politics of the 1991 Canada–United States Agreement on Air Quality. *Policy Studies Journal* 27 (2): 347–359.

Almond, Gabriel A., and Sidney Verba. 1963. *The Civic Culture: Political Attitudes and Democracy in Five Nations*. Princeton: Princeton University Press.

Anderson, Benedict R. 1991. *Imagined Communities: Reflections on the Origin and Spread of Nationalism*. New York: Verso.

Andersson, Krister P., Clark C. Gibson, and Fabrice Lehoucq. 2006. Municipal Politics and Forest Governance: Comparative Analysis of Decentralization in Bolivia and Guatemala. *World Development* 34 (3): 576–595.

Andonova, Liliana B. 2004. *Transnational Politics of the Environment: The European Union and Environmental Policy in Central and Eastern Europe*. Cambridge, Mass.: MIT Press.

Ascher, William. 1999. *Why Governments Waste Natural Resources: Policy Failures in Developing Countries*. Baltimore: Johns Hopkins University Press.

Audley, John J. 1997. *Green Politics and Global Trade: NAFTA and the Future of Environmental Politics*. Washington, D.C.: Georgetown University Press.

Auer, Matthew. 2001. Energy and Environmental Politics in Post-Corporatist Mexico. *Policy Studies Journal* 29 (3): 437–455.

Auer, Matthew, ed. 2005. *Restoring Cursed Earth: Appraising Environmental Policy Reforms in Eastern Europe and Russia*. Lanham, Md.: Rowman & Littlefield.

Axelrod, Robert. 1997. The Dissemination of Culture: A Model with Local Convergence and Global Polarization. *Journal of Conflict Resolution* 41:203–226.

Balsiger, Joerg. 2007. Uphill Struggle: The Politics of Sustainable Mountain Development in the Swiss Alps and California's Sierra Nevada. PhD diss., Department of Environmental Science, Policy and Management, University of California at Berkeley.

Barkdull, John, and Paul Harris. 2002. Environmental Change and Foreign Policy: A Survey of Theory. *Global Environmental Politics* 2 (2): 63–91.

Bates, Robert H. 1981. *Markets and States in Tropical Africa: The Political Basis of Agricultural Policies*. Berkeley: University of California Press.

Bates, Robert, Avner Greif, Margaret Levi, Jean-Laurent Rosenthal, and Barry Weingast, eds. 1998. *Analytic Narratives*. Princeton: Princeton University Press.

Baumgartner, Frank, and Bryan D. Jones. 2009. *Agendas and Instability in American Politics*. 2nd ed. Chicago: University of Chicago Press.

Bednar, Jenna, and Scott Page. 2007. Can Game(s) Theory Explain Culture? The Emergence of Cultural Behavior within Multiple Games. *Rationality and Society* 19 (1): 65–97.

Bennett, Vivienne, Sonia Davila-Poblete, and Maria Nieves Rico. 2005. *Opposing Currents: The Politics of Water and Gender in Latin America*. Pittsburgh: University of Pittsburgh Press.

Benoit, Kenneth. 2004. Models of Electoral System Change. *Electoral Studies* 23 (3): 363–384.

Berkes, F. 2002. Cross-Scale Institutional Linkages: Perspectives from the Bottom Up. In *The Drama of the Commons*, ed. Elinor T. Ostrom, Thomas Dietz, Nives Dolsak, Paul C. Stern, Susan Stonich, and Elke U. Weber, 293–321. Washington, D.C.: National Academy Press.

Betsill, Michele M., and Elisabeth Corell. 2006. NGO Influence in International Environmental Negotiations: A Framework for Analysis. *Global Environmental Politics* 1 (4): 65–85.

Bill, James A., and Robert L. Hardgrave Jr. 1981. *Comparative Politics*. Washington, D.C.: University Press of America.

Birner, Regina, and Heidi Wittmer. 2003. Using Social Capital to Create Political Capital: How Do Local Communities Gain Political Influence? A Theoretical Approach and Empirical

Evidence from Thailand. In *The Commons in the New Millennium: Challenges and Adaptation*, ed. Nives Dolšak and Elinor Ostrom, 291–334. Cambridge, Mass.: MIT Press.

Blackman, Allen. 2008. Can Voluntary Environmental Regulation Work in Developing Countries? Lessons from Case Studies. *Policy Studies Journal* 46 (4): 119–141.

Blaikie, Piers. 1985. *The Political Economy of Soil Erosion in Developing Countries*. New York: John Wiley & Sons, Inc.

Blyth, Mark. 2006. Great Punctuation: Prediction, Randomness, and the Evolution of Comparative Political Science. *American Political Science Review* 100:493–498.

Boix, Carles. 1999. Setting the Rules of the Game: The Choice of Electoral Systems in Advanced Democracies. *American Political Science Review* 93 (3): 609–624.

Börzel, Tanja A. 2002. *States and Regions in the European Union: Institutional Adaptation in Germany and Spain*. New York: Cambridge University Press.

Botcheva, Liliana. 1996. Focus and Effectiveness of Environmental Activism in Eastern Europe: A Comparative Study of Environmental Movements in Bulgaria, Hungary, Slovakia, and Romania. *Journal of Environment & Development* 5 (3): 292–308.

Brady, Henry E., and David Collier, eds. 2004. *Rethinking Social Inquiry: Diverse Tools, Shared Standards*. Lanham, Md.: Rowman and Littlefield.

Brechin, Steven R. 1999. Objective Problems, Subjective Values, and Global Environmentalism: Evaluating the Postmaterialist Argument and Challenging a New Explanation. *Social Science Quarterly* 80 (4): 793–809.

Bryant, Richard. 1992. Political Ecology: An Emerging Research Agenda in Third World Studies. *Political Geography* 11 (1): 12–36.

Bueno de Mesquita, Bruce, and Hilton Root, eds. 2000. *Governing for Prosperity*. New Haven: Yale University Press.

Busch, Per-Olof, and Helge Jörgens. 2005. The International Sources of Policy Convergence: Explaining the Spread of Environmental Policy Innovations. *Journal of European Public Policy* 12 (5): 860–884.

Cardoso, Fernando Henrique, and Enzo Faletto. 1979. *Dependency and Development in Latin America*. Trans. Mattingly Urquidi. Berkeley: University of California Press.

Carmin, JoAnn, and Elizabeth Bast. 2009. Cross-Movement Activism: A Cognitive Perspective on the Global Justice Activities of US Environmental NGOs. *Environmental Politics* 18 (3): 351–370.

Carmin, JoAnn, and Adam Fagan. 2010. Environmental Mobilisation and Organisations in Post-Socialist Europe and the Former Soviet Union. *Environmental Politics* 19 (5): 689–707.

Carmin, JoAnn, and Stacy D. VanDeveer, eds. 2005. *EU Enlargement and the Environment: Institutional Change and Environmental Policy in Central and Eastern Europe*. New York: Routledge.

Carraro, Carlo, and François Lévêque, eds. 1999. *Voluntary Approaches in Environmental Policy*. Boston: Kluwer Academic Publishers.

Carruthers, David. 1996. Indigenous Ecology and the Politics of Linkage in Mexican Social Movements. *Third World Quarterly* 17 (5): 1007–1028.

Carruthers, David. 2001. Environmental Politics in Chile: Legacies of Dictatorship and Democracy. *Third World Quarterly* 22 (3): 343–358.

Cashore, Benjamin, Graeme Auld, and Deanna Newsom. 2004. *Governing through Markets: Forest Certification and the Emergence of Non-state Authority*. New Haven: Yale University Press.

Cass, Loren R. 2006. *The Failures of American and European Climate Policy: International Norms, Domestic Politics, and Unachievable Commitments*. Albany: SUNY Press.

Chilcote, Ronald. 1981. *Theories of Comparative Politics*. Boulder: Westview Press.

Christen, Catherine, Selene Herculano, Kathryn Hochstetler, Renae Prell, Marie Price, and J. Timmons Roberts. 1998. Latin American Environmentalism: Comparative Views. *Studies in Comparative International Development* 33 (2): 58–87.

Clark, Ann Marie, Elisabeth J. Friedman, and Kathryn Hochstetler. 1998. The Sovereign Limits of Global Civil Society: A Comparison of NGO Participation in UN World Conferences on the Environment, Human Rights, and Women. *World Politics* 51 (1): 1–35.

Collier, Ruth Berins, and David Collier. 1979. Inducements versus Constraints: Disaggregating "Corporatism." *American Political Science Review* 73 (4): 967–986.

Cooper, Phillip J., and Claudia Maria Vargas. 2004. *Implementing Sustainable Development: From Global Policy to Local Action*. Lanham, Md.: Rowman and Littlefield.

Cox, Gary W. 1997. *Making Votes Count: Strategic Coordination in the World's Electoral Systems*. New York: Cambridge University Press.

Crepaz, Markus M. L. 1995. Explaining National Variations of Air Pollution Levels: Political Institutions and Their Impact on Environmental Policy-Making. *Environmental Politics* 4 (3): 391–414.

Dahl, Robert Alan. 1961. *Who Governs? Democracy and Power in an American City*. New Haven: Yale University Press.

Dalton, Russell J. 1994. *The Green Rainbow: Environmental Groups in Western Europe*. New Haven: Yale University Press.

Dalton, Russell J., Steve Recchia, and Robert Rohrschneider. 2003. The Environmental Movement and the Modes of Political Action. *Comparative Political Studies* 36 (7): 743–771.

Dawson, Jane I. 1996. *Eco-Nationalism: Anti-nuclear Activism and National Identity in Russia, Lithuania and Ukraine*. Durham: Duke University Press.

de Bruijn, Theo, and Vicky Norberg-Bohm, eds. 2005. *Industrial Transformation: Environmental Policy Innovation in the United States and Europe*. Cambridge, Mass.: MIT Press.

della Porta, Donatella, and Dieter Rucht. 2002. The Dynamics of Environmental Campaigns. *Mobilization: An International Quarterly* 7 (1): 1–14.

DeSombre, Elizabeth R. 2000. *Domestic Sources of International Environmental Policy: Industry, Environmentalists, and US Power*. Cambridge, Mass.: MIT Press.

DeSombre, Elizabeth R. 2006. *Flagging Standards: Globalization and Environmental, Safety and Labor Regulations at Sea*. Cambridge, Mass.: MIT Press.

Dewan, Torun, and Kenneth A. Shepsle. 2008. Recent Economic Perspectives on Political Economy, Part I. *British Journal of Political Science* 38:363–382.

Díez, Jordi. 2006. *Political Change and Environmental Policymaking in Mexico*. New York: Routledge.

Dobson, Andrew, and Derek Bell, eds. 2006. *Environmental Citizenship*. Cambridge, Mass.: MIT Press.

Douglas, Mary. 1986. *How Institutions Think*. New York: Syracuse University Press.

Dove, Michael. 2006. Indigenous People and Environmental Politics. *Annual Review of Anthropology* 35:191–208.

Dryzek, John S., David Downes, Christian Hunold, and David Schlosberg. 2003. *Green States and Social Movements: Environmentalism in the United States, United Kingdom, Germany, and Norway*. New York: Oxford University Press.

Duch, Raymond M., and Randy Stevenson. 2006. Assessing the Magnitude of the Economic Vote over Time and Across Nations. *Electoral Studies* 25 (3): 528–547.

Duffy, Rosaleen. 2000. Shadow Players: Ecotourism Development, Corruption and State Politics in Belize. *Third World Quarterly* 21 (3): 549–566.

Dunlap, Riley E., Kent D. Van Liere, Angela G. Mertig, and Robert Emmet Jones. 2000. New Trends in Measuring Environmental Attitudes: Measuring Endorsement of the New Ecological Paradigm: A Revised NEP Scale. *Journal of Social Issues* 56 (3): 425–442.

Durant, Robert F., Daniel J. Fiorino, and Rosemary O'Leary. 2004. *Environmental Governance Reconsidered: Challenges, Choices and Opportunities*. Cambridge, Mass.: MIT Press.

Eaton, Kent. 2008. Federalism in Europe and Latin America: Conceptualization, Causes, and Consequences. *World Politics* 60 (4): 665–698.

Eckley, Noelle, and Henrik Selin. 2004. All Talk, Little Action: Precaution and European Chemicals Regulation. *Journal of European Public Policy* 11 (1): 78–105.

Economy, Elizabeth. 2004. *The River Runs Black: The Environmental Challenge to China's Future*. Ithaca: Cornell University Press.

Ederington, Josh. 2007. NAFTA and the Pollution Haven Hypothesis. *Policy Studies Journal* 35 (2): 239–244.

Evans, Peter. 1979. *Dependent Development: The Alliance of Multinational, State, and Local Capital in Brazil*. New York: Cambridge University Press.

Farrell, Alex E., and Jill Jäger, eds. 2006. *Assessments of Regional and Global Environmental Risks: Designing Processes for Effective Use of Science in Decisionmaking*. Washington, D.C.: Resources for the Future Press.

Farrell, Alex E., Jill Jäger, and Stacy D. VanDeveer. 2001. Environmental Assessment: Four Under-Appreciated Elements of Design. *Global Environmental Change* 11 (4): 311–333.

Feaver, Peter D. 1999. Civil-Military Relations. *Annual Review of Political Science* 2:211–241.

Finnemore, Martha, and Kathryn Sikkink. 2001. Taking Stock: The Constructivist Research Program in International Relations and Comparative Politics. *Annual Review of Political Science* 4:391–416.

Fox, Jonathan A., and L. David Brown, eds. 1998. *The Struggle for Accountability: The World Bank, NGOs, and Grassroots Movements*. Cambridge, Mass.: MIT Press.

Gadgil, Madhav, and Ramachandra Guha. 1985. *Ecology and Equity: The Use and Abuse of Nature in Contemporary India*. New York: Routledge.

Gamson, William A., and Andre Modigliani. 1989. Media Discourse and Public Opinion on Nuclear Power: A Constructionist Approach. *American Journal of Sociology* 95 (1): 1–37.

Garcia-Johnson, Ronnie. 2000. *Exporting Environmentalism: US Multinational Chemical Corporations in Brazil and Mexico*. Cambridge, Mass.: MIT Press.

Geddes, Barbara. 1999. What Do We Know about Democratization after 20 Years? *Annual Review of Political Science* 2:115–144.

George, Alexander L., and Andrew Bennett. 2005. *Case Studies and Theory Development in the Social Sciences*. Cambridge, Mass.: MIT Press.

Gerring, John. 2007. *Case Study Research: Principles and Practices*. Cambridge: Cambridge University Press.

Gibson, Clark C. 1999. Bureaucrats and the Environment in Africa. *Comparative Politics* 31 (3): 273–293.

Gillroy, John Martin. 1999. American and Canadian Environmental Federalism: A Game-Theoretic Analysis. *Policy Studies Journal* 27 (2): 360–388.

Goldstein, Judith. 1993. *Ideas, Interests, and American Trade Policy*. Ithaca: Cornell University Press.

Goodin, Robert E., and Charles Tilly, eds. 2006. *The Oxford Handbook of Contextual Political Analysis*. New York: Oxford University Press.

Gottlieb, Robert. 2005. *Forcing the Spring: The Transformation of the American Environmental Movement*. Washington, D.C.: Island Press.

Gourevitch, Peter. 1978. The Second Image Reversed: The International Sources of Domestic Politics. *International Organization* 32 (4): 881–912.

Grant, Wyn, Duncan Matthews, and Peter Newell. 2000. *The Effectiveness of European Union Environmental Policy*. New York: St. Martin's Press.

Greif, Avner. 1994. Cultural Beliefs and the Organization of Society: A Historical and Theoretical Reflection on Collectivist and Individualist Societies. *Journal of Political Economy* 102 (5): 912–950.

Grove, Richard. 1993. Conserving Eden: The (European) East India Companies and Their Environmental Policies on St. Helena, Mauritius and in Western India, 1660–1854. *Comparative Studies in Society and History* 35 (3): 318–351.

Gutner, Tamar L. 2002. *Banking on the Environment: Multilateral Development Banks and Their Environmental Performance in Central and Eastern Europe*. Cambridge, Mass.: MIT Press.

Haas, Peter M. 1990. Obtaining International Environmental Protection through Epistemic Consensus. *Millennium: Journal of International Studies* 19 (3): 347–363.

Hall, Peter, ed. 1989. *The Political Power of Economic Ideas—Keynesianism Across Nations*. Princeton: Princeton University Press.

Hall, Peter A. 2003. Aligning Ontology and Methodology in Comparative Research. In *Comparative Historical Analysis in the Social Sciences*, ed. James Mahoney and Dietrich Rueschemeyer, 373–404. New York: Cambridge University Press.

Hall, Peter, and Rosemary Taylor. 1996. Political Science and the Three New Institutionalisms. *Political Studies* 44:936–957.

Harrington, Winston, Richard D. Morgenstern, and Thomas Sterner, eds. 2004. *Choosing Environmental Policy: Comparing Instruments and Outcomes in the United States and Europe*. Washington, D.C.: Resources for the Future Press.

Harris, Paul G. 2000. *Climate Change and American Foreign Policy*. New York: St. Martin's Press.

Harris, Paul, ed. 2005. *Confronting Environmental Change in East and Southeast Asia: Eco-Politics, Foreign Policy, and Sustainable Development*. Tokyo: UN University Press.

Harris, Paul. 2007. *Europe and Global Climate Change: Politics, Foreign Policy and Regional Cooperation*. Cheltenham: Edward Elgar.

Herbst, Jeffrey. 1990. War and the State in Africa. *International Security* 14:117–139.

Hicks, Barbara. 1996. *Environmental Politics in Poland: A Social Movement between Regime and Opposition*. New York: Columbia University Press.

Higley, John, and Michael Burton. 2006. *Elite Foundations of Liberal Democracy*. Lanham, Md.: Rowman & Littlefield.

Hochstetler, Kathryn. 2002. After the Boomerang: Environmental Movements and Politics in the La Plata River Basin. *Global Environmental Politics* 2 (4): 35–57.

Hochstetler, Kathryn, and Margaret E. Keck. 2007. *Greening Brazil: Environmental Activism in State and Society*. Durham: Duke University Press.

Hsiao, Hsin-Huang Michael, On-Kwok Lai, Hwa-Jen Liu, Francisco Magno, Laura Edles, and Alvin Y. So. 1999. Culture and Asian Styles of Environmental Movements. In *Asia's Environmental Movements: Comparative Perspectives*, ed. Yok-shiu F. Lee and Alvin Y. So, 210–229. Armonk, N.Y.: M. E. Sharpe.

Huntington, Samuel P. 1991. *The Third Wave: Democratization in the Late Twentieth Century*. Norman, Okla.: University of Oklahoma Press.

Inglehart, Ronald. 1990. *Culture Shift in Advanced Industrial Society*. Princeton: Princeton University Press.

Jänicke, Martin, and Helge Jorgens. 1998. National Environmental Policy Planning in OECD Countries: Preliminary Lessons from Cross-National Comparisons. *Environmental Politics* 7 (2): 27–54.

Jänicke, Martin, and Helmut Weidner, eds. 1997. *National Environmental Policies: A Comparative Study of Capacity-Building*. Berlin: Springer.

Jasanoff, Sheila. 1990. *The Fifth Branch: Science Advisors and Policy Makers*. Cambridge, Mass.: Harvard University Press.

Jasanoff, Sheila. 2005. *Designs on Nature: Science and Democracy in Europe and the United States*. Princeton: Princeton University Press.

Jasanoff, Sheila, and Marybeth Long Martello, eds. 2004. *Earthly Politics: Local and Global in Environmental Governance*. Cambridge, Mass.: MIT Press.

Jimenez, M. 1999. Consolidation through Institutionalization? Dilemmas of the Spanish Environmental Movement in the 1990s. *Environmental Politics* 8 (1): 149–171.

Johnson, Chalmers A. 1982. *MITI and the Japanese Miracle: The Growth of Industrial Policy, 1925–1975*. Palo Alto: Stanford University Press.

Jordan, Andrew. 2005. *Environmental Policy in the European Union*. 2nd ed. London: Earthscan.

Jordan, Andrew, Rüdiger Wurzel, and Anthony R. Zito. 2003. "New" Instruments of Environmental Governance: Patterns and Pathways of Change. *Environmental Politics* 12 (1): 1–24.

Keck, Margaret E., and Kathryn Sikkink. 1998. *Activists Beyond Borders: Advocacy Networks in International Politics*. Ithaca: Cornell University Press.

Kedar, Orit. 2005. When Moderate Voters Prefer Extreme Parties: Policy Balancing in Parliamentary Elections. *American Political Science Review* 99 (2): 185–199.

Kelemen, R. Daniel. 2004. Environmental Federalism in the United States and the European Union. In *Green Giants? Environmental Policies of the United States and the European Union*, ed. Norman J. Vig and Michael G. Faure, 113–134. Cambridge, Mass.: MIT Press.

Kelemen, R. Daniel, and David Vogel. 2010. Trading Places: The Role of the United States and the European Union in International Environmental Politics. *Comparative Political Studies* 43 (4): 427–456.

Kim, Sunhyuk. 2000. Democratization and Environmentalism: South Korea and Taiwan in Comparative Perspective. *Journal of Asian and African Studies* 35 (3): 287–302.

Kingston, Paul. 2001. Patrons, Clients and Civil Society: A Case Study of Environmental Politics in Postwar Lebanon. *Arab Studies Quarterly* 23 (1): 55–72.

Kitschelt, Herbert. 1989. *The Logics of Party Formation: Ecological Politics in Belgium and West Germany*. Ithaca: Cornell University Press.

Kitschelt, Herbert. 2000. Linkages between Citizens and Politicians in Democratic Polities. *Comparative Political Studies* 33 (6): 845–879.

Knill, Christopher. 2005. Introduction: Cross-National Policy Convergence: Concepts, Approaches and Explanatory Factors. *Journal of European Public Policy* 12 (5): 764–774.

Kopstein, Jeffrey, and Mark Lichbach, eds. 2005. *Comparative Politics: Interests, Identities, and Institutions in a Changing Global Order*. New York: Cambridge University Press.

Laitin, David D. 1998. *Identity in Formation: The Russian-Speaking Populations in the Near Abroad*. Ithaca: Cornell University Press.

Lebel, Louis, Po Garden, and Masao Imamura. 2005. The Politics of Scale, Position, and Place in the Governance of Water Resources in the Mekong Region. *Ecology and Society* 10 (2): 18. http://www.ecologyandsociety.org/vol10/iss2/art18, accessed May 26, 2011.

LeDuc, Lawrence, Richard G. Niemi, and Pippa Norris, eds. 1996. *Comparing Democracies: Elections and Voting in Global Perspective*. Thousand Oaks, Calif.: Sage Publications.

Lee, Yok-shiu F., and Alvin Y. So, eds. 1999. *Asia's Environmental Movements: Comparative Perspectives*. Armonk, N.Y.: M. E. Sharpe.

Le Prestre, Phillipe, and Peter Stoett, eds. 2006. *Bilateral Ecopolitics: Continuity and Change in Canadian-American Environmental Relations*. Aldershot: Ashgate.

Lichbach, Mark Irving, and Alan S. Zuckerman. 1997. *Comparative Politics: Rationality, Culture, and Structure*. New York: Cambridge University Press.

Linz, Juan J. 2000. *Totalitarian and Authoritarian Regimes*. Boulder: Lynne Rienner Publishers.

Lipschutz, Ronnie D. 1992. Reconstructing World Politics: The Emergence of Global Civil Society. *Millennium: Journal of International Studies* 21 (3): 389–420.

Liverman, Diana M., and Silvina Vilas. 2006. Neoliberalism and the Environment in Latin America. *Annual Review of Environment and Resources* 31:327–363.

Lupu, Noam, and Susan Stokes. 2010. Democracy, Interrupted: Regime Change and Partisanship in Twentieth-Century Argentina. *Electoral Studies* 29 (1): 91–104.

Madison, James. [1787] 2003. The Federalist No. 10. In *The Federalist with Letters of Brutus*, ed. Terence Ball, 40–44. New York: Cambridge University Press.

Mahoney, James. 2007. Qualitative Methodology and Comparative Politics. *Comparative Political Studies* 40 (2): 122–144.

Mainwaring, Matthew S. 1997. Juan Linz, Presidentialism, and Democracy: A Critical Appraisal. *Comparative Politics* 29 (4): 449–471.

Maniates, Michael. 2002. Individualization: Plant a Tree, Buy a Bike, Save the World? In *Confronting Consumption*, ed. Thomas Princen, Michael F. Maniates, and Ken Conca, 43–66. Cambridge, Mass.: MIT Press.

March, James G., and Johan P. Olsen. 1966. Institutional Perspectives on Political Institutions. *Governance* 9 (3): 247–264.

March, James G., and Johan P. Olsen. 1989. *Rediscovering Institutions*. New York: Free Press.

Martello, Marybeth Long. 2001. A Paradox of Virtue?: Other Knowledges and Environment-Development Politics. *Global Environmental Politics* 1 (3): 114–141.

McAdam, Doug, and Dieter Rucht. 1993. The Cross-National Diffusion of Movement Ideas. *Annals of the American Academy of Political and Social Science* 528:56–74.

McAdam, Doug, John D. McCarthy, and Mayer N. Zald, eds. 1996. *Comparative Perspectives on Social Movements: Political Opportunities, Mobilizing Structures, and Cultural Framings*. New York: Cambridge University Press.

Migdal, Joel S. 1988. *Strong Societies and Weak States: State-Society Relations and State Capabilities in the Third World*. Princeton: Princeton University Press.

Mitchell, Ronald B., William C. Clark, David W. Cash, and Nancy Dickson, eds. 2006. *Global Environmental Assessments: Information and Influence*. Cambridge, Mass.: MIT Press.

Molina, Oscar, and Martin Rhodes. 2002. Corporatism: The Past, Present, and Future of a Concept. *Annual Review of Political Science* 5:305–331.

Montesquieu, Charles de Secondat, baron de. [1777] 1989. *The Spirit of Laws*, ed. Anne M. Cohler, Basia C. Miller, and Harold S. Stone. Cambridge, UK: Cambridge University Press.

Muller, Edward N., and Mitchell A. Seligson. 1994. Civic Culture and Democracy: The Question of Causal Relationships. *American Political Science Review* 88 (3): 635–652.

Mumme, Stephen P., and Pamela Duncan. 1997–1998. The Commission for Environmental Cooperation and Environmental Management in the Americas. *Journal of Interamerican Studies and World Affairs* 39 (4): 41–62.

Munck, Gerardo L. 1998. Canons of Research Design in Qualitative Analysis. *Studies in Comparative International Development* 33:18–45.

Munck, Gerardo L. 2001. Game Theory and Comparative Politics: New Perspectives and Old Concerns. *World Politics* 53:173–204.

Nash, Roderick. 1967. *Wilderness and the American Mind*. 3rd ed. New Haven: Yale University Press.

Norris, Pippa, Stefaan Walgrave, and Peter Van Aelst. 2005. Who Demonstrates? Antistate Rebels, Conventional Participants, or Everyone? *Comparative Politics* 37 (2): 189–205.

North, Douglass. 1981. *Structure and Change in Economic History*. New York: W. W. Norton.

Obach, Brian K. 2002. Labor-Environmental Relations: An Analysis of the Relationship between Labor Unions and Environmentalists. *Social Science Quarterly* 83 (1): 82–100.

Olson, Mancur. 1968. *The Logic of Collective Action: Public Goods and the Theory of Groups*. New York: Schocken Books.

Olson, Mancur. 2000. *Power and Prosperity: Outgrowing Communist and Capitalist Dictatorships*. New York: Basic Books.

O'Neill, Kate. 2000. *Waste Trading among Rich Nations: Building a New Theory of Environmental Regulation*. Cambridge, Mass.: MIT Press.

O'Neill, Kate, Joerg Balsiger, and Stacy D. VanDeveer. 2004. Actors, Norms and Impact: Recent International Cooperation Theory and the Influence of the Agent-Structure Debate. *Annual Review of Political Science* 7 (1): 149–175.

O'Neill, Kate, and Stacy D. VanDeveer. 2005. Transnational Environmental Activism after Seattle: Between Emancipation and Arrogance. In *Charting Transnational Democracy: Beyond Global Arrogance*, ed. Janie Leatherman and Julie Webber, 195–220. New York: Palgrave MacMillan.

Oreg, Shaul, and Tally Katz-Gerro. 2006. Predicting Proenvironmental Behavior Cross-Nationally: Values, the Theory of Planned Behavior, and Value-Belief-Norm Theory. *Environment and Behavior* 38 (4): 462–483.

Ostrom, Elinor. 1990. *Governing the Commons: The Evolution of Institutions for Collective Action*. New York: Cambridge University Press.

Ostrom, Elinor. 1998. Scales, Polycentricity, and Incentives: Designing Complexity to Govern Complexity. In *Protection of Global Biodiversity: Converging Strategies*, ed. Lakshman D. Guruswamy and Jeffrey A. McNeely, 149–167. Durham: Duke University Press.

Peluso, Nancy Lee. 1992. *Rich Forests, Poor People: Resource Control and Resistance in Java*. Berkeley: University of California Press.

Pierce, John C., Taketsugu Tsurutani, Nicholas P. Lovrich, and Takematsu Abe. 1986. Vanguards and Rearguards and Environmental Politics: A Comparison of Activists in Japan and the United States. *Comparative Political Studies* 18 (4): 419–447.

Powell, G. Bingham Jr. 1986. American Voter Turnout in Comparative Perspective. *American Political Science Review* 80 (1): 17–43.

Powell, G. Bingham, and Guy Whitten. 1993. A Cross-National Analysis of Economic Voting: Taking Account of the Political Context. *American Journal of Political Science* 37 (2): 391–414.

Pralle, Sarah B. 2006. Timing and Sequence in Agenda-Setting and Policy Change: A Comparative Study of Lawn Care Pesticide Politics in Canada and the US. *Journal of European Public Policy* 13 (7): 987–1005.

Press, Daniel. 1998. Local Environmental Policy Capacity: A Framework for Research. *Natural Resources Journal* 38:29–52.

Putnam, Robert. 1971. Studying Elite Political Culture: The Case of "Ideology." *American Political Science Review* 65 (3): 651–681.

Putnam, Robert D. 1988. Diplomacy and Domestic Politics: The Logic of Two-Level Games. *International Organization* 42 (3): 427–460.

Putnam, Robert D. 1993. *Making Democracy Work: Civic Traditions in Modern Italy*. Princeton: Princeton University Press.

Raustiala, Kal. 1997a. Domestic Institutions and International Regulatory Cooperation. *World Politics* 49 (4): 482–509.

Raustiala, Kal. 1997b. States, NGOs, and International Environmental Institutions. *International Studies Quarterly* 41 (4): 719–740.

Revesz, Richard L. 2001. Federalism and Environmental Regulation: A Public Choice Analysis. *Harvard Law Review* 115 (2): 553–641.

Ribot, Jesse C. 2002. *Democratic Decentralization of Natural Resources: Institutionalizing Popular Participation*. Washington, D.C.: World Resources Institute.

Rochon, Thomas. 1998. *Culture Moves: Ideas, Activism, and Changing Values*. Princeton: Princeton University Press.

Rochon, Thomas R., and Daniel A. Mazmanian. 1993. Social Movements and the Policy Process. *Annals of the American Academy of Political and Social Science* 528: 75–87.

Rodrigues, Maria Guadalupe Moog. 2004. *Global Environmentalism and Local Politics: Transnational Advocacy Networks in Brazil, Ecuador and India*. Albany: SUNY Press.

Rogowski, Ronald. 1993. Comparative Politics. In *Political Science: The State of the Discipline II*, ed. Ada W. Finifter, 431–450. Washington, D.C.: American Political Science Association.

Rogowski, Ronald. 1995. The Role of Theory and Anomaly in Social-Scientific Inference. *American Political Science Review* 89:467–470.

Rootes, Christopher A. 1999. The Transformation of Environmental Activism: Activists, Organizations and Policy-Making. *Innovation: The European Journal of Social Sciences* 12 (2): 155–173.

Rose-Ackerman, Susan. 1995. *Controlling Environmental Policy: The Limits of Public Law in Germany and the United States*. New Haven: Yale University Press.

Rucht, Dieter. 1995. Ecological Protest as Calculated Law-Breaking: Greenpeace and Earth First! in Comparative Perspective. In *Green Politics Three*, ed. Wolfgang Rüdig, 66–89. Edinburgh: Edinburgh University Press.

Rueschemeyer, Dietrich. 2003. Can One or a Few Cases Yield Theoretical Gains? In *Comparative Historical Analysis in the Social Sciences*, ed. James Mahoney and Dietrich Rueschemeyer, 305–336. New York: Cambridge University Press.

Rydin, Yvonne, and Nancy Holman. 2004. Re-evaluating the Contribution of Social Capital in Achieving Sustainable Development. *Local Environment* 9 (2): 117–133.

Sabatier, Paul. 1989. An Advocacy Coalition Framework of Policy Change and the Role of Policy-Oriented Learning Therein. *Policy Sciences* 21:129–168.

Sampson, Gary P. 2005. *The WTO and Sustainable Development*. Tokyo: UN University Press.

Schreurs, Miranda. 2002. *Environmental Politics in Japan, Germany, and the United States*. New York: Cambridge University Press.

Schreurs, Miranda A. 2005. Environmental Policy-Making in the Advanced Industrialized Countries: Japan, the European Union and United States of America Compared. In *Environmental Policy in Japan*, ed. Hidefumi Imura and Miranda A. Schreurs, 315–341. Northampton, Mass.: The World Bank/Edward Elgar.

Scruggs, Lyle. 2001. Is There Really a Link Between Neo-Corporatism and Environmental Performance? Updated Evidence and New Data for the 1980s and 1990s. *British Journal of Political Science* 31 (4): 686–692.

Scruggs, Lyle. 2003. *Sustaining Abundance: Environmental Performance in Industrial Democracies*. New York: Cambridge University Press.

Selin, Henrik, and Stacy D. VanDeveer. 2006. Raising Global Standards: Hazardous Substances and E-waste Management in the European Union. *Environment* 28 (10): 6–17.

Selin, Henrik, and Stacy D. VanDeveer, eds. 2009. *Changing Climates in North American Politics*. Cambridge, Mass.: MIT Press.

Shepsle, Kenneth A. 1989. Studying Institutions: Some Lessons from the Rational Choice Approach. *Journal of Theoretical Politics* 1 (2): 131–147.

Sikkink, Kathryn. 1991. *Ideas and Institutions: Developmentalism in Brazil and Argentina*. Ithaca: Cornell University Press.

Skocpol, Theda. 1979. *States and Social Revolutions: A Comparative Analysis of France, Russia, and China*. New York: Cambridge University Press.

Skocpol, Theda. 1984. Emerging Agendas and Recurrent Strategies in Historical Sociology. In *Vision and Method in Historical Sociology*, ed. Theda Skocpol, 356–391. New York: Cambridge University Press.

Social Learning Group. 2001. *Learning to Manage Global Environmental Risks: A Comparative History of Social Responses to Climate Change, Ozone Depletion and Acid Rain*. Volumes 1 and 2. Cambridge, Mass.: MIT Press.

Staniland, Paul. 2010. Cities on Fire: Social Mobilization, State Policy, and Urban Insurgency. *Comparative Political Studies* 43 (12): 1623–1649.

Steinberg, Paul F. 2001. *Environmental Leadership in Developing Countries: Transnational Relations and Biodiversity Policy in Costa Rica and Bolivia*. Cambridge, Mass.: MIT Press.

Steinberg, Paul F. 2003. Understanding Policy Change in Developing Countries: The Spheres of Influence Framework. *Global Environmental Politics* 3 (1): 11–32.

Steinberg, Paul F. 2005. From Public Concern to Policy Effectiveness: Civic Conservation in Developing Countries. *Journal of International Wildlife Law and Policy* 8:341–365.

Stepan, Alfred, ed. 1973. *Authoritarian Brazil: Origins, Policies, and Future*. New Haven: Yale University Press.

Stepan, Alfred. 1988. *Rethinking Military Politics: Brazil and the Southern Cone*. Princeton: Princeton University Press.

Stepan, Alfred, and Cindy Skach. 1993. Constitutional Frameworks and Democratic Consolidation: Presidentialism versus Parliamentarism. *World Politics* 46:1–22.

Takahashi, Wakana. 2000. Formation of an East Asian Regime for Acid Rain Control: The Perspective of Comparative Regionalism. *International Review for Environmental Strategies* 1 (1): 97–117.

Tang, Ching-Ping, and Shui-Yan Tang. 2000. Democratizing Bureaucracy: The Political Economy of Environmental Impact Assessment and Air Pollution Prevention Fees in Taiwan. *Comparative Politics* 33 (1): 81–99.

Tarrow, Sidney. 2005. *The New Transnational Activism*. Ithaca: Cornell University Press.

Taylor, Dorceta E. 2000. The Rise of the Environmental Justice Paradigm: Injustice Framing and the Social Construction of Environmental Discourses. *American Behavioral Scientist* 43 (4): 508–580.

Thelen, Kathleen, and Sven Steinmo. 1992. *Historical Institutionalism in Comparative Analysis*. New York: Cambridge University Press.

Thomas, Craig W. 2003. *Bureaucratic Landscapes: Interagency Cooperation and the Preservation of Biodiversity*. Cambridge, Mass.: MIT Press.

Thorburn, Craig. 2002. Regime Change—Prospects for Community-Based Resource Management in Post–New Order Indonesia. *Society & Natural Resources* 15:617–628.

Tsai, Lily L. 2007. Solidarity Groups, Informal Accountability, and Local Public Goods Provision in Rural China. *American Political Science Review* 101 (2): 355–372.

VanDeveer, Stacy D., and Ambuj Sagar. 2005. Capacity Development for the Environment: Broadening the Focus. *Global Environmental Politics* 5 (3): 14–22.

Verweij, Marco. 2000. Why Is the River Rhine Cleaner than the Great Lakes (Despite Looser Regulation)? *Law & Society Review* 34 (4): 1007–1054.

Vig, Norman J., and Michael G. Faure. 2004. *Green Giants? Environmental Policies of the United States and the European Union*. Cambridge, Mass.: MIT Press.

Vogel, David. 1995. *Trading Up: Consumer and Environmental Regulation in the Global Economy*. Cambridge, Mass.: Harvard University Press.

Wälti, Sonja. 2004. How Multilevel Structures Affect Environmental Policy in Industrialized Countries. *European Journal of Political Research* 43 (4): 599–634.

Wapner, Paul. 1995. Politics beyond the State: Environmental Activism and World Civic Politics. *World Politics* 47 (3):311–340.

Watts, Michael J. 2005. Righteous Oil? Human Rights, the Oil Complex, and Corporate Social Responsibility. *Annual Review of Environment and Resources* 30:373–407.

Weale, Albert, Geoffrey Pridham, Andrea Williams, and Martin Porter. 1996. Environmental Administration in Six European States: Secular Convergence or National Distinctiveness? *Public Administration* 74 (2): 255–274.

Weible, Christopher M., Paul A. Sabatier, and Kelly McQueen. 2009. Themes and Variations: Taking Stock of the Advocacy Coalition Framework. *Policy Studies Journal* 37 (1): 121–140.

Weinthal, Erika. 2002. *State Making and Environmental Cooperation: Linking Domestic and International Politics in Central Asia*. Cambridge, Mass.: MIT Press.

Werksman, Jacob, ed. 1996. *Greening International Institutions*. London: Earthscan.

White, T. Anderson, and C. Ford Runge. 1994. Common Property and Collective Action: Lessons from Cooperative Watershed Management in Haiti. *Economic Development and Cultural Change* 43 (1): 1–41.

Wilkening, Kenneth E. 2004. *Acid Rain Science and Politics in Japan*. Cambridge, Mass.: MIT Press.

Wolmer, William. 2003. Transboundary Conservation: The Politics of Ecological Integrity in the Great Limpopo Transfrontier Park. *Journal of Southern African Studies* 29 (1): 261–278.

Yeo, Andrew. 2010. Ideas and Institutions in Contentious Politics: Anti-US Base Movements in Ecuador and Italy. *Comparative Politics* 42 (4): 435–455.

Young, Oran R. 2002. *The Institutional Dimensions of Environmental Change: Fit, Interplay, and Scale*. Cambridge, Mass.: MIT Press.

II
Greening States and Societies

3

Greening the State?

James Meadowcroft

The constitution of the environmental domain as a distinct sphere of government activity is a comparatively recent phenomenon. It was only in the late 1960s and early 1970s that governments across the developed world moved decisively to put in place the foundations of the system of national environmental controls we know today (Janicke and Weidner 1997; Hanf and Jansen 1998). Since this takeoff phase, environmental government has continued to evolve, as the range of issues with which it is concerned has grown, its linkages with other areas of government activity have extended, and new strategies and instruments have found favor (Lafferty and Meadowcroft 2000; Durant, Fiorino, and O'Leary 2004).

This chapter explores the significance of this development within industrialized democracies.[1] The evolution of the nation-state has long been a focus of research in comparative social science, particularly among historically oriented political scientists, sociologists, and economists (Skocpol 1979; Held 1983; Pierson 1996). The "greening" of states thus provides a clear example of the central argument of this book—that we can gain a better understanding of social responses to environmental problems by availing ourselves of the concepts and subjects of comparative inquiry. The argument is divided into four parts. The first presents a brief history of environmental governance; the second discusses the genesis of the environmental state; the third considers how environmental issues relate to more established governmental concerns; and the fourth examines prospects for further greening of the state.

A Brief History of Environmental Governance

In one sense, states have always been environmental actors. Their actions have helped shape the environments within which their populations live. They regulate entitlements to exploit environmental endowments (soil, water, minerals, timber, game, and so on) through property law. And their interventions (whether directed to economic or military ends) have had significant consequences for the nonhuman natural world (Goudie 2005). We get closer to the modern notion of "environmental policy," however, when we consider governmental action to protect specific natural endowments. Such intervention goes back a long way, but grew more common in industrializing societies during the second half of the nineteenth and first half of the twentieth centuries (Dunlap 1999). But it was only with the genesis of modern "environmental consciousness" in the 1960s and the subsequent passage of framework environmental laws and national air and water pollution regulations, as well as the establishment of environmental ministries and agencies, that modern environmental policy was born.

The late 1960s and early 1970s witnessed remarkable institutional growth in the environmental domain across the Organization of Economic Cooperation and Development (OECD) states. The Swedish Environmental Protection Agency was set up in 1967 and the Swedish Environmental Advisory Council in 1968. Japan adopted its Basic Law for Environmental Pollution Control in 1967 and established its environment agency in 1971. The UK Department of Environment and the UK Royal Commission on Environmental Pollution were created in 1970. The same year saw enactment of the US National Environmental Policy Act and the birth of the US Environmental Protection Agency. In fact, within a few years, every OECD state had a national environmental agency or ministry. This was also a period of intense legislative activity. Figures show that the number of major pieces of environment-related legislation adopted across the OECD rose from an average of 0.8 per year between 1956 and 1960 to 2.0 per year between 1961 and 1965, 3.6 per year between 1965 and 1970, and 6.2 per year in the period 1971–1975 (OECD 2000).

It is convenient to split the era of modern environmental government into two periods, with the transition between them located at the end of the 1980s. The first period featured the establishment of central governmental institutions explicitly concerned with environmental management, an initial effort to bring industrial pollution in the developed countries under control, and a gradual expansion of the environmental agenda, with an associated growth in the scale and complexity of regulatory intervention. The second period has been characterized by more systematic attempts to manage long-term environmental burdens, with increased emphasis on integrating environment and economic decision making, diversifying the range of policy instruments, involving a wider range of social partners in the environmental policy process, and establishing increased international collaboration. One illustration of the shift between the first and second stages is provided by the diffusion of environmental policy instruments. For example, Tews, Busch, and Jörgens (2003) show that the takeoff for ecolabeling, national sustainable development strategies, legislation regarding access to environmental information, and carbon/energy taxes in countries of the OCED and Central and Eastern Europe began in the 1988–1990 period. From an international perspective, the shift from one period to the next coincided with the phase of rapid innovation between the publication of the Report of the World Commission on Environment and Development in 1987 (which popularized the notion of "sustainable development") and the Rio Earth Summit in 1992.[2]

The policy changes that got under way in most developed countries from the late 1980s are often presented as a series of switches: from measures focused on physical media (separate regulation of emissions to air, water, land) to integrated pollution control (considering the overall profile of the plant, firm, or industrial sector); from end-of-pipe treatment and cleanup of accumulated contamination to preventing pollution and transforming production (greening products and processes); from command-and-control regulation to market-based and negotiated approaches;[3] from the environment as the responsibility of one ministry to the integration of environment into the work of all ministries; from reliance on government initiatives to greater involvement of businesses and civil society; from nationally based regulation to international initiatives; and so on (Glasbergen 1996; Lafferty and Meadowcroft 2000). These dichotomies reflect the change in international policy idiom that occurred at that time and suggest the general direction of movement thereafter. But they can also be misleading, for although there are important contrasts between the two periods, there is also an underlying continuity. In the first place, ideas and institutions from the earlier period carried over into the second stage. The regulatory system established in the early years provided the grounding without which subsequent innovation would have been impossible. Second, problems encountered with the initial phase of policy development served to stimulate subsequent departures. Third, elements central to the later period can be found much earlier, even if they were not immediately embedded in policy initiatives (consider, e.g., the ambitious language in the documents from the Stockholm Conference on the Human Environment in 1972 and in the US National Environmental Policy Act of 1969). Fourth, changes in policy idiom from the early 1990s far outran changes in the real practice of environmental governance. Finally, such developments were uneven across the industrialized world. They were most pronounced in a number of northern European states (such as Germany, Sweden, and the Netherlands) and most weakly represented at the national level in the United States (Anderson and Liefferink 1997; Lafferty and Meadowcroft 2000; Driessen and Glasbergen 2002).

Looking at the overall pattern of change across the developed world over the four decades since the birth of the modern environmental era, four broad trends are clear. Most obvious is the vast *expansion of the environmental domain*. This expansion is manifest with respect to the range of issues with which environmental policy is concerned and the temporal and spatial scales over which problems are defined and remedial action organized. It is reflected in the volume of legislative and administrative ordinances, the range of implicated departments, the size of environmental expenditure, and the scope and density of government programs (Janicke and Weidner 1997). There has been a clear growth in the social reach of environmental intervention: more groups and organizations are implicated, and a broader range of actors seek to influence decision making. With this expansion has come increased complexity: environmental policy has ramified into innumerable subfields, and the cross-connections among specialist areas have multiplied. The environmental domain has become more closely entwined with other policy sectors. And the political, economic, legal, and scientific issues that must be weighed in developing governmental responses have become more involved.

There has also been a significant *deepening of state engagement with environmental issues*. It is not just that governments devote more time and energy to managing the environment, but rather that there has been movement toward more sophisticated understandings of environmental problems and more profound engagement with underlying issues. Elements of this deepening are manifest in the policy shifts that began in the late 1980s. Governments have increasingly accepted that environmental policy cannot be divorced from sectoral decision making (e.g., separating habitat protection from forestry or climate change from energy use). Over time, there has been recognition that problems are more profoundly embedded in prevailing economic and social practices than first imagined. And there has been some tentative engagement with preventative strategies and discussion of adjusting patterns of production and consumption to mitigate environmental burdens.[4] But this deepening can be appreciated in other ways. Note, for example, that concepts and policy proposals championed by environmental critics—for example, ecosystem-based management approaches, life cycle analysis, and ecological fiscal reform—gradually have been incorporated into official programs.[5] And over time, approaches to environmental management that take greater account of underlying ecological constraints have gained in strength: consider, for example, the shift in focus from species to ecosystem protection, the definition of critical loads in the Long-Range Transboundary Air Pollution agreement (LRTAP) and the trend toward managing fresh water through catchment-focused institutional designs (as in the European Union Water Directive).[6]

This expanded and deepened environmental management effort has also *become more central to the activities and structure of the state itself*. In part, this development relates to the sheer volume of work—the accretion of regulations, agencies, and programs means that proportionately the environment constitutes a larger share of what states actually do. But there is also the issue of linkages to other policy domains and state priorities. The environmental sphere is now more clearly understood to be important for economic development, public welfare, and even security. Connections to the orientation of key sectors such as energy, transport, construction, and agriculture are explicitly acknowledged. The internationalization of environmental policy has also contributed to states taking it more seriously—they require negotiating positions and must make some effort to implement agreements.[7] And as states have made broader claims about environmental protection, so the legitimacy of governments and the state institutions themselves have become linked to some extent to the successful delivery of environmental commitments.

Each of these changes is closely bound to another development—the emergence of the environment *as a permanent area of political contention*. Public debate and concern help propel the expansion of the policy domain, the deepening of governmental engagement, and the relative strengthening of the environment within the portfolio of state functions. On the other hand, this broader, deeper, more centrally positioned environmental policy domain now generates a steady stream of issues, proposals, and dilemmas that wash back into the political arena. They provoke further media interest and public debate and require some response from officials and politicians. Although specific issues come and go, and the environmental domain as a whole attracts more or less public interest in relation to other political problems, the continuing flow of domestic and international political events and the wide range of concerned interests and perspectives means that one dimension or other of the environment is always hovering near the forefront of political debate.

Genesis of an Environmental State

The character and scale of the transformation that has taken place since the mid-1960s suggests it makes sense to refer to the emergence of an "environmental state." Not because the state has somehow resolved environmental problems, or because it has become the sort of state of which environmental activists would generally approve (Eckersley 2004; Barry and Eckersley 2005), but rather because states have become irreducibly enmeshed in the management of environmental problems and their politics is continuously marked by environmental controversy. Environmental management has now become an essential component of state activity. It is publicly recognized as a fundamental part of what a civilized state should do.

Both policy phases defined previously were critical to the genesis of this environmental state. If the first step created an independent environmental policy realm, the second strengthened linkages to broader state concerns. Indeed, the two phases can be understood as point and counterpoint, reflecting something of the underlying way environmental problems manifest themselves in modern societies, for, on the one hand, environmental problems come to be understood as specific problems, which must be addressed by specialized organizations. And, on the other hand, they are connected intimately to broader patterns of social activity (WCED 1987). So environmental management must be linked to general economic and political decision making. Yet when the environment is integrated into more general decision making, it is always in danger of being overwhelmed by more immediate interests. So one is led back again to the need for specialized custodians of environmental values. Thus both "moments"—specialist attention and generalized interest, differentiated focus and integration with broader issues of economy and society—are required. And the foundations for these two dimensions of the environmental state were laid during the final decades of the twentieth century.

The argument to this point has implied that there has been a clear direction in the evolution of state engagement with the environment since the emergence of a distinct policy domain in the late 1960s. It has been movement from a limited to a more extensive intervention; from a relatively simple to a more sophisticated approach; and from according the environment a peripheral position within the state's portfolio of tasks to assigning it a more central location. In fact, the claim made here goes somewhat further: The move toward this wider, deeper, and weightier involvement was to some extent implicit from the moment the state first explicitly accepted responsibility for environmental management. The grand objectives (but limited reach) of the first generation of environmental policies introduced in the 1960s and 1970s were bound to be partially frustrated because they were based on a (necessarily) imperfect appreciation of the true dimensions of the challenge. Political leaders and government officials made commitments to deal with specific problems (air pollution, industrial effluent, and so on) while offering grand declarations about protecting "the environment." So they raised expectations and opened the door to wider claims. Moreover, underlying economic, social, and political pressures (for economic growth, expanded consumption, and so on) were actually accelerating the environmental degradation that had initially prompted the call for governmental intervention. This is not to suggest that particular perspectives, concepts, or policies were inevitable. But it is to say that once "the environment" emerged as a politically salient category, and national governments accepted this as an area in which they should intervene, the pressures were bound to grow for further, deeper, and more sophisticated intervention.

Clearly, this is not the only way to interpret the evolution of governmental engagement with the environment over recent decades (Hanf and Jansen 1998; van Tatenhove, Arts, and Leroy 2001). And it is worth pausing briefly to consider perspectives that are less sanguine about these developments. For example, some have emphasized the "issue-attention cycle," suggesting that the preoccupation with environment is cyclical: events conspire to focus the attention of publics and politicians; some measures are implemented, but soon other issues rise to the top of the pile, and the environment loses political saliency (Downs [1972] 1998). Alternatively, emphasis can be placed on the late 1960s and the early 1970s as a phase of social contestation and innovation when the growth logic of modern states was explicitly challenged by critics. But with the rhetorical reconciliation of growth and environment secured by the turn toward "sustainable development," the radical environmental critique was tamed and the movement coopted. The changing ideological climate of the 1980s and 1990s (in which the state was to be rolled back and a greater place left for markets), rather than any appeal to policy learning, can be invoked to explain the newfound enthusiasm for market-based instruments and the reticence to employ regulatory initiatives. And the decline in state capacity (attendant upon economic and political globalization, and the increased reliance on the private sector), as well as the relative weakness of international environmental institutions (in comparison to those dealing with trade and security), can be added to the equation.

Yet the issue-attention cycle is not really in contradiction with the story told here, as long as certain things are kept in mind. First, the environment is not one issue but an envelope for a whole series of subissues (acid rain, toxics, climate change, habitat conservation, and so on), and each of these subissues may also rise and fall on the political agenda. Second, when considering the overall impact on state activities the effect is less that of a cycle and more that of a ratchet—measures taken in each period of innovation have consequences long after they are no longer in the headlines. Ramifications of these policy initiatives continue to percolate through the governance structure: programs pass from design to implementation, agencies extend their work to adjacent areas, case law accumulates around the new practices, expenditures become entrenched, unintended impacts force adjustment in related spheres, and so on. And over time, the accretions and interactions grow. The biggest cycles of international public/political interest correspond with the onset of the two phases identified above. And there is some evidence that we have recently experienced a third upswing in attention—this time largely focused on climate change. So if we are to talk of cycles, we should recognize that like the turning of a crank, the cycles gradually accomplish work.

With respect to the idea that the innovations that got underway in the 1990s simply represent a cooptation of the environmental movement, and an extension of a "profits first" mentality, it should be remembered that the radical antigrowth environmentalism of the 1960s never seriously penetrated the policy realm. So, from the perspective of state orientation, there was no "retreat." On the contrary, as the decades have advanced, the state has been forced to accept that an ever more profound transformation of economic activity and of political and legal obligations will be required if environmental problems are to be managed. Indeed, even as a serious economic downturn took hold in 2008–2010, governments in many countries were attempting to give a green twist to economic stimulus packages and talking of using the opportunity to leverage climate-friendly change and build more sustainable infrastructure.

Two further perspectives on the evolution of environmental governance that offer alternative interpretations to the one presented here can be introduced at this point: the first refers to the emergence of "ecological modernization" and the second emphasizes the global consolidation of a neoliberal political economy. Initially, the concept of ecological modernization was applied to a phase of societal development in which the environment emerged from its economic integument to constitute an independent social sphere, and industrial production was being readjusted on ecological lines. An outgrowth of modernization theory, it highlighted the adaptive capacities of contemporary societies (Mol and Spaargaren 1993; Spaargaren 1997). But the term also came to denote a policy stance that presented the environment as an opportunity agenda—for accelerating innovation, creating jobs, conquering new markets, increasing profits, and so on—rather than simply a cost imposed on the economy (Weale 1992). Thus ecological modernization could be characterized as a discourse that promoted environmental reform but stopped short of fundamental structural change (Hajer 1995). In subsequent debates, some analysts teased out a distinction between more or less radical versions of ecological modernization, contrasting existing incremental and probusiness variants with the potential for more reflexive approaches that might deepen the greening of contemporary societies (Christoff 1996).

Thus ecological modernization represents not so much an integrated theory as a common idiom to approach evolving responses to environmental problems in contemporary societies (Meadowcroft 2005a). And this literature has contributed interesting studies around themes such as ecoindustrial adjustment, the changing roles of states and markets in environmental governance, shifts in the discursive strategies of environmental contestation, and the limits of current reform orientations (Young 2000; Mol and Sonnenfeld 2000; Mol 2001).

Although neoliberalism also has a wide range of meanings, it is typically associated with policies to promote market-based solutions to societal problems and to roll back the "interferences" of the state. Privatization, marketization, the import of private sector management techniques into the public service, and the transfer of social responsibilities from government to the corporate or voluntary sectors are typical of this orientation. It is argued that from early forms in Thatcher's Britain and Reagan's America, the neoliberal current became ascendant in international organizations (the "Washington consensus") and subsequently was exported around the globe. In fact, neoliberalism can be presented as a coherent project to restructure political and social relations and facilitate accumulation; it is, in short, the latest phase of capitalist development (Castree 2007; Heydnen et al. 2007). Evolving patterns of environmental governance are to be understood within this broader narrative as attempts to manage crises and contradictions generated by accumulation imperatives.

Although neoliberalism has been invoked in a wide range of interesting studies of conflicts over resource management and environmental policy, it becomes more problematic when elevated to a master narrative to explain the evolution of state engagement with environmental issues over the past thirty years. Here the emphasis on a neoliberal "order" (or "project," "settlement," "regime," or "hegemony") tends to reduce the complex adjustment of social institutions to emerging perceptions of environmental problems to a monist struggle between neoliberalizers and resistance movements of the oppressed. Major differences among political currents are obscured—for example, the "New Right" and the "Third Way" are presented as different neoliberal variants (Peck and Tickell 2002). Moreover, it is deeply misleading to reduce the history of the past thirty years to a systematic dismantling of social programs and the erosion of regulatory regimes. Welfare states have been reorganized and readjusted, but their core significance in developed countries remains (Pierson 1998; Gough 2008). Above all, in the environmental domain, the overall scope of governmental and social controls on individual and corporate behavior has continued to grow. Remember, market-based measures such as emissions trading systems or environmental taxes may be "business-friendly," but they are just as firmly grounded in regulatory intervention as are permits and prohibitions. Although "voluntary" environmental programs may appear as no more than mechanisms for public authorities to avoid responsibility, they may often also be part of a process of experimentation ("softening up") that ultimately leads to tighter societal controls. Many of these nuances in the evolution of state-business relations in environmental management are discussed by Gallagher and Weinthal (chapter 6, this volume) in their analysis of the evolution of corporate social responsibility.

Although the literatures of ecological modernization are largely complementary to the analysis developed here, the perspectives of some of the more intransigent critics of neoliberal ascendancy may not be—largely because of their tendency to dismiss moves to green the public power as marginal adjustments to an apparatus that exists to further private accumulation imperatives.

Changing Patterns of State Activity

Modern democratic governments are now involved in a vast array of activities, but—setting aside the issue of the environment—three areas lie at their core. The first relates to the very existence of the state, to its *capacity to maintain internal order* (civil peace and the integrity of its institutions) and to deal with external threats. Bodies associated with this function include the armed forces and security services, the police, the apparatus for the administration of justice, and the corresponding ministries and agencies. The second area relates to *national prosperity, economic growth, and financing the state.* Key institutions include the ministry of finance and tax authorities, regulatory agencies such as the central bank, competition authorities, and organizations concerned with industrial and trade policy. The third domain concerns the *organization of welfare services*, including education, insurance against accident and unemployment, pensions, and health care. Each of these broad domains—the security state, the prosperity state, and the welfare state— is critical to the successful operation, legitimacy, and ultimately the survival of contemporary states. They mark out what modern governments are expected to achieve, and politicians who fail to deliver order, continued economic prosperity, and viable welfare provision are unlikely to be forgiven by the electorate.

Although there is considerable continuity, the detailed content of governmental activity in these areas has varied considerably over time. Practices considered appropriate at one point give way to new structures and initiatives. There is a more or less continual struggle among different political forces to influence the profile of intervention. And much of the content of democratic politics consists of adjustments and reforms to the policy stance in these three areas.[8]

Though each policy domain is distinct, there are complex interdependencies among them, and practices in one area can complement, but also contradict, those in other areas. Specialized bodies serve each functional area, but the core structures and decision-making routines of the state (constitution, executive, legislature, judiciary, etc.) operate across all domains. Thus the security, prosperity, and welfare states are not so much separate structures (although they are this as well), as different manifestations of a multifaceted structure.

In one sense, there is an underlying logical hierarchy that runs from security, to economy, to welfare. Without stability the economy cannot prosper, and without a successful economy there will be few resources to apply to public welfare. Yet it is also true that in the long run, order and security depend upon economic success and that good economic performance can be disrupted by a failing welfare system. Thus each domain is in some sense crucial to the long-term development of the state and to the welfare of its population. But there are also tensions among these domains and the requirements and orientation of policies in one may interfere with those in another. Resources are limited, and those applied in one area cannot be applied elsewhere. Beyond that, measures taken to secure one set of objectives may undercut policies directed to other ends: enhanced border security may dampen economic activity; welfare initiatives that require higher marginal tax rates may discourage inward investment; and so on.

As the environment emerges as a fourth core domain of activity, the potential significance of interactions with each of the other domains comes to be acknowledged. With respect to security, there are concerns (a) that serious environmental disruption might generate security threats (mass population movements, the collapse of vulnerable states, conflicts over resources such as water, and so on), and (b) that security policies can generate environmental impacts (production and use of weapons systems, training practices, and so on). But the most crucial linkages are to the economy: on the one hand, there is worry about distortions caused by the failure to include environmental commons in economic calculus and about the eventual economic consequences of eroding the environmental base, and on the other hand, there is concern about the costs and competitiveness impacts of implementing environmental measures. At a later point, there is also recognition of the economic potential (jobs, exports) of green technologies. Because there is never only one way to define problems or to construct solutions and the distribution of costs and benefits (among geographic areas, economic sectors, classes, and across time) varies, the direction and orientation of adjustment among the domains is the object of continued political argument and struggle. Some of the interactions among these four areas of state activity are presented in table 3.1.

It is interesting to note that there are significant historical parallels between the growth of the modern environmental state and the emergence of the welfare state that began to take form from the final quarter of the nineteenth century and expanded dramatically over the course of the twentieth century (Ashford 1986; Flora and Heidenheimer 1981). Although welfare states take distinct forms in different national contexts and are periodically reconfigured, they are a fundamental feature of contemporary developed democratic polities. Their growth can be understood as a response to long-term social and economic change (industrialization, urbanization) and the subsequent expansion of political rights (democratization). The much more recent emergence of the environmental state, summarized in the first section of this chapter, can be seen as a parallel-but-lagged response to the rise of industrial civilization because it takes time—for environmental impacts to accumulate (as technology becomes more disruptive of natural systems and diffuses globally, and human numbers rise); for science to map impacts and establish causal mechanisms; for critical thinkers to interrogate established socioenvironmental practices; and for democratic and bureaucratic responses to mature. As with the earlier emergence of the welfare state, the timing and character of developments in particular countries differ, and the resultant structures, policies, and programs vary from state to state as new functions are grafted onto existing political practices and cultures.[9]

At present, there is no elegant typology of environmental states equivalent to the well know classification of welfare states (Esping-Andersen 1990). In part, this may be because the environmental state is a comparatively recent creation. And it is one that has been layered on top of (a) well-established economic variants (forms of capitalism), (b) political-institutional setups, and (c) welfare state types. In short, national environmental states are strongly colored by what has gone before, and it may be difficult to divide them into a small number of types.[10]

Table 3.1
Interactions among core state functions

Impacts on other functional domains

Action in functional domain	Order (Security state)	Economy (Prosperity state)	Welfare (Welfare state)	Environment (Environmental state)
Order (Security state) national defense public order system of constitutional, criminal, and civil law		– Favorable or unfavorable context for economic activity – Economic costs of security and administration of justice – Scale of security and defense industries	– Competition for expenditure – Potential equity implications	– Favorable or unfavorable context for environmental protection – Potential obstacles to collective action – Impacts of security apparatus (weapons, etc.)
Economy (Prosperity state) financial stability economic growth competitiveness fiscal and monetary policy industrial policy	– Wealth or lack of wealth for security spending – Reduced or increased social tensions – Resource vulnerabilities – Trade relations		– Wealth or lack of wealth for welfare spending – Potential equity implications	– Wealth or lack of wealth for environmental spending – Quantity and quality of economic growth may accelerate or reduce environmental pressures – Technical innovation to address environmental issues

Welfare (Welfare state) welfare provision income transfers poverty alleviation equity promotion	– May enhance or reduce social tensions	– May accelerate or slow economic growth – May enhance or reduce international competitiveness		– May raise, lower, or alter character of mass consumption – May raise or lower exposure to environmental goods and bads – May facilitate interventionist state and/or environment-driven economic restructuring
Environment (Environmental state) protection of natural environment pollution control resource management	– May reduce or increase security threats – May introduce new rights/ obligations/crimes – Competition for expenditure	– May enhance or slow economic growth or change its character – Promote or slow technological innovation – Stimulate or slow emergence of green industries	– May increase or decrease wealth for welfare spending – Potential equity implications	

Today, the environment remains the most vulnerable of these core domains of state activity because it is the newest and least institutionally embedded. Economic interests and bureaucratic institutions tied to the extension of environmental protection are weaker than those in the other fields. And features of environmental problems consistently cited in the policy literature (diffuse impacts, long time frames, scientific and technical complexity, distributional implications, and so on) make it difficult to maintain political coalitions to effect change. On the other hand, the seriousness of environmental concerns—in terms of impacts on public health, economic activity, and ecosystem services—have already prompted states to take action with significant economic costs even in the face of considerable political resistance.

Greening the State

I have argued that over the past forty years, we have witnessed the genesis of an "environmental state." This does not mean that managing human interactions with the environment has eclipsed other state functions. It means that states now have to devote significant resources (money, personnel, attention of political leaders and of law-making and judicial bodies) to managing environmental issues. And at times, the demands of environmental policy moderates claims made for action in other domains. I have also suggested that we have witnessed a two-step movement over this period, reflecting a gradual deepening of the societal understanding of the character of environmental difficulties.

Many factors will influence the future evolution of this environmental state. But some indications of where it needs to go, if it is to get a grip on emerging problems, can be provided by experience to date—particularly if we look not just at policy outputs, but also at policy outcomes.

Overall, the environmental policy field has been characterized by remarkable success and remarkable failure. On the one hand, in the developed countries environmental policy has been successful in managing specific identified burdens. And an "absolute decoupling" of economic activity from certain environmental stresses has been observed in specific countries over defined periods.[11] The control of SO_x emissions, lead, mercury, and ozone-depleting substances in developed states are cases in point (EEA 2002). Air and water quality in many countries have improved (OECD 2001). On the other hand, viewed from a broader perspective, environmental policy has not succeeded in containing the growth in the total burden humans impose on global ecosystems. Even within the developed states, gains in efficiency and pollution abatement are often overwhelmed by the growth of production and consumption (OECD 2001; EEA 1999). And many environmental burdens have been displaced to the developing world as production has moved offshore. Difficulties are particularly evident with respect to climate change, but unsustainable practices continue in many fields, including patterns of land use, chemical releases, the nitrogen cycle, and harvesting of potentially renewable resources such as forests and fisheries. Studies such as the Millennium Ecosystem Assessment (2005) suggest that these formidable pressures are set to increase dramatically in coming decades.

The broad outlines of many of the policy measures and institutional changes that will be required are already known. Indeed, many are being tried today in different jurisdictions. The case for abolishing subsidies for environmentally destructive behavior (e.g., fossil fuel production and consumption) and shifting the tax system to encourage green practices (ecological fiscal reform) has been laid out by international organizations such as the OECD (OECD 2006). The importance of planning for the environment and sustainable development (Steurer and Martinuzzi 2005; Meadowcroft 2007a), green public procurement (Bouwer et al. 2005), enhancing the strategic reach of environment ministries, and improving the monitoring and measurement of social environmental interactions and policy interventions (Niestroy 2005; Meadowcroft 2007b) are also clear. Other approaches include constitutional embedding of environmental values and entitlements, the definition of citizen rights to environmental information, and the creation of advocates for the environment and sustainable development.[12] Above all, the goal of integrating environmental objectives into sectoral policy making has been a critical component of the discourse on sustainable development from the outset (WCED 1987; OECD 2002). And although change has been slow, some progress is beginning to be made in countries that are recognized as environmental leaders (Lenschow 2002; Lafferty 2004; Nilsson and Eckerberg 2007).

Yet something more is required if the environmental state is to grapple with the problems that confront it. It is a *transformative* orientation: a focus on altering established societal practices in order to reduce the burden that production and consumption impose on the global ecosphere. Such a transformative orientation is focused deliberately on altering received ways of doing things, changing the frontiers of social acceptability, and reconstructing the production/consumption complexes that constitute the social economy. Of course, specific policies are needed to resolve specific problems. But these need to be understood as part of a broader narrative about societal change—the recasting of social practices and social relations so that they no longer lead to acute environmental burdens.

If the maxim of the first phase of the environmental state was "clean up pollution and protect the environment," and that of the second phase has been "promote sustainable development," then the new motto needs to be something like "transform societal practices to respect ecological limits." Of course, this third maxim—which couples an emphasis on societal transformation with a renewed concern with limits—does not replace the other two. Each completes the others. We need to protect the environment. And we need to ensure that development is sustainable. Indeed, only by linking environment and development in decision making (by accounting for the environment as we define a development trajectory) is it possible to consistently protect the environment. But to these principles must be added a further insight—that in light of the unsustainable social trajectory to which we are practically committed, a set of *deliberate societal changes* is required in order to produce human communities that can protect the environment and that can realize a sustainable development trajectory. And the environmental state should be understood as a mechanism for helping secure this type of long-term societal adjustment.

In one sense, this *transformative* orientation is immanent within the original environmental critique, and it more clearly approaches the surface in the discussion of sustainable development. After all, why would we need to talk about sustainable development if such development were produced spontaneously by the operation of markets and politics? But in the struggle over the interpretation of what sustainable development actually entails, there is a tendency to rob it of its radical impulse, to assimilate it with the quest for all good things (a better "quality of life"), and to avoid the conclusion that many of our institutions and practices must deliberately be altered (Meadowcroft 2007c). In fact, sustainable development points to the need for a radical discontinuity with existing routines. And in the developed countries, the dramatic reduction of imposed environmental burdens lies at the heart of sustainable development. Of course, sustainable development also has economic and social pillars. But the problem is not that developed states have failed to achieve economic advance or failed to establish systems of welfare provision—though of course more could always be done. The problem is rather that *they have been unable to secure economic and social advance without continuing environmental degradation*. And changing this situation requires a major transformation of existing social practices. Just how deep this transformation needs to go remains to be seen. Certainly it requires shifts in technology, the social organization of production and consumption, acquired rights and duties of individuals and corporations, as well as substantial innovations in international governance. But it is only as these transformations advance, and as further social and ecological feedbacks accumulate, that it will be possible to define more clearly exactly what they will entail.

Climate change provides a good example of the kind of environmental challenge to which the transformative orientation of the state will need to be directed. Achieving emissions reductions on the scale that now appears necessary (perhaps 80 percent cuts in developed states by midcentury, with emissions declining to a few percent of existing levels by the end of the century) will require a radical restructuring of energy systems (Schellnhuber et al. 2006). There is no simple technological fix to this issue, although the deployment and development of new technologies will be critical. Instead it will have profound and subtle implications for politics and economics, production and consumption (Meadowcroft 2007d). Already, states are formulating goals and establishing policy frameworks for mitigation and adaptation with timescales broader than any that have been contemplated before. The scale of change implicit in the European Union's new climate targets, and its goal of becoming a leader in low-carbon energy systems, are an order of magnitude more ambitious than any earlier environmental goals and rival the scope of major state-led economic development efforts (such as those of the Asian tigers in the 1960s and 1970s). Of course, defining a target is not effecting a transformation. But if climate leaders such as Germany, the United Kingdom, and Sweden follow through with further policy initiatives, they will achieve a fundamental transformation of their energy systems within a few decades.

Nor is climate change the only domain in which such transformative orientations will be required. Greening the materials system (Geiser 2001); reforming agricultural production to reverse long-term soil loss, bring the nitrogen cycle back into balance, and make water usage sustainable; and putting an end to the unsustainable exploitation of biological resources will all demand attention in coming decades.

To assume such a transformative mantle, states will require appropriate decision-processes—to involve stakeholders, establish reform coalitions, and make strategic choices. They will need to devise and implement effective policies and to operate feedback mechanisms to allow adjustments in mid course. They will need to mobilize resources to implement appropriate solutions and to buy off powerful opponents of change. They will need to prove adept at operating at the domestic, regional, and international levels. And they will need to develop a powerful ideological underpinning to support a new relationship between humans and the natural world and to legitimate their interventionist role (Meadowcroft 1999).

Much of the initial thrust of environmental policy—the establishment of permitting systems, protected areas, and resource harvest quotas, the introduction of environmental impact assessments, management procedures, development controls, and so on—was predicated upon systems of routine bureaucratic administration setting general standards to protect environmental quality (Paehlke and Torgerson 2005). Moreover, the system was by definition largely *reactive*: when evidence of harm was produced, remedial measures could be set in place; when a development proposal came forward, an impact assessment could be carried out and necessary amendments introduced; when a species was threatened, essential habitat could be defined and protected; and so on. Sustainable development policy making has emphasized balancing economic, social, and environmental factors at an earlier phase of decision making. But the transformative impulse—breaking with how things are currently done—is too often lost. And the "balancing" can easily degenerate into a bureaucratic routine of "box ticking."

Of course, to say that states should assume a transformative mantle is not to argue that they are the underlying force behind such change. On the contrary, broader societal movements and pressures, such as those reviewed in Kate O'Neill's essay (chapter 5, this volume), are required to underpin such an interventionist posture of the public power.

Lest it be thought that this image of the state is hopelessly idealistic, it should be noted that a number of governments are in fact already moving in this direction—particularly in relation to coming to terms with climate change. The Swedish Social Democrats have spoken of building the "Green welfare state" (Lundqvist 2004), and the government has reaffirmed the commitment to ending fossil fuel dependence by 2020. Moreover, the country's ambitious system of national environmental objectives, developed after extensive stakeholder consultation, involves an integrated plan extending to all levels of government to eliminate transferred environmental burdens within a generation. The Dutch government has invoked the concept of "transition management" in relation to the necessary transformation of dysfunctional societal subsystems, most particularly to ensure the emergence of a carbon neutral energy sector (NEEP4 2002; Rotmans, Kemp, and van Asselt 2001). Germany has embarked on a major campaign to transform the energy system, extending wind and solar photovoltaic generation, district heating, and biomass. Even in the United Kingdom (which twenty years ago was known as "the dirty man of Europe"), ambitious targets on climate change and energy and the high-level discussion of changing patterns of production and consumption are increasingly placing societal transformation in the political realm. A new Climate Change Act, for example, gives long-term emissions reduction targets a statutory basis and establishes a cycle of national carbon budgets with independent monitoring and annual reporting to Parliament.

In passing, it should be noted that a major gap in the comparative environmental politics literature (and thus a significant opportunity for future research) concerns the greening of states in developing and postcommunist countries. Outside of the industrialized democracies discussed in this chapter, the politics of state reform is typically cast by researchers in terms of specific legal and institutional reforms, with only weak ties to literatures on state building and political development. We should not expect the greening of states in these regions to resemble that of industrialized democracies, with their decades of institutional stability and high regulatory capacity. Yet the question of whether and how states embrace environmental protection and sustainable development among their core responsibilities is at least as pressing, and probably much more so, in developing and postcommunist countries. Processes of democratization present critical junctures for the institutionalization of environmental capacities, while the trend toward decentralizing power from state capitals to subnational bodies raises important questions. How do central and regional governments negotiate the division of resources and responsibilities, strategically augmenting or shedding roles? More generally, how does greening differ across various types of states in the developing world? How are these processes affected by transnational relations with foreign organizations promoting various environment and development agendas? How are environmental ideas employed by states that struggle for legitimacy amid contentious state-society relations stemming from legacies of colonialism and authoritarian rule? What does greening look like in very small countries, where governments lack many of the fundamental capacities associated with state building?

Within the developed world, it is clear that different societies (with their distinct political cultures and institutional arrangements) may be more or less enthusiastic about the type of activist state implied by the transformational logic discussed previously. Polities with traditions of interventionist government, "consensus politics," and an elaborate welfare state may be more comfortable with the public power assuming a direct role in orienting societal advance. On the other hand, even the more litigious and liberal societies do not hesitate to turn to the state when problems become acute. Various mixes of policy tools (that may be more or less acceptable to different ideological currents) can be deployed to effect similar sorts of results. And very different narratives can be constructed to legitimate reform. It is possible to tell a "technological story" (e.g., about modernizing energy supply through a massive infrastructure investment in solar power) or an "energy security story" (about weaning a country off oil imported from volatile regions), as well as an "environmental responsibility story" (about saving the planet for future human generations and nonhuman nature), and an "internationalist story" (about controlling our environmental impacts to advance international cooperation or to make room for higher living standards for peoples in developing countries).

In one sense, the further development of the environmental state is inevitable: governments are enmeshed in a web of contradictions and pressures that requires further action. And that action adds to the reach and complexity of environmental controls already in place. On the other hand, there is no guarantee that this action will successfully engage underlying problems. It is possible for states to continue to react to environmental crises as they emerge in a piecemeal fashion. It is possible for them to eschew long-term planning, focus on immediate issues, and pretend that the social adjustments provoked by changed ecological and economic circumstances (as well as by the impacts of policy intended to address these realities) are the result of "natural" processes. And of course, they can continue to displace burdens of a deteriorating environment beyond their borders, or forward in time, or onto specific classes of their own citizens. Ultimately, it will be a question of political struggle that determines just how much that turns out to be the case.

It is within the context of these political struggles that the challenges of international environmental policy making can best be understood. For those who approach global environmental politics from the perspective of international relations, this analysis carries a number of implications. Over the long haul, the impact of international treaties and organizations and the influence of transnational NGOs will be a function not merely of one-off events, projects, and policy initiatives focusing on specific environmental problems. The real question is whether they contribute to the decades-long process of the greening of states and societies. International environmental policy making, whether pursued through multilateral channels like the European Union (EU) and the United Nations or through bilateral initiatives, provides support for the idea that environmental protection is an essential part of what it means to be a modern state. To the extent that international actors contribute to the process of broadening and deepening of state commitments, they can help to create the self-reinforcing dynamic discussed earlier, which pushes states toward incorporating green concerns alongside traditional emphases on security, prosperity, and welfare. In non-OECD countries, leaders are being asked, by both international actors and domestic environmental constituencies, to expand into green concerns when they have not yet secured the core functions of security (versus internal upheaval and external threats), economic growth (and concomitant financial flows for the state), and the provision of services for social welfare. Politicians in these countries cannot (and do not) ignore these other functions when they are asked to address environmental concerns. The success of global environmental initiatives will be enhanced to the extent that they help domestic actors to simultaneously address these multiple state imperatives.

Notes

I would like to thank the Canada Research Chairs for supporting the research program on which this chapter is based.

1. On the challenges of state reform within developing countries, see the chapters by Sowers (9) and Steinberg (10) in this volume.

2. Outcomes from the Rio conference included the Rio Declaration on Environment and Development, signature of the United Nations Convention on Biodiversity and the United Nations Framework Convention on Climate Change, and Agenda 21.

3. On negotiated approaches, see, for example, Mol, Lauber, and Liefferink 2000 and De Clercq 2002.

4. Consider, for example, Sustainable Consumption Roundtable 2006.

5. Thus ecosystem-based management has been formally adopted as the a cornerstone of Australian fisheries policy, life-cycle analysis of carbon emissions of transportation fuel is central to California's attempt to control greenhouse gas emissions, and ecological fiscal reform has begun to be implemented in Sweden, Germany, and the Canadian province of British Columbia.

6. Developments in the European Union (see Andonova and VanDeveer, chapter 11, this volume; Selin and VanDeveer, chapter 13, this volume) are pertinent to the environmental state on two levels: on the one hand, EU law must be implemented in (indeed, can *only* be implemented *by*) member states, and on the other, member states (or specified majorities of them) must agree to initiatives if they are to be adopted as EU policy. The EU is not a nation-state, but it is more than an international organization. It lacks independent tax raising powers and military force. But it has directly elected representative institutions, a significant bureaucracy, and courts that can overrule member states. And this suggests a third level of pertinence: to some extent the EU is emerging as a collective "public power," acting in the total territory of its member states' jurisdictions.

7. Note how environmental issues have increasingly become a staple of G8 meetings, with climate change now emerging as the most persistent and challenging issue.

8. A different account of these state functions is given by Dryzek et al. 2003, who include a "legitimation" function related to representative democracy as a distinct sphere.

9. A more detailed comparison of the historical parallels between the welfare and environmental states can be found in Meadowcroft 2005b.

10. But for an interesting discussion of variations in environmental states, see Duit 2008.

11. An "absolute decoupling" of economic activity for a given environmental stress implies that even as economic activity continues to rise (GDP growth is positive), the environmental stress declines in absolute terms. This relationship contrasts with "relative decoupling," in which a growth in economic activity leads only to a reduction in the rate at which environmental pressure is growing.

12. For the first, consider the French Environmental Charter; for the second, the Aarhus Convention on Access to Information, Public Participation in Decision-making and Access to Justice in Environmental Matters; and for the third, the Canadian Commissioner for the Environment and Sustainable Development and the New Zealand Parliamentary Commissioner for the Environment.

References

Anderson, Mikael S., and Duncan Liefferink. 1997. *European Environmental Policy: The Pioneers*. Manchester, UK: Manchester University Press.

Ashford, Douglas. 1986. *The Emergence of the Welfare States*. Oxford, UK: Basil Blackwell.

Barry, John, and Robyn Eckersley, eds. 2005. *The State and the Global Ecological Crisis*. Cambridge, Mass.: MIT Press.

Bouwer, Maarten, Klaas de Jong, Margo Jonk, Tanya Berman, Raffaella Bersani, Helmut Lusser, Ari Nissinen, Katriina Parikka, and Péter Szuppinger. 2005. Green Public Procurement in Europe 2005—Status Overview. Virage Milieu & Management bv, Korte Spaarne 31, 2011 AJ Haarlem, the Netherlands. http://ec.europa.eu/environment/gpp/pdf/Stateofplaysurvey 2005_en.pdf, accessed May 20, 2011.

Castree, Noel. 2007. *Neoliberal Environments: A Framework for Analysis*. Manchester Papers in Political Economy, April 2007. Manchester, UK: University of Manchester, Centre for the Study of Political Economy.

Christoff, Peter. 1996. Ecological Modernization, Ecological Modernities. *Environmental Politics* 5:476–500.

De Clercq, Marc, ed. 2002. *Negotiating Environmental Agreements in Europe.* Cheltenham, UK: Edward Elgar.

Downs, Anthony. [1972] 1998. Up and Down with Ecology: The "Issue-Attention Cycle." In *Political Theory and Public Choice, Collected Works of Anthony Downs,* vol. 1, 100–112. Northampton, UK: Edward Elgar.

Driessen, Peter, and Peter Glasbergen, eds. 2002. *Greening Society: The Paradigm Shift in Dutch Environmental Politics.* Dordrecht: Kluwer Academic.

Dryzek, John, David Downes, Christian Hunold, David Schlosberg, with Hans-Kristian Hernes. 2003. *Green States and Social Movements: Environmentalism in the United States, United Kingdom, Germany, and Norway.* Oxford, UK: Oxford University Press.

Duit, Andreas. 2008. *The Ecological State: Cross-National Patterns of Environmental Governance Regimes.* EPIGOV Paper No. 39. Berlin: Ecologic–Institute for International and European Environmental Policy.

Dunlap, Thomas. 1999. *Nature and the English Diaspora: Environmental History in the United States, Canada, Australia and New Zealand.* Cambridge, UK: Cambridge University Press.

Durant, Robert, Daniel Fiorino, and Rosemary O'Leary. 2004. *Environmental Governance Reconsidered.* Cambridge, Mass.: MIT Press.

Eckersley, Robyn. 2004. *The Green State: Rethinking Democracy, and Sovereignty.* Cambridge, Mass.: MIT Press.

EEA (European Environment Agency). 1999. *Environment in the European Union at the Turn of the Century.* Copenhagen: European Environment Agency.

EEA (European Environment Agency). 2002. *Environmental Signals.* Copenhagen: European Environment Agency.

Esping-Andersen, Gøsta. 1990. *Three Worlds of Welfare Capitalism.* Cambridge, UK: Polity Press.

Flora, Peter, and Arnold Heidenheimer, eds. 1981. *The Development of Welfare States in Europe and America.* London: Transaction Books.

Geiser, Kenneth. 2001. *Materials Matter: Toward a Sustainable Materials Policy.* Cambridge, Mass.: MIT Press.

Glasbergen, Peter. 1996. Learning to Manage the Environment. In *Democracy and the Environment: Problems and Prospects,* ed. William Lafferty and James Meadowcroft, 175–193. Cheltenham: Edward Elgar.

Goudie, Andrew. 2005. *The Human Impact on the Natural Environment: Past Present and Future.* 6th ed. Oxford, UK: Blackwell.

Gough, Ian. 2008. European Welfare States: Explanations and Lessons for Developing Countries. In *Inclusive States: Social Policy and Structural Inequalities,* ed. Anis Dani and Arjan de Haan, 39–72. Washington, D.C.: World Bank.

Hajer, Maarten. 1995. *The Politics of Environmental Discourse: Ecological Modernization and the Policy Process.* Oxford, UK: Clarendon Press.

Hanf, Kenneth, and Alf-Inge Jansen, eds. 1998. *Governance and Environment in Western Europe: Politics, Policy and Administration*. Harlow, UK: Longman.

Held, David, ed. 1983. *States and Societies*. Oxford, UK: Blackwell.

Heydnen, Nik, James McCarthy, Scott Prudham, and Paul Robbins, eds. 2007. *Neoliberal Environments*. London: Routledge.

Janicke, Martin, and Helmut Weidner, eds. 1997. *National Environmental Policies: A Comparative Study of Capacity Building*. Berlin: Springer.

Lafferty, William. 2004. From Environmental Protection to Sustainable Development: The Challenge of Decoupling through Sectoral Integration. In *Governance for Sustainable Development*, ed. William Lafferty, 191–220. Cheltenham: Edward Elgar.

Lafferty, William, and James Meadowcroft, eds. 2000. *Implementing Sustainable Development: Strategies and Initiatives in High Consumption Societies*. Oxford, UK: Oxford University Press.

Lenschow, Andrea, ed. 2002. *Environmental Policy Integration: Greening Sectoral Policies in Europe*. London: Earthscan.

Lundqvist, Lennart. 2004. *Sweden and Ecological Governance: Straddling the Fence*. Manchester, UK: Manchester University Press.

Meadowcroft, James. 1999. Planning for Sustainable Development: What Can be Learned from the Critics? In *Planning for Sustainability*, ed. Michael Kenny and James Meadowcroft, 12–38. London: Routledge.

Meadowcroft, James. 2005a. Environmental Political Economy, Technological Transitions and the State. *New Political Economy* 10:479–498.

Meadowcroft, James. 2005b. From Welfare State to Ecostate? In *The State and the Global Ecological Crisis*, ed. John Barry and Robyn Eckersley, 3–23. Cambridge, Mass.: MIT Press.

Meadowcroft, James. 2007a. National Sustainable Development Strategies: A Contribution to Reflexive Governance? *European Environment* 17:152–163.

Meadowcroft, James. 2007b. Public Monitoring, Assessment and Review of Government Initiatives for the Environment and Sustainable Development: An Overview and Guide. Report prepared for the Best Practice Network for Sustainable Development, Ottawa.

Meadowcroft, James. 2007c. Who Is in Charge Here? Governance for Sustainable Development in a Complex World. *Journal of Environmental Policy and Planning* 9:299–314.

Meadowcroft, James. 2007d. Governing the Transition to a New Energy Economy. In *Energy . . . Beyond Oil*, ed. Fraser Armstrong and Katherine Blundell, 197–214. Oxford, UK: Oxford University Press.

Millennium Ecosystem Assessment. 2005. *Ecosystems and Human Well Being: A Synthesis*. Washington, D.C.: Island Press.

Mol, Arthur. 2001. *Globalization and Environmental Reform: The Ecological Modernization of the Global Economy*. Cambridge, Mass.: MIT Press.

Mol, Arthur, Volkmar Lauber, and Duncan Liefferink. 2000. *The Voluntary Approach to Environmental Policy: Joint Environmental Policy Making in Europe*. Oxford, UK: Oxford University Press.

Mol, Arthur, and David Sonnenfeld. 2000. *Ecological Modernization Around the World: Perspectives and Critical Debates*. London: Frank Cass.

Mol, Arthur, and Gert Spaargaren. 1993. Environment, Modernity and Risk Society: The Apocalyptic Horizon of Environmental Reform. *International Sociology* 8:432–459.

NEEP4 (Fourth National Environmental Policy Plan of the Netherlands). 2002. *Where There's a Will There's a World*. The Hague: Ministry of Housing Spatial Planning and the Environment.

Niestroy, Ingeborg. 2005. *Sustaining Sustainability*. Utrecht, The Netherlands: EEAC.

Nilsson, Mans, and Katarina Eckerberg. 2007. *Environmental Policy Integration in Practice: Shaping Institutions for Learning*. London: Earthscan.

OECD (Organisation for Economic Cooperation and Development). 2001. *OECD Environmental Strategy for the First Decade of the 21st Century*. Paris: OECD.

OECD (Organisation for Economic Cooperation and Development). 2002. *Improving Policy Coherence and Integration for Sustainable Development: A Checklist*. Paris: OECD.

OECD (Organisation for Economic Cooperation and Development). 2006. *The Political Economy of Environmentally Related Taxes*. Paris: OECD.

OECD (Organisation for Economic Cooperation and Development) and Bill L. Long. 2000. *International Environmental Issues and the OECD 1950–2000: An Historical Perspective*. Paris: OECD.

Paehlke, Robert, and Douglas Torgerson. 2005. *Managing Leviathan: Environmental Politics and the Administrative State*. 2nd ed. New York: Broadview Press.

Peck, Jamie, and Adam Tickell. 2002. Neoliberalizing Space. *Antipode* 34 (3): 380–404.

Pierson, Christopher. 1996. *The Modern State*. London: Routledge.

Pierson, Christopher. 1998. *Beyond the Welfare State: The New Political Economy of Welfare*. 2nd ed. Cambridge, UK: Polity Press.

Rotmans, Jan, Rene Kemp, and Marjolein van Asselt. 2001. More Evolution than Revolution: Transition Management in Public Policy. *Foresight* 3:15–31.

Schellnhuber, Hans Joachim, Wolfgang Cramer, Nebojsa Nakicenovic, Tom Wigley, and Gary Yohe. 2006. *Avoiding Dangerous Climate Change*. Cambridge, UK: Cambridge University Press.

Skocpol, Theda. 1979. *States and Social Revolutions*. Cambridge, UK: Cambridge University Press.

Spaargaren, Gert. 1997. *The Ecological Modernization of Production and Consumption*. Wageningen, The Netherlands: Wageningen University.

Steurer, Reinhard, and André Martinuzzi. 2005. Towards a New Pattern of Strategy Formation in the Public Sector: First Experiences with National Strategies for Sustainable Development in Europe. *Environment and Planning C: Government & Policy* 23:455–472.

Sustainable Consumption Roundtable. 2006. Looking Back, Looking Forward. UK Sustainable Development Commission. http://www.sd-commission.org.uk/publications/downloads/Looking_back_SCR_2.pdf, accessed May 20, 2011.

van Tatenhove, Jan, Bas Arts, and Pieter Leroy, eds. 2001. *Political Modernisation and the Environment: The Renewal of Environmental Policy Arrangements*. Dordrecht: Kluwer Academic.

Tews, Kerstin, Per-Olof Busch, and Helge Jörgens. 2003. The Diffusion of New Environmental Policy Instruments. *European Journal of Political Research* 42 (4): 569–600.

WCED (World Commission on Environment and Development). 1987. *Our Common Future.* Oxford, UK: Oxford University Press.

Weale, Albert. 1992. *The New Politics of Pollution.* Manchester, UK: Manchester University Press.

Young, Stephen C., ed. 2000. *The Emergence of Ecological Modernisation: Integrating the Environment and the Economy.* London: Routledge.

4

The Globalization of Environmental Concern

Riley E. Dunlap and Richard York

Conventional wisdom has long held that widespread citizen awareness of environmental problems and support for environmental protection were phenomena limited to wealthy, highly industrialized, and primarily Northern Hemisphere nations. The early emergence of environmentalism and green parties in North America and Northern European countries lent support to this view, as did the wary reaction of poorer nations to the 1972 UN Conference on the Human Environment in Stockholm (see, e.g., Carnegie Endowment for International Peace 1972). Shortly after Stockholm, a prominent conservative economist captured conventional thinking when he wrote, "Poor people will naturally have a greater incentive to give priority to more goods and services than to the environment in general. In the same way, poor countries . . . would be foolish to make heavy sacrifices of economic progress in the interests even of their own environment, let alone that of the world in general" (Beckerman 1974, 89).

In chapter 1, Steinberg and VanDeveer argue that comparative research can provide clearer insight into the causal processes driving environmental outcomes, such as the formation of state interests and the likelihood that societies will embrace environmental concerns. If the conventional wisdom is true—if it is unrealistic to expect poorer countries to make a priority of environmental protection—this causal model carries important implications for the conduct of international environmental relations (whether by official treaty-making bodies or transnational NGOs), which would need to provide education and incentives to motivate action from reluctant leaders and societies that would rather focus attention and resources elsewhere. If, on the other hand, the conventional wisdom is mistaken—if leaders and publics in the developing world are no less concerned about these issues than their counterparts in industrialized countries—the implications are profound. Scholars and practitioners of global environmental politics would need to revisit long-standing assumptions and open new areas of inquiry. The negotiating positions of developing countries at environmental summits would need to be understood in a new light. New research would be needed on the origin and impact of environmental citizens' movements and policy initiatives in the developing world to better understand how international actors and institutions might contribute to these processes. When physical environmental outcomes in poor countries are positive, we could not attribute it to a simple lack of industrialization or pandering for foreign aid. When environments are degraded, we could no longer assume that it is due to a lack of concern; other factors (such as political power, institutions, state-society relations, and other long-standing interests of comparative politics) would need to enter the equation.

Are poorer countries indeed less concerned about the environment? The more enthusiastic participation of poor nations in the 1992 United Nations Conference on Environment and Development (UNCED) in Rio de Janeiro,[1] and the huge representation of developing country environmental NGOs at the accompanying Global Forum (Fisher 1993), should have signaled that conventional wisdom needed revision—particularly because the vast number of NGOs in Rio reflected the spread of environmental activism throughout the poorer regions of the world (Steinberg 2001; Durning 1989). Yet the efforts in Rio of representatives from poor nations to tie environmental protection to increased economic aid seemed to reinforce the image held by those in wealthy nations that people in poor countries cared more about development than the environment (Broad and Cavanagh 1993). Thus, a couple years later, a famous Marxist historian proclaimed, "It is no accident that the main support for ecological policies comes from the rich countries and from the comfortable rich and middles classes.... The poor, multiplying and under-employed, want more 'development,' not less" (Hobsbawm 1994, 570).

Guha and Martinez-Alier suggest that "wisdom may be deemed conventional when it unites ideologues of the left and right, scholars as well as journalists" (1997, xv), and indeed even today one can find journalists expressing the views shared by Beckerman and Hobsbaw (see, e.g., Tierney 2009). We would add, however, that conventional wisdom becomes most important when adopted by policy makers, as has the assumption that people in poor nations are not concerned about environmental protection (Brechin and Kempton 1994; Broad and Cavanagh 1993). A superb example occurred months prior to Rio when Lawrence Summers, then chief economist for the World Bank, issued an internal memo on December 12, 1991, that generated considerable controversy by suggesting that the World Bank should be encouraging *more* migration of "dirty industries" to the least developed countries (LDCs) for three reasons: (1) the health costs of pollution will be less because labor is cheaper in LDCs, (2) many LDCs (especially African nations) are "under-polluted," and thus increasing pollution levels will have minimal effect, and (3) the demand for a clean environment is low among poor people because such demand has "high income elasticity" (see Guha and Martinez-Alier 1997, 37–38).

Summers's assumption of the lack of concern for environmental quality among residents of poor nations not only expressed conventional wisdom unabashedly, but was consistent with the perspective of mainstream, neoclassical economics in which environmental amenities are viewed as "luxury goods" of concern mainly to those whose more basic needs for food, housing, and survival are adequately met (Baumol and Oates 1979). And interestingly, social science theorizing about environmentalism has served to reinforce conventional economic and popular thinking, which Steinberg terms "theories of environmental privilege" (2001, 27–45). In particular, sociologists have tended to view environmentalism as an exemplar of the "new social movements"—including the peace, antinuclear, and feminist movements—that have arisen within wealthy postindustrial societies in pursuit of lifestyle and quality-of-life issues rather than class-based economic interests (Buttel 1992). Similarly, political scientists have argued that environmentalism stems from the emergence of "postmaterialist values" among residents of wealthy nations during the post–World War II decades of affluence, especially among members of the "New Class" who are well educated but hold jobs in the service and information sectors rather than the core industrial and market sectors of the economy (Inglehart 1990).

The perspectives from economics, sociology, and political science are interrelated and mutually reinforcing, as relatively affluent members of the New Class espousing postmaterialist values are seen as the core constituency of New Social Movements such as environmentalism (Sutton 2000, 168–169). Nonetheless, it is the theory of postmaterialist values developed by Ronald Inglehart (1977, 1990, 1997) that has been most widely used to account for the emergence of environmentalism, green political parties, and citizen concern for the environment in social science analyses of these phenomena. Indeed, Guha and Martinez-Alier (1997, xiv) suggest that it has developed "hegemonic status" as an explanation of environmentalism, a view shared by others (e.g., Brechin and Kempton 1994; Lowe and Rudig 1986).

We will therefore focus primary attention on Inglehart's theory as we examine the results of cross-national surveys of citizen attitudes toward environmental issues to evaluate the validity of conventional wisdom and social science theorizing about potential differences between residents of poor and wealthy nations. Our goal is to determine the degree to which existing data support the widespread assumption that residents of poor nations are significantly less concerned about environmental problems and supportive of environmental protection than are their counterparts in the rich nations, as predicted by the postmaterialist explanation of environmental concern. To achieve it, we will present results from four large multinational surveys conducted between 1990 and 2001, including one that focused specifically on environmental issues and three others that each included several environmental items.

The Theory of Postmaterialist Value Change

Inglehart's theory of value change draws upon Maslow's theory of a hierarchy of human needs and Mannheim's theory of generations in arguing that within the wealthy, industrialized nations, those generations that have reached adulthood during post–World War II affluence have experienced a major shift in their basic values. Specifically, he combines a Maslowian-derived "scarcity hypothesis" that holds that individuals place most emphasis on "those things in short supply" with a Mannheimian-derived "socialization hypothesis" that holds that "one's basic values reflect the conditions that prevailed during one's pre-adult years" (Inglehart 1990, 68). Combining these two hypotheses leads Inglehart to theorize a widespread shift from materialist values such as economic and physical security to "postmaterialist" values such as freedom of speech, citizen participation, and quality of life among the generations that have reached adulthood during the affluent postwar decades—beginning prominently with the revolutionary "sixties generation." He further argues that the growing prevalence of postmaterialist values within the wealthy nations resulting from generational cohort replacement is the primary factor that has stimulated the emergence of progressive social movements such as the peace, feminist and environmental movements along with a host of other fundamental social changes (Inglehart 1977, 1990, 1997).

Inglehart's theory of value change provides important insights into basic social changes over the past several decades, and despite various criticisms, it has become a widely used perspective in comparative politics. Our goal is not to evaluate the overall theory, but rather its ability to account for the emergence of environmentalism and widespread concern for environmental quality at the international level. As noted earlier, the growth of postmaterialist values has been used to explain the emergence of environmental activism and concern in European, North American, and other wealthy nations—often rather successfully in empirical analyses (Inglehart 1990, 1997; Lowe and Rudig 1986). The specific issue we are concerned with, however, is the degree to which the theory of postmaterialist values can account for international patterns of citizen concern for environmental quality. As Guha and Martinez-Alier put it, "The theory of postmaterialism . . . provides a clear and in many respects persuasive explanation for the development and popularity of the environmental movement in the North. [But] it appears that the postmaterialist framework does not allow for the expression of environmental concern in the less developed world" (1997, viv).

The presumed lack of widespread concern for the environment in LDCs follows from Inglehart's (1990) assumption that environmental quality is a higher-order, quality-of-life value that poor people who are struggling to meet basic needs cannot afford to endorse. As such, Inglehart's theory provides strong support for conventional wisdom regarding the lack of citizen concern for the environment within the poor nations of the world (Brechin and Kempton 1994). Although Inglehart's theory depends on value change among individuals and is thus ideally tested via individual-level data, it clearly implies a link between national affluence and citizen attitudes and behaviors. His theory posits that being raised in affluence influences individuals' values and that values in turn influence attitudes (and behaviors) on specific issues such as the environment. Because postmaterialist values are far more prevalent in affluent than in poor nations, it follows that residents of rich nations should express higher levels of concern for environmental quality than do residents of poor nations (Brechin 1999; Brechin and Kempton 1997; Dunlap and Mertig 1997).

Challenges to the Postmaterialist Explanation of Environmental Concern

The growing awareness of environmental activism within poor nations (e.g., Steinberg 2001; Durning 1989), greatly enhanced by the huge number of grassroots organizations from such nations participating in the Global Forum in Rio in 1992 (Fisher 1993), began to raise questions about the assumed absence of environmental awareness and concern in Third World nations (Brechin and Kempton 1994). Yet whether such activism was highly atypical within poor nations or reflected a widespread concern for environmental quality among citizens of such nations remained unclear. It was left to a 1992 international environmental survey conducted by the Gallup International Institute (Dunlap, Gallup, and Gallup 1993) to provide the evidence required to examine the conventional view that citizen concern for the environment depended upon affluence and the subsequent spread of postmaterialist values.

The Health of the Planet (HOP) Survey was conducted in twenty-four economically and geographically diverse nations by members of the worldwide network of Gallup affiliates. The twenty-four nations (from five continents) in the HOP survey included six classified as "low" income, seven as "medium" income, and eleven as "high" income nations by the World Bank on the basis of per-capita gross national product (Dunlap, Gallup, and Gallup 1993). This was a far more diverse set of nations than those used in previous cross-national surveys obtaining data on environmental issues (e.g., Inglehart 1990), which were typically limited to Europe and North America.

Each affiliate translated the questionnaire into the appropriate language(s), and the Gallup International Institute had them "back-translated" into English to ensure comparability. The surveys were conducted via face-to-face and in-home interviews (thus minimizing problems of illiteracy), and all were completed during the first four months of 1992. Nationally representative samples were used in all nations but India, where rural areas and regions experiencing terrorism were underrepresented, with samples sizes ranging from 770 in Finland to 5,000 in India. Most were in the 1,000–1,500 range, yielding margins of error of approximately 3 percent for the respective national populations.

The HOP survey examined a wide range of environmental issues (Dunlap, Gallop, and Gallop 1993; Dunlap 1994). It drew upon relevant opinion and attitude research to ensure that key facets of "environmental concern"—defined as concern about environmental problems and support for environmental protection—were included (Dunlap and Jones 2002). A diverse set of fourteen different variables, including three multiple-item measures, were used to examine the linkage between national affluence and citizen concern for the environment (Dunlap and Mertig 1995, table 2). Aggregate national-level scores on each variable were created by computing the mean of all responses within each country, and these scores were then correlated with national affluence as measured by gross national product per capita.

The HOP results clearly called into question affluence-based, postmaterialist values as the key source of citizen concern for the environment. Of the fourteen different measures of environmental concern employed, eleven were found to be significantly correlated with national affluence—but surprisingly, seven were *negatively* related, indicating higher levels of concern among residents of poor nations! Citizens of poorer nations were significantly more likely to (1) express personal concern about environmental problems, (2) rate the quality of their national environments as poor, (3) rate the quality of their community environments as poor, (4) perceive environmental problems as health threats at present and (5) in the future, (6) rate six community-level environmental problems as serious, and (7) express support for six governmental environmental protection programs. In contrast, citizens of wealthier nations were more likely to (1) perceive environmental problems as serious *relative to* other national problems, (2) rate the quality of the world environment as poor, (3) express a preference for environmental protection over economic growth, and (4) express a willingness to pay higher prices for environmental protection. The three variables that were *not* significantly related to national affluence included (1) perceiving environmental problems in the nation as serious, (2) perceiving environmental problems as health threats in the past, and (3) rating seven global-level environmental problems as serious.

Given that the postmaterialist values explanation of environmental concern and the conventional wisdom it supports would predict consistently positive relationships between national affluence and indicators of citizen concern for the environment, the results of the HOP survey offered a strong disconfirmation of both (Dunlap and Mertig 1995). Obviously, widespread citizen concern for environmental problems and support for environmental protection were *not* confined to the wealthy nations, but if anything seemed stronger among the poorer nations in the HOP survey where—of course—the postmaterialist values assumed to be a prerequisite for environmental concern are known to be rare (Dunlap and Mertig 1997, 24). Overall, the HOP results suggested that citizen concern for environmental quality has become a worldwide phenomenon, *not* one limited to wealthy nations.

Brechin and Kempton (1994) published an article highly critical of the postmaterialist explanation of environmental concern using preliminary results from twenty-two nations covered in an early report on the HOP survey prepared for distribution at the 1992 Global Forum. Brechin later captured the importance of the HOP findings and the concomitant growth in awareness of environmental activism in developing countries when he wrote:

> Prior to 1992, the convention for explaining public formation of environmental concern . . . had been economic wealth. . . . The convention was first challenged through the 1980s and 1990s by many transnational environmental organizations and academic researchers with their reports on the environmental protests and activities of many local grassroots groups in poor developing countries. . . . The second and most devastating blow, however, came in 1992 with the *Health of the Planet* survey. (1999, 794)

Scholarly proponents of widely endorsed theoretical perspectives, like lay proponents of conventional wisdom, do not readily give up their views in the face of evidence to the contrary. It is not surprising, therefore, that a major debate over the utility of postmaterialist values in explaining citizen concern for the environment was stimulated by Brechin and Kempton's 1994 article (see, in particular, Kidd and Lee 1997; Brechin and Kempton 1997; Dunlap and Mertig 1997). Interestingly, while several critics and defenders of Inglehart's theory participated in this debate, Inglehart used another avenue to offer his own position on the utility of postmaterialist values for explaining international patterns of environmental concern.

Revising the Postmaterialist Explanation of Environmentalism

In 1995 Inglehart published an article on "public support for environmental protection" based on results from the 1990–1993 World Values Survey (WVS), the first wave to have near worldwide coverage with more than forty nations encompassing approximately 70 percent of the world's population included. It covered a wide range of nations in terms of geography (although, like the HOP survey, it included only one African nation—Nigeria) and, particularly, levels of affluence. In a rather unsystematic fashion, Inglehart (1995) reported national-level, aggregate responses to five environmental items, one dealing with "approval of the Ecology Movement" and four allegedly reflecting willingness to make economic sacrifices for environmental protection, which he combined into an "Environmental Protection Index." Although Inglehart never reported correlations between a measure of national affluence and aggregate-level attitudes across the nations, relying instead on tables showing percentages providing pro-environmental responses to the items for each nation, the overall patterns were clear—there was little relationship between afflu-ence and expressions of environmental concern within this large sample of nations.

Inglehart was not fazed by these findings, however, and offered an explanation of the high levels of citizen concern for the environment found in many of the poor nations covered by the WVS: "As one would expect, mass support for environmental protection tends to be greatest in countries that have relatively severe objective problems (as indicated by levels of air pollution and water pollution). This finding fits a 'challenge-response' model, which is the interpretation a naive environmental-ist would probably emphasize: people are concerned about the environment because they face serious objective problems" (1995, 57).

Not surprisingly, however, Inglehart continued by noting "this is only part of the story" and then argued, "Public support for environmental protection is also shaped by subjective cultural factors"—specifically "postmaterialist values" (1995, 57). He pointed out that countries with high levels of postmaterialist values also rank rela-tively high in public support for environmental protection (which of course his theory had always predicted), and concluded by arguing, "Objective problems and subjective predispositions are both involved; the available evidence indicates that both of these factors are about equally important" (57).

Put simply, Inglehart (1995) provided a post hoc explanation for the surprisingly high levels of public concern for the environment in poor nations, and, for example, the fact that citizens in nations as diverse as Norway, Turkey, Brazil, and Bulgaria indicated similar levels of willingness to pay higher taxes for environmental protec-tion. In the process, he created a two-factor explanation that Brechin aptly termed the *objective problems-subjective values* or *OPSV* explanation of global environ-mentalism: "In the South, it is derived from citizens experiencing directly pollution and other environmental degradation. In the North, it is derived from citizens expe-riencing a shift in their subjective or cultural values" (1999, 794). The problem with this explanation is that it is basically nonfalsifiable, for if environmental concern is found to be higher among residents of wealthy nations, it is attributed to their postmaterialist values, whereas if it is found to be higher (or at least as high) among residents of poor nations, it is attributed to their reactions to high levels of pollu-tion. Finally, Inglehart's OPSV explanation for the increasingly global spread of citizen concern for the environment is surprising in its emphasis on the importance of objective environmental conditions, as these were downplayed in his earlier analyses of the emergence of environmentalism in wealthy nations (Inglehart 1990, 372).

The wording of the four items Inglehart combined into his "Environmental Pro-tection Index" made us skeptical that they can legitimately be treated as a unidi-mensional measure. We also discovered that the 1990–1993 WVS included three additional environmental items, and as we are aware that analysts of environmental concern have long argued that it "makes a difference" how the construct is measured (Dunlap and Jones 2002), we decided to conduct our own analysis of the 1990–1993 data as well as data from the subsequent 1995–1998 and 1999–2001 waves of the WVS. Our goal is to provide an analysis of these three surveys that is sensitive to the potential existence of multiple dimensions of environmental concern within each one and to then employ the results to make systematic comparisons between them and those of the HOP survey in terms of the relationship between national affluence and citizen concern for the environment.

Analyses of the WVS Data Sets

The WVS surveys represent a monumental effort at international collaboration, relying on a worldwide network of social scientists obtaining funding for the surveys within their own nations. The 1990–1993 WVS was conducted in more than forty nations, the 1995–1998 WVS in more than fifty, and the 1999–2001 WVS in more than sixty, yielding unprecedented cross-national data on citizen attitudes, values, and behaviors on a range of issues. Yet the voluntary collaborative nature of the WVS surveys creates inevitable problems, one being that—unlike the HOP survey—they are not implemented at the same time, and in a few countries are conducted two or three years later than in the majority. Second, not all items are used in every nation, probably for cost reasons. Finally, it is difficult to find information on sampling procedures for each nation, raising further questions about comparability. Nonetheless, the WVS network appears to consist of experienced survey researchers, and the data are widely employed and accepted in the social science community.

We were able to find adequate data on the environmental items in a majority of the nations in each of the three waves of the WVS, and our analyses are obviously limited to these nations (see lists in the appendices in Dunlap and York 2008). All three include a very wide range of nations, both in terms of geography (Nigeria, covered in the first WVS, was joined by Ghana and South Africa in the second and then several more African countries in the third to give Africa improved, if still inadequate, representation) and national affluence. This makes the WVS data sets ideal for testing the widely assumed link between affluence and citizen concern for the environment, thereby providing replications of the HOP results.

1990–1993 WVS Results

As noted earlier, Inglehart (1995) and Kidd and Lee (1997) used four items from the 1990–1993 WVS to create an Environmental Protection Index, and Inglehart also reported national-level frequencies for "approval of the ecology movement." However, we found that the survey included two additional environmental attitude items, and following is the resulting list of seven items along with the "pro-environment" response for each one. Note that the first six were preceded by the statement, "I am now going to read out some statements about the environment. For each one I read out, can you tell me whether you agree strongly, agree, disagree or strongly disagree."

1. I would be willing to give part of my income if I were sure that the money would be used to prevent environmental pollution (agree).

2. I would agree to an increase in taxes if the extra money is used to prevent environmental pollution (agree).

3. The government should reduce environmental pollution, but it should not cost me any money (disagree).

4. Protecting the environment and fighting pollution is less urgent than often suggested (disagree).

5. If we want to combat unemployment in this country, we shall just have to accept environmental problems (disagree).

6. All the talk about pollution makes people too anxious (disagree).

7. There are a number of groups and movements looking for public support. For each of the following movements, . . . can you please tell me whether you approve or disapprove of this movement? . . . Ecology movement or nature protection (approve).

Inglehart (1995, 61) combined the first four items into a single index, and then reported the percentages within each nation who scored "high" on it by agreeing with the first two and disagreeing with the second two. However, although the first three clearly involve willingness to make economic sacrifices, the fourth does not. In fact, the fourth and sixth items appear to measure—albeit rather ambiguously— the perceived seriousness of environmental pollution, which past research suggests is likely to be a separate dimension distinct from economic sacrifice (Dunlap and Jones 2002). And, of course, the seventh item dealing with perception of the "ecology movement" is quite distinct in content. In addition, the third item is troubling because it is inherently double-barreled, in that it is easy to imagine respondents who are strongly pro-environmental agreeing with the first part but disagreeing with the second.

Besides being skeptical about Inglehart's four-item measure, we wanted to make use of all seven items if possible. We therefore examined the possibility that different dimensions of environmental concern are being tapped by these seven items and assessed whether the patterns are consistent across the thirty-six nations for which data are available. Specifically, for each national sample, a factor analysis was employed to investigate the relation among the seven items, and the results revealed three distinct dimensions (i.e., clusters of questions that tend to elicit similar responses) that were reasonably stable across all nations (see Dunlap and York 2008, 540). On this basis, we created three variables for the 1990–1993 WVS survey: (1) willingness to make economic sacrifices for environmental protection (items 1 and 2), (2) perceived seriousness of environmental pollution (items 4, 5, and 6), and (3) approval of the ecology movement (item 7). These results demonstrate that the four-item index used by Inglehart (1995) and Kidd and Lee (1997) is flawed, including three items tapping two distinct dimensions as well as a fourth (the double-barreled number 3) that behaves unpredictably.[2]

We next constructed national-level, aggregate scores for each country based on citizens' responses to the items constituting each variable. That the various items clearly tap distinct dimensions is apparent from the fact that the three variables we created are *not* significantly correlated with one another at the national level.[3] Use of these three variables allows us to examine the relationship between citizen concern for the environment and national affluence more fully and systematically than did Inglehart (1995), and in a fashion comparable to that used by Dunlap and Mertig (1995) in reporting the HOP results. Specifically, we ran statistical correlations between national-level scores on the three variables described earlier and two measures of national affluence, per capita gross domestic product and the log of GDP/capita for 1990. We used both measures because although the theory of postmaterialist values and conventional wisdom predict a positive relationship between national affluence and citizen concern for the environment, the precise nature of the relationship is unclear. It could be linear, or it could be that there is a rapid increase in environmental concern after nations reach a reasonable level of affluence, allowing for provision of basic needs to their citizens and then a leveling of such concern at high levels of affluence (Brechin and Kempton 1994, 257; Dunlap and Mertig 1995, 127). Because the latter approximates a logistic relationship, we computed Pearson's correlation coefficients between national scores on the environmental concern variables and both GDP/capita to test the linear increase hypothesis and the logarithm of GDP/capita to test the logistic function hypothesis.

The results of our analyses are reported in table 4.1, where in order to maximize information, we report the correlations between national affluence and the composite variables we created as well as each of the individual seven items in the 1990–1993 WVS. Several findings are worth noting. First, the results obtained for GDP/capita and log GDP/capita tend to be very similar (as was the case for the HOP), and thus we confine our discussion to the former. Second, the degree and direction of the relationships vary substantially, both for the composite variables and the individual items—again emphasizing that the WVS items are tapping distinct dimensions of environmental concern.

Table 4.1

Correlations between national affluence (GDP per capita) and measures of environmental concern[a]—1990–1993 World Values Survey (36 Nations)

Willingness to make economic sacrifices	GDP per capita 1990	Log (GDP per capita) 1990
Give income	−0.47**	−0.49**
Pay taxes	−0.33*	−0.36*
Not cost	0.39*	0.24
Willingness Index[b]	−0.41*	−0.44**
Perceived Seriousness of Environmental Problems		
Unemployment	0.33**	0.37**
Too anxious	0.43**	0.37*
Not urgent	0.46**	0.59**
Seriousness Index[c]	0.46**	0.50**
Ecology Movement		
Approve of movement	−0.47**	−0.35*

Notes: *$p < 0.05$ (two-tailed test); **$p < 0.01$ (two-tailed test)
[a]All items/measures are coded so that higher scores indicate a "pro-environment" position.
[b]Sum of first two items.
[c]Sum of all three items.

Most notably, the two items dealing with willingness to make economic sacrifices for environmental protection both correlate *negatively* with national affluence, as does the composite index formed by them, as the latter correlates—0.41 ($p < 0.05$) with GDP/capita. (In contrast, the double-barreled "not cost" item correlates positively with national affluence, further evidence that it does not tap the same dimension as the other two economic items and perhaps indicative of its inherent ambiguity.) This finding diverges sharply with the HOP, in which willingness to pay higher prices for environmental protection and a preference for environmental protection over economic growth were positively correlated with national affluence (Dunlap and Mertig 1995, 129). The WVS results not only directly contradict Inglehart's theory of postmaterialist values as a key source of environmental concern but also challenge the conventional wisdom as expressed by Lawrence Summers's assumption that people in poor nations do not value environmental quality. Given that people in poorer nations clearly have less ability to pay for environmental quality in monetary terms, these results are frankly perplexing.

In contrast, the three items tapping the perceived seriousness of environmental pollution, as well as the composite index formed by them, are all positively and significantly correlated with national affluence (the latter 0.46, $p < 0.01$), meaning that residents of richer nations are expressing *more* concern than are their counterparts in the poorer nations. Again, this finding contrasts with the HOP and perhaps stems from the fact that whereas the HOP tended to have respondents rate the seriousness of specific environmental problems, the WVS includes rather vague items (Neumayer 2002). Specifically, respondents who *disagree* that talking about pollution makes people too anxious, that protecting the environment is less urgent than often suggested, and that environmental problems need to be accepted to combat unemployment (which might be expected to load on the economic sacrifice dimension, but does not), are classified as seeing environmental problems as serious. Although one can argue that these results support conventional wisdom and the theory of postmaterialist values, they ironically contradict Inglehart's more recent emphasis on the importance of objective conditions stimulating environmental concern within poor nations or the OPSV explanation of global environmentalism (Brechin 1999). Obviously, residents of poor nations experiencing high levels of pollution should be more likely to feel that fighting pollution is urgent.

The third variable consists of the single item measuring approval of the ecology (environmental) movement, a reasonable indicator of a pro-environmental orientation. Here we again find a strong negative relationship ($r = -0.47$, $p < 0.01$), indicating that citizens in poor nations have a more positive view of the ecology movement than do their counterparts in rich nations. This finding suggests that not only has environmental activism become common in many poor nations (see, e.g., Steinberg 2001; Durning 1989; Fisher 1993; Guha and Martinez-Alier 1997; Pellow 2007) but also that it tends to be viewed favorably by citizens within those nations.

In sum, the results of the 1990–1993 WVS yield a mixed and surprising set of findings. The two multiple-item composite indexes we created on the basis of factor analyses—measures that should have greater validity and reliability than single-item indicators—yield opposite and unintuitive findings: willingness to make economic sacrifices on behalf of environmental protection is negatively related to national affluence, while perceiving environmental problems as serious is positively related. Both findings, and their opposition to those produced by the HOP, suggest the need for replication. Nonetheless, when approval of the ecology movement, which is negatively related to affluence, is also taken into account it is clear that the overall pattern of findings from the 1990–93 WVS is at odds with expectations from conventional wisdom and the theory of postmaterialist values. On two of the three variables residents of poorer nations—where postmaterialist values are rare—are found to be bold more pro-environmental views than do their counterparts in rich nations, where postmaterialist values are far more prevalent.

1995–1998 WVS Results

The 1995–1998 wave of the WVS included several new environmental items and only one from the prior wave. We again factor-analyzed the items for each nation, and again the results were generally consistent, with four distinct dimensions emerging (Dunlap and York 2008, 543–544).

The first set of items deals with willingness to make economic sacrifices for environmental protection, including the "pay taxes" item used in the first wave. The three items, which were introduced with the same statement as in the first wave (and the "pro-environmental" response for each), are:

1. I would agree to an increase in taxes if the extra money were used to prevent environmental damage (agree).

2. I would buy things at 20 percent higher than usual prices if it would help protect the environment (agree).

3. Here are two statements people sometimes make when discussing the environment and economic growth. Which of them comes closer to your own point of view?

   a. Protecting the environment should be given priority, even if it causes slower economic growth and loss of some jobs (this choice).

   b. Economic growth and creating jobs should be given the top priority, even if the environment suffers to some extent.

The first two form a distinct dimension across a majority of the nations, but the third one (a broad trade-off item similar to the one used in the HOP survey) behaves less consistently. Although it tends to load on the same dimension, it does so with a lower magnitude and less consistency, and we therefore formed a composite index consisting only of the first two items. The similarity of this Willingness Index to that used in the first wave offers an important opportunity for replication.

The next two dimensions emerged from a set of five self-reported behaviors given to respondents after they were asked, "Which, if any, of these things have you done in the last twelve months out of concern for the environment?" In each case, a "yes" is indicative of a pro-environmental response. The five include:

1. Have you chosen household products that you think are better for the environment?

2. Have you decided for environmental reasons to reuse or recycle something rather than throw it away?

3. Have you tried to reduce water consumption for environmental reasons?

4. Have you attended a meeting or signed a letter or petition aimed at protecting the environment?

5. Have you contributed to an environmental organization?

In addition to the well-known weakness of self-reported (as opposed to observed) behaviors, we feel that this is a very problematic set of items for use in a cross-national survey covering numerous poor nations.

These behaviors are representative of what Guha and Martinez-Alier (1997) term the "full-stomach" environmentalism of wealthy nations, largely inapplicable to the "empty-belly" environmentalism of poorer nations, and strongly biased in favor of residents of the affluent, largely Northern Hemisphere countries. People living in poverty-stricken nations reuse and recycle and conserve water out of necessity, and it is difficult to imagine how they would respond to these items. Even the two politically oriented items are worded with "Northern environmentalism" in mind, as environmentalists in developing countries are less likely to protest in writing or to make financial contributions to environmental groups than are their rich-nation counterparts. Despite their obvious bias, we included these items rather than relying solely on the economic-environment dimension and single confidence item described earlier. Across the majority of nations, these five items formed two distinct dimensions, with the first three loading heavily on a "green consumerism" factor and the last two on an "environmental activism" factor.

We employed composite measures tapping these three dimensions, along with an individual item measuring "confidence in the Green/Ecology movement," to examine the relationship between public concern for the environment and national affluence among all nations with sufficient data, ranging between thirty-six and forty-four countries, depending on the specific variable. As with the first wave of the WVS, we ran Pearson correlation coefficients between these various indicators of pro-environmental attitudes/behaviors and both GDP/capita and log GDP/capita; to maximize information, we report the correlations between the composite variables we created as well as each of the individual nine items in the 1995–1998 WVS.

As was the case for the 1990–1993 WVS, the results obtained for GDP/capita and log GDP/capita tend to be very similar, and thus we confine our discussion to the former. Second, like the earlier wave, the relationships vary substantially across the various measures, emphasizing that the 1995–1998 indicators are also tapping distinct dimensions of environmental concern and cautioning against combining individual items into indexes without first conducting necessary analyses to establish the appropriateness of doing so.

Perhaps the most notable finding reported in table 4.2 is that the Willingness Index is not significantly related to national affluence (−0.14). Interestingly, although this composite and its two constituent items (both clearly tapping individuals' willingness to make economic sacrifices, via higher taxes and prices, respectively) are negatively related to national affluence, the more generalized economic growth versus environmental protection trade-off item ("protect environment") is positively related, reinforcing our decision not to include the latter in the index. Although the

Table 4.2
Correlations between national affluence (GDP per capita) and measures of environmental concern[a]—1995–1998 World Values Survey (36–44 Nations)[b]

Willingness to make economic sacrifices	GDP per capita 1995	Log (GDP per capita) 1995
Pay taxes	−0.12	−0.15
Higher prices	−0.15	−0.05
Protect environment	0.12	0.24
Willingness Index[c]	−0.14	−0.11
Green Consumerism		
Household products	0.69**	0.72**
Reuse/recycle	0.78**	0.76**
Reduce water use	0.10	0.19
Green Consumerism Index[d]	0.67**	0.71**
Environmental Activism		
Meeting/letter/petition	0.42**	0.44**
Contributed to organization	0.27	0.10
Environmental Activism Index[e]	0.39*	0.31*
Ecology Movement		
Confidence in movement	−0.11	0.13

Notes: *$p < 0.05$ (two-tailed test); **$p < 0.01$ (two-tailed test)
[a]All items/measures are coded so that higher scores indicate a "pro-environment" position.
[b]For Willingness Index, N = 43; for Green Consumerism Index, N = 36; for Environmental Activism Index, N = 41; and for Confidence in Ecology Movement, N = 43. For "Pay taxes" and "Protect environment," N = 44.
[c]Sum of first two items.
[d]Sum of all three items.
[e]Sum of both items.

lack of statistical significance for the index and its two items make these findings less counterintuitive than those that emerged in the 1990–1993 WVS, the direction of their relationships with national affluence is still surprising and—more important— at odds with conventional wisdom and the theory of postmaterialist values. Clearly, residents of poor nations are no less likely than their counterparts in wealthy nations to support environmental protection, even when doing so entails personal cost.

In contrast—and unsurprisingly, given our earlier argument that the self-reported behavioral items appear heavily biased in favor of Northern environmentalism— there are strong positive correlations between national affluence and both green consumerism and environmental activism. Residents of the wealthier nations are far more likely to report engaging in green consumerism (0.67, $p < 0.01$) and considerably more likely to report engaging in environmental activism (0.39, $p < 0.01$) than are their counterparts in the poorer nations. The former seems inevitable to us, given that the items used to measure green consumerism are essentially irrelevant to many people in poor nations who engage in such behaviors out of necessity and not due to a conscious effort to protect the environment, and the latter is unsurprising given that the items tap written protests and presumably financial contributions to organizations—quintessential Northern forms of activism of less relevance in poor nations (Guha and Martinez-Alier 1997). Combined with the fact that consumption practices are often *household* rather than individual decisions, and that self-reports of either respondent or household behavior have questionable validity, we feel that the strongly positive correlations between national affluence and citizens' pro-environmental behaviors should be viewed with considerable caution.

Finally, the level of confidence in the Green/Ecology movement is not significantly related to national affluence (−0.11). This item is also a weak indicator of pro-environmental orientation in our view, lacking the clarity of the item measuring approval/disapproval of the movement used in the prior wave. Nonetheless, combining it with the three composite measures tapping the distinct dimensions found among the other attitudinal/behavioral items results in another mixed set of results. Overall, the 1995–1998 WVS yields two measures of environmental concern—the willingness to make economic sacrifices dimension and confidence in the Green/Ecology movement—that are unrelated to national affluence, and two others—(self-reported) green consumerism and environmental activism—that are strongly positively related to affluence.

In our view, the economic sacrifice dimension is the most crucial, both because the WVS items tapping it are clear-cut indicators of pro-environmental attitudes and because it is on this dimension that both conventional wisdom and proponents of postmaterialist values place most emphasis (Inglehart 1995, 59). Keeping in mind that conventional wisdom and the theory of postmaterialist values would predict consistently positive correlations between national affluence and all indicators of citizen concern for the environment, we conclude that like its 1990–1993 predecessor, the 1995–1998 WVS yields evidence that calls both into question.

1999–2001 WVS Results

The third wave of the WVS included fewer environmental items than did the prior two; unfortunately, one was the flawed, double-barreled item ("not cost") used in the first wave. It also included the two items ("give income" and "pay taxes") used in the Willingness [to Make Economic Sacrifices] Index constructed for that wave and reported in table 4.1, along with the environmental protection versus economic growth trade-off item ("protect environment") used in the second wave and reported in table 4.2. Because the double-barreled item did not load with the other two

Table 4.3
Correlations between national affluence (GDP per capita) and measures of environmental concern[a]—1999–2001 World Values Survey (32–55 Nations)[b]

Willingness to make economic sacrifices	GDP per capita 2000	Log (GDP per capita) 2000
Give income	−0.25	−0.32*
Pay taxes	−0.14	−0.30*
Not cost	0.38**	0.22
Protect environment	0.21	0.25
Willingness Index[c]	−0.20	−0.32*
Ecology Movement		
Confidence in movement	−0.07	−0.08

Notes: *p < .05 (two-tailed test); **p < .01 (two-tailed test)
[a]All items/measures are coded so that higher scores indicate a "pro-environment" position.
[b]For "Give income," "Pay taxes," "Not cost," and Willingness Index, N = 55; for "Protect environment," N = 36; for "Confidence in movement," N = 32.
[c]Sum of first two items.

economic sacrifice items in the first wave and is inherently ambiguous, we again examine its relationship to national affluence separately rather than include it in the Willingness Index in the third wave. Similarly, because the trade-off item did not load consistently on the Willingness Index constructed for the second wave *and* because it was not asked in many of the nations in the third wave, we also examine it separately.

The 1999–2001 WVS also included an item measuring degree of confidence in "the Environmental Protection movement" similar to the one used in the second wave, albeit for only a small majority of the nations participating in the survey, and we report the relationship between responses to it and national affluence in table 4.3 as well.

Table 4.3 reports the results obtained from correlating aggregate, national-level scores on the four individual economic-oriented items and the two-item Willingness Index along with the item on confidence in the Environmental Movement with national affluence. Unlike results for the prior two WVS waves, there are consistent differences in the significance levels (but not directions) of the relationships depending on whether GDP/capita or log GDP/capita is employed as the indicator of affluence, and these will be noted.

As was true for the first wave of the WVS, the two individual items providing straightforward indicators of willingness to make economic sacrifices for environmental protection—"give income" and "pay taxes"—are negatively related to national affluence, as is the composite Willingness Index constructed by combining them. In contrast to the first-wave results, however, for the third wave only the log GDP/capita correlations are statistically significant: –0.32 ($p < 0.05$) and –0.30 ($p < 0.05$) for the individual items and –0.32 ($p < 0.05$) for the composite index. The double-barreled item, "not cost," is again positively and significantly correlated (0.38, $p < 0.01$) with national affluence (measured by GDP/capita), as in the first wave, reemphasizing that it is not tapping the same dimension as are the first two items and/or is hopelessly ambiguous. Likewise, the environmental tradeoff item—used in only thirty-two nations—is also positively (0.21) but not significantly related to national affluence, as was the case in the second wave, again indicating that having respondents choose between environmental protection and economic growth produces different results than asking if they are personally willing to pay higher taxes or give part of their income for environmental protection. Finally, confidence in the Environmental Protection movement (used in only thirty-six nations) is nonsignificantly—but negatively—related (–0.07) to affluence, comparable to the finding for the similar item in the second wave.

In short, the relatively limited set of relationships between indicators of pro-environmental attitudes available for the third wave of the WVS are, overall, consistent with those found in the first two waves. Most notable, in our view, is that responses to the items that provide the most direct and unambiguous indicators of *personal* willingness to make economic sacrifices on behalf of environmental protection (including a two-item index that should possess better validity and reliability than the single-item measures) are negatively related to national affluence, exactly the opposite of what both the theory of postmaterialist values and conventional wisdom predict.

Summary

Our primary goal has been to compare the results of the 1990–1993, the 1995–1998, and the 1999–2001 waves of the World Values Survey—each encompassing diverse and ever larger sets of nations—with those of Gallup's 1992 Health of the Planet Survey. Readers may interpret our WVS findings (three significant negative correlations, two insignificant correlations, and three significant positive correlations when focusing on the composite measures and single "ecology/environmental movement" items) in various ways. The crucial issue in our mind is that both conventional wisdom and social science explanations of environmental concern as stemming from postmaterialist values would predict consistently positive relationships between citizen concern for the environment and levels of national affluence, and clearly the three waves of the WVS do not produce supportive evidence for either. When one considers that many of the WVS items seem biased in favor of yielding more pro-environmental responses among the publics of wealthy than poor nations, the results become even more noteworthy. Given the emphasis that both spokespersons for conventional wisdom such as Summers and of postmaterialism such as Inglehart place on public willingness to pay for environmental protection, and that the most straightforward indicators of such willingness are consistently (if not always significantly) *negatively* correlated with national affluence, the WVS results are particularly damaging—and even puzzling.

On the other hand, those who have followed the rapidly accumulating evidence of citizen action on behalf of environmental protection in poor and developing nations around the would (as documented in Steinberg 2005; Fisher 1993; Guha and Martinez-Alier 1997; Martinez-Alier 2002; Pellow 2007) will not be surprised that environmental activism in these countries is often reflective of widespread public sentiment. Clearly, both environmental activism and public support for environmental protection have become global phenomena and are no longer—if they ever were—limited to the wealthy nations of the world.

Implications for Policy Making and Social Science Theory

Although it may take different shapes, concern for the environment has obviously spread well beyond wealthy nations, and it is time for both policy makers and social scientists to revise their views accordingly. To conceptualize environmental quality as something that only the wealthy can afford, and that is of little concern to the poor, does violence to the facts. This should have been apparent already at the 1992 Earth Summit in Rio, where poor nations were asking for financial and technical assistance to help protect their environments and wealthy nations were not only stingy with such assistance, but in some cases (notably the United States under the first Bush administration) openly hostile to international environmental agreements (Vaillancourt 1993). This pattern was even more apparent a decade later at the 2002 World Summit on Sustainable Development in Johannesburg, where the United States under the second Bush administration led the way in blocking or weakening virtually every significant proposal—often with the help of a few other wealthy countries such as Australia and Japan (Speth 2003). In a world in which a handful of rich nations are often the major impediments to effective international environmental protection treaties, and many treaties neglect or exacerbate current inequities (Roberts and Park 2006), it is disingenuous to continue to blame residents of poor nations (or their leaders) for the lack of progress in protecting the global environment.

Furthermore, the conventional notion that people in poor countries cannot afford to be concerned about environmental protection leads to simplistic and ineffective policies to stimulate economic growth within those nations. Policy proposals from international institutions such as the World Bank and International Monetary Fund typically call for unleashing market forces by privatizing natural resources and encouraging their exportation (Goldman 2005). These proposals not only ignore the inequitable consequences of such "development" but also the deleterious socio-economic and ecological impacts of privatizing common property resources and rapidly depleting the natural resource base of poor nations (Goldman 1998).

The assumption that affluence is a prerequisite for efforts to address environmental problems is embedded in the *environmental Kuznets curve (EKC)* hypothesis, which posits that nations will start to curb their environmental impacts only after a certain level of national income is exceeded (Dinda 2004). The EKC, which implicitly shares many of the assumptions of the postmaterialist values thesis (Dietz, Fitzgerald, and Shwom 2005, 361), is often uncritically accepted among social scientists, policy makers, and journalists as true (Broad and Cavanagh 1993; Tierney 2009), even though it is empirically supported in only a limited set of circumstances (Cavlovic et al. 2000) and is clearly invalid when considering global environmental problems (York, Rosa, and Dietz 2003).

In short, recognizing that citizens of poorer nations—particularly those whose livelihoods depend directly upon available natural resources—are motivated to protect the environment can help both national and international governmental bodies design more effective policies. Rather than pushing narrowly for economic growth and hoping that it will result in increased affluence and thus citizen concern for the environment, policies that recognize the inherent link between ecological and economic sustainability may prove more popular as well as efficacious. Although "sustainable development" has often been primarily a rhetorical device (Goldman 2005), our results suggest that programs that promote ecologically and economically sound "livelihoods" may have strong appeal to residents of poor nations (Martinez-Alier 2002).

What can be called the globalization of citizen concern for the environment also poses a direct challenge to social science theorizing about the origins and social bases of environmentalism. Explanations highlighting the role of the New Class and their postmaterialist values may have been useful for explaining the emergence of modern environmentalism in North America and Europe but are clearly inadequate for explaining the global spread of environmental activism and concern. There are many factors involved in stimulating awareness, concern, and activism regarding environmental issues within and particularly across different nations, and it is unlikely that universalistic explanations will prove adequate in accounting for the diverse sources and nature of environmental concern worldwide.

In a world in which environmental concern and activism have become commonplace—prevalent in poor as well as rich nations, with aims ranging from pollution prevention to maintenance of subsistence resources to preservation of aesthetic values, and with foci encompassing the local to global levels—it is necessary to go beyond the quest for parsimonious explanations that highlight single factors like postmaterialist values as the source of activism and concern. It is also time to lay to rest the assumption that environmental quality is a luxury good of concern only to the affluent.

Notes

This chapter is a shortened version of Dunlap and York 2008. The article provides more detail on data analyses and appendices listing the nations included in the three waves of the World Values Survey (including their GDP per capita and sample sizes) for which results are reported herein.

1. This is not to deny that there were major divisions between rich and poor nations in Rio, but their differences were more over diagnoses of the causes of environmental problems and policies and funding for environmental protection rather than over the seriousness of environmental problems (see, e.g., Haas, Levy, and Parson 1992).

2. The inadequacy of Inglehart's (1995) four-item index is reflected by the fact that at the national level it correlates +0.73 with the Willingness Index (with which it shares two items) but only +0.37 with the Seriousness Index and −0.20 with approval of the ecology movement.

3. The Pearson's correlation coefficient for the relationship between economic sacrifice and perceived seriousness (when coded so that high scores indicate "pro-environment" responses) is −0.20 (not significant), for economic sacrifice and approval of the ecology movement it is 0.07 (not significant), and for perceived seriousness and approval of the ecology movement it is −0.19 (not significant).

References

Baumol, William J., and Wallace E. Oates. 1979. *Economics, Environmental Policy, and Quality of Life*. Inglewood Cliffs, N.J.: Prentice-Hall.

Beckerman, Wilfred. 1974. *Two Cheers for the Affluent Society*. New York: St. Martin's Press.

Brechin, Steven R. 1999. Objective Problems, Subjective Values, and Global Environmentalism: Evaluating the Postmaterialist Argument and Challenging a New Explanation. *Social Science Quarterly* 80:793–809.

Brechin, Steven R., and Willet Kempton. 1994. Global Environmentalism: A Challenge to the Postmaterialism Thesis? *Social Science Quarterly* 75:245–269.

Brechin, Steven R., and Willet Kempton. 1997. Beyond Postmaterialist Values: National versus Individual Explanations of Global Environmentalism. *Social Science Quarterly* 78:16–23.

Broad, Robin, and John Cavanagh. 1993. Beyond the Myths of Rio. *World Policy Journal* 10:65–72.

Buttel, Frederick H. 1992. Environmentalization: Origins, Processes, and Implications for the Rural Social Change. *Rural Sociology* 56:461–474.

Carnegie Endowment for International Peace. 1972. Environment and Development: The Founex Report. *International Conciliation*, no. 586.

Cavlovic, Therese A., Kenneth H. Baker, Robert P. Berrens, and Kishore Gawande. 2000. A Meta-analysis of Environmental Kuznets Curve Studies. *Agricultural and Resource Economics Review* 29:32–42.

Dietz, Thomas, Amy Fitzgerald, and Rachel Shwom. 2005. Environmental Values. *Annual Review of Environment and Resources* 30:335–372.

Dinda, Soumyananda. 2004. Environmental Kuznets Curve Hypothesis: A Survey. *Ecological Economics* 49:431–455.

Dunlap, Riley E. 1994. International Attitudes toward Environment and Development. In *Green Globe Yearbook—1994*, ed. Helge Ole Bergesen and Georg Parmann, 115–126. Oxford and New York: Oxford University Press.

Dunlap, Riley E., George H. Gallup Jr., and Alex M. Gallup. 1993. Of Global Concern: Results of the Health of the Planet Survey. *Environment* 35 (November): 7–15, 33–39.

Dunlap, Riley E., and Robert Emmet Jones. 2002. Environmental Concern: Conceptual and Measurement Issues. In *Handbook of Environmental Sociology*, ed. Riley E. Dunlap and William Michelson, 482–524. Westport: Greenwood Press.

Dunlap, Riley E., and Angela G. Mertig. 1995. Global Concern for the Environment: Is Affluence a Prerequisite? *Journal of Social Issues* 51:121–137.

Dunlap, Riley E., and Angela G. Mertig. 1997. Global Environmental Concern: An Anomaly for Postmaterialism. *Social Science Quarterly* 78:24–29.

Dunlap, Riley E., and Richard York. 2008. The Globalization of Environmental Concern and the Limits of the Postmaterialist Values Explanation: Evidence from Four Multinational Surveys. *Sociological Quarterly* 49 (3): 529–563.

Durning, Alan. 1989. Mobilizing at the Grassroots. In *State of the World 1989*, ed. Lester R. Brown, 154–173. New York: Norton.

Fisher, Julie. 1993. *The Road from Rio: Sustainable Development and the Nongovernmental Movement in the Third World*. Westport, Conn.: Praeger.

Goldman, Michael. 1998. *Privatizing Nature: Political Struggles for the Global Commons*. New Brunswick, N.J.: Rutgers University Press.

Goldman, Michael. 2005. *Imperial Nature: The World Back and Struggles for Social Justice in the Age of Globalization*. New Haven: Yale University Press.

Guha, Ramachandra, and Joan Martinez-Alier. 1997. *Varieties of Environmentalism: Essays North and South*. London: Earthscan.

Haas, Peter, Marc A. Levy, and Edward A. Parson. 1992. Appraising the Earth Summit: How Should We Judge UNCED's Success? *Environment* 34 (8): 6–11, 26–33.

Hobsbawm, Eric. 1994. *The Age of Extremes*. London: Michael Joseph.

Inglehart, Ronald. 1977. *The Silent Revolution: Changing Values and Political Styles among Western Publics*. Princeton: Princeton University Press.

Inglehart, Ronald. 1990. *Culture Shift in Advanced Industrial Society*. Princeton: Princeton University Press.

Inglehart, Ronald. 1995. Public Support for Environmental Protection: Objective Problems and Subjective Values in 43 Societies. *PS: Political Science & Politics* 28:57–72.

Inglehart, Ronald. 1997. *Modernization and Postmodernization: Cultural, Economic, and Political Change in 43 Societies*. Princeton: Princeton University Press.

Kidd, Quentin, and Aie-Rie Lee. 1997. Postmaterialist Values and the Environment: A Critique and Reappraisal. *Social Science Quarterly* 78:1–15.

Lowe, Philip D., and Wolfgang Rudig. 1986. Review Article: Political Ecology and the Social Sciences—The State of the Art. *British Journal of Political Science* 16:513–550.

Martinez-Alier, Joan. 2002. *The Environmentalism of the Poor*. Cheltenham, UK: Edward Elgar.

Neumayer, Eric. 2002. Do We Trust the Data? On the Validity and Reliability of Cross-National Surveys. *Social Science Quarterly* 83:332–340.

Pellow, David N. 2007. *Resisting Global Toxics: Transnational Movements for Environmental Justice*. Cambridge, Mass.: MIT Press.

Roberts, J. Timmons, and Bradley C. Parks. 2006. *A Climate of Injustice: Global Inequality, North–South Politics, and Climate Policy*. Cambridge, Mass.: MIT Press.

Speth, James Gustave. 2003. Perspectives on the Johannesburg Summit. *Environment* 45:24–29.

Steinberg, Paul F. 2001. *Environmental Leadership in Developing Countries: Transnational Relations and Biodiversity Policy in Costa Rica and Bolivia*. Cambridge, Mass.: MIT Press.

Steinberg, Paul F. 2005. From Public Concern to Policy Effectiveness: Civic Conservation in Developing Countries. *Journal of International Wildlife Law and Policy* 8:341–365.

Sutton, Philip W. 2000. *Explaining Environmentalism: In Search of a New Social Movement*. Aldershoot, UK: Ashgate.

Tierney, John. 2009. Use Energy, Get Rich and Save the Planet. *New York Times* (Science Times), April 21, p. D1.

Vaillancourt, Jean-Guy. 1993. Earth Summits of 1992 in Rio. *Society & Natural Resources* 6:81–88.

York, Richard, Eugene A. Rosa, and Thomas Dietz. 2003. Footprints on the Earth: The Environmental Consequences of Modernity. *American Sociological Review* 68 (2): 279–300.

III
Nonstate Actors and Social Mobilization

5

The Comparative Study of Environmental Movements

Kate O'Neill

For almost twenty years, the Goldman Environmental Prize has been awarded annually to individuals from six continents engaged in environmental activism in their native countries. Recent winners include a Russian working to protect Lake Baikal from pollution, a Belgian who helped establish that country's first national park, a Mexican working with indigenous agricultural techniques to restore farmland, a musician from Mozambique bringing basic education and sanitation technology to remote areas, and two Ecuadorians fighting for reparations from the oil multinational Chevron. As of 2010, the prize had been awarded to 126 individuals from different parts of the world, illustrating both the truly global reach of environmentalism and the great diversity of activities, campaigns, and struggles encompassed under the environmentalist label. Although the prize is awarded to individuals, these winners are supported in their activities by communities, organizations, and networks, either close by or spanning national borders.

The sheer scope and diversity of individuals and groups around the world engaged in environmental activism makes environmental movements a rich source for comparative scholarship in the social sciences. Indeed, it is almost impossible to understand contemporary environmentalism and its impact on the world without making comparisons—across borders, across movements and movement organizations, or across issue areas. Likewise, few studies of comparative environmental politics fail to include environmental movements in their analysis, given the importance of environmental activism in raising awareness of problems and pushing them onto political agendas. The field of global environmental politics, especially research on the implementation of multilateral agreements and initiatives, can also benefit from a deeper understanding of the comparative politics of environmentalism, particularly given the role that environmental movement organizations play in creating governance partnerships, implementing environmental agreements, and raising awareness about global problems (O'Neill 2009). The study of how and in which political contexts NGOs can work effectively to further global agendas carries important lessons for political actors at the international level.

This chapter outlines some of the major themes in the comparative study of environmental movements. First, I outline the emergence of and diversity within the environmental movement. I then examine environmental movements in relation to social movement theory. Social movement theory covers a broad range of theoretical literatures that seek to explain the emergence, organization, and impacts of collective action by civil society groups, including environmental movements. Its insights have been applied to environmental movements across industrialized and developing countries, democracies, and authoritarian states, and countries in political and economic transition. It helps us understand in a systematic way why environmental movements look the way they do or have differing political and social impacts across and within these different categories of nation state. I then address the impact that the burgeoning literature on transnational social movements and networks has had on the comparative study of environmental movements. It is very hard these days to study movements in isolation from their transnational networks or from the influence of ideas originating elsewhere. However, national and local perspectives on environmental movements have far from withered, instead taking on a new sort of importance in understanding our more globalized world. The chapter concludes with a brief review of some of the more recent questions shaping work on comparative environmental movements.

Environmental Movements: A Brief Introduction

At the most basic level, environmentalists are concerned with altering the relationship between human society and the natural world, changing human behavior to halt or slow down environmental degradation of all types (Mauch et al. 2006, 1). Their actions may be for the immediate benefit of communities losing access to resources they have used for centuries or threatened by the toxic emissions of a factory or power plant or waste facility. They may also be in the interests of the natural world itself, through preserving biodiversity, for example, or in the interests of future generations, as in the struggle to slow down climate change.

When environmentalists and others start working together to achieve common goals, they form movement organizations. Some environmental movement organizations, such as Greenpeace International or Friends of the Earth, are global in scope and cover multiple issues. Others, such as the Quincy Library Group in the United States or the Chipko Movement in India, are far more localized. Collectively, these organizations make up environmental movements. In comparative politics, we often talk about the German, or the Australian, or the North American environmental movement as a sort of shorthand that brings together groups that share and are shaped by particular national contexts. It is also possible to talk about the climate change movement, the anti-toxics movement, or the rainforest movement, bringing together groups united (and sometimes divided) by a common environmental cause.

Environmentalism of all sorts is and always has been deeply political. In fact, most collective action around environmental issues (in other words, the formation of movement organizations) has been in order to gain strength against opposing interests and to convince the uncommitted of the value of the cause. Sometimes these conflicts are played out in the streets, sometimes in the halls of government, corporate boardrooms, the courts, or the press. In extreme situations, environmental activists may be putting their own lives and liberty on the line. In fact, one function of the Goldman Prize is to draw international attention and acclaim to the awardees, which may help protect them from such threats. Relatively few environmental campaigns have involved this level of conflict or risk to participants. But from wilderness protection campaigns in North America to anti-dam movements in Asia or Latin America, environmental activists frequently come up against powerful opposing interests and perspectives.

Table 5.1 maps out some of the major arenas of environmental activism: wilderness and species preservation, access to and use of natural resources, responses to

Table 5.1
Mapping arenas of environmental activism

---

1. **Wilderness and species preservation**
   Biodiversity conservation (habitat, species, genetic diversity)
   Parks movements
   Deep ecology

2. **Access to and use of natural resources**
   Land, forests, water, plants, and animals
   Property rights and common pool resources
   Food security
   Community-based conservation
   Multistakeholder participation

3. **Responding to industrial and technological risks**
   Industrial, agricultural production—toxics, air pollution, pesticide use, land degradation
   Mining and resource extraction
   Large scale construction—dams, roads, power plants, factories
   Waste disposal
   Nuclear weapons and power
   Genetically modified organisms and biotechnology
   Climate change

4. **Communitarian green movements**
   Critiques of free-market capitalism, state socialism, neoliberal globalization
   Promotion of alternative lifestyles within predominant systems
   Promotion of alternative economic systems

---

industrial and technological risks, and communitarian green movements. Each of the four categories encompasses very diverse sorts of movement organizations, some of which overlap strongly with other categories and indeed with other sorts of movements altogether.

For example, wilderness and species preservation movements include members of the conservation biology community who are dedicated to scientific methods of conserving species and habitats, as well as deep ecology movements, such as Earth First! (Taylor 1995b), which advocate more radical ways of reducing the human footprint on the environment. Anti-toxics movements include both environmental justice organizations, whose emphasis is on protecting poor or otherwise marginalized communities from bearing the greatest burden of polluting activities, and "Not In My Back Yard" (NIMBY) movements, who focus primarily on their own neighborhoods, rich or poor. Organizations focusing on access to and use of natural resources are among some of the earliest environmental organizations (Edelman 2001, 294–295, citing the work of Grove), though more recently, the issues that have generated activism concern newer problems like water privatization or access to genetic resources. These movements are very likely to frame their concerns in broader terms, connecting often to indigenous or landless rights, and to broader human rights movements. Interconnections are also rife. Food security movements, formed initially to protect agriculture-dependent communities and encourage smaller-scale farming, are increasingly confronting the multinational biotechnology sector (Shiva 2004). Even the climate change movement, which began as a relatively elite movement designed to inform policy makers of climate science and convince them of the need for action, has recently become far more populist, aiming to change people's lifestyles (particularly in wealthy countries) and provide help for the most vulnerable communities.

The comparative study of environmental movements draws on and contributes to a number of wider literatures, including social movement theory, theories of political institutions, and political theory and philosophy. Broadly, there are three main threads to the comparative environmental movements literature. First is the study of the history, emergence, and varieties of environmental movements around the world: their ideological bases, the events prompting the emergence of collective action, and their broad trajectories over time. Second, an expansive social science literature examines movements themselves: the variables that explain their organizational form, their choice of tactics, their scope, their targets, and specific trajectories of movements and movement organizations. Third, what are the actual impacts of environmental movements? Do they succeed in meeting their goals? In influencing policy outcomes? Do they, or can they, contribute to broader political and societal transformations?

A cross-national or comparative perspective sheds important light on all of these questions. For example, how do different political contexts and institutions shape the form or the impacts of environmental movements? Why, and how, do the ideological bases of environmental movements differ across countries? How are movement organizations themselves able to take advantage of available resources or of ideas and images in order to further their goals? We begin with the first theme: the emergence of, and varieties of, environmentalism.

Varieties of Environmentalism

The study of environmental movements began with the emergence of a new wave of environmental activism in Europe and America in the 1960s and early 1970s. Much of the early literature started from the assumption that environmentalism was largely the concern of wealthy elites, a set of concerns that became salient only when pressing material needs—food, shelter, work—had been taken care of (Inglehart 1982). As Dunlap and York discuss (chapter 4, this volume), this interpretation of environmentalism as a top-down, postmaterialist phenomenon has since been challenged (to a very large part by comparative work), and it is now widely studied as a phenomenon that occurs across class, racial, and ethnic divides.

Ramachandra Guha (2000) identifies two waves of global environmentalism, focusing on ideas about and perceptions of the environment. The first wave, a nineteenth-century response to the industrial revolution, emphasized nature and countryside preservation (with an emphasis on the purity of rural life, which he associates with Ruskin and Morris in England, and Mahatma Gandhi in India), "scientific conservation" (particularly as practiced in the colonies, notably in early notions of scientific forestry), and wilderness preservation (in the colonies—notably Africa—but also in the United States, with John Muir and the national parks movement).

Guha identifies the second wave as a period in which environmentalism gained wide popular support around the world, as both a child of the 1960s and a grandchild of the 1860s. In this second wave, he differentiates between the environmentalism of affluence and the environmentalism of poverty (along with an illuminating chapter on environmentalism under state socialism). In the environmentalism of affluence, associated largely with the industrialized North, he focuses on the importance of the work of Rachel Carson and others in raising awareness in the United States of the risks posed by unregulated chemicals, the rise of the great membership organizations, and crises such as Love Canal—all of which focused attention on creating agencies and legislation to regulate environmental quality. In Europe, closer links can be drawn between the student movements and antinuclear movements of the late 1960s as the second wave's immediate precursors and a concomitant emergence of environmentalism at this time as part of a much broader social (even socialist) platform rather than a purely "environmental" movement. As the movement progressed over the following years, environmental movement organizations professionalized and became more part of mainstream politics on both sides of the Atlantic, and we saw the emergence of organizations such as the Sierra Club or Friends of the Earth, which employ a professional staff and rely on a large membership and foundation funding, and the rise of green parties in Europe, competing with established parties for political representation. At the same time, radical environmentalism remained strong, with the emergence of Earth First! and, more recently, the Earth Liberation Front in the United States and the split in the German Green Party between the Realo ("realist") and Fundi ("fundamentalist") wings of the party, analyzed by Michael O'Neill (chapter 7, this volume).

Guha illustrates the "environmentalism of the poor" with some examples from the 1980s and 1990s that are fairly well known in the West: struggles in India over the Sardar Sarovar dam, peasant opposition (mobilized by Buddhist priests) to the conversion of forests to plantations in Thailand, the execution of Ogoni activist Ken Saro Wiwa in Nigeria, and Waangari Matthai's Green Belt Movement in Kenya. These movements—and similar examples that can be traced much further back—share characteristics that identify them as a form of environmentalism distinct from that in the North and that in some respects "masked" them from Northern scholars as environmental movements. These characteristics include a commitment to social justice and the struggles of poor communities to maintain their livelihoods in the face of state or multinational corporation-led efforts to appropriate land and natural resources (see also Haynes 1999). In fact, many of these groups may not even label themselves as "environmentalist," unless used in a strategic fashion to gain support from organizations in wealthier countries.

This distinction between Northern and Southern environmentalism has been adopted and built upon by scholars in different ways, and it is relatively common these days to see global surveys of environmentalism that cover both North and South (e.g., Mauch, Stoltzfus, and Weiner 2006; Doyle 2005). In a world in which environmentalists are often labeled as wealthy elitists, such surveys emphasize the diversity of "the" global environmental movement.

Many of these same studies also effectively deconstruct the North–South environmental dichotomy. Doyle (2005) differentiates between "majority" and "minority" worlds in his study of environmental campaigns, a distinction not defined by national borders, as the "majority world" encompasses those who live in relative poverty while the "minority world" are the relatively affluent. Thus, environmental justice movements in the United States or Aboriginal land rights movements in Australia, which fit more closely with the "majority" category, become more visible than they do in a simple "North–South" distinction. In an introduction to a special issue of the journal *Environmental Politics*, Doherty and Doyle (2006, 707) identify three broad environmentalist frames: postmaterialist, postindustrial, and postcolonial. Postmaterialist environmentalism—found, for example, in the United States—focuses on nonhuman nature, such as the preservation of wilderness and protection of species. Postindustrial environmentalism—common in Europe—"challenges the excesses of the industrialist project; the rights of corporations to pollute and degrade, and the dwindling of the earth's resources as they are fed into the advanced industrial machines" (Doherty and Doyle 2006, 707). Postcolonial environmentalism focuses attention on the legacy (and continuing forms of) empire, disparities between rich and poor, and the structural inequalities inherent in the global system. These frames can coexist and even intersect within the same movement or sector, though, they argue, each dominates particular parts of the world.

Comparisons of environmentalism around the world are characterized by additional cross-cutting frames and debates. A distinction can be drawn among environmental movements and movement organizations that are issue-specific or universal (or communitarian, see Kousis, Della Porta, and Jiménez 2008, 1636). Issue-specific movements include those that focus on toxics, or climate change, or endangered species protection—retaining a specific focus on those issues—though they may work with other sorts of groups. Universalist movements, by contrast, promote a green political ideology that challenges how society is organized—either human society itself (an ideological approach taken by most green parties) or humanity's relationship with nature, which characterizes many "deep ecologists." Most environmental movement organizations do not evolve to take on a more holistic critique of industrial or capitalist societies, but some do. The European green parties trace their origins back to the antinuclear movement but have also taken on a broader platform, in part because of the influence of their founders and of particular branches of political theory (Kelly 1994; Kemp and Wall 1990). If there is one recent movement or set of movement organizations that has the potential to do this, it is the climate change movement, given the extent to which the actions needed to address climate change touch all sectors of human activity—but to date, this has not happened.[1]

A final distinction can be drawn between those groups that espouse radical, or confrontational tactics in achieving their goals, and those that prefer more conciliatory or cooperative tactics. As shall be discussed shortly, often the choice of "radical" versus "reformist" strategies is dictated by the political context within which groups operate: a group facing a closed and hostile government is more likely to adopt street protests and similar forms of action than one that has the opportunity to talk to and persuade state actors or other target groups.[2] There has been greater attention paid in recent years, particularly in the aftermath of the sometimes highly disruptive antiglobalization protests of the 1990s, to the use of violent tactics by environmentalist groups, though such actions are used by a tiny minority of environmentalists. However, "unconventional" tactics by more mainstream environmental activists have come under scrutiny in a post-9/11 world, as efforts by many governments to beef up anti-terrorism laws have caught other sorts of "nonstate actors," not just foreign terrorists, in their sights.[3] At the same time, some groups known more for hewing to lobbying and other actions associated with the professionalized wing of the movement occasionally embrace nonviolent protest as a means of reaching a broader audience (O'Neill and VanDeveer 2005).

Organizational Forms, Trajectories, and Impacts: Social Movement Theory and Environmental Movements

In explaining differences and similarities in the trajectories, impacts, and organizational forms of environmental movements, many analysts draw on insights from social movement theory. Social movement theory cuts across the disciplines of political science, sociology, and anthropology.[4] Its rise was fueled by the political turbulence of the 1960s: the civil rights movement in the United States; student movements worldwide; and the emergence of environmental, feminist, and gay rights movements whose actions were (at least most visibly) characterized by tactics of violent and nonviolent contention. A social movement can be defined, very broadly, as "an association or set of associations organized around a common interest that seeks to influence collective outcomes without obtaining authoritative offices of government" (Dryzek et al. 2003, 2). Within this rubric, environmental movements are "broad networks of people and organizations engaged in collective action in pursuit of environmental benefits" (Rootes 1999, 2). The main strength of using social movement theory in the analysis of environmental movements and organizations is that it brings a theoretical structure—established debates, concepts, and methods—to what could be overly ad hoc or descriptive accounts of movement organizations and their impacts. Where there has been some disconnect between the study of social movements in general and environmental movements in particular has been in applying predominantly Western theoretical concepts to a broader range of political systems to which they may not easily apply and in integrating the broader range of players (such as corporations, experts, and knowledge holders) in political outcomes who may be less present in analyses of other sorts of movements. In turn, these are some of the important ways in which the study of environmental movements has contributed to the parent field of social movement theory.

"New social movements," which include environmental, feminist, gay rights, and civil rights movements, were initially identified—at least by European social scientists—in reaction to Marxist theories of social action. It had become clear by the 1960s and 1970s that the labor-industrialist divide was not the only source of social conflict; further, opportunities for "upward mobility" challenged Marxist determinism and opened the possibility of other (coexisting and cross-cutting) causes of social stratification such as race or gender (Della Porta and Diani 1999, 11–13). Other characteristics of the "new" social movements include resistance to the state or market in the interests of personal development and autonomy, greater attention to social rather than economic goals, informal networks and organization, and ideological fluidity (Della Porta and Diani 1999, citing the works of influential theorists Alberto Melucci and Claus Offe).[5] Early work on social movements by US scholars, on the other hand, focused on more material or strategic variables such as resource mobilization (the ability of actors to engage in collective action by mobilizing material, human, and other resources) and political processes, or state-society relations, broadly defined (Edelman 2001, 289–291). Only in the 1990s did some sort of transatlantic synthesis emerge (McAdam, McCarthy, and Zald 1996; Della Porta and Diani 1999; Edelman 2001).

The nature of social movement theory lends itself easily to comparisons (McAdam, McCarthy, and Zald 1996). Even if collective action by civil society actors in different countries or other settings is triggered by similar, shared grievances, such as institutionalized discrimination on the basis of race or gender, or a crisis, such as an environmental accident or a new law, what happens after the emergence of a movement or movement organization differs extensively across national borders, across movements, and over time. Scholarly interest has focused on two broad sets of variables. First, they are interested in explaining the movements themselves: their organizational forms, their resource base and membership, their choice of tactics, their trajectory over time, and so on. Second, they examine the various impacts that movements have, whether goal attainment or more intangible impacts such as the creation and spread of new societal norms. Of course, these two sets of variables are not unrelated, although sometimes the nature of their relationship can be hard to predict. Table 5.2 illustrates some of the dependent (outcome-related) variables relative to movements. Table 5.3 illustrates a broad range of impact-related dependent variables and associated research questions.[6]

From a comparative perspective, these variables generate many important questions for exploring differences or similarities across borders, or for illuminating a single-country case study (e.g., Schlosberg and Bomberg 2008; Bomberg and Doyle 2008). For example, why do green parties take hold and gain significant political representation more readily in some countries than in others? What factors foster the rise of a professionalized NGO sector in some countries but not in others? Why does a movement-sponsored issue like climate change or dam construction gain political traction in one country and not in another? What factors enable some environmental movements to grow and remain strong over time, while others fade away?

Social movement theorists have identified a range of independent, or explanatory, variables that can be applied across national contexts to answer some of these questions, which connect quite strongly to the broader themes of comparative politics

Table 5.2
Movement-related dependent variables

Movement-related variables	Examples
Organizational form	Green party
	Professional movement organization
	Ad hoc, community-based organization
	Ongoing, issue-specific organization
	Organizational network
Membership and resource bases	Large, national
	Single community
	Membership dues or philanthropic funding
	Volunteer initiatives
Scope	Local, regional, national
	Global or transnational
	Single issue or multiple issues
Tactics	Lobbying
	Information provision
	Protest or other nonviolent confrontational tactics
	Partnership, instruction
	Violent confrontation, such as sabotage
Targets	The state
	The corporate sector
	Public opinion
	International organizations
Mobilizing events, issues, and causes	Single triggering cause (e.g., a proposed road, dam, or hazardous waste facility)
	Broad environmental cause (e.g., biodiversity conservation, climate change, or nuclear power)
	System (e.g., global capitalism)
Ideology	Ecocentric vs. anthropocentric
	Environmental/social justice
	Conservation
	Greening capitalism
Trajectory	Institutionalization (e.g., from oppositional to mainstream)
	Dissolution
	From single group to network
	From narrow to broader scope
Alliances and networks	Extra-movement alliances (e.g., other civil society movements, the state, the church, the corporate sector)
	Intra-movement alliances (e.g., with other environmental groups, within the country or across borders)

Table 5.3
Impact-related dependent variables

Impact-related variables	Examples of research questions
Goal attainment	Proximate goals: Does the movement succeed in halting dam or power plant construction? Longer-term goals: Does the movement help open up political processes?
Policy change	Do policy makers respond to movement demands? Can the influence of the movement on policy be determined?
Problem solving	Does the movement improve or solve a given problem, such as rates of deforestation?
Attitude changing	What impact does the movement have on public or official opinion on the environment?
Movement cohesion and extension	Does the movement or movement organization contribute to the overall strength of the environmental movement? Does the movement generate links with other sorts of movements? To what extent does the movement create shared identity among its members?
Political transformation	To what extent do movement actions contribute to broader political transformations—including institutional reform (e.g., an environment ministry or new decision-making process) and transforming underlying norms and political-economic structures (e.g., institutionalizing sustainable development)?
Negative or unintended consequences	Does the movement trigger a backlash that worsens environmental conditions? Do movement activities trigger an increase in repressive actions by the state, such as greater police powers?

outlined in chapter 2. Table 5.4 illustrates three of these sets of variables: political contexts and institutions, the capacity of movements to mobilize resources and use them effectively over time, and the role of ideas and identity in movements and movement action. Although each set of variables has its own adherents, some argue that they are best seen as complementary, rather than as alternative explanations (McAdam, McCarthy, and Zald 1996).

Environmental Movements and Comparative Politics: Political Contexts and Opportunities

Comparative studies of environmental movements have generated significant findings in recent years. In studying these movements, researchers have to make some

Table 5.4
Explaining patterns of social movement actions and outcomes: Independent variables

1. Political contexts and opportunities[a]	Examples
Nature of regime	Democracy
	Authoritarian
	Transitional
	Stable or unstable
Political institutions and access to the policy process	Electoral system
	Means of interest representation
	• Informal channels: lobbying, advisory panels
	• Formal representation: corporatism
	Judicial system: open or closed to environmental lawsuits?
	Media and press: open or closed?
Allies and opponents	Allies within the state
	Elite allies, such as corporate sector or churches
State's capacity for repression	High/low

2. Movement-based variables	
Resources, mobilization ability	Financial (and from what source?)
	Membership and volunteers
	Information and expertise
	Organizational base (communities, churches, workplaces)
Support networks	Community support: broad or shallow?
	Friends, family, work-based associations or others?
Leadership	Charismatic, hierarchical, consensual, entrepreneurial
Tactical repertoires	Available tactics: range and type
	Tactics agreed upon by movement members
	Adaptability to changing situations

3. Ideational variables	
Framing	Creation of shared meanings, problem definitions, solutions
	Ability to transmit framings beyond movement
	Ability to maintain relevance of framing or concerns over time
Identity	Creation and maintenance of movement identities, both collective and individual

[a]Note that political opportunity-related variables were constructed with the state as the primary target; however, they can be adapted to apply to other movement targets, from large corporations to international organizations.

important methodological choices. One of the first choices concerns the appropriate unit of analysis—whether to compare nationwide phenomena (e.g., the British and Australian environmental movements), categories of movement organizations (such as the role of green parties or NGOs across different national contexts), or movements focused on particular issue areas or sectors (such as climate change or anti-dam movements), right down to the study of individual organizations. Doyle (2005), for example, employs a combination of three units of analysis—national movements, campaign-specific movements, and individual organizations—to compare environmental movements in "majority" and "minority" worlds. As interest in transnational movement dynamics grows, another possible approach is to examine the operation of the same transnational organization (such as Conservation International or the Rainforest Action Network) in different countries.

Research methods and modes of data collection also vary widely, from ethnographic or other field-based research to archival work, news and media analysis, social network analysis (Saunders 2007), and surveys across large numbers of cases.[7] Thus the literature ranges from small-N qualitative studies that are the result of intensive fieldwork to large-N statistical analyses of environmental movements (e.g., Scruggs 2003). Sometimes the environmental movement or movement organization is the prime object of study while in other instances the researcher is looking at environmental activism as one of a suite of variables determining particular outcomes (O'Neill 2000). Finally, this is a field with a large amount of activist-scholar participation, and many of those who research environmental movements have normative as well as analytical goals. Although exclusion of one in favor of the other may result in only a partial understanding of the dynamics of environmental movements, this choice largely depends on the researcher's target audience (see also Bevington and Dixon 2005).

Studies based on political contexts, opportunities, and constraints have dominated research on environmental movements within the field of comparative politics, although not wholly (see, e.g., Pralle 2006). Although these concepts have been criticized for being used too broadly (McAdam, McCarthy, and Zald 1996) or for being too static or deterministic, careful identification of relevant variables across countries has generated important insights into why the forms, actions, and impacts of movements vary across and within national contexts.[8]

A focus on political contexts in particular enables us to explain variation along these dimensions (Kitschelt 1986). Very similar movements can experience different outcomes in a political system that is closed to societal input—for example, an authoritarian system—than one that is open, as is the case in most democracies. Within these broad systems, there are wide variations in, for example, channels of access for societal actors to influence the policy process and other political institutions. A political system that is unstable or in transition can provide additional opportunities for social movement actions (as witnessed, e.g., during the fall of communism in Europe in the late 1980s, and as is discussed by Steinberg in chapter 10, this volume), or it can trigger oppressive actions by embattled political elites. We now move on to look at how political contexts shape, or are shaped by environmental movements, taking as examples some of the leading studies in this field.

Studies of environmental movements across advanced industrialized democracies demonstrate how institutional differences—across electoral systems or systems of interest mediation, for example—can have quite large impacts on the organizational form or level of success of environmental movements. In one of the classic articles in the field, Kitschelt (1986) explains variations in the impacts of antinuclear movements across France, Sweden, the United States, and West Germany (all democracies) by the relative openness or closure of each political regime to societal demands and the capacity of each to translate movement demands into policy. More broadly, Dryzek et al. (2003) examine how state structures in the United States, Norway, Germany, and the United Kingdom shape each country's environmental movement: how, for example, in Britain, during the Thatcher years and beyond, an "actively exclusionist" state helped close off options for movement action not only through established political channels but also by heavily policing protests and other sorts of civil action. In the United States, by contrast, a "passively inclusionist" state allowed for the development of a highly professionalized environmental sector equipped to lobby Congress and use the judicial system to address grievances. Dryzek and colleagues take their analysis a few steps further, asking which of these states are most likely to be shaped by environmental movements, taking on a "green" imperative as one of the state's functions along the lines described by Meadowcroft (chapter 3, this volume). They find that Germany most closely approximates this ideal and that the United States, where economic interests still defined themselves in opposition to environmentalism, lags furthest behind.

In my own work, examining the propensity of industrialized democracies to import hazardous wastes (O'Neill 2000), I find (among a range of other institutional variables) that countries that are net importers of hazardous wastes are those in which industrial interests have more privileged access to the policy process relative to the environmental movement and in which environmental movements have less of a coherent voice. Schreurs (2002) examines the trajectories of environmental movements in a comparative study of environmental politics and climate policy in Japan, Germany, and the United States. She explores how state structures and access to the policy process shaped movement trajectories in each country, including the failure of the Japanese environmental movement to mobilize beyond the grassroots. Focusing on institutions and on the interactions among groups of societal actors, she also notes that a strong environmental movement does not always translate into strong environmental regulations (as with climate policy in the United States). More recently, Hall and Taplin (2007) examine why climate NGOs enjoyed more legitimacy on the political scene in the United Kingdom compared with Australian NGOs, who faced a more politically powerful fossil fuel industry and a government (under then–Prime Minister John Howard) that actively marginalized the NGO sector, restricting the sorts of activities that they could undertake to receive funding.

Another example of institutionalized environmentalism, green parties exist in roughly one hundred countries. The question of why they gain political power and representation at the national level in some countries (such as Germany) but remain marginalized in others (such as the United States) has generated important insights about the impacts of electoral systems (Müller-Rommel 1998; Rüdig 2002). In systems with some form of proportional representation in which at least part of the parliament is allocated according to the number of votes received, smaller parties that represent particular interests are more likely to gain representation and even to take part in coalition governments. Germany has such a system, and from 1998 to 2005, the German Greens were part of the governing coalition with the Social Democrats. The United States, on the other hand, has a system that is not only "winner takes all"—rewarding all of a district's votes to the candidate who wins the majority—but requires political parties to achieve a massive level of national organization in order to gain significant representation. Therefore, although the US Green Party has achieved some small success at local levels, activists invest far more of their energy in the NGO sector and in lobbying, rather than participating directly in the process of government.

There are fewer comparative studies of environmentalism under authoritarian rule; single-country studies tend to dominate what research exists on this phenomenon.[9] Yet, despite the lack of free and vibrant civil societies and public space in which to organize, environmental movements have developed in several authoritarian states, and indeed different varieties of authoritarianism have led to distinctly different forms of environmental movements. Doyle and Simpson (2006) compare Burma—a closed, highly authoritarian military dictatorship—with Iran, a more politically and economically complex theocracy. In Burma, environmental groups exist, but are nearly always resistance-based, with groups struggling (often in a losing battle) against large-scale energy and deforestation projects. These groups, too, are often from the most marginalized sectors of Burmese societies—ethnic minorities such as the Karen or the Shan. The Iranian government, on the other hand, has encouraged a state-sanctioned environmental movement: groups that are organized around environmental issues but do not challenge the state in any way. Groups that do challenge the status quo—and they do exist—are quickly repressed. Interestingly, they note that the state-sanctioned green movement is one of the few spaces in Iran in which young women are allowed to participate in large numbers in public life (Doyle and Simpson 2006, 63).

Social movement theorists have always been interested in the role of movement organizations in periods of political and economic transition—times when established orders are changing rapidly and there may be more opportunities for societal actors to act—or to help shape final outcomes. Environmental movements often emerge in response to the impacts of rapid industrialization. This phenomenon is particularly clear in East Asia (Lee and So 1999). Environmental groups also played a pivotal role in the downfall of communist regimes in the Soviet Union and Eastern Europe (Jancar-Webster 1998; see also Hochstetler [chapter 8, this volume] and Andonova and VanDeveer [chapter 11, this volume]). One of the triggers for social action was the growth in elite and popular impressions of severe environmental degradation that became the hallmark of highly industrialized state socialism. Environmental movements began to emerge and proliferate across the Soviet Bloc in the 1980s, starting in the more "liberal" states of Poland and Yugoslavia. Given the closed nature of the regimes they faced, they were largely protest-based organizations. By 1989, groups such as Ecoglasnost (Bulgaria) and the Danube Circle (Czechoslovakia) had become well known in the West and attracted a lot of social support within Eastern Europe. Activists on both sides of the Iron Curtain rapidly began to draw connections between the state of the environment and the broader state socialist system (Pavlínek and Pickles 2004).

Environmentalism in many ways worked as a good vehicle for social revolution. It was supported by religious organizations and could be aided by the West without being seen as too politically interfering (at least at first). But, as Dawson (1996) points out, the relative safety of environmental activism as a form of political activity allowed the movement to act as a "cloak" for more nationalist interests. Although antinuclear movements were very strong across the USSR and its immediate neighbors before 1991, they rapidly declined thereafter. Dawson argues that this is due largely to the way that antinuclear activism masked (in a cynical sense) or represented (more benignly) a desire for greater local self-determination on the part of these regions—a goal that was largely achieved.

In the years since the fall of the Soviet Union, however, environmental movements in Central and Eastern Europe and Central Asia have failed to reach their potential, and in many cases have declined significantly in number and in influence, although there is strong regional variation. While in Russia and Central Asia, civil society organizations have remained weak and dependent on the state (see Luong and Weinthal 1999; Weinthal 2002), in countries that have recently joined the European Union, environmental organizations—though weaker than those in Western Europe—are typically stronger than their Russian and Central Asian counterparts (a fact not independent of the process of acceding to the EU).[10] Taking a longer time frame, and a slightly different set of transitional countries, Kousis, Della Porta, and Jiménez (2008) find that environmental movements in Southern European countries (such as Spain, Greece, and Portugal) are in fact stronger than some analysts had predicted. Although they lack the same organizational capacity and state support as some of their Northern European counterparts, still, in the years since those countries transitioned from dictatorship and/or joined the EU, their environmental movements have expanded and become more institutionalized.

In our final example of the role of political contexts and opportunities in the study of environmentalism, the movements and movement organizations in the global South, even in democracies, have more in common with the literature on postcommunist transitions than with studies of advanced industrialized democracies. In part that is because political processes are more informal, political systems are more weakly institutionalized in many developing countries, and political and economic conditions tend to alter more rapidly. Professionalized NGOs are relatively rare and are often supported by transnational activist groups as well as—or sometimes instead of—local civil societies. Environmental groups face very different sorts of political challenges than their Western counterparts and often utilize different frames of reference to mobilize support (Haynes 1999; Guha 2000). Khagram (2004) compares the dynamics of large dam construction across India, Brazil, China, South Africa, and Indonesia.[11] Social mobilization—the ability of movements (not only environmental movements, but also indigenous and others) to mobilize against large dam construction, which typically carries high social and environmental costs—has been a critical variable in the viability of large-scale development projects. Even more important has been the ability of movement organizations to convey their demands to higher political levels and to have them met. Khagram finds that two sets of variables matter the most: the presence of democratic institutions (and the relative maturity of democratic transition) and levels of social mobilization. The countries whose dam construction plans have altered the least are those with authoritarian regimes (China), less complete or more recent democratic institutions (Indonesia), or low levels of social mobilization (as in South Africa, where social activism declined after the transition to democracy and has only recently started to rebuild).

Direct comparisons of environmental movements in Northern and Southern countries, even among democracies, are scarce. This scarcity may be due to the (often mistaken) perception that differences between them are too wide to provide enough grounds for a valid comparison. Two areas that do bridge the North–South gap, however, are studies of grassroots, or radical, environmental movements (Taylor 1995a; Peluso and Watts 2001) and campaign-based studies (Doyle 2005). Grassroots organizations the world over face similar challenges and employ similar sets of resources, such as local community support, volunteer workers, and protest tactics to achieve their goals, given their relative lack of access to state or corporate institutions. Further, the North–South connections that have been made across different issue areas such as biotechnology or toxics have fostered the rise of transnational networks of activist groups that work together on these issues (such as Pesticide Action Network) and analytical work linking these issues across national borders (Pellow 2007). One area in which we are beginning to see some progress is in interrogating power and resource differences among environmental groups and how that may shape their relationship in sometimes less than functional and benign ways (Fox and Brown 1998; O'Neill and VanDeveer 2005).

In sum, the comparative study of environmental movements has helped illuminate some important questions around the emergence, organization, and impacts of social movements and how political institutions and state-society relations can shape collective action by civil society actors. In turn, the studies cited thus far have helped answer some important questions in the field of comparative environmental politics, and comparative politics more broadly—for example, why climate change movements have been more successful in some countries than others, or why some countries make the environmental policy choices they do. Specifically, the environmental movements literature has made some strong contributions to social movement theory, over and above providing a useful set of cases. The great diversity and multiple interpretations of what environmentalism itself is, and how movements and movement organizations manifest themselves and operate over time and space, forming and reforming around different problems as they arise, provides a continual challenge for movement theorists—and helps ensure that the field's insights and progress do not stagnate. Finally, this literature and the examples it discusses provide opportunities for environmental movements to learn from what similar groups have attempted and achieved in other countries. We turn now to what has become a major agenda in the field of environmental studies and political science more generally: the emergence and growth of transnational social movements and the impact of this phenomenon on the comparative study of environmental movements.

Comparing Environmental Movements in a Globalizing World

One of the most active research areas in the field of social movement studies in general, and of environmental movements in particular, is that of transnational or global movement politics. There are many reasons why transnational factors have shaped environmental movements worldwide. Pressures of globalization and the knowledge that most environmental problems have transboundary or even global dimensions mean that targeting national governments or other actors no longer suffices for a movement to be successful. Further, the availability of transnational communication and networking abilities have made it far easier than ever for environmental groups to work together across national borders.

To some extent, it is possible to question the continued utility of a comparative perspective on environmental movements, as ideas, tactics, and organizational networks become more global and, in many cases, more focused on global issues. But in practice, domestic political processes are as relevant as ever, and thus a comparative politics approach provides essential insights into the nature of environmental movements. First, not all environmental politics are global—many political campaigns and issues remain firmly grounded in local and national arenas. Second, global and comparative analytic frameworks can complement one another, together providing a fuller explanation of environmental movements than is possible using either in isolation. In transnational networks made up of allied groups from various countries, differences across national political contexts and in the capacities of movement actors shape movement actions, trajectories, and outcomes in important ways. And bringing in a transnational dimension to cross-national comparisons of environmental movements can play an important supplemental role in explaining outcomes and impacts. These days, it is harder than ever to understand the emergence of environmental movements in developing and transitional countries without looking at the role of transnational actors, from movement organizations in other countries to foreign government actors wanting to foster a "healthy civil society."

Environmental movements have become more global in several ways. First, many groups have started to directly target international actors and political processes through lobbying, protest, and participation in international political debates. Many NGOs now attend international environmental negotiations on issues ranging from climate change to biodiversity to hazardous waste trading, achieving varying degrees of access and success (Betsill and Corell 2007; Princen and Finger 1994). In the 1990s, a global antiglobalization protest movement emerged, targeting meetings of key global economic organizations such as the World Bank, the World Trade Organization (WTO), and the International Monetary Fund (IMF) (O'Neill 2004). More generally, environmentalism is often seen as a key part of an emerging global civil society (Wapner 1996).

Second, there is growing evidence that movement ideas, strategies, and tactics have long diffused across national borders. The choices a movement makes in one country can profoundly influence movement choices in a different country (McAdam and Rucht 1993; Chabot and Duyvendak 2002). The emergence of green parties around the world from the 1970s onward, which share similar (if not identical) party platforms is one example; the use of particular protest tactics, such as nonviolent civil disobedience, is another. Paul Steinberg (2001) develops the concept of "bilateral activism" to delineate the ways in which environmental actors (in his cases, from Bolivia and Costa Rica) work simultaneously in international and domestic settings to influence policy developments in their home countries.

Third, transnational networks of activists and movement organizations have become a dominant feature of the landscape of movement politics across many countries (Keck and Sikkink 1998; Khagram, Riker, and Sikkink 2002). From opposing dam construction or pesticide use to protecting old-growth forests, environmental movements in different countries have found common cause and strength in numbers as they work together to address shared problems.

Social movement theory—with its focus on ideas, strategies, and the political contexts that shape movement actions and outcomes—has provided important insights and theoretical frameworks for understanding transnational movements, although not without some important modifications as the operational field for movements is scaled up or extended across borders (e.g., Smith, Chatfield, and Pagnucco 1997; McAdam 1998). For example, analyses that focus on channels of access to decision-making processes can help us understand, even at a global level, why some movements resort to protest (when facing, e.g., the WTO or IMF, which are highly immune to input from nonstate actors), while others are able to translate lobbying and the provision of information effectively to the global level. For example, the United Nations Environment Programme and other organizations coordinating environmental negotiations have been quite open to allowing accredited NGOs to attend most of their meetings. In their study of transnational movements, Keck and Sikkink (1998) develop the "boomerang" model to show how groups working in a closed political context can enlist help from allies in other countries who push for change in the first country. This model has been extended to show how shareholder activist networks can use a boomerang-type strategy to target multinational corporations (McAteer and Pulver 2009).

To return to our earlier question, if it is the case that environmental movements are becoming more globalized, what if any continued utility does the comparative politics lens on movement organizations have? The answer is, quite a lot. First, the very nature of transnational activism means that activists from different national settings and political contexts have to learn to work together, even though the goals, practices, and strategies they have learned and adopted at home may differ significantly. For example, a lot of work in this field focuses on North–South dynamics within transnational activist coalitions (Fox and Brown 1998). Second (and conversely), how transnational networks operate in one or another country can be fundamentally shaped by national contexts. The sorts of practices adopted, the targets selected, and the appropriate tactics used to gain political influence have to be learned, and cannot be assumed, by an outside group. An international NGO that works on the same problem in, say, China and Eastern Europe could experience radically different outcomes if it does not learn to adapt to the politics of each country or region and to understand where and when it can show visible support for local activist groups. Cashore, Auld, and Newsom (2004) demonstrate how the

Forest Stewardship Council, a transnational certification organization with high NGO involvement, has had to adapt in order to be adopted in different countries.

Some recent studies in the field have synthesized comparative and transnational perspectives to understand the impacts of environmental movements. Chester's 2006 study examines two cross-border alliances for biodiversity conservation in North America. One, the International Sonoran Desert Alliance (ISDA), operates across the US-Mexico border, and the other, the Yellowstone to Yukon (Y2Y) conservation initiative, operates across the US-Canada border. National political contexts—and the interaction of activists across these national borders—turn out to be an important set of factors affecting the relative success of each movement. The ISDA, for example, had to contend with the weak Mexican government, as well as a US government that was turning away from international conservation initiatives. It also had to deal with a much more contentious set of border politics, with issues such as drug smuggling and illegal immigration making it virtually impossible to establish a transboundary conservation region. By comparison, Y2Y had far fewer (or far less extreme) cultural, economic, and political differences to contend with.

Ultimately, it is hard to separate comparative and transnational perspectives on environmental movements, and it would be unwise to do so: few environmental movements operate in a national or local vacuum. Good syntheses can truly enhance our understanding of both. For example, in a (perhaps paradoxical) way, globalization and the growing ability even of small groups to forge transnational connections has increased the visibility of local movements and their challenges and opportunities, raising their profile as examples of larger transnational mobilizations rather than purely as components of national movements (Diani and Rambaldo 2007).

Future Research Agendas

Where is the comparative study of environmental movements headed? As we can see from the previous analysis, environmental movement organizations remain the subject of intense scholarly interest and remain politically relevant in most countries around the world. This section identifies some of the more pressing themes of ongoing and future research in the comparative study of environmentalism. The first is the continued synthesis of transnational and comparative movement studies; environmental problems are now viewed as fundamentally global, but how specific movements and movement organizations address political challenges and opportunities within and across borders needs further study. This, too, is an area to which the field of global environmental politics needs to pay attention, given the important role that environmental groups play in negotiating and implementing international environmental agreements and in raising local awareness of problems that are addressed at the global level, such as climate change or biodiversity loss (Betsill and Corell 2007).

Second, as noted previously, there has been a resurgence of interest in the study of contentious politics in the wake of the antiglobalization protests of the 1990s and early 2000s, and the attempts to transform that protest movement into a global network for change (e.g., in the World Social Forum). This new focus on protest mirrors in some ways earlier work on protest cycles that came out of the 1960s but adds a transnational dimension. Conca (2006), for example, examines how protest movements become networked and more institutionalized over time, looking at transnational antidam movements and at the anti–water privatization movement across South Africa and Latin America as a more nascent form of transnational network.

Third, there is growing interest not only in how environmental movement organizations interact with each other and with the state but also in their interactions with other sorts of actors—corporations, local and regional government agencies, and social movements in other arenas, such as health and human rights. In other words, the unit of analysis has expanded beyond just the movement or movement organization to include the range of organizations interacting over a given issue area. This field of study may include, for example, the comparative politics of certification regimes (such as the Forest Stewardship Council and other certification organizations, fair trade movements, and so on) (Espach 2006; Cashore, Auld, and Newson 2004), or, more formally, the study of "organizational fields"—the collection of state and nonstate actors working in a given issue area (Balsiger 2007). There is a growing literature on how movements interact with private actors, for instance, the tactics and dilemmas in working with the corporate world (McAteer and Pulver 2009; Trumpy 2008) or with the private foundations that provide a good portion of their funding (Bartley 2007). How environmental movements interact with scientists' organizations and other expert groups or knowledge holders is also a promising area of study, especially in the context of climate change and linkages between health and environmental movements (Jasanoff and Martello 2004).

Let me conclude this overview by highlighting two points. First, environmentalism is political: environmentalists have to engage with powerful political actors, from the state to multinational corporations, and must work within particular political contexts (both stable and rapidly changing) to achieve their goals. If there is one thing that the works cited thus far have in common, it is that the most interesting type of environmentalism from the perspective of comparative politics is less about changing individual behavior, or being a "green consumer," than it is about challenging existing political structures. The second point is that a lot can be learned from looking at environmentalism through a comparative lens. The global nature of environmental challenges should, at the very least, discourage a parochial view. More to the point, a comparative perspective allows us to see the diversity of environmental movements around the world, in terms of issues, movement types, strategies, and impacts—a diversity that encourages curiosity and continues to engage many different scholars and activists in attempts to understand and learn from it.

Notes

1. On the potential for the environmental movement to create a "green public sphere," see Torgerson 1999.

2. On the choice of protest as a movement tactic, see Barkan 1979. For comparative studies of radical environmentalism, see for example Taylor 1995a and Wall 1999.

3. See Grigoriadis 2006 on the "rise and fall" of eco-radicalism in the United States.

4. For major overviews, see Della Porta and Diani 1999; McAdam, McCarthy, and Zald 1996; Dalton and Kuechler 1990; Edelman 2001; Giugni 1998; Pichardo 1997; and Tarrow 1998.

5. See, for example, Melucci 1996 and Offe 1985.

6. See also Rucht 1999. More generally on movement impacts, see Giugni 1998, and Rochon and Mazmanian 1993.

7. For an overview of methodological choices in social movement theory, see Klandermans and Staggenborg 2002.

8. For a debate on the continued utility of political opportunity structures, see Goodwin and Jasper 1999 and other essays in the same issue of *Sociological Forum*.

9. See, for example, the burgeoning literature on environmentalism in China (e.g., Ho 2001, 2006), and on other authoritarian regimes (e.g., Sowers 2007 on Egypt and Carruthers 2001 on Chile).

10. See, for example, the essays by Hallstrom (2004), Bell (2004), and Hicks (2004) in a special issue of *Environmental Politics*.

11. Other comparative studies of environmental movements in the South include Haynes 1999, Hirsch and Warren 1998, and Bennett, Davila-Poblete, and Rico 2005. Studies that situate environmental movements in broader contexts include Hirsch and Warren 1998 and Doyle and Risely 2008. Other important volumes that are composed primarily of single case studies woven more loosely together in terms of comparative analysis include Díez and Dwivedi 2007 and Mauch, Stoltzfus, and Weiner 2006.

References

Balsiger, Jörg. 2007. Uphill Struggles: The Politics of Sustainable Mountain Development in the Swiss Alps and California's Sierra Nevada. Ph.D. diss., Department of Environmental Science, Policy and Management, University of California at Berkeley.

Barkan, Steven E. 1979. Strategic, Tactical and Organizational Dilemmas of the Protest Movement against Nuclear Power. *Social Problems* 27 (1): 19–37.

Bartley, Tim. 2007. How Foundations Shape Social Movements: The Construction of an Organizational Field and the Rise of Forest Certification. *Social Problems* 54 (3): 229–255.

Bell, Ruth Greenspan. 2004. Further Up the Learning Curve: NGOs from Transition to Brussels. *Environmental Politics* 13 (1): 194–215.

Bennett, Vivienne, Sonia Davila-Poblete, and Maria Nieves Rico, eds. 2005. *Opposing Currents: The Politics of Water and Gender in Latin America*. Pittsburgh: Pittsburgh University Press.

Betsill, Michele M., and Elisabeth Corell, eds. 2007. *NGO Diplomacy: The Influence of Nongovernmental Organizations in International Environmental Negotiations*. Cambridge, Mass.: MIT Press.

Bevington, Douglas, and Chris Dixon. 2005. Movement-Relevant Theory: Rethinking Social Movement Scholarship and Activism. *Social Movement Studies* 4 (3): 185–208.

Bomberg, Elizabeth, and Timothy Doyle. 2008. US Environmentalism in Comparative Perspective. *Environmental Politics* 17 (2): 337–348.

Carruthers, David. 2001. Environmental Politics in Chile: Legacies of Dictatorship and Democracy. *Third World Quarterly* 22 (3): 343–358.

Cashore, Benjamin, Graeme Auld, and Deanna Newsom. 2004. *Governing through Markets: Forest Certification and the Emergence of Non-state Authority*. New Haven: Yale University Press.

Chabot, Sean, and Jan Willem Duyvendak. 2002. Globalization and Transnational Diffusion between Social Movements: Reconceptualizing the Dissemination of the Gandhian Repertoire and the "Coming Out" Routine. *Theory and Society* 31:697–740.

Chester, Charles C. 2006. *Conservation across Borders: Biodiversity in an Interdependent World*. Washington, D.C.: Island Press.

Conca, Ken. 2006. *Governing Water: Contentious Transnational Politics and Global Institution Building*. Cambridge, Mass.: MIT Press.

Dalton, Russell J., and Manfred Kuechler. 1990. *Challenging the Political Order: New Social and Political Movements in Western Democracies*. New York: Oxford University Press.

Dawson, Jane I. 1996. *Eco-nationalism: Anti-nuclear Activism and National Identity in Russia, Lithuania, and Ukraine*. Durham: Duke University Press.

Della Porta, Donatella, and Mario Diani. 1999. *Social Movements: An Introduction*. Oxford, UK: Blackwell Publishers.

Diani, Mario, and Elisa Rambaldo. 2007. Still the Time of Environmental Movements? A Local Perspective. *Environmental Politics* 16 (5): 765–784.

Díez, Jordi, and O. P. Dwivedi, eds. 2007. *Global Environmental Challenges: Perspectives from the South*. Peterborough, Ontario, Canada: Broadview Press.

Doherty, Brian, and Timothy Doyle. 2006. Beyond Borders: Transnational Politics, Social Movements and Modern Environmentalisms. *Environmental Politics* 15 (5): 697–712.

Doyle, Timothy. 2005. *Environmental Movements in Majority and Minority Worlds: A Global Perspective*. New Brunswick, N.J.: Rutgers University Press.

Doyle, Timothy, and Melissa Risely, eds. 2008. *Crucible for Survival: Environmental Security and Justice in the Indian Ocean Region*. New Brunswick, N. J.: Rutgers University Press.

Doyle, Timothy, and Adam Simpson. 2006. Traversing More Than Speed Bumps: Green Politics under Authoritarian Regimes in Burma and Iran. *Environmental Politics* 15 (5): 750–767.

Dryzek, John S., David Downes, Christian Hunold, and David Schlosberg. 2003. *Green States and Social Movements: Environmentalism in the United States, United Kingdom, Germany, and Norway.* New York: Oxford University Press.

Edelman, Marc. 2001. Social Movements: Changing Paradigms and Forms of Politics. *Annual Review of Anthropology* 30:285–317.

Espach, Ralph. 2006. When Is Sustainable Forestry Sustainable? The Forest Stewardship Council in Brazil and Argentina. *Global Environmental Politics* 6 (2): 55–84.

Fox, Jonathan A., and L. David Brown, eds. 1998. *The Struggle for Accountability: The World Bank, NGOs and Grassroots Movements.* Cambridge, Mass.: MIT Press.

Giugni, Marco G. 1998. Was It Worth the Effort? The Outcomes and Consequences of Social Movements. *Annual Review of Sociology* 24:371–393.

Giugni, Marco, Doug McAdam, and Charles Tilly, eds. 1999. *How Social Movements Matter.* Minneapolis: University of Minnesota Press.

Goodwin, Jeff, and James M. Jasper. 1999. Caught in a Winding, Snarling Vine: The Structural Bias of Political Process Theory. *Sociological Forum* 14 (1): 27–53.

Grigoriadis, Vanessa. 2006. The Rise and Fall of the Eco-radical Underground. *Rolling Stone* (August 10): 73–77, 104–107.

Guha, Ramachandra. 2000. *Environmentalism: A Global History.* New York: Longman.

Hall, Nina L., and Ros Taplin. 2007. Solar Festivals and Climate Bills: Comparing NGO Climate Change Campaigns in the UK and Australia. *Voluntas* 18:318–338.

Hallstrom, Lars K. 2004. Eurocratizing Enlargement? EU Elites and NGO Participation in European Environmental Policy. *Environmental Politics* 13 (10): 175–193.

Haynes, Jeff. 1999. Power, Politics, and Environmental Movements in the Third World. In *Environmental Movements: Local, National and Global,* ed. Christopher Rootes, 222–242. London: Frank Cass.

Hicks, Barbara. 2004. Setting Agendas and Shaping Activism: EU Influence on Central and Eastern European Environmental Movements. *Environmental Politics* 13 (1): 216–233.

Hirsch, Philip, and Carol Warren, eds. 1998. *The Politics of Environment in Southeast Asia: Resources and Resistance.* London: Routledge.

Ho, Peter. 2001. Greening without Conflict? Environmentalism, NGOs and Civil Society in China. *Development and Change* 32:893–921.

Ho, Peter. 2006. Sprouts of Environmentalism in China? Government-Organized NGOs and Green Organizations in Disguise. In *Shades of Green: Environmental Activism around the Globe,* ed. Christof Mauch, Nathan Stoltzfus, and Douglas R. Weiner, 135–160. Lanham, Md.: Rowman & Littlefield.

Inglehart, Ronald. 1982. *Changing Values and the Rise of Environmentalism in Western Societies.* Berlin: International Institute for Environment and Society.

Jancar-Webster, Barbara. 1998. Environmental Movement and Social Change in the Transition Countries. *Environmental Politics* 7 (1): 69–90.

Jasanoff, Sheila, and Marybeth Long Martello, eds. 2004. *Earthly Politics: Local and Global in Environmental Governance.* Cambridge, Mass.: MIT Press.

Keck, Margaret E., and Kathryn Sikkink. 1998. *Activists Beyond Borders: Advocacy Networks in International Politics*. Ithaca: Cornell University Press.

Kelly, Petra E. 1994. *Thinking Green! Essays on Environmentalism, Feminism, and Nonviolence*. Berkeley: Parallax Press.

Kemp, Penny, and Derek Wall. 1990. *A Green Manifesto for the 1990s*. London: Penguin Books.

Khagram, Sanjeev. 2004. *Dams and Development: Transnational Struggles for Water and Power*. Ithaca: Cornell University Press.

Khagram, Sanjeev, James V. Riker, and Kathryn Sikkink, eds. 2002. *Restructuring World Politics: Transnational Social Movements, Networks, and Norms*. Minneapolis: University of Minnesota Press.

Kitschelt, Herbert P. 1986. Political Opportunity Structures and Political Protest: Anti-nuclear Movements in Four Democracies. *British Journal of Political Science* 16:57–85.

Klandermans, Bert, and Suzanne Staggenborg, eds. 2002. *Methods of Social Movement Research*. Minneapolis: University of Minnesota Press.

Kousis, Marian, Donatella Della Porta, and Mauel Jiménez. 2008. Southern European Environmental Movements in Comparative Perspective. *American Behavioral Scientist* 51 (11): 1627–1647.

Lee, Yok-shiu F., and Alvin Y. So, eds. 1999. *Asia's Environmental Movements: Comparative Perspectives*. Armonk, N.Y.: M. E. Sharpe.

Luong, Pauline Jones, and Erika Weinthal. 1999. The NGO Paradox: Democratic Goals and Non-Democratic Outcomes in Kazakhstan. *Europe-Asia Studies* 51 (7): 1267–1284.

Mauch, Christof, Nathan Stoltzfus, and Douglas R. Weiner, eds. 2006. *Shades of Green: Environmental Activism around the Globe*. Lanham, Md.: Rowman and Littlefield.

McAdam, Doug. 1998. Conclusion: The Future of Social Movements. In *From Contention to Democracy*, ed. Marco G. Giugni, Doug McAdam, and Charles Tilly, 229–246. Lanham, Md.: Rowman and Littlefield.

McAdam, Doug, John D. McCarthy, and Mayer N. Zald, eds. 1996. *Comparative Perspectives on Social Movements: Political Opportunities, Mobilizing Structures, and Cultural Framings*. Cambridge, UK: Cambridge University Press.

McAdam, Doug, and Dieter Rucht. 1993. The Cross-national Diffusion of Movement Ideas. *Annals of the American Academy of Political and Social Science* 528:56–74.

McAteer, Emily, and Simone Pulver. 2009. The Corporate Boomerang: Shareholder Transnational Advocacy Networks Targeting Oil Companies in the Ecuadorian Amazon. *Global Environmental Politics* 9 (1): 1–30.

Melucci, Alberto. 1996. *Challenging Codes: Collective Information in the Information Age*. Cambridge, UK: Cambridge University Press.

Müller-Rommel, Ferdinand. 1998. Explaining the Electoral Success of Green Parties: A Cross-national Analysis. *Environmental Politics* 7 (4): 145–154.

Offe, Claus. 1985. New Social Movements: Changing Boundaries of the Political. *Social Research* 52:817–868.

O'Neill, Kate. 2000. *Waste Trading among Rich Nations: Building a New Theory of Environmental Regulation*. Cambridge, Mass.: MIT Press.

O'Neill, Kate. 2004. Transnational Protest: States, Circuses, and Conflict at the Frontline of Global Politics. *International Studies Review* 6:233–251.

O'Neill, Kate. 2009. *The Environment and International Relations*. Cambridge, UK: Cambridge University Press.

O'Neill, Kate, and Stacy D. VanDeveer. 2005. Transnational Environmental Activism after Seattle: Between Emancipation and Arrogance. In *Charting Transnational Democracy: Beyond Global Arrogance*, ed. Janie Leatherman and Julie A. Webber, 195–220. New York: Palgrave MacMillan.

Pavlínek, Petr, and John Pickles. 2004. Environmental Pasts/Environmental Futures in Post-Socialist Europe. *Environmental Politics* 13 (1): 237–265.

Pellow, David Naguib. 2007. *Resisting Global Toxics: Transnational Movements for Environmental Justice*. Cambridge, Mass.: MIT Press.

Peluso, Nancy Lee, and Michael Watts, eds. 2001. *Violent Environments*. Ithaca: Cornell University Press.

Pichardo, Nelson A. 1997. New Social Movements: A Critical Review. *Annual Review of Sociology* 23:411–430.

Pralle, Sarah B. 2006. *Branching Out, Digging In: Environmental Advocacy and Agenda Setting*. Washington, D.C.: Georgetown University Press.

Princen, Thomas, and Matthias Finger. 1994. *Environmental NGOs in World Politics: Linking the Local and the Global*. London: Routledge.

Rochon, Thomas R., and Daniel A. Mazmanian. 1993. Social Movements and the Policy Process. *Annals of the American Academy of Political and Social Science* 528: 75–87.

Rootes, Christopher, ed. 1999. *Environmental Movements: Local, National and Global*. London: Frank Cass Publishers.

Rucht, Dieter. 1999. The Impact of Environmental Movements in Western Societies. In *How Social Movements Matter*, ed. Marco Giugni, Doug McAdam, and Charles Tilly, 204–224. Minneapolis: Minnesota University Press.

Rüdig, Wolfgang. 2002. Between Ecotopia and Disillusionment: Green Parties in European Government. *Environment* 44 (3): 20–33.

Saunders, Clare. 2007. Using Social Network Analysis to Explore Social Movements: A Relational Approach. *Social Movement Studies* 6 (3): 227–243.

Schlosberg, David, and Elizabeth Bomberg. 2008. Perspectives on American Environmentalism. *Environmental Politics* 17 (2): 187–199.

Schreurs, Miranda. 2002. A. *Environmental Politics in Japan, Germany and the United States*. Cambridge, UK: Cambridge University Press.

Scruggs, Lyle. 2003. *Sustaining Abundance: Environmental Performance in Industrial Democracies*. Cambridge, UK: Cambridge University Press.

Shiva, Vandana. 2004. The Future of Food: Countering Globalization and Recolonization of Indian Agriculture. *Futures* 36:715–732.

Smith, Jackie, Charles Chatfield, and Ron Pagnucco, eds. 1997. *Transnational Social Movements and Global Politics: Solidarity Beyond the State*. Syracuse: Syracuse University Press.

Sowers, Jeannie. 2007. Nature Reserves and Authoritarian Rule in Egypt: Embedded Autonomy Revisited. *Journal of Environment & Development* 16 (4): 375–397.

Steinberg, Paul F. 2001. *Environmental Leadership in Developing Countries: Transnational Relations and Biodiversity Policy in Costa Rica and Bolivia*. Cambridge, Mass.: MIT Press.

Tarrow, Sidney. 1998. *Power in Movement: Social Movements and Contentious Politics*. 2nd ed. Cambridge, UK: Cambridge University Press.

Taylor, Bron, ed. 1995a. *Ecological Resistance Movements: The Global Emergence of Radical and Popular Environmentalism*. Albany: SUNY Press.

Taylor, Bron. 1995b. Earth First! and Global Narratives of Popular Ecological Resistance. In *Ecological Resistance Movements: The Global Emergence of Radical and Popular Environmentalism*, ed. Bron Taylor, 11–34. Albany: SUNY Press.

Torgerson, Douglas. 1999. *The Promise of Green Politics: Environmentalism and the Public Sphere*. Durham: Duke University Press.

Trumpy, Alexa J. 2008. Subject to Negotiation: The Mechanisms behind Co-optation and Corporate Reform. *Social Problems* 55 (4): 480–500.

Wall, Derek. 1999. *Earth First! and the Anti-Roads Movement: Radical Environmentalism and Comparative Social Movements*. London: Routledge.

Wapner, Paul. 1996. *Environmental Activism and World Civic Politics*. Albany: State University of New York Press.

Weinthal, Erika. 2002. *State Making and Environmental Cooperation: Linking Domestic and International Politics in Central Asia*. Cambridge, Mass.: MIT Press.

6

Business-State Relations and the Environment: The Evolving Role of Corporate Social Responsibility

Deborah Rigling Gallagher and Erika Weinthal

In both environmental studies and comparative political economy, the corporation is a central actor affecting political and economic outcomes (for excellent overviews, see Kraft and Kamieniecki 2007; Haggard, Maxfield, and Schneider 1997). A large body of literature assumes that in developed and developing countries alike, business interests can capture the state and shape institutional outcomes so as to promote their narrow economic interests and personal gain (see, e.g., Hellman et al. 2000; Kang 2002; Keohane, Revesz, and Stavins 1998). Yet the field of comparative environmental politics shows that regulatory policy in the twenty-first century is much more multifaceted than previously conceptualized in the literature on business-state relations. It is no longer simply about whether business gets its way (see Kamieniecki 2006); nor is it about merely having a strong state with enough autonomy and capacity to formulate and implement environmental regulations irrespective of economic interests.[1] Rather, it is about corporations engaging in voluntary environmental programs (VEPs) and increasingly playing a proactive role in influencing environmental outcomes, both within the nation-state and beyond, by establishing priorities for environmental best practices. As economic trade becomes ever more transnational and supply chains even more elongated, corporations are increasingly filling a void in the global economy as the suppliers of regulatory governance (Büthe 2010). Firms are taking advantage of opportunities for voluntary participation offered by state institutions seeking to promote "beyond compliance" behavior and eager to increase the capacity for environmental stewardship. Through their participation in voluntary initiatives, corporations are the creators of social knowledge about the pairing of economic growth and environmental governance.[2]

This transformation is apparent in the actions of Sir Richard Branson, who announced on September 21, 2006, at the annual meeting of the Clinton Global Initiative that his company, Virgin Group Limited, would invest all profits from its travel companies over the next ten years in the fight to stop global warming, boldly signaling Virgin's commitment to a new form of corporate social responsibility (CSR). Rather than just engaging in the well-practiced philanthropy of providing financial support to address social problems,[3] Branson put forth a new approach whereby the creation of shareholder value and responsible environmental citizenship are increasingly compatible: "I believe we need to make a virtue out of investing in clean technology and renewable energy and not be ashamed to want to make profits out of it," he said.[4] An estimated $3 billion will be directed to a new investment unit—Virgin Fuels—to support the development of biofuels as an alternative to the dirtier fossil fuels.[5]

The current focus of CSR is embodied in the definition offered by the World Business Council for Sustainable Development: "the commitment of business to contribute to sustainable economic development, working with employees, their families, the local community and society at large to improve their quality of life" (Fox, Ward, and Howard 2002, 1). The study of CSR is a relatively new field that brings together scholars of environmental policy with those who have traditionally studied the firm as a creator of shareholder value (for a survey, see, e.g., Vogel 2005 and Prakash 2007). Firms have long been viewed as the economic engines of nation states (Chandler, Almatori, and Ikino 1997), bringing prosperity to citizens through employment and supporting government initiatives through taxation, all the while producing undesirable environmental impacts. Most corporate wealth is, however, channeled to powerful shareholders. Thus business scholars have focused attention on the strategies firms use to increase shareholder value, including strategies to minimize wasteful behaviors that lead to environmental pollution.

This merger of strange bedfellows—businesses and environmental groups—was frowned upon in the early days of the environmental movement in the United States, when environmental agency capture by powerful firms was a significant concern (Sabatier 1975). In a well-known piece in the *New York Times* in 1970, Milton Friedman chided General Motors for pondering the notion of social responsibility, especially in the realm of pollution and safety, which he referred to as "pure and unadulterated socialism"—that is, decisions driven by political objectives rather than the market.

Friedman's apprehension was unwarranted, as transportation and energy companies proved notoriously resistant during the 1970s to mounting pressure from activists for environmental stewardship. Most automakers continue to work against environmental regulations (Luger 1995), as evidenced by a 2004 lawsuit to overturn California's 2002 Clean Cars program and to impede the state's energy and efficiency standards. But as Sir Richard Branson has sought to demonstrate, an increasing number of corporate managers—even in the transportation industries—no longer eschew social responsibility objectives or engage in regulatory capture. Indeed, other companies have followed suit: Tesco, the British food giant, has assumed a leadership position in the food sector by vowing to assess the carbon footprint of its products and to drastically cut energy consumption (Specter 2008; see also Fuchs and Kalfagianni 2010). The list of industry leaders continues to grow. Xerox, a major producer of printers and copiers, is seeking ways to help companies reduce the consumption of paper (Lyons 2008). Walmart, the world's largest retailer, has announced goals to use 100 percent renewable energy, produce no waste, and bring sustainable products to the market (Lazlo 2008). General Electric, an oft-cited polluter of lakes and streams,[6] has refashioned itself through its "ecoimagination" initiative, investing billions of dollars into clean energy research and development and promising to reduce greenhouse gas emissions (Kappler 2005).

Signaling this transformation, in early 2007 the *Harvard Business Review* awarded its 2006 McKinsey Award for the year's most significant article to Michael Porter and Mark Kramer, who describe CSR behavior in "Strategy and Society: The Link Between Competitive Advantage and Corporate Social Responsibility" as a strategic firm resource.[7] Porter and Kramer suggest that firms should minimize negative impacts of their operations and build positive relationships with key societal stakeholders. Strategic actions such as these, the authors assert, can improve competitive advantage through cost savings and reputation building.

As the command-and-control environmental compliance and enforcement paradigm has been complemented by voluntarism[8], corporations are increasingly independent of the state and autonomous in their ability to engage in environmental best practices. At the same time, their behavior is increasingly constrained by other nonstate actors and in particular by the growth in environmental transnational advocacy groups since the 1980s (Keck and Sikkink 1998), which have pushed corporations to embrace the particular values associated with CSR. Thus some of the most interesting developments in environmental governance are taking place outside of governmental institutions with the legal authority for environmental policy making and in the realm of non-state-led environmental governance (O'Neill 2010). Especially in developing countries, global actors including both multinational corporations and international NGOs exert tremendous influence across a large number of economic sectors by diffusing new norms and business practices that bring about changes in corporate behavior even in the absence of a strong regulatory culture (see also Pulver 2007a; Najam, Runnalls, and Halle 2007). These actors also have the capacity to devote financial resources to environmental governance and social welfare in the countries where they operate (Jones Luong and Weinthal 2010). As a result, there is a push toward greater convergence and harmonization of standards across developed and developing countries, despite their different institutional settings and regulatory cultures (Busch and Jörgens 2005; Garcia-Johnson 2000; Weinthal 2002; Cashore, Auld, and Newsom 2004).

This chapter takes stock of these important trends, exploring the potential for comparative research to shed light on the greening of corporations and examining the multitude of influences shaping the adoption of strategic corporate environmental management practices in both developed and developing countries and across different sectors of the economy. The rest of the chapter proceeds as follow. First, we turn to the literature on interest groups to provide the historical context for explaining how business-state relations have traditionally been studied in the field of comparative politics. Next, we describe the domestic origins of CSR in advanced industrialized countries. We argue that although firms in developed economies continue to participate in the long-standing command-and-control regulatory framework and remain motivated by existing and pending regulations, they increasingly seek to fulfill social demands for environmental stewardship by participating in voluntary programs that promote beyond-compliance behavior and burnish reputational assets. We then explain the domestic origins of CSR in a small number of developing countries where environmental governance structures are comparatively weak and environmental regulations are few, albeit not entirely absent. In these settings, domestic firms that participate in VEPs to gain experience often become leaders once regulatory structures are in place. Although some firms may embrace CSR initiatives to gain access to markets or in response to civil society pressure, many developing country firms are pulled by the state to participate voluntarily in programs focused on creating a public perception of environmental compliance. Participation protects the firms from ad hoc enforcement actions and enables them to push back against subsequent development of more stringent regulation. In contrast, firms in developed countries are pulled to participate in government-sponsored voluntary programs operating in conjunction with existing regulations, and rather than pushing back against regulation, they push for new programs, having gained inimitable strategic resources from being early adopters.

This push-pull of regulation versus voluntarism is seen in figure 6.1. Finally, we examine the global diffusion of CSR across a number of sectors, with particular attention to extractive industries and developing countries, showing how transnational advocacy groups have caused multinational and domestic corporations to embrace the particular values associated with CSR.

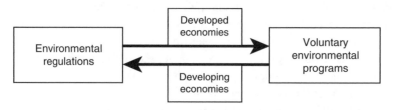

Figure 6.1
Push-pull of regulation vs. voluntarism

Business-State Relations

The study of interest groups has been central to the development of the field of comparative politics generally and to explanations of business-state relations specifically. With origins dating back to the *Federalist Papers*, concern over the role of factionalism as an impediment to the public good has long informed studies of pluralism and interest group theories.[9] In the 1950s and 1960s, American scholars of pluralism reasoned that political power was shared by a variety of interest groups, owing to the many points of access in the American political system that fostered spirited competition in the decision-making process (Truman 1951; Dahl 1961). Others, however, have deplored the disproportionate influence that some interest groups—primarily business—have had on liberal democracy (Lowi 1969). Researchers emphasizing collective action have shown that the business sector can shape policy to further its interests at the expense of the public good because it is better organized than other social groups; unlike larger disconnected groups of citizens, business is able to marshal resources and lobby government officials (Olson 1965). Today there is a perception by many that business continues to hold a privileged position in society, allowing it to subvert the democratic process by pressing Congress to pass special interest legislation (for an overview, see Kraft and Kamieniecki 2007). During the 2007 Democratic presidential debates, Barack Obama, for example, vociferously stressed that "we push against the special interests that are holding us back."[10] These concerns have a long pedigree, and the US government has a history of seeking to limit the influence of business through the legislative process, marked by the passage of the Sherman Antitrust Act of 1890 that authorizes the government to outlaw "every contract, combination or conspiracy in restraint of trade" and "monopolization" (cited in Kovacic and Shapiro 2000, 43). President Theodore Roosevelt used this act to bring suit against Standard Oil in 1906, charging it with conspiring to restrain trade.

Outside of US politics, the literature on comparative political economy has also emphasized the disproportionate impact of business on international economic relations (Evans 1979) and on economic reform in transition economies (Hellman 1998). For instance, the greatest obstacle to the progress of economic reform in Russia came from enterprise insiders and commercial bankers who sought to preserve their early gains from the reform process and ultimately "capture" the state (Hellman 1998; Hellman et al. 2000). In the developing world, similar concerns have been articulated through dependency theory and scholarly and popular writings on the "neocolonial" practices of multinational firms seeking to control natural resources in the tropics through means ranging from economic inducements to political manipulation and violence (Dos Santos 1970; Cardoso and Falleto 1979)—concerns given new life amid current debates surrounding state regulatory capacity and public welfare in an age of globalization (Ó Riain 2000; for an informative overview of business-state relations in developing countries, see Maxfield and Schneider 1997). As a result of these concerns, a good deal of attention in the field of comparative politics has concentrated on how best to insulate the state from corporate interests in order to ensure that the state is able to carry out its policy agenda (Evans 1992, 1995). Elsewhere, scholars have found the creation of an autonomous technocratic elite to be necessary to shield the state from interest group pressures (Johnson 1982). These insulated technocrats, relying upon their economic skills, manage the country's resources for the public good rather than to promote private benefits (Williamson 1994, 12). The primary objective has been to curb rent-seeking behavior on the part of the state and its bureaucrats and to rein in business so as to preclude clientele capture.

When we turn to the literature on interest groups and environmental policy, similar arguments follow. For example, environmentalists perceive that businesses not only resist any form of regulations that would impose new costs, but that they seek to capture the policy-making process, leveraging their disproportionate power to impede the formulation and implementation of environmental standards (see Kamieniecki 2006, 9). The extraordinary influence of the business sector was evident during the George W. Bush administration, when Vice President Dick Cheney led the Energy Task Force to design a national energy plan. Pressure from environmental groups to release documents under the Freedom of Information Act exposed numerous meetings and close ties between the Department of Energy and industry representatives, while environmental groups were continuously rebuffed.[11]

Traditionally, the literature on business and the environment has also argued that businesses in industrialized countries will engage in "industrial flight" and relocate to countries that lack strict environmental regulations. At the same time, it is widely perceived that developing country firms have no reason to ratchet up their environmental credentials. Others have found these explanations wanting. Pulver (2007a) documents how firms in developing countries often serve as leaders in environmental innovation, contrary to the assumption that they are "locked into a single, polluting trajectory" (Pulver 2007a, 192). Birdsall and Wheeler (1993) find little evidence that poor countries set low regulatory standards to attract foreign investment (the so-called pollution haven hypothesis). David Vogel (1997) has also challenged this assumption, arguing that a "California effect" may take place, in which a wealthier country applies stricter environmental regulations that forces its trading partners to ratchet up their standards in order to maintain their export markets.

As we argue shortly, the role of the business sector in the environmental realm is much more complex than the conventional story of powerful interests always getting their way. Although we do not go as far as market liberals who see stronger growth translating into more corporate funds for environmental protection (for a discussion, see Clapp and Dauvergne 2005), we do contend that business is playing a more dynamic role in policy making than that suggested by much of the comparative politics literature on business-state relations. The story is less about the state reining in business groups and increasingly about changes taking place within the private sector in both industrialized and developing countries pertaining to CSR. In the rest of the chapter, we explore the domestic and international influences that drive the greening of corporate strategy and motivate firms to move "beyond compliance" (see, e.g., Green 2010; Hoffman 2000; Press and Mazmanian 2006; Pulver 2007a).

The Domestic Origins of Corporate Social Responsibility in Advanced Industrialized Countries

Bowen's classic 1953 work *Social Responsibilities of the Businessman* laid out the rudiments of the concept of CSR, which he defined as "the obligations of businessmen to pursue those policies, to make those decisions or to follow those lines of action which are desirable in terms of the objectives and values of our society" (Bowen 1953, 6). Bowen spurred a business movement and sparked a sharp retort characterized best by Friedman's declaration that "there is one and only one social responsibility of business—to use its resources and engage in activities designed to increase its profits" (1970, 126). Friedman did, however, recognize that businesses must play by the rules of the game, which were rapidly changing in an era of expansive environmental regulation.

What were the circumstances prompting business to change its behavior within specific countries? In the early 1970s, few US corporations voluntarily embraced better environmental practices. After initially clashing with governmental regulators, corporations were forced to adhere to new environmental standards mandated by the 1970 Clean Air Act and 1972 Clean Water Act, for instance (Kraft and Kamieniecki 2007, 10–11). Their commitment to the environment was a direct response to legislation that required industry to adopt the "best available technology" and to provide an "adequate margin of safety" to protect public health (Andrews 1999).

During this time, firms in Europe faced similarly strict regulatory actions designed to constrain business behavior (for an overview, see Majone and Baake 1996). Business was forced to develop the operational and managerial capacity to protect the environment while still providing economic value to shareholders. Businesses also began to see their nascent environmental management competency in strategic terms, however, and learned that moving beyond basic compliance could offer attractive advantages, such as setting high standards for laggard peers to follow and developing technological competencies that provided competitive advantage (Jaffe et al. 1995; Porter and van der Linde 1995). For example, in 1978, faced with regulations to phase out chlorinated fluorocarbons that were found to damage the ozone layer, firms were able to reduce operating costs and boost performance through the use of alternative solvents (Porter and van der Linde 1995).

This approach to environmental governance, in which business developed environmental management capacity as a defensive posture, was framed by a contentious relationship between industry and government regulators in states with strong institutions such as the US Environmental Protection Agency and the UK's Environment Agency. Significant government resources were dedicated to surveillance of business operations and to enforcement actions. It was in the best interest of the business community to develop compliance capacity and resources to lobby against potential further regulation of business operations. From the late 1970s through the early 1990s, many multinational corporations were developing corporate-level environmental affairs organizations (Lyon and Maxwell 1999) whose efforts focused squarely on influencing future regulatory policies. In later years, however, their efforts were moving away from direct opposition to a more measured response. Hoffman describes the period from 1988 to 1993 as one in which companies such as Shell were practicing "strategic environmentalism," developing new and expanded strategic environmental management resources to respond to escalating environmental regulations in countries such as the United States and the United Kingdom (1997, 13).

This sophisticated business response was predicated on the existence of a strong business climate in these countries. Because of the ability of US and European businesses to successfully compete in the increasingly global economy, firm resources were available to be channeled back to these nascent strategic operations. Multinational corporations then took on leadership roles in promoting the wider diffusion of environmental practices they had applied in their own organizations. For example, in 1990, leaders of firms such as Eastman Kodak, DuPont, and Proctor and Gamble, which maintained a significant number of employees in their corporate environmental affairs and environmental management organizations, created the Global Environmental Management Initiative, "dedicated to fostering environmental, health and safety excellence worldwide through the sharing of tools and information in order for business to help business achieve environmental excellence."[12]

In the late 1980s, as businesses were gaining expertise in strategically managing environmental impacts of their operations, the tenor of business-government relationships was changing in advanced industrialized countries. No longer was government's sole response to newly perceived environmental problems one of instating new regulatory requirements. Command-and-control government regulation of environmental activities diminished in the United States as it was accompanied by market-based and voluntary programs. By the late 1990s businesses in the United

States could participate in more than fifty voluntary environmental programs and European firms had signed on to over three hundred voluntary agreements (Morgenstern and Pizer 2007). Most successful businesses in industrialized countries came to be simultaneously "pushed" (through state enforcement) to a baseline of compliance with existing regulations and "pulled" toward the acquisition of additional expertise through voluntary participation in government-led beyond-compliance initiatives.

Businesses, furthermore, sought to apply their environmental protection competencies strategically through industry sector sponsored programs such as the Chemical Manufacturer Association's Responsible Care program, which required participating companies to adhere to strict standards of environmental stewardship. Prakash (2000) argues that chemical manufacturers engaged in these voluntary practices to generate good will for the industry, fearing a strong regulatory response after the tremendous negative press surrounding the 1984 Union Carbide Bhopal tragedy, in which an explosion at a pesticide manufacturing facility released toxic gases, killing more than 8,000 people and injuring an additional 120,000 (Prakash 2000). In 1986, their fears materialized when strict regulations governing disclosure of toxic chemical emissions were imposed on US firms through the EPA's Toxics Release Inventory, a program the agency describes as directly linked to the tragedy (Jasanoff 2007).

Although in the United States in the 1980s environmental groups were experiencing backlash from the Reagan administration's antiregulatory stance, it was still clear that companies could not overlook the concerns of civil society pressure, particularly from environmental NGOs (see Wapner 1995). As a result, they were forced to engage in relationships with stakeholders not only as a defensive posture, as when McDonalds and the Environmental Defense Fund worked together to reduce the company's packaging,[13] but also to obtain a competitive advantage. Firms' capacity for engaging in productive relationships with NGO stakeholders can be leveraged as a strategic resource (Gallagher and Gallagher 2007).

In this atmosphere of social concern alongside government reluctance to impose direct regulation, US agencies responded to industry trade association efforts to help members improve environmental stewardship behavior by initiating a broad-based series of voluntary environmental programs (for an overview of VEPs, see Press and Mazmanian 2006).[14] These programs were designed to motivate firms to go beyond traditional compliance measures so as to pollute far less or to confront issues such as transportation impacts, energy use, and climate change. The motivation behind these programs was to create a policy environment that pulls businesses into new directions such that they consider the environmental and social costs of production while pursuing economic growth. Such programs also allowed a modicum of progress on environmental protection amid the backlash against command-and-control policy making. This orientation carried over into the Clinton administration with its focus on "reinventing government" to incorporate competition and client-oriented practices from the private sector. VEPs promoted an atmosphere of cooperation between business and the public sector as opposed to relations based largely on government coercion. This is not to say that an era of pure government-business cooperation had arrived. Kraft and Kamieniecki (2007) describe a US policy environment in which businesses continue to allocate significant resources to lobby for policies that serve their interests and of which NGOs remain skeptical.[15] Nonetheless, policies supported by business lobbying that focus on public-private partnerships and voluntarism can promote high levels of environmental stewardship and are seen by some scholars as indications of a broader "greening of industry."[16]

Because VEPs promised to promote rather than hinder economic growth, they were an appropriate response to the regulatory backlash of the 1980s. These programs are essentially a form of self-regulation whereby firms voluntarily agree to take on challenges that were not envisioned by the designers of the traditional command-and-control regulation incorporated in the early Clean Air and Clean Water Acts (Andrews 1998). However, they often operate in the shadow of public regulation, in that there may come a time when regulatory action is necessary to address an impending environmental crisis. For example, leading US firms currently participate in VEPs such as the Environmental Protection Agency (EPA) Climate Leaders and the Chicago Climate Exchange, which allow firms to gain experience tracking and managing greenhouse gas emissions in advance of the expected contentious congressional debate on federal carbon cap-and-trade requirements. An early VEP, the US EPA's 33/50 program, operated in the shadow of increased regulatory enforcement of the Emergency Planning and Community Right to Know Act (Innes and Sam 2008) and provided participating firms with desirable publicity about their efforts to decrease emissions of toxic pollutants.[17]

VEPs offer a number of mechanisms to motivate firms to move beyond basic compliance. The government publicizes successful efforts and partners with firms to train employees and engage in research and development of new technologies, but without mandating specific behavioral change. Prakash surmises that one of the benefits of turning to voluntary programs over regulations is that voluntary codes "make laws less adversarial between regulators and firms and hence lessen the recourse to judicial settings" (2000, 185). VEPs were a first step for the US government to redefine its relationships with the business sector to be more conciliatory.

In contrast to the adversarial business-state relations in the United States, corporatist institutional structures in Europe that regulate government consultations with employers and unions have facilitated a different trajectory for corporate social responsibility.[18] Despite the predominance of command-and-control regulations in Europe throughout the 1980s and 1990s, close ties between the business community and governments account for the strength of new policy instruments that include voluntary agreements (Jordan et al. 2003). The UK's voluntary Climate Change Agreements, for example, were negotiated with a wide variety of trade associations and provide quantitative goals for participating firms' energy use reduction. European governments have, likewise, introduced ecolabels (starting with Germany's Blue Angel label in 1978), which rely not upon regulatory coercion but upon market incentives and moral suasion, providing consumers with information on the environmental impact of specific goods and services (Jordan, Würzel, and Zito 2003, 11).[19] Moreover, the widely accepted principle of cooperation (*Kooperationsprinzip*) together with the precautionary principle (*Vorsorgeprinzip*) has facilitated a more conciliatory regulatory style in Germany than in the United States since the 1970s (Würzel et al. 2003).

Domestic Origins of Corporate Social Responsibility in Developing Countries

Although the bulk of scholarly attention has focused on the evolution of CSR in companies in industrialized countries, a burgeoning literature is assessing the determinants of CSR in developing country firms, particularly in the realm of environmental sustainability (Pulver 2007a). In contrast to the prevailing assumption that developing countries' firms are environmental laggards, civil society mobilization, government regulation, and market forces are propelling firms to embrace sustainable practices and simply not engage in a race to the bottom (Pulver 2007a). Scholars such as Simone Pulver—through her study of Mexico's national oil company, PEMEX—have challenged the notion that all developing country firms are environmental laggards. Entrepreneurial managers within PEMEX identified climate change as a strategic priority for the company and imported global best practices in the climate sector (Pulver 2007b). In his study of community-driven regulation in Vietnam, Dara O'Rourke (2004) has also shown that developing-country firms, many of which are notorious polluters, may be responsive to civil society and environmental agency pressure.

Developing country firms are thus increasingly embracing voluntary initiatives aimed at improving their environmental track records (Pulver 2007a). Voluntary environmental programs are being designed and implemented in Latin America; Mexico, for example, currently operates more than fifteen VEPs and Colombia more than fifty (Blackman, Lyon, and Sisto 2006). In South Africa, the "Proudly South African" label provides an example of governments facilitating the proliferation of "voluntary product labels." Developed under the auspices of the National Economic Development and Labor Council, a business-government institution that seeks to build consensus on economic and social policy, Proudly South African was established to support South African economic development through business certification (see Fox, Ward, and Howard 2002, 5).[20] More than 2,000 South African businesses—most of which are small in size and geographic reach—are now authorized to display the Proudly South African label, signifying their commitment to established standards of in-country production, fair labor and employment, and basic environmental management practices.

What then can be said about differences in the use of voluntary programs in developing and developed economies? In countries where regulatory development and enforcement infrastructure is weak, voluntarism is offered as a solution for achieving compliance with existing, basic environmental regulations (Blackman and Sisto 2006). In Mexico, Blackman describes policymakers as using VEPs to "remedy rampant noncompliance with mandatory regulation" (2008, 120). In developing countries with a nascent regulatory culture, such as South Africa, Egypt, and Costa Rica, voluntary initiatives are more likely to have domestic origins. They serve to build upon and enhance existing institutional capacity. Examples include Costa Rica's voluntary Certification for Sustainable Tourism program (Rivera 2004) and the Egyptian Pollution Abatement Project (Hamed and El Mahgary 2004). In each of these cases, a state-sponsored platform existed prior to the inception of VEPs. In contrast, in those developing countries where an institutional structure for environmental compliance and enforcement is lacking, the origins of CSR are more likely to be international, as discussed in the next section. Where environmental regulations are rare or nonexistent, firms experience the push-pull of regulation versus voluntarism differently than firms in industrialized states. Firms are pulled by the state to participate voluntarily in government programs focused on establishing a high rate of basic compliance. Participation then provides them with a modicum of protection from enforcement actions, using their "clean" status to push back against subsequent government development of more stringent regulation.

For situations in which there is some interest and capacity among government agencies to launch VEPs, as in Mexico, the programs largely focus on demonstrating to the public that an acceptable rate of basic compliance exists. In these cases, only a small number of elite firms participate in program design. This limited participation contrasts sharply with the origins of CSR in many industrialized countries, where VEPs are developed with broad industry involvement and reward beyond compliance behavior. For example, Mexico's Clean Industry Program, which was initiated in 2002, is administered directly by the Federal Environmental Attorney General's office with the goal of boosting basic compliance rates. Designed with minimal business input, the program requires participating firms to undergo independent environmental audits of their operations and to agree in writing to address all violations within a specified date in exchange for not being penalized. Firms able to meet the requirements are issued a clean certificate and avoid regulatory inspections for two years. Leading firms are thus provided flexibility to experiment with creative alternatives to strict compliance behavior and thus push back on the development of more stringent regulations.

Industry has also translated some of its domestic initiatives into international ones, allowing for greater convergence in the environmental practices of businesses operating abroad (Gallagher et al. 2005). Industry organizations have designed and implemented broad-based environmental certification schemes such as the International Organization for Standardization's ISO 14001 environmental management system standard, requiring participating firms to adhere to standardized protocols and to undergo regular third-party audits to maintain certification. Globally, more than 46,000 firms have been certified as ISO 14001–compliant to date. The United States and Japan are leaders in terms of certified firms, with an increasing number of Chinese businesses obtaining certification (ISO 2003).

As ISO 14001 and other international certification schemes such as SA8000 (which uses a management system framework to address human rights and labor issues[21]) have been adopted by firms across the globe, they have served as frameworks for government-led initiatives in those developing countries with some limited regulatory capacity. For example, the Egyptian Environmental Policy Program has employed an ISO 14001 platform to develop environmental governance institutions and regulatory policies. South Africa's National Responsible Tourism Guidelines and Costa Rica's Certification for Sustainable Tourism program are also modeled after these international standards, but seek to operate in the tourism sector as part of an overall national business development strategy.

Few studies to date, however, have explored why firms in developing countries adopt ISO 14001. Sowers (2003) concludes that in Egypt, managers comply with VEPs not only for public relations purposes but also based on the belief that they will be required for entry to developed markets.[22] Access to markets has also served as a driver for the growth in certification labels in the agricultural sector in developing countries for organic and fair trade labels (Calo and Wise 2005). These labels ostensibly guarantee customers in markets far from the source of production that agricultural products and other tradable commodities are produced according to strict social and environmental standards, including a fair labor standards, direct trade, community development, and environmental sustainability (Starobin and Weinthal 2010). In the coffee sector, growers of shade-grown and organic coffee have introduced these labels as a way to capture a high-end market and accordingly higher prices paid to small producers in developing countries (Bacon 2004).

CSR as a Global Movement

As we saw in the previous section, many VEPs have important transnational dimensions. Here we consider these in greater detail and explore more fully the international origins of CSR in countries experiencing a regulatory deficit. In particular, some research on global implementation of ISO 14001 indicates that multinational corporations operating in developing countries depend on voluntary self-regulation to promote environmental stewardship behavior in the absence of strong regulatory institutions (Christmann and Taylor 2001). Without such frameworks, managers of production facilities would not necessarily be inclined to dedicate significant resources to environmental protection.[23] Companies that export products to consumers in developed countries are especially sensitive to the need to employ the well-respected ISO 14001 brand to build reputational assets and signal their "greenness" (King et al. 2005). This behavior is a logical extension of the common business practice of using third-party certification schemes to signal best practices and cultivate customer trust along the supply chain. ISO 14001 thus addressed two needs—providing guidance on procedures and processes to assist firms seeking to understand and comply with increasingly complex environmental regulations (Darnall, Gallagher, and Andrews 2001) and, in what has become the standard's primary role, signaling an environmental stamp of approval (King, Lenox, and Terlaak 2005).

While governments in developed countries applaud corporations adopting ISO 14001, governments in developing countries often lack the desire or ability to pressure corporations to adhere to CSR. In countries with weak environmental regulations and governance mechanisms, corporations have largely been unregulated, leading some observers to suggest that multinational firms seek out "pollution havens," relocating industries abroad to take advantage of the absence of strict environmental regulations (for an overview, see Porter 1999). For instance, China's weak environmental regulatory culture has facilitated the relocation of many steel-producing firms from Germany's Ruhr Valley to Hebei Province in China, such that the "outsourcing of [Germany's] polluting industries has given them cleaner air and water," while China's air quality continues to deteriorate.[24] The violent protests that erupted in Seattle during the 1999 meeting of the World Trade Organization were in part fueled by concerns that the expansion of the global economy was having a negative impact on people and the environment in developing countries, as corporations were moving their operations abroad to reap the benefits of cheaper inputs (i.e., labor and natural resources).

Over time, comparative research has countered arguments that multinational corporations are responsible for weak environmental standards in developing countries. Garcia-Johnson (2000) argued that owing to the expansion of free trade, corporations going abroad have served as the torch bearers for better environmental practices. The above-mentioned Responsible Care program has enabled the US chemical industry to export improved environmental practices in its operations. This stronger role for corporations as agents of change contrasts strongly with the way that CSR developed in many industrialized economies—that is, as a retort to government regulations and civil society pressure. Rather, corporations operating in countries where regulations are weak or absent may push governments to create basic compliance-based VEPs, which allows them to secure the competitive advantage of being among the first to leverage environmental compliance expertise. In these settings, CSR can be seen as a natural response to a governance deficit. Firms in the global marketplace rush in to institutionalize "good" practices like environmental stewardship or protection of human rights, which governments in developing countries have limited capacity to provide through regulation, monitoring, and enforcement (Grayson and Marsden 2007).

Although critics of CSR may perceive such efforts as just symbolic or as a corporate relations ploy, some multinational corporations have exhibited higher levels of CSR in their operations abroad than they do at home. This phenomenon raises the question: under what conditions will corporations self-regulate in the absence of a domestic regulatory threat? We argue that this change in behavior can be linked to the growth in environmental transnational advocacy groups like those discussed in Kate O'Neill's chapter in this volume. CSR as a global movement has been spurred by pressure from international and local NGOs that diffuse new norms for corporate behavior throughout the international system.[25] Especially in developing countries with weak environmental and labor regulations, local actors have relied on transnational linkages to international NGOs to alter the behavior of corporations (Keck and Sikkink 1998). O'Rourke's (2004) study of environmental regulation in Vietnam also demonstrates how advocacy networks between international and local NGOs forced a Korean-owned Nike factory to change its environmental practices. Nike was particularly vulnerable because of the value it placed upon retaining ISO 14000 certification, in contrast to many other firms in Vietnam and the developing world. By targeting Nike, a coalition of local and international activists changed the practices of its subcontractor to ensure compliance with the law and a commitment to further improve environmental management.

When transnational linkages exist between international and local NGOs, a firm operating in a country where lax environmental standards prevent access to clean water for production and employee health may, out of self-interest, promote the diffusion of practices that protect water supplies. For example, while in early 2003 environmental activist groups such as the India Resource Center rightly scrutinized Coca Cola's use of water in India, the firm was working to improve water efficiency and water supply protection practices in its Indian bottling plants in response to an ongoing drought (Hills and Welford 2005).

Since the 1990s, international NGO advocacy campaigns have increased the accountability and transparency of corporations operating in the extractive industries and in conflict zones (see, e.g., Ballentine and Nitzschke 2005). In this sector, owing to the regulatory deficit in many developing countries, international NGOs have chosen at times to bypass fledgling governments and instead directly target corporations, especially large multinationals that can no longer ignore the influence of CSR on their bottom line.[26] For example, in some instances, international NGOs have relied on litigation to force companies to introduce CSR programs that take into account human rights, environmental conditions, and the social welfare needs of local populations in the areas where they operate. One such case is the lawsuit brought against Talisman Energy, an independent oil and gas company with its headquarters in Canada, for violating the human rights of Christian and other non-Muslim minorities in Sudan as part of its energy operations (for details, see Kobrin 2005). The protracted class action suit filed against ChevronTexaco in the US courts in 1993 is another case in which a transnational alliance between international NGOs and local communities has sought to hold corporations accountable for negligent environmental practices (Sawyer 2006; Watts 2005).

One way that businesses, especially in the extractive industries, have sought to improve their public image then is through the deepening of these nascent alliances with NGOs. In fact, a shift has taken place. Where once environmentalists were stuck in a vicious struggle against corporate power, over time corporations have reached out to NGOs to involve them in their programs. BP, for example, regularly consults stakeholders such as Human Rights Watch, Amnesty International, Oxfam, Christian Aid, Global Witness, IUCN, and WWF (Skjærseth 2004). Corporations such as BP and Shell subcontract out some of their CSR programs to provide greater information to local populations and the NGO community about their business practices. It is now common for NGOs and the business community to sit at the same table to discuss the promotion of CSR, rather than for NGOs to exert pressure solely through protests on the street.

This is not to say that there is complete agreement that all corporations have adhered to CSR or that CSR is the appropriate strategy for promoting better environmental governance and social welfare. Some argue that this change in behavior may only be a form of "green wash" (Barkan 2004; Frankental 2001; Frynas 2005). But although corporations may not have gone into CSR as the agents of transformation, in the last few decades their power in the global economy has created a new space for them to serve as major influences on human rights and the environment in the countries in which they operate. Bennett argues that international NGOs are pushing multinational corporations to "bear some responsibility for the effects of their operations on the local environment and populations" (2002, 394). In short, corporations especially in the extractive industries have been forced to deal with societal and environmental pressures (Jones Luong and Weinthal 2010). Many corporate leaders in the petroleum sector argue that "oil companies can never assume the responsibility of political institutions, or become substitutes for such institutions" (Olsen 2002, 15). But in countries with weak political institutions, corporations are nonetheless seen by international and domestic NGOs as a way to bring about political, social, and environmental change and hence to force governments to become more accountable and transparent in their actions. Outside of the extractive industries, Webersik (2005) argues in his analysis of Somalia's banana plantation economy that multinational corporations could play a more constructive role in promoting peace and security in the postconflict phase.

The creation of new certification and transparency initiatives provides some additional evidence of the impact of international NGO activism on countries with extractive industries and on the multinational firms operating within them. Corporations have been accused for decades of reinforcing the corrupt practices of governments and of complicity with states or warring factions that disregard basic human rights and protection of the natural environment. In the late 1990s, the international NGO Global Witness publicized the diamond industry's contribution to the illegal trade in diamonds, which was generating revenue to finance civil conflicts in Sierra Leone and Angola (Grant and Taylor 2004; Global Witness 1998). Following international boycotts and information campaigns by NGOs, corporations and governments have succumbed to international pressure to sign onto new international initiatives demanding CSR. Charges of connivance in Angola's civil war led De Beers and other companies that procure diamonds from conflict-prone areas to endorse a voluntary certification scheme known as the Kimberley Process.[27] The result of a concerted effort by a broad coalition of international NGO efforts in the late 1990s to bring conflict diamonds to the attention of the world community (see Smillie 2005), the Kimberley Process came into effect on January 1, 2003. It brings together more than thirty governments, the diamond industry, and NGOs seeking to ensure that the industry's diamonds are identified as "conflict-free" (Fox, Ward, and Howard 2002). The Kimberley Process, as Kantz points out, clearly demonstrates the "discursive power of NGOs and like-minded governments" (2007, 2) to create new CSR interests within the business community. Vogel describes these NGO initiatives as "civil regulations," which others refer to as "non-state" or "market-based regulatory frameworks" (2006, 5) that also include the Forest Stewardship Council's labeling program to promote sustainably harvested wood. In contrast to prior decades, when governments would regulate industries operating within the nation-state, such NGO-led initiatives have had a profound impact on industry behavior at the global level by forcing corporations to become more transparent in the way they conduct business with developing countries.[28]

Another example in which nonstate actors are pushing companies to adopt CSR in countries with regulatory deficits is the United Nations Global Compact, launched in 1999 as a partnership among the United Nations, labor unions, and NGOs. In a press conference on the UN Global Compact, former UN Secretary General Kofi

Annan justified his decision to promote CSR: "You don't need to wait for a government to pass laws before you ensure that your operations do not pollute the lake or water that produces fish for the people. You don't need to wait for government to pass laws before you pay a decent wage. You don't need to wait for governments to pass laws before you refuse to employ children. We are asking them to tell us what they are doing."[29]

What is striking is that the UN—an organization that deals extensively with nation-states at all levels of its organization—recognizes that it is not only nation-states and NGOs that play a vital role in environmental governance but also the private business sector. Especially for those developing countries that lack the capacity to regulate industry and to govern effectively, the UN is relying on the influence of large corporations to lead by example. The Global Compact calls upon companies to self-regulate by adhering to ten universal principles related to human rights, labor standards, and the environment, especially for companies operating in conflict zones.[30] According to John Ruggie, one of its architects, the Global Compact has embraced a "learning approach" to influence corporate behavior, with firms submitting case studies describing what they have done to adopt best practices of CSR in their everyday operations (Ruggie 2002).

Over time, as a result of intense pressure from both international and domestic NGOs and a shift in international norms regarding the best practices of multinational corporations, public-private initiatives have emerged that bring together a coalition of businesses, governments, international financial institutions, and civil society. Through the leadership of former Prime Minister Tony Blair, the Extractive Industries Transparency Initiative (EITI) was initiated in 2002 at the World Summit on Sustainable Development in Johannesburg. Unlike efforts by transnational advocacy networks to change business practices, this particular private-public initiative also aims to enhance governance in countries with extractive industries through improved transparency and accountability.[31] Corporations are central to this mission through their disclosure of the payments they make to governments (e.g., for concession contracts), which provides civil society with information about government revenues.

Conclusion: From VEPs and Certification to Sustainability

The global spread of corporate social responsibility both reflects and contributes to changing interactions between state, societal, and transnational actors. Whereas in industrialized countries CSR often developed as a defensive response to the regulatory pressures of the state, over time many businesses have embraced self-regulation and in the process have fostered a change in the way states approach environmental governance. In developing countries, where multinational corporations have often been forces of social exploitation and environmental damage, growing numbers of firms seeking to maintain their competitive advantage and reputations have pursued CSR policies even absent the threat of regulation. Through our discussion of the diffusion of CSR across firms in both developed and developing countries, we conclude that business-state relations within the study of comparative politics can no longer be viewed merely as a powerful interest group trying to impede environmental policies and to capture the policy-making process, but also as a potential partner in promoting environmental sustainability.

What then does the future of CSR hold in store? Since the late 1990s, CSR has evolved from a focus on moving beyond compliance through voluntarism and certification to an emphasis on "sustainability" at both the national and international levels. Multinational firms motivated by a desire to "do well by doing good" see a new CSR framed by the concept of sustainability as a means of increasing shareholder value and as a source of competitive advantage (Vogel 2005). A fundamental premise of this movement is that meaningful relationships with stakeholders are critical and that an expansive definition of "stakeholder" is required, incorporating not only managers and shareholders but also employees, community members, NGOs, and the environment itself. When operating under a strategy grounded in sustainability, firms work closely with interest groups and NGOs to better understand and develop responses to critical social issues. Because firms increasingly engage in productive relationships with stakeholders not as a defensive posture, but to build a competitive advantage, there is less likelihood for regulatory capture than interest group theorists once presumed (e.g., Lowi 1969).

Though most of the literature seeking to explain the diffusion of CSR has examined changes taking place within the firm, or has focused on the ability of business to capture the state, our analysis suggests that more research is needed on the actual effects of CSR, especially on state institutions in developing countries. This is an especially appropriate line of inquiry in light of the tenth anniversary of the UN Global Compact, which has served as a mechanism for more than 7,000 firms and NGOs in both developed and developing countries to engage in learning and dialog focused on the creation of social norms grounded in CSR (Kell 2005). Will CSR contribute to better governance in developing countries as more firms join NGOs in demanding greater accountability and transparency on the part of governments? That CSR constitutes a global movement is indisputable; that domestic politics and transnational actors have influenced corporate behavior is also undeniable. Yet the effects on governance are still ambiguous and will require the sustained attention of scholars and activists interested in comparative environmental policies as they develop over the coming decades.

Notes

Authorship is based on alphabetical order and the authors share equal responsibility for the content and analysis herein. We thank David Vogel and the other participants in the Comparative Environmental Politics workshop at UC Berkeley in March 2008 for comments.

1. For an overview of the debates on the relationship between state and society, see Skocpol 1985.

2. In many ways, this observation is similar to Barnett and Finnemore's (1999) work on international organizations.

3. For a discussion of firm motivations to move from a primary focus on philanthropy to a more strategic approach integrating broader citizenship behavior, see Porter and Kramer 2006.

4. Sir Richard Branson Interview with Saab Automobile UK, August 3, 2007, http://www.saabhistory.com/2007/04/23/sir-richard-branson-interview-with-saab-automobile-uk, accessed June 28, 2008.

5. See Revkin 2006 and Miller 2010.

6. For a discussion of GE's contamination of the Hudson River, see Kamieniecki 2006, chapter 6.

7. In this chapter, we apply the term "strategic" to mean contributing to sustained competitive advantage, as do business scholars such as Porter (1980).

8. The historical evolution of state regulatory responses is discussed by Meadowcroft (chapter 3, this volume).

9. The issue of factions was raised by Madison in Paper No. 10. Aiming to counter the power of factions, the US government was thus divided into three separate branches of government (executive, legislative, and judicial) with sufficient checks and balances on each branch to ensure the dispersion of power.

10. The Democratic Debate on MSNBC. *New York Times*, October 30, 2007, http://www.nytimes.com/2007/10/30/us/politics/30debate-transcript.html, accessed May 23, 2011.

11. Van Natta and Banerjee 2002.

12. For details, see http://www.gemi.org, accessed June 28, 2008.

13. In the 1990s, one of the most successful attempts to influence industry behavior was a campaign organized to force the McDonald's Corporation to stop producing its hamburger box made of foam and plastic and switch to paper wrapping. Bending to activist pressure, McDonald's agreed to change its packaging, although the firm did not believe that the decision made ecological or economic sense (see also Wapner 1995).

14. These are described by Lyon and Maxwell as "public voluntary programs" (2008, 723).

15. Furthermore, Kamieniecki (2006) concludes that when business interests participate in environmental policy debates, they do not always sway policy decisions.

16. See especially Press and Mazmanian 2006 for a discussion of voluntary policies to promote environmental stewardship by firms.

17. The 33/50 program had virtually no impact on reducing emissions (Vidovic and Khanna 2007); firms received positive publicity for emissions reductions already taken. The program's

most significant effect was to communicate to firms that there is value in participating in VEPs.

18. On the effects of corporatism on the environment in Germany, see Würzel et al. 2003.

19. Other ecolabels in Europe that ensued include the Nordic Swan and the European Flower. On the issue of credible information associated with eco-labeling schemes, see Starobin and Weinthal 2010.

20. For more information, see also http://www.proudlysa.co.za, accessed June 28, 2008.

21. SA8000, a global auditable certification standard based on the UN Universal Declaration of Human Rights, Convention on Human Rights of the Child and various international labor organization policy recommendations, was developed by Social Accountability International (SAI). As of January 1, 2008, more than 1,500 facilities worldwide were certified to SA8000.

22. The Egyptian Environmental Affairs Agency also favors these international VEPs because it allows them to downplay their poor environmental performance with respect to industrial pollution (Sowers 2003).

23. Consumer and community pressure is also a significant factor in pushing firms to comply. For examples set in Brazil and Mexico, respectively, see da Motta 2006 and Gangadharan 2006.

24. *New York Times*, December 21, 2007. For an overview of China's weak responses to its growing environmental problems, see also Economy 2004.

25. See also Najam, Runnalls, and Halle 2007 on the diffusion of ideas.

26. Dalton, Recchia, and Rohrschneider (2003) point out that there is a larger repertoire of actions that environmental NGOs may pursue, from contacting media organizations to fostering links with officials in political parties and/or parliamentary committees. Steinberg (2005), furthermore, shows that in other economic sectors, it is not always the case that NGOs bypass governments, and also that under particular circumstances NGOs may enable governments to provide public goods and enhance national policy.

27. For more information, see http://www.kimberleyprocess.com, accessed May 23, 2011.

28. Although it is beyond the scope of this chapter to evaluate the effectiveness of different certification schemes, Vogel (2005) sheds light on their variation. Besides the Kimberley Process, the Forest Certification Schemes (FSC) has also been moderately effective in regulating sustainably harvested timber. See especially Cashore, Auld, and Newson 2004 for a discussion of FSC.

29. Transcript of Press Conference by Secretary-General Kofi Annan at Headquarters, http://www.unis.unvienna.org/unis/pressrels/2000/sg2619.html, accessed June 28, 2008.

30. For more information, see http://www.unglobalcompact.org, accessed June 10, 2011.

31. For details, see http://eiti.org, accessed June 10, 2011.

References

Andrews, Richard N. L. 1998. Environmental Regulation and Business Self-Regulation. *Policy Sciences* 31 (3): 177–197.

Andrews, Richard N. L. 1999. *Managing the Environment, Managing Ourselves: A History of American Environmental Policy*. New Haven: Yale University Press.

Bacon, Christopher. 2004. Confronting the Coffee Crisis: Can Fair Trade, Organic, and Specialty Coffees Reduce Small-Scale Farmer Vulnerability in Northern Nicaragua? *World Development* 33 (3): 497–511.

Ballentine, Karen, and Heiko Nitzschke, eds. 2005. *Profiting from Peace: Managing the Resource Dimensions of Civil War*. Boulder: Lynne Rienner Publishers.

Barkan, Joel. 2004. *The Corporation: The Pathological Pursuit of Profit and Power*. New York: Free Press.

Barnett, Michael N., and Martha Finnemore. 1999. The Politics, Power, and Pathologies of International Organizations. *International Organization* 54:699–732.

Bennett, Juliette. 2002. Multinational Corporations, Social Responsibility and Conflict. *Journal of International Affairs* 55 (2): 393–410.

Birdsall, Nancy, and David Wheeler. 1993. Trade Policy and Industrial Pollution in Latin America: Where Are the Pollution Havens? *Journal of Environment & Development* 2 (1): 137–149.

Blackman, Allen. 2008. Can Voluntary Environmental Regulation Work in Developing Countries? Lessons from Case Studies. *Policy Studies Journal* 36 (1): 119–143.

Blackman, Allen, Thomas P. Lyon, and Nicholas Sisto. 2006. Voluntary Environmental Agreements When Regulatory Capacity Is Weak. *Comparative Economic Studies* 48:682–702.

Blackman, Allen, and Nicholas Sisto. 2006. Voluntary Environmental Regulation in Developing Countries: A Mexican Case Study. *Natural Resources Journal* 46 (4): 1005–1042.

Bowen, Howard R. 1953. *Social Responsibilities of the Businessman*. New York: Harper and Row.

Busch, Per-Olof, and Helge Jörgens. 2005. The International Sources of Policy Convergence: Explaining the Spread of Environmental Policy Innovations. *Journal of European Public Policy* 12 (5): 860–884.

Büthe, Tim. 2010. Private Regulation in the Global Economy: A (P)Review. *Business and Politics* 12 (3): Article 2. http://www.bepress.com/bap/vol12/iss3/art2/, accessed June 10, 2011.

Calo, Muriel, and Timothy A. Wise. 2005. *Revaluing Peasant Coffee Production: Organic and Fair Trade Markets in Mexico*. Medford, Mass.: Global Development and Environment Institute.

Cardoso, Fernando Henrique, and Enzo Faletto. 1979. Dependency and Development in Latin America. Trans. Marjory Mattingly Urquidi. Berkeley: University of California Press.

Cashore, Benjamin, Graem Auld, and Deanna Newsom. 2004. *Governing through Markets: Forest Certification and the Emergence of Non-state Authority*. New Haven: Yale University Press.

Chandler, Alfred, Franco Almatori, and Takahashi Ikino, eds. 1997. *Big Business and the Wealth of Nations*. New York: Cambridge University Press.

Christmann, Petra, and Glen Taylor. 2001. Globalization and the Environment: Determinants of Firm Self-Regulation in China. *Journal of International Business Studies* 32 (3): 439–458.

Clapp, Jennifer, and Peter Dauvergne. 2005. *Paths to a Green World: The Political Economy of the Global Environment*. Cambridge, Mass.: MIT Press.

Dahl, Robert A. 1961. *Who Governs? Democracy and Power in an American City*. New Haven: Yale University Press.

Dalton, Russell J., Steve Recchia, and Robert Rohrschneider. 2003. The Environmental Movement and the Modes of Political Action. *Comparative Political Studies* 36 (7): 743–771.

da Motta, Ronaldo Seroa. 2006. Analyzing the Environmental Performance of the Brazilian Industrial Sector. *Ecological Economics* 57 (2): 269–281.

Darnall, Nicole, Deborah Gallagher, and Richard N. L. Andrews. 2001. ISO 14001: Greening Management Systems. In *Greener Manufacturing and Operations: From Design to Delivery and Back*, ed. Joseph Sarkis, 178–190. Sheffield, UK: Greenleaf.

Dos Santos, Theotonio. 1970. The Structure of Dependence. *American Economic Review* 60 (2): 231–236.

Economy, Elizabeth C. 2004. *The River Runs Black: The Environmental Challenge to China's Future*. Ithaca: Cornell University Press.

Evans, Peter. 1979. *Dependent Development: The Alliance of Multinational, State, and Local Capital in Brazil*. New York: Cambridge University Press.

Evans, Peter. 1992. The State as Problem and Solution: Predation, Embedded Autonomy, and Structural Change. In *The Politics of Economic Adjustment*, ed. Stephan Haggard and Robert R. Kaufman, 139–181. Princeton: Princeton University Press.

Evans, Peter. 1995. *Embedded Autonomy: States and Industrial Transformation*. Princeton: Princeton University Press.

Fox, Tom, Halina Ward, and Bruce Howard. 2002. *Public Sector Roles in Strengthening Corporate Social Responsibility: A Baseline Study*. Washington, D.C.: World Bank.

Frankental, Peter. 2001. Corporate Social Responsibility—A PR Invention? *Corporate Communications: An International Journal* 6 (1): 18–23.

Friedman, Milton. 1970. The Social Responsibility of Business Is to Increase Its Profits. *New York Times Magazine* (September 13): 32–33, 122–126.

Frynas, Jedrzej George. 2005. The False Developmental Promise of Corporate Social Responsibility: Evidence from Multinational Oil Companies. *International Affairs* 81 (3): 581–598.

Fuchs, Doris, and Agni Kalfagianni. 2010. The Causes and Consequences of Private Food Governance. *Business and Politics* 12 (3). http://www.bepress.com/bap/vol12/iss3/art5/, accessed June 10, 2011.

Gallagher, Deborah R., Richard N. L. Andrews, Achara Chandrachai, and Kaewta Rohitratana. 2005. Environmental Management Systems in the US and Thailand: A Case Comparison. *Greener Management International* 46:41–56.

Gallagher, Deborah R., and John W. Gallagher. 2007. Stakeholder Relationship Management: A Strategic Resource for Sustainability. *Finance Marketing and Production* 3:28–38.

Gangadharan, Lata. 2006. Environmental Compliance by Firms in the Manufacturing Sector in Mexico. *Ecological Economics* 59 (4): 477–486.

Garcia-Johnson, Ronie. 2000. *Exporting Environmentalism: US Multinational Chemical Corporations in Brazil and Mexico*. Cambridge, Mass.: MIT Press.

Global Witness. 1998. A Rough Trade: The Roles of Companies and Governments in the Angolan Conflict. http://www.globalwitness.org/media_library_detail.php/90/en/a_rough_trade, accessed June 27, 2008.

Grant, J. Andrew, and Ian Taylor. 2004. Global Governance and Conflict Diamonds: The Kimberley Process and the Quest for Clean Gems. *Round Table* 93 (375): 385–401.

Grayson, David, and Chris Marsden. 2007. The Business of Business Is . . . ? Unpicking the Corporate Responsibility Debate. Paper of the Doughty Centre for Corporate Responsibility at Cranfield University School of Management, UK. http://dspace.lib.cranfield.ac.uk/handle/1826/2312, accessed June 10, 2011.

Green, Jessica F. 2010. Private Standards in the Climate Regime: The Greenhouse Gas Protocol. *Business and Politics* 12 (3). http://www.bepress.com/bap/vol12/iss3/art3/, accessed June 10, 2011.

Haggard, Stephan, Sylvia Maxfield, and Ben Ross Schneider. 1997. Theories of Business and Business-State Relations. In *Business and the State in Developing Countries*, ed. Sylvia Maxfield and Ben Ross Schneider, 36–60. Ithaca: Cornell University Press.

Hamed, M. M., and Y. El Mahgary. 2004. Outline of a National Strategy for Cleaner Production: The Case of Egypt. *Journal of Cleaner Production* 12 (4): 327–336.

Hellman, Joel. 1998. Winners Take All: The Politics of Partial Reform in Postcommunist Transitions. *World Politics* 50 (2): 203–234.

Hellman, Joel, Geraint Jones, Daniel Kaufmann, and Mark Schankerman. 2000. Measuring Governance, Corruption, and State Capture: How Firms and Bureaucrats Shape the Business Environment in Transition Economies. World Bank Policy Research Working Paper 2312. Washington, D.C.: World Bank.

Hills, Jonathan, and Robert Welford. 2005. Coca Cola and Water in India: A Case Study. *Corporate Social Responsibility and Environmental Management* 12:169–177.

Hoffman, Andrew J. 1997. *From Heresy to Dogma: An Institutional History of Corporate Environmentalism*. San Francisco: The New Lexington Press.

Hoffman, Andrew J. 2000. Integrating Environmental and Social Issues into Corporate Practice. *Environment* 42 (5):22–33.

Innes, Robert, and Abdoul G. Sam. 2008. Voluntary Pollution Reductions and the Enforcement of Environmental Law: An Empirical Study of the 33/50 Program. *Journal of Law & Economics* 51:271–296.

ISO (International Organization for Standardization). 2003. The ISO Survey of ISO 9000 and ISO 14001 Certificates. ISO, Geneva, 12th cycle. http://www.iso.org/iso/iso_catalogue/management_standards/certification/the_iso_survey.htm, accessed March 5, 2010.

Jaffe, Adam B., Steven R. Peterson, Paul R. Portney, and Robert N. Stavins. 1995. Environmental Regulation and the Competitiveness of US Manufacturing: What Does the Evidence Tell Us? *Journal of Economic Literature* 33 (1): 132–163.

Jasanoff, Sheila. 2007. Bhopal's Trials of Knowledge and Ignorance. *Isis* 98:344–350.

Johnson, Chalmers A. 1982. *MITI and the Japanese Miracle: The Growth of Industrial Policy, 1925–1975*. Palo Alto: Stanford University Press.

Jones Luong, Pauline, and Erika Weinthal. 2010. *Oil Is Not a Curse: Ownership Structure and Institutions in Soviet Successor States*. New York: Cambridge University Press.

Jordan, Andrew, Rüdiger K. W. Würzel, and Anthony R. Zito. 2003. *'New' Instruments of Environmental Governance? National Experiences and Prospects*. London: Frank Cass.

Kamieniecki, Sheldon. 2006. *Corporate America and Environmental Policy: How Often Does Business Get Its Way?* Palo Alto: Stanford University Press.

Kang, David. 2002. *Crony Capitalism: Corruption and Development in South Korea and the Philippines*. Cambridge, UK: Cambridge University Press.

Kantz, Carola. 2007. The Power of Socialization: Engaging the Diamond Industry in the Kimberley Process. *Business and Politics* 9 (3): Article 2. http://www.bepress.com/bap/vol9/iss3/art2/, accessed June 10, 2011.

Kappler, Ralph. 2005. Imaginative Energy? GE's Drive to Accelerate Investments in Clean Energy and Energy Efficiency Measures. *Refocus* 6 (6): 49–51.

Keck, Margaret E., and Kathryn Sikkink. 1998. *Activists beyond Borders: Advocacy Networks in International Politics*. Ithaca: Cornell University Press.

Kell, George. 2005. The Global Compact: Selected Experiences and Reflections. *Journal of Business Ethics* 59:60–79.

Keohane, Nathaniel, Richard L. Revesz, and Robert N. Stavins. 1998. The Choice of Regulatory Instruments in Environmental Policy. *Harvard Environmental Law Review* 22:313–367.

King, Andrew A., Michael J. Lenox, and Ann Terlaak. 2005. The Strategic Use of Decentralized Institutions: Exploring Certification with the ISO 14001 Management Standard. *Academy of Management Journal* 48 (6): 1091–1106.

Kobrin, Stephen. 2005. Multinational Enterprise, Public Authority, and Public Responsibility: The Case of Talisman Energy and Human Rights in Sudan. In *International Business and Government Relations in the 21st Century*, ed. Robert Grosse, 191–216. New York: Cambridge University Press.

Kovacic, William E., and Carl Shapiro. 2000. Antitrust Policy: A Century of Economic and Legal Thinking. *Journal of Economic Perspectives* 14 (1): 43–60.

Kraft, Michael E., and Sheldon Kamieniecki. 2007. Analyzing the Role of Business in Environmental Policy. In *Business and Environmental Policy: Corporate Interests in the American Political System*, ed. Michael E. Kraft and Sheldon Kamieniecki, 3–32. Cambridge, Mass.: MIT Press.

Laszlo, Chris. 2008. *Sustainable Value: How the World's Leading Companies Are Doing Well by Doing Good*. Palo Alto: Stanford University Press.

Lowi, Theodore J. 1969. *The End of Liberalism: The Second Republic of the United States*. New York: W. W. Norton & Company.

Luger, Stan. 1995. Market Ideology and Administrative Fiat: The Rollback of Automobile Fuel Economy Standards. *Environmental History Review* 19:77–93.

Lyon, Thomas P., and John W. Maxwell. 1999. Corporate Environmental Strategies as Tools to Influence Regulation. *Business Strategy and the Environment* 8:189–196.

Lyon, Thomas P., and J. W. Maxwell. 2008. Corporate Social Responsibility and the Environment: A Theoretical Perspective. *Review of Environmental Economics and Policy* 2 (2): 240–260.

Lyons, Daniel. 2008. Enterprise Strategies: The Paper Chasers. *Newsweek* (December 1).

Majone, Giandomenico, and Pio Baake. 1996. *Regulating Europe.* London: Routledge.

Maxfield, Sylvia, and Ben Ross Schneider, eds. 1997. *Business and the State in Developing Countries.* Ithaca: Cornell University Press.

Miller, Claire C. 2010. In Backing Clean Energy Start-Ups, Fund Looks for Longer Résumés. *New York Times,* May 9.

Morgenstern, Richard D. and William A. Pizer. 2007. *Reality Check: The Nature and Performance of Voluntary Environmental Programs in the United States, Europe, and Japan.* Washington, D.C.: Resources for the Future.

Najam, Adil, David Runnalls, and Mark Halle. 2007. *Environment and Globalization: Five Propositions.* Winnipeg: International Institute for Sustainable Development.

Olsen, Willy H. 2002. Petroleum Revenue Management—An Industry Perspective. Presentation at the Workshop on Petroleum Revenue Management, Washington, D.C., October 23–24.

Olson, Mancur. 1965. *The Logic of Collective Action: Public Goods and the Theory of Groups.* Cambridge, Mass.: Harvard University Press.

O'Neill, Kate. 2010. *The Environment and International Relations.* Cambridge, UK: Cambridge University Press.

Ó Riain, Seán. 2000. States and Markets in an Era of Globalization. *Annual Review of Sociology* 26:187–213.

O'Rourke, Dara. 2004. *Community-Driven Regulations: Balancing Development and the Environment in Vietnam.* Cambridge, Mass.: MIT Press.

Porter, Gareth. 1999. Trade Competition and Pollution Standards: "Race to the Bottom" or "Stuck at the Bottom"? *Journal of Environment & Development* 8 (2): 133–151.

Porter, Michael. 1980. *Competitive Strategy.* New York: The Free Press.

Porter, Michael E., and Claas van der Linde. 1995. Toward a New Conception of the Environment-Competitiveness Relationship. *Journal of Economic Perspectives* 9:97–118.

Porter, Michael E., and Mark R. Kramer. 2006. Strategy and Society: The Link between Competitive Advantage and Corporate Social Responsibility. *Harvard Business Review* (December): 1–14.

Prakash, Aseem. 2000. Responsible Care: An Assessment. *Business & Society* 39 (2): 183–209.

Prakash, Aseem. 2007. Corporate Environmentalism: Problems and Prospects. *Global Environmental Politics* 7 (3): 130–135.

Press, Daniel, and Daniel A. Mazmanian. 2006. The Greening of Industry: Combining Government Regulations and Voluntary Strategies. In *Environmental Policy.* 6th ed., ed. Norman J. Vig and Michael E. Kraft, 264–287. Washington, D.C.: CQ Press.

Pulver, Simone. 2007a. Introduction: Developing-Country Firms as Agents of Environmental Sustainability? *Studies in Comparative International Development* 42:191–207.

Pulver, Simone. 2007b. Importing Environmentalism: Explaining Petroleos Mexicanos' Cooperative Climate Policy. *Studies in Comparative International Development* 42:233–255.

Revkin, Andrew C. 2006. Branson Pledges Billions to Fight Global Warming. *New York Times,* September 21.

Rivera, Jorge. 2004. Institutional Pressures and Voluntary Environmental Behavior in Developing Countries: Evidence from the Costa Rican Hotel Industry. *Society & Natural Resources* 17:779–797.

Ruggie, John Gerard. 2002. The Theory and Practice of Learning Networks: Corporate Social Responsibility and the Global Compact. *Journal of Corporate Citizenship* 5:27–36.

Sabatier, Paul. 1975. Social Movements and Regulatory Agencies: Toward a More Adequate –and Less Pessimistic—Theory of "Clientele Capture." *Policy Sciences* 6 (3): 301–342.

Sawyer, Suzana. 2006. Disabling Corporate Sovereignty in a Transnational Lawsuit. *PoLAR: Political and Legal Anthropology Review* 29 (1): 23–43.

Skjærseth, Jon Birger. 2004. *Limits to Corporate Social Responsibility: A Comparative Study of Four Major Oil Companies. Report 7/2004.* Polhøgda, Norway: Fridtjof Nansen Institute.

Skocpol, Theda. 1985. Bringing the State Back In: Strategies of Analysis in Current Research. In *Bringing the State Back In*, ed. Peter B. Evans, Dietrich Rueschemeyer, and Theda Skocpol, 3–37. Cambridge, UK: Cambridge University Press.

Smillie, Ian. 2005. What Lessons from the Kimberley Process Certification Scheme? In *Profiting from Peace: Managing the Resource Dimensions of Civil War*, ed. Karen Ballentine and Heiko Nitzschke, 47–68. Boulder: Lynne Rienner Publishers.

Sowers, Jeannie Lynn. 2003. Allocation and Accountability: State-Business Relations and Environmental Politics in Egypt. Unpublished doctoral dissertation. Politics Department, Princeton University, Princeton, N.J.

Specter, Michael. 2008. Big Foot: A Reporter at Large. *New Yorker* 84 (2): 25.

Starobin, Shana, and Erika Weinthal. 2010. The Search for Credible Information in Social and Environmental Global Governance: The Kosher Label. *Business and Politics* 12 (3): Article 8. http://www.bepress.com/bap/vol12/iss3/art8/, accessed June 10, 2011.

Steinberg, Paul. 2005. From Public Concern to Policy Effectiveness: Civic Conservation in Developing Countries. *Journal of International Wildlife Law and Policy* 8:341–365.

Truman, David B. 1951. *The Governmental Process: Political Interests and Public Opinion.* New York: A. Knopf.

Van Natta, Don, Jr., and Neela Banerjee. 2002. Bush Energy Paper Followed Industry Push. *New York Times*, March 27.

Vidovic, Martina, and Neha Khanna. 2007. Can Voluntary Pollution Prevention Programs Fulfill Their Promises? Further Evidence from the EPA's 33/50 Program. *Journal of Environmental Economics and Management* 53 (2): 180–195.

Vogel, David. 1997. *Trading Up: Consumer and Environmental Regulation in a Global Economy.* Cambridge, Mass.: Harvard University Press.

Vogel, David. 2005. *The Market for Virtue: The Potential and Limits of Corporate Social Responsibility.* Washington, D.C.: Brookings.

Vogel, David. 2006. The Private Regulation of Global Corporate Conduct. Center for Responsible Business. Working Paper Series. Paper 34. http://repositories.cdlib.org/crb/wps/34, accessed March 5, 2010.

Wapner, Paul. 1995. Politics beyond the State: Environmental Activism and World Civic Politics. *World Politics* 47 (3): 311–340.

Watts, Michael J. 2005. Righteous Oil? Human Rights, the Oil Complex, and Corporate Social Responsibility. *Annual Review of Environment and Resources* 30:373–407.

Webersik, Christian. 2005. Fighting for Plenty: The Banana Trade in Southern Somalia. *Oxford Development Studies* 33 (1): 81–97.

Weinthal, Erika. 2002. *State Making and Environmental Cooperation: Linking Domestic and International Politics in Central Asia*. Cambridge, Mass.: MIT Press.

Williamson, John. 1994. Search of a Manual for Technopols. In *The Political Economy of Policy Reform*, ed. John Williamson, 11–28. Washington, D.C.: Institute for International Economics.

Würzel, Rüdiger K. W., Andrew Jordan, Anthony R. Zito, and Lars Brückner. 2003. From High Regulatory State to Social and Ecological Market Economy? "New" Environmental Policy Instruments in Germany. In *New Instruments of Environmental Governance? National Experiences and Prospects*, ed. Andrew Jordan, Rudiger Würzel, and Anthony R. Zito, 115–136. London: Frank Cass.

7

Political Parties and the "Meaning of Greening" in European Politics

Michael O'Neill

From Social Movement to Party Politics

The first deputy to win a seat in a national parliament anywhere in the world under green party colors did so in Switzerland in October 1979. By the end of the millennium, green parties had secured representation in almost every western European legislature. There has also been a bloc of greens in the European Parliament since the elections of 1984. The rise of green parties was one response to rising anxieties over problems affecting the global commons, from resource depletion to nuclear accidents, climate change, energy shortfalls, and water shortages. What began as localized citizen action developed over time into new left and green parties (Lowe, Clifford, and Buchanan 1980, 26–28; see also Rüdig 1985; Poguntke 1987; and Kitschelt 1993). Radicals of the baby-boomer generation were as disconcerted about "old" left politics as they were dismissive of the center-right, seeing it as faux radicalism in its preoccupation with economic growth, nuclear energy, and the installation of American strategic weapons on native soil (Parkin 1968; Rochon 1989).

New politics movements likewise objected to the old left's authoritarian and elitist approach to politics. How politics is conducted is as important for greens as why. According to Porritt and Winner, green radicalism "seeks nothing less than a nonviolent revolution to overthrow our whole polluting, plundering and materialistic industrial society and, in its place, to create a new economic and social order which will allow human beings to live in harmony with the planet" (1988, 9). Accordingly, the greens claim that their movement is "the most radical and important cultural force since the birth of socialism" (9). From the start, greens have defined themselves as harbingers of a wholly new politics, not merely conservation-minded or environmental politics but one concerned with "deep" ecology.[1] And a movement that "can properly take its place alongside other political ideologies [for] ecologism cannot be seen as simply embedded in other political ideologies—it is a political ideology in its own right" (Dobson 1990, 3).

Localized green movements became political parties almost everywhere in western Europe (see table 7.1), a transformation that has presented them with ideological and organizational challenges.[2] Party politics makes demands on political discipline and requires compromises with radical predilections, making for dilemmas that radical activists find ideologically objectionable and even ethically repugnant. How the greens should "do" politics has been problematic for green parties from the outset. The nature of these dilemmas and their consequences, what it means to be "green," and whether these parties represent a new politics or are merely familiar radical wine decanted into a new left bottle are matters for ongoing inquiry (see, e.g., Poguntke 1987; Müller-Rommel 1982; 1985a; 1985b; 1985c; Hulsberg 1988, 10; and Müller-Rommel and Poguntke 1989).

This chapter reviews the ideological and strategic predicaments that have confronted western Europe's green parties as they have sought to address the challenge of building party organizations and consolidating a small but nevertheless growing electoral constituency since the late 1960s. The study of political parties occupies an important role in the field of comparative politics because of their centrality in political organization and social change. Political parties are arenas for ideological conflict and agencies of political participation in the modern nation state. They bring together competing ideas and—for some activists—represent visions of the ends of politics. Parties are more than merely passive agencies channeling ideological preferences or mediating cultural values between civil society and the state. They are key agencies for democratic governance, legitimizing what would otherwise be top-down governance and providing a medium for political communication educating citizens about what is feasible given the constraints that apply to public policy.

For the emergent field of comparative environmental politics, research on green parties demonstrates the advantage of approaching environmental questions from the vantage point of comparative politics. The strength of green parties has been widely acknowledged in the global environmental politics literature as an important predictor of national support for environmental treaties (Sprinz and Vaahtoranta 1994). Therefore it is worth taking a closer look at where these parties come from and the challenges they face when attempting to inject new values and political practices into well-established party systems. For those who wish to understand cross-national variation in state support for environmental goals, the comparative study of green parties reveals that this question is considerably more complex than one of variance, across countries and over time, in social values and physical conditions—though these certainly play a part. This chapter demonstrates that the fate of the greens—and more broadly, the ways in which values and interests are articulated and aggregated into authoritative political decisions—must be understood as a complex causal narrative in which party leaders respond strategically to opportunities shaped by historical contingency and by political structures

Table 7.1
Western Europe's principal green parties, 1973–1997

Symbol used in figures 7.1 and 7.2	
AGALEV	Flemish Green Party (Belgium)
ALO	Alternative Liste Österreichs (Austria)
AREV	Alternative Rouge et Verte (France)
AVL	Alternative Verde/Los Verdes (Spain)
B90/DG	Bundnis 90/Die Grünen (Germany)
CG	Comhaontas Glas (Ireland)
CLV	Confederación de los Verdes (Spain)
DM	Denmarks Miljopartiet (Denmark)
DE/GR	De Groenen (The Netherlands)
DG	Die Grünen (Germany)
DGa	Dée Gréng Alternativ (Luxembourg)
DGA	Die Grüne Alternative (Austria)
DGe	De Grønne (Denmark)
ECOLO	Wallonian Green Party (Belgium)
ERG	Enhedaliste de Rod Gronne (Denmark)
EP	Ecology Party (Finland)
EAL	Ecologists Alternatives List (Greece)
EL/AL	Ecological Left (German)
FEO	Federation of Ecological Associations (Greece)
GAZ	Grüne Aktion Zukunft (former green party in West Germany)
GE	Génération Écologie (France)
GL	GroenLinks (The Netherlands)
GPA	Groen Progressief Akkoord (The Netherlands)
GPN	Groene Partij Nederlands (The Netherlands)
GL-EI	Gréng Lëscht-Ekologesch Initiativ (Luxembourg)
GPS/FPE	Föderation der Grünen Parteien der Schweiz (Switzerland)
GP	Green Party (UK)
Les V	Les Verts (France)
LVD	Liste Verdi: La Federazione delle Liste Verdi (Italy)
Los V	Los Verdes (Spain) (formerly Alternative Verde)
MEI	Mouvement Écologiste Indépendant (France)
MGN	Miljøpartiet de Grønne (Norway)
MgS	Miljöpartiet de Gröna (Sweden)
ODP	Ökologisch-Demokratische Partei (former West Germany)
OV	Os Verdes (Portugal)
PE	Parti Écologiste (Switzerland)
P/EP	People's/Ecology Party (UK)
VERDE	Vértice Español de Reivindicación y Desarrollo Ecológico (Spain)
VGO	Vereinte Grüne Österreichs (Austria)
VL	Vihreä Liitto (Finland)

including electoral rules, the structure of party systems, and broader shifts in social conditions.

Strategic and Ideological Predicaments

Radicals who operate inside party and governance systems confront both a strategic and an ideological predicament. Whether and how far green parties adjust to the demands of mainstream politics says much about the dynamics of party politics. The varied responses of Europe's greens to these challenges ranges from outright resistance to reluctant accommodation; some parties embrace the rules of the game, and others engage in virtual civil war over what many see as critical tests of radical commitment.

Strategy: The Radical Dilemma of Fundamentalism versus Realism

The first critical distinction on this spectrum of political dispositions is between militancy and moderation. On one side of this particular issue are so-called fundamentalists, a faction in most European green parties usually described as "fundis," who put principle before pragmatism. On the other side are the so-called realists ("realos" as they are known in Die Grünen, the German green party), who accept the need for strong party organization, political discipline, and hierarchic leadership so as to improve effective performance in elections and exert influence in the policy process.

This dilemma sooner or later confronts every radical movement that opts for party politics; indeed, conflicts over political organization have occurred in most green parties. Socialist parties confronted the very same choices when they competed for parliamentary seats, as discussed by Robert Michels in his classic account of Germany's Social Democratic Party (1962, 364–371). One can quite see why, for these parties have their origins in single-issue politics and alternativist social movements composed of activists who abjure the compromises of "bourgeois" politics.

Among green parties, radical ecologists are less inclined to trust conventional political procedures and more disposed to principled detachment from what many activists regard as entrapment in a politics they deem responsible for exploiting mankind and despoiling nature. As they see it, there can be no compromise with "old" politics and its "failed" parties (Mushaben 1989). These radical greens tend then to be hostile to green realists who engage with "normal" politics (Kitschelt 1989). The radical predicament is less acute for realos, and more a matter of politics as the art of the possible—of practicalities rather than principles. Accordingly, they have sought to consolidate an electoral base in order to compete for political power, to lobby government by winning representation in parliaments or other elected assemblies, and thence to influence public policy (Foss and Larkin 1986). Some red-green parties or factions within them have claimed success in these terms, playing parliamentary politics to advantage, making alliances with other parties and even participating in governance.

Wherever green parties stand on the realo-fundi issue, they have all faced difficulties engaging with supposedly "failed" and "corrupted" politics (Bürklin 1985a). There have been spectacular fallouts between pragmatists and fundamentalists, which have cost them dearly at the polls. Austria's greens, for example, split over these issues into a pure green VGO and a red-green ALO. Much the same happened in the Netherlands, France, Sweden, and Denmark, though intraparty rivalry here was more about policy preferences and political strategy than ideology. Elsewhere, these issues have been less disruptive, though not entirely absent. This issue is critical for its impact on these parties' public image and thus how they perform at the ballot box and, in particular, whether green parties can compete for a growing progressive constituency with other new and radical parties (Bürklin 1985b). For many green parties, this dilemma has never been quite resolved, though electoral success and political survival has for the most part mitigated the febrile and occasionally self-destructive nature of these issues in the early days.

Ideology: Cucumbers versus Watermelons

The second axis on a notional map of green party politics tracks ideological preferences—in effect, where greens stand in relation to the old left: whether and how far they stand outside the traditional right-left cleavage, defining politics in terms of new ideas, as old versus new, as postmaterial versus productionism, pure ecology versus red-green preferences. Ideological positioning is quite a different matter from that of party organization and political strategy, though ideology does have implications for strategy. The fact that socialist parties have begun to take green issues on board has certainly sharpened conflict over ideas of what it means to be green. This conflict too affects the greens' prospects as agents for change.

Realos tend to be red-greens (so-called watermelons—green on the outside but red beneath the skin) with some ideological affinity with socialism. The red-green issue has preoccupied many European green parties, not least the issue of ecosocialism, a debate that covers a wide ideational spectrum from post-Keynesian social democracy to eco-anarchism. (See, e.g., Bookchin 1982; Sale 1985; Bahro 1986; Roszak 1978; and Goldsmith 1988. For a critique of these narratives, see Paehlke 1986.) Just as there are varied responses to the strategic dilemma of whether to engage with mainstream politics, red-greens are by no means uniform in ideology, and there are wide variations from green social democrats to militant ecosocialists and anarchists. The spillback from these ideological squabbles has at times brought some green parties to virtual civil war, and even where this has been avoided, these conflicts have dissipated scarce political energy.

"Pure" greens who resist the linkage of ecology and socialism (described by some commentators as the "cucumber" tendency because they are green all the way through) have mostly avoided alliances with old left parties. For them ecology is politics sui generis, quite distinct from ideology geared toward "outmoded" class-based politics. They refute the notion of politics as a left-right cleavage, the dynamic famously identified by Lipset and Rokkan (1967) as the principal descriptor of European party politics since the industrial and democratic revolutions of the nineteenth century. Pure greens are concerned primarily about humanity's failed stewardship of the natural world, and this outlook appeals to many realos and fundis alike.

The juxtaposition of strategic and ideological preference is useful then for locating green parties on a grid that facilitates comparison both cross-nationally and over time. (See, and compare, the shifting positions of green parties in figures 7.1 and 7.2.) Correlating these two axes shows the range of possibilities for "being green." The map is, by and large, what we might expect: more watermelons than cucumbers, and a tendency for most green parties toward realism over fundamentalism as they adapt to the challenges of playing party politics. This mapping exercise also shows that the strategic and ideological dimensions of party politics are separate though connected. Ideology has been a significant factor in determining whether and how greens have adapted to party politics. A new party seeking to consolidate and to engage with the policy process must make alliances, and these are more likely to be with leftist parties than those of the right, though in some countries (e.g., Ireland and the Netherlands), pure greens have participated in center-right governments. The idea of the global commons, subscribed to by both pure and red greens, is rather more compatible with the left's preference for collectivism than the libertarianism and neoliberalism of the right. The European left has certainly been more receptive to green ideas than have center-right parties, even though they compete with greens for a quite limited radical constituency. Common values, a sense of solidarity on progressive causes, and concern about nuclear energy and associated risks to human health and welfare have been the basis for cooperation, the most successful political outcome so far being the red-green coalition that governed Germany between 1998 and 2005.

There have nevertheless been some less predictable linkages emerging from these two defining issues, such as the link between pure greens and right-wing libertarians. A notable example is that of Herbert Gruhl, a disenchanted German Christian Democrat who had flirted with Die Grünen in its formative period and before it took an eco-left direction, who founded the German Ecological Democratic Party (ODP). The ODP had right-wing credentials similar to those of its conservative predecessor, the German Action Future (GAZ) also founded by Gruhl. The Austrian Alternative Liste Österreichs (ALO) and the Swiss Grünen Parteiten der Schweiz (GPS) likewise embraced a pure green and rightist orientation (Poguntke 1987).

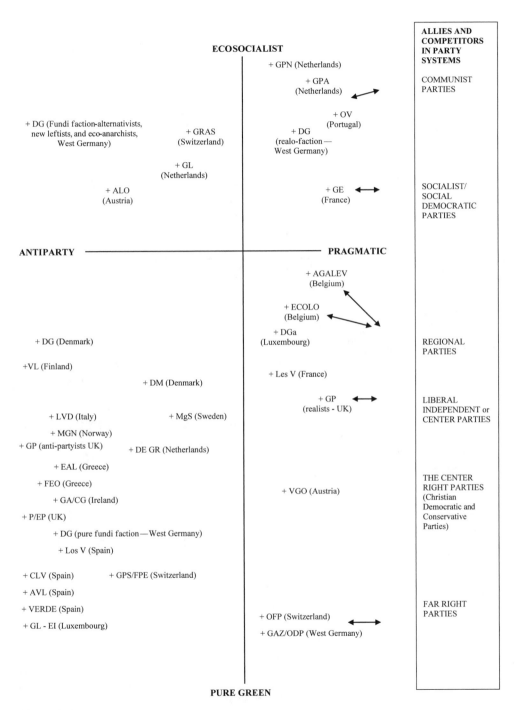

Figure 7.1
Mapping European green parties: the formative phase, 1973–1989

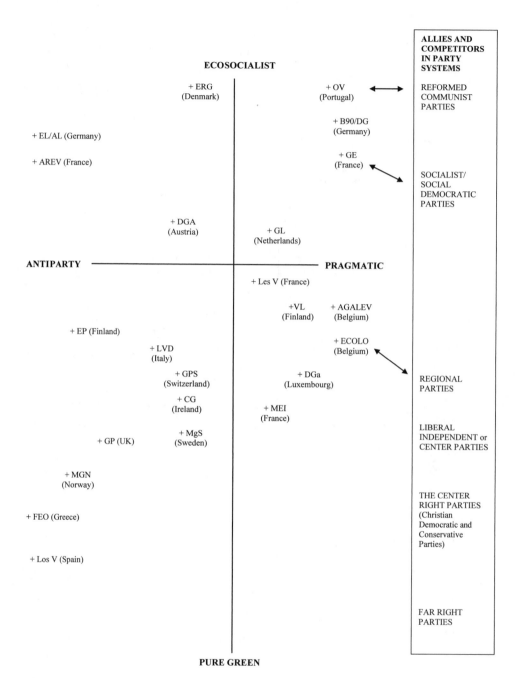

Figure 7.2
Mapping green parties in contemporary western Europe

The map of green parties also reveals shades of red, particularly differences between left-oriented realists prepared to make alliances of convenience with the moderate left (who can be described as "pink"), and fundis of the left ("dark red"), who prefer direct action and militancy. Left-oriented fundis have mostly been as reticent as pure green fundis about making overtures to the mainstream left, both sharing a strong antiparty disposition.

This mapping exercise is important for understanding the dynamics of green party politics and can be applied to the ideological and strategic positioning of every type of political party (center-left, center-right, or liberal) in Europe, or indeed elsewhere. But this is only part of the theoretic task of this chapter. To explain the "meaning of greening" in these terms raises the broader question of the nature of contemporary political change that has given rise to this "new" politics.

Explaining the Rise of Green Politics

Explaining political change is as challenging to scholars now as it was when Plato addressed social and political development in the *Laws* some twenty-four centuries ago. Change remains the critical problematic of the social sciences, and the rise of green parties offers a lens on the problematic of change in contemporary politics—a useful gauge of what is often described as "new" politics.

"New" in this sense implies an alternative paradigm of politics and public policy, an indictment of supposed failures of established parties, and the perceived futility of current policy in the face of unprecedented global challenges. Green parties do indeed project themselves as agencies of new politics, though the term should be treated with circumspection, not least the facile assumption of an inexorable shift in European political culture. Moreover, old and new politics coexist rather than compete within western Europe's party systems. The old politics is far from being defunct, and the mainstream parties that are its primary agencies are resilient, continuing to dominate politics. Established parties have repositioned and in some cases reinvented themselves in response to the challenge of the new. Accordingly, new politics is much less a direct challenge to the established order than militant fundis might prefer. This does not mean that new politics is sham politics. These handicaps notwithstanding, the "new" does have political salience, and even where greens have compromised, it has been far from an abject surrender of principles. This much is clear when we consider what is really new about the new politics, as discussed in the following brief review of some academic accounts of the rise of the European greens.

Political Change as Culture Shift

One influential narrative cites value shifts as the principal cause of change, seeing normative preferences as the primary determinant of political behavior. Two broad value sets supposedly shape political preferences in contemporary advanced societies. Dalton identifies these normative drivers as follows:

Many political issues, such as economic security, law and order, and national defense, tap underlying sustenance and safety needs. . . . In a time of depression or civil unrest, for example, security and sustenance needs undoubtedly receive substantial attention. If a society can make significant progress in addressing these goals, then the public's attention can shift to higher-order values. These higher-order goals are reflected in the issues of individual freedom, self expression, and participation. (1988, 81–82; see also Hildebrandt and Dalton 1978 and Baker, Dalton, and Hildebrandt 1981)

The most influential account of the impact of value shifts is the opus of Ronald Inglehart. (Among his most influential works are Inglehart 1977; 1979; 1981; 1984; 1987; 1990.) As is discussed by Dunlap and York (chapter 4, this volume), Inglehart separates value preferences into materialist and postmaterialist sets. Old politics is shaped by materialistic or security concerns, economic growth, public order, welfare in the broad sense, national security, and so on. The public's preferences are confronted by postmaterial values, emphasizing a policy agenda and normative preferences that are outside the normal material and distributive/redistributive frame of reference that defines conventional party politics and that are also promoted by social and political actors with quite different priorities, the result of novel experiences, expectations, and ethical codes related to public policy. In these circumstances, new values and postmaterial preferences challenge the established political and cultural order. Postmaterialism thus confronts old politics, bringing about what Inglehart (1977) has described as a "silent revolution."

The explanation of why change occurs here is "firmly anchored in the socialization processes of individual value orientations, and slowly growing by generational turnover" (Inglehart 1990, 76). Other writers have followed Inglehart's theoretic lead. Chandler and Siaroff, for instance, favor a similarly sociological narrative, introducing so-called period effects, such as distinctive socialization experiences that accompany wars or prolonged periods of peace, economic depression, or prosperity. Such formative experiences change popular perceptions, alter attitudes to politics and not least political preferences (Chandler and Siaroff 1986, 304). This narrative connects longer-term social and structural developments to shorter or medium-term shifts in values and attitudes about public policy, forming patterns that—as these writers see it—explain political change. New politics is a direct consequence of this process of zeitgeist or culture shift, though a conditional one in as much as its outcome is potentially reversible.

One conclusion from Inglehart's trawl of available social data is that there is potential for consolidating a green electorate, though he tempered bold prediction with due caution, noting that the greens were not "about to become one of the major political forces in Western Europe overnight" (Inglehart and Rabier 1986,

467). Developments since this research was published have borne out such reticence. Inglehart acknowledged that cultural "revolution" in advanced societies is much less the wholesale replacement of one social or ideological order than it is about political actors making trade-offs between principles and pragmatism. He noted the greens' reluctance to compromise principles, and likewise the resource constraints that handicap them as newcomers to politics, but was convinced nevertheless that political change was underway in as much as "the rise of post-materialism has placed existing party systems under chronic stress." Consequently, partisan alignment is reshaping European politics, and the left-right axis no longer corresponds "to the social bases of support for changes, or to polarization over the most heated (green and related) issues" (Inglehart 1990, 76).

The postmaterialist narrative does give some insight into the current state of European politics, but it is at best a partial account of political change, notwithstanding Inglehart's impressive scholarship. This narrative has been criticized on a number of fronts, and rightly so (see, e.g., Böltgen and Jagodzinski 1985; Bürklin 1984, 216–220; and Dunlap and York, chapter 4, this volume). Here I review some of its principle shortcomings while highlighting components of a more complex but ultimately more satisfactory account of the rise of the greens. First, the postmaterialist narrative relies unduly on pre-adult socialization as the principal determinant of values, ignoring other socialization experiences such as the impact of higher education, the workplace, or adult experience in shaping political and social preferences (Eckersley 1989, 218). Second, it is silent on the relationship between social values and political change, ignoring factors such as the intervening influence of contingent historical events; the strategic actions of social movement leaders working with the political resources and opportunities available to them in diverse political settings; and structural factors such as electoral rules and party systems.[3]

Toward a More Complex Account of Environmental Values

Early socialization is only part of the story of where values come from, and some basic facts show the limitations of this narrow narrative. For instance, many greens—whether activists or voters—are neither radical nor leftists, and their politics cannot be neatly explained as the outcome of a "silent revolution," of value shifts, let alone those shaped by early socialization. William Tucker (1980), for example, identifies competing value sets within America's environmental movement, and though environmentalism is usually seen as a liberal movement, this simply cannot be assumed a priori. Neither can postmaterial values be attributed exclusively to pre-adult socialization.

In America, as elsewhere in the developed world, environmentalism has conservative as well as radical roots and reflects not just early socialization but unalloyed self-interest—a reflex of a privileged middle class attracted to anti-industrial, anti-productionist preferences insofar as these suit their material interests. As Tucker argues, under cover of seemingly principled support for environmental causes,

America's upper-middle class has learned to suspect technological change, to look askance at economic growth, to place "spiritual values" over "material progress," and to start looking down on industry and commercial activity as something vulgar and distasteful. All of these, of course, are ancient, well-tuned aristocratic attitudes. . . . The quality of self-interest in the environmental movement is something which the press [and seemingly, academic commentators too] has found absolutely impossible to grasp. (1980, 145–146)

For Tucker, environmentalism can represent the "protection of entrenched privilege. . . . People who have reached a certain level of affluence and privilege in society inevitably turn their efforts away from the accumulation of more wealth and privilege, and towards denying the same benefits to others" (Tucker 1980, 146). What he is describing here is plainly "nimbyism," green issues resonating with the socially and politically conservative. The greens on this reading are by no means harbingers of a silent revolution, giving voice to postmaterial values acquired during early socialization.

Furthermore, similar value sets may have higher or lower salience in some political cultures than in others or within one polity over time. Any plausible explanation of political change must take account of such diversity. Accordingly, explanations of new politics in general and of green politics in particular that posit values as the critical independent variable are less than convincing. They fail to explain why particular value preferences—for instance, propensities for pacifism or cosmopolitan or humanist values—are expressed as support for green politics, or why similar value sets in one society equate with ecological preferences, whereas in others they give rise to quite different ideological propensities. In his perceptive critique of this theoretic narrative, Claus Offe notes that "the supposedly predominant need [of postmaterialism] for self-actualization could equally well lead to new and unconventional, but entirely *private* lifestyle and consumption patterns, rather than to new *politics*" (1987, 84; emphasis in original). Why, for instance, did the 1960s beatnik and the 1980s new age movements show a greater receptiveness to ecological politics than the hippies of the seventies?

Catalysts and Contingency

The rise of green parties, and political change more generally, entails complex causal processes shaped as much by catalysts and contingency as by values. Singular events—the 1986 Chernobyl accident that released radiation across much of Europe is the obvious example—have been significant for determining the electoral prospects of many green parties, and no less for radicalizing erstwhile apathetic citizens. Affigne's (1990) study of the Swedish Miljöpartiet identified that horrific accident as a significant reason for the green party's breakthrough in the 1988 general election. Protests against nuclear energy also raised the greens' profile throughout the continent during the 1970s (see Kitschelt 1986). Local events too have played a part—the lake Koijarvi protest in Finland, the campaign to stop the building of Disneyland Paris, and the Sellafield issue in Ireland are cases in point.

However, rising support for the greens has depended on more than singular events. Other catalysts, some more structural than contingent, have contributed too—not least, tensions caused by demographic and generational changes, especially among a new generation of students during the late 1960s and early 1970s, who rejected what they regarded as complacent consensus between the old left and new right. Concern about what might be called "life chances" (flanking issues such as jobs and perceived threats to economic well-being), as much as the emergence of postmaterial norms, had an impact on European political culture. If a process is complex and its outcomes are ambiguous, they hardly amount to a straightforwardly new politics. National history, generational shifts, disjunctions caused by war, and economic and technological development all contribute to refashioning public and political preferences.

Structures and Movements

Values are important for explaining political change, but as Max Weber ([1904] 1992) showed in his classic studies of social change, they are only a partial explanation. They inform and are in turn informed by structural factors—the more enduring aspects of political life and social organization. Structural narratives of change seek to avoid these methodological shortcomings by iterating a medley of variables as the basis for comparative research, not least the significance of socioeconomic organization and institutional arrangements. Structural factors mediate individual experience, determining how and indeed which values an individual acquires, and they shape in turn both personal and collective affiliation and behavior (Chandler and Siaroff 1986, 303). Individuals acquire the cognitive imprint of the structural and cultural milieus in which they learn and play out their social roles. New politics is one response to these structural prompts, though by no means the only one. And although this narrative does not discount the function of values per se for confirming ideological and political preferences, it does place greater explanatory weight on values as outcomes to be explained rather than causal variables.

What structural factors can help account for the rise of the greens? Some writers focus, for instance, on the political resources available to political activists and those opportunity structures that facilitate or otherwise hinder the prospects for new politics (see Kate O'Neill's discussion in chapter 5, this volume, as well as Zucker 1987; Jahn 1993; Zald and McCarthy 1987; and Klandermans 1990). The interaction between available political resources and action when activists make strategic choices figures notably in Kitschelt's account of Europe's new parties, including the greens. The critical variable here is less a general cultural propensity to change based on "propitious" values, "something in the political air," than the potent mix of circumstance, the availability of political resources, and no less structural factors and cultural triggers conducive to change. This "mix" determines how and how much radical potential is generated, and in what particular forms. There is nothing preordained, let alone inevitable, about the political outcome in this narrative, for as Kitschelt argues, "Grievances and institutional change are endemic in most societies, but they rarely translate into collective political action." Rather, "the actors' skills and resources and the broader institutional opportunity structures determine when individuals are able to engage in collective mobilization. In particular, the choice of a specific vehicle of mobilization, such as a party, can be explained only in terms of actors' resources and opportunities" (Kitschelt 1988b, 196–197).

Electoral Rules and Party Systems

The rules of the electoral system comprise a political opportunity structure with significant bearing on whether greens (or any other radical movement party) are effective change agents—indeed, whether they opt to play party politics or remain detached from it. Clearly, electoral systems based on plurality (first-past-the-post) are not favorable to representation for small and new parties, as the experience of the British and to a lesser degree the French greens confirms, and for that matter green parties in North America. It is hardly coincidence that in these polities green parties have had a harder time winning legislative seats than in those where the electoral rules are more favorable to small niche parties. Whatever their value preferences, many voters resist "wasting" their vote, and tend not to support parties that are unlikely to win legislative seats. The modest impact of greens on party and electoral politics in these countries is more a testament to these structural constraints than it is to the absence or presence of cultural values conducive to postmaterialism. These and other national opportunity structures—whether party funding is available from the public purse, broadcasting regulations, and so on—affect both party strategy and electoral prospects.

The origin and fate of green parties is affected not only by electoral rules per se but also by the system of political parties in which they must compete. This in turn is shaped by sociological and historical legacies, the social cleavages and ideological preferences that fashion political culture. These factors determine, for instance, the number of parties and where they fit on the ideological spectrum. And this affects in turn interparty cooperation and by extension the bargaining essential for coalition making. As Müller-Rommel puts it, the greens' "electoral success is not so much dependent upon the strength of new movements in a given country as upon the type of party system in which they operate" (1990, 225). Green parties may be either constrained or helped by these systemic conditions, and there is no singular pattern here.

Established parties (the usual governing parties) are for practical reasons more likely to be receptive to the new politics in multiparty systems, or at least disposed to making bargains with newcomers in order to make or sustain governing coalitions. The prospects for the greens and indeed for other new politics parties in these circumstances are improved, with established parties more amenable to assimilating new ideas into their policy programs, if only for short-term tactical reasons—the cases of the receptiveness of Italy's and Germany's center-left and of Ireland's center-right to the greens are cases in point. In contrast, in multiparty systems dominated by two dominant party blocs (usually conservative/liberal and social democrat/socialists), the logics and no less the culture of party competition suggests that mainstream parties will concentrate their efforts on securing the center ground, being less likely to need the support of smaller parties. (Greens in Britain, France, or Spain, for instance, have notably fared far worse than in Italy, Germany, and Ireland.) Where the electoral arithmetic makes established parties less dependent for a parliamentary majority on the support of minor parties, greens and other minor parties are more likely to be marginalized. Some party systems are more accommodating of new and small parties than others—or at least less hostile to them. As Müller-Rommel maintains, "in polarized multi-party systems [Italy, Denmark and the Netherlands] with a proportional representation electoral law, the movement followers' vote is distributed among several small left-wing parties, but also among larger parties" (1990, 225).

For Raschke, parties are important mediatory agencies, "bearers of societal interests, which are transformed into programmes by party organizations halfway democratized, and therefore they are of lasting political influence" (1983, 110). This is accurate as far as it goes, but it is an unduly generalized (possibly even tautological) account of parties as agents of change. If parties were merely reactive agencies that adjust to external events, there would be little point to studying them. Parties help shape events rather than merely respond to them: leadership strategies, factionalism, organizational arrangements, and available resources all matter with regard to how parties fare at the polls, affecting their parliamentary credibility and whether they attract or alienate potential coalition partners.

Of course, the importance of endogenous factors by no means invalidates Raschke's point that external as much as internal factors are significant for explaining the greens' prospects. The performance of Europe's green parties, as he sees it, confirms that public opinion—not least rising discontent with the old politics—has helped green parties to get their message across and to build a constituency. There has been growing instability in Western Europe's party systems, and the mass parties (*volksparteien*) that dominated postwar politics "have touched the limits of their effectiveness" (Raschke 1983, 113). These established parties have been less than adaptive to change, and this in turn "prevents them from becoming vehicles of future-orientated, active change . . . renders them increasingly incapable of representing the variety of qualitative societal interests" (113). Moreover, these parties suffer from "over-institutionalization, which has estranged them from the participatory, and also expressive, needs of a growing number of citizens" (113). As such, they are experiencing "overstrain as a result of no longer meeting the expectations which they themselves have created as well as those held by others" (113).

This is a damning indictment of old politics, but it is overgeneralized, for a putative crisis of old politics is hardly the same thing as the triumph of the new. No particular outcome can be assumed from changes in popular attitudes toward the mainstream parties, despite discernible evidence of partisan dealignment. The point is, however, that though new parties are not entirely masters of their own destiny, they certainly have a hand in shaping it. And this is where the predicaments discussed previously—those strategic dilemmas and ideological choices that confront radical newcomers—are so crucial for determining outcomes. Some green parties have responded well to challenges; others less so. But these choices do matter, not least for outcomes. Parties are important change agents in their own right, mediating social and cultural change, giving expression to new and radical voices, and bringing novel issues onto the policy agenda. How a party connects with and how far it represents or otherwise alienates emergent social and cultural forces does have significant bearing on its political fate.

Conclusions: Whither the Greens?

To what extent have the greens had a meaningful impact on party politics in Western Europe, and what does the future hold in store? New politics has indeed emerged alongside the old, modifying if not quite refashioning national party systems and to a degree influencing how politics is played. The old politics has begun to come to terms with the green challenge and is more discomfited by it than established parties and politicians might care to acknowledge. The green agenda is now part of mainstream politics, and green parties are a presence in national politics and even in government, with surely more to contribute as policy makers everywhere face global challenges that threaten mankind and nature head on. Even so, new politics has modified rather than replaced the old and has been superimposed on rather than replaced the left-right cleavage identified by Lipset and Rokkan (1967) as the primary dynamic shaping Europe's party systems.

The greens are nothing if not a force for change, but they have not brought about the fundamental realignment of politics prescribed by green ideologues and anticipated by party activists—at least, not yet. "New politics" has certainly contributed to the reinvigoration of party politics and has affected the policy agenda, though the outcome has hardly been the transformative politics anticipated by greens and other radicals. Although the greening of European politics is significant, its impact as measured by electoral success falls somewhat short of the dramatic shift in the continent's political and cultural fabric anticipated by Inglehart and others, who saw the greens as the leading agency for a new politics. For all that, green parties are here to stay, and comparative political science must account for their impact, track their progress, and monitor how they respond to the dilemmas outlined in this chapter.

What does this situation signify for the future of party politics in Europe, or indeed, for the study of radical and postnationalist politics further afield, whether in Europe's new democracies, in established democracies beyond the European continent, or even in the developing world? As a contribution to the field of comparative environmental politics, research on the origin and fate of green parties in Europe may carry important lessons for the rest of the world. Yet our knowledge of the greening of party systems in the developing world in particular is practically nonexistent. Research into the fate of green parties (and of environmental agendas generally) in party systems outside the OECD is likely to yield results quite novel from those described here. Such knowledge would be to the benefit of political theory and environmental practice alike and takes on particular urgency given the surge in electoral contestation accompanying the wave of democratization that has swept through non-OECD countries over the past forty years. What determines whether reformers pursue the greening of traditional parties versus the creation of new ones? What are the prospects for green parties, or for the greening of traditional parties, in political systems dominated by patronage, political instability, or ethnic rivalries? Do parties on the left adopt environmental agendas more readily than those on the right? If so, why? To what extent, and through what channels, do similar parties in different countries share environmental ideas? How do the electoral prospects of new parties evolve throughout the process of democratic consolidation? These are questions that cry out for further research by students and scholars of comparative environmental politics and would connect well with the research agendas on environmental movements and democratization discussed in this volume by Kate O'Neill (chapter 5) and Kathryn Hochstetler (chapter 8).

For Western Europe, the theoretic narratives reviewed in this chapter identify green parties as a political response to changing values, demographic shifts, and the combination of historical contingency and structural parameters present in different countries at different junctures. To merely list such factors—some broadly favorable to political change, others specific to particular societies—does not amount to a satisfactory explanation of causality, the critical benchmark of heuristic theorizing. Commendable work has been done to identify and track contributory factors, if not yet to fashion them into useful theory that accounts for the rise and explains the significance of green parties. More detailed and comparative work needs to be done here to turn these indicative variables into heuristic theory. What Kitschelt and those who follow his theoretic lead offer are useful insights into what is an immensely complex process. He identifies, for instance, some key indicators that as he sees it determine prospects for left-libertarian parties, including the greens, inter alia: high per-capita GNP and social security expenditure, because these issues appeal to a radical constituency; levels of industrial unrest (especially labor strikes); a significant role for left parties in national politics; and a high intensity of controversy over the nuclear issue (Kitschelt 1988b). The list is by no means exhaustive or necessarily reliable, for these indicators are time-specific—more relevant to events in the 1970s and 1980s than to the present global age. But it is a start as a useful template for further research. The art of comparative theorizing is to assemble a toolkit of explanatory approaches to be utilized as a collection, rather than exclusively, to get an altogether better fix on the political issues under review.

Thus explaining the rise of the greens, and understanding what exactly is new about supposedly new politics, requires that we look at how parties respond to their social environment. Critical questions for empirical research are as follows: which social constituencies do these parties most appeal to, whether as voters or activists? How do new parties perform at the polls, and how do they deal with antipartyism in their ranks once they opt for parliamentary politics? What are their particular programmatic choices, and do radical ideological or policy preferences accelerate or hinder partisan dealignment and political realignment in national politics?

For more than a generation, new politics has survived, even if it has hardly flourished, and it continues to challenge old politics on its own turf. The critical question surely is: how durable is the challenge of the new over the longer term? Time may seem to be on the side of greens, as accelerating climate change enhances the salience of sustainability for a wider audience. The policy community—and no less the public at large—may be better disposed to the greens' message, but whether these parties can capitalize on this development to reshape the policy agenda depends on how they respond to the predicaments that have dogged them from the start. Whether green parties will modulate principles and adapt to a politics they regard as both corruptive and complacent so as to consolidate their electoral base is the critical issue here, as it has been from the outset. The greens' preference for the global commons over possessive individualism, for ecologically sustainable economics and public goods over conspicuous consumption, putting biosphere above unfettered production, may well be at the center of the policy discourse as public preferences change. Yet these objectives are by no means easy to promote, let alone to deliver in Europe's hedonistic societies.

Some commentators are unconvinced that the greens can remotely rise to this challenge. Jens Alber, for instance, sees the greens as still peripheral in contemporary politics, a merely reactive protest by an inchoate counter elite, for the most part iconoclasts or dilettantes, and in sociological terms "victims" of what Durkheim famously called anomie—those massive structural shifts underway in Western Europe since the 1970s (see Alber 1985, 1989). Self-interest for Alber is the primary driver of radical protest as much as for any other politics, in this case propelled by a well-educated minority concerned about its deteriorating life chances, albeit disguised as idealism. A similar perspective informs Bürklin's view. He too identifies particular social groups as key actors in new politics, in particular younger and well educated graduates. Bürklin concludes that the greens' challenge to the established political order is thus unsustainable over the duration (1984, 216–220). Such radical instincts will be dissipated by improvements in personal circumstances, such as opportunities afforded by well-paid employment (careers to be made), and the personal responsibility (e.g., families to nurture) that comes with maturity. (See Bürklin 1984, 1985a, 1987, and 1988. For a similar theoretical approach, see also Hines 1989.) In this account, greens are ephemeral—a mere political fad or a temporary radical itch.

Social marginality and the personal anomie that give rise to protest politics in this rather patronizing narrative will supposedly pass with exposure to social mobility. Discontented and marginalized activists possessing resources for self-improvement and social mobility—notably education and other transferable skills—will have experiences that over time blunt radical instincts, green or otherwise. For Alber, Bürklin, and those who share this reductive view of radical motivation, new politics simply cannot sustain the support base necessary for a sustained radical challenge, though these groups may have some influence en passant. The greens in this narrative are a temporary irritant to the political establishment, but they hardly threaten to shift the tectonic plates of European politics.

This narrative bears little resemblance to events on the ground, for green parties have survived in most European countries, even if they have not exactly thrived. Several studies show that their support base is by no means confined to the disaffected or socially marginalized, or not entirely so: green parties attract support too from those with above-average job security and material prosperity. Green voters and activists alike tend to be middle class, and many are middle-aged, having made successful careers in the public sector, the arts and education, and similar liberal professions. And though they do experience improvement in their life chances over time, many continue to profess radical values (Kitschelt 1988a; and Bürklin's rejoinder in Bürklin 1988). On this basis, we might reasonably conclude that relative deprivation is hardly a compelling explanation for green politics.

After a generation and more of national and transnational activity, one might well conclude that Europe's green parties are here to stay, at least for the foreseeable future. Shifts in the balance of economic power and no less in the scale of economic organization as capitalism has been transformed by globalization, the exponential expansion of postindustrial (tertiary and service) sectors delivering public goods and new types of private goods in an interdependent world, and the attendant problems of resource depletion are all factors more likely than not to sustain a green constituency. One might reasonably anticipate that the corporate greed exposed by the global financial crisis that began in 2008 can only deepen disenchantment with the old politics. Far from being a fad of the baby boomer generation, the greens have tapped into a postmaterial constituency, not just of the young or marginalized but also of new socioeconomic groups. At the same time, they have retained the political allegiance of many of those aging radicals with postmaterial preferences who were first attracted to the greens in their youth.

Chandler and Siaroff, among other commentators, remain upbeat about the greens' political resilience, especially impressed by Germany's Die Grünen, observing that the "growing awareness of new policy dilemmas and redefinitions of issue priorities" suggests that the greens "should not be viewed as a short-term manifestation of cyclical protest but rather as an indicator of an enduring social and political transformation" (Chandler and Siaroff 1986, 322–323). Of course, political survival cannot be taken for granted; it depends on how green parties continue to address the ideological and organizational challenges outlined previously.

Those parties that have developed effective party organization and adjusted to the demands of routine politics have generally fared better than those that have flunked these tests, and this is likely to continue to be the case. Yet far from departing the political scene, the greens have staked out a distinctive turf, some even making alliances with other parties that have brought some of them into government. More often than not, they have been transformed in the process, from protest parties reluctant to compromise radical principles to established if not establishment actors, and in the process reconciled to conducting their politics by rules not of their making nor much to their liking. To this extent, Europe's green parties have come a long way, and in a relatively short time.

Notes

1. The transformation of ecologism was much influenced by seminal work such as Rachel Carson's *Silent Spring* (1962), Barry Commoner's *Science and Survival* (1966) and *The Closing Circle* (1972), and Edward Goldsmith's *A Blueprint for Survival* (1972).

2. The German green party (Die Grünen) was founded in 1980 by an alliance of radical social movements and alternative groups. An eclectic mix of radical Christians and alternativists in Flemish-speaking Belgium coalesced into a political party (AGALEV) in 1982 following the lead of Wallonian or French-speaking Belgians who had formed a regional green party to contest the 1974 elections. The prospect of the 1984 European elections led to green party lists in the Netherlands—the Groen Progressief Akkoord (GPA). A youth ecology movement

(Jeunes et Environnement) emerged in Luxembourg on the back of the antinuclear campaign at the end of the 1970s. This movement subsequently formed Dée Gréng Alternativ party in 1983. Local campaigns also launched two Austrian green parties (Vereinte Grüne Österreichs, or VGO, and Alternative Liste Österreichs, or ALO) in 1982, which coalesced into Die Grüne Alternative in 1987. Swiss environmentalists and more radical groups formed the Groupement pour la Protection de l'Environnement (GPE) party in 1979 alongside several localized or cantonal green parties.

The first national "ecology list" anywhere in Europe was formed in France prior to the 1974 presidential elections. After factional infighting, a unified green party, Les Verts—Confédération Écologiste, Parti Écologiste, was established in 1984. Italian green politics remained dispersed and localized during the late 1970s and early 1980s but formed an unstable green federation in 1986 (Liste Verdi) in order to coordinate their forces for the 1987 elections. The Greek greens followed a similar path, although these disparate groups (more than ninety of them) did coalesce into a loosely organized party, the Alternative Ecologist movement. Spanish and Portuguese green politics were delayed by the experience of dictatorships that prevented the conditions favoring the emergence of libertarian and new left politics. Even after democracy was restored, radical or antisystem politics was heavily discounted. Nevertheless, the ecological banner is carried in Spain by Los Verdes, formed in 1984. In Portugal, ecological politics was subsumed under the flag of the PPM (an antidictatorship party) and the MDP (a neo-Marxist party) although a semi-independent party, Os Verdes, did emerge in 1987. Britain boasts the oldest European ecological party—the People's Party (1973)—which metamorphosed several times to become the Green Party in 1986. The Ecology Party of Ireland (EPI) was established in 1981, changed its name to the Green Alliance (Comhaontas Glas) in 1983, and to the Green Party in 1989. The Finnish Greens began to show in local elections as early as 1976, formed a national list in 1983 and eventually established a Green Association (Vihreä Liitto) in 1987. In Denmark, a national green party, De Grønne, was established in 1983. The Swedish green party, Miljöpartiet de Gröna, was founded in 1981. The Norwegian greens (Miljøpartiet de Grønne) adopted national party status only in 1989.

3. Inglehart responded to his critics by taking greater account in subsequent work of both structural and contingent factors as determinants of changing values and behavior in politics. Though timely, these revisions were grafted onto the same pre-adult socialization paradigm.

References

Affigne, Anthony. 1990. Environmental Crisis, Green Party Power: Chernobyl and the Swedish Greens. In *Green Politics One*, ed. Wolfgang Rüdig, 115–132. Edinburgh: University of Edinburgh.

Alber, Jens. 1985. Modernisierung, neue Spannungslinien und die politishchen Chancen der Grünen. *Politische Vierteljahresschrift* 26 (3): 211–226.

Alber, Jens. 1989. Modernization, Cleavage Structures and the Rise of Green Parties and Lists in Europe. In *New Politics in Western Europe: The Rise and Success of Green Parties and Alternative Lists*, ed. Ferdinand Müller-Rommel, 195–210. Boulder: Westview Press.

Bahro, Rudolf. 1986. *Building the Green Movement*. London: New Society Publishers.

Baker, Kendall L., Russell J. Dalton, and Kai Hildebrandt. 1981. *Germany Transformed: Political Culture and the New Politics*. Cambridge, Mass.: Harvard University Press.

Böltgen, Ferdinand, and Wolfgang Jagodzinski. 1985. In an Environment of Insecurity: Postmaterialism in the European Community, 1970 to 1980. *Comparative Political Studies* 17 (4): 453–484.

Bookchin, Murray. 1982. *The Ecology of Freedom: The Emergence and Dissolution of Hierarchy*. Palo Alto: Cheshire Books.

Bürklin, Wilhelm P. 1984. *Grüne Politik: Ideologische Zyklen, Wähler und Parteiensystem*. Opladen: Westdeutscher Verlag.

Bürklin, Wilhelm P. 1985a. The German Greens: The Post-industrial Non-established and the Party System. *International Political Science Review* 6 (4): 463–481.

Bürklin, Wilhelm P. 1985b. The Split between the Established and Non-established Left in Germany. *European Journal of Political Research* 13 (3): 283–293.

Bürklin, Wilhem P. 1987. Why Study Political Cycles? *European Journal of Political Research* 15 (2): 131–143.

Bürklin, Wilhelm P. 1988. A Politico-Economic Model Instead of Sour Grapes Logic: A Reply to Herbert Kitschelt's Critique. *European Sociological Review* 4 (2): 161–166.

Carson, Rachel. 1962. *Silent Spring*. Boston: Houghton Mifflin.

Chandler, William M., and Alan Siaroff. 1986. Postindustrial Politics in Germany and the Origins of the Greens. *Comparative Politics* 18 (3): 303–325.

Commoner, Barry. 1966. *Science and Survival*. New York: Viking Press.

Commoner, Barry. 1972. *The Closing Circle*. New York: Knopf.

Dalton, Russel J. 1988. *Citizen Politics in Western Democracies: Public Opinion in the United States, Great Britain, West Germany, and France*. Chatham, UK: Chatham House Publishers.

Dobson, Andrew. 1990. *Green Political Thought*. London: Routledge.

Eckersley, Robyn. 1989. Green Politics and the New Class: Selfishness or Virtue? *Political Studies* 37 (2): 205–223.

Foss, Daniel A. and Ralph Larkin. 1986. *Beyond Revolution: A New Theory of Social Movements*. South Hadley, Mass.: Bergin & Garvey.

Goldsmith, Edward. 1972. *A Blueprint for Survival*. Boston: Houghton.

Goldsmith, Edward. 1988. *The Great U-Turn: De-industrialising Society*. Bideford, UK: Green Books.

Hildebrandt, Kai, and Russell J. Dalton. 1978. Political Change or Sunshine Politics? In *Elections and Parties: German Political Studies*, vol. 3, ed. Max Kaase and Klaus von Beyme, 69–96. London: Sage.

Hines, K. 1989. Green Voters in the Federal Republic of Germany and France: A Comparative Analysis. Hovedoppgave (Thesis), Institute for Comparative Politics. University of Bergen, Norway.

Hulsberg, Werner. 1988. *The German Greens: A Social and Political Profile*. London: Verso.

Inglehart, Ronald. 1977. *The Silent Revolution: Changing Values and Political Styles among Western Publics*. Princeton: Princeton University Press.

Inglehart, Ronald. 1979. Political Action: The Impact of Values, Cognitive Level and Social Background. In *Political Action: Mass Participation in Five Western Democracies*, ed. Samuel H. Barnes and Max Kasse, 343–380. London: Sage.

Inglehart, Ronald. 1981. Post-materialism in an Environment of Insecurity. *American Political Science Review* 75 (4): 880–900.

Inglehart, Ronald. 1984. The Changing Structure of Political Cleavages in Western Society. In *Electoral Change in Advanced Industrial Democracies*, ed. Russel J. Dalton, Scott C. Flanagan, and Paul Allen Beck, 25–69. Princeton: Princeton University Press.

Inglehart, Ronald. 1987. Value Change in Industrial Societies. *American Political Science Review* 81 (4): 1289–1319.

Inglehart, Ronald. 1990. *Culture Shift in Advanced Industrial Societies*. Princeton: Princeton University Press.

Inglehart, Ronald, and Jacques-Rend Rabier. 1986. Political Realignment in Advanced Industrial Society: From Class-Based Politics to Quality of Life Politics. *Government and Opposition* 21:456–479.

Jahn, Detlef. 1993. The Rise and Decline of New Politics and the Greens in Sweden and Germany: Resource Dependence and New Social Cleavages. *European Journal of Political Research* 24:177–194.

Kitschelt, Herbert P. 1986. Political Opportunity Structures and Political Protest: Anti-nuclear Movements in Four Democracies. *British Journal of Political Science* 16 (1): 57–85.

Kitschelt, Herbert P. 1988a. The Life Expectancy of Left-Libertarian Parties: Does Structural Transformation or Economic Decline Explain Party Innovation? A Response to Wilhelm P. Bürklin. *European Sociological Review* 4 (2): 155–160.

Kitschelt, Herbert P. 1988b. Left-Libertarian Parties: Explaining Innovation in Competitive Party Systems. *World Politics* 40 (2): 194–234.

Kitschelt, Herbert P. 1989. *The Logics of Party Formation: Structure and Strategy of Belgian and West German Ecology Parties*. Ithaca: Cornell University Press.

Kitschelt, Herbert P. 1993. The Green Phenomenon in Western Party Systems. In *Environmental Politics in the International Arena: Movements, Parties, Organizations and Policy*, ed. Sheldon Kamieniecki, 93–112. Albany: State University of New York Press.

Klandermans, Bert. 1990. Linking the "Old" and "New" Movement Networks in the Netherlands. In *Challenging the Political Order*, ed. Russel J. Dalton and Manfred Kuechler, 122–136. Oxford, UK: Oxford University Press.

Lipset, Seymour M., and Stein Rokkan. 1967. *Party Systems and Voter Alignments: Cross-National Perspectives*. New York: Free Press.

Lowe, Phillip, Jane Clifford, and Sarah Buchanan. 1980. The Mass Movement of the Decade. *Vole* 3 (4): 26–28.

Michels, Robert. 1962. *Political Parties: A Sociological Study of the Oligarchical Tendencies of Modern Democracy*. New York: Free Press.

Müller-Rommel, Ferdinand. 1982. Ecology Parties in Western Europe. *West European Politics* 5 (1): 68–74.

Müller-Rommel, Ferdinand. 1985a. The Greens in Western Europe: Similar but Different. *International Political Science Review* 6 (4): 483–498.

Müller-Rommel, Ferdinand. 1985b. Social Movements and the Greens: New Internal Politics in Germany. *European Journal of Political Research* 13:53–67.

Müller-Rommel, Ferdinand. 1985c. New Social Movements and Smaller Parties. A Comparative Perspective. *West European Politics* 8:41–54.

Müller-Rommel, Ferdinand. 1990. New Political Movements and "New Politics" Parties in Western Europe. In *Challenging the Political Order*, ed. Russel J. Dalton and Manfred Kuechler, 209–231. Oxford, UK: Oxford University Press.

Müller-Rommel, Ferdinand, and Thomas Poguntke. 1989. The Unharmonious Family: Green Parties in Western Europe. In *The Greens in West Germany: Organisation and Policy Making*, ed. Eva Kolinsky, 11–29. Oxford, UK: Berg.

Mushaben, Joyce M. 1989. The Struggle Within: Conflict, Consensus, and Decisionmaking among National Coordinators and Grass-Roots Organizers in the West German Peace Movement. In *Organizing for Change*, ed. Bert Klandermans, 267–298. Greenwich, UK: JAI Press.

Offe, C. 1987. Challenging the Boundaries of Institutional Politics: Social Movements since the Sixties. In *Changing Boundaries of the Political*, ed. Charles S. Maier, 63–106. Cambridge, UK: Cambridge University Press.

Paehlke, Robert. 1986. *Bucolic Myths: Towards More Urbanist Environmentalism*. Toronto: Centre for Urban and Community Studies.

Parkin, Frank. 1968. *Middle Class Radicalism: The Social Bases of the British Campaign for Nuclear Disarmament*. New York: Praeger.

Poguntke, Thomas. 1987. New Politics and Party Systems: The Emergence of a "New Type of Party"? *West European Politics* 10 (1): 76–88.

Poguntke, Thomas. 1989. The New Politics Dimension in European Green Parties. In *New Politics in Western Europe: The Rise and Success of Green Parties and Alternative Lists*, ed. Ferdinand Müller-Rommel, 195–210. Boulder: Westview Press.

Porritt, Jonathon, and David Winner. 1988. *The Coming of the Greens*. London: Fontana/Collins.

Raschke, Joachim. 1983. Political Parties in Western Democracies. *European Journal of Political Research* 11 (1): 109–114.

Rochon, Thomas. 1989. *Mobilizing for Peace: Anti-nuclear Movements in Western Europe*. Princeton: Princeton University Press.

Roszak, Theodore. 1978. *Person/Planet: The Creative Disintegration of Industrial Society*. Garden City, N.Y.: Anchor Press/Doubleday.

Rüdig, Wolfgang. 1985. The Greens in Europe: Ecological Parties and the European Elections of 1984. *Parliamentary Affairs* 38 (1): 56–72.

Sale, Kirkpatrick. 1985. *Dwellers in the Land: The Bioregional Vision*. San Francisco: Sierra Club Books.

Sprinz, Detlef, and Tapani Vaahtoranta. 1994. The Interest-Based Explanation of International Environmental Policy. *International Organization* 48 (1): 77–105.

Tucker, William. 1980. Environmentalism: The Newest Toryism. *Policy Review* 14:141–152.

Weber, Max. [1904] 1992. *The Protestant Ethic and the Spirit of Capitalism*. London: Routledge.

Zald, Mayer N., and John D. McCarthy, eds. 1987. *Social Movements in an Organizational Society: Collected Essays*. New Brunswick: Transaction Books.

Zucker, Lynne G. 1987. Institutional Theories of Organization. *Annual Review of Sociology* 13:443–464.

IV

Institutional Effectiveness across Political Systems

8

Democracy and the Environment in Latin America and Eastern Europe

Kathryn Hochstetler

Environmental politics is not just a technical policy area that operates the same way in all countries. Instead, one of the most important insights that the study of *comparative* environmental politics brings to research on the global environment is that the nature of the larger political system that surrounds environmental policymaking is critical for the kinds of environmental policies that are made, who makes them, how well they will be carried out—and even if they will exist at all. This chapter argues that whether political institutions are democratic or authoritarian affects how well the environment is protected. Why would this be the case? To offer just a few examples of institutional differences that might affect environmental politics, democracies give much bigger political roles to ordinary citizens than authoritarian governments do and typically have freer media and access to information. Whether these obvious differences improve or limit environmental protections is the central question of this chapter.

Similar studies have asked whether corporatist democracies are better or worse than pluralist democracies in achieving environmental protection (Crepaz 1995; Matthews 2001) or how different types of authoritarian systems respond to environmental problems (Sowers, chapter 9, this volume). All of these questions share the same basic comparative politics argument that political institutions matter for political outcomes, including in the environmental issue area.

The environmental performance of democracies and authoritarian regimes is a topic ideally suited to this volume's goal of bringing the comparative study of environmental politics into closer conversation with the wider field of comparative politics. For scholars of comparative politics, democracy and democratization have been major topics of interest for the last twenty-five years. From 1989 to 2004, more than three-quarters of the articles published in major comparative politics journals were about political regimes, regime transition, and democratic institutions (Munck and Snyder 2007, 9). This interest followed the political transitions that brought democracy to an unprecedented number of the world's citizens in the 1980s and 1990s. In the study of environmental politics, this real-world development coincided with theoretical debates about which kind of government—democratic or authoritarian—was most conducive to environmental protection. In this chapter, I take up these topics in several forms.

I begin with the debates among political philosophers and others about which form of government should be expected to perform better. I then review the small number of quantitative studies that have tried to find an association between democracy and levels of environmental protection, and discuss why firm, consistent findings have been elusive. In the final and largest section of the chapter, I look more directly at how democratization—the process of establishing democratic institutions—may affect levels of environmental protection, especially in the former Soviet bloc and Latin America. Overall, I argue that countries that have opted for democratic political systems generally have better environmental protections than do authoritarian regimes.

Thinking Theoretically about Environment and Democracy

Several early and influential publications spurred the debate about democracy and the environment by arguing strongly that democracy was incompatible with environmental protection. Ophuls's ([1974] 2004, 56) "scarcity society" was one in which resource use would inevitably have to be governed by "an all-powerful Leviathan—perhaps benign, perhaps not" because individuals seemed inclined to unsustainable self-indulgent use of resources. In making this argument, Ophuls drew on Hardin's (1968) analysis of the tragedy of the commons, in which resource use that is rational from an individual point of view leads to collectively irrational (and suboptimal) results. Hardin called for "mutual coercion mutually agreed upon" (Hardin 1968, 1247) to prevent this tragedy, especially with respect to population growth. Although decisions "mutually agreed upon" suggest democratic decision making, the tone of the article leaves clear that mutual coercion—or perhaps just coercion—is the more critical piece of environmental protection. Heilbroner (1974) makes this argument explicit, prescribing centralization of power and authoritarian decision making to preserve the environment and human life.

Press (1994) describes these ideas as a "centralist" position, one of two poles of thought on the relationship between environment and democracy. The centralist position endorses centralizing power, taking it from the large number of citizens influential in democracies and giving it to a small number of expert decision makers. The most extreme advocates of this view argue that a full authoritarian regime is necessary; less extreme proponents simply argue that environmental regulation should be carried out without mass public input. Centralists believe that imminent environmental crisis will show that democracy is too slow and uncertain for environmental protection. Instead, centralists favor "enlightened authoritarian regimes

[that] could merge ecological awareness with swift, forceful, and comprehensive action to restore ecosystems and restrain human appetites for unsustainable growth" (Press 1994, 12). A related set of arguments emphasizes the importance of technocratic expertise in modern, complex systems (Fischer 2000). Participation by ordinary citizens is devalued not just for its slowness, but because centralists see most people as ignorant and self-indulgent, hardly likely to make good choices. In turn, because democratic leaders are dependent on popular support for reaching office, they are unlikely to be willing and able to impose constraints on individuals' choices about how they drive cars, make a living, or raise their families—even when those choices harm the environment and the long-term survival needs of the human species.

Against these authoritarian centralists who are skeptical of democracy as a model for ensuring environmental protection, a second pole of thought is represented by two different groups of thinkers who claim that democratic institutions and practices are actually a solution to environmental degradation. Though both favor democracy, they have different understandings of what democracy is—liberal or participatory—which affects their analyses. "Liberal" is used here in the classic philosophical sense that stresses individual freedom of choice; as an approach to democracy, it emphasizes individual choice and expression in politics through acts like voting. Participatory democracy, in contrast, considers the most effective democratic practices to be those processes of respectful discussion in which citizens not only express their preferences, but also listen to the preferences of others and seek consensus. These kinds of respectful and deliberative discussions may occur fairly naturally in local communities where people know each other, or they may be purposefully established to bring together people who perhaps share an environmental resource or interest but have not previously sought a collective solution to their problems.

The liberal variant of the prodemocracy argument challenges the assumption that individual liberty, expressed in individual votes and market choices, is incompatible with environmental protection. Payne (1995, 42–44) begins with the observation that liberal electoral democracy—characterized by individual rights to assembly, to have information, to choose one's leaders, and to lobby government—results in governments that are more likely to respond to criticisms and demands from their citizens. All of these characteristics, he argues, enable environmentalists and scientists in democracies to push for environmental protection, influence public opinion, and monitor governments. They can use the information they have to criticize powerful political and economic actors. These processes produce greater environmental protection through the actions of governments, who ultimately must respond to their voting publics in elections. In addition, democracies are more likely to learn from the policy successes and failures of other democracies, spreading innovations internationally, and more sensitive to transnational pressures for environmental cooperation (Payne 1995, 44–48).

Payne is joined by other scholars in his assertion that liberal electoral democracy offers opportunities for environmental protection that are not matched by authoritarian regimes, especially because historically authoritarian governments have rarely prioritized the environment as Ophuls and Hardin suggest they should (Eckersley 1996; Paehlke 1995). Some of these scholars agree with Payne's final point, that the market economies that have historically accompanied liberal democracy also offer additional tools for environmental preservation. He argues that markets can protect the environment if green consumers demand environmentally sound products and governments consider market-based alternatives to regulation (Payne 1995, 48–51).

The participatory set of prodemocracy responses agrees with the centralists that individual choices on their own are unlikely to lead to good collective environmental outcomes and that liberal democracy is therefore an inadequate response to environmental dilemmas. However, these participatory democratic theorists believe that the solution is *more* democracy than liberal democracy offers, rather than the authoritarian recourse of the centralists (Press 1994). For one group of these theorists, called decentralists, the solution is to move geographically away from centralized governments of all kinds to local settings in which participants in decision making will have direct knowledge of the environments they seek to govern—and of each other.[1]

Another current of thought in the participatory democratic tradition holds that the decision process used is more important than the geographical level. Intimate and participatory decision-making sessions of both state and societal actors will allow participants to educate each other through "reasoned argument and public reflection" (Meadowcroft 2004, 184). Then outcomes will reflect collective long-term interests rather than the short-term individual interests that would otherwise dominate politics (e.g., Baber and Bartlett 2005; Doherty and de Geus 1996; Dryzek 1997; Eckersley 2004; Fischer 2000; Lafferty and Meadowcroft 1996). This literature draws on the insights of deliberative democratic theory, rather than the liberal strains. It is a perspective shared by a significant number of practitioners, who have launched experiments such as community forest programs that bring together many different stakeholders to make decisions collectively about uses of their local forests (e.g., Baker and Kusel 2003; Hulme and Murphree 2001; Weber 2000) or other environmental dilemmas. Colombia has experimented with similar stakeholder-based discussions to set fees for discharges of pollutants into waterways. The Colombian example does highlight some of the potential pitfalls of deliberative processes, as industrial interests apparently were able to dominate many of the discussions there, and proponents of environmental interests were "quite weak or altogether nonexistent" (Blackman 2005, 14).

As outlined so far, the terms of this debate focus on the question of which political institutions—authoritarian/centralized or democratic (liberal or participatory)—are most conducive to environmental protection. However, another side of the debate is equally relevant: just what constitutes "better environmental protection"? The two general answers here partially correspond to the three institutional arguments. Virtually all the centralists and some of the two kinds of democrats prefer to understand environmental protection in terms of *physical* environmental outcomes, such as deforestation rates, emissions of CO_2 per capita, and the like. This is obviously a very direct measure of environmental outcomes and environmental protection.

Other democrats, however, focus instead on *political* outcomes, such as the establishment of environmental agencies or participatory processes, the presence of environmental movements, or the writing of legislation. The literature on effectiveness, which distinguishes political (sometimes called commitment) from environmental (physical) effectiveness, acknowledges there is no automatic translation from the former to the latter (Kütting 1999; Wettestad 2006). However, there is often no physical improvement without preexisting political changes, so democracy adherents cite the appearance of those initial steps as evidence that democracy improves environmental outcomes. In addition, they point out that physical environmental outcomes have many causes beyond political regimes, from fluctuations in global economies to local wind patterns. Political outcomes, in contrast, are much more directly attributable to political regimes (Neumayer 2002).

Comparative politics scholars enter these theoretical debates with enthusiasm, offering a number of studies that use countries around the world to test arguments about which kinds of political institutions produce which kind of environmental outcomes. The remainder of this chapter reviews these empirical studies, with close attention to how they conceive of both the explanatory variables (political regimes and institutions as causal forces) and outcome variables (environmental institutions and physical conditions).

Thinking Quantitatively about Environment and Democracy

A few scholars have used large quantitative datasets to assess whether liberal democracies as a group do in fact have better environmental outcomes than do nondemocracies. Using a wide variety of definitions, indicators, and statistical techniques, three studies come to similar overall conclusions: democracies, on balance, outperform nondemocracies in their environmental achievements. However, the advantage of democracy is usually small and uneven (Gleditsch and Sverdrup 2002; Li and Reuveny 2006; Neumayer 2002). In contrast to this positive assessment of democracy's performance, Midlarsky (1998) concludes that democracies have insignificant or negative physical environmental effects and Pellegrini and Gerlagh (2006) find the impact of democracy disappears when measures of corruption are included. To help sort through the complexity of the arguments and measures, table 8.1 summarizes the basic approach and conclusions of the articles. In this section, I present these conclusions in more detail, noting that it is difficult to come to any simple conclusions about the relationship between democracy and the environment based on these studies. I conclude with a critique of their shared research design, which is inappropriate for understanding environmental outcomes in transitional regimes—countries in which the political system changes from authoritarian to democratic or vice versa.

This literature follows an extensive tradition in quantitative political science that investigates the presumed beneficial effects of liberal democracy on social and political outcomes such as economic development (Lipset 1959; Marks and Diamond 1992) and peaceful international relations (Ray 1995; Russett 1993). The initial step of such analyses is to divide the world's countries into basic political categories such as "democratic" and the usually residual "nondemocracies," which can contain many types of political systems.[2] Comparative politics scholars have spilled a great deal of ink assessing the merits of existing indexes that categorize countries (e.g., Mainwaring, Brinks, and Pérez-Liñán 2001). The Freedom House measures of democracy used by many economists studying democracy and environment in the 1990s, for example, have been largely discredited as politically biased and inconsistent from year to year (Mainwaring, Brinks, and Pérez-Liñán 2001). All of the various indicators focus on liberal rather than participatory components of democracy, so they are all effectively measures of the argument that liberal democracy improves environmental protection.[3]

In these quantitative studies about environmental outcomes, it appears that the choice of index of democracy probably does not make a great deal of difference in the results. The two articles that find the most straightforward positive links between democracy and physical environmental degradation such as greenhouse gas emissions (Gleditsch and Sverdrup 2002; Li and Reuveny 2006) both use the Polity indexes, which identify democracies largely by the presence of institutionalized elections.[4] The other articles use multiple measures of democracy, all including the Polity indexes. Midlarsky (1998) finds that the Polity index and a political rights index from Freedom House yield different results, primarily in the level of statistical significance rather than in the actual direction of the relationship. However, Neumayer (2002) and Pellegrini and Gerlagh (2006) both find that their results are insensitive to the particular measure of democracy, although the two studies reach opposite conclusions.

The differences among these studies are not limited to their measures of the explanatory variable, democracy. In fact, the different measures of environmental

Table 8.1
Summary of the quantitative literature on the relationship between democracy and environmental outcomes

Authors	Outcome variables	Explanatory variables	Major findings on relation of democracy and environment
Gleditsch and Sverdrup (2002)	Physical and political	Democracy Standard controls[a]	Positive relationships between democracy and political outcomes, not physical outcomes
Li and Reuveny (2006)	Physical	Democracy Standard controls[a]	Positive relationships between democracy and physical outcomes
Midlarsky (1998)	Physical plus protected land area (political)	Democracy Standard controls[a]	Positive relationship between democracy and protected land area only, not physical outcomes
Neumayer (2002)	Political (willingness to make commitments)	Democracy Standard controls[a]	Positive relationships between democracy and political outcomes
Pellegrini and Gerlagh (2006)	Political (policy stringency)	Democracy standard controls[a] Corruption	No relationship between democracy and political outcomes once levels of corruption are included

[a] All of the studies used standard control variables, including factors like levels of socioeconomic development, population, and level of urbanization.

outcomes are more important. On this issue Neumayer (2002) and Pellegrini and Gerlagh (2006) stand apart, as they examine democracy's impact on countries' willingness to undertake environmental policy commitments, such as signing and ratifying treaties or creating National Councils on Sustainable Development (Neumayer) or several measures of policy stringency (Pellegrini and Gerlagh). Such measures form one part of the Gleditsch and Sverdrup (2002) study, which they call "solution-oriented indicators"; Midlarsky (1998) includes protected land area, also a policy measure. Otherwise, the authors use physical environmental outcomes as their outcome variables.

Although the results of the studies are not directly comparable, the commitment indicators appear to have the strongest and most positive associations with liberal democracy. Neumayer's political results are strongly positive; Gleditsch and Sverdrup see stronger positive relationships for their commitment indicators (which they call solution-oriented measures) (2002, 60–61); and protected land area is the *only* indictor for which Midlarsky finds a strong, positive relationship with democracy (1998, 354). Pellegrini and Gerlagh (2006) also find a positive, significant relationship between democracy and environmental policy stringency—but only until they include measures of corruption and other control variables, at which point the democracy variable's importance and significance disappear. Finally, Li and Reuveny (2006) find generally positive associations between democracy and their physical indicators, but they do so in part because they have an unusually large number of control variables that help to sort out the many confounding causes. In this final study, democracies have lower levels of environmental degradation, whether measured as carbon dioxide emissions, nitrogen dioxide emissions, deforestation, land degradation, or organic pollution in water. The most democratic countries in the world are also among the wealthiest, and the two factors typically work together to produce the positive environmental outcomes associated with democracy in these studies.

On the basis of these quantitative studies of the democracy-environment relationship, it seems safe to conclude that liberal democracies are more likely to make commitments to policies and institutions intended to protect the environment than are nondemocracies. However, the gap between those policies and institutions and the intended physical environmental outcomes may be large, as is seen in the complex, weak, or negative relationships with physical variables. Returning to the competing institutional arguments, then, the quantitative studies do weakly support the liberal democrats over the centralists. Because they do not distinguish between democratic countries that have significant decentralization and participatory processes and those that do not, they provide little evidence to adjudicate between the two variants of democratic arguments.

Notwithstanding all their differences, these five studies share a basic research design of a cross-sectional "snapshot"; that is, they pick a particular year in which to sort countries into the democratic or nondemocratic categories, take single measures of the various outcome variables, and evaluate the statistical relationship between those measures. This is a strategy that works well enough for countries that are of one or the other regime type for long periods. It is much more problematic for countries in transition, for which the choice of years can greatly affect the results. Gleditsch and Sverdrup (2002) acknowledge the problem and resolve it by dropping all transitional cases. Midlarsky (1998) does not discuss the issue and chooses years that probably maximize the measurement problem: he measures democracy in 1980, but the data for his outcomes variables come from at least a decade later. For the Latin American countries, many of which underwent regime transitions in the 1980s, democratic outcome values thus end up associated with regimes labeled as nondemocracies. This gap is a special problem for fast-changing outcomes such as deforestation rates. Slow-changing outcomes can also be misleading, as when a new democracy might show problematic physical data for issues like water quality that are really inheritances from previous regimes (Pavlínek and Pickles 2004).

In short, global quantitative analyses based on cross-sectional research designs are likely to stumble over the time dimension that is central in transitional regimes. Fortunately, other research designs are especially appropriate and possible for transitional regimes. In these studies, the outcomes of democratic and nondemocratic regimes can be compared over time—pre- and post-transition—in one country (or in a series of them), providing a kind of natural experiment that effectively holds many national characteristics constant. In the final part of this chapter, I examine how levels of environmental protection in Latin American and Central and Eastern European countries changed as their political systems were transformed in the so-called third wave of democratization.

Thinking Qualitatively about Environment and Democracy over Time: Democratization in Latin America and Eastern Europe

Between 1978 and 1994, fourteen Latin American countries left military government behind for civilian rule. As their wave of democratization reached its end, the former Soviet bloc underwent its own political transition, from one-party Communist states dominated by the Soviet Union to varying levels of political competition in a region that increasingly looked to Western Europe for political and economic models (see Andonova and VanDeveer, chapter 11, this volume). The countries that are discussed here all acquired the most basic component of democracy—regular competitive elections. Many also experimented with decentralization and participatory measures. Thus their experiences can shed light on the environmental impact of both kinds of institutional changes.

Several factors do complicate the task of evaluating this impact. Transitions appear to be inherently uneven—institutions frequently change before values, for example, and there may be advances in some areas such as legislation, while others, such as judicial development and the rule of law, commonly lag. In both regions, democratization was joined with simultaneous market-oriented economic reforms, leaving entangled causal relationships. Because of these many dimensions, most studies of the impact of democratization have been qualitative. Notwithstanding these difficulties, however, almost all of the countries assessed do show clear improvements in their institutions and policies for the environment following the transition to democracy. The former Soviet bloc also shows improvements in many physical indicators of environmental quality, while the Latin American results are more mixed.

The Impact of Transition in Central and Eastern Europe

For scholars of environmental politics in postcommunist Central and Eastern Europe, studies of the impact of the political and economic transitions on the environment are common. Most find improved environmental institutions and legislation after the transitions, although implementation has been slower. Experiments in decentralization have been less successful either at actually shifting power and resources to local levels or at improving environmental outcomes there. Environmental movements have made the least progress, with their fate affected by serious erosion in public support for and attention to environmental protection. Fewer scholars have examined the physical environmental outcomes systematically, but those who have see real improvement post-transition coupled with new problems. Table 8.2 summarizes the regional environmental outcomes and can serve as a guide through this section of the chapter.

Notwithstanding their poor environmental reputation, the communist regimes began to put environmental institutions and legislation in place beginning in the 1950s and 1960s. The most effective of these, like nature preserves, worked well across the region. Some 30 percent of the region's lands were "pristine" ecosystems at the time of transition (Pavlínek and Pickles 2004, 241–243). Antipollution initiatives were much less successful under the communist regimes. Immediately after the transitions to postcommunist regimes, countries across the region built many new environmental institutions and filled in numerous legislative gaps, although other problems remained. Poland is the only country where environmental institutions have remained substantially unchanged, albeit with some new legislative and other tools that make it more effective (Auer 2004, 11–12). The new initiatives in the region focused on pollution mitigation and regulation (Baker and Jehlicka 1998, 14–15; Glushenkova 1999). European countries provided some 3.5 billion euros for

Table 8.2
Impact of democratic transitions on environmental outcomes in the former Soviet bloc

Environmental outcomes	Former Soviet bloc as a whole	EU-aspirants (Czech Republic, Estonia, Hungary, Poland, Slovenia)	Non-EU-aspirants (Albania, Bulgaria, Russia, Ukraine)
Political outcomes			
Institutions and laws	Immediate improvements, except for Poland	Second wave of improvements to meet EU requirements	Institutions critically weak
Environmental movements	Declined	Declined; Hungary, Poland partial exceptions	Some strength in Albania and Bulgaria
Decentralization	Little improvement	Little improvement; Hungary a partial exception	No improvement
Physical outcomes			
Water/air pollution	Greatly improved	Improved emissions/unit	Improved only with economic decline; emissions per GDP still high
Consumption-based problems	Worsened	Worsened	Worsened, but less than in wealthier EU aspirants
Deforestation	Probably worsened	Probably worsened	Probably worsened

pollution remediation from 1990 to 1995, much of it in loans (Carmin and VanDeveer 2004, 10).

This early wave of activity died down quickly, before real implementation took place. Only the set of countries joining the EU have participated in a second wave of institutional and legal capacity building in order to bring their national frameworks in line with European ones, as required for membership (Carmin and VanDeveer 2004; Pavlínek and Pickles 2004). Although this second wave occurred after the transition, it is in important ways not a reflection of national democratic processes: the impetus comes from outside the countries rather than from their own citizens and policy makers, and the countries' representatives did not participate in the formulation of the framework (Carmin and VanDeveer 2004). Darst (1997) argues that Russia's international motivations to protect the environment were actually strongest before the transition, when environmental cooperation was an easy bright spot in Cold War relations. Because it has not tried to join the EU, the international dimension was subsequently reduced to a combination of bribery and blackmail—we'll clean up our dirty problems only if you give us money and vice versa—which largely disappeared after the 1990s.

Whatever their origins, all of these formal institutions coexist with old informal institutions that often undercut their new official powers. The Soviet-style bureaucratic mentality has been harder to shake than its formal institutional structures (Assetto, Hajba, and Mumme 2003; Auer 2004; Baker and Jehlicka 1998). In addition, environmental institutions are often critically weak when compared to economic production institutions, inside and outside the government. This ranking reflects public preferences: as Auer notes, societal environmental norms not only do not precede environmental policy implementation—as they often do in Western Europe—they often do not even follow it (1994, 23). Economic concerns are at the forefront and may be growing more important. In 1993, 58.5 percent of Russians indicated a willingness to pay the costs of environmental protection, a stance held by only 38.1 percent of Russians in 2001 (Whitefield 2003, 101).

Similar dynamics have led to the one development that most directly contravenes both prodemocracy arguments: citizen-based environmental movements have actually declined since the transition, rather than flourishing in democracy. In a large-scale study of 1,700 environmental nongovernmental organizations in the region, 1990–1992 were peak years for founding organizations. In contrast, only five were created in 1994 (Massam and Earl-Goulet 1997, 139) and many have disappeared since. Numerous authors have traced the ways that the final years of communism allowed unusual opportunities for citizen mobilization, with the numbers swelled by the fact that other kinds of regime opposition were not allowed (e.g., Auer 2004; Baker and Jehlicka 1998; Berg 1999; Botcheva 1996).

Post transition, environmental movements lost their grassroots connections as society moved to focus on economic concerns and as the movements themselves drew on newly available international financing to formalize their own organization—a development not well received by the populations (Baker and Jehlicka 1998). In addition, environmental NGOs were largely unable to develop new roles in the still-centralized state institutions. Hungarian and, to a lesser extent, Polish NGOs are an exception to these generalizations, with comparatively strong links both to state and society (Auer 2004; Baker and Jehlicka 1998; Botcheva 1996). Interestingly, environmental NGOs are also comparatively strong in some of the weakest regional states, doing most of what environmental protection gets done in Albania and Bulgaria (Auer 2004, 20).

Decentralization and participation initiatives have foundered for many of the reasons already outlined. Heavily promoted by EU officials and by international development agencies of all kinds, these depend on citizens who are not only active and engaged but also interested in promoting and monitoring environmental protection. In addition, local level governments need environmental capacity and experience, which simply does not exist (Carmin and VanDeveer 2004). Such initiatives rest uneasily within the larger heritage of centralized administrative and political cultures and are not strongly promoted from above (Baker and Jehlicka 1998). Local governments in Russia have been more inclined to use their control over resources for political power or economic growth than for sustainable development (Glushenkova 1999; Kotov and Nikitina 1993).

Even Hungary has seen few positive outcomes from one of the region's most extensive decentralization experiments. Environmental regulations still come from the center, leaving little local flexibility. Overwhelmed local administrations under serious economic and personnel restraints often have not established the local environmental committees they are empowered to create; when they do, they staff them with local council members and environmental experts rather than citizens (Assetto, Hajba, and Mumme 2003).

As the iron curtain rose, early reports on physical environmental conditions in the region stressed the unexpectedly severe pollution that had resulted from Soviet-era economic policies (e.g., Berg 1999; Fagin 1994). Over time, observers have noted that the actual environmental heritage was much more mixed, with pockets of highly polluted areas but also numerous bright spots, as in the successful reserves noted above (Auer 2004; Baker and Jehlicka 1998, 6; Carmin and VanDeveer 2004, 8; Pavlínek and Pickles 2004, 241). In one of the few regional studies of physical environmental conditions that presents quantitative pollutant data over time, Pavlínek and Pickles (2004) find the emissions of water and air pollutants had actually begun to decline in the 1980s, before the transition, although the pace and scope of the decline increased afterwards. This study provides strong evidence that political transition contributes to a cleaner environment. A study of just Russia is not nearly so positive and shows that Russia lacks good data that would allow a full assessment of its environmental problems (Oldfield 1999).

In the immediate post-transition years, any physical environmental improvements were "passive" (Auer 2004, 6) or "cleanup by default" (Pavlínek and Pickles 2004, 243). That is, economic collapse was the primary cause of improved emissions numbers in the early years. Later in the decade, the post-transition institutional and legal changes took effect in the more economically successful countries, along with many new investments with cleaner technology. One way to trace whether improvements are passive or active is to look at emissions per unit of economic activity (emissions per GDP). These actually rose during the years of economic collapse in the Czech Republic, Slovakia, and Hungary (Auer 2004, 6) before dropping. Emissions per GDP remain high in the poorer countries of Ukraine, Bulgaria, and Russia, which continue to have policies that allow high pollution per GDP. These have economic decline as their only source of reduced pollution in the 1990s (Auer 2004, 9).

It is the wealthier countries in the region, however, that are also in the forefront of developing "new" environmental problems. Western chain retailers and car culture have come to them, creating new resource consumption and waste issues. The whole region shares other new challenges "typical of deregulated market capitalism" (Pavlínek and Pickles 2004, 252). Newly privatized forests are probably less secure than before, and some of the region's new market investors continue to make "dirty" investments, especially in light of the continuing regulation gaps. Elected governments have hesitated to regulate these new problems associated with individual choice in more affluent conditions.

The overall picture then leads to a conclusion that political transition in Central and Eastern Europe has led to better, albeit uneven, environmental outcomes, with two major comments. The first is that the EU has been a much more active cause of improved environmental protection than any of the domestic-regime arguments would suggest, first as a lender and then as an institutional draw that used environmental conditionality to prod would-be members into improvements. Political transition, of course, was crucial for turning the countries of Eastern Europe from the Soviet Union to the European Community as a model.

The second is that the postcommunist countries appear to be divisible into two groups that share whole clusters of attributes. Countries like Poland, the Czech Republic, Hungary, Slovenia, and Estonia are more fully democratic, have been more economically successful, have a stronger rule of law and civil society, and recently joined the EU. They also have stronger environmental protection, but the exact causes would be hard to trace. In the poorer Central and Eastern European countries—Ukraine, Bulgaria, and Russia—all of those factors are comparatively absent.

The experiences of the former Soviet bloc best support the arguments of the liberal democrats. The pre-transition authoritarian regimes fared better in only one measure of environmental outcomes, that of numbers and influence of environmental movements, and that was only at the very end of these regimes' existence. In other regards, liberal democracies fared at least as well as or were better and faster in making environmental improvements than their predecessors. In addition, countries in the region that progressed further as liberal democracies also progressed further in their environmental protections. This region simply has not successfully initiated enough of the decentralized and participatory kinds of political changes to fully evaluate the arguments of the participatory democratic theorists. Its experiences suggest that those are more difficult changes to make, especially in postauthoritarian situations.

The Impact of Transition in Latin America

Comparatively few scholars have directly assessed the impact of political transition on environmental protection in Latin America. Of the fourteen transitional countries in the region, only Brazil (Hochstetler 2005; Hochstetler and Keck 2007; Hochstetler and Mumme 1998), Chile (Carruthers 2001; Silva 1996–1997) and Mexico (Auer 2001; Mumme and Korzetz 1997) have been the subject of extended studies of democratization's impact on environmental protection.[5] Major overviews of Latin American environmental politics both at the time of the transitions (Goodman and Redclift 1991) and more recently (Roberts and Thanos 2003) focus on economic development issues and global economic dynamics rather than political changes in domestic politics.

Many of the causes of environmental destruction that this literature discusses—such as highly inequitable land and power distributions, aggressive extraction of natural resources for foreign sale, and international indebtedness—have indeed been largely untouched by formal political transition and continue to cause a variety of problems for the region. At the same time, however, applying this chapter's multifaceted conception of democracy to recent Latin American environmental developments will show that the political transition did make a difference, especially in putting environmental institutions, legislation, and actors in place. Table 8.3 summarizes environmental outcomes in Latin America since the democratizing transition and provides a guide through this section of the chapter.

Table 8.4, which relates the years of political transition, creation of national environmental agencies, and writing of general environmental laws for Latin American democratizers, helps to explain the lack of focus on political transition in the region. On average, the fourteen recently transformed political systems took 7.8 years to create environmental agencies and 9.8 years to write broad cross-sectoral

Table 8.3
Impact of democratic transitions on environmental outcomes in Latin America

Environmental outcomes	Latin America as a whole	Southern Cone (Argentina, Brazil, Chile, Paraguay, Uruguay)	Andean Region (Bolivia, Colombia, Ecuador, Peru, Venezuela)	Central America and Mexico
Political outcomes				
Institutions and laws	Generally improved, although not immediately	Improved—spending and personnel up	Improved	Improved
Green parties and voters	Weak or nonexistent	Weak (Brazil, Chile)	None notable	Weak (Mexico)
Environmental movements	Improved	Improved—new participatory initiatives in Argentina, Brazil, and Chile	Little information	Little information except for Mexico, where new participatory initiatives
Decentralization	Mixed—new initiatives with mixed success	Mixed	Mixed	Mixed
Physical outcomes				
Climate change emissions	Largest have improved emissions/unit; no baseline data	Mixed; Brazil has improved emissions/unit	Continuing greenhouse gas emissions	Mixed; Mexico has improved emissions/unit
Deforestation	Continuing deforestation; no baseline data	Continuing deforestation	Continuing deforestation	Many new protected areas, but continuing deforestation

Table 8.4
Second and third wave democracies in Central and South America and years of creation of national environmental agencies and laws

Country	First year of democratic regime[a]	Year of first national environmental agency (ministry)[b]	Years to create agency	Year of general national law on environment	Years to law
Third wave			7.8[d]		9.8[d]
Argentina	1983	1991	8	2002	19
Bolivia	1982	1994	12	1992	10
Brazil	1985	1973 (1985)	−12	1981	−4
Chile	1990	1990	0	1994	4
Ecuador	1979	1984	5	1994	15
El Salvador	1984	1994 (1997)	10	1998	6
Guatemala	1986	2000	14	1986	0
Honduras	1982	1984	2	1993	11
Mexico	1988	1982 (1994)	−6	1972; 1988	−16
Nicaragua	1984	1995	11	1996	14
Panama	1990	1998	8	1998	8
Paraguay	1989	2000	11	—	—
Peru	1980[c]	—	−2	1990	10
	1995	1994		2005	
Uruguay	1985	1990	5	2000	15
Second wave			30.0		28.3
Colombia	1958	1993	35	1993	35
Costa Rica	1949	1986	37	1981	32
Venezuela	1958	1976	18	1976	18

Sources: Mumme and Korzetz 1997, 42; Palacio Jiménez 2005, 37; government websites from countries included here. (A full list of websites is available from the author upon request.)
Notes:
[a]Classifications of political regimes are from Mainwaring, Brinks, and Pérez-Liñán (2001, 49). Although these authors divide regimes into authoritarian, democratic, and semidemocratic, I treat both democratic and semidemocratic regimes as democratic in order to simplify the discussion.
[b]Dates in parentheses indicate when an earlier subministerial agency was replaced by a ministerial level agency.
[c]Peru was under authoritarian rule from 1992 to 2000.
[d]These are average figures for the third wave, which do not include the countries that created agencies and wrote laws before the political transition.

environmental laws. Only Chile displays the former Soviet pattern of a transitional regime that immediately moved to update its institutional and legal infrastructure to protect the environment. The early democratizers took even longer, waiting decades.

Nonetheless, these data also help to support the overall argument about the importance of liberal democracy for policy commitments to the environment: only three of seventeen Latin American authoritarian regimes created national environmental agencies of any kind. Even when authoritarian regimes initiated some environmental institutions, democratization brought considerable expansion and opening to them. Brazil's environmental agency had just three employees in 1973, a number that had swelled to over 6,000 by 1989, post transition (Hochstetler and Keck 2007, 27, 36). In Chile, environmental spending quintupled between the last military government and the first civilian one (Silva 1996–1997, 20). From 1990 to 2000, Chile's CONAMA increased its number of personnel from 6 to 370, with 4,758 total public environmental personnel at the end of the decade. CONAMA's budget increased over the same time period from US$76,000 to US$21 million (Asenjo et al. 2002, 46). Together, NAFTA and the decline of corporatist institutions have pushed the Mexican environmental bureaucracy to be steadily more responsive to the public (Auer 2001, 438, 443), although Mumme stresses continuing blocks to environmental activism (Hochstetler and Mumme 1998; Mumme and Korzetz 1997).

Similar dynamics mark the writing of environmental legislation. As noted, there was often a delay in crafting cross-sectoral environmental laws. However, the legislative histories on the agency websites of every country in the region show the very same pattern: initial sectoral environmental legislation appeared sparingly in the authoritarian period and then accumulated quickly, if not immediately, in the democratic period. Even the Brazilian military government—a regular outlier in this discussion for its comparative attention to environmental issues—saw its efforts dwarfed by those of the ensuing civilian governments (Hochstetler and Keck 2007).

Although these gradual changes did not have the direct international motivation for improving environmental protections that the drive for EU membership gave East and Central Europe, democratization in Latin America did increase regional openness to accepting international environmental norms and assistance, as Payne (1995) suggests. International normative pressure to create environmental institutions has been concentrated in two time periods (Friedman, Hochstetler, and Clark 2005). The first, at the time of the first global conference on the environment in Stockholm, Sweden, in 1972, was largely ignored by the region's mostly authoritarian governments. In the case of Argentina, a national environmental agency was created during a three-year democratic interlude from 1973 to 1976 but was dismantled by the incoming military regime. The second period of international normative pressure came twenty years later at the United Nations Conference on

Environment and Development, and Latin America's new democracies were much more receptive to this wave. For example, the transitional countries of South America began to accept Inter-American Development Bank funding to create environmental institutions and laws during this time (Hochstetler 2005). The greater role of international funding can also be traced to potential funders' increased willingness to financially support the governments of democratic countries, as Steinberg (2001) reports for Bolivia.

Taken together, this evidence suggests that democratization has been necessary, but not sufficient, as a driving force behind environmental protection activities in Latin America. One reason for this is that electoral democracy has not been a particularly strong transmission belt for environmental ideas and demands. The region's green parties and candidacies have generally been weak. The best reported outcome for any green party was the Chilean party's 5.5 percent in the 1994 election (Mumme and Korzetz 1997, 48). It and the Brazilian Green Party have received enough votes to seat federal deputies. In Brazil, these and a few other environmentally oriented legislators from other parties have been crucial for some of the legislative gains there, including in the 1988 constitution (Hochstetler and Keck 2007). Auer (2001, 251–252) reports that urban voters in Mexico City have made environmental issues important in some campaigns there.

In the Andean countries of the region, indigenous movements have gained major currency in national politics post-transition, including electing the region's first indigenous presidents after 2000 (Maybury-Lewis 2002; Van Cott 1994). Notwithstanding the tendency of outsiders to associate indigenous and environmental politics, these political/party movements rarely address environmental issues directly. Other indigenous movements are still shut out of the policy-making process in Latin America (Carvalho 2000; Sawyer 2004).

With little assistance from electoral democracy, environmentalists have found organizing through autonomous organizations—social movements, NGOs, transnational alliances—to be the most reliable ways to bring their issues onto the political agenda. Here again, the contrast with Central and Eastern Europe is stark. In Chile (Silva 1996–1997, 10) and Mexico (Auer 2001), some analysts noted that the authoritarian governments found environmental issues to be a way to make minor concessions to opponents. However, the former-Soviet reverse phenomenon— wherein regime opponents found environmental issues to be a useful frame for demanding political as well as policy changes—is almost absent from Latin America. Only one major mobilization, Brazil's first national initiative to preserve the Amazon in 1978–1979, took this form (Hochstetler and Keck 2007, 157–160). Otherwise, environmentalists were not widely recognized as an identifiable part of the movements for regime change. Thus the transitions brought them strikingly new political settings to manage, but did not lead to their rapid eclipse and decline.

There are no reliable regional figures for how numbers of environmentalists have changed over time in Latin America. One survey finds that there were nine hundred environmental NGOs in Brazil and one hundred in Mexico by the end of the 1980s, while twenty-four were counted in Ecuador by 1992 (Mumme and Korzetz 1997, 44–45). Data from the World Values Survey for Argentina, Brazil, Chile, and Mexico shows a sharp increase in the percentage of survey respondents in all of these countries who said that they participated as active members in environmental organizations. Mexico ranked just behind the United States in 1995–1997, with 9.4 percent of respondents claiming active participation (Steinberg 2005, 350–351, 365). The number of environmental organizations in Brazil has continued to grow, with new and continuing organizations pushing the total to 1,593 in 2002. All but a few hundred of these were formed after the 1985 political transition (Instituto Brasileiro de Geografía e Estatistica 2004, table 16; see also Hochstetler and Keck 2007). Numerous case studies also provide evidence for the growing importance of environmental NGOs, showing a rise in mobilization without permitting quantification of this gain (e.g., Haughney 2006; Roberts and Thanos 2003; Sawyer 2004; Steinberg 2001). As in Eastern Europe, they often are especially important in countries and times when formal environmental bureaucracies are weak. The assertion of rising NGO importance should not be interpreted to mean that environmentalists always win. Instead, it is a claim that they continue to be present and active.

In addition, NGOs have an increasing number of tools at their disposal, with most of them inspired by liberal and/or participatory conceptions of democracy. Brazilians have acquired perhaps the most extensive set of these; a partial list would include the right to bring legal suits in defense of collective interests, public environmental impact assessments, participatory environmental councils at all levels of government, and a strong new public ministry with a record of challenging governmental and private actors. The participatory councils began under the military government, but were greatly expanded afterwards. All of the other tools originated in civilian government and have allowed environmental activists to be central players there, inside and outside the government (Hochstetler and Keck 2007).

Other countries tend to have fewer of these mechanisms (Grupo Y'Guazú 1995), although they are being put in place in a piecemeal fashion. Chileans gained a consultative council that gives them a small role and a newly public environmental impact report process (Silva 1996–1997, 18). The Mexican government gave citizens the right-to-know and grievance procedures in environmental impact assessments in the late 1990s, albeit with little publicity (Auer 2001, 449). Similar provisions exist in the city of Buenos Aires, although not in the rest of Argentina, and activists complain that they are hardly guaranteed in practice. As Steinberg notes, such mechanisms can greatly improve not just the process of environmental decision making, but also the physical outcomes, as citizens give governments site-specific information and can closely monitor and advocate for effective implementation. In this way, participation should be seen as potentially building state capacity, rather than as always an alternative to it (Steinberg 2005).

Other Latin American experiments have taken the form of decentralization efforts. Mexico's began in 1983, well before its final transition to competitive government. It has not been a particularly successful effort, not least because responsibilities have been moved to local levels without corresponding increases in resources (Assetto, Hajba, and Mumme 2003, 260). The study also blames both local sides: local governments that do not seek participation and local populations who do not want to participate. Other decentralization experiments show more potential. Decentralization of forestry controls in Bolivia "shows that strengthening the role of local governments in forest management can lead to greater equity and even more sustainable resource use. It also shows that these outcomes are by no means assured" (Kaimowitz et al. 1998, 57; see also Agrawal, chapter 12, this volume). Similarly, decentralized and participatory water basin management in Brazil only sometimes achieves both greater participation and better management, depending on the character and level of support of the resulting policy networks (Lemos and de Oliveira 2004).

A program in Peru has joined decentralization and participation efforts, using Environmental Dialogues at all levels of government to develop and prioritize environmental agendas (Andean Center for Economics in the Environment 2001, 34). The Lula administration did the same thing in Brazil, with 65,000 community representatives (most of them not environmentalists) participating in consultations leading to the First National Conference on the Environment in 2003—only to be enraged when their central demand to block legalization of genetically modified organisms did not become administration policy (Hochstetler 2004).

So far, I have focused on the political and policy measures of environmental effectiveness, which generally show improvement in Latin America after the transition to democracy. Whether and how those political improvements translate into improvements in physical measurements of environmental protection is a separate issue. In general, the failure to translate promising new institutions into actual practices is a common feature of post-transition Latin America. Environmental activists spend much of their time demanding they be allowed to exercise rights that are formally guaranteed (e.g., Carruthers 2001; Hochstetler and Keck 2007; Mumme and Korzetz 1997). From the institutional point of view, the problem is that the "anti-establishment vision" of environmentalist discourses needs to be completed by "more propositional visions" (Asenjo et al. 2002, 27). However, both sides would agree that formal political changes have not yet really taken hold and should thus not yet be expected to lead to dramatic improvements in environmental quality.

A full assessment of the impact of political transition on the Latin American physical environment will never be known. This is because most countries in the region simply do not have extensive baseline environmental data for the pretransition years. The most comprehensive assessments of the region's environmental outcomes were done for the Inter-American Development Bank in 2002, primarily covering the years from 1990 to 2000. Here I highlight these reports' conclusions about two important clusters of issues—deforestation and climate change emissions—to show general regional patterns and subregional variations. Overall, these reports thus allow us to draw conclusions about how Latin America's new democracies have handled environmental issues, even though we often lack the data to say if they are more or less effective than the previous authoritarian regimes. The fact that many of the numbers given below worsen over the 1990s and 2000s means the new democracies are not managing to solve many of their environmental problems and are even losing ground.

Per-capita carbon dioxide emissions rose steadily in Central America and Mexico until the 1980s before dropping sharply and only slowly climbing back to levels near the historic highs (Pratt and Girot 2002, 24). Mexico's emissions peaked in 1982 when its debt crisis sparked economic problems in all of Latin America; as its economy has recovered, emissions remain below that peak, suggesting a decline in emissions per GDP. In the rest of the subregion, the lack of significant industrial development means that emissions are half those of Mexico, but they struggle with a different set of environmental problems including worsening urban environmental conditions and inadequate risk management for the disasters that regularly hit Central America (Pratt and Girot 2002, 28).

Following their transitions to democracy, countries of the subregion have experienced less contentious international relations, allowing them to cooperate on a series of initiatives that are meant to protect forests and address climate change, such as the Mesoamerican Biological Corridor (Pratt and Girot 2002, 31, 38–40). Overall in the region, transition has led to real institutional improvements that are not yet reflected in systematic physical improvements. To cite one especially stark example, the amount of land in protected areas rose from 3.4 percent in 1989 to 10.2 percent in 1997. Nicaragua and Guatemala increased protected area by a startling 3,681 percent and 2,084 percent, respectively (Pratt and Girot 2002, 35). Nonetheless, the region lost 1.5 percent of its forest coverage annually between 1990 and 2000 (Pratt and Girot 2002, 10); the lack of data means we do not know how these compare to earlier, pre-transition years.

All the countries of the Andean subregion (Bolivia, Colombia, Ecuador, Peru, and Venezuela) also lost forest coverage post-transition, losing an average of 0.75 percent per year from 1990 to 1995 (Andean Center for Economics in the Environment 2001, 5). A failure by some countries in the region to follow basic legislation with specific regulations has contributed to the resulting threats to biodiversity (9–10). Deforestation has a second cost, as land use change makes one of the largest contributions to the Andean subregion's greenhouse gas emissions, along with fossil fuels produced in the region. Per-capita carbon dioxide emissions are near Central American levels, except for Venezuela, which tops even Mexico, Latin America's other historic oil producer (73–74).

The Southern Cone (Argentina, Brazil, Chile, Paraguay, Uruguay) shows similar patterns. Deforestation is continuing, and it affects other important environmental issues like greenhouse gas contributions and biodiversity loss (Asenjo et al. 2002, 14). In Paraguay, the rate of forest loss increased from 290,000 hectares per year before its political transition to 327,000 hectares per year afterwards. Brazil, in contrast, has seen deforestation-based CO2 emissions drop from 1,400 million tons in pre-transition 1980 to 969 in 1990 and 850 in 1995 (Asenjo et al. 2002, 22). In São Paulo, CO_2 emissions per unit of gross state product (and per capita) rose until 1999, but they have since dropped to levels below the beginning of the time series in 1990 (Reid et al. 2005, 13). A largely successful effort to reign in industrial pollution in São Paulo has been stymied by a corresponding rise in automobile-source pollution (Hochstetler and Keck 2007), and Brazil as a whole has had rising industrial emissions (Asenjo et al. 2002, 22). Other big cities in this subregion (which is heavily urbanized, with the exception of Paraguay) are increasingly able to control some sources of atmospheric contamination, although levels remain very high and smaller cities lag (21). There are no calculations of emissions per GDP for the Andean region or Southern Cone or any systematic pre-transition data.

Drawing broader Latin American patterns from this brief survey, deforestation is an ongoing problem, despite regime change, formal protection initiatives, and a generation of international attention. Brazil is the only country with a documented drop in deforestation since the military years, but it continues to have very serious deforestation problems (Hochstetler and Keck 2007). Although these figures are just occasional snapshots, three in-depth studies of conservation policies in five Latin American countries also found no systematic improvement crossing the line of political transition (Foresta 1991; Hopkins 1995; Steinberg 2001). Only the biggest and most industrialized Latin American countries, Brazil and Mexico, can document a drop in emissions per GDP. With Chile, they also have had some of the region's only policies that limit individuals' use of personal cars, suggesting that development may be as important as democracy for such regulatory capacities. The others, beginning from much lower economic and industrial levels, are likely to see growing emissions as—or if—they develop economically.

It is not clear that the results could be different. As Goodman and Redclift noted at the time of transition, Latin American development patterns have huge environmental costs, but the region continues to need to develop because adequate living standards are unavailable for so many (1991, 13). They call for a change in development models, noting that conventional development in Latin America hurts the environment without helping the poor, for whom the environment *is* important (Goodman and Redclift 1991, 21; see also Dunlap and York, chapter 4, this volume). So far, Latin America's democratic regimes have not found the magic model that achieves growth and equity without hurting the environment. They "probably will not be worse" than their predecessors (Kaimowitz et al. 1998, 46), but how much they can and will be better is still unknown, notwithstanding a generation of political improvements.

Conclusion

Does democratic government improve environmental protection? A variety of quantitative and qualitative data show clearly that liberal democracy improves political measures of environmental outcomes. All the data from these two regions show that liberal democracies write environmental legislation and create and support environmental agencies in ways that authoritarian governments have not, suggesting that liberal democracy may be at least a necessary condition for adequate environmental protection. Qualitative analyses of Latin American countries before and after their political transitions show that they also have found much more room for environmental activists and for a series of decentralization and participatory initiatives, although the institutional changes there have not been as immediate as in Central and Eastern Europe.

These kinds of political changes provide a presumed foundation for improved environmental quality, although actual outcomes vary. The quantitative measures find mixed results on the question of whether liberal democracies actually leave more trees standing or have more breathable air than do authoritarian governments. The ambiguity of these results are matched in Latin America, where new democracies struggle with ongoing high rates of deforestation and mixed emissions results. Decentralization and participatory efforts there sometimes give better results than either authoritarian or liberal arrangements, but the evidence is scanty and never firm. In the former Soviet bloc, the countries that achieved more successful liberalizing transitions also show the strongest improvements in physical environmental outcomes—without significant participation or decentralization. Thus whether liberal democracy can be *sufficient* for all kinds of environmental improvements, or whether liberal democratic results might themselves be improved by more participation and decentralization, cannot be determined with the evidence at hand.

The work surveyed here, though extensive, does not exhaust the possible areas of interest for future research. One next step would be to move beyond simply looking at the effects of democracy to examine the effects of particular subtypes of democracy. There is a small existing literature on whether corporatist or pluralist forms of democratic interest representation are more successful at addressing environmental problems (Matthews 2001; Scruggs 2001). This line of investigation could be extended to the transitional regimes and also theoretically expanded to include more analysis of the alternative deliberative styles of interest representation.

Another area for future research would be to begin more cross-regional studies using qualitative case selection techniques (Hochstetler and Laituri 2005) to understand the implications of regional variations without going to the highly aggregated levels of the quantitative studies discussed here. This research would allow comparison of other kinds of democratic subtypes and their effects, such as the presidential regimes of Latin America, the semipresidential regimes of much of the former Soviet bloc, and the parliamentary systems of others in Europe. It will also be interesting to see whether the Latin American or post-Soviet experiences—or neither—provide the best roadmap for understanding the impact of democratization in regions of Asia and Africa. Now is the right time to gather baseline data and develop hypotheses on this central issue.

This chapter also demonstrates the value of comparative analysis for the study of global environmental politics. The interplay of international and national governance appears frequently in this chapter, especially in discussing the transitional regimes. International governance can both help and hinder the establishment of democratic regimes, just as it can both promote and impede the establishment of policies that protect the environment. The international level—and specifically the influence of the EU and its requirements for membership—was profoundly important for understanding environmental developments in the subset of former Soviet bloc countries seeking EU membership (see, for example, Andonova and VanDeveer, chapter 11, this volume). Without this external motivation, it is likely that the political outcomes in these countries would have been more like those of the rest of the region—and decidedly weaker. In fact, citizens in the region might well have preferred to use scarce governmental resources and attention for other purposes, suggesting that it was *not* democratic mechanisms that improved environmental protections there. In Latin America, international pressures were not as direct, but they also interacted with democratization to bring about improved environmental protections. Understanding these relationships more systematically is a promising area for future collaboration between scholars of international relations and comparative politics.

Finally, all attempts to understand the impact of democracy on other political outcomes are confounded by the historical and possibly necessary link between stable, long-lasting democracy and high levels of economic development. Wealthy stable democracies led the development of global concern with environmental protection and innovated a set of mechanisms for addressing environmental problems (once they had destroyed many of their own natural resources and consumed a great deal of those of the rest of the world). The quantitative studies surveyed here show that high *levels* of both wealth and democracy are linked to greater environmental protection, but the qualitative studies of Latin America and the post-Soviet bloc show that the *processes of development and democratization*—the processes of moving additional countries to such high levels—often carry at least some environmental costs. This is especially true in the comparatively poor Latin American region and in the poorest subregions within both Latin America and the post-Soviet bloc. These observations raise questions about just how to parse the relationships between democracy, development, and the environment; the questions are both empirical and normative. *What are* the relationships among them and *what should* they be? The answers are beyond the scope of this chapter and so far have proven to be beyond the scope of current global problem solving.

Notes

I would like to thank the editors as well as James Meadowcroft and the other authors of this book for helpful comments on earlier versions of this chapter. Any remaining errors of fact or interpretation are, of course, my responsibility.

1. See the analysis by Agrawal (chapter 12, this volume). Some noncentralist authors argue strongly against the wisdom of such moves, noting that especially rural local authorities in postcolonial settings may have very little accountability to local populations (e.g., Ribot 1999).

2. All of the studies considered in detail here include control variables for factors such as socioeconomic levels of development, population, and level of urbanization.

3. In principle, quantitative analysis could be used to assess the participatory arguments, but would require knowledge about individual cases—such as information about subnational levels of government and deliberative processes—which is not included in existing democracy datasets.

4. The Polity indexes were created by academic researchers who have rated most of the world's political regimes from 1800 to 2007 (Polity IV) for their level of democracy from full autocracies to full democracies, on a score of −10 to 10. See http://www.systemicpeace.org/polity/polity4.htm. The NGO-created Freedom House index, which assesses the political rights and civil liberties of every country, can be found at http://www.freedomhouse.org.

5. Hochstetler (2005) also briefly considers Argentina, Paraguay, and Uruguay; Mumme and Korzetz (1997) include a short study of Ecuador, Brazil, and Mexico.

References

Andean Center for Economics in the Environment. 2001. *Executive Profile of Environmental Management Andean Region*. Washington, D.C.: Inter-American Development Bank.

Asenjo, Rafael, Guillermo Espinoza, Fernando Valenzuela, and J. Jure. 2002. *Regional Policy Dialogue on Environmental Executive Profile of Environmental Management Subregion South Cone: Argentina, Brazil, Chile, Paraguay, Uruguay.* Washington, D.C.: Inter-American Development Bank.

Assetto, Valerie J., Eva Hajba, and Stephen P. Mumme. 2003. Democratization, Decentralization, and Local Environmental Policy Capacity: Hungary and Mexico. *Social Science Journal* 40 (2): 249–268.

Auer, Matthew. 2001. Energy and Environmental Politics in Post-corporatist Mexico. *Policy Studies Journal* 29 (3): 437–455.

Auer, Matthew R. 2004. Lessons from Leaders and Laggards: Appraising Environmental Reforms in Central and Eastern Europe and Russia. In *Restoring Cursed Earth: Appraising Environmental Policy Reforms in Eastern Europe and Russia,* ed. Matthew R. Auer, 1–35. Lanham, Md.: Rowman and Littlefield.

Baber, Walter F., and Robert V. Bartlett. 2005. *Deliberative Environmental Politics: Democracy and Ecological Rationality.* Cambridge, Mass.: MIT Press.

Baker, Mark, and Jonathan Kusel. 2003. *Community Forestry in the United States: Learning from the Past, Crafting the Future.* Washington, D.C.: Island Press.

Baker, Susan, and Petr Jehlicka. 1998. Dilemmas of Transition: The Environment, Democracy and Economic Reform in East Central Europe—An Introduction. *Environmental Politics* 7 (10): 1–27.

Berg, Marni. 1999. Environmental Protection and the Hungarian Transition. *Social Science Journal* 36 (2): 227–251.

Blackman, Allen. 2005. Colombia's Discharge Fee Program: Incentives for Polluters or Regulators? Discussion Paper 05–31. Washington, D.C.: Resources for the Future.

Botcheva, Liliana. 1996. Focus and Effectiveness of Environmental Activism in Eastern Europe: A Comparative Study of Environmental Movements in Bulgaria, Hungary, Slovakia, and Romania. *Journal of Environment & Development* 5 (3): 292–308.

Carmin, Joann, and Stacy D. VanDeveer. 2004. Enlarging EU Environmental: Central and Eastern Europe from Transition to Accession. *Environmental Politics* 13 (1): 3–24.

Carruthers, David. 2001. Environmental Politics in Chile: Legacies of Dictatorship and Democracy. *Third World Quarterly* 22 (3): 343–358.

Carvalho, Georgia O. 2000. The Politics of Indigenous Land Rights in Brazil. *Bulletin of Latin American Research* 19 (4): 461–478.

Crepaz, Markus M. L. 1995. Explaining National Variations of Air Pollution Levels: Political Institutions and their Impact on Environmental Policy-Making. *Environmental Politics* 4 (3): 391–414.

Darst, Robert G. 1997. The Internationalization of Environmental Protection in the USSR and its Successor States. In *The Internationalization of Environmental Protection,* ed. Miranda A. Schreurs and Elizabeth C. Economy, 97–133. Cambridge: Cambridge University Press.

Doherty, Brian, and Marius de Geus, eds. 1996. *Democracy and Green Political Thought: Sustainability, Rights, and Citizenship.* London: Routledge.

Dryzek, John S. 1997. *The Politics of the Earth: Environmental Discourses.* Oxford, UK: Oxford University Press.

Eckersley, Robyn. 1996. Greening Liberal Democracy: The Rights Discourse Revisited. In *Democracy and Green Political Thought: Sustainability, Rights, and Citizenship*, ed. Brian Doherty and Marius de Geus, 212–236. London: Routledge.

Eckersley, Robyn. 2004. *The Green State: Rethinking Democracy and Sovereignty*. Cambridge, Mass.: MIT Press.

Fagin, Adam. 1994. Environment and Transition in the Czech Republic. *Environmental Politics* 3 (3): 479–494.

Fischer, Frank. 2000. *Citizens, Experts, and the Environment: The Politics of Local Knowledge*. Durham: Duke University Press.

Foresta, Ronald. 1991. *Amazon Conservation in the Age of Development: The Limits of Providence*. Gainesville: University Press of Florida.

Friedman, Elisabeth Jay, Kathryn Hochstetler, and Ann Marie Clark. 2005. *Sovereignty, Democracy, and Global Civil Society: State-Society Relations at UN World Conferences*. Albany: SUNY Press.

Gleditsch, Nils Petter, and Bjørn Otto Sverdrup. 2002. Democracy and the Environment. In *Human Security and the Environment: International Comparisons*, ed. Edward A. Page and Michael Redclift, 45–70. Cheltenham, UK: Edward Elgar.

Goodman, David, and Michael Redclift, eds. 1991. *Environment and Development in Latin America: The Politics of Sustainability*. Manchester, UK: Manchester University Press.

Glushenkova, Helena I. 1999. Environmental Administrative Change in Russia in the 1990s. *Environmental Politics* 8 (2): 157–164.

Grupo Y'Guazú. 1995. *Bases para la Armonización de Exigencias Ambientales en el Mercosur*. Buenos Aires: FARN.

Hardin, Garrett. 1968. The Tragedy of the Commons. *Science* 162:1243–1248.

Haughney, Diane. 2006. *Neoliberal Economics, Democratic Transition, and Mapuche Demands for Rights in Chile*. Gainesville: University Press of Florida.

Heilbroner, Robert L. 1974. *An Inquiry into the Human Prospect*. New York: Norton.

Hochstetler, Kathryn. 2004. Civil Society in Lula's Brazil. Working Paper CBS-57-04. Oxford, UK: Centre for Brazilian Studies, University of Oxford.

Hochstetler, Kathryn. 2005. Race to the Middle: Environmental Politics in the Mercosur Free Trade Agreement. In *Handbook of Global Environmental Politics*, ed. Peter Dauvergne, 348–361. Cheltenham, UK: Edward Elgar.

Hochstetler, Kathryn, and Margaret E. Keck. 2007. *Greening Brazil: Environmental Activism in State and Society*. Durham: Duke University Press.

Hochstetler, Kathryn, and Melinda Laituri. 2005. Methods in International Environmental Politics. In *Palgrave Advances in International Environmental Politics*, ed. Michele M. Betsill, Kathryn Hochstetler, and Dimitris Stevis, 82–109. Basingstoke, UK: Palgrave MacMillan.

Hochstetler, Kathryn, and Stephen P. Mumme. 1998. Environmental Movements and Democracy in Latin America. In *Assessing Democracy in Latin America*, ed. Philip Kelly, 37–53. Boulder: Westview Press.

Hopkins, Jack W. 1995. *Policymaking for Conservation in Latin America: National Parks, Reserves, and the Environment*. Westport, Conn.: Praeger.

Hulme, David, and Marshall Murphree, eds. 2001. *African Wildlife and Livelihoods: The Promise and Performance of Community Conservation.* Oxford, UK: James Currey Ltd.

Instituto Brasileiro de Geografia e Estatistica. 2004. Fundações Privadas e Asociações. http://www.ibge.gov.br/home/estatistica/economia/fasfil/2005/default.shtm, accessed May 25, 2011.

Kaimowitz, David, Cristian Vallejos, Pablo B. Pacheco, and Raul Lopez. 1998. Municipal Governments and Forest Management in Lowland Bolivia. *Journal of Environment & Development* 7 (1): 45–59.

Kotov, Vladimir, and Elena Nikitina. 1993. Russia in Transition: Obstacles to Environmental Protection. *Environment* 35 (10): 10–20.

Kütting, Gabriela. 1999. *Environment, Society and International Relations—Towards More Effective International Agreements.* London: Routledge.

Lafferty, William, and James Meadowcroft, eds. 1996. *Democracy and the Environment: Problems and Prospects.* Cheltenham, UK: Edward Elgar.

Lemos, Maria Carmen, and João Lúcio Farias de Oliveira. 2004. Can Water Reform Survive Politics? Institutional Change and River Basin Management in Ceará, Northeast Brazil. *World Development* 32 (12): 2121–2137.

Li, Quan, and Rafael Reuveny. 2006. Democracy and Environmental Degradation. *International Studies Quarterly* 50 (4): 935–956.

Lipset, Seymour Martin. 1959. Some Social Requisites of Democracy: Economic Development and Political Legitimacy. *American Political Science Review* 53 (1): 69–105.

Mainwaring, Scott, Daniel Brinks, and Aníbal Pérez-Liñán. 2001. Classifying Political Regimes in Latin America, 1945–1999. *Studies in Comparative International Development* 36 (1): 37–65.

Marks, Gary, and Larry Diamond, eds. 1992. *Reexamining Democracy: Essays in Honor of Seymour Martin Lipset.* Newbury Park, Calif.: Sage Publications.

Massam, Bryan H., and Robert Earl-Goulet. 1997. Environmental Nongovernmental Organizations in Central and Eastern Europe: Contributions to Civil Society. *International Environmental Affairs* 9 (2): 127–147.

Matthews, Mary M. 2001. Cleaning Up Their Acts: Shifts of Environmental and Energy Policies in Pluralist and Corporatist States. *Policy Studies Journal* 29 (3): 478–499.

Maybury-Lewis, David, ed. 2002. *The Politics of Ethnicity: Indigenous Peoples in Latin American States.* Cambridge, Mass.: Harvard University Press.

Meadowcroft, James. 2004. Deliberative Democracy. In *Environmental Governance Reconsidered: Challenges, Choices, and Opportunities*, ed. Robert F. Durant, Daniel J. Fiorino, and Rosemary O'Leary, 183–217. Cambridge, Mass.: The MIT Press.

Midlarsky, Manus I. 1998. Democracy and the Environment: An Empirical Assessment. *Journal of Peace Research* 35 (3): 341–361.

Mumme, Stephen P., and Edward Korzetz. 1997. Democratization, Politics, and Environmental Reform in Latin America. In *Latin American Environmental Policy in International Perspective*, ed. Gordon J. MacDonald, Daniel L. Nelson, and Marc A. Stern, 40–59. Boulder: Westview.

Munck, Gerardo, and Richard Snyder. 2007. Debating the Direction of Comparative Politics: An Analysis of Leading Journals. *Comparative Political Studies* 40 (1): 5–31.

Neumayer, Eric. 2002. Do Democracies Exhibit Stronger International Environmental Commitment? A Cross-Country Analysis. *Journal of Peace Research* 39 (2): 139–164.

Oldfield, Jon. 1999. The Environmental Impact of Transition: A Case Study of Moscow City. *Geographical Journal* 165 (2): 222–231.

Ophuls, William. [1974] 2004. The Scarcity Society. In *Green Planet Blues: Environmental Politics from Stockholm to Johannesburg*, 3rd ed., ed. Ken Conca and Geoffrey D. Dabelko, 54–60. Boulder: Westview Press.

Paehlke, Robert. 1995. Environmental Values for a Sustainable Society: The Democratic Challenge. In *Greening Environmental Policy: The Politics of a Sustainable Future*, ed. Frank Fischer and Michael Black, 129–144. New York: St. Martin's Press.

Palacio Jiménez, María Cecilía. 2005. *Compilación de Normas Nacionales e Regionales sobre Medio Ambiente desde 1980 en Bolivia y Diagnóstico Sobre su Complimiento ante Autoridades Judiciales.* La Paz, Bolivia: Centro Boliviano de Estudios Multidisciplinarios.

Pavlínek, Petr, and John Pickles. 2004. Environmental Pasts/Environmental Futures in Post-Socialist Europe. *Environmental Politics* 13 (1): 237–265.

Payne, Rodger A. 1995. Freedom and the Environment. *Journal of Democracy* 6 (3): 41–55.

Pellegrini, Lorenzo, and Reyer Gerlagh. 2006. Corruption, Democracy, and Environmental Policy: An Empirical Contribution to the Debate. *Journal of Environment & Development* 15 (3): 332–354.

Pratt, Lawrence, and Pascal O. Girot. 2002. *Executive Profile for Regional Dialogue on the Environment: The Mesoamerican Sub-region.* Washington, DC: Inter-American Development Bank.

Press, Daniel. 1994. *Democratic Dilemmas in the Age of Ecology: Trees and Toxics in the American West.* Durham: Duke University Press.

Ray, James L. 1995. *Democracy and International Conflict: An Evaluation of the Democratic Peace Proposition.* Columbia: University of South Carolina Press.

Reid, Walter V., Osvaldo Lucon, Suani Teixeira Coelho, and Patricia Guardabassi. 2005. *No Reason to Wait: The Benefits of Greenhouse Gas Reduction in São Paulo and California.* Menlo Park, Calif.: Hewlett Foundation.

Ribot, Jesse C. 1999. Decentralisation, Participation and Accountability in Sahelian Forestry: Legal Instruments of Political-Administrative Control. *Africa* 69 (1): 23–65.

Roberts, J. Timmons, and Nikki D. Thanos. 2003. *Trouble in Paradise: Globalization and Environmental Crises in Latin America.* London: Routledge.

Russett, Bruce M. 1993. *Grasping the Democratic Peace: Principles for a Post–Cold War World.* Princeton: Princeton University Press.

Sawyer, Suzana. 2004. *Crude Chronicles: Indigenous Politics, Multinational Oil, and Neoliberalism in Ecuador.* Durham: Duke University Press.

Scruggs, Lyle. 2001. Is There Really a Link Between Neo-corporatism and Environmental Performance? Updated Evidence and New Data for the 1980s and 1990s. *British Journal of Political Science* 31 (4): 686–692.

Silva, Eduardo. 1996–1997. Democracy, Market Economics, and Environmental Policy in Chile. *Journal of Interamerican Studies and World Affairs* 38 (4): 1–33.

Steinberg, Paul F. 2001. *Environmental Leadership in Developing Countries: Transnational Relations and Biodiversity Policy in Costa Rica and Bolivia*. Cambridge, Mass.: MIT Press.

Steinberg, Paul F. 2005. From Public Concern to Policy Effectiveness: Civic Conservation in Developing Countries. *Journal of International Wildlife Law and Policy* 8 (4): 341–365.

Van Cott, Donna Lee, ed. 1994. *Indigenous Peoples and Democracy in Latin America*. New York: St. Martin's Press and the Inter-American Dialogue.

Weber, Edward P. 2000. A New Vanguard for the Environment: Grass-Roots Ecosystem Management as a New Environmental Movement. *Society & Natural Resources* 13 (3): 237–259.

Wettestad, Jørgen. 2006. The Effectiveness of Environmental Policies. In *Palgrave Advances in International Environmental Politics*, ed. Michele M. Betsill, Kathryn Hochstetler, and Dimitris Stevis, 299–328. Basingstoke, UK: Palgrave MacMillan.

Whitefield, Stephen. 2003. Russian Mass Attitudes Towards the Environment, 1993–2001. *Post-Soviet Affairs* 19 (2): 95–113.

9

Institutional Change in Authoritarian Regimes: Water and the State in Egypt

Jeannie Sowers

Egypt's Ministry of Water Resources and Irrigation is an imposing, multistory concrete building in Cairo, on the bank of the Nile River, surrounded by gates, with a small lawn and fountain on the interior.[1] It towers above the surrounding neighborhood of Imbaba, a densely populated district that attained notoriety in 1992 when the Mubarak regime besieged Islamic militants in its narrow streets. In the aftermath, the government tried to upgrade the area, providing piped water and sewage lines in a bid to forestall further unrest.

Egypt's irrigation system is one of the oldest in the world and has long required hierarchical public institutions to administer an extensive system of canals and dams dependent upon the flow of the Nile River. Centralized water management to sustain irrigated agriculture sparked a tradition in Western social science associating "hydraulic societies" with centralized bureaucracies and authoritarian rule (see, e.g., Wittfogel 1957). In the eighteenth and nineteenth centuries, social theorists from Montesquieu to Weber discussed governance in the Middle East and Asia in terms of "oriental despotism," while Marx termed the elaborate bureaucracies that evolved alongside extensive irrigation works the "Asiatic mode of production." Under such broad categories, Western social theorists lumped together irrigation-governance systems across what is now modern-day China, India, Iraq, and Egypt.

Until the uprisings that swept the Middle East and North Africa in early 2011, most social science accounts of politics in the Arab world focused on the centralization of decision making by ruling families, presidents, parties, or monarchs. State control over natural resources—whether oil or water—figured centrally in explanations for why political regimes sustained centralized, repressive rule over their societies.

If we step inside Egypt's Ministry of Water Resources and Irrigation, however, the dominant position of the ministry over the neighborhood, and of the central government over society in general, becomes less apparent. As in many other government agencies, resources and salaries are limited. Only a few elevators function, and government employees queue in the heat to avoid climbing flights of stairs.

Following the mass street protests that forced President Hosni Mubarak to resign, the faded portraits of Egypt's thirty-year ruler that long graced ministerial offices were removed, leaving battered furniture and tattered rugs. Even in the heat of summer, only the offices of high officials supported by international donor projects are air-conditioned and equipped with computers. Much of the work of ministry employees is not conducted in this building in Cairo, but is spread throughout the provinces as part of what we might term the "local state."[2]

As a glimpse inside the ministry suggests, an analytical focus confined to the central government is not adequate to capture the politics of environmental protection, which typically involves new forms of political coalitions and networks across different scales and multiple landscapes. As the editors of this volume argue, the creation and maintenance of environmental regulatory regimes typically involves multilevel governance shaped by institutions and networks within the state itself, between the state and various social groups, and across international institutions and transnational networks. This has also been the case in the authoritarian regimes of the Arab world, but has been less apparent given the opaque nature of policy making in these states.

Although authoritarian leaders have sometimes played dominant roles in shaping policy agendas, it is easy to "overstate the Arab state," attributing more authority and effectiveness in policy implementation than is actually warranted (Ayubi 1995). State bureaucracies have typically been overextended and underfunded, and local outcomes have rarely resembled those envisioned in the reams of centralized directives, plans, and reports issued in Cairo and other capitals. Ironically, then, though some scholars call for "reinstating the state" in the study of environmental politics (Barry and Eckersley 2005, ix), students of Middle East environmental politics must look beyond the central government to a broader range of actors and processes.

To understand environmental policy change in the region, we must disaggregate the state, paying attention to its manifestations at local levels and within the high ranks of the political elite and how both respond to popular mobilization and activism. Many developing countries have experimented with decentralization and devolution of governance to local communities, particular for resource management (Agrawal and Ostrom 2001; Ribot 2002; Agrawal, chapter 12, this volume). This chapter explores why efforts to promote more participatory and decentralized forms of water management in Egypt have stalled despite a long-term commitment to reform by international donors and leading Egyptian water experts.

From the standpoint of comparative environmental politics, Egypt poses some intriguing puzzles. Egypt has extensive laws and institutions for water management compared with other states in the Arab world and Africa (Gomaa 1997; Genena 2003, 17–18). Although these have been inadequate for addressing environmental problems, the causes for weak environmental capacities do not simply flow from weak institutions, a lack of funding, or an absence of commitment from top officials, as many analyses of environmental politics in developing countries tend to suggest.

Instead, Egypt's weak environmental performance shows that environmental reforms entail political challenges associated with the restructuring of existing rights and institutions. The problem is one of re-regulation and facilitating participation, rather than simply the creation of new forms of administrative capacity. Building environmental capacities is a recurring theme in the global environmental politics literature, especially in connection with developing countries (Haas, Keohane, and Levy 1993). Yet capacity-building efforts often encounter significant obstacles, in part because international donors underestimate the "stickiness" of existing institutional arrangements and the relations of power that these represent.

A growing literature has highlighted the catalytic role played by networks of environmental experts in setting environmental agendas (Haas 1990; Keck and Sikkink 1998; Steinberg 2001). These experts diagnose environmental harm and often propose specific solutions. But as the case of irrigation reform in Egypt shows, the elaboration and institutionalization of technical knowledge often abruptly encounters communities and agents of the local state, who often do not share the interests and policy preferences of leading officials and environmental experts. Thus the picture of monolithic authoritarian states with strong capacities to regulate society or even control the state apparatus is a poor starting point for understanding the dynamics of environmental politics in the Middle East.

Before analyzing the evolution of Egypt's water reforms in greater depth, this chapter situates the study of Middle East environmental politics in the broader context of comparative environmental politics. I discuss why empirical cases of Middle Eastern environmental politics have been largely absent from this emerging field of inquiry, even as the political and economic effects of natural resource exploitation have figured centrally in studies of Middle Eastern political economy.

Bringing the Middle East into Comparative Environmental Politics

The study of Middle East politics and environmental politics have danced past each other, preoccupied with different questions, approaches, and concerns. This lack of engagement stems from developments in the region and within the respective disciplines. The early and enduring focus of comparative environmental politics on social movements, green parties, and "postmaterial" green attitudes (discussed by Michael O'Neill in chapter 7 and Riley Dunlap and Richard York in chapter 4, this volume) did not travel well to the seemingly durable authoritarian regimes of the Middle East. In many Middle Eastern states, environmental social movements, reliable public opinion data, and transparent elections have been lacking. Governments repressed, contained, and where possible co-opted popular forms of collective action, while Islamists and other social movements framed popular mobilization as a quest for authenticity, social welfare, and freedom from external intervention. For environmental scholars, these concerns did not mesh with the postmaterial themes that characterized early environmental scholarship focused on the experiences of Europe and the United States.

An expanding literature on environmental politics in developing countries has likewise excluded much of the region. The growing numbers of case studies and regional surveys of environmental politics in Latin America, South Asia, and East Asia[3] has not been matched by equivalent work on the Middle East. Research in political ecology has drawn on agrarian studies and environmental history in sub-Saharan Africa and Southeast Asia, with little parallel in the Middle East.[4] Similarly, the lack of democratization in the Middle East has meant that the region has been overlooked in the burgeoning literature on the role of environmental movements in the democratic transitions of Central and Eastern Europe, the former Soviet Union, and Latin America.[5] Although emerging global environmental discourses such as "integrated water resource management" have figured prominently in environmental management efforts in the Middle East, studies of the diffusion and implementation of these ideas have generally excluded Middle Eastern cases.[6]

Sustained authoritarian rule, war, external interventions, and sanctions have limited access and information for researchers of Middle Eastern environmental politics. As a result, only a few countries in the region—including Israel, Egypt, Turkey, Tunisia, and Lebanon—attract and sustain significant communities of social scientists. Domestic restrictions on research inhibit field-based social and political inquiry, and regimes often deny or delay research clearances, forcing researchers to seek nongovernmental funding sources and to conduct research without official permission.

Environmental studies of the Middle East are further hindered by inflexible and overburdened education systems in much of the Arab world. In Egypt, for instance, university enrollments are allocated through a set of uniform secondary school exams (*thanawiyya amma*). Talented students are typically channeled into science and engineering, while spaces in the humanities and social sciences are filled with students who score less well. Social science as a discipline is generally neglected in publicly funded universities, in stark contrast with some other developing countries, such as India, where local scholars working in the field of subaltern and postcolonial studies successfully set new global agendas in the social sciences and humanities by the early 1980s.

There have been some recent and welcome exceptions to the lack of studies in Middle Eastern environmental politics. For Israel, the Palestinian territories, and Turkey, lively transnational communities and diasporas of scholars have produced interesting studies of environmental politics and history (Tal 2002; Alatout 2006;

Weinthal and Parag 2003; Adaman and Murat 2005). Egypt has seen some studies of environmental policy, environment and poverty in rural areas, and the politics of protected areas (Kishk 1997; Gomaa 1997; Henawi 2001; Zetter and Hassan 2002; Sowers 2007). Environmental historians have begun to mine rich colonial archives; Diana Davis, for instance, shows how French narratives of desertification and deforestation shaped post-colonial resource management in Morocco and North Africa (Davis 2004; 2006; 2007).

Although Middle Eastern cases are generally absent from the field of environmental studies, the relationship between natural resources and governance institutions has been an influential trend in comparative political studies of the Middle East. Flowing from political economy approaches—which illuminate how political power and institutions shape economic activity and class structure, and how economic structure and the distribution of wealth shape political processes—some scholars have focused on the political-economic consequences of the Middle East's endowments of ample oil and scarce water.

In 1970, Mahdavy published an influential article describing the deleterious effects of oil revenues on economic development in Iran. His study of Iran as a "rentier state"—that is, a state relying heavily on the export of natural resources as a principal source of income—marked one key focus of Middle East political study for the next three decades.[7] As the Middle East became the epicenter of the oil revolution, serving as the principal energy supplier for the industrialized countries in the decades after World War II, oil revenues generally went directly to the coffers of the state and to the elite that controlled it. State access to oil revenues was facilitated by direct ownership of the companies responsible for extraction, processing, and distribution of the resource or through royalty agreements with multinational consortiums.

The postwar period and creation of oil economies also saw the consolidation of authoritarian regimes across much of the Middle East. Some of these regimes were based on military rule, others on dominant political parties, and others adapted family and dynastic rule to modern states.[8] These new political regimes rapidly expanded the role and scope of the state in the economy and in the management of natural resources, following the Soviet model and the Keynesian interventions of the United States and Britain (Vitalis and Heydemann 2000). States such as Egypt, Algeria, Tunisia, and Iraq nationalized much of their private sectors, establishing state-owned sectors that dominated the economy. Oil-exporting states with small populations, including Saudi Arabia, Libya, and the small Gulf states, used oil revenues to rapidly acquire the organizational infrastructure of modern states in the course of decades rather than centuries.

Most scholars studying these trends in governance and revenue argue that oil rent helped sustain authoritarian rule. Income from oil fueled the creation of patronage networks loyal to the regime, freed rulers from bargaining with social groups over taxation, and financed the rapid expansion of state bureaucracies that crowded out private sector activity (Luciani 1990; Beblawi 1990; Crystal 1990; Karl 1997). Others, however, point out that the recycling of oil revenues in domestic and international economies helped create larger, well-capitalized private sectors. These business groups have played an increasing role in setting policy agendas through parliaments, informal networks, and formal associations (Okruhlik 1999; Moore 2004; Luciani 2005).

In the field of comparative politics, research soon expanded beyond the borders of the Middle East and beyond a focus on the oil sector. Oil revenues are only one form of rentier income; rulers capture rent from foreign aid, strategic location, and other resources such as timber, natural gas, and diamonds. Studies of the "resource curse" began to explore the impact of such rents in sub-Saharan Africa, Latin America, Russia, and Central Asia. This literature included broad cross-national comparisons using statistical techniques (Ross 2001a), in-depth comparative studies of selected cases using primarily qualitative approaches (Ross 2001b; Dauvergne 1997, 2001) and studies drawing on mixed methodologies (Luong and Weinthal 2006). Because the price of natural resource commodities is often volatile and resources such as timber can be rapidly exhausted, many of these studies found that cycles of boom and bust in resource revenues weakened efforts at building robust institutions and encouraged firms and state elites alike to rapidly and unsustainably exploit resources (Dauvergne 1997, 2001; Ross 2001b).

Back in the Middle East, scholars also focused on the politics of another natural resource: scarce water. Most studies of hydropolitics linked state interests with regional prospects for cooperation and conflict, analyzing interstate relations around the Jordan, the Nile, and the Tigris-Euphrates river basins (Waterbury 1979; Lowi 1993; Elmusa 1998; Waterbury 2002). Scholars also clarified how water scarcity is shaped by economic and institutional development: wealthier countries can afford to pursue solutions to water scarcity such as desalination, large-scale water transfer, and the purchase of "virtual water" through imports, while poorer countries have few alternatives (Allan 1994, 2001). Some scholars, drawing on postmodern approaches and the experience of the Israeli-Palestinian conflict, showed how technocratic discourses about water, ecology, and technology helped constitute unequal relations of power and unequal access to water (Selby 2003; Alatout 2006).

One recurrent question asked in the hydropolitics literature was why even relatively capable states seemed unable to proactively reform water management in the face of rising populations and static water supplies (Allan 2001; Ayeb 2004). The entwining of irrigated agriculture with ideologies of nationalism and state building provided one answer. State elites in Turkey, Israel, Egypt, Libya, Iraq, and Saudi Arabia have long portrayed land reclamation—the conversion of desert land to agriculture through irrigation—as an essential element of modern nationhood (Sowers 2011). Thus, instead of shifting water out of the agricultural sector, the largest sectoral consumer of water, many regimes continued to pursue new irrigation schemes.

In the study of Middle Eastern comparative politics, then, the politics and economics of natural resource management have received some attention from scholars interested in understanding domestic politics and interstate relations. However, even these scholars have generally overlooked emerging state and social interest in environmental issues. From the 1980s onward, shifts in the priorities of international donors, deteriorating air and water quality, and the interventions of environmental scientists introduced environmental discourses and regulatory practices to the Middle East. As Meadowcroft demonstrates (chapter 3, this volume), around the world states created new legal regimes, new environmental institutions, and new areas of policy intervention under the rubric of protecting the environment. Yet the politics of creating new environmental policy domains and restructuring "old" strategies of resource exploitation in the Middle East remains largely uncharted. In the remainder of the chapter, I analyze one such area of reform: attempts to restructure water management from state-controlled institutions toward more participatory user associations. International donors and Egyptian water planners have been at the forefront of articulating the need for such a shift. An examination of these reform efforts offers insights into the challenges of institutional reform in authoritarian and transitional regimes.

This chapter is based largely on material gathered through fieldwork in Egypt. I draw on interviews with water experts, ministry employees, and international donors intimately acquainted with policy reform efforts. I also rely upon unpublished reports, surveys, conference papers, and documents created by international donors, governmental ministries, and nongovernmental associations, in addition to published research.

Egypt's Water Dilemmas

Egypt's water situation has long attracted international attention because of its Malthusian combination of relatively fixed water supplies, a rapidly growing population, and increasing demands for water from a variety of users. Sources of freshwater are largely limited to the Nile River and renewable aquifers recharged by the river, which provides 96 percent of Egypt's water resources. Unlike more water-scarce areas of the Middle East, such as Yemen, Jordan, and Gaza and the West Bank, control over the Nile has allowed Egypt to avoid generalized water shortages, though localized shortages from distribution problems are frequent.

The construction of the Aswan High Dam, completed in 1970, enabled the central government to capture virtually the entire flow of the Nile River in the reservoir of

Lake Nasser and release it downstream in a controlled manner throughout the year. The dam provided Egypt with a semblance of water security, as Cairo controlled Nile discharge independently of other states and regularized flow through periods of flood and drought (Ayeb 2002).

The limits of this water regime, however, are rapidly approaching. Demand for water continues to increase from greater numbers of people and higher levels of consumption. Egypt's per-capita water availability is expected to decline from 845 m^3 per person per year in 2000 to 590 m^3 per person per year in 2025 (Sowers, Weinthal, and Vengosh 2010). Egypt's population is projected to increase from 80.4 million in 2010 to an estimated 103.6 million in 2025 (Population Reference Bureau 2011).

Irrigated agriculture claims approximately 86 percent of total water distributions, with 6 percent consumed by municipalities and 8 percent by industry. Agricultural production for some crops results in the highest yield per acre in the world, yet each year Egypt loses significant quantities of highly productive agricultural land in the Nile Delta due to urbanization. In the greater Cairo area, these losses have averaged 1,040 acres annually from 1972 to 2003 (Hereher 2006). Egypt has become the world's largest importer of wheat; food imports are the main source of virtual water and are essential to the survival of the population (Allan 2001). Skyrocketing food prices in 2007–2008 reinforced the Egyptian government's commitment to both reforming water institutions and pushing ahead with land reclamation schemes.

As per-capita water supplies diminish, water quality has also rapidly deteriorated. Between the Aswan High Dam and the outfalls to the Mediterranean Sea, the Nile river basin is essentially a closed system (Seckler 1992; Seckler and Moore 1993). In a closed hydrological basin, pollutants, pesticides, fertilizers, and salts accumulate as water is reused for a variety of activities. Thus contamination upstream affects multiple users and communities downstream. The principal sources of contamination to Egypt's fresh surface and groundwater sources are untreated municipal and industrial wastewater discharged to canals and agricultural drains, solid waste accumulation in and around waterways, and agricultural discharges from irrigation and agriculture. Egypt's success in extending water supplies to a growing population has intensified its water quality problems. Investments in wastewater treatment facilities for industry and municipal use have not kept pace, and pilot projects for unconventional treatment have not been widely supported (Zawahri, Sowers, and Weinthal 2011).

Irrigation "Reform," Institutional Change, and the Local State

Since the early 1980s, leading Egyptian water officials and international donors have highlighted the need to establish water user associations as part of broader packages of institutional reform for the irrigation and drainage system. Involving farmers in the operation of irrigation systems can increase the efficiency of irrigation deliveries, generate more reliable information about crop selection and water consumption, and help cover the operation and maintenance costs of irrigation and drainage infrastructure (Lowdermilk 1986; Ostrom 1990; World Bank 2007). Creating effective and sustainable user associations, however, has proven difficult in many countries (Groenfeldt and Svendsen 2000). Most early studies of the benefits of user associations focused on small-scale irrigation systems in relatively homogenous communities, not irrigation systems of the scale or level of complexity found in Egypt. Egypt's irrigation and drainage system is extensive and multilayered, supplying not only the agricultural sector but also the needs of major cities and industrial enterprises. The network includes 31,000 km of state-owned canals, 80,000 km of privately owned field channels, and 17,000 km of public drains (Abu Zeid 1995, 39).

Boone (2003) suggests a useful way to categorize governance institutions connecting the central government to the periphery. Following public policy studies, she distinguishes between the extent of spatial concentration or deconcentration of the state apparatus to localities and the extent to which authority is actually decentralized to local powerbrokers. The institutional arrangements governing Egypt's irrigation system have long been spatially deconcentrated to Egypt's provinces, with decision-making authority hierarchically administered through the various layers of the irrigation ministry and little participation from local users. Water releases from the Aswan High Dam to major canals are decided in Cairo, while in the subsidiary irrigation district (*markaz al-rai*), the irrigation engineer (*muhandis al-rai*) and local water gatekeeper (*bahari*) control releases of water to private canals at preset levels and on a fixed rotation schedule (Radwan 1997, 1998; Moustafa 2007).

The Ministry of Water Resources and Irrigation is supposed to fulfill numerous central and local functions beyond the allocation of water. Distinct departments cover irrigation, drainage, groundwater, mechanical work, and electrical work. Each department, in turn, subdivides the country geographically into hierarchically descending units of general directorates, inspectorates, and districts. The boundaries of these "local" units of irrigation administration are not coterminous across different ministerial departments, nor do they correspond with the provincial designations used by central government for purposes of planning and financial transfers.

The ministry, like other government agencies in Egypt, is overstaffed and underfunded, resulting in underinvestment in the irrigation and drainage system. State expenditures in the water sector have been reduced as part of the government's goal of contracting public investment to address financial deficits. In recent years, public financing for operation and maintenance within the irrigation sector amounted to

4 percent of total public expenditures in Egypt, and measures for "cost recovery" from irrigation users have figured increasingly on the government's agenda (World Bank 2007, 14).

The "liberalization" of the agricultural sector undertaken during the 1980s posed new and acute challenges for centralized water management. The government stopped issuing directives on what farmers could grow and at what price, with the exception of quotas for water-intensive crops such as cotton, rice, and sugarcane. The government withdrew from setting crop prices and acreage quotas, slashed subsidies for inputs such as fertilizer and pesticides, and eliminated controls on land rents and tenancy arrangements. These policy measures created significant variations in cropping patterns, in turn producing highly variable demands for irrigation water. Legal restrictions on rental prices for land, designed to grant small farmers security in tenancy, were also lifted. The result has been reconsolidation of land holdings and dispossession of small-scale tenant farmers (Bush 2002).

At the same time that water demands from users changed in ways that the ministry could not accurately predict, extreme variability in climate and Nile flows exacerbated water management challenges. A prolonged drought during the 1980s in upstream states led to critically low Nile flow. In contrast, record high Nile flows in the second half of the 1990s forced water planners to release excess water from behind the Aswan High Dam into Egypt's western desert.

The rigid and centralized structure of the irrigation system was thus increasingly unable to deliver adequate water, at the right times, to the *fellahiin* (peasants) or to agribusiness, leading to costly losses in the agricultural sector. As one Egyptian resource economist described the management system, the ministry's management tools "relied on structural works and forced quotas to run a complex system with rigid supply even to handle severe drought, rising needs, deteriorating irrigation-drainage networks, lack of proper utilization, and degenerating water quality" (Khouzam 1994, 3.1). Many farmers increasingly used mobile diesel pumps to access poor-quality water in shallow aquifers and drainage canals in an attempt to compensate for variable, polluted, and inadequate water supplies (Abu Zeid and Abdel-Meguid 2007).

In response to these problems, bilateral and multilateral donors sponsored a number of pilot projects to rehabilitate the irrigation network and involve user associations in maintaining and operating upgraded infrastructure.[9] During the 1980s, for instance, the US Agency for International Development sponsored the "Irrigation Improvement Project" in selected areas of the Nile Delta, which initially focused on the level of privately owned field channels (USAID 1999). The goal was to provide farmers with a continuous flow of water in the canals, new technology to access and control this flow, and the creation of user associations to negotiate local distribution schedules and arbitrate conflicts. The *mesqa* associations, which included up to two hundred farmers, were considered to have performed well in improving both efficiency and equity of water deliveries (Ministry of Water Resources and Irrigation 2005, 20). This approach—investing in the rehabilitation of the irrigation and drainage system while creating user associations—was extended to other agricultural areas in projects funded by the World Bank and the Japanese International Cooperation Agency (Shalby, Gamal and Ali 2004, 115).

Donors and top officials at the ministry also began to promote the notion of integrated water resource management (IWRM). Integrated water management emphasizes expert coordination among different users and sectors, the decentralization of water management to the lowest practical level (the principle of subsidiarity), and the valuation of water according to multiple social, ecological, and economic criteria. Over the past two decades, IWRM has become the dominant global paradigm for water management (Conca 2006). Egyptian water planners, such as former Minister of Irrigation Mahmoud Abu Zeid, figured prominently in diffusing international norms of IWRM (Sowers 2008).

By the early 1990s, donors and leading officials at the Ministry of Water Resources and Irrigation attempted to apply IWRM by undertaking pilot projects to establish water user associations at higher levels of the irrigation system—from the local *mesqa* (field channel) associations to larger branch canal associations. Branch canals serve large, heterogeneous communities of users, ranging from one thousand to ten thousand persons. For the branch canal elections, donors focused on establishing transparent electoral processes that included the representation of industrial and municipal sectors as well as agricultural interests. By 2011, Egyptian and international consultancies, financed by the international donors, established approximately one thousand user associations (or "water boards") at the branch canal level, as shown in table 9.1.

Table 9.1
Egypt's irrigation system and user associations

Canal (from smallest to largest)	Ownership	User associations
marwa (field ditch)	private (individual/family)	N/A
mesqa (field channel or tertiary canal)	private (communal)	Estimated 9,900 user associations in 2009
branch/secondary canal (covering 500–700 hectares)	public (Ministry of Water Resources and Irrigation)	1,000 elected water boards for branch canals established between 1995 and 2009
main/primary canal	public (Ministry of Water Resources and Irrigation)	6 pilot boards established by 2009 for primary canals

Elected Associations in an Authoritarian System

Elections for the branch canal associations took place in a political system that the Mubarak regime manipulated to ensure dominance of the government's National Democratic Party. Parliamentary elections were marred by fraud and violence, and participation declined as voters became disenchanted with the government's flagrantly rigged outcomes. Elections for branch canal associations were thus exceptional exercises in relatively open democratic contestation during the Mubarak period. As one consultant involved in establishing user associations recalled in 2008, "The water board elections exposed the supposedly 'democratic' elections put on by the regime. There were lots of sly jokes comparing the water board elections with the lack of true elections at the local, parliamentary, and national levels."[10]

The contrasts between water user elections and the government's staging of national and municipal elections were stark. Second and third rounds of elections for the branch canals produced significant rotations of power; in some branch canals, voters ousted two-thirds of the existing delegates and the leadership.[11] Moreover, women often won seats reserved for municipal representation on the branch canal boards. These delegates raised issues of water pollution long considered outside the customary purview of local irrigation officials. These concerns included the accumulation of trash in canals and the lack of alternative disposal sites for solid waste, criticism of municipalities for discharging sewage directly into drainage canals, and requests for funds to repair septic tanks, finance hand pumps, and dig deeper wells to avoid contaminated water supplies.[12]

Donor projects focused on building the organizational capacity of these associations, partly through incentives to sustain interest and participation from farmers. Consultants urged the irrigation ministry to contract directly with users associations—rather than with private contractors unconnected to the locality—for operation and maintenance tasks. They also helped the ministry employ association members as record keepers and violation inspectors. Farmers in branch canal associations began to use their elected boards to resolve conflicts over irrigation deliveries (Abu Zeid and Abdel-Meguid 2007, 17).

By 2006, however, donor assessments of the branch canal associations identified a disturbing trend. Although elected water boards demonstrated specific organizational capacities (retention of members, contributions of work and time, record keeping, transparency of funds and operations), the ministry did not include them in irrigation and drainage decisions (Radwan, Bron, and Barakat 2006, 12). These findings held across all areas of irrigation decision-making, including maintenance, water distribution, finance, and administration, even though in some regions user associations had been in operation for more than a decade.

Encountering the "High" State and the "Local" State

Why did efforts to promote participatory management in irrigation falter? Water experts and donors focused on creating incentives for water users to participate in associations, but could not overcome resistance from two key groups within the state: the political elite at the Cabinet level, and representatives of the "local state"—the mid- and lower-level employees of the ministry deconcentrated throughout the provinces. Neither of these was interested in shared, substantive participatory devolution of authority to elected user associations. As one irrigation engineer observed in May 2011, "The government still doesn't trust sharing power with user associations." Experiments in participatory management could also not overcome significant institutional barriers that segregated different aspects of water governance under different government ministries. To give but one example, while the Ministry of Water Resources and Irrigation was responsible for irrigation deliveries, water quality was the province of the Ministry of Housing and its affiliated sanitation and drinking water companies.

The legal foundation for establishing water user associations was initially established by an administrative decree from the Minister of Water Resources and Irrigation, a common approach in Egypt for promulgating administrative law.[13] User associations at the *mesqa* level were later legally ratified as juridical persons through parliamentary vote, which granted them authority to collect fees from members and sanction violations (World Bank 2004). Donors and the ministry sought similar amendments to recognize branch canal associations as legal entities.[14] Although work on the relevant legislative amendments began in 1998, by 2011 the revisions to Law 12/1984 had still not been issued by Egypt's Parliament, the *Majlis al-Sha'ab*. Instead, the revised legislation was stalled in opaque inter-ministerial and Cabinet discussions. One long-term Egyptian consultant to the ministry concluded that "the government sees the water users associations as threatening because they are elected, they constitute institutions that could rival local political/administrative structures, particularly because water is becoming an increasingly scarce resource."[15]

As legal recognition of branch canal associations remained stalled, another set of obstacles emerged from the perceptions and practices of local and midlevel employees of the ministry. In theory, irrigation officials could engage the elected water boards in various forms of irrigation participation (notifying, consulting, or negotiating specific decisions with user associations) even without legal recognition. Yet assessments revealed that water boards were rarely informed, let alone consulted, by irrigation officials (Radwan et al. 2006).

In surveys and workshops convened by the ministry, provincial officials suggested that the role of water boards was primarily to serve the ministry by carrying out mundane, labor-intensive tasks. In the words of one project staff member, these officials considered the water boards "unpaid labor for the ministry."[16] Lower-level officials frequently expressed mistrust of the user associations, arguing that they lacked technical expertise and sometimes organized against actions and decisions taken by the ministry itself (Radwan et al. 2006, 18). This mobilization was seen as "irresponsible," indicative of users' ignorance, inexperience, and particularistic interests, rather than as a legitimate function for representatives of community-based organizations.[17]

The devolution of authority to the water user associations thus stalled in spite of sustained donor funding, well-staffed projects, and strong commitment from leading water officials. Reform efforts focused on creating incentives for farmer participation, but little attention was given to restructuring incentives for employees of the local state, building political support within the cabinet, or establishing mechanisms for other ministries to take seriously the input of the water boards. While the upper echelons of the ministry and donor agencies regarded water associations as a step toward broader institutional reform and future "partners in resource management," these perceptions were not shared by mid- and lower-level irrigation officials (Radwan et al. 2006, 13). They were also not shared by the Mubarak regime, which was threatened by the creation of more participatory institutions. Branch canal associations, designed to represent larger, more diverse electoral constituencies than the small *mesqa* associations, represented more democratic contestation than the government was prepared to countenance.

Conclusion

Environmental issues in the Middle East are part of daunting developmental challenges. The region's environmental problems are acute and extend far beyond water scarcity, the most widely recognized environmental problem in the region. Desertification, climate change, the diminishing quantity and quality of water and agricultural land, increasing population, hazardous levels of urban air pollution, inadequate sanitation, and insufficient controls on industrial pollution all have significant consequences for human health, economic growth, and the functioning of ecosystems. Egypt and other Middle Eastern countries thus have significant incentives to enact substantive environmental reforms. Yet little research has explored the formulation and implementation of environmental initiatives in the region. This dearth of research mirrors the lack of attention to public policy and the politics of everyday governance in the Arab world more generally.

Just as Egypt has encountered many of the shared ecological challenges facing the Middle East, it has also shared in a broader regional "architecture" of authoritarian rule (United Nations Development Program 2005, 15–18). As in many other states in the region, this architecture has consisted of concentrated power in the executive apparatus of the state, controlled by a relatively small circle of decision makers. In practice, however, centralized directives and plans have rarely matched outcomes, influenced instead by different layers of the state apparatus, a variety of informal networks, and local mobilizations.

In this chapter, I have argued that attempts to restructure Egypt's irrigation system provide an illuminating case to explore institutional reform under systems of authoritarian rule. Despite long-term commitments by external donors and environmental experts to participatory irrigation management, user associations foundered in light of opposition from the highest levels of the government and from employees of the local state. Authority over irrigation and drainage remained vested in a spatially deconcentrated structure that relied on hierarchical decision making exercised by local state agents. Moreover, although leading officials in the Ministry of Irrigation and Water Resources promoted integrated resource management, water governance remains fragmented into sectors such as potable water, sanitation, and water quality, under the authority of other governmental ministries and agencies. These institutions have little incentive to engage with user associations promoted by international donors through the water ministry.

These outcomes were part of a broader pattern in the region. States like Egypt sought to enhance their formal environmental capacities, often through the assistance of international donors, in ways that accommodated the central institutions of authoritarian rule.[18] These accommodations, in turn, undermined and constrained the efficacy of top-down environmental reforms (Sowers 2007). Understanding these dynamics of institutional reform requires focusing our analytical attention upward and outward—upward to the highest level of the regime, and outside the capital to appreciate the ways in which the state apparatus is articulated in the provinces.

As this chapter has shown, environmental reforms are often best understood as complex projects of re-regulation—taking place in settings that are crowded with institutional commitments and associated power struggles—rather than as novel regulatory initiatives. The expansion of bureaucratic power that characterized the development of Middle Eastern authoritarian regimes in the 1950s and 1960s led to extensive, inefficient bureaucracies and increasing demands on limited state resources. As a result, state and donor initiatives in subsequent decades emphasized institutional transformation under the rubrics of decentralization, privatization, and other kinds of state contraction, yet without disrupting the political logics of patrimonial rule embedded in these institutions.

Egypt's experience in promoting user associations highlights the limitations of relying on external aid, interventions, and experts to produce substantive institutional change. Much of the literature in global environmental politics rather reflexively calls for capacity building without clarifying under what conditions aid interventions can be sustainable and appropriate. The small but growing literature evaluating the effectiveness of environmental aid has begun to offer correctives (Keohane and Levy 1996; Weinthal and Parag 2003; Hicks, Parks, Roberts, and Tierney 2008). One such condition is an enabling external environment. Unlike the situation in Eastern Europe and Turkey, where the EU accession process ensured external pressure for civil rights and upward harmonization of environmental standards (Cook 2007; Andonova and VanDeveer, chapter 11, this volume), donors working in the poorer countries of the Arab world did not impose environmental conditionalities. Instead, environmental aid served as another form of external income, or rent, to selected institutions within the government (Sowers 2003). As is emphasized in the literature on rentier states, forms of external income, whether from natural resources or foreign aid, often sustain exclusionary forms of policy-making by financing projects that require little local engagement.

At the same time, comparative politics approaches to the Middle East would benefit greatly from engagement with emerging avenues of inquiry in environmental politics. Most political analysis of the Middle East has been preoccupied with the prospects for and hindrances to democratization, focusing on how regimes limited contestation and participation in formal political institutions. This scholarly preoccupation, though important in its own right, has crowded out inquiry about the formulation and implementation of public policies that broadly affect populations in the Middle East. Insights from comparative environmental politics can encourage Middle East scholars to focus on emerging multilevel forms of governance and the role of nonstate actors—such as communities, advocacy organizations, firms, and activist networks—in shaping policy agendas and the provision of public services.

The popular uprisings that spread across the region in the spring of 2011 threw such issues into sharp relief. Following popular protests in Tunisia that resulted in the flight of long-time ruler Zine Ben Ali, Egypt saw eighteen days of mass street protest that forced the resignation and detention of Mubarak and the assumption of power by a military council. These events catalyzed a process of political transformation in which the fundamental character of the political regime is in question. The January 25 revolution, as it is termed in Egypt, swept away entrenched fear and deference, not only toward the despised internal security apparatus of the state, but also toward the circles of elite officials and businessmen that had previously seemed above accountability. With arrests of high-profile businessmen, the dissolution of the government's ruling party, and promised elections for the parliament and presidency, forms of political engagement have proliferated across the country.

One promising area of inquiry for Middle East scholars may thus be comparative environmental movements, reviewed by Kate O'Neill (chapter 5, this volume). Environmental protest, like other forms of mobilization, was constrained under the Mubarak regime by the insecurity of civil and political rights under draconian Emergency Laws. Nevertheless, as with other forms of protest, environmental campaigns had begun to take root in Egypt before the uprisings. In 2008, for instance, protest against a large fertilizer plant to be built by foreign investors in Egypt's port city of Damietta spread to an unusually broad coalition of social and governmental actors ranging from local businessmen to journalists to parliamentarians (Elmusa and Sowers 2009).

As activists experiment with a variety of formal and informal strategies of political engagement, we can expect several kinds of environmental politics to become more salient. The first is local contestation around issues that affect the everyday quality of life in urban neighborhoods and the urbanizing countryside. Environmental issues will emerge in terms of demands for critical public services such as solid waste collection, sanitation, and equitable water provision. The need for effective conflict resolution and coordination mechanisms at various levels of the irrigation system will only intensify.

The second will be broader calls for restructuring systems of rent allocation derived from natural resources such as land, water, and fossil fuels. One of the most important means of generating revenue in Egypt has been the sale and transfer of land, particularly land provided with water infrastructure. One of the first actions of Egypt's military junta was to halt and review major allocations of land, part of a broader attempt to respond to popular anger over crony capitalism while shielding the junta's own personnel from scrutiny in fostering speculative land markets. Environmental politics in the Middle East will continue to be shaped by the politics of rent generation and allocation, but rent more broadly conceived in terms of land and water assets. The intersection of expanded participatory politics and restructured systems of rent will ensure that Middle Eastern environmental politics remains a fascinating field of inquiry for students of comparative politics.

Notes

1. The ministry has undergone a number of name changes over the years but is popularly known as *Wizarat al-Rai*, the Ministry of Irrigation.

2. This term has a long trajectory in political geography and public administration (Duncan and Goodwin 1988; Goodwin, Duncan, and Halford 1993); here I use it to refer to the local presence of central government ministries at the provincial (governorate) and municipal levels, rather than local governments.

3. In a rapidly growing field, see the excellent books by Gadgil and Guha (2001); Economy (2004); and Hochstetler and Keck (2007).

4. For an overview of political ecology, including a compilation of key field studies, see Robbins 2004.

5. For a sample of this literature, see the discussions by Hochstetler (chapter 8) and Andonova and VanDeveer (chapter 11) in this volume, as well as Auer 2004; Hochstetler and Mumme 1998; Carruthers 2001; Pavlinek and Pickles 2000; and Carmin and VanDeveer 2005.

6. For instance, Conca's book *Governing Water* (2006) includes extensive case studies of Brazil and South Africa yet no discussion of the Middle East, the most water-scarce region in the world.

7. Some of the most interesting studies of rentier states in the Middle East include Beblawi 1990; Crystal 1990; Karl 1997; Chaudhry 1997; Okruhlik 1999; and Luciani 1990 and 2005.

8. The growth of authoritarian regimes and expansion of bureaucratic power is summarized nicely in relevant chapters of Richards and Waterbury 2007; Ayubi 1995; and Owen 2004.

9. Primary funders of Egypt's irrigation "reforms" have included the United States Agency for International Development, the World Bank, the Royal Dutch Embassy, and the German aid agency GTZ.

10. Author's interview with consultant, Branch Canal Water Boards Project, the Ministry of Water Resource and Irrigation, Cairo, June 5, 2007.

11. Author's interview with consultant, Branch Canal Water Boards Project, the Ministry of Water Resource and Irrigation, Cairo, June 8, 2007.

12. Author's interview with project manager, Branch Canal Water Boards Project, Ministry of Water Resource and Irrigation, Cairo, June 6, 2007.

13. For branch canals, see Ministerial Decree No. 28, January 28, 1999.

14. The two primary laws concerned with irrigation and drainage are Law No. 12 of 1984 and Law No. 312 of 1994.

15. Author's interview with consultant, Branch Canal Water Boards Project, the Ministry of Irrigation and Water Resources, Cairo, June 5, 2007.

16. Author's interview with project manager, Branch Canal Water Boards Project, Ministry of Irrigation and Water Resources, Cairo, June 6, 2007.

17. Author's interview with consultant, Branch Canal Water Boards Project, Ministry of Irrigation and Water Resources, Cairo, June 5, 2007.

18. Heydemann (2004, 2007) provides a good overview of how Arab regimes have adapted economic and political liberalization to "upgrade" the institutions of authoritarian rule.

References

Abu Zeid, Khaled, and Amr Abdel Meguid. 2007. *Water Conflicts and Conflict Management Mechanisms in the Middle East and North Africa.* Cairo: Centre for Environment and Development for the Arab Region and Europe.

Abu Zeid, Mahmoud. 1995. Major Policies and Programs for Irrigation Drainage and Water Resources Development in Egypt. *Options Méditerranéennes*, Sér. B, No. 9, Egyptian Agriculture Profile. http://ressources.ciheam.org/om/pdf/b09/CI950934.pdf, accessed May 25, 2011.

Adaman, Fikret, and Arsel Murat. 2005. *Environmentalism in Turkey: Between Democracy and Development?* Burlington, Vt.: Ashgate.

Agrawal, Arun, and Elinor Ostrom. 2001. Collective Action, Property Rights, and Decentralization in Resource Use in India and Nepal. *Politics & Society* 29 (4): 485–514.

Alatout, Samer. 2006. Towards a Bio-territorial Conception of Power: Territory, Population, and Environmental Narratives in Palestine and Israel. *Political Geography* 25 (6): 601–621.

Allan, John Anthony. 1994. Evolving Water Demands and National Development Options. In *The Nile: Sharing a Scarce Resource*, ed. Paul Howell and John Allan, 301–311. Cambridge, UK: Cambridge University Press.

Allan, John Anthony. 2001. *The Middle East Water Question: Hydropolitics and the Global Economy*. London: I. B. Tauris.

Auer, Matthew, ed. 2004. *Restoring Cursed Earth: Appraising Environmental Policy Reforms in Eastern Europe and Russia*. New York: Rowman and Littlefield.

Ayeb, Habib. 2002. Hydraulic Politics: The Nile and Egypt's Water Use: A Crisis for the Twenty-first Century? In *Counter-revolution in Egypt's Countryside*, ed. Ray Bush, 76–100. London: Zed Books.

Ayeb, Habib. 2004. Free-market Water Management: The Egyptian Hydraulic Crisis Amidst Peasant Poverty. In *Securing Land and Resource Rights in Africa: Pan-African Perspectives*, ed. Munyaradzi Saruchera, 75–84. Belleville, South Africa: University of the Western Cape.

Ayubi, Nazih. 1995. *Overstating the Arab State*. London: I. B. Tauris.

Barry, John, and Robin Eckersley. 2005. *The State and the Global Ecological Crisis*. Cambridge, Mass.: MIT Press.

Beblawi, Hazem. 1990. The Rentier State in the Arab World. In *The Arab State*, ed. Giacomo Luciani, 85–98. Berkeley: University of California Press.

Boone, Catherine. 2003. *Political Topographies of the African State*. Cambridge: Cambridge University Press.

Bush, Ray. 2002. Land Reform and Counter-Revolution. In *Counter-Revolution in Egypt's Countryside*, ed. Ray Bush, 3–31. London: Zed Books.

Carmin, JoAnn, and Stacy D. VanDeveer, eds. 2005. *EU Enlargement and the Environment: Institutional Change and Environmental Policy in Central and Eastern Europe*. New York: Routledge.

Carruthers, David. 2001. Environmental Politics in Chile: Legacies of Dictatorship and Democracy. *Third World Quarterly* 22 (3): 343–358.

Chaudhry, Kiren. 1997. *The Price of Wealth*. Ithaca: Cornell University Press.

Crystal, Jill. 1990. *Oil and Politics in the Gulf: Rulers and Merchants in Kuwait and Qatar*. Cambridge: Cambridge University Press.

Conca, Ken. 2006. *Governing Water: Contentious Transnational Politics and Global Institution Building*. Cambridge, Mass.: MIT Press.

Cook, Steven. 2007. *Ruling But Not Governing: The Military and Political Development in Egypt, Algeria, and Turkey*. Baltimore: Johns Hopkins University.

Dauvergne, Peter. 1997. *Shadows in the Forest: Japan and the Politics of Timber in Southeast Asia*. Cambridge, Mass.: MIT Press.

Dauvergne, Peter. 2001. *Loggers and Degradation in the Asia-Pacific*. Cambridge: Cambridge University Press.

Davis, Diana. 2004. Desert "Wastes" of the Maghreb: Desertification Narratives in French Colonial Environmental History of North Africa. *Cultural Geographies* 11:359–387.

Davis, Diana. 2006. Neoliberalism, Environmentalism, and Agricultural Restructuring in Morocco. *Geographical Journal* 172 (2): 88–105.

Davis, Diana. 2007. *Resurrecting the Granary of Rome: Environmental History and French Colonial Expansion in North Africa*. Athens: Ohio University Press.

Duncan, Simon, and Mark Goodwin. 1988. *The Local State and Uneven Development*. Cambridge: Polity Press.

Economy, Elizabeth. 2004. *The River Runs Black: The Environmental Challenge to China's Future*. Ithaca: Cornell University Press.

Elmusa, Sharif. 1998. *Water Conflict: Economics, Politics, Law and Palestinian-Israeli Water Resources*. Washington, D.C.: Institute for Palestine Studies.

Elmusa, Sharif, and Jeannie Sowers. 2009. Damietta Mobilizes for Its Environment. *Middle East Report Online*. http://www.merip.org/mero/mero102109, accessed June 8, 2011.

Gadgil, Madhav, and Ramachandra Guha. 2001. *The Use and Abuse of Nature*. Oxford, UK: Oxford University Press.

Genena, Tareq. 2003. A Consultant Report on the Country Environmental Analysis. Unpublished manuscript, EcoConserve Consulting, Cairo.

Gomaa, Salwa Sharawi. 1997. *Environmental Policy-Making in Egypt*. Cairo: The American University in Cairo.

Goodwin, Mark, Simon Duncan, and Susan Halford. 1993. Regulation Theory, the Local State and the Transition of Urban Politics. *Environment and Planning. D, Society & Space* 11 (1): 67–88.

Groenfeldt, David, and Mark Svendsen. 2000. *Case Studies in Participatory Irrigation Management*. Washington, D.C.: World Bank.

Haas, Peter. 1990. *Saving the Mediterranean*. New York: Columbia University Press.

Haas, Peter, Robert Keohane, and Marc Levy, eds. 1993. *Institutions for the Earth: Sources of Effective International Environmental Protection*. Cambridge, Mass.: MIT Press.

Henawi, Essam. 2001. *Qadiyaat al-Bii'a wal Tanmiyya fi Misr*. Cairo: Dar Al-Shurouq.

Hereher, Mohamed El-Desoky. 2006. Monitoring Spatial and Temporal Changes of Agricultural Lands in the Nile Delta and Their Implications on Soil Characteristics Using Remote Sensing. Unpublished PhD dissertation. Department of Soil, Water, and Environmental Science, University of Arizona.

Heydemann, Steven. 2004. *Networks of Privilege in the Middle East: The Politics of Economic Reform Revisited*. New York: Palgrave.

Heydemann, Steven. 2007. *Upgrading Authoritarianism in the Arab World*. Washington, D.C.: Saban Center for Middle East Policy, Brookings Institution.

Hicks, Robert, Bradley Parks, J. Timmons Roberts, and Michael J. Tierney. 2008. *Greening Aid? Understanding the Environmental Impacts of Development Assistance*. Oxford: Oxford University Press.

Hochstetler, Kathryn, and Margaret Keck. 2007. *Greening Brazil: Environmental Activism in State and Society*. Durham: Duke University Press.

Hochstetler, Kathryn, and Stephen Mumme. 1998. Democracy and the Environment in Latin America. In *Assessing Democracy in Latin America*, ed. Philip Kelly, 37–53. Boulder: Westview Press.

Karl, Terry. 1997. *The Paradox of Plenty: Oil Booms and Petro-States*. Berkeley: University of California Press.

Keck, Margaret E., and Kathryn Sikkink. 1998. *Activists Beyond Borders: Advocacy Networks in International Politics*. Ithaca: Cornell University Press.

Keohane, Robert, and Marc Levy, eds. 1996. *Institutions for Environmental Aid*. Cambridge, Mass.: MIT Press.

Khouzam, Raouf. 1994. Strategic Water Planning: An Exercise Case Study of Egypt. Paper presented at VIII IWRA World Congress on Water Resources, November 21–25, Cairo.

Kishk, Mohamed Atef. 1997. Poverty of Environment and Environment of Poverty. Proceedings of the National Symposium on Poverty and Environmental Degradation in Rural Egypt, October 20–22, Cairo.

Lowdermilk, Max K. 1986. Improved Irrigation Management: Why Involve Farmers? In *Irrigation Management in Developing Countries: Current Issues and Approaches*, ed. Kenneth C. Nobe and Rajan K. Sampath, 427–456. Boulder: Westview.

Lowi, Miriam. 1993. *Water and Power: The Politics of a Scarce Resource in the Jordan River Basin*. Cambridge, UK: Cambridge University Press.

Luciani, Giacomo. 1990. Allocation Versus Production States: A Theoretical Framework. In *The Rentier State*, ed. Hazem Beblawi and Giacomo Luciani, 65–84. London: Croom Helm.

Luciani, Giacomo. 2005. Oil and Political Economy in the International Relations of the Middle East. In *International Relations of the Middle East*, ed. Louise Fawcett, 81–102. New York: Oxford University Press.

Luong, Pauline Jones, and Erika Weinthal. 2006. Rethinking the Resource Curse: Ownership Structure, Institutional Capacity, and Domestic Constraints. *Annual Review of Political Science* 9 (1): 241–263.

Mahdavy, Hossein. 1970. The Patterns and Problems of Economic Development in Rentier States: The Case of Iran. In *Studies in the Economic History of the Middle East*, ed. M. A. Cook, 428–467. London: Oxford University Press.

Ministry of Water Resources and Irrigation. 2005. *Integrated Water Resources Management Plan for Egypt*. Cairo: Ministry of Water Resources and Irrigation.

Moore, Peter. 2004. *Doing Business in the Middle East: Politics and Economic Crisis in Jordan and Kuwait*. Cambridge, UK: Cambridge University Press.

Moustafa, Tamir. 2007. *The Struggle for Constitutional Power: Law, Politics, and Economic Development in Egypt*. Cambridge: Cambridge University Press.

Okruhlik, Gwenn. 1999. Rent Wealth, Unruly Law, and Rise of the Opposition: Political Economy of Oil States. *Comparative Politics* 3 (3): 295–315.

Ostrom, Elinor. 1990. *Governing the Commons: The Evolution of Institutions for Collective Action*. New York: Cambridge University Press.

Pavlinek, Petr, and John Pickles. 2000. *Environmental Transitions: Transformations and Ecological Defense in Central and Eastern Europe*. London: Routledge.

Population Reference Bureau. 2011. http://www.prb.org/Datafinder/Geography/Data.aspx?category=10&region=10&region_type=2, accessed June 1, 2011.

Radwan, Lutfi. 1997. Farmer Responses to Inefficiencies in the Supply and Distribution of Irrigation Requirements in Delta Egypt. *Geographical Journal* 163 (1): 78–92.

Radwan, Lutfi. 1998. Water Management in the Egyptian Delta: Problems of Wastage and Inefficiency. *Geographical Journal* 164 (2): 129–138.

Radwan, Hanan, Jan Bron, and Essam Barakat. 2006. *Report on Preliminary Field Workshops*. Cairo: Water Boards Project, Ministry of Water Resources and Irrigation.

Ribot, Jesse. 2002. *Democratic Decentralization of Natural Resources: Institutionalizing Popular Participation*. Washington, D.C.: World Resources Institute.

Richards, Alan, and John Waterbury. 2007. *A Political Economy of the Middle East*. 3rd ed. Boulder: Westview Press.

Robbins, Paul. 2004. *Political Ecology: A Critical Introduction*. Malden, Mass.: Wiley-Blackwell.

Ross, Michael. 2001a. Does Oil Hinder Democracy? *World Politics* 53:325–361.

Ross, Michael L. 2001b. *Timber Booms and Institutional Breakdown in Southeast Asia*. Cambridge: Cambridge University Press.

Seckler, David. 1992. *Irrigation Policy, Management, and Monitoring in Developing Countries*. Arlington, VA: Winrock International Institute for Agricultural Development.

Seckler, David, and David Moore, eds. 1993. *Water Scarcity in Developing Countries: Reconciling Development and Environmental Protection*. Arlington, Va.: Winrock International Institute for Agricultural Development.

Selby, Jan. 2003. *Water, Power, and Politics in the Middle East: The Other Israeli-Palestinian Conflict*. London: I. B. Tauris.

Shalby, R., F. El Gamal, and H. Ali. 2004. Participatory Water Management in Egypt: Country Review. Proceedings of the 1st Participatory Water Saving Management and Water Cultural Heritage Workshop. Options Méditerranéennes, Series B, Studies and Research, Number 48. Paris: International Centre for Advanced Mediterranean Agronomic Studies.

Sowers, Jeannie. 2003. Allocation and Accountability: State-Business Relations and Environmental Politics in Egypt. Unpublished PhD dissertation. Politics Department, Princeton University, Princeton, N.J.

Sowers, Jeannie. 2007. Nature Reserves and Authoritarian Rule in Egypt: Embedded Autonomy Revisited. *Journal of Environment & Development* 16 (4): 375–397.

Sowers, Jeannie. 2008. Transnational Networks and the Political Geography of Water Projects in Egypt. Paper presented at the 9th Annual Mediterranean Research Meeting, European Union Institute, Montecatini Terme, Italy, March 12–15.

Sowers, Jeannie. 2011. Re-mapping the Nation, Critiquing the State: Environmental Narratives and Desert Land Reclamation in Egypt. In *Environmental Imaginaries in the Middle East: History, Policy, Power, and Practice*, ed. Diana K. Davis and Edmund Burke III. Athens: Ohio University Press.

Sowers, Jeannie, Erika Weinthal, and Avner Vengosh. 2010. Climate Change, Water Resources, and the Politics of Adaptation in the Middle East and North Africa. *Climatic Change* 104 (3–4): 599–627.

Steinberg, Paul. 2001. *Environmental Leadership in Developing Countries: Transnational Relations and Biodiversity Policy in Costa Rica and Bolivia*. Cambridge, Mass.: MIT Press.

Tal, Alon. 2002. *Pollution in a Promised Land*. Berkeley: University of California Press.

United Nations Development Program. 2005. *Arab Human Development Report 2004: Towards Freedom in the Arab World*. New York: United Nations Development Program.

Vitalis, Robert, and Steven Heydemann. 2000. War, Keynesianism and Colonialism: Explaining State-Market Relations in the Postwar Middle East. In *War, Institutions and Social Change in the Middle East*, ed. Steven Heydemann, 100–145. Berkeley: University of California Press.

US Agency for International Development (USAID). 1999. Establishment of Branch Canal Water User Associations in the Egyptian Irrigation System. Agricultural Policy Reform Program-Water Policy Activity, Report No. 17. Cairo: US Agency for International Development and Ministry of Public Works and Water Resources.

Waterbury, John. 1979. *Hydropolitics of the Nile Valley.* Syracuse: Syracuse University Press.

Waterbury, John. 2002. *The Nile Basin: National Determinants of Collective Action.* New Haven: Yale University Press.

Weinthal, Erika, and Yael Parag. 2003. Two Steps Forward, One Step Backward: Societal Capacity and Israel's Implementation of the Barcelona Convention and the Mediterranean Action Plan. *Global Environmental Politics* 3 (1): 51–71.

Wittfogel, Karl. 1957. *Oriental Despotism: A Comparative Study of Total Power.* New Haven: Yale University Press.

World Bank. 2004. Balancing Productivity and Environmental Pressure in Egypt: Toward an Interdisciplinary and Integrated Approach to Agricultural Drainage. Agriculture & Rural Development Working Paper 13. Washington, D.C.: World Bank.

World Bank. 2007. *Making the Most of Scarcity: Accountability for Better Water Management Results in the Middle East and North Africa. MENA Development Report #5.* Washington, D.C.: World Bank.

Zawahri, Neda, Jeannie Sowers, and Erika Weinthal. 2011. Water and Sanitation in the Middle East and North Africa: A Critique of the MDG Assessments. Paper presented at the International Studies Association Annual Meeting, Montreal, Canada, March 17.

Zetter, Roger, and Al-Moataz Hassan. 2002. Urban Economy or Environmental Policy: The Case of Egypt. *Journal of Environmental Policy and Planning* 4 (2): 169–184.

10

Welcome to the Jungle: Policy Theory and Political Instability

Paul F. Steinberg

Environmental politics is fundamentally about social change—in values, behaviors, patterns of economic activity and, crucially, in political institutions. The transformative aspirations of environmental politics are part of what makes this such an exciting arena for students and social reformers alike and a fertile opportunity for pairing the substantive concerns of environmental studies with the analytic tools of comparative political inquiry.

A crucial part of this social transformation is policy change, including the creation and reform of environmental laws, regulations, agencies, and government programs. Environmental problems are often the result of market failures and collective action problems, and their resolution typically requires confronting powerful economic interests. As a result, it is no exaggeration to say that changes in government policy are a prerequisite for large-scale improvement in environmental conditions (see Barry and Eckersley 2005; Steinberg 2005). With policy change figuring prominently on the agendas of environmental movements throughout the world (Dalton, Recchia, and Rohrschneider 2003), it comes as little surprise that the canonical studies of policy change in industrialized democracies draw heavily on environmental cases (Baumgartner and Jones 1993; Kingdon 1984; Sabatier 1988; Sabatier and Jenkins-Smith 1993; Downs 1972).

Yet when we look more closely at the meaning of policy change, and that of institutional change generally, it becomes clear that the concept of "change" refers simultaneously to two quite distinct phenomena. First, change entails moving away from a previous arrangement deemed by reformers to be unsatisfactory. In the context of environmental policy, this move typically requires passing new laws and creating new bureaucratic structures for the control of industrial pollution and the provision of goods ranging from drinking water to national parks. Second, the new arrangement must endure. Endurance is central to the very meaning of institutions, described by Hughes as "relative permanence of a distinctly social sort" (Hughes 1936, 180, as cited in Clemens and Cook 1999). Or as March and Olsen put it, "An institution is a relatively enduring collection of rules and organized practices, embedded in structures of meaning and resources that are relatively invariant in the face of turnover of individuals and relatively resilient to the idiosyncratic preferences and expectations of individuals and changing external circumstances" (2006, 3). Institutional rules create the order and predictability necessary for collective action (Ostrom 1999). Institutional reform, in turn, is designed to project a new pattern of social interaction into the future, to preserve a moment of political creativity for posterity. The proper metaphor for institutional change is that of switching tracks, not continuous reversals in course. Captured in terms like "lasting change," "a permanent shift," and "the revolutionary legacy," these two dimensions of the process of institutional change—switching and sticking—suggest two distinct categories of causal mechanisms that together are necessary conditions for meaningful reforms in public policies and other state institutions.

This chapter focuses on the second dimension of this challenge—the long-term stability of reforms in government institutions, particularly in developing and post-communist countries.[1] Research on institutional stability gained an unfortunate reputation in an earlier generation of comparative politics research, as it often focused on the durability of regimes irrespective of their commitment to human rights (see, e.g., Huntington 1965; for a critique of stability studies, see Jourde 2007, 487–489). Authoritarian regimes commonly invoke stability as justification for their rule, while global powers have often used the rhetoric of stability as a rationale for supporting dictators to their liking. Following global trends toward democratization, however, institutional stability has received renewed attention as a legitimate focus of comparative politics research on topics such as the survival of fragile new democracies and the long-term consolidation of institutional reforms (Schedler 1998).

As part of a larger research agenda on comparative environmental politics, institutional stability merits closer attention for at least three reasons. First, major reforms in public policy—be it the development of a modern welfare state, the overhaul of a nation's health-care system, or the establishment of an effective air quality management system—take place over a period of decades (Meadowcroft 2005). This time is required for experimentation and learning on the part of policy reformers and for the creation of social constituencies in support of the new institutions. Meaningful policy reform cannot be achieved in a context of perpetual turnover in programs, personnel, and practices. Second, institutional continuity is vital for environmental governance in particular, given the potential for irreversible harm (notably species extinction and the destruction of ecosystems) and in light of the long time horizons required for sound management of resources like forests, fisheries, and watersheds (Steinberg 2009).

Third, the durability of institutional arrangements is important because it stands in stark contrast to the institutional instability characteristic of most of the world's nations, which are subject to frequent regime changes, runaway inflation, military coups and countercoups, constitutional crises, ethnic clashes, guerrilla warfare, breakaway republics, booms and busts in export revenues, budgetary crises, corruption scandals, electoral fraud, crackdowns on civil liberties, and heightened vulnerability to natural disasters, among other disruptive forces. I call these *stochastic* political systems, employing the term normally used to describe statistical variance to emphasize how inhospitable these political environments can be for the consolidation of policy reforms.

For those readers who have spent their lives in stable industrialized democracies, it may be difficult to appreciate either the pervasiveness or the everyday ramifications of social instability in most of the world's nations. The consequences of this instability for environmental institutions are often profound. In the course of hundreds of interviews with environmental policy reformers from a wide range of developing countries over the past fifteen years, I have encountered innumerable instances in which promising new environmental policies have been swept aside, time and again, with each change in political administration. In Ecuador, where an environmental agency was established in 1996, Environment Minister Yolanda Kakabadse led a successful effort to attract international funds and to increase coordination with the agriculture and energy sectors on issues like climate change and biodiversity—until, two years into her tenure, her government was ousted in a military coup. In Bolivia, conservationists pioneered the use of national environmental endowments, an innovative institutional arrangement designed to "dampen funding oscillations" associated with government sources (Quintela 2003, 15). After raising upward of 100 million dollars from international donors, the Bolivian fund was dismembered following the 1993 presidential election.

A similar phenomenon can be observed in a wide range of countries. Michael Ross documents how, during the post–World War II period, the Philippines established an exemplary forestry agency "with a well-trained staff, a considerable degree of political independence, a policy of promoting sustained-yield forestry, and a reputation for avoiding the corruption and patronage that plagued many other government agencies" (2001, 54). In the mid-1950s, however, fluctuation in timber exports destroyed the agency, making it the target of political leaders seeking access to surging revenues. In Bulgaria, in the wake of the transition from Soviet rule, Baker and Baumgartl (1998, 194) cite "instability at the apex of government, in particular at the ministerial level, making it difficult to ensure policy continuity." In an analysis of sustainable forestry and antipollution initiatives in Argentina, Espach concludes that "feckless and unstable state agencies have created an institutional environment unfavorable even for private initiatives aimed at bypassing government interference" (2005, 1). In Brazil, Hochstetler and Keck report, "As new chief executives (at federal or state levels) seek to put their stamp on government, they move environmental agencies from one jurisdiction to another, change their attributions, create new departments, and eliminate others. When frequent reshuffling occurs, it becomes almost as surprising when there is policy continuity as when there is not" (2007, 224). In Nepal, Heinen and Shrestha report (2006, 51) that the political upheaval of the past decade has brought conservation policy reforms to a standstill. Foreign tourism is notoriously susceptible to political and economic instability (Clements and Georgiou 1998), and in Eastern Africa, events such as the 1998 embassy bombings and widespread civil unrest in Kenya in 2007 caused the collapse of tourist-based conservation projects throughout the region.[2]

How can one create effective environmental institutions in political systems characterized by pervasive instability? This is the central question of this chapter, and I argue that it should occupy a more central place in our thinking about the prospects for effective environment governance around the globe. Institutional stability has been largely overlooked in comparative research on environmental policy making, which has focused almost exclusively on stable industrialized democracies, mirroring the geographic bias of policy studies generally. Representative journals such as *Policy Sciences*, *Policy Studies Review*, and the *Policy Studies Journal* are strongly oriented toward the United States in particular, building theories of policy change on the experiential basis of a country with a degree of political stability that is almost unparalleled by world standards. If we wish to expand our geographic horizons to include most of the world's political systems—and in order to remain relevant, policy research must do precisely this—then the durability of reforms can no longer be taken for granted.

The long-term fate of policy reforms in chaotic institutional environments raises important questions for the study of comparative politics. When political regimes change, do regulatory arrangements change in kind? How resilient are institutions vis-à-vis shifts in social conditions? We know, on the one hand, that the institutional impacts of political and economic change can be profound. Yet surely not every coup or crisis reorders the institutional landscape from scratch. What changes and what endures? What is the relation between political form and function? This topic also carries important ramifications for the study and practice of global environmental politics. Institutions for global cooperation seek to protect biodiversity, stem damage to forests and oceans, and mitigate climate change over the next several decades. How can such tasks ever be accomplished without a greater understanding of the dynamics of policy reform and institution building in non-OECD countries, the site of most of the planet's people, natural resources, and future economic growth? By examining the endurance of policies across regimes—governance across governments—we can gain insights into the social processes underlying successful reform efforts in a wider range of national settings and can better understand the microfoundations of institutional stability in unstable systems.

The argument proceeds in three parts. First, I situate this investigation in the existing literature on policy change and institutional stability. I argue that external shocks—the very factors identified in the literature as major drivers of policy change in stable industrialized democracies—can have the opposite effect when present in excess, inhibiting policy change by preventing the consolidation of reforms. Next, I document major sources of instability in stochastic political systems, drawing together a number of quantitative indicators and historical illustrations. The remainder of the discussion focuses on mechanisms of endurance. Cognizant of their tenuous hold on power, policy reformers in stochastic political systems have at their disposal a number of strategies for increasing the odds that reforms will last. This section draws on ongoing field research in Costa Rica and Bolivia, on interviews with environmental policy practitioners from fifteen developing countries conducted between 2001 and 2003, and on insights and case material from the literatures on regime change, democratization, comparative public administration, and environmental policy. I conclude by considering the implications of this line of inquiry for the study and practice of environmental governance, and for broader efforts to join the fields of environmental policy and comparative politics.

Conceptualizing Policy Change

Under what conditions do countries adopt policies conducive to environmental protection? This question occupies a central place in the global environmental politics literature and is often tied to questions regarding support for international environmental regimes and compliance with treaty commitments (Sprinz and Vaahtoranta 1994; Mitchell 1994; Haas 1990). As argued in chapter 1, this work would benefit from more thorough engagement with research on domestic policy processes, which comprises an impressive and diverse body of literature.[3] In reviewing theories of policy change, Lowry (2006, 314) notes that "most dominant causal explanations of significant policy change over time involve unplanned factors arising from outside the policy system."[4] The seminal works on policy change—notably research by Sabatier (1988), Kingdon (1984), and Baumgartner and Jones (1993)—all report that these exogenous shocks are frequently the impetus behind major policy reforms. Sabatier's advocacy coalition framework focuses on domestic policy subsystems (such as the subsystem governing air quality in a given locale) that are targets of advocacy by competing coalitions holding divergent policy beliefs. Sabatier concludes that events external to the policy subsystem—such as changes in socioeconomic conditions, in governing coalitions, and in decisions from other policy subsystems—are the primary drivers of major reforms (Sabatier 1988, 134). These external changes influence the policy subsystem either by changing the beliefs of its dominant coalition or by replacing one coalition with another.

The same conclusion emerges from Baumgartner and Jones's (1993) work on punctuated equilibrium theory. Focusing again on the United States, these authors argue that seemingly stable political arrangements dominating a policy area, such as iron triangles of interest groups and their congressional and bureaucratic allies, ultimately depend on the existence of powerful social institutions. Therefore macrolevel changes in social institutions—such as growth in the influence of NGOs, changes in the organization of legislative bodies, or shifts in federal power-sharing arrangements—can produce rapid and profound changes in policy. They find that large-scale external changes, such as the OPEC-induced energy crisis or the election of Ronald Reagan and his antiregulatory agenda, create the conditions for major policy shifts.

In what is probably the most influential book written on policymaking processes, John Kingdon (1984) likewise identifies large-scale social change as a dominant force driving policy reforms. Kingdon's model emphasizes the role of policy entrepreneurs who join together three distinct processes, or streams—the availability of policy solutions, the recognition of policy problems by decision makers, and windows of opportunity for change. Examples of windows of opportunity include the installation of a new administration, a new legislature or committee chair, or swings in national mood. Kingdon concludes that these windows, which appear briefly and with rarity in the American system, are the precipitating events for sweeping changes in public policies. Large-scale political change has played an equally important role in the reform of domestic environmental policies in Europe, as the expansion of EU regulatory authority has increased the influence of the "greener" member states through regulatory competition and policy diffusion (Vogel 2003; Andonova and VanDeveer, chapter 11, this volume).

In sum, large-scale changes in national conditions provide important opportunities for creative efforts to reform policy. But what about when there is "too much" change? In nations characterized by pervasive crises and perennial shifts in political power, one would expect that there exist ample opportunities for the initiation of new policy endeavors, but that these might not last beyond the next large-scale social disruption. That is, the very factors that in moderation promote policy change in industrialized democracies may, in excess, inhibit it in other societies. After all, exogenous shocks provide a window of opportunity for opponents of environmental regulation as well, such as the logging company eager to extract timber from a newly protected area, the factory forced to reduce toxic emissions, or the fishing fleet affected by catch limits. Even without actual reversals of policy, major political and economic developments can distract public attention to the extent that previous initiatives are underfunded or otherwise fall to the wayside (Downs 1972).

The challenge that pervasive social disruptions pose for the consolidation of policy reforms has been missed by researchers comparing the policy responsiveness of industrialized democracies. Tsebelis (1995) among others compares presidential and parliamentary systems with respect to their ability to respond to new social challenges, weighing factors such as the impact of federalism and different configurations of party politics. By focusing exclusively on the initiation of policy reforms (such as the passage of laws) rather than their long-term consolidation, this literature fails to distinguish between the switching and sticking dimensions of policy change. The implementation of policy is no trivial matter even in established industrialized democracies (see Patashnik 2008). But in these countries, significant policy reforms are accompanied by a process of institutionalization associated with a modern professional bureaucracy. New environmental laws and regulatory bodies soon constitute a force to be reckoned with, bolstering the case against future reversals by documenting environmental and health conditions and by producing visible improvements in environmental quality and public services. This situation stands in sharp contrast to the prevailing conditions in stochastic political systems, where there are ample opportunities to initiate policy, but these new innovations are easily overturned. Often the result is "policy churn," described by O'Toole and Meier (2003, 47) as "the adoption of frequently changing reforms without leaving sufficient time for implementation."

Sources of Instability

From 1970 to 2009, there were 182 successful military coups around the world. From 1946 to 2003, 229 armed conflicts, mostly internal, took place in 148 countries. From 1970 to 2006, thirty-nine countries experienced triple-digit annual inflation in consumer prices for more than one year. Between 1951 and 1990, the average lifespan of a democracy was eighteen years for countries with per capita income between $1,001 and $3,000 and six years for those under $1,000. Within the past seventy-five years—roughly the lifespan of a macaw—there have been changes in constitutional regimes in all of Latin America, Africa, Asia, and the Middle East, and almost all of Europe. In the entire world, only five countries with populations over a million (Canada, Australia, the Netherlands, the United Kingdom, and the United States) have constitutional regimes that have lasted for a century— roughly the time required for a clear-cut forest to recover minimal ecological functions.[5]

Political change is clearly endemic to modern society and is indeed a necessary condition for human betterment. But in many countries, political turnover has reached epidemic proportions. The data in figure 10.1 confirm the widely appreciated point that political instability is spread unevenly throughout the world. This figure, based on data from the Cross-National Time Series Data Archive, shows only the most extreme type of political change—the adoption of a new national

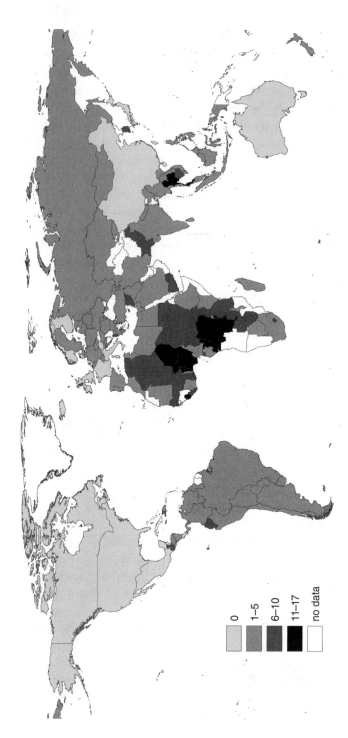

Figure 10.1
Constitutional changes, 1960–2003

constitution. Although some leaders may adopt a new constitution for ceremonial purposes with little impact on the existing political order, these data are broadly representative of the frequency of significant shifts in the rules of the political game. Constitutions, as the rules for rule making, lay down fundamental precepts for political representation, civil-military relations, legal process, the distribution of power and resources between the central government and regions, civil liberties, relations among branches of government, and patterns of participation by ethnic, religious, and other social sectors.

What does sustainable forestry look like in a country that has experienced an average of one constitutional regime change per decade? Why should a factory owner take seriously air pollution regulations issued by a government agency unlikely to last through the next election or coup? As Deacon argues, "If the institutions of government are weak or short-lived, proposals for long-term investment in government-owned assets [such as national forests] will lack credibility since the segments of society making the initial sacrifice will have no guarantee of receiving the ultimate reward" (1994, 423). Quite apart from the regulatory uncertainty that results from frequent shifts among governments with competing policy priorities, the periods of transition from one regime to the next present serious challenges for any effort to govern effectively. Research on democratization has documented the notoriously unstable nature of transitional regimes—nascent democracies following periods of anarchy or authoritarian rule, or regimes that otherwise fall somewhere in between poles of democracy and authoritarianism (Goldstone et al. 2005).

The comparative politics literature on these topics has focused almost exclusively on macrolevel considerations—operationalizing definitions of regime types, measuring trends in democratization and political stability, and offering theories to explain change at this level of analysis. This literature has paid considerably less attention to the implications of regime transitions for the day-to-day business of governance—a task described by scholars of postcommunist states as akin to "rebuilding the ship at sea" (Elster, Offe, and Preuss 1998). Deacon (1994) reports that political instability is empirically correlated with increases in deforestation, a finding consistent with research on the relationship between political stability and economic growth (Evans and Rauch 1999). In interviews with policy reformers in developing countries, I find that the institutional fluidity associated with regime change poses serious challenges for those trying to create effective environmental institutions. Energy policy makers in Mexico, for example, report that with the downfall of the single-party system dominated by the Institutional Revolutionary Party (PRI), it has become exceptionally difficult for federal policy makers to implement reforms on a national scale. Under the old regime, state governors followed presidential directives because this was a prerequisite for advancing their own political careers. In the post-PRI period, this incentive is no longer available, yet there is nothing to replace it, as a new system governed by the impersonal rule of law and a functioning court system has yet to take shape. A similar phenomenon is reported by Stern and colleagues with respect to the postcommunist countries of Europe, where "old norms, rules, organizations, routines and other public sense-making structures have been abolished, compromised, or have otherwise abruptly lost their binding character before any alternative structures have settled" (2002, 527). The pains of regime transition are equally apparent in South Africa, where environmental officials report in interviews that the expulsion of experienced Afrikaners from the diplomatic corps, which accompanied the country's transition to democracy, has denied South Africa the long-term interpersonal relationships with foreign diplomats that are often crucial for problem solving during international environmental negotiations.

The sources of institutional instability around the world are not limited to political transitions. Figure 10.2 shows national experiences with periods of extreme inflation, measured as the average of the three highest years of inflation in consumer prices reported by the International Monetary Fund's International Financial Statistics database. Runaway inflation poses a direct threat to many environmental policies and practices. What are the prospects for sustainable agriculture, for example, under 500 percent annual inflation in food prices? These inflationary periods are also a source of political instability in regimes with a tenuous hold on power. Grindle and Thomas note: "In the absence of established systems and traditions, constitutional or other, reinforced by adherence over time, that regulate political competition and changes of power, the legitimacy of state actions is always open to dispute. Challenges to the right of regimes to remain in power can emerge easily" (1991, 57). Runaway inflation creates a social environment in which collective action for long-term goals is highly improbable. O'Donnell writes:

Anyone who has lived under these circumstances understands this is a harsh, nasty world . . . the longer and the deeper this crisis, and the less the confidence that the government will be able to solve it, the more rational it becomes for everyone to act: at highly disaggregated levels, especially in relation to state agencies that may solve or alleviate the consequences of the crisis for a given firm or sector; with extremely short time horizons; and with assumptions that everyone else will do the same. A gigantic—national level—prisoner's dilemma holds. (1993, 1363)

Apart from inflation per se, price volatility places serious strains on environmental institutions in many developing countries, which are as a rule heavily dependent on natural resources for export revenues and concentrate on one or a small number of commodities, such as oil, coffee, timber, or minerals. The lack of diversification combined with the inherent volatility of natural resource commodity prices creates boom-and-bust cycles with significant negative impacts on budget cycles, capital investments, and exchange rates (Ross 2001).

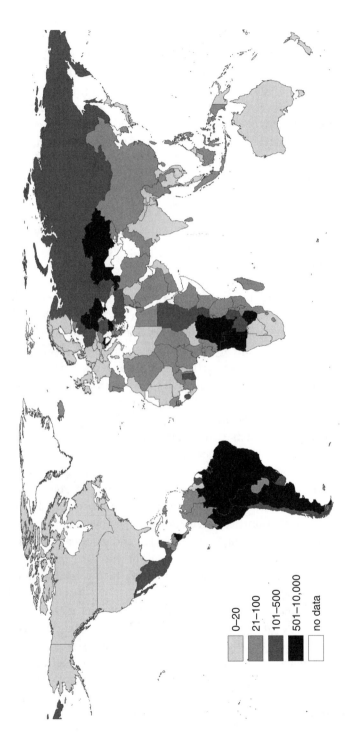

Figure 10.2
Inflation: highest three years, 1970–2006 (average)

Many of the same countries that have experienced chronic political turnover and economic instability have also been the sites of significant military conflicts. From 1946 to 2003, there were 112 wars, defined as conflicts with 1,000 battle deaths or more (Eriksson and Wallensteen 2004). In addition to the devastating human toll, a collateral victim of these conflicts are national parks and other protected areas, which are frequently used by refugee populations, guerrilla armies, and government forces during times of conflict and as a source of revenues for patronage during reconstruction. Donovan, de Jong, and Abe (2007, 2) report that more than 40 percent of the world's tropical forest area is located in countries plagued by violent conflict, where munitions and overharvesting take a toll on wildlife and habitats (Dudley et al. 2002; McNeely 2003). Policies that benefit rural peoples in areas such as agricultural extension, water access, and rural electrification suffer when government employees stay away because of imminent danger or their lack of regulatory authority in regions ruled by competing forces.

These three sources of instability—political, economic, and military—often reinforce one another, as military conflicts and economic crises increase the fragility of regimes, and unstable regimes are less capable of resolving crises. Compounding these challenges are two sources of policy instability that do not stem from macro-level changes, but are nonetheless significant factors in developing and postcommunist countries. The first is the discontinuity that results from foreign aid, which often constitutes a significant proportion of the budgets of environmental agencies in these countries. Trends in the donor world come and go, and the project orientation of international assistance impedes coordinated long-term planning and institutional consolidation. The expatriate experts who assume leadership positions in these projects typically have a residence time in the host country of about two or three years before moving on to a new project in another country. These experts constitute a large fraction of the top-level technical managers in many countries receiving environmental aid, so this turnover comes at a significant cost. Finally—and perhaps most important—in most countries, environmental policies and institutions are quite new and lack the long-standing constituencies and political weight of established ministries in agriculture, planning, and development. In periods of political and economic change, it is precisely the newer and less firmly established institutions that are most prone to collapse.

In sum, over much of the planet's surface, the public institutions governing environmental quality are in a state of near-constant flux. Having brought this broadly intuitive point to the analytic foreground, the question remains as to how, if at all, environmental governance can be achieved under these trying circumstances. My aim is not to paint a hopeless picture, but merely to revise some of the default assumptions undergirding comparative environmental policy research. By way of analogy, it was only after collective action theorists pointed out the inherent difficulties of cooperation—changing our default assumption to one of noncooperation—that every instance of coordinated social action became a puzzle, a subject worthy of inquiry. Likewise, there are environmental policy successes in stochastic political systems, and these require explanation. Bolivia, for example, has emerged as a global leader in biodiversity conservation policy despite its history as one of the least politically stable countries in the world, having experienced well over one hundred changes of government since independence (Steinberg 2001). In Brazil, disparate environmental organizations that had maintained a low profile during military rule were united and animated during the transition to democracy, helping to draft the environmental chapter of the new national constitution in 1985–1988 (Hochstetler 1997). Regime transitions provided similar opportunities for environmental mobilization in East Asia (Lee and So 1999) and Central and Eastern Europe (see Andonova and VanDeveer, chapter 11, and Hochstetler, chapter 8, this volume).

This observation raises a larger point, namely that knowledge of the structural conditions shaping an action arena provides only a partial understanding of the dynamics of change. As David Dessler argues, we should think of structure not as a "container" but as a "medium" for action in light of the "capacities and liabilities of the agents who respond to those conditions of action" (1989, 467, 444). Making the most of constraints is the essence of entrepreneurship, including creative efforts at policy change undertaken by reformers with decades of political experience in a given country. Let us then consider in greater detail the puzzle and the possibility of establishing lasting environmental institutions in stochastic political systems.

Sources of Durability in Stochastic Political Systems

The extent to which mainstream policy theory is detached from the conditions prevalent in most developing and postcommunist countries is apparent in the fact that "basic constitutional structure" appears, in Sabatier's advocacy-coalition framework (Sabatier 1988, 132), within the category of "relatively stable" parameters affecting policy change (compare to figure 10.1). When the durability of political institutions is no longer the default assumption for theories of change, we encounter a very interesting and important question: what are the mechanisms at play that can account for institutional resilience in conditions of social stochasticity? Research on national policy styles shows that the characteristic manner of producing policy in a given country—construed along dimensions such as conflict resolution processes and the organization of scientific input—persists across administrations (Howlett 2002; Brickman, Jasanoff, and Ilgen 1985). But few studies have considered whether and under what conditions the actual substance of policy persists over the long term.[6]

Countervailing the sources of instability documented in the preceding section are a number of forces favoring policy continuity. Research on path dependence demonstrates that "established institutions generate powerful inducements that reinforce their own stability and further development" (Pierson 2000, 255). Richard Rose observes: "Policy makers are inheritors before they are choosers . . . new programs cannot be constructed on green field sites. Instead, they must be introduced into a policy environment dense with past commitments" (1993, 78). To the extent that environmental policies become embedded in organizational routines and provide benefits (such as drinking water, clean air, jobs, urban beautification, and recreational opportunities) that are valued by politically vocal members of society, it becomes more difficult to overturn them (Steinberg 2009). To understand why some policy reforms become part of the fabric of a society while others are discarded, we can draw on insights from historical institutionalism, specifically Kathleen Thelen's emphasis on the "mechanisms of reproduction" that sustain an institution. As Thelen expresses the challenge, "We need to know exactly who is invested in particular institutional arrangements, exactly how that investment is sustained over time, and perhaps how those who were not invested in the institution are kept out" (1999, 391). Causal mechanisms can be understood as recurring complexes of cause-and-effect relationships found in wide range of social settings (see Tilly 2001). These mechanisms interact with other (sometimes countervailing) mechanisms in different combinations in different places and historical junctures. Thus, an emphasis on causal mechanisms allows cumulative, cross-national comparisons without requiring unrealistic assumptions of uniformity or determinism.

What are the mechanisms sustaining policy reforms in systems characterized by pervasive social instability? This is a large and unexplored topic, and my intention is to broach the question rather than settle it. Let us begin with the observation that policy reformers in stochastic political systems are acutely aware of the tenuous nature of their influence and frequently pursue strategies with this limitation in mind. In countries wracked by ongoing institutional upheaval, reformers can often be found attaching numerous tethers to their new policy initiatives, much like the owners of boats at dock do in anticipation of an approaching storm. Often the political storm makes a mockery of these attempts, tossing the institutional structure onto the rocky shoals. In other instances these efforts are successful, achieving a measure of consolidation over time. Here I consider three categories of tethering mechanisms: bureaucratic institutionalization, the role of nonstate actors, and the establishment of horizontal and vertical linkages outside the policy subsystem.

Bureaucratic Politics

The concept of a modern Weberian bureaucracy, as a distinct organizational form oriented toward the provision of long-term public goods, is intimately tied with the notion of stability (see O'Toole and Meier 2003). To the extent that public agencies approximate the Weberian ideal of professionalism and insulation from the whims of patronage politics, they can offer a measure of continuity across regimes, providing incoming rulers with information about a problem and with the competencies needed for effective governance. Even military rulers typically rely on civilian expertise to run most of a country's affairs, as military organizations are considerably more adept at capturing power than in actually governing. Environmental policies are invariably associated with bureaucratic structures such national park systems, environment ministries, and new units devoted to climate change mitigation projects, water quality monitoring, and other functions. The fate of environmental bureaucracies across changes in regimes and political administrations thus serves as a logical point of departure for investigation into the potential sources of policy continuity in stochastic political systems.

For a policy reform to last, there must be at least a modicum of consistency in agency personnel. How much turnover occurs in agency personnel following changes in political administration? Turnover must be considered at three distinct levels: agency leaders and other high-level political appointees; midlevel professional managers (career civil servants in modern bureaucracies) who run much of the day-to-day business of an agency; and the front-line staff who are responsible for service delivery, often interacting directly with the public. Because heads of state typically rule for relatively short periods, continuity in agency staff is largely a function of the autonomy of the procedures governing civil service personnel selection and promotion. According to Meyer-Sahling, "The recent literature on politician-bureaucrat relations in Western democracies suggests that the politicization of personnel policy is widespread, that the modes, the degree and the depth of politicization differ across countries and time, and that the virtual absence of political intervention into civil service affairs, as in the United Kingdom, is an exception" (2008, 4). Although the notion of a truly autonomous bureaucratic personnel system may be more myth than reality, there are significant cross-national disparities. Meyer-Sahling observes that in Hungary, "by international standards, personnel turnover is very high . . . changes of government trigger almost a complete substitution of personnel in the senior ranks of the ministerial bureaucracy" (2008, 2). This finding is consistent with those for postcommunist countries generally, in which "the prevailing pattern in these states is still one of the top echelons of the civil service changing with each election, or, in worse cases, government reshuffles" (Verheijen and Robrenovic 2001, 441, cited in Meyer-Sahling 2008; see also Goetz 2001).

A number of East Asian countries benefit from highly professional bureaucracies that serve as a buffer against the effects of turnover and crisis. The role of state-led development in East Asia under the guidance of competent administrators under both authoritarian and democratic regimes has been widely documented (Haggard

2004; Evans and Rauch 1999). Elsewhere, however, bureaucracies provide at best a thin thread of continuity across administrations, as personnel turnover appears to often reach well into the ranks of middle-level managers. Grindle finds that "where patronage defines who is appointed to office, organizations are susceptible to rapid turnover of staff and their leaders are highly vulnerable to political changes" (1997, 483). Sloan reports that the predominance of personalistic rule and patronage-based appointments in Latin American bureaucracies results in high levels of turnover and job insecurity: "Hence, too many Latin American bureaucracies do not accumulate the institutional memories from trial and error experiences necessary to enlarge administrative capabilities required to perform the tasks and to improve efficiency in carrying out old functions" (1984, 141). (For a contrary example, see McAllister 2008; see also Klingner 1996.)

One unexplored dimension of bureaucratic stability concerns the fate of front-line agency staff during periods of instability and regime change. What becomes of the factory inspector or forestry official during times when it is unclear who is in charge, what the directives are, or even whether the government employee still has a job? Do front-line staff continue to perform their duties, even without pay, until things are put in order, or do they abandon their posts until the new boss arrives? We might expect uninterrupted fidelity to institutional roles when there is a strong sense of esprit de corps within an agency that is confident about its long-term prospects. Likewise, to the extent that employees have a normative commitment to the institutional mission or derive social status from their positions, we might expect them to act in a semi-official role during these transition periods. As Heclo observes, "History offers compelling examples of societies surviving through devastating cataclysms by virtue of ordinary people simply carrying on with appointed duties" (2006, 738). Future work on this topic could tap into research on the evolution of institutions in semilawless circumstances, such as Dudziak and Volpp's (2006) analysis of the US-Mexico border during the transition to American rule in the latter half of the nineteenth century.

In stochastic political systems, state agencies often lack the professional autonomy needed to protect against policy reversals motivated by patronage, corruption, or whim. Cognizant of these threats, policy reformers use a variety of alternative tethering strategies to help their institutional creations to survive the coming political storms. Clark Gibson provides insight into the challenge of governance across governments in his study of the strategies used by conservation agency officials under one-party rule in Zambia:

Politics makes the exercise of public authority temporary. This uncertainty drives the creators of public agencies to choose institutional designs they would never select if pursuing administrative efficiency alone. Since political victory allows incumbents only temporary control over political authority, they attempt to protect their agency from their political opponents, who could in the future gut or eliminate the agency. The fleeting nature of political control may even motivate incumbents to insulate the agency by hobbling their own exercise of public authority. (1999, 275)

Efforts to insulate institutions against future reversals of fortune are common in stable democracies (Moe 1990), but tethering strategies can reasonably be expected to proliferate in proportion to their proponents' perception of future threats of change. Looming instability, or even a tradition of instability, provides incentives to institutionalize. In studies of Mexico, Chile, and South Africa, Boylan observes that "where authoritarian elites fear the populism that may be endemic to new democracies and know that a regime change is imminent, they can be expected to create autonomous central banks to lock in a commitment to price stability over the long haul" (2001, 5). A similar strategy was deployed by the last British governor of Hong Kong, Christopher Patten, who pushed reforms to bolster the independent power of the legislature before ceding control to authoritarian China in 1997 (Husock 1998).

One tethering strategy entails the creation of a quasistate agency, an entity that has a government-sanctioned public function but enjoys considerable autonomy in its hiring and management practices and is less susceptible to manipulation by political leaders (see Bouckaert and Peters 2004). Quasistate agencies have proliferated in developing countries in recent decades, partly in response to concerns about patronage and corruption. But their autonomy comes at a cost. In addition to raising questions about public accountability, autonomy can compromise the effectiveness of an agency that has a transformative mission requiring it to confront powerful entrenched interests—a task that requires high-level political support. The designers of Costa Rica's environment ministry debated this issue at length in the 1980s, ultimately deciding that only a cabinet-level government agency would have the political clout needed to take on traditional ministries focused on resource extraction and development (Steinberg 2001). Other strategies include institutional designs such as Bolivia's forestry superintendency, created as part of the country's innovative forestry law reforms of 1996. To reduce the risk of political manipulation, the superintendent is nominated by the Senate and approved by the president. To promote policy consistency over time, the superintendent's appointment lasts for six years, spanning two four-year political administrations. Yet another tethering strategy can be found in environmental trust funds, which have been created in numerous developing and post-communist countries to "provide sustained funding, mitigating risks of unexpected stoppage of funds due to political changes, budget cuts, economic austerity programs, etc." (Conservation Finance Alliance 2003).

Nonstate Actors

The creation and implementation of environmental policy depends heavily on nonstate actors, from university scientists to investigative journalists, public interest law firms, organic farmers, professional associations, and grassroots advocacy groups. These nonstate actors can serve as an important source of policy continuity in stochastic political systems. At the broadest level, an important mechanism for durability is the rise of a policy culture—an enduring set of social expectations concerning government action in a particular issue area (Steinberg 2001, 153–191). With the rise of environmental movements in many non-Western countries and associated efforts to raise public awareness and reform state institutions, political leaders of all stripes are increasingly expected to address environmental issues (see, e.g, Lee and So 1999). In the Philippines, for instance, an alliance of environmental NGOs sponsors the Green Electoral Initiative, surveying politicians on their environmental views and practices and publishing their relative rankings in voter guides. When broad swaths of society desire and eventually expect government action on certain issues, it is less likely that policies affecting those issues will be cast aside as a consequence of political change. Where there exists a strong environmental policy culture, it is also more likely that political leaders have been exposed to environmental ideas through mass media, school curricula, peer groups, and civil society organizations.

The consolidation of policy reforms is a long-term undertaking, and therefore the success of reform efforts depends on the long-term presence of legal reformers who can doggedly pursue a cumulative effort across projects and across administrations. But where do reformers go after their political party or government is removed from power? An institutional landscape composed of diverse nonstate actors devoted to environmental goals allows reformers to stay involved over the long haul, as these organizations provide employment, networking opportunities, and venues for sustained intellectual creation, discussion of proposals, and even policy influence during periods when political shifts prevent reformers' direct participation in government.

Environmental NGOs often promote policy continuity across administrations through their continued advocacy, over many years, of a coherent set of policy ideas. The 1998 Global Environmental Organizations Survey, which polled 248 organizations in 59 countries, found that environmental groups routinely interact with government officials (Dalton, Recchia, and Rohrschneider 2003). The institutional memory provided by nongovernmental organizations with respect to environmental laws (many of which they helped to design) is important because the judicial system is often deficient in this regard. In many developing countries, it is common for judges and law enforcement officials to be unfamiliar with the environmental laws on the books. Environmental NGOs such as CEDARENA in Costa Rica have produced compendia of laws and have provided formal training to judges, police, and even newly installed legislators and cabinet members. In many countries, NGOs have government-sanctioned roles in managing national parks, monitoring pollution, and working with local communities on projects related to coastal management and community forestry (Steinberg 2005). These groups may approach newly installed political leaders and agency officials to bring them up to speed on long-standing efforts, advocating continued financial and political support, and offering their technical services.

Public employee unions and professional societies, whose members constitute the technical staff of government agencies, provide another potential source of continuity across regimes and administrations, especially when they share a common set of normative commitments and management outlooks associated with their professions (see Haas 1990). Economic constituencies can likewise provide a thread of continuity across administrations. Policies that provide income streams to those who protect natural resources—through ecotourism, community forestry, organic agriculture standards, or payment for protection of watersheds—create not only economic incentives for sustainable behavior but political incentives to voice objections to any attempts to overturn these policies (Steinberg 2009).

Another mechanism of endurance in stochastic political systems is the existence of alliances among environmental reformers affiliated with a spectrum of political parties. When one or another party is installed in power, informal networks among environmentalists can help ensure that members of the network provide a consistent source of advocacy for given policies and programs across successive administrations. These alliances have proven to be an important source of continuity in Costa Rica, where bargains have been struck among prospective environment ministers in the country's two major political parties in advance of an election to ensure collaboration regardless of the outcome. Boards of directors of environmental NGOs in Costa Rica and quasi-state organizations (such as the National Biodiversity Institute) are often explicitly multipartisan in their composition to bolster the organizations' long-term prospects. In contrast, Guatemalan policy reformers attempting to create the institutional architecture for climate change mitigation projects report that in the absence of a broad consensus on environmental issues spanning the political spectrum, their efforts are stymied by jarring policy discontinuities associated with frequent changes in top administrative officials.

Establishing Linkages Outside the Policy Subsystem

When creating new policies, if reformers establish meaningful linkages outside the environmental policy subsystem in question—spreading regulatory responsibilities and building constituencies across numerous agencies and levels of government—they can increase the prospects for the long-term consolidation of reforms. The challenge for reformers in stochastic political systems is to create conditions favorable to path dependence—to begin a process that will generate incentives, expectations, routines, and relationships that reinforce the stability of the new institutional arrangement. Pierson emphasizes that "path dependent processes will often be most powerful not at the level of individual organizations or institutions but at a more macro level that involves complementary configurations of organizations and institutions" (2000, 255). Some of these other institutions, such as traditional government ministries, may simply be stronger and therefore better able to withstand social upheaval generally, as a result of better funding, long-standing political support, a well-established policy culture, and other elements of path dependence. Moreover, institutions outside the environmental policy subsystem may not be exposed to the same political and economic fluctuations; the pressures they experience may be of different sorts and may occur at different times. When there are numerous institutions involved, even if they individually have the same degree of exposure to social turbulence and similar types of vulnerabilities, as a collection the odds are greater that not all of them will fold.

Linkages established outside an environmental policy subsystem may be horizontal or vertical in nature. Horizontally, the prospects for the consolidation of policy reforms improve to the extent that the normative goals and regulatory routines of new policies are mainstreamed rather than confined to a small environmental agency, with its few dozen employees looking anxiously toward the next election or coup. Kathryn Sikkink's excellent study of the institutionalization of new economic development policies in Brazil and Argentina is instructive in this regard. In Argentina, the new economic model ("developmentalism," associated with Raúl Prebisch and other Latin American economists) did not take hold. "Its only true institutional home was the political party apparatus associated with [President] Frondizi . . . and many policies were undermined and revised as soon as Frondizi left office" (Sikkink 1991, 25), a problem compounded by turnover in the Argentinean bureaucracy. In Brazil, in contrast, developmentalism was embraced by industry associations and became embedded in the organizational routines of the National Development Bank, the Development Council, and parts of the Banco do Brasil and the Foreign Ministry. "As part of the institutional identity of these organizations, developmentalist ideas were transmitted in training programs and embodied in laws, procedures, and publications" (Sikkink 1991, 25).

Environmental reformers have pursued similar strategies, seeking horizontal linkages with agencies outside of their particular policy subsystem. In interviews, a top environmental official in the Philippines recounted his efforts to mainstream interest in climate change by inviting his counterpart in the energy ministry to meet with international environmental donors and to directly solicit project funds. Horizontal linkages with ministries of foreign affairs can have a similar effect, as occurred in South Africa under President Mbeki with the establishment of a cabinet-level committee bringing together seventeen agency leaders to coordinate international policy initiatives in support of sustainable development. According to a senior official involved in the process, "The environmental ministries around the world have had a traditional place in the cabinet: very low down. . . . In the Mbeki administration this has changed. Environmental concerns are becoming more and more of a discussion around market access and international trade relations, so it's a different vibe."[7]

Strategies for building vertical linkages include the creation of local constituencies and the partial devolution of regulatory responsibilities to local governments. In recent years, dozens of developing countries have decentralized important features of natural resource policy and management (Ribot 2002). Similar to the dynamic seen with NGOs, when a town or regional government has a vested interest in the long-term viability of a protected area (for watershed protection or local tourism, for example), its leaders can be expected to push for protection of that area despite shifts in national leadership. This arrangement in turn enhances the governing capacity and associated legitimacy of the state because each new agency leader, regardless of political longevity, can "preside" over an intact park system due to local diligence. Hart and colleagues (1997) report that in the course of Rwanda's devastating civil war in the early 1990s, local community support for gorilla conservation resulted in considerably less poaching than would have been expected given the suspension of functioning government institutions. In contrast, in the political turmoil afflicting Uganda in the 1970s, communities that had recently been deprived by the central government of tradition rights to local forests allowed the degradation of forest resources (Turyahabwe and Banana 2008). Strengthening vertical linkages through decentralization also carries risks. Local governments are highly susceptible to the influence of resource extraction industries and other powerful economic actors, and local politicians may prioritize short-term income-generating opportunities and their associated political benefits (Andersson, Gibson, and Lehoucq 2006). But even the most ardent proponents of democratic decentralization of natural resource management, such as Ribot (2002), argue that decentralization must be accompanied by national regulatory standards.

Vertical linkages established "upward" with international actors and institutions include treaty commitments, participation in transnational advocacy networks, and support from international donors. Because foreign organizations such as the World Bank, the United Nations Development Program, and Conservation International operate outside the domestic political system in question, they are not subjected to the same sources of variance threatening domestic environmental institutions. As is often the case with domestic NGOs and local constituencies, leaders of these international organizations routinely approach newly installed national officials to educate them about ongoing projects and about the social and environmental problems motivating those projects.

Membership in the European Union represents one extreme within the range of vertical relationships. It is difficult to imagine circumstances in which a newly installed leader in an EU member state experiencing instability could ignore the long-standing environmental commitments of his or her predecessors. The European Union example suggests that a nation's propensity to respect previous treaty commitments—which is crucial to international law and a potentially important source of continuity in stochastic political systems—will be animated to the extent that the country has incentives to comply.

Conclusions

O'Toole and Meier observe: "Few ideas these days seem as retrograde as the quaint notion that stability can be helpful in the world of public administration. . . . Nothing seems hotter than novelty" (2003, 43–44). Institutional stability is integral to the very meaning of policy change, yet the history of environmental governance in much of the world resembles a growing heap of novelties that have been jettisoned by successive administrations in a context of pervasive political and economic upheaval. Still, many policy innovations have endured. By studying the mechanisms of institutional endurance in chaotic political environments, we can gain a better appreciation for the structural challenges facing environmental policy reformers in non-Western societies and the strategies they deploy to advance environmental agendas in very trying circumstances.

Although the purpose of this analysis is largely exploratory, let me conclude with a prediction, a prescription, and an exhortation. I predict that, on the whole, countries with chronic political and economic instability are less likely to see the consolidation of environmental institutions than are countries experiencing lower levels of social turbulence, though I have also pointed to many contrary examples. I also predict that in these societies, more so than in relatively stable social settings, one will find numerous and explicit efforts at institutional tethering, either through novel institutional designs, multipartisan alliances, or the establishment of linkages outside the policy subsystem. When tethering does not occur in these countries, policy change efforts will fail with greater frequency than in those instances where there is extensive tethering. These tethers can be identified both ex post and ex ante. Looking backward, one can identify through interviews and archival research the most significant threat faced by a given policy initiative and how that threat was countered. Looking to the future, the researcher can pose questions to knowledgeable practitioners using hypothetical scenarios: what would happen if there were an economic collapse, or a shift in the ruling party? Who would likely speak out against future reversals in fortune? It is during these moments of crisis, either real or counterfactual, that mechanisms of continuity become visible.

This analysis has prescriptive implications as well. Although tethering is a common strategy, it is not universally appreciated or practiced in countries experiencing chronic instability. Activists and policy reformers on the front lines of environmental struggles are often so preoccupied with putting out the latest brush fire—a legislative proposal that has stalled in the senate, a company illegally harvesting timber from a park—that they fail to reflect on the long-term prospects of environmental institutions. The same is true of the international organizations funding environmental projects in these countries. This analysis suggests that more explicit attention should be given to issues such as the design of state agencies (including personnel policies), the role of policy-oriented nonstate actors, and strategies for establishing horizontal and vertical linkages outside of environmental policy subsystems. Strategic environmental assessment, which has been developed in the European Union to incorporate environmental considerations into national planning efforts, provides one promising model for mainstreaming environmental concerns throughout diverse institutions of government. At local levels, environmental proponents can identify specific high-value resources that require long-term management and can design institutions with social instability in mind (Steinberg 2009).

Finally, this analysis points to the need for closer collaboration between scholars of environmental policy and comparative politics. Environmental policy studies have a lot to learn from comparative politics, with its focus on long-term processes and its vast literature on the non-Western world, in contrast to the highly constrained geographical focus of policy studies. Over two decades after Horowitz (1989) asked, "Is there a third world policy process?" our understanding of policy change in non-OECD countries remains in its infancy. This is a topic that cries out for greater attention from the field of comparative politics. Comparative politics research, in turn, stands to benefit from closer engagement with theories of policy change (see Scharpf 2000). Hall and Taylor argue that "fundamental to any institutional analysis" is "how to explain the process whereby institutions originate or change," including "explanations for why the regularized patterns of behaviour that we associate with institutions display continuity over time" (1996, 937, 939). Research on institutional consolidation in the unsettled political and economic climates of non-OECD countries can offer important insights into the social mechanisms that promote or hinder institutionalization. This topic lends itself to study from each of the three major theoretical perspectives of comparative politics, described in chapter 2. From an interest-based perspective, one can study the incentives that encourage or dissuade social actors from thinking about the long term (see Stein and Tommasi 2008; Hovi, Sprinz, and Underdal 2009). From a constructivist view, investigators can explore how cultural norms lead actors to sustain or abandon social practices across changes in formal rules. From the perspective of historical institutionalism, one can identify the processes that promote path dependence toward the fulfillment of public-spirited goals. The study of governance across governments brings together the theoretical and the practical, simultaneously focusing attention on the broad social structures and the microlevel mechanisms that shape the evolution of environmental institutions around the globe.

Notes

The author wishes to thank George Busenberg, Paul Butler, Ted Robert Gurr, Stephanie McKinney, James Meadowcroft, Miranda Schreurs, and Stacy VanDeveer for their helpful feedback at various stages of this research. Rachel-Mikel ArceJaeger and Warren Roberts provided essential assistance with data collection and Geographic Information Systems (GIS) database management, respectively.

1. A third component of policy change concerns the need for new institutions to continue evolving in response to changing social conditions (Social Learning Group 2001). The present analysis focuses on the enduring components of institutional reforms, both for conciseness and because it is an important and largely unexplored challenge for environmental governance.

2. Nick Menzies, Executive Director, Asia Institute, University of Los Angeles, personal communication. Paul Butler, Vice President of Global Programs, RARE, personal communication.

3. One strand of this literature focuses on agents of change, exploring the conditions under which NGOs, social movements, and reformers within government have an impact on policy (Rochon and Mazmanian 1993; Barzelay 1992; Grindle and Thomas 1991). Another strand examines the impact of state structures on policy processes and outcomes, including assessments of presidential versus parliamentary systems, administrative styles, voting rules, and bureaucratic structures (Vogel 2003; Jasanoff 1990; Scharpf 2000; Howlett 2002; Egeberg 1999). At the intersection of the two are studies examining the reciprocal influence of state structures and social organizations (Dryzek et al. 2003; Migdal 1987). Neofunctionalist accounts of policy change examine how state structures arise in response to social needs (North 1981) and the ways in which resource endowments make policy reform more or less likely (Silva et al. 2002). Still others show how the sequence and timing of events shape the prospects for change (Pralle 2006; Pierson 2000). The influence of focusing events (Birkland 1997), cross-national diffusion of policy ideas (Busch and Jörgens 2005; Hall 1989), and Europeanization (Cowles, Caporaso, and Risse 2001; Knill 2001) have all attracted attention.

4. Lowry argues that the literature has paid too little attention to forces for change originating within policy subsystems, but he does not contest the fundamental importance of exogenous shocks.

5. Data on coups calculated from *Polity IV: Regime Authority Characteristics and Transitions Datasets 1800–2010* (Center for International Development and Conflict Management, University of Maryland, College Park). Includes only countries with population over 500,000. Available at http://www.systemicpeace.org/inscr/inscr.htm. Regime change calculation is based on data from Banks 2011. Inflation figures are calculated from the International Monetary Fund's International Financial Statistics database. The figures on armed conflicts are from Eriksson and Wallensteen 2004. Figures on the lifespan of democracies are from Przeworski 2005.

6. Within the policy implementation literature, authors such as Patashnik (2008) and Mazmanian and Sabatier (1983) consider the long-term fate of policy reforms in the United States.

7. Interview with author, December 4, 2001.

References

Andersson, Krister P., Clark C. Gibson, and Fabrice Lehoucq. 2006. Municipal Politics and Forest Governance: Comparative Analysis of Decentralization in Bolivia and Guatemala. *World Development* 34 (3): 576–595.

Baker, Susan, and Bernd Baumgartl. 1998. Bulgaria: Managing the Environment in an Unstable Transition. *Environmental Politics* 7:183–206.

Banks, A.S. 2011. *Cross-national Time-Series Data Archive.* Jerusalem: Databanks International.

Barry, John, and Robin Eckersley, eds. 2005. *The State and the Global Ecological Crisis.* Cambridge, Mass.: MIT Press.

Barzelay, Michael, with the collaboration of Babak J. Armajani. 1992. *Breaking through Bureaucracy: A New Vision for Managing in Government.* Berkeley: University of California Press.

Baumgartner, Frank, and Bryan D. Jones. 1993. *Agendas and Instability in American Politics.* Chicago: University of Chicago Press.

Birkland, Thomas. 1997. *After Disaster.* Washington, D.C.: Georgetown University Press.

Bouckaert, Geert, and B. Guy Peters. 2004. Symposium on State Autonomous Agencies—Guest Editors' Preface. *Public Administration and Development* 24 (2): 89.

Boylan, Delia M. 2001. Democratization and Institutional Change in Mexico: The Logic of Partial Insulation. *Comparative Political Studies* 34 (1): 3–29.

Brickman, Ronald, Sheila Jasanoff, and Thomas Ilgen. 1985. *Controlling Chemicals: The Politics of Regulation in Europe and the United States.* Ithaca: Cornell University Press.

Busch, P.-O., and H. Jörgens. 2005. The International Sources of Policy Convergence: Explaining the Spread of Environmental Policy Innovations. *Journal of European Public Policy* 12 (5): 860–884.

Clemens, Elisabeth S., and James M. Cook. 1999. Politics and Institutionalism: Explaining Durability and Change. *Annual Review of Sociology* 25:441–466.

Clements, M. A., and A. Georgiou. 1998. The Impact of Political Instability on a Fragile Tourism Product. *Tourism Management* 19 (3): 283–288.

Conservation Finance Alliance. 2003. Conservation Finance Guide, Environmental Trust Funds (Section 1.4). Washington, D.C.: Conservation Finance Alliance.

Cowles, Maria Green, James Caporaso, and Thomas Risse. 2001. *Transforming Europe: Europeanization and Domestic Change.* Ithaca: Cornell University Press.

Dalton, Russell J., Stephen Recchia, and Robert Rohrschneider. 2003. The Environmental Movement and the Modes of Political Action. *Comparative Political Studies* 36 (7): 743–771.

Deacon, Robert T. 1994. Deforestation and the Rule of Law in a Cross-Section of Countries. *Land Economics* 70 (4): 414–430.

Dessler, David. 1989. What's at Stake in the Agent-Structure Debate? *International Organization* 43 (3): 441–473.

Donovan, Deanna, Wil de Jong, and Ken-Ichi Abe. 2007. Tropical Forests and Extreme Conflict. In *Extreme Conflict and Tropical Forests*, ed. Wil De Jong, Deanna Donovan, and Abe Ken-ichi, 1–15. Berlin: Springer.

Downs, Anthony. 1972. Up and Down with Ecology—The "Issue-Attention Cycle." *Public Interest* 28:38–50.

Dryzek, John S., David Downes, Christian Hunold, and David Schlosberg. 2003. *Green States and Social Movements: Environmentalism in the United States, United Kingdom, Germany, and Norway*. New York: Oxford University Press.

Dudley, Joseph P., Joshua R. Ginsberg, Andrew J. Plumptre, John A. Hart, and Liliana C. Campos. 2002. Effects of War and Civil Strife on Wildlife and Wildlife Habitats. *Conservation Biology* 16 (2): 319–329.

Dudziak, Mary L., and Leti Volpp, eds. 2006. *Legal Borderlands: Law and the Construction of American Borders*. Baltimore: Johns Hopkins University Press.

Egeberg, Morten. 1999. The Impact of Bureaucratic Structure on Policy Making. *Public Administration* 77 (1): 155–170.

Elster, Jon, Claus Offe, and Ulrich K. Preuss. 1998. *Institutional Design in Post-Communist Societies: Rebuilding the Ship at Sea*. Cambridge: Cambridge University Press.

Eriksson, Mikael, and Peter Wallensteen. 2004. Armed Conflict, 1989–2003. *Journal of Peace Research* 41 (5): 625–636.

Espach, Ralph. 2005. Private Regulation Amid Public Disarray: An Analysis of Two Private Environmental Regulatory Programs in Argentina. *Business and Politics* 7 (2): Article 3. http://www.bepress.com/bap/vol7/iss2/art3, accessed May 25, 2011.

Evans, Peter, and James E. Rauch. 1999. Bureaucracy and Growth: A Cross-National Analysis of the Effects of "Weberian" State Structures on Economic Growth. *American Sociological Review* 64 (5): 748–765.

Gibson, Clark C. 1999. Bureaucrats and the Environment in Africa. *Comparative Politics* 31 (3): 273–293.

Goetz, Klaus H. 2001. Making Sense of Post-Communist Central Administration: Modernization, Europeanization or Latinization? *Journal of European Public Policy* 8:1032–1051.

Goldstone, Jack A., Robert H. Bates, Ted Robert Gurr, Michael Lustik, Monty G. Marshall, Jay Ulfelder, and Mark Woodward. 2005. A Global Forecasting Model of Political Instability. Paper presented at the Annual Meeting of the American Political Science Association, September, Washington, D.C.

Grindle, Merilee S. 1997. Divergent Cultures? When Public Organizations Perform Well in Developing Countries. *World Development* 25 (4): 481–495.

Grindle, Merilee S., and John W. Thomas. 1991. *Public Choices and Policy Change: The Political Economy of Reform in Developing Countries*. Baltimore: Johns Hopkins University Press.

Haas, Peter M. 1990. Obtaining International Environmental Protection through Epistemic Consensus. *Millennium: Journal of International Studies* 19 (3): 347–363.

Haggard, Stephan. 2004. Institutions and Growth in East Asia. *Studies in Comparative International Development* 38 (4): 53–81.

Hall, Peter, ed. 1989. *The Political Power of Economic Ideas—Keynesianism across Nations*. Princeton: Princeton University Press.

Hall, Peter, and Rosemary Taylor. 1996. Political Science and the Three New Institutionalisms. *Political Studies* 44:936–957.

Hart, Terese, John A. Hart, Cheryl Fimbel, Robert Fimbel, William F. Laurance, Carrie Oren, Thomas T. Struhsaker, et al. 1997. Conservation and Civil Strife: Two Perspectives from Central Africa. *Conservation Biology* 11 (2): 308–314.

Heclo, Hugh. 2006. Thinking Institutionally. In *The Oxford Handbook of Political Institutions*, ed. R. A. W. Rhodes, Sarah A. Binder, and Bert A. Rockman, 731–742. New York: Oxford University Press.

Heinen, Joel T., and Suresh K. Shrestha. 2006. Evolving Policies for Conservation: An Historical Profile of the Protected Area System of Nepal. *Journal of Environmental Planning and Management* 49 (1): 41–58.

Hochstetler, Kathryn. 1997. The Evolution of the Brazilian Environmental Movement and Its Political Roles. In *The New Politics of Inequality in Latin America: Rethinking Participation and Representation*, ed. Douglas A. Chalmers, Carlos M. Vilas, Katherine Hite, and Scott B. Martin, 192–216. New York: Oxford University Press.

Hochstetler, Kathryn, and Margaret E. Keck. 2007. *Greening Brazil: Environmental Activism in State and Society*. Durham: Duke University Press.

Horowitz, Donald L. 1989. Is There a Third-World Policy Process? *Policy Sciences* 22 (3–4): 197–212.

Hovi, Jon, Detlef F. Sprinz, and Arild Underdal. 2009. Implementing Long-Term Climate Policy: Time Inconsistency, Domestic Politics, International Anarchy. *Global Environmental Politics* 9 (3): 20–39.

Howlett, Michael. 2002. Understanding National Administrative Styles and Their Impact upon Administrative Reform: A Neo-institutional Model and Analysis. *Policy and Society* 24 (4): 1–23.

Hughes, Everett C. 1936. The Ecological Aspect of Institutions. *American Sociological Review* 1:180–189.

Huntington, Samuel P. 1965. Political Development and Political Decay. *World Politics* 17 (3): 386–430.

Husock, Howard. 1998. *Executive-Led Government and Hong Kong's Legislative Council: Debating Harbor Protection. Case Study 1431.0*. Cambridge, Mass.: Kennedy School of Government, Harvard University.

Jasanoff, Sheila. 1990. *The Fifth Branch: Science Advisors and Policy Makers*. Cambridge, Mass.: Harvard University Press.

Jourde, Cédric. 2007. The International Relations of Small Neoauthoritarian States: Islamism, Warlordism, and the Framing of Stability. *International Studies Quarterly* 51 (2): 481–503.

Kingdon, John W. 1984. *Agendas, Alternatives, and Public Policies*. Boston: Little, Brown & Co.

Klingner, Donald E. 1996. Public Personnel Management and Democratization: A View from Three Central American Republics. *Public Administration Review* 56 (4): 390–399.

Knill, Christoph. 2001. *The Europeanisation of National Administrations: Patterns of Institutional Change and Persistence*. New York: Cambridge University Press.

Lee, Yok-shiu F. and Alvin Y. So, eds. 1999. *Asia's Environmental Movements: Comparative Perspectives*. Armonk, N.Y.: M. E. Sharpe.

Lowry, William. 2006. Potential Focusing Projects and Policy Change. *Policy Studies Journal* 34 (3): 313–335.

March, James G., and Johan P. Olsen. 2006. Elaborating the "New Institutionalism." In The Oxford Handbook of Political Institutions, edited by R. A. W. Rhodes, Sarah A. Binder, and Bert A. Rockman, 3–20. New York: Oxford University Press.

Mazmanian, Daniel A., and Paul A. Sabatier. 1983. *Implementation and Public Policy*. Glenview, Ill.: Scott, Foresman.

McAllister, Lesley K. 2008. *Making Law Matter: Environmental Protection and Legal Institutions in Brazil*. Palo Alto: Stanford University Press.

McNeely, Jeffrey. 2003. Conserving Forest Biodiversity in Times of Violent Conflict. *Oryx* 37 (2): 142–152.

Meadowcroft, James. 2005. From Welfare State to Ecostate. In *The State and the Global Ecological Crisis*, ed. John Barry and Robin Eckersley, 3–23. Cambridge, Mass.: MIT Press.

Meyer-Sahling, Jan-Hinrik. 2008. The Changing Colours of the Post-Communist State: The Politicisation of the Senior Civil Service in Hungary. *European Journal of Political Research* 47 (1): 1–33.

Migdal, Joel. 1987. *Strong Societies and Weak States: State-Society Relations and State Capabilities in the Third World*. Princeton: Princeton University Press.

Mitchell, Ronald B. 1994. *Intentional Oil Pollution at Sea: Environmental Policy and Treaty Compliance*. Cambridge, Mass.: MIT Press.

Moe, Terry. 1990. The Politics of Structural Choice: Toward a Theory of Public Bureaucracy. In *Organization Theory: From Chester Bernard to the Present and Beyond*, ed. Oliver E. Williamson, 116–153. New York: Oxford University Press.

North, Douglass C. 1981. *Structure and Change in Economic History*. New York: W.W. Norton.

O'Donnell, Guillermo. 1993. On the State, Democratization and Some Conceptual Problems: A Latin American View with Glances at Some Postcommunist Countries. *World Development* 21 (8): 1355–1369.

Ostrom, Elinor. 1999. Institutional Rational Choice: An Assessment of the Institutional Analysis and Development Framework. In *Theories of the Policy Process*, ed. Paul A. Sabatier. Boulder: Westview Press.

O'Toole, Laurence J., Jr., and Kenneth J. Meier. 2003. Plus ça Change: Public Management, Personnel Stability, and Organizational Performance. *Journal of Public Administration: Research and Theory* 13:43–64.

Patashnik, Eric M. 2008. *Reforms at Risk: What Happens after Major Policy Changes Are Enacted*. Princeton: Princeton University Press.

Pierson, Paul. 2000. Increasing Returns, Path Dependence, and the Study of Politics. *American Political Science Review* 94 (2): 251–267.

Pralle, Sarah B. 2006. Timing and Sequence in Agenda-Setting and Policy Change: A Comparative Study of Lawn Care Pesticide Politics in Canada and the US. *Journal of European Public Policy* 13 (7): 987–1005.

Przeworski, Adam. 2005. Democracy as an Equilibrium. *Public Choice* 123 (3–4): 253–273.

Quintela, Carlos E. 2003. In Workshop Proceedings, Building a Secure Financial Future: Finance and Resources, Fifth IUCN World Parks Congress, Durban, South Africa, September 8–17. Washington, DC: Conservation Finance Alliance.

Ribot, Jesse C. 2002. *Democratic Decentralization of Natural Resources: Institutionalizing Popular Participation*. Washington, DC: World Resources Institute.

Rochon, Thomas R., and Daniel A. Mazmanian. 1993. Social Movements and the Policy Process. *Annals of the American Academy of Political and Social Science* 528:75–87.

Rose, Richard. 1993. *Lesson-Drawing in Public Policy*. London: Chatham House Publishers.

Ross, Michael L. 2001. *Timber Booms and Institutional Breakdown in Southeast Asia*. New York: Cambridge University Press.

Sabatier, Paul A. 1988. An Advocacy Coalition Framework of Policy Change and the Role of Policy-Oriented Learning Therein. *Policy Sciences* 21 (2–3): 129–168.

Sabatier, Paul A., and Hank Jenkins-Smith, eds. 1993. *Policy Change and Learning: An Advocacy Coalition Approach*. Boulder: Westview Press.

Scharpf, Fritz W. 2000. Institutions in Comparative Policy Research. *Comparative Political Studies* 33 (6/7): 762–790.

Schedler, Andreas. 1998. What Is Democratic Consolidation? *Journal of Democracy* 9 (2): 91–107.

Sikkink, Kathryn. 1991. *Ideas and Institutions: Developmentalism in Brazil and Argentina*. Ithaca: Cornell University Press.

Silva, Eduardo, David Kaimowitz, Alan Bojanic, Francois Ekoko, Togu Manurung, and Iciar Pavez. 2002. Making the Law of the Jungle: The Reform of Forest Legislation in Bolivia, Cameroon, Costa Rica, and Indonesia. *Global Environmental Politics* 2 (3): 63–97.

Sloan, John W. 1984. *Public Policy in Latin America: A Comparative Survey*. Pittsburgh: University of Pittsburgh Press.

Sprinz, Detlef, and Tapani Vaahtoranta. 1994. The Interest-Based Explanation of International Environmental Policy. *International Organization* 48 (1): 77–105.

Stein, Ernesto, and Mariano Tommasi. 2008. *Policymaking in Latin America: How Politics Shapes Policies*. Cambridge, Mass.: Harvard University.

Steinberg, Paul F. 2001. *Environmental Leadership in Developing Countries: Transnational Relations and Biodiversity Policy in Costa Rica and Bolivia*. Cambridge, Mass.: MIT Press.

Steinberg, Paul F. 2005. From Public Concern to Policy Effectiveness: Civic Conservation in Developing Countries. *Journal of International Wildlife Law and Policy* 8:341–365.

Steinberg, Paul F. 2009. Institutional Resilience amid Political Change: The Case of Biodiversity Conservation. *Global Environmental Politics* 9 (3): 61–81.

Stern, Eric, Bengt Sundelius, Daniel Nohrstedt, Dan Hansén, Lindy Newlove, and Paul 't Hart. 2002. Crisis Management in Transitional Democracies: The Baltic Experience. *Government and Opposition* 37 (4): 524–550.

Social Learning Group. 2001. *Learning to Manage Global Environmental Risks: A Comparative History of Social Responses to Climate Change, Ozone Depletion and Acid Rain*. Vols. 1 and 2. Cambridge, Mass.: MIT Press.

Thelen, Kathleen. 1999. Historical Institutionalism in Comparative Politics. *Annual Review of Political Science* 2:369–404.

Tilly, Charles. 2001. Mechanisms in Political Processes. *Annual Review of Political Science* 4:21–41.

Tsebelis, George. 1995. Decision Making in Political Systems: Veto Players in Presidentialism, Parliamentarism, Multicameralism, and Multipartyism. *British Journal of Political Science* 25:289–385.

Turyahabwe, Nelson, and Abwoli Y. Banana. 2008. An Overview of the History and Development of Forest Policy and Legislation in Uganda. *International Forestry Review* 10:641–656.

Verheijen, T., and A. Robrenovic. 2001. The Evolution of Politico-Administrative Relations in Post-Communist States: Main Directions. In *Politico-Administrative Relations: Who Rules?* ed. T. Verheijen, 410–426. Bratislava: NISPAcee.

Vogel, David. 2003. The Hare and the Tortoise Revisited: The New Politics of Consumer and Environmental Regulation in Europe. *British Journal of Political Science* 33 (4): 557–580.

V

Comparative Multilevel Governance

11

EU Expansion and the Internationalization of Environmental Politics in Central and Eastern Europe

Liliana B. Andonova and Stacy D. VanDeveer

The countries of Central and Eastern Europe (CEE) have experienced a profound integration in international and regional institutions in the last twenty years. Environmental cooperation was an important aspect of the long journey from the relative isolation of the former communist countries from the Western world to full membership in the European Union and participation in hundreds of multilateral treaties and institutions. What has been the impact of international cooperation on domestic environmental politics? Under what conditions does international cooperation contribute to converging trends in domestic environmental policies and institutions? Under what conditions does divergence persist?

This chapter examines the international and domestic aspects of environmental politics in CEE in comparative perspective. International environmental influences were particularly strong in the context of postcommunist transition for several reasons. From Western perspectives, the end of communism uncovered massive environmental damage, some of it with transboundary impacts that required immediate attention and regional cooperation. At the same time, environmental movements played important roles as dissident movements in bringing down communist regimes. Environmental cooperation was also instrumental in facilitating a gradual détente between the former Soviet Union and the United States, and it was perceived as a relatively neutral, scientific arena in which to advance cooperative relations quickly (Botcheva 1996; Hicks and Kaminski 1995; Jancar-Webster 1993; Vari and Tamas 1993; VanDeveer 1997).

The newly democratized governments and societies of CEE promised to provide fertile ground for environmental ideas and policies developed abroad. Indeed many international actors perceived postcommunist states—as it turns out, not quite correctly—as tabula rasa for environmental management. Consequently, multiple programs of regional and global East–West environmental cooperation were launched and instituted (Andonova 2005; Connolly, Gutner, and Bedarff 1996; VanDeveer and Carmin 2006). This history provides a perfect opportunity to examine in comparative perspective how environmental politics are affected by international cooperation and how these policies evolve in a multilevel institutional context (Andonova 2004; Andonova, Mansfield, and Milner 2007; Carmin and VanDeveer 2005; Auer 2004).

This chapter shows that international cooperation has contributed to a trend of "diverging convergence" in the environmental politics of Central and Eastern European states, much as in other policy arenas (Bruszt 2002). There is a high degree of normative convergence in the principles that guide environmental policies in these states as well as formal regulatory convergence resulting from EU membership and the adoption of environmental laws. At the same time, we observe a persistent divergence in domestic environmental institutions, particularly with respect to the implementation of international and national policies. To explain these patterns of convergence and divergence, we examine environmental politics in CEE by looking at the interplay among international and domestic political actors, institutions, and processes and their influence on policy and institutional outcomes. The chapter first outlines three mechanisms of international environmental influence. It then examines these mechanisms and their interaction with domestic political outcomes across CEE countries in the context of the Environment for Europe Process, cooperation for regional commons, and in the process of EU accession.

Sources of International Influence

Following the broader literature on the interplay between international and domestic politics, we distinguish three types of influences of international cooperation and European integration in CEE: (1) normative and cognitive influence, (2) regulatory influence, and (3) the capacity-building influences of international institutions.

The diffusion of norms, consensual knowledge, and information is one of the most widely discussed mechanisms of international environmental influence. As elaborated in chapters 1 and 2, the spread of environmental norms and scientific information is facilitated by international regimes and materializes through multiple channels, including nongovernmental networks, scientific communities, and governmental elites and policy networks (Haas 1989; Knill and Lehmkuhl 1999; Keck and Sikkink 1998; Litfin 1994; O'Neill, Balsiger, and VanDeveer 2004). Indeed, in the early years of the postcommunist transition, there were a number of initiatives of East-West environmental cooperation that placed a strong emphasis on linking democratic and environmental norms and spreading both scientific and policy-relevant knowledge on environmental management (Andonova 2005; Pavlínek and Pickles 2000; VanDeveer 2004, 2005, 2006). Suasion, normative diffusion, and learning are also important aspects of the process of European integration and the resulting "Europeanization" of policies in the CEE states (Andonova 2005; Schimmelfennig and Sedelmeier 2005; Linden 2002; Carmin and VanDeveer 2005).

International regulatory commitments represent a second mechanism of international environmental influence, and an important contribution of this volume is to illuminate the domestic impacts of international regulation through a comparative lens. In CEE, the importance of this mechanism of international influence grew over time, particularly with EU accession (Andonova 2004; Schimmelfennig and Sedelmeier 2005; VanDeveer and Carmin 2006). The literature on international environmental institutions has emphasized the importance of international rules as a commitment mechanism to advance or strengthen policies that countries would not otherwise adopt or comply with in the absence of institutionalized collective action and monitoring. International regulations can also influence domestic politics through issue linkages as well as through redistribution of costs, benefits, and risks across sectors of society (Andonova 2004; Haas, Keohane, and Levy 1993; Mitchell 1994). Studies of international environmental regulation typically examine states as units of analysis and focus on their interaction with each other and on their overall level of compliance and implementation (Victor, Raustiala, and Skolnikoff 1998)

A third source of international influence, capacity building, is only rarely discussed in the literature as a separate mechanism. Capacity-building efforts generally seek to change or enhance the efficiency, effectiveness and/or normative content of a target organization (such as a state, local government, or NGO) or a defined population (such as an expert community or a subset of public servants) (Grindle 1997; Sagar 2000; VanDeveer and Dabelko 2001; VanDeveer and Sagar 2005; Sissenich 2007). Capacity-building programs are vehicles both for transferring norms and for the implementation of international commitments, because they are often tied closely to a particular norm or a particular international agreement. Typically, compliance and effectiveness studies view capacity-building programs as "management" mechanisms to prevent involuntary non-compliance (Haas, Keohane, and Levy 1993; Tallberg 2002). Yet capacity building may seek to change behaviors and institutional structures within target organizations and populations, and it is useful to examine it as a distinct mechanism of international influence separate from those of norms, knowledge, and specific international commitments.

Impacts of Internationalization: Convergence or Divergence?

How have CEE societies and governments adjusted to the multiple pressures and incentives associated with international environmental cooperation? We examine the extent to which the three mechanisms of international environmental influence elaborated above have resulted in convergence in environmental responses across CEE states. The presence of dense regional institutions, strong EU conditionality, and assistance for environmental reforms might lead us to expect fairly uniform convergence in the environmental norms, institutions, and regulations of CEE countries (Holzinger, Knill, and Sommerer 2009). But despite some degree of normative and regulatory convergence, considerable divergence in environmental practices and institutions persists across the region (Andonova 2004). We seek to account for this "converging divergence" by focusing on the interplay between domestic conditions and international influences.

The constructivist literatures on international norms and European integration emphasize several conditions for successful norm diffusion and internalization across member states, including the compatibility between domestic and international norms and practices and the presence of communities interested and able to facilitate norm and knowledge uptake domestically (Haas 1989; Knill and Lehmkuhl 1999; Schimmelfennig and Sedelmeier 2005). On the basis of this logic, the conditions for diffusion were particularly ripe in CEE at the very beginning of the transition period, when there was a great willingness domestically to link norms of democratization, international integration, and environmental stewardship. We should therefore expect normative convergence to be facilitated by institutions such as the Environment for Europe process and by regional programs, which were established early in the transition period and emphasized the creation of communities of knowledge that share and promote across Europe a normative linkage among democracy, European integration, and environmental protection.

Turning to the second category of international influence – regulatory commitments – we anticipate that the effects of European regulatory commitments depend on multiple interactions between international and domestic interests and institutions, producing areas of policy convergence as well as persistent divergence (Andonova 2004; Holzinger, Knill, and Sommerer 2009). Although the EU required full adoption of EU environmental regulations as a condition for accession, there has been considerable space left for differential paths of adoption of EU norms and diverse institutional designs for implementing these regulations. The literature on EU integration and regulatory harmonization identifies several conditions under which the interplay of domestic and international processes facilitates environmental convergence. When large lucrative markets are at stake, failure to adopt specific environmental regulations can serve as a trade barrier, creating strong incentives for regulatory mimicking and convergence (Vogel 1995; Andonova 2004). Regulatory convergence is also facilitated by an increasing number of transnational associations and NGOs operating simultaneously at domestic, regional, and international levels (Schreurs, Selin, and VanDeveer 2009). We call this "network-induced" convergence, and we would expect that policy arenas characterized by relatively dense regional and transnational organization and associated networks are more likely to facilitate some institutional and regulatory convergence. The presence of significant negative cross-border spillover effects is another factor likely to increase international pressure for convergence as a consequence of concerns about high negative externalities associated with failure in cooperation and compliance (Botcheva and Martin 2001). However, even in the presence of negative spillovers, domestic veto actors or institutions can still interfere with the extent to which convergence is achieved. International regulatory commitments that impose significant costs that are not offset by market benefits or by transnational pressure are more likely to produce divergent policies (Andonova 2004; Börzel 2002a).

We expect that capacity building, the third mechanism of international influence discussed previously, is likely to produce divergent adjustment of institutional practices as international programs interact with established domestic institutions and bureaucratic culture. If we understand transition politics not as a blank slate but as processes embedded in distinct domestic institutions and traditions, we would expect persistent divergence despite early international efforts to promote a consistent set of environmental policy instruments and institutions across CEE (Andonova 2004; Andonova, Mansfield, and Milner 2007). In the context of EU accession, capacity building has been extensive and has relied on "twinning programs" of cooperation between Western European and CEE bureaucracies to facilitate trans-European networks and to help establish adequate implementation institutions (Sissenich 2007). Capacity building may facilitate the convergence of norms and regulations even while institutional differences persist across a range of environmental policies. In the following empirical sections, we apply a comparative perspective to assess the extent to which specific capacity-building programs have fostered such convergence.

Table 11.1 summarizes this chapter's framework. It includes the three sources of international influence on environmental politics in CEE and lists cases of cooperative institutions (discussed shortly) in which one or more mechanisms of international influence are embedded. The table also specifies expectations regarding the conditions for convergence or divergence. The following sections examine these impacts empirically across three cases of regional environmental cooperation in Europe. First, we consider the Environment for Europe Process, instituted shortly after the end of the Cold War primarily as a platform for normative diffusion, with some capacity-building efforts to support institutional innovation. Second, we consider programs for governing regional commons, such as international cooperation centered on the Convention on Long-Range Transboundary Air Pollution (CLRTAP) and the Helsinki Conventions governing marine pollution in the Baltic Sea. These programs have strong knowledge diffusion and regulatory functions. Finally, we analyze the process of EU accession and its impact on environmental regulations as the most significant dimension of international regulatory, normative and capacity-building influence in the region. We use process tracing to illustrate the mechanisms of international influence within each of these forums for cooperation and to assess the conditions for convergence and divergence. This analysis draws on policy documents, the academic

Table 11.1
Sources of international influence in CEE environmental politics and their anticipated effects

Mechanisms of international influence	Exemplary cases	Convergence vs. divergence
Normative action Knowledge diffusion	Environment for Europe EU accession CLRTAP Helsinki Conventions	Normative convergence likely
Regulatory commitment	CLRTAP Helsinki Conventions EU accession	Regulatory convergence if (1) credible international commitment and pressure; (2) associated with market benefits and networks; (3) low cost of implementation Regulatory divergence if (1) high domestic cost of implementation; (2) blocking domestic interests; (3) weak domestic institutions
Capacity building	Environment for Europe EU accession	Contributes to normative, epistemic, and regulatory convergence Institutional divergence likely to persist

literature, and on the authors' interviews with policy makers, environmental NGOs, and economic interest groups.

Environment for Europe

The Environment for Europe Process was launched in 1991 to advance environmental cooperation between the newly democratized CEE countries and their West European counterparts. The first Ministerial Environment for Europe conference was proposed by Josef Vavrousek, the Czechoslovak Minister of the Environment and a former dissident, who hosted the meeting in the Dobris Castle near Prague in 1991. Ministerial meetings followed from 1993 to 2007 in Lucerne, Sofia, Aarhus, Kiev, and Belgrade. The overarching objective was to foster East-West environmental cooperation as a prerequisite for the reintegration of Europe and to increase the profile of environmental issues. Through these high-level meetings, the Environment for Europe Process aimed to advance a set of constitutive environmental principles, to diffuse policies and, to a lesser extent, to build capacity. Norm and knowledge diffusion was the primary mechanism of influence and was accomplished through a network of government officials, policy experts, environmental NGOs, and international organizations. Although there were some capacity-building efforts to help countries experiment with policy instruments such as economic taxes and fees, these efforts remained largely limited to knowledge diffusion.

Central and East European participants hoped that Environment for Europe would generate significant financial assistance and contribute to the better coordination of aid, but these hopes were soon disappointed (Andonova 2005; Connolly, Gutner, and Bedarff 1996). Efforts to increase aid commitments produced weak results, and donors preferred to maintain greater control over the allocation of aid by using bilateral channels. International financial institutions prioritized assistance according to their own standard operating procedures, rather than coordinating it within a broader international forum (Connolly, Gutner, and Bedarff 1996; Gutner 2002). This cooperative program thus did little to generate financial resources for dealing with environmental problems associated with the communist past of CEE countries or to strengthen domestic institutions. It did play some role in orienting the attention of development assistance programs toward environmental problems such as regional water management, hot spots (including the Black Triangle region between Germany, Poland, and the Czech Republic), and air pollution, which was identified as a prevalent problem across the region.

The failure of Environment for Europe to generate significant financial resources did not, however, compromise the broader agenda of diffusing norms and knowledge. Two of the principles promoted by the Environment for Europe program—access to environmental information and the use of economic instruments for environmental finance—illustrate how convergence in norms (and associated policies) developed alongside persistent institutional divergence in the region.

The conditions for policy convergence through norm diffusion, identified in table 11.1, were particularly ripe in the sphere of public access to environmental information. The principle of access to information was embraced by domestic advocacy groups and featured in regional and bilateral capacity-building initiatives. Arguably the largest and most enduring impact of international cooperation within the Environment for Europe forum was the legitimacy and support it lent to domestic actors seeking to embed environmental rights (particularly access to environmental information) in the new legislative frameworks developed in the aftermath of communism. This support was facilitated by Environment for Europe's unique characteristics (relative to other cooperative programs) that promoted interaction among high-level officials, international financial institutions, and NGOs, particularly those supported by the Regional Environmental Center. The Regional Environmental Center, with headquarters in Hungary, was funded with US assistance to support environmental NGOs and public participation in the region (Francis, Klarer, and Petkova 1999). The link between the domestic objectives of democratization and environmental protection in the early postcommunist period ensured that the principle of access to information diffused and became institutionalized relatively quickly across the region. Furthermore, many former environmental dissidents joined the first postcommunist administrations, in which they served as a transmission belt for ideas and policy proposals between the international and domestic arenas. Bulgaria's Ecoglasnost, for example—which led numerous environmental protests against the communist government in the 1980s—gained parliamentary seats in the first democratic elections, as did green movements in Poland, Czechoslovakia, and Hungary (Andonova 2004; Botcheva 1996). These developments produced a close correspondence between the norms promoted through Environment for Europe and the deep-rooted concerns of advocates and expert communities across CEE countries regarding democratization and access to environmental information.

By the middle of the 1990s, virtually all CEE countries had adopted the principles of citizens' right to information and the right to a healthy environment in their postcommunist constitutions and in framework legislation on environmental protection. According to a 1995 survey conducted by the Regional Environmental Center, of the ten countries that are now members of the EU, only Estonia had refrained from including the right to a healthy environment in its constitution or environmental policy documents (REC 1995). These countries also adopted laws and ordinances requiring environmental impact assessment (EIA) in the early 1990s, long before EIA regulation was established as a formal condition for compliance with EU regulations as part of the accession process.

Despite these trends toward convergence in the early 1990s, the legislative mechanisms used to establish the rules for EIA and the extent of public participation in the process differed considerably across countries. A 1995 comparative assessment of EIA procedures and practices in the region revealed that some countries, such as Slovakia and the Czech Republic, had already adopted elaborate legislation to facilitate EIA implementation, including public access to the process and to the information generated, and that other countries were just beginning to consider the adoption of a relevant legislative framework (REC 1995). In Hungary, vague regulatory language resulted in inconsistent application of the approach, and an analysis of EIA procedures in Latvia concluded that "lack of information inhibits public participation. Enterprises often ignore the requirements of the EIA and the public does not always realize the possible impact on human health and the social consequences of certain activities" (REC 1995, 85). International cooperation enabled domestic NGOs to publicize inconsistent application of the access to information principle and to generate transnational pressure on their governments. Environmental NGOs in Bulgaria, for example, raised awareness about a proposed 1995 amendment to the Environmental Protection Law, which could reverse EIA requirements in instances where "vital interests of the population are at stake." The NGOs used international conferences and commitments to pressure the Bulgarian government to uphold the original EIA legislation. Environmental NGOs in Poland and the

Czech Republic worked to expand the scope of EIA procedures and information access beyond that required by EU and domestic legislation, to include areas such as chemical safety and transportation. These NGOs were supported by a network of local REC offices, which served as focal points for coordination, expertise, and increasing the voice of civil society domestically and in the Environment for Europe process.

As is anticipated by our theoretical framework, the interplay between domestic advocacy and the international norms supported by Environment for Europe resulted in high levels of convergence and, over time, compliance with the principle of access to information. A 1996 study by the Regional Environmental Center (REC 1996), conducted prior to any formal preparation for EU accession, revealed that by the mid-1990s there was already a relatively high level of convergence between EU law and the policy frameworks adopted in CEE countries. Normative convergence and its embodiment in domestic law were further strengthened by the adoption in 1998 of the Aarhus Convention, considered one of the crowning achievements of Environment for Europe. The convention established a binding pan-European agreement both for the EU and CEE to "guarantee the rights of access to information, public participation in decision-making, and access to justice in environmental matters."[1] The Aarhus Convention was the result of years of work by networks of NGOs, policy makers, and environmental bureaucracies, supported by the Environment for Europe framework and the Regional Environmental Center.

The Environment for Europe process also instituted modest capacity-building activities, intended primarily to institutionalize national environmental management strategies, the use of market-based environmental policies, and the creation of extra-budgetary environmental endowments to support environmental investments. Capacity building was undertaken primarily by the Organization for Economic Cooperation and Development (OECD), which provided technical and managerial experience and assistance in the institutional design of environmental funds. The environmental funds were intended to address the gap between the high investment needs for environmental improvements and limited private and public resources in postcommunist countries. This institutional innovation was developed first by a few leading reformers, such as Poland, and promoted across the region and in the former Soviet Union by experts from international financial institutions. The funds drew income mostly from domestic sources, such as pollution taxes, penalties, and in some instances budget allocations, complemented by some foreign assistance. With active support and capacity building from Environment for Europe, the fund system was adopted by virtually all CEE countries.

Despite convergence in the form of these policy instruments, considerable divergence remained in the ability of national environmental administrations to institutionalize and endow environmental funds (Andonova, Mansfield, and Milner 2007;

Francis, Klarer, and Petkova 1999). In Poland, there was a close match between the concept of environmental investment funds and a turn in the country's environmental policy toward greater use of economic instruments. Early in the postcommunist transition period, the Polish government instituted high pollution taxes and penalties and a strict system of enforcement through national and regional inspectorates. This system became the source of revenues for a well-endowed National Environmental Fund as well as regional environmental funds, reflecting the relatively high degree of autonomy enjoyed by regional governments in the management of environmental resources. This approach facilitated the creation of a network of regional environmental funds that were instrumental in supporting local environmental priorities.

The Czech Republic also established a strong national environmental fund, although its environmental policies did not emphasize market-based instruments, instead earmarking resources from the privatization process and maintaining a high collection rate for water, air, and waste charges. In both Poland and the Czech Republic, the institutionalization of environmental funds was facilitated by synergies between the policy instruments supported by international actors and the domestic political priorities and institutional traditions of CEE countries. Those countries that lacked supportive policy frameworks and institutional traditions also created environmental funds with international support, but these were poorly endowed and less effective in promoting environmental investments. The 1997 income of the National Environmental Fund of Bulgaria and of Estonia were US$10 million and US$8 million, respectively, and the income of the Environmental Fund of Hungary was US$81 million and that of the Czech Environmental Fund was US$167 million. These disparities reflect variation in domestic policy commitments to institute tough economic instruments for the environment and the capacity to collect penalties, taxes, and fees (Andonova, Mansfield, and Milner 2007). This variation suggests that institutional innovations promoted through capacity-building programs are more likely to stick if they find a receptive policy environment and domestic policy entrepreneurs who can take advantage of international commitments and translate their principles in particular domestic contexts.

In sum, the Environment for Europe Process influenced state practices primarily through the transmission of norms, fostering (alongside the efforts of domestic advocates) normative convergence on the dual objectives of democracy and environmental stewardship. However, the domestic impact of capacity-building efforts was variable. The use of environmental funds has been highly variable and has been shaped by cross-national divergence in institutional contexts and in state commitments to administer environmental taxes and penalties. Countries that, for domestic purposes, emphasized strong implementation and enforcement were able to build on these policies and establish strong and well-endowed environmental funds. Low political interest and domestic capacity to enforce and collect environmental taxes and fees translated into relatively weak environmental funds.

Regional Commons Cooperation

Europe is home to a host of influential regional environmental cooperation arrangements (Balsiger and VanDeveer 2010), particularly institutions constructed to protect and improve environmental quality around the continent's many regional seas, such as the Baltic and Mediterranean (Brooks and VanDeveer 1997; VanDeveer 2000) and the set of pan-European air pollution agreements within the United Nations Economic Commission for Europe (UNECE) and under CLRTAP (Andonova 2004, 2006a; Selin and VanDeveer 2003; VanDeveer 2004, 2005, 2006). This dense network of regional agreements and related organizations includes numerous forums in which state compliance is periodically assessed and reported. Ongoing implementation reviews tend to increase the prospects of state implementation and compliance (Victor, Raustiala, and Skolnikoff 1998). Regulatory commitments are the primary mechanism through which these "regional commons" regimes influence domestic institutions in CEE, although capacity building and norm diffusion have also played a supporting role. As discussed shortly, and as anticipated by our theoretical framework, these regulatory commitments produced variable impacts on domestic policies and institutions, both over time and across countries. This variation reflects the changing interplay between domestic and international regulatory incentives, institutional practices, and knowledge.

State engagement in regional seas cooperation has varied substantially across Central and Eastern Europe. Marine pollution control efforts are most robust around the Baltic Sea, including strong regional treaties and dozens of mutually agreed-upon, voluntary recommendations for pollution control, monitoring, and assessment. Over the course of the 1990s, EU member states in the Baltic region (especially Finland, Germany, and Sweden) led efforts to harmonize regional commitments with EU environmental policy (Selin and VanDeveer 2004; VanDeveer 2011). As such, CEE states that were candidates for EU membership (and then eventual members) had overlapping incentives to implement policy changes to combat marine pollution. The secretariat for Baltic Sea marine pollution cooperation is the Helsinki Commission (HELCOM), which has emerged as a central node of regional cooperation in environmental science and politics (VanDeveer 2000, 2002). States such as Estonia, Latvia, Lithuania, and Poland have achieved reasonably high rates of environmental policy change and implementation of HELCOM commitments (Selin and VanDeveer 2004). Policy makers looked to HELCOM recommendations and to EU laws and regulations as they instituted domestic environmental policy reforms in the 1990s (VanDeveer 1997, 2002). Where marine pollution policies are concerned, Estonia and Latvia successfully integrated international assistance for pollution cleanup projects with broader public and NGO sector capacity building to completely reform domestic environmental policies, organizations, and practices. New institutions to monitor and assess environmental quality and policy implementation were established, and detailed regulations were issued that implemented many HELCOM recommendations.

Larger states such as Poland (on the Baltic Sea) and Romania (on the Black Sea) have found the tasks of environmental policy change and implementation more difficult than in smaller states such as Estonia, Latvia, and Croatia. The large states have enacted legislative and regulatory change, but building the domestic capacity to implement and enforce these changes has proven difficult. Country size (and the related size of the state itself) may be important in influencing outcomes simply because the scale of bureaucratic, personnel, and normative change differs, though this relationship needs further research. In another trend related to country size, environmental monitoring and enforcement has been decentralized in both Poland and Romania—delegated to local or regional authorities around the country, often to organizations and personnel who lack the capacity to accomplish the tasks assigned to them. Decentralization of authority was an idea pushed by international organizations of various kinds in the wake of communism's collapse, and the stability and results of these reforms varied widely across the region (Yoder 2003).

Comparing the effects of regional seas cooperation across the region—around the Baltic, Mediterranean, and Black Seas, for example—suggests that more institutionalized, well-funded, and active regional cooperation initiatives are more likely to affect domestic norms, laws and behaviors (VanDeveer 2000). For example, in all three marine regions, regional cooperation has enhanced transnational scientific and technical cooperation. Experts around all three seas have more contact with one another, share more data, engage in more joint research, and develop more consensual knowledge about the state of each sea and what should be done about it than they could in the absence of regional cooperation institutions (VanDeveer 2000). In the Baltic region, however, more intensive and extensive cooperation around detailed policies and procedures has yielded more discernable domestic political impacts than can be seen in the Mediterranean and Black Sea regions. The integration of pollution prevention and sustainable development discourses into domestic politics and regulation can be seen in all of the CEE states. However, the degree to which these discourses have been incorporated into environmental policy varies greatly, at least partly in response to differences in the capabilities of state and local actors to develop and implement environmental policy (VanDeveer 1997, 2000). In other words, the ability of policy makers and state organizations to convert environmental discourses into laws, policies, and programmatic activities depends, at least in part, on the capacities of public sector institutions and personnel. Where capacities are robust, ideational and normative changes promoted through international cooperation can be acted upon and institutionalized to a greater extent than is the case when public sector capacity is limited.

Turning our attention to air pollution cooperation institutions, the process of East-West cooperation with CLRTAP has a history dating back to the Cold War, when it was viewed as a convenient platform to foster détente through scientific and environmental cooperation (Haas, Keohane, and Levy 1993; Levy 1995). Initially, the main mechanism of international influence was knowledge-based. By raising awareness about air pollution and strengthening the prominence and voice of the domestic scientific community, CLRTAP cooperation supported the growth of environmental awareness and its linkage to the anticommunist movement in communist Europe.

From the late 1980s through much of the 1990s, CLRTAP cooperation clearly enhanced scientific and technical knowledge and transnational engagement around air pollution issues across most of the CEE region (VanDeveer 2005, 2006), although states with the most developed air pollution research programs, such as Poland and the Czech Republic, were clearly the most engaged. Great differences persisted, however, in the impacts of this knowledge on domestic policy across the region. First, institutional connections among domestic scientific and technical air pollution experts were slow to develop in the postcommunist period. Communist regimes often lacked institutions designed to bring scientific and technical critiques to bear on policy making. Such input and review processes do not just spring from the ground when authoritarian governance ends; they must be built over time. Second, the technical and modeling information generated within CLRTAP bodies tended to be used in CEE countries to assess implementation costs rather than to directly inform environmental regulation or lawmaking.

The regulatory impact of CLRTAP was initially minimal. The governments of communist countries signed the agreement to advance their foreign policy goals, without implementing policy for the reduction of air pollutants causing regional acidification. In the early postcommunist period, CEE governments anticipated a greater "bite" for CLRTAP standards, as compliance was likely to be a condition for European reintegration. They bargained hard for more lenient standards or financial transfers, and when none materialized, it was anticipated that CEE countries would have difficulty implementing the regulations embedded in the Second Sulfur Protocol and in subsequent protocols regulating nitrogen oxides, volatile organic compounds, and the multiple pollutants covered by the 1999 Gothenburg Protocol (Levy 1995; McCormick 1998). This series of protocols imposed emission limits on all CEE countries on the basis of their contribution to acidification and other transboundary air pollution problems in Europe and required them to implement costly desulfurization technologies compatible with "best available technology" standards.

By 2007, however, virtually all CEE states were complying with the standards mandated by CLRTAP protocols (Andonova 2006b). This high level of convergence can be attributed to several factors. The initial economic decline and restructuring in CEE countries contributed to reduced air pollution. More important, however, was that CEE states adopted air pollution policies to support EU accession and as a consequence maintained low levels of acidifying emissions even after the mid-1990s, when their economies grew rapidly (Andonova 2004; 2006b). International air pollution regulations, including CLRTAP standards and related EU directives, served as commitment mechanisms for domestic reformers, allowing them to push forward and implement national regulations. The environmental administrations of Bulgaria and the former Czechoslovakia, for example, used (in 1995 and 1991, respectively) the CLRTAP conventions and associated international negotiation events to argue in their national parliaments that the adoption of air pollutions standards compatible with European regulations was a necessary condition for advancing their ultimate foreign policy objective of reintegration in Europe. These arguments were made prior to the pre-accession agreements with the EU and referred primarily to CLRTAP regulations, which were already formally binding for the two countries (Andonova 2004). The relatively high level of convergence in compliance was thus initially facilitated by economic restructuring and subsequently sustained by anticipatory policy adaptation to West European standards for which CLRTAP was taken as a benchmark early in the transition process.

Behind the high level of convergence in adopting CLRTAP and EU air pollution standards, however, there was considerable divergence in the pace of institutional reforms that CEE countries adopted to implement these standards. Some countries, such as the Czech Republic and Slovakia, adopted stringent, technology-based standards early in the transition processes, assuring anticipatory overcompliance even with subsequent regional or EU regulations. In the Czech Republic, what mattered most was the broad commitment mechanisms that a reform-seeking administration used to revamp air pollution policy (Andonova 2004; Ministry of the Environment of the Czech Republic 1995).

In Poland, the institutional approach to air pollution regulation was completely different, emphasizing (as noted earlier) green investment and market-based regulatory instruments, which often clashed with the best available technology model institutionalized under CLRTAP and EU acidification regulations (Andersson 1999). The Polish emphasis on market instruments was motivated by several domestic factors, including a strongly unionized coal sector that could block regulatory approaches negatively affecting the economy. This situation provided an incentive for the government to experiment with instruments carrying fewer direct economic impacts and for which the cost of regulation could be extended more readily to consumers. Poland's first postcommunist environmental strategy thus emphasized cost-effective improvements in ambient standards rather than immediate implementation of costly technology-based standards (Andersson 1999; Andonova 2004). This emphasis implied considerably greater institutional adaptation, more liberal interpretation of the CLRTAP best available technology requirement, and longer transition periods to adopt some of the most stringent EU regulations on acidification. Indeed, the Polish government, in cooperation with its power sector, produced multiple economic analyses to identify the most liberal interpretation of CLRTAP and EU standards and regulatory approaches to allow maximum flexibility (Andersson 1999; Andonova 2004, 2006a). The Polish government also used its strong system of environmental funds to support the implementation of desulfurization technology, reducing the cost and thereby avoiding opposition from the energy sector.

Bulgaria exemplifies another approach to regulatory adaptation to EU and CLRTAP regulatory standards on acid rain. In a context of limited domestic institutional capacity and the absence of strong international capacity building or transfer programs for acid rain, the Bulgarian government initially adopted the European standards, but did so without an institutional infrastructure for implementation or the capacity to offset the cost of regulation (as in the case of Poland). In 1996, the government adopted regulations that conformed to the spirit of CLRTAP regulations, but left a loophole for temporary regulatory exemption for firms facing economic hardship (National Assembly of the Republic of Bulgaria 1995). With the privatization and restructuring of the power sector, however, the obligation to comply with CLRTAP and similar EU standards was passed from the state to the new owners and operators of power plants. This change provided a mechanism for going beyond mere legislative harmonization toward greater implementation of CLRTAP and EU air pollution standards (Andonova 2002, 2004). These examples demonstrate that despite the presence of strong and dual sources of international influence on domestic acid rain policies (CLRTAP and EU directives), the persistence of divergent domestic responses and institutions can be anticipated in regulatory arenas that require considerable institutional adjustment.

EU Accession

Membership in the EU has entailed profound political and institutional transformations in candidate countries, both prior to and since the 2004 accession of the Czech Republic, Estonia, Hungary, Latvia, Lithuania, Poland, Slovakia, and Slovenia and the 2007 accession of Bulgaria and Romania. After the collapse of Communist rule in 1989, international engagement and foreign assistance to CEE states and societies gradually shifted from an initial emphasis on abandoning Soviet-style governance toward a focus on assisting CEE states in their quest to integrate into the EU and other Western institutions. The accession process involved years of international-level negotiations among officials from the EU, the member states, and each of the candidate countries, as well as years of effort within each candidate country to "harmonize" domestic laws and policies with those of the EU. Environmental policy harmonization was one of the areas requiring sweeping domestic changes and the dedication of substantial resources within CEE states and societies (Andonova 2004; Carmin and VanDeveer 2005; Börzel 2009). The accession process was so ambitious and broad in its scope that it entailed all three of the mechanisms of international influence discussed in this chapter: normative action and knowledge diffusion, regulatory commitments, and capacity building. Each of these mechanisms is addressed in the growing "Europeanization" research literature, which is briefly reviewed in this short case study of CEE accession to EU membership.

Environment-related foreign assistance often seeks to remediate environmental problems themselves and/or to support the creation of new environmental organizations, policies, and initiatives. In CEE countries, during the first ten to fifteen years of the transition era, international environmental assistance initiatives often explicitly sought to develop environment-related capacities of states and NGOs (Carmin and VanDeveer 2005). While building capabilities, such assistance programs may also diffuse Western environmental norms, values and expertise among state and nonstate officials and organizations, thereby shaping institutional development (Linden 2002; VanDeveer 1997, 2002). Environmental remediation and the building of new institutions in Central and Eastern Europe were heavily influenced by foreign aid through technical capacity-building programs (VanDeveer and Carmin 2006) and by initiatives that adopted a more expansive approach to capacity-development seeking to more substantially transform aspects of the public, private, and civil society sectors (Sagar 2000; VanDeveer and Sagar 2005). As a consequence, the process of making environmental law and regulations was reshaped in important ways in the formerly communist states, strengthening the role of environmental bureaucracies and seeking to advance monitoring and enforcement organizations and procedures.

EU accession processes involved a vast number of complex pathways through which knowledge and norms could potentially diffuse into CEE states and societies, in part because it paralleled rapid political, economic, and social integration of CEE states and societies with those in the EU. EU actors commissioned repeated assessments of each CEE state's progress toward harmonization with EU law and policy. Such assessment involved hundreds of consultants, public officials, and NGOs in EU and candidate countries (see, e.g., Andonova 2006a; Ecotech 2001a, 2001b; European Commission 2001; Kruger and Carius 2001). Many of these same actors participated in a host of non-EU forums, including OECD and UNECE, conducting similar reviews (OECD 2000; UNECE 1996, 1998, 1999, 2000a, 2000b, 2001). Such assessment efforts built networks, raised awareness, and improved knowledge about EU policies and expectations within CEE, while apprising EU officials and NGOs of progress toward accession and challenges to harmonization (Carmin and VanDeveer 2005; VanDeveer 2005, 2006).

The large social science research literature seeking to define, measure, and assess the "Europeanization" of domestic policies demonstrates the dramatic expansion of EU authority and the significant influence of the EU on its member states and societies (Börzel 2002a; 2002b; Jordan and Liefferink 2005; Knill 2001; Knill and Lenschow 2000; Ladrech 2010). Although this "Europeanizing" turn in social science research originally focused on the relationship between EU institutions and member states, it has been also applied to EU enlargement and subsequent influence on new member states (Andonova 2004; Carmin and VanDeveer 2005; Börzel 2009).

Europeanization research has explored (1) "top-down" dynamics of EU influence on such factors as the content of member state policy, policy-making styles, state structures, and political processes; (2) the movement of policy competencies "up" to the EU level from member states; and (3) the dynamic interaction of EU and member state institutions and debates (Jordan and Liefferink 2005). The domestic adjustments needed to implement EU policies (a generally top-down approach) is clearly relevant to EU expansion in CEE, because the EU required that CEE states enact the *acquis*—the total body of EU law—in order to gain admission. This approach to EU influence proceeds from the assumption that member and candidate states must change (at least in part) to accommodate EU policy decisions. In the CEE accession process, this was clearly the case, as CEE officials and citizens did not participate in building the environmental *acquis* that they were required to adopt to gain admission.

Europeanization scholarship analyzes EU-induced domestic adjustment through various causal pathways (Knill and Lehmkuhl 1999). The first, a hierarchical institutional model, suggests that subordinate units adjust domestic institutions when required to do so by EU policy-making processes or policy outcomes. Another path of EU influence entails altering domestic opportunity structures, whereby incentives for domestic political actors in member or candidate states are changed as a result of EU political debate and policy making. Changes in incentives might, for example, result from changing market incentives within the EU's single market (Andonova 2004). They might also result from attempts by domestic environmental officials to leverage EU environmental policy debates or requirements into greater domestic political influence. Lastly, Europeanization scholarship posits that actors may well change more than strategies and interests. Rather, their beliefs, values, and expectations are also changed as a result of Europeanization processes. For example, environmental concern and awareness among citizens or policy makers may be increased by EU policy debates, procedures, and dictates. Rather than merely influence their material interests or interest calculations, Europeanization may alter actors' underlying preferences and beliefs regarding policy and environmental quality (Knill 2001; Knill and Lehmkuhl 1999).

As such, EU-driven domestic changes call attention to the strategic behavior of various actors, including that of government officials, NGOs, and firms, and to potential changes in values, norms, and expectations. While EU officials attempt to exercise power directly over CEE states during accession negotiations and via international aid programs, incentives for domestic actors and these actors' values and beliefs also change in response to EU actions and to transformations brought about by political and economic transitions. As property rights and ownership patterns change across the region, for example, so have the incentives for private sector and state actors. Furthermore, civil society actors have continued to push for greater participation in policy making and greater access to information.

Consistent with top-down expectations, CEE officials moved to enhance national legal, administrative, and human resource capacities associated with environmental policy in response to EU directives and regulations that require a host of specific laws, procedures, standards, and regulatory functions. Many CEE state initiatives in environmental policy occurred because the EU required them as part of accession obligations and capacity-building efforts. EU officials and consultants regularly assessed how well each candidate state was progressing in its attempts to harmonize its laws and regulations with those of the EU, highlighting problematic areas and publicizing concerns. In responses, CEE officials and institutions were expected to act to bring identified problems into accord with EU expectations. EU officials can file complaints with the European Court if they believe any member state is failing to comply with EU requirement.

Changing domestic incentives are visible in a variety of areas, including the involvement of environmental actors (state officials and civil society groups) in domestic policy making, the impacts of EU assistance programs, the cofinancing requirements of international donors, and the changing practices of consumers and private sector actors amid market liberalization and privatization (Andonova 2004; Carmin and VanDeveer 2005; Börzel 2010). These changes can affect environmental outcomes, such as reductions in industrial pollution emissions and/or increases in household wastes, traffic, and urban sprawl (Carmin and VanDeveer 2005). Thus, these variable outcomes may all make CEE states and societies more European, even when they do not result in improved environmental protection or greater sustainability.

With respect to norms and knowledge diffusion, the institutionalization of EU norms and the impact of EU decisions and discourses on the beliefs and expectations of domestic actors is evident across the region. For example, norms associated with

NGO involvement in policy making attempt to apply concepts such as pollution prevention, the precautionary principle, and polluter pays approaches (manifest in pollution taxes, for example) to policy processes and outcomes in CEE states. All suggest changing norms and ideas about environmental governance across the CEE region (Carmin and VanDeveer 2005; Börzel 2009). Examination of both the material and ideational aspects of Europeanization (or EU-driven change) is essential for explaining the resulting variation in political outcomes.

At one level, Europeanization processes affect applicant states through the same pathways that shape long-standing member states. Yet merely asking how domestic institutions adjust to accommodate EU policy, as is common in contemporary "top-down" Europeanization research, misses a number of important dynamics. First, it may underestimate the influence of domestic agents and institutions on policy and behavioral outcomes. Domestic NGOs and public sector actors—sometimes in cooperation with a non-EU international actor such as a foundation—are important determinants of domestic CEE policy and environmental quality outcomes. Second, top-down Europeanization approaches appear to underestimate the interactive learning processes that take place under the guise of EU harmonization and implementation. For example, the Europeanization of CEE environmental policy has revealed problems and limitations with EU policy in numerous areas of environmental, transport, agricultural, investment, and energy policies (Carmin and VanDeveer 2005). In other words, in the process of trying to apply EU policy in CEE states and societies, changes and/or greater flexibility in EU policies may occur, calling into question the unidirectional assumptions of the top-down approaches.

In sum, partly because EU accession and harmonization of new member states' policies and procedures is so expansive in its goals and requirements, all three of this chapter's mechanisms of international influence are identifiable in Europeanization processes and scholarship. As Europeanization research demonstrates, normative action and knowledge diffusion, regulatory commitments, and capacity-building programs all shape the structure and content of accession states and their environmental policies. Though international influence is substantial across all CEE states, this does not (and should not be expected to) produce exactly the same policy or institutional outcomes. CEE states' and societies' distinct institutions interact with these international influences in particular ways and in unique combinations, leaving institutional differences and some divergence in policy and in implementation outcomes.

Conclusions

The postcommunist countries of CEE present a case of profound internationalization of domestic environmental politics. Several mechanisms explored in this chapter—norm diffusion, regulatory commitments, and capacity building—interact with domestic norms, actors, and policy institutions to influence environmental policy in the region. This high degree of internationalization is in some ways unique to Europe due to the high degree of regional and supranational cooperation in the region. Nevertheless, the presence of multiple cases and multiple paths of adjustment to these international forces allows us to disentangle the mechanisms of international influence and to trace their interplay with domestic politics in comparative perspective.

Several important and broadly generalizable observations can be made on the basis of this analysis. The multiple mechanisms of international influence examined in this chapter are often considered to be in competition with one another, according to different theoretical perspectives in international relations. A comparative analysis demonstrates, however, that normative, epistemic, regulatory, and capacity-building mechanisms of European influence often coexist and interact with each other and have a greater impact on national policies when they encounter favorable domestic conditions. For example, the diffusion of norms and regulations regarding environmental impact assessment and access to information was facilitated by the early willingness of CEE administrations to link democratization and environmental protection and by the international programs and institutions established to promote these dual objectives.

The high degree of compliance with CLRTAP standards was also facilitated by favorable domestic conditions including economic restructuring, high concern about air pollution, and the ability of environmental administrations across the region to use CLRTAP regulations as a commitment mechanism to advance new domestic air pollution legislation. CLRTAP implementation was also accelerated by growing links and harmonization efforts between EU policy and CLRTAP. However, the air pollution case also demonstrates that despite the high level of internationalization of environmental politics in CEE, considerable institutional divergence persists in regulatory areas that involve significant implementation costs and institutional adjustment. Capacity-building efforts sometimes do mitigate these adjustment costs, resulting in some degree of institutional convergence. Although capacity-building contributes to policy convergence, it cannot be expected to erase the institutional differences among CEE states.

The size and institutionalization of capacity-building efforts and the significant variance among capacity-building programs deserve more attention. The early financial transfer and institutional strengthening programs targeted primarily environmental "hot spots"—localized areas of severe environmental contamination. These programs were effective in mitigating particular environmental problems but were weakly coordinated and not well institutionalized (Connolly, Gutner, and Bedarff 1996). By contrast, later EU assistance for institutional strengthening through expert "twinning" and transfer of managerial and investment resources has been relatively centralized and much larger in size (Sissenich 2007; VanDeveer and Carmin 2006). Clearly EU assistance has often sought to transform the structure of state and non-state institutions more broadly, not just enhance the technical abilities of particular actors (Börzel 2009).

Paradoxically, EU enlargement produces both greater diversity and more European unity. Consequently, it is clear that simply asking "How do domestic institutions and actors change in response to EU action?" is too narrow a question to capture the diversity of factors shaping environmental policy change and environmental outcomes across the CEE region. European politics is changing, not just "expanding" its territory (Carmin and VanDeveer 2005). CEE state and NGO actors have responded to many revolutionary changes, not merely those engendered by the *acquis*. The changes in environmental institutions and outcomes driven by EU accession cannot be explained without attention to larger changes in political and economic structures and shifts in the roles and expectations of state officials, citizens, and civil society groups. In other words, although EU accession drove the environmental policy agendas in CEE states for over a decade, it is not the only factor that significantly shapes policy outcomes.

EU foreign assistance programs and EU foreign policy increasingly seek to shape state structures and policies around the EU periphery across former Soviet republics and parts of the Mediterranean region. Our study suggests that such efforts, coupled with other international and bilateral programs, are likely to produce variable but notable influence through the diffusion of norms, regulations, capacity, and epistemic networks. Further study of these impacts in countries with close European cooperation but no formal membership accession processes is needed to illuminate the patterns of internationalization of domestic environmental politics. Such studies might better isolate the influence of formal EU membership from the dense set of internationalizing institutions that characterizes European cooperation.

A final point about greater legal and environmental policy convergence can be drawn from the CEE experience—namely, that increased convergence of state and social institutions does not necessarily produce homogeneity. States and societies can move in the same directions, enact many similar policies, and reshape public institutions in similar ways and still retain specific regulatory styles and institutional characteristics. International actors and institutions interact with domestic actors and institutions in highly complex ways. CEE states and societies suggest that "converging divergence" often results.

Note

1. Article 1, Aarhus Convention, http://www.unece.org/env/pp/documents/cep43e.pdf, accessed June 8, 2011.

References

Andersson, Magnus. 1999. *Change and Continuity in Poland's Environmental Policy.* Boston: Kluwer Academic Publishers.

Andonova, Liliana B. 2002. The Challenges and Opportunities for Reforming Bulgaria's Energy Sector. *Environment* 44 (10): 8–19.

Andonova, Liliana B. 2004. *Transnational Politics and the Environment: EU Integration and Environmental Policy in Central and Eastern Europe.* Cambridge, Mass.: MIT Press.

Andonova, Liliana B. 2005. The Europeanization of Environmental Policy in Central and Eastern Europe. In *The Europeanization of Central and Eastern Europe*, ed. Frank Schimmelfennig and Ulrich Sedelmeier, 135–155. Ithaca: Cornell University Press.

Andonova, Liliana B. 2006a. Structure and Influence of International Assessments: Lessons from Eastern Europe. In *Global Environmental Assessments: Information and Influence*, ed. Ronald B. Mitchell, William C. Clark, David W. Cash, and Nancy M. Dickson, 151–173. Cambridge, Mass.: MIT Press.

Andonova, Liliana B. 2006b. Acid Rain in a Wider Europe. In *Acid in the Environment: Lessons Learned and Future Prospects*, ed. Gerald R. Visgilio and Diana M. Whitelaw, 151–174. Berlin: Springer.

Andonova, Liliana B., Edward D. Mansfield, and Helen V. Milner. 2007. International Trade and Environmental Policy in the Post-Communist World. *Comparative Political Studies* 40 (10): 1–27.

Auer, Mathew R., ed. 2004. *Restoring Cursed Earth: Appraising Environmental Policy Reforms in Central and Eastern Europe and Russia.* Lanham, Md.: Rowman & Littlefield.

Balsiger, Joerg, and Stacy D. VanDeveer. 2010. Regional Governance and Environmental Problems. In *International Studies Encyclopedia*, vol. 9, ed. Robert A. Denemark, 6179–6200. Malden, Mass.: Blackwell Publishing.

Börzel, Tanja. 2002a. *States and Regions in the European Union: Institutional Adaptation in Germany and Spain.* Cambridge, UK: Cambridge University Press.

Börzel, Tanja A. 2002b. Improving Compliance Through Domestic Mobilization? New Instruments and the Effectiveness of Implementation. In *Implementing EU Environmental Policy: New Directions and Old Problems*, ed. Christopher Knill and Andrea Lenschow, 222–250. Manchester, UK: Manchester University Press.

Börzel, Tanja. 2009. *Coping with Accession to the European Union: New Modes of Environmental Governance.* New York: Palgrave Macmillan.

Börzel, Tanja A., ed. 2010. Civil Society on the Rise? EU Enlargement and Societal Mobilization in Central and Eastern Europe. Special issue of *Acta Politica* 45 (1–2): 1–270.

Bruszt, Laszlo. 2002. Making Markets and Eastern Enlargement: Diverging Convergence? *West European Politics* 25 (2): 121–140.

Botcheva, Liliana. 1996. Focus and Effectiveness of Environmental Activism in Eastern Europe. *Journal of Environment & Development* 5 (3): 292–308.

Botcheva, Liliana, and Lisa Martin. 2001. Institutional Effects on State Behavior: Convergence and Divergence. *International Studies Quarterly* 45:1–26.

Brooks, Anathea, and Stacy D. VanDeveer. 1997. *Saving the Seas: Values, Scientists and International Governance*. College Park, Md.: Maryland Sea Grant College.

Carmin, JoAnn, and Stacy D. VanDeveer. 2005. *EU Enlargement and the Environment: Institutional Change and Environmental Policy in Central and Eastern Europe*. London: Routledge.

Connolly, Barbara, Tamar Gutner, and Hildegard Bedarff. 1996. Organizational Inertia and Environmental Assistance in Eastern Europe. In *Institutions for Environmental Aid*, ed. Robert O. Keohane and Marc Levy, 281–323. Cambridge, Mass.: MIT Press.

Ecotech. 2001a. Administrative Capacity for Implementation and Enforcement of EU Environmental Policy in the 13 Candidate Countries. DGENV Contract: Environmental Policy in the Candidate Countries and their Preparations for Accession. Birmingham, UK.

Ecotech. 2001b. The Benefits of Compliance with the Environmental Acquis for Candidate Countries. DGENV Contract: Environmental Policy in the Candidate Countries and their Preparations for Accession. Birmingham, UK.

European Commission. 2001. Regular Reports on Progress towards Accession. Brussels: European Commission. http://ec.europa.eu/enlargement/press_corner/key-documents/index_ en.htm, accessed June 8, 2011.

Francis, Patrick, Jurg Klarer, and Nelly Petkova. 1999. *Sourcebook on Environmental Funds in Economies in Transition*. Paris: OECD.

Grindle, Merilee S. 1997. *Getting Good Government: Capacity Building in the Public Sector of Developing Countries*. Cambridge, Mass.: Harvard University Press.

Gutner, Tamar L. 2002. *Banking on the Environment: Multilateral Development Banks and Their Environmental Performance in Central and Eastern Europe*. Cambridge, Mass.: MIT Press.

Haas, Peter. 1989. Do Regimes Matter? Epistemic Committees and Mediterranean Pollution Control. *International Organization* 43 (3): 377–403.

Haas, Peter, Robert Keohane, and Marc Levy. 1993. *Institutions for the Earth*. Cambridge, Mass.: MIT Press.

Hicks, James K., and Bartomiej Kaminski. 1995. Local Government Reform and the Transition from Communism: The Case of Poland. *Journal of Developing Societies* 9 (1): 1–20.

Holzinger, Katharina, Christoph Knill, and Thomas Sommerer. 2009. Environmental Policy Convergence: The Impact of International Harmonization, Transnational Communication, and Regulatory Competition. *International Organization* 62 (4): 553–587.

Jancar-Webster, Barbara. 1993. *Environmental Action in Eastern Europe: Responses to Crisis*. Armonk, N.Y.: M. E. Sharpe.

Jordan, Andrew, and Duncan Liefferink. 2005. *Environmental Policy in Europe: The Europeanization of National Environmental Policy*. London: Routledge.

Keck, Margaret, and Kathryn Sikkink. 1998. *Activists Beyond Borders: Advocacy Networks in International Politics*. Ithaca: Cornell University Press.

Knill, Christoph. 2001. *The Europeanisation of National Administrations: Pattern of Institutional Change and Persistence*. Cambridge, UK: Cambridge University Press.

Knill, Christoph, and Dirk Lehmkuhl. 1999. How Europe Matters: Different Mechanisms of Europeanization. *European Integration On-Line Papers (EIoP)* 3 (7). http://eiop.or.at/eiop/ comment/1999-007c.htm, accessed June 5, 2011.

Knill, Christoph, and Andrea Lenschow. 2000. *Implementing EU Environmental Policy: New Directions and Old Problems*. Manchester, UK: Manchester University Press.

Kruger, Christine, and Alexander Carius. 2001. *Environmental Policy and Law in Romania: Towards EU Accession*. Berlin: Ecologic.

Ladrech, Robert. 2010. *Europeanization and National Policy*. New York: Palgrave-Macmillan.

Levy, Marc. 1995. International Cooperation to Combat Acid Rain. In *Green Globe Yearbook of International Co-operation on Environment and Development*, ed. Helge O. Bergesen and Georg Parmann, 59–68. Oxford, UK: Oxford University Press.

Linden, Ronald H. 2002. *Norms and Nannies: The Impact of International Organizations on the Central and Eastern European States*. Lanham, Md.: Rowman & Littlefield.

Litfin, Karen. 1994. *Ozone Discourses. Science and Politics in Global Environmental Cooperation*. New York: Columbia University Press.

McCormick, John. 1998. Acid Pollution. *Environment* 40 (3): 16–20.

Ministry of the Environment of the Czech Republic. 1995. State Environmental Policy. Document approved by the Government of the Czech Republic on August 23.

Mitchell, Ronald B. 1994. *Intentional Oil Pollution at Sea: Environmental Policy and Treaty Compliance*. Cambridge, Mass.: MIT Press.

National Assembly of the Republic of Bulgaria. 1995. Proektozakon za Chistotata Na Atmosfernia Vazduh 1995. Proektozakon za Chistotata Na Atmosfernia Vazduh. Draft Clean Air Law.

OECD (Organisation for Economic Cooperation and Development). 2000. Environmental Performance Reviews (1st Cycle): Conclusions and Recommendations: 32 Countries (1993–2000). OECD Working Paper on Environmental Performance. Paris: OECD.

O'Neill, Kate, Jörg Balsiger, and Stacy D. VanDeveer. 2004. Actors, Norms and Impact: Recent International Cooperation Theory and the Influence of the Agent-Structure Debate. *Annual Review of Political Science* 7:149–175.

Pavlínek, Petr, and John Pickles. 2000. *Environmental Transitions: Transformation and Ecological Defence in Central and Eastern Europe*. London: Routledge.

REC (Regional Environment Center for Central and Eastern Europe). 1995. *Status of Public Participation Practices in Environmental Decisionmaking in Central and Eastern Europe*. Budapest: REC.

REC (Regional Environment Center for Central and Eastern Europe). 1996. *Approximation of European Union Environmental Legislation*. Budapest: REC.

Sagar, Ambuj. 2000. Capacity Development for the Environment: A View from the South, A View from the North. *Annual Review of Energy and the Environment* 25:377–439.

Schreurs, Miranda A., Henrik Selin, and Stacy D. VanDeveer, eds. 2009. *Transatlantic Environmental and Energy Politics: Comparative and International Perspectives*. Aldershot, UK: Ashgate.

Schimmelfennig, Frank, and Ulrich Sedelmeier, eds. 2005. *The Europeanization of Central and Eastern Europe*. Ithaca: Cornell University Press.

Selin, Henrik, and Stacy D. VanDeveer. 2003. Mapping Institutional Linkages in European Air Pollution Politics. *Global Environmental Politics* 3 (3): 14–46.

Selin, Henrik, and Stacy D. VanDeveer. 2004. Baltic Hazardous Substances Management: Results and Challenges. *AMBIO: Journal of the Human Environment* 33 (3): 353–360.

Sissenich, Beate. 2007. *Building States without Society: European Union Enlargement and the Transfer of Social Policy to Poland and Hungary*. Lanham, Md.: Lexington Books.

Tallberg, Jonas. 2002. Paths to Compliance: Enforcement, Management, and the European Union. *International Organization* 56 (3): 609–643.

UNECE (United Nations Economic Commission for Europe). 1996. *Environmental Performance Review of Estonia*. Geneva: UNECE.

UNECE (United Nations Economic Commission for Europe). 1998. *Environmental Performance Review of Lithuania*. Geneva: UNECE.

UNECE (United Nations Economic Commission for Europe). 1999. *Environmental Performance Review of Croatia*. Geneva: UNECE.

UNECE (United Nations Economic Commission for Europe). 2000a. *Environmental Performance Review of Bulgaria*. Geneva: UNECE.

UNECE (United Nations Economic Commission for Europe). 2000b. *Environmental Performance Review of Lithuania: Report on Follow-Up, Estonia*. Geneva: UNECE.

UNECE (United Nations Economic Commission for Europe). 2001. *Environmental Performance Review of Romania*. Geneva: UNECE.

VanDeveer, Stacy D. 1997. Normative Force: The State, Transnational Norms and International Environmental Regimes. PhD. diss., Department of Government and Politics, University of Maryland, College Park, Md.

VanDeveer, Stacy D. 2000. Protecting Europe's Seas: Lessons after 25 Years. *Environment* 42 (6): 10–26.

VanDeveer, Stacy D. 2002. Environmental Cooperation and Regional Peace: Baltic Politics, Programs and Prospects. In *Environmental Peacemaking*, ed. Ken Conca and Geoffrey D. Dabelko, 23–60. Baltimore: Johns Hopkins University Press/Woodrow Wilson Center Press.

VanDeveer, Stacy D. 2004. Ordering Environments: Organizing Knowledge and Regions in European International Environmental Cooperation. In *Earthly Politics: Local and Global in Environmental Governance*, ed. Sheila Jasanoff and Marybeth Long-Martello, 309–334. Cambridge, Mass.: MIT Press.

VanDeveer, Stacy D. 2005. European Politics with a Scientific Face: Framing, Asymmetrical Participation and Capacity in LRTAP. In *Assessments of Regional and Global Environmental Risks: Designing Processes for Effective Use of Science in Decisionmaking*, ed. Alex E. Farrell and Jill Jäger, 25–63. London: Resources for the Future.

VanDeveer, Stacy D. 2006. Assessment Information in European Politics: East and West. In *Global Environmental Assessments: Information and Influence*, ed. Ronald B. Mitchell, William C. Clark, David W. Cash, and Nancy Dickson, 113–150. Cambridge, Mass.: MIT Press.

VanDeveer, Stacy D. 2011. Networked Baltic Environmental Cooperation. *Journal of Baltic Studies* 42 (1): 37–55.

VanDeveer, Stacy D., and JoAnn Carmin. 2006. Sustainability and EU Accession: Capacity Development and Environmental Reform in Central and Eastern Europe. In *The Environment and Sustainable Development in the New Central Europe*, ed. Zbigniew Bochniarz and Gary B. Cohen, 45–58. New York: Berghahn Books.

VanDeveer, Stacy D., and Geoffrey D. Dabelko. 2001. It's Capacity Stupid: National Implementation and International Assistance. *Global Environmental Politics* 1 (2): 18–29.

VanDeveer, Stacy D., and Ambuj Sagar. 2005. Capacity Building for the Environment: North and South. In *Global Challenges: Furthering the Multilateral Process for Sustainable Development*, ed. A. Churie Kallhauge, Gunnar Sjöstedt, and Elisabeth Corell, 259–273. London: Greenleaf.

Vari, Anna, and Pal Tamas. 1993. *Environment and Democratic Transition: Policy and Politics in Central and Eastern and Europe*. Dordrecht: Kluwar Academic Publishers.

Victor, David G., Kal Raustiala, and Eugene B. Skolnikoff. 1998. *The Implementation and Effectiveness of International Environmental Commitments: Theory and Practice*. Cambridge, Mass.: MIT Press.

Vogel, David. 1995. *Trading Up*. Cambridge, Mass.: Harvard University Press.

Yoder, Jennifer. 2003. Decentralisation and Regionalisation after Communism: Administrative and Territorial Reform in Poland and the Czech Republic. *Europe-Asia Studies* 55 (2): 263–286.

12

Local Institutions and the Governance of Forest Commons

Arun Agrawal

In the past two decades, scholarly writings on commons and common property have led to one of the more productive research programs in the social sciences. This program comprises thousands of peer-reviewed articles, new research on collective action, social-ecological systems, and cross-scale sociopolitical interactions, a solid body of findings based on rigorous investigations and thriving debates, and translation of these findings into new resource management policies that cover the developing world. The principal exponent of this work, Elinor Ostrom, won the Nobel Prize in the Economic Sciences in 2009, in striking testimony to the enduring importance of this research. This chapter reviews the core of the work on one stream of common property—forest commons—to examine its relevance to comparative environmental politics and to continuing debates on natural resources, environmental governance, institutional analysis, and policy studies.

Forest commons are patches of forests used collectively by many different people. The boundaries of the forest, the identity of the user groups, and the property rights that determine who benefits from the forest are all well defined. Their users have a stake in improving governance and outcomes, and central governments formally or informally recognize local interests and claims over such forests. From an environmental standpoint, understanding how forest commons can be better governed is important because they constitute nearly a quarter of the forest area in the developing world and provide benefits to literally hundreds of millions of users around the globe. From the perspective of comparative politics, the study of forest commons offers new insights into institutions, collective action, and governance (Chhatre and Agrawal 2008, 13286) and takes up the methodological challenge of analyzing multiple outcomes, which are characteristic of many of the subjects of comparative research (Chhatre and Agrawal 2009). Cross-national comparisons of the politics of forest governance can generate better social theories across the social sciences (Jessup and Peluso 1986; Arnold and Stewart 1991; Gibson, McKean, and Ostrom 2000; Peluso 1992; Sivaramakrishnan 1999).

Forest commons are no mere historical curiosity, the remnants of a time long gone. They are a modern-day phenomenon—indeed, as a result of decentralization reforms undertaken by governments in the Global South, forest area under community governance has increased from less than 200 million hectares in 1980 to more than 450 million hectares today. They are of central relevance to policy debates surrounding biodiversity conservation, livelihoods of the poor, and, increasingly, carbon sequestration in terrestrial ecosystems. Natural resource governance around the world has witnessed a significant shift away from centralized administration (Andersson, Gibson, and Lehoucq 2006; Brooks et al. 2006; Pretty 2003). This shift has meant greater involvement by local populations in resource governance through community- and district-level organizations; recourse to private, market-based incentives to promote sustainable resource use; and the involvement of NGOs as partners and monitors in resource conservation. In Bolivia, Ecuador, and Brazil, for example, indigenous communities have gained control over millions of hectares of forest land (Sunderlin, Hatcher, and Liddle 2008). In Nepal, India, and the Philippines, among other countries in Asia, local communities have devised new rules to manage millions of hectares of forests earlier controlled by central government forest departments.

Decentralization is occurring because central governments are under pressure from a number of sources to extend rights to govern natural resources (Nygren 2005; Lemos and Agrawal 2006; Wittman and Geisler 2005). These pressures include fiscal deficits, aid from international donors that is conditional upon local participation, pressures from communities and indigenous groups for greater control over their lands, and evidence that local actors have the capacity to protect and use forest resources sustainably and at lower costs than government agencies. The continued growth in forest area controlled by local actors significantly increases the relevance of research on institutional arrangements shaping user incentives and actions. The ensuing review, however, focuses less on the policy relevance of a fast-changing field and more on research findings that will remain important as policy innovations connect local and global concerns and mediate the relationship between private and social interests—all enduring themes in the comparative study of environmental politics.

These connections stem from the fact that forests yield multiple products. They contribute to local livelihoods through fodder, firewood, timber, and nontimber forest products, yet are also essential for global biodiversity and carbon sequestration. Diverse stakeholders assert competing claims to these benefits. Governments are interested in revenues they can derive from forests, as indeed are many timber companies. Local users are interested in subsistence benefits and, where possible, cash incomes. Many NGOs and central governments are interested in the conservation of species and ecosystems and the mitigation of global climate change.

In common with research on other types of common-pool resources, research on forest-based commons has focused primarily on how variations in institutional arrangements shape resource-related outcomes. Signal contributions to this work have explored principles of institutional design (Ostrom 1999), the need for fit between institutions—the collections of rules governing forest resources—and their political-ecological context (Dietz, Ostrom, and Stern 2003, Ribot 1999), the ways in which institutions mediate population and market pressures (Agrawal and Yadama 1997), the importance of local enforcement of rules (Agrawal 2005; Gibson, Ostrom, and Williams 2005), possibilities of social resistance (Guha 1989; Peluso 1992), the necessity of broad-based participation in institutionalized governance (Ribot 2002), the relationship between indigenous peoples and forests (Rangan and Lane 2001), and how forest conditions are affected by local factors ranging from elevation to distance to markets and gender relations (Agrawal and Chhatre 2006).

Much of this essay focuses on the diversity of conclusions emanating from research on forest commons, with the goal of highlighting some of the leading edges and unresolved questions in this exciting field of research. Lest this leave the impression that the field lacks consensus or a cumulative body of conclusions, it is important to indicate at the outset some areas in which this scholarship has already substantially advanced our understanding of the issues. Three such contributions are evident. The first is the demonstration that local populations and communities can manage their forests effectively and sustainably, often more so than government or private sector actors. Somanathan, Prabhakar, and Mehta (2005) show, for example, that in the Indian Himalaya local users protect their forests as effectively as government agencies managing forests through strict controls, but do so at a lower cost and with greater subsistence benefits. The second major contribution is the identification of specific factors at the community level that have a close association with and likely a causal impact on more effective governance. Chief among these is local enforcement of community rules. Regular monitoring and sanctioning of rules has been found in numerous studies to be closely associated with improved outcomes related to forest conditions (Gibson, Ostrom, and Williams 2005; Chhatre and Agrawal 2008). Finally, studies by scholars such as Ostrom (1990) and Baland and Platteau (1996) have identified a relatively small set of institutional and other factors that improve forest commons outcomes (to be discussed shortly). Given the complexity of the conditions under which forest commons are managed, identifying a small set of relevant variables is in itself a major accomplishment. Collectively, these contributions constitute a remarkable step toward improving our understanding of how resources can be governed better, addressing many of the central concerns of comparative environmental politics and identifying ways in which theoretical inquiry can have significant practical relevance.

In the rest of this chapter, I first demonstrate the pervasiveness of commons arrangements through an empirical examination of how forest ownership rights are distributed in different parts of the world. I then survey some of the central findings of research on forest commons, noting its relevance to forest policy and governance. This research clarifies the importance of property rights arrangements, local levels of use and management, and the community relationships that frame local governance. The subsequent section examines gaps related to data, theory, and methods in the study of forest-based commons. The conclusion outlines some pressing and exciting new areas for future research.

Forests and Common Property

Forest commons are forests used and managed collectively by a group of people. Forest commons are similar to common-pool resources broadly in that benefits harvested from them are not available to others and it is difficult to exclude users from harvesting benefits (Ostrom, Gardner, and Walker 1994).[1] Forest commons make up nearly 18 percent of global forest area (White and Martin 2002; Agrawal 2007). As noted previously, they make crucial contributions to global and local well-being. Indeed, their contributions to local livelihoods far exceed their territorial extent—more than a billion people are estimated to depend at least partially on different kinds of benefits drawn from forest commons, from watershed protection to fuel wood, fodder, green manure, medicinal plants, and wild foods. Although the total forest area in the world continues to decline, that under forest commons has increased substantially over the past two decades as a result of political and administrative shifts toward greater local control.

Most of the world's forests are owned by governments. But private and other forms of ownership are increasing, and governments often set aside areas for use by communities, even in developed countries. In Australia, for example, indigenous protected areas that allow for joint management of biodiversity and forests add up to nearly a quarter of the Australian National Reserve System.[2] Institutional solutions to competing claims on forest resources are always complex and political because of the simultaneous importance of forests for global conservation and local livelihoods. Any solution is also provisional and subject to ongoing revisions as a result of demographic shifts, developmental processes, changes in landscapes, and political alliances, among other forces. As Dietz, Ostrom, and Stern remark, "Successful commons governance requires that rules evolve" (2003, 1907). The shift toward community-based commons is itself an example of this statement. But at a finer level of institutional organization, commons arrangements themselves change over time. The fascinating interplay among institutions, ecology, and social change has inspired a great deal of research on forests, both within and outside of the field of common property.[3] The size, variety, and depth of this body of research reflects the many ways in which forests have been, and continue to be, central to human survival, livelihoods, and prosperity.

Table 12.1 lists the estimated area under major forms of tenure for the thirty countries in the developing world with the highest forest cover and an additional six developed nations with large areas under forest cover (FAO 2005; White and Martin 2002; Agrawal, Chhatre, and Hardin 2008). Collectively these countries represent more than 80 percent of officially recognized forests.[4] Because the areas listed for different countries draw from official statistics between the years 2000 and 2005, the figures in table 12.1 are at best approximations—indeed, there are no accurate numbers in existence. The numbers in the table were calculated using the information from the UN Food and Agriculture Organization (FAO) (2005) as a starting point, supplemented with a literature search for documented forest area statistics available in each of the listed countries and with figures in the published report from the Rights and Resources Initiative (Sunderlin, Hatcher, and Liddle 2008). The table indicates that a nontrivial area of forests is either collectively managed through community-level institutions or is designated as owned by community-level actors.

The numbers in table 12.1 certainly underrepresent the impact of private/corporate and community-level actors in forests. Case study evidence from these and other African countries demonstrates the presence of community-based governance in forests even when official agencies report a different story to international organizations. The data also conceal the practice of governments granting logging concessions to private corporations operating in state-owned forests. Case study evidence and national reports from Cameroon, Central African Republic, Democratic Republic of Congo, Gabon, Indonesia, and Myanmar show significant levels of logging in forests nominally under government control.[5] According to some estimates, close to 10 percent of the global forest area is currently enrolled in sustainable harvest certification programs, a form of governance typically spearheaded by nonprofit and private sector organizations (Peña-Claros, Blommerde, and Bongers 2009).

Despite potential inaccuracies, the numbers in the table indicate that common property arrangements are far more common, so to speak, in the developing than the developed world. The greater prevalence of forest commons in the developing world explains in part the geographic focus of much of the literature on the topic (Haenn 2006; Maskey, Gebremedhin, and Dalton 2006; Pagdee, Kim, and Daugherty 2006). These data confirm that government agencies own most of the world's forests—nearly 82 percent. Globally, private and communal/indigenous tenure cover 11.9 and 8.3 percent, respectively. But in the developing world, the position of communal and indigenous actors is far stronger. Private actors possess

Table 12.1
Ownership of forest and other wooded lands (2005, in millions of hectares)

| Region | Public | | Private | | Total |
	Government-administered	Community-administered	Community/Indigenous	Individual/Firm	
Africa[a]	670.8 (96%)	4.2 (0.6%)	11.9 (2%)	9.8 (1.5%)	696.7
Asia[b]	296.4 (71%)	15.1 (3.5%)	101.4 (24%)	5.2 (1.5%)	418.5
Latin America[c]	777.6 (74%)	106.5 (10%)	66.7 (6%)	106.5 (10%)	1057.3
Developed[d]	1443.3 (80%)	20.0 (1%)	0	344.6 (19%)	1737.9
Developing	1744.8 (80%)	125.8 (6%)	180.0 (8%)	121.5 (6%)	2172.1
Total	3188.1 (81%)	145.8 (4%)	180.0 (5%)	466.1 (10%)	3910.0

Sources: FAO 2005 and White and Martin 2002.
[a]Includes Angola, Botswana, Cameroon, Central African Republic, Democratic Republic of Congo, Gabon, Mali, Mozambique, Nigeria, South Africa, Sudan, Tanzania, and Zambia.
[b]Includes China, India, Indonesia, Lao PDR, Malaysia, Myanmar, and Papua New Guinea.
[c]Includes Argentina, Bolivia, Brazil, Chile, Colombia, Guyana, Mexico, Paraguay, Peru, and Venezuela.
[d]Includes Australia, Canada, Japan, the Russian Federation, Sweden, and the United States.

only about 5.6 percent in contrast to the 14.1 percent of forests characterized by communal tenure.

Table 12.2 shows how claims and tenure rights over forests have changed since the 1990s. The table shows that the area of forests governed through common property institutions has increased substantially in the past two decades. Much of this shift has occurred because of new legislation and policy initiatives. The total area transferred to a community tenure regime in the past twenty years may be as much as 200 million hectares (White and Martin 2002; ITTO 2005; Sunderlin, Hatcher, and Liddle 2008). The increasing area under community-oriented tenure regimes can be seen as an implicit admission by national- or provincial-level decision makers that local community actors can govern their resources quite effectively when they have the opportunity to do so.

What Factors Lead to Successful Governance of Forest Commons?

Theoretical work on forest commons has concrete implications for policy because it explores how institutions affect forest conditions and related social outcomes. Those writing on the subject look at many types of outcomes, including contributions to livelihoods, sustainability of governance, and improvements in forest conditions measured in terms of biodiversity or biomass. This multifaceted approach is not surprising because forests are a multiple-use, multiple-benefit resource. Although this diversity in outcome variables makes comparisons across studies more difficult, forest commons research nonetheless offers important lessons for practitioners. To take just one example, consider the question of whether forest commons can be managed more effectively if local people have greater autonomy in deciding how to use them. Chhatre and Agrawal (2009), analyzing data on eighty forest commons in ten countries across Asia, Africa, and Latin America, conclude that when local communities own forest commons and have significant rule-making autonomy, they restrict their consumption of forest products, leave more trees standing, and enjoy greater benefits.

When examining the relationship between institutions and outcomes, forest commons research must control for many variables potentially affecting outcomes in a given case, from the physical characteristics of the resource to the broader social context in which resource management takes place. Typically, scholars find that institutions mediate the impact of factors such as user group characteristics, demographic pressure and change, market penetration, levels of community participation, state policies, and democratic competition. For example, although road-building often leads to tropical deforestation, research suggests that if governments enforce forest protection effectively, roads are also important for ensuring forest protection. Roads have little net effect on forest conditions in the presence of

Table 12.2
Major community tenure reforms in the developing world since 1985

Country	Area in million hectares		Year of reform	Nature of legal reform
	Community administration	Community ownership		
Bolivia	16.6	2.8	1996	Ancestral rights of community groups have precedence over concessions; municipal governments gain control over forest lands; indigenous groups have reserves over which they exercise governance rights.
Brazil	74.5	0.0	1988	Ancestral rights of indigenous groups and communities recognized.
Colombia	0.0	24.5	1991	Framework for collective territorial rights of indigenous groups and Afro-Colombians.
India	11.6	N/A	1989	Joint Forest Management with state forest agencies recognizing community governance.
Indonesia	0.6	N/A	2000	Regulatory process for customary ownership and community concessions.
Mozambique	N/A	N/A	1997	Titles for customary tenure available.
Nepal	1.2	N/A	1996	Community forestry legislation to recognize governance rights.
Philippines	N/A	N/A	1997	Constitution protects ancestral domain rights; 1997 legislation recognizes indigenous tenure.
Peru	8.4	22.5	1999	Rights of communities recognized by law.
Sudan	0.8	N/A	N/A	
Tanzania	0.4	N/A	1999	Customary tenure available and protected.
Uganda	N/A	N/A	2000	2000 draft under revision; strong program to promote devolution.
Zambia	N/A	N/A	1995	Customary tenure recognized but titles not available.
Total	114.1	49.8		

Sources: Agrawal 2004, ITTO 2005, White and Martin 2002, and Wily 2001.

Notes: These data have been collected from several different sources; therefore, the numbers may not be strictly comparable across countries. In addition to the countries listed here, the following countries either have plans to recognize community rights to administer or manage forests, or already do so at least on paper: Botswana, Cameroon, Central African Republic, Mali, Kenya, Senegal, Nigeria, Guatemala, Guyana, Mexico, Paraguay, Venezuela, Bhutan, Lao PDR, Malaysia, and Thailand.

effective institutions (Agrawal and Yadama 1997; Agrawal and Chhatre 2006). But absent strong institutions, roads translate into higher levels of deforestation (Chomitz 2007; Wilkie et al. 2000).

Building on earlier work (Agrawal 2001b), I describe in the remainder of this chapter key findings from research on the factors affecting outcomes in forest commons categorized for convenience into characteristics of the resource system, characteristics of user groups, institutional arrangements, and the influence of the external social environment. This overview is followed by discussion of additional relevant variables emerging from the literature and the strategies that researchers are using to grapple with these complex causal relationships.

Characteristics of the Resource System

Systems for governing forest resources are shaped by a broad set of biophysical variables. These are the boundary conditions within which humanly devised rules of the game must be situated. Following Ostrom's (2005) lead, a number of researchers have explored how specific elements of the natural environment shape the likelihood of successful commons governance. Agrawal and Chhatre (2006), for example, test common property theory using a dataset covering ninety-five forest governance institutions from Himachal Pradesh in India and conclude that altitude is an important cause of variation in the condition of local forest resources. Other characteristics relevant to effective governance include the size and boundaries of the resource system, whether the resource is mobile, the extent to which resource units can be stored, the rate and predictability of the flow of benefits, and the ease of monitoring resource conditions. Thus, small patches of forest commons may be easier to govern than small fisheries because fish are mobile and invisible and because fluctuation in their stocks is less predictable than is the case for forests. Institutional arrangements and technological changes can alter some of the biophysical features of resource systems. For example, it may be possible to increase the size of the forest available to a group of users or to change the boundaries of a local forest. But other biophysical characteristics—the rate at which forests grow, the soils on which a given forest common is located, and so forth—may be beyond human capacities to alter or excessively costly to engineer.

Even as the broader literature on deforestation and changes in forest condition has documented the importance of biophysical variables such as soils, topography, fire, and pests (Geist and Lambin 2001, 14; Tole 2001), research on forest-based commons has been less attentive to these factors (Gibson, Lehoucq, and Williams 2002; Tucker 1999; but see Tucker, Randolph, and Castellanos 2007). This point is of more general relevance to research on comparative environmental politics. The basic issue is simple: do biophysical processes play an important role in shaping environmental outcomes, thus requiring careful analysis by social scientists researching environmental outcomes? Or can environmental research largely ignore biophysical forces? If the natural environment and its problems provide no more than "local color" for the more "enduring questions of comparative politics," questions of interdisciplinarity and familiarity with environmental sciences become relatively unimportant.

Certainly for research on forest commons, far more work is needed to integrate the analysis of causal impacts produced by biophysical, social, and institutional factors (Agrawal and Chhatre 2006). The literature on adaptive management has made important contributions in this regard, and research on forest commons can draw on these efforts (Cumming, Cumming, and Redman 2006; Klooster 2002; Mutimukuru, Kozanayi, and Nyirenda 2006; Reed and McIlveen 2006). For example, researchers affiliated with the Resilience Alliance and the Santa Fe Institute have developed a "thresholds database" with information on more than 270 cases of interactions between different components of social-ecological systems.[6] Such cross-disciplinary work is likely to broaden the dimensions along which commons researchers assess institutional outcomes. The forest commons literature typically evaluates outcomes in terms of forest conditions, and sometimes rural livelihoods and equity-related issues (Berkes 2004; Turner, Davidson-Hunt, and O'Flaherty 2003). In contrast, research on adaptive systems and complexity also considers the resilience and robustness of ecosystems shaped by human activities to be important criteria for evaluating institutional effectiveness.

One biological factor that has received substantial attention is a forest's ability to yield multiple products, which can often be harvested to yield significant economic benefits for users without adverse effects on the forest. Salafsky, Dugelby, and Terborgh (1993), in an influential paper, argue that forest users in Guatemala and Indonesia were able to use forests to meet their daily needs in a manner consistent with tropical forest preservation. Those interested in valuation of tropical forests have similarly found that the benefits of nonwood forest products (NWFPs) are often higher than the value from clear-felling the forest. A report from the UN FAO (2005) recognizes that NWFPs are one of the most important benefits that forests provide at a global scale and are grossly undervalued. By highlighting the multiple benefits arising from forests, research on forest commons has helped to address concerns about equity and livelihoods as well as sustainable forest management.[7]

Characteristics of Users

A second major determinant of outcomes in forest commons concerns the characteristics of the communities who use them. Researchers often draw on the literature on collective action as their starting point for evaluating the impact of user group characteristics, examining issues related to the size of the group, whether group boundaries are clearly defined, heterogeneity among group members, the extent of interdependence among them and their dependence on the resource, and whether the group possesses sufficient resources to meet the costs of initiating and maintaining collective action (Poteete and Ostrom 2004; Ostrom 1999; Agrawal and Goyal 2001). Despite the wealth of work on these issues, there is considerable debate over the ways in which these variables influence collective action and the condition of forests.

The nature of the disputes is clear when one examines the role of group size. Agrawal and Goyal (2001) conclude that monitoring costs rise disproportionately as group size increases because there are more resources to protect and more potential users to monitor. Moreover, there is "lumpiness" in the effects of monitoring—for example, there is a threshold of monitoring frequency (such as patrols by a forest guard) below which monitoring has no effect. The result is that, contrary to the assertions made by Mancur Olson (1965) in his canonical work on collective action, medium-sized groups are found to be more likely than small or large groups to provide third-party monitoring (see also Ostrom 1999).

Similar debates surround group heterogeneity. Most resources are managed by groups divided along multiple axes such as ethnicity, gender, religion, wealth, and caste (Agrawal and Gibson 1999). Different dimensions of social, political, and economic heterogeneity have potentially different impacts on resource governance (Baland and Platteau 1999, 773; Bowles and Gintis 1998, 4). For example, Baland and Platteau observe:

The relation between wealth distribution and outside opportunities is actually ambiguous. Indeed, on the one hand, rich people usually have easier access to alternative opportunities due to their better endowments in human and social capital and access to financial markets. On the other hand, owing to their low resource base, poor people may be forced to actively seek outside employment. When taking up outside occupations, however, rich and poor people still behave differently with regard to the CPR [common-pool resource]. Indeed, the employment prospects for the poor are often so uncertain that they are keen to preserve the local CPR as a hedge against the risk of unemployment. (1999, 775)

It is difficult to know which dimensions of heterogeneity are relevant in a given context and for what reasons. These difficulties are compounded by challenges in generating measures of heterogeneity that capture its different dimensions and their potentially divergent effects on resource governance outcomes.

Recognizing the complex effects of heterogeneity on the governance of the commons, Baland and Platteau (1996) provide an initial attempt to classify group heterogeneity into three types: endowments, interests, and identities. They hypothesize that heterogeneities of endowments have a positive effect on resource management, whereas heterogeneities of interests and identities create obstacles to collective action. This work draws on Olson (1965) and Hardin (1982), who show that heterogeneous groups with a small number of extremely well-off individuals may be able to overcome the problem of collective action if it is in their strong interest to provide a collective good. Simply put, when users have substantial endowments, they can afford the costs of collective action. On the other hand, when users have divergent interests and identities, they also differ in the goals they seek through cooperation.

Baland and Platteau's efforts need further analysis and discussion. For example, the categories into which they classify heterogeneities are not mutually exclusive. Heterogeneities of interests or identities may lead to different types of economic specialization and different levels of endowments, which could in turn lead to mutually beneficial exchange. Nor is it clear that heterogeneities in identities and interests are necessarily obstacles to collective action. Other scholars have noted that heterogeneity can facilitate the emergence of collective action but hinder its maintenance. Finally, Poteete and Ostrom (2004) suggest that it is difficult to identify direct relationships between heterogeneities and resource governance outcomes because these are mediated by institutions, yet relatively little research on the subject has attempted to identify these effects. Despite strong caste divisions in many parts of India, for example, forest-dependent communities are often able to manage forests well because they have been supported by government policies to develop strong local institutions for their forests (Berkes, Davidson-Hunt, and Davidson-Hunt 1998; Blair 1996). The impact of within-group heterogeneities on the distribution of benefits from forests may be more analytically tractable (Adhikari 2005). Research suggests that group members with higher economic and political standing often gain a larger share of benefits from a resource. For example, Agarwal (1997) finds that women are often denied an equitable share in benefits from forest commons in India and Nepal.

Poverty is another user group characteristic that has been the subject of considerable research. Poverty directly relates to the capacity of users to protect and regulate common-pool resources. But precisely what this truism means for the success of institutionalized protection and allocation of resource-based benefits is still uncertain. The poor often rely more on the commons, as Jodha (1986) identified in one of the earlier studies of the commons, using evidence from villages across India. But greater dependence on commons can lead either to higher levels of harvesting and degradation or to incentives to manage the resource for the long term. Indeed, there is some debate over whether the poor actually benefit more from the commons than those who are better off. These debates notwithstanding, one major contribution of research of forest-based commons has been to highlight the importance of poverty and equity in the regulation and use of commons.

Whether the relationship between user group characteristics and forest outcomes is negative, positive, or curvilinear seems to depend on a range of other contextual and mediating factors, not all of which are clearly understood (Agrawal 2001b). Broadly speaking, smaller, more homogeneous, relatively well-off groups whose members' depend on each other as well as on benefits from forest commons, and who have not suffered volatility in their demands upon the forest, are more likely to be successful in creating institutions that help regulate forest commons.

Institutional Arrangements

The impact of institutions on forest conditions has been an intense focus of investigation from the very beginnings of research on the commons and thus ties in well with cross-cutting concerns in the field of comparative environmental politics. This research has produced a number of generalizations regarding the effects of rules on user incentives and behavior. These insights, several of which had long been asserted in case studies of the commons, were first explored systematically by McKean (1992) and Ostrom (1990) and more recently by Dietz, Ostrom, and Stern (2003, 1910). McKean examines the historical management of forests in Japan; Ostrom analyzes a number of cases from around the world; and Dietz and colleagues focus on forests under a variety of property rights arrangements. Despite their different empirical referents, their findings are very similar. Rules that are easy to understand and enforce, locally designed and accepted, take into account differences in types of violations, help manage conflicts, and hold users and officials accountable are most likely to lead to effective governance (Ostrom 2009).

Although these findings are highly relevant to policy, they must undergo further translation before they are adopted in specific settings. Consider an example: it may appear that a statement such as "rules should be locally created and enforced" is quite transparent. The import of the statement lies in the recognition that (1) local users and their organizations have a great deal of knowledge about the resource, about other users, and about environmental conditions, and (2) local users are best equipped to use this knowledge to create institutional arrangements more suited to governing forests effectively. But what this statement means in practice is open to interpretation because of ambiguities in the meanings of every operant word in the phrase: rule, local, creation, and enforcement. For this statement to be useful as an operational guide, we need more clarification about types of rules, meanings of "local," and forms of enforcement. This is perhaps true of all efforts to translate scholarly research into operational guidelines. Ostrom (2005) suggests that there may be literally hundreds of thousands of different rule combinations from which decision makers can choose. The interpretation of seemingly clear and concrete recommendations runs headlong into this plethora of possibilities.

In some situations, for example, rules may be better designed by those not at the local level. When levels of deforestation are very high and the need to conserve trees even greater, it may be simpler for national governments to design rules that prevent felling of trees and timber. But when the situation is more complex, and variation in local conditions is high, local input into rule formation and implementation becomes more important—and in these situations, the meaning of "local" must be clarified (Raffles 1999). "Local" can be defined in terms of birth, residency, geographic proximity, degree of dependence on the resource, contributions to the creation of a local institution, and so forth. Those charged with creating and modifying rules may be elected (through a variety of rules), nominated, or appointed (by many potential authorities), and may adopt rules in many different ways. The economy of expression found in policy prescriptions emanating from institutional research is thus a function of heroic abstraction from the context that scholars of the commons take for granted.

External Social Environment

As is the case for comparative environmental politics research generally, the objects of forest commons research—such as the configuration of common property arrangements, common-pool resources, and user groups—must be understood in the broader social environments in which they are located. Demographic, cultural, technological, and market-related factors, the nature of state agencies, involvement by actors such as NGOs, and international aid flows have been studied by researchers interested in deforestation. Scholars of forest commons have been less attentive to these extremely important variables structuring outcomes in the commons.

Research on the commons has begun to address these contextual variables in the past few years, but they often receive less attention than institutional factors. The result is an intriguing disjuncture in the research findings of those interested in explaining deforestation versus those explaining the condition of forest-based commons. Population and market pressures, for example, appear as critically important causal factors in the deforestation literature (Young 1994), yet commons scholars often conclude that roads and population pressures are relatively unimportant influences on resource conditions. This inconsistency may well have to do with differences between the two literatures in the levels of analysis, regional focus, and the use of cross-sectional versus time-series data. This inconsistency also suggests productive avenues of dialog between those who focus on issues such as markets, market institutions, and demographic shifts as critical influences on commons governance and those who focus primarily on community institutions (Bray, Antinori, and Torres-Rojo 2006; Brown 2000; Clark 2004; Goeschl and Igliori 2006; Power 2006). The development of market institutions often has important political dimensions, and state officials can become closely involved in the privatization of commons and the selling of resources previously held under common property arrangements (Rangarajan 1996; Sivaramakrishnan 1999; Skaria 1999). It is especially important to study how market institutions mediate the impact of new arenas of exchange in relation to carbon and watershed services (Taylor 2005). Similarly, demographic and broader economic shifts have been taken by a number of scholars as harbingers of forest transitions in which deforestation trends have given way to growing forest area in some countries and regions (Kauppi et al. 2006; Victor and Ausubel 2000).

Another important dimension of the external social environment concerns the technological means available to use and harvest the commons. Technological innovations that transform the cost-benefit ratios of harvesting are likely to undermine the institutions needed to govern them as well as the resources themselves. Technological changes can disrupt not only the mechanisms of coordination (around mobility, storage, and exchange of resources) that serve users of the commons, but the very nature of the political and economic calculation that goes into inventing and defining common property. For example, new techniques to catch fish more efficiently, or in the dark, or at long distances from the coast can disrupt institutions designed to restrict fishing effort.

The current trend toward decentralization is a powerful example of how outcomes in forest commons are shaped by forces external to the commons themselves. The current landscape of tenure transformations is highly complex, to say the least. The state, as the ultimate guarantor of property rights arrangements, has long played a central role in determining the changing area of forests available to communities (Peluso and Vandergeest 2001). But in the past two decades, an increasing number of governments have decentralized control over natural resources to local user groups. The community forestry program in Nepal and the joint forest management program in India are good examples (Sundar 2001). These countries have created thousands of new forest user groups at the local level, through which more than a quarter of forests in these countries are now being used and managed. In these situations, the forest department, together with local users, defines how forests should be managed. Similarly, debates around the role of forest conservation in reducing atmospheric carbon dioxide (notably the emphasis on Reducing Emissions from Deforestation and Degradation, known as REDD+, under the climate change regime) create a new arena of contestation affecting forest commons (Phelps, Webb, and Agrawal 2010). Research on decentralization of forest policy and management has begun to explore these issues (Palmer and Engel 2007; Lynch and Talbott 1995). But more systematic examination of the outcomes of these reforms is needed. It is only by integrating central policy concerns with the theoretical issues featured in commons research that this literature will gain greater visibility and interest.

Dealing with Complexity

Steinberg and VanDeveer argue in chapter 1 that a core challenge of research in comparative environmental politics is "the need to convey an appreciation for complexity without becoming overwhelmed by it." This is certainly true of forest commons research, in which efforts to integrate the dynamic, long-term effects of biophysical variables alongside the many socioeconomic, political, institutional, and contextual factors that affect outcomes on the commons (see, e.g, Ostrom 2007) produces an explosion in the number of variables that must be considered. In addition to the factors mentioned previously, researchers have identified dozens of variables shaping the success of forest governance. In their comprehensive work on adaptive governance, Dietz, Ostrom, and Stern (2003) posit seven distinct requirements for successful governance in complex systems such as forest-based commons: availability of necessary information; conflict management; compliance with rules; provision of technical, institutional, and physical infrastructure; and the ability to adapt and change. These requirements, when applied to particular situations, translate into a far larger number of variables.

It should be evident that there are many factors that must be taken into account in comparative analyses of the forces affecting forest commons. This is a familiar problem in comparative politics, and one that scholars of forest commons have handled in a number of ways—by identifying specific variables that are relevant under one set of contextual conditions but not in others, by applying new methods and approaches (especially those related to the analysis of complex systems), and through the more conventional route of multivariate statistical analysis. Although much of the earlier research on forest commons relied on case studies, increasingly scholars of the commons are using statistical approaches to take into account the potential effects of multiple causal variables (Bardhan and Dayton-Johnson 2002). The rise of statistical approaches in the study of the commons has been facilitated in part by the resolutely local scale of the subject matter. In contrast to the many areas of comparative environmental studies that focus on national and macrolevel politics, commons research tries to explain how microsocial and political processes influence outcomes on relatively small patches of forests at the local level, affording researchers the luxury of an extraordinarily large number of units of analysis for assessing the importance of the numerous variables affecting outcomes.

Directions for Future Research

Recent reviews of research on deforestation and other undesirable environmental outcomes have been forced to recognize the critically important role of institutions and governance (Geist and Lambin 2001; Kaimowitz and Angelson 1998). Interventions by scholars of commons and community forests are responsible in no small measure for this trend. Institutions are the units of which governance is made, and the work on forest commons and common property institutions provides highly elaborated examples of how institutions affect politics, are shaped by it, and in turn affect environmental outcomes.

The previous discussion also suggests a number of areas in which far more work remains to be done. For example, Dietz, Ostrom, and Stern (2003, 1908) show that different institutional configurations of private ownership, communal tenure, and government control are each compatible with improvements, declines, and stability in forest conditions. This important finding hints at the significance of context, but we still need to track down exactly how context matters for commons governance in complex social situations. The following discussion focuses specifically on knowledge gaps along three dimensions: data, theory, and methods. These interdependent domains constitute the three legs on which scientific knowledge rests. Admittedly, this attempt to identify research priorities is provisional and unstable—as befits a three-legged stool. But that is surely the character of all scientific advancement.

Data Related to Forest-Based Commons

There are two data-related gaps in the study of forest commons. The first gap concerns its conventional focus on institutions. Commons researchers have long complained about the absence of reliable cross-sectional and longitudinal datasets on governance strategies at the local level. New research is beginning to address this data gap along several dimensions. Scholars associated with the International Forestry Resources and Institutions (IFRI) Program are collecting data on local institutions, their variations, and how they change over time. Research associated with the Center for International Forestry Research (CIFOR) is harder to categorize because of its variety, but focuses greater attention on the role of the external social environment in deforestation. Researchers at the World Resources Institute have advanced our understanding of decentralization initiatives related to forest policy, particularly in African countries.

There are other areas in which knowledge about forest-based commons remains quite poor. One critical gap concerns basic descriptive information: we have very little knowledge even about the area under common property regimes in different countries. The figures in table 12.1 are based on relatively scattered sources of information and are highly tentative. Even within nations, the quality of information is poor. This state of affairs is reflected in the UN FAO's most recent global Forest Resource Assessment (FAO 2005), in which the agency located all community-based tenure in the category "other"! We understand too little about the spatial distribution of forest commons and about the ways in which governance institutions vary within this broad category. We also know far too little in the aggregate—either at the national or global level—about *why* institutional arrangements vary from one place to the next and the effects of this variation. Finally, those studying forest commons can vastly expand their contributions by drawing on research that may not go under the name of commons, but shares similar concerns and investigative foci. There is a substantial literature, as this review has pointed out, on indigenous peoples and forests, on the importance of markets and market institutions for forest-related outcomes, and on the ways in which forest-related outcomes are affected by interactions between biophysical, social, and institutional variables. These literatures provide important avenues for commons scholars to broaden the scope of their investigations, enrich their substantive concerns, and increase the impact of their contributions.

Theories of Forest-Based Commons Governance

Research on forest-based commons would be greatly advanced if researchers were to distinguish more clearly among the major outcomes that commons institutions shape. This survey does not distinguish among such outcomes as sustainability of resource use, equity in allocation of benefits, management efficiency, resilience of resource systems, or conservation effectiveness because the literature itself does not do so. Indeed, the review does not distinguish among different substantive arenas of outcomes—for example, livelihoods, forest cover, and biodiversity. It is easy to imagine that these different outcomes may be positively or negatively associated with one another, depending on the context and the focus of governance institutions. In some situations, a focus on the resilience of a resource system and its institutional arrangements may be compatible with improvements in the equitable allocation of benefits. But where the social context is one of extreme inequality, efforts to improve equity may undermine institutional resilience or other performance goals. However, we do not know if it actually does so.

New data can shed light on questions of governance, but theoretical development is equally urgent. Theoretical contributions from studies of forest-based commons can substantially advance comparative social science on a number of fronts. Here I wish to emphasize three of them: the relationship between institutions and identities, cross-level analysis of the effectiveness of governance arrangements, and dynamic social-ecological relationships characterized by feedbacks, discontinuities, and irreversibilities.

The ways in which new institutions generate worldviews has been a major focus of research since the founding of the social sciences, even if the language used to talk about this relationship varies across disciplines, which describe it in terms of rules and preferences, subjectivities and norms, and perceptions and practices. In relation to forest governance, the question is basic: do different institutions of governance have different effects on the way people view forests and the environment? In a study of changing forestry institutions in northern India, Agrawal (2005) finds that forest users came to care about forests more and to protect them better as they were given more responsibilities and powers to manage them, in part because they depended on these forests and could witness the ill effects of high levels of illegal harvests on forest condition. Thus institutions are not just the product of existing preferences—they also generate new preferences. And in turn, the ways in which people think about forest use, conservation, and management shape the possibility of effective governance. However, scholars of forest-based commons have scarcely attended to the relationship between institutions and identities. Reviewing the research on forest-based commons, one might infer that no such relationship exists, but this impression merely reflects the absence of theoretical lenses that permit researchers to imagine this possibility and to collect the data to investigate it. Pursuing this question theoretically would make a major contribution to research on the commons and to comparative environmental politics generally.

The second theoretical gap surrounds a question that is already in the sights of those researching forest-based commons but needs more careful development: how do interactions among the processes at multiple social and institutional levels affect forest governance? Progress on this issue is hobbled by the slow development of theoretical approaches that can take advantage of existing data at multiple levels. We need a better understanding of the conditions under which macrolevel processes structure what happens at the local level and, conversely, of instances when local processes overwhelm the influence of more macrolevel phenomena.

The third set of theoretical issues—understanding stability and change in social-ecological systems—has been far more difficult to address. Forest commons are by definition coupled social and natural systems: they are forests governed by humanly crafted social institutions, situated in larger social and ecological systems. These systemic relationships evolve over time as elements in these relationships change in response to shifts in other elements of the system, and many such changes are non-linear. Although the behavior of these coupled systems may be stable for long periods of time, system stability can shift drastically and irreversibly if some of the structuring processes shift. Thus, forest commons may be in equilibrium for extended periods, but with the emergence of substitutes for forest products, better communications and transportation, in- or out-migration, new technologies, or rapid population growth, the system might undergo a precipitous decline. Or it might not—we do not know, because most theories of forest commons address dynamic system processes in a static framework. They therefore fail to provide predictions about how and under what conditions changes in structuring conditions will be absorbed by particular commons systems, and when other systems will collapse.

The Search for Appropriate Methods

The conventional strategy of case-based research and comparative case analysis, which has been so central to forest commons research, is likely to retain an important position given the specific geographic interests of many of those who research the commons. Case-based methods can also be used to good effect when analyzing data across levels of analysis and to fill many of the gaps identified in this review.

But to effectively use new data in light of new theories, it will also be necessary to use new methodological approaches. We are already witnessing an upsurge in research that takes advantage of large datasets using quantitative techniques, marking a departure from the predominant case approaches of the 1980s and 1990s.

Some possibilities in this direction include complex systems research and analytic models, including agent-based approaches. Others may lie in advanced statistical models that can analyze nested data or that incorporate spatial features of the data more explicitly into the analysis. The application of new methods to incorporate agent heterogeneity, feedbacks, dynamic processes, and nonlinear relationships will facilitate new theoretical insights. Given the extraordinary richness of the existing case-based work on forest commons, new methods for meta-analyses that compare findings across case studies can prove extremely useful.

Conclusion

Research on forest-based commons has helped to identify the institutional factors that promote sustainable resource governance. However, the influence of this body of research on global approaches to forest governance remains an open question (but see Nepstad et al. 2006). For example, in the most recent Global Forest Resources Assessment (FAO 2005)—which is arguably the most visible and influential publication on global forests—there is little discussion of research on commons or of the importance of institutions and property rights in shaping forest-related outcomes. Despite the significant proportion of forests that are governed under communal or community-based arrangements, the assessment fails to include a single reference from the field of commons research. Similarly, there is little mention of work by commons scholars in Jeffrey Sachs's *The End of Poverty*, one of the most widely read recent publications on poverty and development (2005). Despite widespread knowledge about the extent to which poor households rely on forest commons for significant aspects of their livelihoods, those focusing primarily on poverty have remained inattentive to the contributions of commons research.

Such a disjuncture—between the focus of research on forest-based commons and the pressing questions related to forests—is partly a result of the nearly single-minded concentration of commons scholarship on institutions and property rights. Future research needs to incorporate more explicitly the additional dimensions of institutional effectiveness, the role of biophysical factors, the relationship between research and policy effectiveness, interactions between various levels of analysis, and the extent to which corruption and violence may undermine the sustainability of resource governance. Scholars of forest commons also need to integrate their research more insistently with substantive concerns about indigenous peoples, social heterogeneities and inequalities, local livelihoods and poverty, and the effectiveness of international aid. A closer pairing of the theory and practice of forest governance will advance the goal of "doubly engaged social science" that Theda Skocpol (2003) has articulated and that comparative environmental politics research is ideally suited to fulfill (see Steinberg and VanDeveer, chapter 14, this volume).

The interdisciplinary nature of comparative environmental work suggests the need for greater attention to biophysical processes. The study of environmental politics cannot be reduced to the study of environment, and of politics, undertaken separately. Such reductions run the risk of misunderstanding the nature of environmental politics in relation to any given environmental problem. Nor should environmental politics simply be about the application of cutting-edge techniques from political science and comparative politics to the field of environmental studies. Using the best available methodologies is critically important, but mainstream methods from the toolbox of comparative political science are inadequate. Game theory and regression analysis—two of the most commonly used tools in comparative politics and political science more broadly—are poorly suited to understanding feedbacks, complexity, nonlinearities in causal relationships, and the emergent nature of environmental outcomes as the consequence of interactions between human and nonhuman agents.

Studies of forest commons have begun to grapple with issues of nonlinearities in causal processes, heterogeneous agent behavior, dynamics of system processes, and, in general, complexity in social-environmental relationships over time. More satisfying treatments of comparative environmental politics may also need to take the complexity of their subject matter more seriously. Rational choice models, game theory, and statistical treatments of human interactions—in which the physical environment is no more than a container for essentially political dynamics that are invariant with respect to their physical surroundings—will need to be supplemented with modeling and analytical approaches that take the complexity of environmental processes more seriously than is feasible through mainstream political science approaches. Without openness to such shifts, a deeper understanding of coupled natural and social systems is going to be extraordinarily difficult, if not impossible.

Understanding the dynamic properties of forest commons—and indeed, those of other topics within comparative environmental politics—will depend upon new and simultaneous advances in data, theories, and methods. New knowledge will demand the collection of not just more data, but new kinds of data. It will require new theories that bring into focus those properties and relationships that have been obscured by static, cross-sectional analyses of forest commons. Testing these new theories using new data will require the development and application of new methods and approaches, perhaps initially borrowed from other disciplines, but ultimately adapted to the needs of the specific fields and problems to which they are applied. Doing so will be critical to the development of the field of study focusing on the forest commons. It will also be central to developing insights into the character of coupled social and natural systems and to advancing the sciences of sustainability.

Notes

1. For example, the rights of villagers in forests in Kumaon, India, were formalized and recognized by the government in the 1930s. Villages have created rules to protect and manage their forests, but there are times when forest products are extracted by others who are not part of the group entitled to forest benefits (Agrawal 2005).

2. See http://www.environment.gov.au/indigenous/ipa/index.html, accessed April 2, 2010.

3. It is worth remembering in this context that most schools of the environment at American universities today started out as schools of forestry.

4. "Officially recognized forests" refers to the area of land classified as forests by forest departments and environment ministries in a given country. Forests and trees can exist on land that is not officially classified as forests, and some areas with this official designation do not in fact have forest cover. Globally, data are available only on officially recognized forests and their classification under different property regimes.

5. See White and Martin 2002, 9. Global Forest Watch has produced a number of reports making essentially the same point; see http://www.globalforestwatch.org/english/about/publications.htm, accessed May 27, 2011.

6. See http://www.resalliance.org/index.php/thresholds_database, accessed May 27, 2011.

7. It is worth noting that a number of scholars question the extent to which nonwood forest products can be important in alleviating poverty (Arnold and Ruiz Pérez 2001; Neumann and Hirsch 2000; Wunder 2001).

References

Adhikari, Bhim. 2005. Poverty, Property Rights and Collective Action: Understanding the Distributive Aspects of Common Property Resource Management. *Environment and Development Economics* 10:1–25.

Agrawal, Arun. 2001b. Common Property Institutions and Sustainable Governance of Resources. *World Development* 29 (10): 1649–1672.

Agrawal, Arun. 2004. Decentralization of Resource Policies in the Developing World, 1980–2005. Paper presented at the CHAOS–Cambridge University Press seminar series at University of Washington, Seattle, June.

Agrawal, Arun. 2005. *Environmentality: Technologies of Government and the Making of Subjects*. Durham: Duke University Press.

Agrawal, Arun. 2007. Forests, Governance, and Sustainability: Common Property Theory and Its Contributions. *International Journal of the Commons* 1 (1): 111–136.

Agrawal, Arun, and Ashwini Chhatre. 2006. Explaining Success on the Commons: Community Forest Governance in the Indian Himalaya. *World Development* 23 (1): 149–166.

Agrawal, Arun, Ashwini Chhatre, and Rebecca Hardin. 2008. Changing Governance of the World's Forests. *Science* 320 (5882): 1460–1462.

Agrawal, Arun, and Clark Gibson. 1999. Enchantment and Disenchantment: The Role of Community in Natural Resource Conservation. *World Development* 27 (4): 629–649.

Agrawal, Arun, and Sanjeev Goyal. 2001. Group Size and Collective Action: Third-party Monitoring in Common-Pool Resources. *Comparative Political Studies* 34 (1): 63–93.

Agrawal, Arun, and Gautam Yadama. 1997. How Do Social Institutions Mediate Market and Population Pressures on Resources? Forest Panchayats in Kumaon India. *Development and Change* 28:435–465.

Agarwal, Bina. 1997. Environmental Action, Gender Equity and Women's Participation. *Development and Change* 28 (1): 1–44.

Andersson, Krister P., Clark C. Gibson, and Fabrice Lehoucq. 2006. Municipal Politics and Forest Governance: Comparative Analysis of Decentralization in Bolivia and Guatemala. *World Development* 34 (3): 576–595.

Arnold, J. E. M., and M. Ruiz Pérez. 2001. Can Non-timber Forest Products Match Tropical Forest Conservation and Development Objectives? *Ecological Economics* 39:437–447.

Arnold, J. E. M., and W. C. Stewart. 1991. *Common Property Resource Management in India.* Oxford, UK: Oxford Forestry Institute, University of Oxford.

Baland, Jean-Marie, and Jean-Philippe Platteau. 1996. *Halting Degradation of Natural Resources: Is There a Role for Rural Communities?* Oxford, UK: Clarendon Press.

Baland, Jean Marie, and Jean-Philippe Platteau. 1999. The Ambiguous Impact of Inequality on Local Resource Management. *World Development* 27 (5): 773–788.

Bardhan, Pranab, and Jeff Dayton-Johnson. 2002. Unequal Irrigators: Heterogeneity and Commons Management in Large-Scale Multivariate Research. In *The Drama of the Commons,* ed. Elinor Ostrom, Thomas Dietz, Nives Dolšak, Paul C. Stern, Susan Stovich, and E. U. Weber, 87–112. Washington, D.C.: National Academy Press.

Berkes, Fikret. 2004. Rethinking Community-Based Conservation. *Conservation Biology* 18 (3): 621–630.

Berkes, Fikret, Iain Davidson-Hunt, and Kerril Davidson-Hunt. 1998. Diversity of Common Property Resource Use and Diversity of Social Interests in the Western Indian Himalaya. *Mountain Research and Development* 18 (1): 19–33.

Blair, Harry W. 1996. Democracy, Equity and Common Property Resource Management in the Indian Subcontinent. *Development and Change* 27 (3): 475–499.

Bowles, Samuel, and Herbert Gintis. 1998. Effective Redistribution: New Rules of Markets, States, and Communities. In *Recasting Egalitarianism: New Rules for Communities, States, and Markets,* ed. Eric Olin Wright, 3–71. London: Verso.

Bray, David Barton, Camille Antinori, and Juan Manuel Torres-Rojo. 2006. The Mexican Model of Community Forest Management: The Role of Agrarian Policy, Forest Policy and Entrepreneurial Organization. *Forest Policy and Economics* 8 (4): 470–484.

Brooks, Jeremy S., Margaret A. Franzen, Christopher M Holmes, Mark N. Grote, and Monique Borgerhoff Mulder. 2006. Testing Hypotheses for the Success of Different Conservation Strategies. *Conservation Biology* 20 (5): 1528–1538.

Brown, Gardner M. 2000. Renewable Natural Resource Management and Use without Markets. *Journal of Economic Literature* 38 (4): 875–914.

Chhatre, Ashwini, and Arun Agrawal. 2008. Forest Commons and Local Enforcement. *Proceedings of the National Academy of Sciences of the United States of America* 105 (36): 13286–13289.

Chhatre, Ashwini, and Arun Agrawal. 2009. Trade-offs and Synergies between Carbon Storage and Livelihood Benefits from Forest Commons. *Proceedings of the National Academy of Sciences of the United States of America* 106 (42): 17667–17670.

Chomitz, Kenneth. 2007. *At Loggerheads: Agricultural Expansion, Poverty Reduction, and Environment in the Tropical Forests*. Washington, D.C.: World Bank.

Clark, Judy. 2004. Forest Policy for Sustainable Commodity Wood Production: An Examination Drawing on the Australian Experience. *Ecological Economics* 50 (3–4): 219–232.

Cumming, Graeme S., David H. M. Cumming, and Charles L. Redman. 2006. Scale Mismatches in Social-Ecological Systems: Causes, Consequences, and Solutions. *Ecology and Society* 11 (1): 14. http://www.ecologyandsociety.org/vol11/iss1/art14, accessed May 27, 2011.

Dietz, Thomas, Elinor Ostrom, and Paul C. Stern. 2003. The Struggle to Govern the Commons. *Science* 302:1907–1912.

Food and Agriculture Organization (FAO). 2005. *Global Forest Resources Assessment*. Rome: Food and Agriculture Research Organization.

Geist, Helmut J., and Eric F. Lambin. 2001. What Drives Tropical Deforestation? A Meta-Analysis of Proximate and Underlying Causes of Deforestation Based on Subnational Case Study Evidence. Land-Use and Land-Cover Change (LUCC) Project Report Series No. 4. Louvain-la-Neuve, Belgium: University of Louvain, Department of Geography, LUCC International Project Office.

Gibson, Clark, Margaret A. McKean, and Elinor Ostrom, eds. 2000. *People and Forests: Communities, Institutions, and Governance*. Cambridge, Mass.: MIT Press.

Gibson, Clark C., Fabrice E. Lehoucq, and John T. Williams. 2002. Does Privatization Protect Natural Resources? Property Rights and Forests in Guatemala. *Social Science Quarterly* 83 (1): 206–225.

Gibson, Clark, Elinor Ostrom, and John T. Williams. 2005. Local Enforcement and Better Forests. *World Development* 33 (2): 273–284.

Goeschl, Timo, and Danilo Camargo Igliori. 2006. Property Rights for Biodiversity Conservation and Development: Extractive Reserves in the Brazilian Amazon. *Development and Change* 37 (2): 427–451.

Guha, Ramchandra. 1989. *The Unquiet Woods: Ecological Change and Peasant Resistance in the Himalaya*. New Delhi: Oxford University Press.

Haenn, Nora. 2006. The Changing and Enduring Ejido: A State and Regional Examination of Mexico's Land Tenure Counter-reforms. *Land Use Policy* 23 (2): 136–146.

Hardin, Russell. 1982. *Collective Action*. Baltimore: Johns Hopkins University Press.

International Tropical Timber Organization (ITTO). 2005. *Status of Tropical Forest Management. ITTO Technical Series N. 24.* Yokohama: ITTO.

Jessup, Timothy C., and Nancy L. Peluso. 1986. Minor Forest Products as Common Property Resources in East Kalimantan, Indonesia. In *Proceedings of the Conference on Common Property Resource Management*, edited by the National Research Council, 501–531. Washington, D.C.: National Academy Press.

Jodha, N. S. 1986. Common Property Resources and Rural Poor in Dry Regions of India. *Economic and Political Weekly* 21:1169–1181.

Kaimowitz, David, and Arild Angelson. 1998. *Economic Models of Tropical Deforestation: A Review.* Bogor, Indonesia: Center for International Forestry Research (CIFOR).

Kauppi, Pekka E., Jesse H. Ausubel, Jingyun Fang, Alexander S. Mather, Roger A. Sedjo, and Paul E. Waggoner. 2006. Returning Forests Analyzed with the Forest Identity. *Proceedings of the National Academy of Sciences of the United States of America* 103:17574–17579.

Klooster, Daniel James. 2002. Toward Adaptive Community Forest Management: Integrating Local Forest Knowledge with Scientific Forestry. *Economic Geography* 78 (1): 43–70.

Lemos, Maria C., and Arun Agrawal. 2006. Environmental Governance. *Annual Review of Environment and Resources* 31:297–325.

Lynch, Owen J., and Kirk Talbott. 1995. *Balancing Acts: Community-Based Forest Management and National Law in Asia and the Pacific.* Washington, D.C.: World Resources Institute.

Maskey, Vishakh, Tesfa G. Gebremedhin, and Timothy J. Dalton. 2006. Social and Cultural Determinants of Collective Management of Community Forests in Nepal. *Journal of Forest Economics* 11 (4): 261–274.

McKean, Margaret. 1992. Success on the Commons: A Comparative Examination of Institutions for Common Property Resource Management. *Journal of Theoretical Politics* 4 (3): 247–281.

Mutimukuru, Tendayi, Witness Kozanayi, and Richard Nyirenda. 2006. Catalyzing Collaborative Monitoring Processes in Joint Forest Management Situations: The Mafungautsi Forest Case, Zimbabwe. *Society & Natural Resources* 19 (3): 209–224.

Nepstad, D., S. Schwartzman, B. Bamberger, M. Santilli, D. Ray, P. Schleisinger, P. Lefebvre, et al. 2006. Inhibition of Amazon Deforestation and Fire by Parks and Indigenous Lands. *Conservation Biology* 20:65–73.

Neumann, Roderick P., and Eric Hirsch. 2000. *Commercialization of Non-timber Forest Products: Review and Analysis of Research.* Bogor, Indonesia: Center for International Forestry Research.

Nygren, Anja. 2005. Community-based Forest Management within the Context of Institutional Decentralization in Honduras. *World Development* 33 (4): 639–655.

Olson, M. 1965. *The Logic of Collective Action: Public Goods and the Theory of Groups.* Cambridge, Mass.: Harvard University Press.

Ostrom, Elinor. 1990. *Governing the Commons.* New York: Cambridge University Press.

Ostrom, Elinor. 1999. Self Governance and Forest Resources. Occasional Paper No. 20, Center for International Forestry Research, Bogor, Indonesia. http://www.cifor.cgiar.org/publications/pdf_files/OccPapers/OP-20.pdf, accessed May 27, 2011.

Ostrom, Elinor. 2005. *Understanding Institutional Diversity*. Princeton: Princeton University Press.

Ostrom, Elinor. 2007. A Diagnostic Approach for Going beyond Panaceas. *Proceedings of the National Academy of Sciences of the United States of America* 104 (39): 15181–15187.

Ostrom, Elinor. 2009. A General Framework for Analyzing Sustainability of Social-ecological Systems. *Science* 325:419–422.

Ostrom, Elinor, Roy Gardner, and James Walker. 1994. *Rules, Games, and Common Pool Resources*. Ann Arbor: University of Michigan Press.

Pagdee, Adcharaporn, Yeon-Su Kim, and P. J. Daugherty. 2006. What Makes Community Forest Management Successful: A Meta-study from Community Forests throughout the World. *Society & Natural Resources* 19 (1): 33–52.

Palmer, Charles, and Stefani Engel. 2007. For Better or For Worse? Local Impacts of the Decentralization of Indonesia's Forest Sector. *World Development* 35 (12): 2131–2149.

Peluso, Nancy Lee. 1992. *Rich Forests, Poor People*. Berkeley: University of California Press.

Peluso, Nancy Lee, and Peter Vandergeest. 2001. Genealogies of the Political Forest and Customary Rights in Indonesia. *Journal of Asian Studies* 60 (3): 761–812.

Peña-Claros, Marielos, Stijn Blommerde, and Frans Bongers. 2009. *Assessing the Progress Made: An Evaluation of Forest Management Certification in the Tropics*. Tropical Resource Management Papers No. 95. Wageningen, The Netherlands: Wageningen University and Research Centre, Department of Environmental Sciences Forest Ecology and Forest Management Group.

Phelps, Jacob, Edward Webb, and Arun Agrawal. 2010. Does REDD+ Threaten to Recentralize Forest Governance? *Science* 328:312–313.

Poteete, Amy, and Elinor Ostrom. 2004. Heterogeneity, Group Size, and Collective Action: The Role of Institutions in Forest Management. *Development and Change* 35 (3): 435–461.

Power, Thomas Michael. 2006. Public Timber Supply, Market Adjustments, and Local Economies: Economic Assumptions of the Northwest Forest Plan. *Conservation Biology* 20 (2): 341–350.

Pretty, Jules. 2003. Social Capital and the Collective Management of Resources. *Science* 302 (5652): 1912–1914.

Raffles, Hugh. 1999. "Local Theory": Nature and the Making of an Amazonian Place. *Cultural Anthropology* 14 (3): 323–360.

Rangan, Haripriya, and Marcus Lane. 2001. Indigenous Peoples and Forest Management: Comparative Analysis of Institutional Approaches in Australia and India. *Society & Natural Resources* 14 (2): 145–160.

Rangarajan, Mahesh. 1996. *Fencing the Forest: Conservation and Ecological Change in India's Central Provinces, 1860–1914*. New Delhi: Oxford University Press.

Reed, Maureen G., and Kirsten McIlveen. 2006. Toward a Pluralistic Civic Science? Assessing Community Forestry. *Society & Natural Resources* 19 (7): 591–607.

Ribot, Jesse C. 1999. Decentralization, Participation, and Accountability in Sahelian Forestry: Legal Instruments of Political-Administrative Control. *Africa* 69 (1): 23–65.

Ribot, Jesse C. 2002. Democratic Decentralization of Natural Resources: Institutionalizing Popular Participation. Working Paper. Washington, D.C: World Resources Institute.

Sachs, Jeffrey. 2005. *The End of Poverty*. New York: Penguin.

Salafsky, Nick, Barbara L. Dugelby, and John W. Terborgh. 1993. Can Extractive Reserves Save the Rain Forest? An Ecological and Socioeconomic Comparison of Nontimber Forest Product Extraction Systems in Peten, Guatemala, and West Kalimantan, Indonesia. *Conservation Biology* 7 (1): 39–52.

Sivaramakrishnan, K. 1999. *Modern Forests: Statemaking and Environmental Change in Colonial Eastern India*. Palo Alto: Stanford University Press.

Skaria, Ajay. 1999. *Hybrid Histories: Forests, Frontiers, and Wildness in Western India*. New Delhi: Oxford University Press.

Skocpol, Theda. 2003. Doubly Engaged Social Science: The Promise of Comparative Historical Analysis. In *Comparative Historical Analysis in the Social Sciences*, ed. James Mahoney and Dietrich Rueschemeyer, 407–429. New York: Cambridge University Press.

Somanathan, E., and R. Prabhakar. and B. S. Mehta. 2005. Does Decentralization Work? Forest Conservation in the Indian Himalayas. Discussion Paper 05–04. New Delhi: Indian Statistical Institute.

Sundar, Nandini. 2001. Is Devolution Democratization? *World Development* 29 (12): 2007–2023.

Sunderlin, William D., Jeffrey Hatcher, and Megan Liddle. 2008. *From Exclusion to Ownership? Challenges and Opportunities in Advancing Forest Tenure Reform*. Washington, D.C.: Rights and Resources Initiative.

Taylor, Peter Leigh. 2005. A Fair Trade Approach to Community Forest Certification? A Framework for Discussion. *Journal of Rural Studies* 21 (4): 433–447.

Tole, Lise. 2001. Jamaica's Disappearing Forests: Physical and Human Aspects. *Environmental Management* 28 (4): 455–467.

Tucker, Catherine M. 1999. Private versus Common Property Forests: Forest Conditions and Tenure in a Honduran Community. *Human Ecology* 27 (2): 201–230.

Tucker, C. M., J. C. Randolph, and E. J. Castellanos. 2007. Institutions, Biophysical Factors and History: An Integrative Analysis of Private and Common Property Forests in Guatemala and Honduras. *Human Ecology* 35 (3): 259–274.

Turner, Nancy J., Iain J. Davidson-Hunt, and Michael O'Flaherty. 2003. Living on the Edge: Ecological and Cultural Edges as Sources of Diversity for Social-Ecological Resilience. *Human Ecology* 31 (3): 439–461.

Victor, David G., and Jesse H. Ausubel. 2000. Restoring the Forests. *Foreign Affairs (Council on Foreign Relations)* 79:127–144.

White, Andy, and Alejandra Martin. 2002. *Who Owns the World's Forests? Forest Tenure and Public Forests in Transition*. Washington, D.C.: Forest Trends and Center for International Environmental Law.

Wilkie, David, Ellen Shaw, Fiona Rotberg, Gilda Morelli, and Philippe Auzel. 2000. Roads, Development, and Conservation in the Congo Basin. *Conservation Biology* 14 (6): 1614–1622.

Wily, Liz Alden. 2001. Reconstructing the African Commons. *Africa Today* 48 (1): 77–99.

Wittman, Hannah, and Charles Geisler. 2005. Negotiating Locality: Decentralization and Communal Forest Management in the Guatemalan Highlands. *Human Organization* 64 (1): 62–74.

Wunder, Sven. 2001. Poverty Alleviation and Tropical Forests—What Scope for Synergies? *World Development* 29:1617–1633.

Young, Kenneth R. 1994. Roads and the Environmental Degradation of Tropical Montane Forests. *Conservation Biology* 8 (4): 972–976.

13

Federalism, Multilevel Governance, and Climate Change Politics across the Atlantic

Henrik Selin and Stacy D. VanDeveer

Introduction

Human activities and their many byproducts are changing the climate of our planet. These changes, like the contributions of different countries and communities to climate change, vary substantially around the world. Every year, the average US citizen pushes almost 20 tons of carbon into the atmosphere while Europeans, Chinese, and Indians average about 8.5, 5.7, and 1.4 tons, respectively (Netherlands Environmental Assessment Agency 2009). Political systems respond very differently to climate change issues. Some countries and local communities have acted to slow and reverse their greenhouse gas (GHG) emissions; others have ignored the problem or refused to act. Often, those who take action use different policy options, as climate change related decisions occur at every level of human organization, from choices made by individuals when purchasing a product to every level of public sector governance (cities, states and provinces, national governments, and international organizations). Comparative politics research offers tools for examining this complex set of outcomes.

The dominant discourse about "global warming" and "global climate change" sometimes leads analysts and observers to think of climate change politics and policy making predominantly in global terms, as does media coverage of the United Nations climate change regime. Yet the dynamics and outcomes of climate change politics at the global, regional, national, and local levels result from a huge number of factors cutting across these governance scales (Andonova and Mitchell 2010; Schreurs 2010; Koehn 2010; Selin and VanDeveer 2009a). Some of these factors are ecological; many others are political, economic, social, and cultural. The significance of this large number of factors is evidenced by the varied national and subnational political responses to climate change and energy challenges all over the world. These complex combinations of political processes and the results they produce are the stuff of comparative political analysis.

Two geographical regions and political systems that have responded differently to the threats posed by climate change are Europe and North America; this despite the fact that the European Union and the United States share many basic political values and have similar levels of economic development and economies of about the same size. Since the early 1990s, the EU has repeatedly enacted more aggressive policies to induce energy efficiency, expand renewable energy production, and reduce greenhouse gas emissions than has the United States. Furthermore, EU officials seek to maintain a global leadership role on climate change and energy issues while the United States became an infamous climate change laggard under the George W. Bush administration. Though the Obama administration brought US and EU climate change rhetoric into greater accord, climate change policies did not rapidly converge across the Atlantic.

The complexities of transatlantic climate change politics are illustrated by the fact that the city of Portland, Oregon, and the state of California are widely recognized for their innovative and aggressive sets of policies to increase energy efficiency and renewable energy use and to reduce GHG emissions from the transportation, building, and energy production sectors (Gore and Robinson 2009; Farrell and Hanemann 2009). Yet both are located within a county known for its national government's failure to enact meaningful GHG reduction policies despite being among the world's top emitters and energy users. At the same time, European energy and climate change policy leaders like Germany, Sweden, and the United Kingdom have reduced their emissions substantially via different combinations of economic changes and policy measures, while some other EU states have seen significant increases in their emissions since 1990. In many respects, California's climate change and energy policies more closely approximate those of the EU than those of the US federal government, and Germany's political responses are closer to California's than to those in Italy, Greece, or Romania (Schreurs, Selin, and VanDeveer 2009).

The EU and the United States both have federalist systems of government. Some EU member states, such as Belgium and Germany, are themselves federal and the United States shares a continent and the North American Free Trade Agreement with its Canadian and Mexican federalist neighbors. Although specific definitions in the literature vary, a federalist system is one with rules that divide public policy authority among national and subnational governments (Scheberle 2004). Jenna Bednar (2009, 18–19) specifies requirements for "robust federation," including firm boundaries of territory and authority that cannot be unilaterally abolished by the constituent states and national government. However, authority over taxation, pollution regulation, natural resource management, national security, criminal justice, health care, education, and a host of other issue areas is shared and distributed quite differently across various federations. The study of differences and similarities across federal systems—and their causes and ramifications—is known as comparative federalism (Burgess 2006). Comparative federalism has a long tradition in comparative politics, but is a much newer area of inquiry among those interested in international environmental politics.

Comparative politics scholars have long been interested in the influence of governance systems on politics and policymaking, as discussed in the introductory chapters of this volume. This chapter combines approaches associated with comparative federalism scholarship with the multilevel governance literature as it explores climate change politics in North America and Europe. This combination of analytical approaches remains rare. Comparative federalist research tends to ignore the international level of governance—that is, it ignores the institutions "above" the national level—focusing instead on national-subnational relationships. Yet climate change policy making happens at every level of government within the US and EU federalist systems, making it well suited for the combination of approaches used in this chapter. Such combinations further illustrate the untapped potential for knowledge creation by bringing comparative politics, environmental studies, and global environmental politics closer and into more sustained conversation.

In short, this chapter argues that sweeping statements—many of them oversimplifications—of transatlantic differences cannot satisfactorily explain US and EU divergence on climate change policy (and many other environmental issues). In fact, many discussions of transatlantic politics greatly overstate the divergence, in part because they focus exclusively on a single level of government on each side of the Atlantic (Schreurs, Selin, and VanDeveer 2009). Instead, to understand why the EU has enacted so many policies related to climate change and energy over the last twenty years while US federal policy in these areas has changed little since 1990, it is necessary to focus careful attention on the structure and operation of the different systems of government on each side of the Atlantic and the different political dynamics these federal systems induce. Rather than assuming, for example, that Europeans care more about the environment or that Americans distrust government too much to enact serious government regulation (claims belied by public opinion data and the fact that Americans have quite a bit of government regulation in many realms), it is essential to understand how the EU and the United States are governed.

The chapter begins by outlining transatlantic differences on climate change, embedding them in a larger debate surrounding political differences between the United States and the EU on environmental issues. This is followed by a discussion of the chapter's two primary concepts: multilevel governance and federalism. Next, US and EU responses to climate change are compared, demonstrating that substantial differences at the federal levels mask significant commonality and interaction at lower levels of governance among US states and municipalities and European national governments and municipalities. This more nuanced picture of comparative transatlantic climate politics shows the importance of institutional structures in shaping political dynamics and policy outcomes. The chapter concludes by taking comparative climate politics global, arguing that many research opportunities exist to study how the growing set of countries with federalist systems[1] respond to climate change.

Why Transatlantic Differences?

The well-documented divergence between Europe and the United States on climate change is part of a broader pattern of divergence on environmental issues. Much ink has been spilled describing and trying to explain past and ongoing transatlantic differences around a host of issues, including biotechnology and genetically modified organisms, food safety, chemicals management, asbestos regulation, waste reduction and disposal policies, support for sustainable development, environmental standards used by export credit agencies, hazardous waste exports, the promotion of renewable energy, agricultural subsidies, and dozens of product and accounting standards (Schreurs, Selin, and VanDeveer 2009; Jasanoff 2005; Vig and Faure 2004; Harrington, Morgenstern, and Sterner 2004; Vogel 2003). Given the many areas of transatlantic cooperation and competition on the environment, climate change policy divergence serves as a window into a much larger set of domestic and international political processes. Many other issues could be studied through the lenses of comparative federalism and multilevel governance dynamics.

In the 1960s and 1970s, many environmental policy ideas and regulations diffused across the Atlantic, particularly from the United States to Europe, in areas such as vehicle emission standards and controls of hazardous substances (Vogel 1995; Jänicke and Weidner 1997; Lafferty and Meadowcroft 2000; Schreurs 2002). The European Union and the United States also cooperated in the establishment of several multilateral environmental agreements. This pattern of collaboration changed as different policy approaches came to dominate on the two sides of the Atlantic starting in the 1980s. Whereas in Europe a regulatory role for the state in environmental protection is well accepted, in the United States a regulatory intervention by the state for conservation and pollution control has often been challenged (Kraft and Kamieniecki 2007; Klyza and Sousa 2008). There has also been a transatlantic rift in relation to global environmental treaties; the EU has ratified nearly every one since the early 1990s, but the United States has refused to ratify most of them (Schreurs, Selin, and VanDeveer 2009). Thus, the transatlantic divide on climate change is a high profile example of a larger set of issues.

Why, when transatlantic economies and societies are increasingly integrated, are the accompanying politics so often discordant? With the growing influence of global environmental norms, international expert communities, multinational corporations, international organizations, and international environment and trade agreements, all coming together under the umbrella of "economic globalization," should not environmental policy differences between Europe and America be narrowing instead of expanding? Given that the forces of economic globalization are alleged to be strong and bringing countries closer together, why in the past decades have the EU and the United States diverged on so many important policy issues? Analysts have offered a host of plausible explanations for transatlantic divergences on the environment. Five commonly invoked sets of explanations are discussed here, including explanations that focus on overlapping (sometimes contradictory, sometimes complementary) factors.

One set of explanations focuses on the importance of diverging societal and cultural norms with respect to protection of the environment and human health, including climate change (Martinelli 2007; Guehlstorf and Hallstrom 2002). Such norms include higher levels of acceptance of concepts such as the precautionary principle and sustainable development in European countries compared with the United States (Grant, Matthews, and Newell 2000; Vig and Faure 2004; Sadeleer 2007). These kinds of explanations often stress that a stronger European commitment to the social welfare state may help to explain why Europeans overall have seemed more prepared to absorb a share of GHG reduction costs than their US counterparts. As the EU, national European governments, and many citizens believe that the threat from climate change is serious and that someone has to take the lead, Europeans—more used to paying taxes and incurring costs as the price for the security afforded them by the social welfare state—believe that this is an area where the EU should take on a regional and global leadership role.

A second set of explanations claim that European public opinion is more informed or more supportive of environmental protection and climate change than in the United States. Some related scholarship points out that green parties and environmental advocacy groups in Europe have been more influential in domestic and regional politics than has the US environmental movement (Bomberg 1998; Burchell 2002; Müller-Rommel and Poguntke 2002). Dunlap and McCright (2008) show that self-identified Democrats and Independents have become more informed and concerned about climate change over time and that Republicans have not. These trends help to explain the continuing and bitter partisan differences in the United States, a phenomenon both less common and less pronounced in Europe. However, the growing fissure in American public opinion may also be a product of partisan division, rather than the cause of it. Rabe and Borick's (2010) public opinion work demonstrates that Americans' awareness of and concern about climate change has grown over the last decade, as has their support for policy actions to address climate change, but there remains substantial reluctance to pay the additional costs associated with potential new policies.

A third set of explanations proposes that transatlantic differences over environmental policy emerged as a political artifact tied to the rise in influence of the Republican Party in the different branches of US politics since the 1980s, as it seeks to reduce the size of government and limit intervention in the private sector. The Republican Party has traditionally been a stronger supporter of business interests than environmental ones, which recently have been more the domain of the Democratic Party. The Republican Party, with the backing of the George W. Bush administration, favored industrial, mining, land use, and energy interests (Kraft and Kamieniecki 2007; Klyza and Sousa 2008). In Europe, the rise of green parties influencing the stands of social democratic, liberal, and Christian democratic parties may help to explain the greater acceptance of environmental regulation in Europe relative to the United States. However, the influence of political parties within democratic systems can be explained only with attention to the structure of the political institutions in which they operate (see Michael O'Neill, chapter 7, this volume).

A fourth set of explanations points toward the ability of interest groups to influence environmental policy making in different political systems. This approach suggests that the neoliberal and neoconservative revolution that began under the Reagan administration, was strengthened with the 1994 appointment of Newt Gingrich as Speaker of the House of Representatives, and solidified with the George W. Bush administration resulted in deep institutional changes such as the weakening of the US Environmental Protection Agency (EPA), the empowerment of conservative think tanks, the increased voice of industry-related lobby groups in Washington, D.C., and state capitals, and the decline of environmentally activist courts. Collectively, these changes put environmental advocacy groups on the defensive and encouraged a search for nonregulatory approaches to pollution control and environmental protection, such as voluntary agreements and public-private partnerships that are less likely to result in an all-out assault from entrenched private sector interests (Morgenstern and Pizer 2007; Klyza and Sousa 2008; see also the discussion by Gallagher and Weinthal, chapter 6, this volume).

A fifth set of explanations focuses on the expanding legal and political role of EU organizations, leading to important developments in European environmental policy making. Beginning in the 1980s, a series of treaty-based changes to the legal basis of the EU expanded the authority of the European Commission, the European Parliament, and the European Council at the expense of national parliaments across most environmental issue areas. Working with green leader states, these EU institutions strengthened a host of regulatory standards. They also provided new avenues for environmental and other societal interests to influence policy making in Brussels and elsewhere, as new environmental advocacy groups formed all over Europe, shaping local and regional policy development. Furthermore, concepts of sustainable development and the precautionary principle became deeply embedded in EU laws and treaties, shaping both European debates and policy making (Baker et al. 1997; Hunter and Smith 2005; Baker 2006).

Although all five sets of factors have some discernable influence in different environmental policy areas, this chapter focuses attention on federalist structures and multilevel governance. The last twenty years have witnessed substantial centralization of environmental policymaking authority in the EU, while US states and municipalities continue to be the laboratories of environmental policy innovation on their side of the Atlantic and organized interests that are generally hostile to or skeptical of environmental regulation remain influential in the US congressional and executive branches. Our analysis highlights these dynamics while integrating aspects of the five rather ad hoc explanations into a framework that focuses on institutions of governance, which can explain transatlantic climate change differences and can be applied to (and tested with) other issue areas and other national and regional comparisons.

From Global Regimes to Multilevel Governance and Federalism

Scholars have long been interested in how states, intergovernmental organizations (IGOs), and nongovernmental organizations (NGOs) interact to create and maintain global and regional institutions to manage specific issues. There are many definitions of "institutions" in the social science literature, but most scholars view them as socially created and maintained structures that in different ways shape interactions, constrain activity, and define what is regarded as "appropriate" and "permitted" behavior of actors operating within these institutions (Krasner 1983; Keohane 1989). Early institutional analysis often focused on the role of states and larger IGOs in creating and maintaining these kinds of structures, but there has been a large expansion in the literature focusing on the influence and activities of NGOs and social movements in international politics over the past several decades (see Kate O'Neill, chapter 5, this volume).

Within the broad field of international institutional analysis, regime analysis is often used in studies of particular environmental issue areas (Young 1989; Haas, Keohane, and Levy 1993; Levy, Young, and Zürn 1995; Hasenclever, Mayer, and Rittberger 1997; Breitmeier, Young, and Zürn 2006; Young, King, and Schroeder 2008; Selin 2010). An international regime is commonly defined in the international relations literature as consisting of "sets of implicit and explicit principles, norms, rules and decision-making procedures around which actors' expectations converge in a given area of international relations" (Krasner 1983, 2). Regimes, as issue-specific social institutions, define acceptable behavior and shape perceptions within a particular policy area. In more formalized regimes, many regulatory and management components are codified in one or several legal multilateral instruments, as in the case of the climate change regime.

The two main climate change agreements are the 1992 United Nations Framework Convention on Climate Change (UNFCCC) and the 1997 Kyoto Protocol. In 2009, the Copenhagen Accord was created by a group of national leaders, and global climate change politics are set to continue for a long time. However, climate change politics are not simply about United Nations–sponsored treaties and high-profile multilateral negotiations. In fact, global commitments are considerably less stringent than many policies and standards developed at regional, national, and local levels, which are integral parts of climate change politics (Andonova and Mitchell 2010). "Global" climate change politics happens at multiple levels of human organization, from United Nations–sponsored negotiations in which almost two hundred countries are formally represented to national, state, and provincial legislatures and city council meetings. This multiscale climate governance includes governing bodies and institutions at various levels of government as well as the civil society and private sector actors engaging these organizations and institutions.

Drawing on concepts from institutional analysis, research on multilevel governance studies how politics and policy-making efforts are linked within and across governance scales (Young 2002; Bache and Flinders 2004; Finger, Tamiotti, and Allouche 2006; Selin 2010). Issues of multilevel governance—involving multiple public and private sector actors operating across horizontal and vertical levels of social organization and jurisdictional authority—have become increasingly important across many issue areas as policy is developed simultaneously in multiple forums ranging across global, regional, national, and local scales. Multilevel governance was first studied mostly by scholars of European governance (Hooghe and Marks 2001) but has since been applied to multiscale policy making outside Europe (Betsill and Bulkeley 2006; Harrison and Sundstrom 2007, 2010; Selin and VanDeveer 2009a; Schreurs 2010).

Multilevel environmental governance, including in the area of climate change, is typically characterized by horizontal and vertical linkages. Horizontal linkages operate among instruments and programs at similar levels of social organization (e.g., among city governments). Vertical linkages exist among different levels of social organization (such as national governments and multilateral forums). Climate change governance in Europe and North America includes extensive horizontal and vertical interaction among federal, state, provincial, and municipal policy makers, private sector leaders, and civil society representatives. Analysis of political dynamics in multilevel systems often focuses on authority and outcomes within and among different levels of jurisdiction. Although such issues may be highly contested, many multilevel systems include formal structures that proscribe official relationships between different governance levels. This is, of course, also true of federal systems in which policy making authority is dispersed across levels of government.

Federalism is a major theme in comparative politics and an important component of the field's interest in governance structures. Research on the influence of federalism focuses on topics such as institutional structure, authority, and power, and how federalist institutions aggregate, centralize, or decentralize interests, social mobilization, and other political activities. Analysis of comparative federalism has a rich history, expanding as the list of states with federalist structures has grown over time and with growing interest in varieties of "fiscal federalism" (Burgess 2006; Hueglin and Fenna 2005; Watts 2008). Today, this work is a subset of comparative institutionalist research. But federalist concepts trace back to the ancient Greeks and were further developed by theorists such as Aquinas, Kant, Hume, Spinoza, Montesquieu, Althusius, and Rousseau (Ward and Ward 2009). These theorists, and many others, influenced the thinking of the early American federalists and their extensive debates with the "antifederalists" and other critics.

Federalist governance and government is dynamic over time, as some of the rules for division of authority and responsibility change and as new areas of policy are added to the system (such as poverty alleviation, healthcare access and delivery, and natural resource conservation or pollution regulation) (Erk and Swenden 2010; Breton et al. 2009). But federalist systems do not necessarily change in similar ways over time. Some increase centralization on some issues, and others may decentralize authority on similar issues (Weibust 2009). Dimensions for comparative analysis include similarities or differences across countries in policy practices and the allocation of authority, as well as on explaining variation across time and across issues areas. Also, as the number of federalist systems has grown, a growing number of comparative research opportunities exist across a host of continents, levels of economic development, cultures, and national histories (see table 13.1).

Table 13.1
Selected federalist systems

Argentina	Iraq
Australia	Malaysia
Belgium	Mexico
Brazil	Pakistan
Canada	Russia
European Union	Spain
Germany	Switzerland
India	**United States**

As James Meadowcroft describes in his contribution to this volume (chapter 3), the quantity of environmental policy has grown over time at every level of government on both sides of the Atlantic. As the diversity of environmental issues and policy instruments has increased, and as states and societies have grappled with questions about the centralization or decentralization of regulatory and decision-making authority, a scholarly subfield of environmental federalism has emerged (Anderson and Hill 1997; Weibust 2009). US and European contributors to this research are interested in how the cooperative, collaborative, and/or dysfunctional nature of relations among levels of government authority impact the implementation of environmental policy (Scheberle 2004). This research often focuses on institutional models that can improve implementation by engendering greater collaboration among levels of government (what public policy scholars refer to as "intergovernmental relations"). Multilevel governance scholars often focus on similar themes, asking how to achieve effective governance across levels of authority and among increasingly diverse governmental, civil society, and private sector actors.

Kelemen (2000, 2004) treats the EU as a federalist structure, despite the frequent objection to this usage in European political circles. He notes that although some characteristics of the EU are unlike other federalist systems, EU environmental policy operates in ways consistent with federalism. Kelemen often quips that some EU scholars and policy makers are uncomfortable "using the F word," instead calling the EU quasi-federal or federal-like. Despite this reluctance, he argues that the EU has the basic attributes of a federal system. We agree with Kelemen's assessment, given the diversity of federalist structures in the EU and its divisions of authority across many issues. Kelemen points to several EU and US similarities, including the fact that both political systems centralize considerable policy making authority while assigning much of the funding, implementation, and enforcement activity to constituent states. In both systems, actors pursue litigious and coercive strategies to increase or to limit state discretion.

Transatlantic Comparisons

The 2001 decision by the George W. Bush administration to withdraw US support for and participation in the Kyoto Protocol strained the transatlantic relationship. But national-level leaders and public policies in the United States have often been at odds with their European counterparts for many years, both at the EU and national levels. For example, although renewable energy is still a small share of total energy in both the EU and the United States and both sides of the Atlantic introduced energy conservation measures in response to the 1973 and 1979 oil shocks, Europe persisted with these efforts at the supranational level far more aggressively than did the United States. In 2001, the EU introduced a directive with the goal of meeting

12 percent of energy demand with renewable sources by 2010, and in 2007, EU officials and member states proposed to increase the goal to 20 percent by 2020. In the United States, several states promote renewable energy with more or less ambitious goals and means, but national standards and programs remain limited in both scope and stringency (Rabe 2004, 2010; Selin and VanDeveer 2005, 2006, 2009a, 2009b).

This difference illustrates a general pattern across the Atlantic. Europe has increasingly centralized climate and energy policymaking at the EU level, sometimes leaving member states broad discretion in the implementation of these goals, but the US federal government has enacted virtually no serious GHG regulation in more than twenty years.[2] As such, climate change policy has developed very differently within the EU and US federal systems. The EU has taken a top-down approach, although European environmental leader states have also been very active in trying to shape pan-European policy. Climate policy activity has occurred over the same period of time that EU member states have continued to invest greater authority in EU institutions.

In contrast, US federalist climate change politics are characterized by bottom-up dynamics. The US government has been largely inactive and has even worked actively against several domestic efforts to set GHG regulations. While debates about US policy have raged among NGOs and firms and in congressional commit-tees in Washington, years of contentious politics have produced no policies designed to alter the country's GHG emissions. In this policy vacuum, subnational entities— states and municipalities—have sometimes stepped in and developed their own climate change policies and standards. As highlighted in what follows, states and cities have also built collaborative institutions to assist them in their joint efforts to curb emissions and to push for more federal policy making.

EU Climate Change Politics: Brussels in the Drivers Seat

The EU, which began with six members in the 1950s, consists of twenty-seven member states, and more countries may join in the future. The population of the EU-27 is close to 500 million, so roughly one in fourteen people in the world live in the EU. EU climate change policy has a relatively long history compared to deci-sion making in other regions, dating back to at least 1991, when the climate change issue began to gain salience and member states responded by adopting collective measures to limit carbon dioxide (CO_2) emissions and improve energy efficiency (Jordan et al. 2010). Current policies are guided by a set of "20-20-20" goals adopted in 2007 to be met by 2020: reduce GHG emissions by 20 percent, increase the share of renewable energy to 20 percent, and improve energy efficiency by 20 percent. The EU also formulated a goal to increase the share of petrol and diesel consumption from biofuels to 10 percent.

"Brussels" is the apex of much European climate change politics (Jordan et al. 2010; Oberthur and Pallemaerts 2010). EU climate change policy is formulated by the European Commission (the administrative bureaucracy), the Council of Ministers (government officials from each member state), and the European Parliament (members elected directly by citizens in each member state). Legislative proposals put forward by the European Commission are negotiated and passed by the Council of Ministers and the European Parliament through a process requiring several iterations of negotiations between and within each of the three institutions. The Council of Ministers takes most decisions on new environmental policies via a "qualified majority" of member states. The requirements for this qualified majority have changed over the last decade as EU membership has expanded and decision-making procedures have changed as a result of treaty revisions. The current system for qualified majority decision making is scheduled to change in 2014, in accordance with the 2007 Lisbon Treaty.

EU legislative acts come in the form of directives and regulations. Directives stipulate standards that must be achieved, but leave most aspects of implementation to individual member states to carry out. Regulations contain more uniform and detailed requirements for implementation, leaving only limited room for member states to take individual action. Both the Council of Ministers and the European Parliament became more important venues for climate change policy development in the 2000s, when Council and Parliament leaders repeatedly advocated for more ambitious policies and pushed for European leadership in international negotiations (Oberthur and Pallemaerts 2010). Each member state is responsible for implementing EU legislation. When a member country fails to meet its obligations or commitments, the European Commission can (and often does) seek to have it found derelict by the European Court of Justice and ordered by the Court to meet its obligations.

EU policy is explicitly linked to multilateral agreements formulated within the global climate change regime. Under the Kyoto Protocol, after extensive negotiations the then 15 EU member states (EU-15) took on a collective target of reducing CO_2 emissions 8 percent below 1990 levels by 2012. Eight of the ten countries that joined the EU after the Kyoto Protocol was adopted also have individual Kyoto targets. The EU-15 divided up their Kyoto target in a 1998 burden-sharing agreement under which several relatively wealthy members took on more aggressive commitments so that less wealthy member states could increase their GHG emissions as part of their efforts to expand industrial production and economic growth. The GHG reduction goal for 2020 is expected to be implemented largely through the EU Emission Trading System (ETS), the world's first public, mandatory GHG emissions trading scheme, modeled in part on US trading schemes for SO_2 and NO_x emissions.

The EU ETS was launched in 2005 with a three-year pilot phase and a second phase from 2008 to 2012. It covers more than 11,500 major energy-intensive installations across all member states, although most are located in a few larger ones (Germany has more than 20 percent of all ETS allowances). The ETS third phase (2013–2020) plans to gradually shrink the EU-wide cap, incorporate more emission sources (including aviation) and greenhouse gases (nitrous oxide and perfluorocarbons), and increase national auctioning of emission allowances, which have hitherto largely been given away for free to participating installations. The ETS has also been expanded to include participation by non-EU members such as Norway and Lichtenstein. This trading scheme illustrates the growing centralization in EU climate and energy policy making, as member state discretion on enforcement and implementation is quite limited and participating firms and installations trade allowances in pan-European (not national) markets within pan-European institutions.

Oberthur and Pallemaerts (2010) argue that the 1990s served as both an agenda-setting stage for EU climate change politics and an era in which the EU's global climate change initiatives outstripped its abilities to meet its goals. Climate change leadership offered EU officials and institutions opportunities to further the ongoing project of deepening European integration and to position themselves as global leaders in environmental politics. In the early 1990s, an EU carbon tax proposed by the European Commission failed to achieve the required unanimous support from member states and was never formally introduced (although some member states have domestic carbon taxes). By the early 2000s, the EU's global leadership on climate change was not matched in its internal policies, yielding a "credibility gap." For example, EU GHG emissions were still growing in the late 1990s and early 2000s. After the United States rejected the Kyoto Protocol and EU policy makers decided to implement the agreement following its entry into force, more aggressive policy action was required to meet their Kyoto commitments.

In the 2000s, the European Council (of national, member state political leaders) and successive (rotating) EU presidencies instituted a set of expert groups, negotiating teams, and lead negotiators (in cooperation with the European Commission) for climate change and energy issues. The result is a substantial increase in negotiating and analytical capacity for the EU and the construction of a consistent body of knowledge within the EU leadership teams and institutions, as they participate simultaneously in global climate change negotiations and EU policymaking (Oberthur and Pallemaerts 2010). As regional consensus increased around the need to take the climate change issue seriously, the earlier reluctance of some member states to enact common policies declined, resulting in the adoption of the ETS and a host of other initiatives. These include directives and regulations on product design, energy efficiency, biofuels, and renewable energy. In 2007, the 20–20–20 policy goals noted previously were initiated, seeking to bring together a wide set of policies toward a clear set of goals and timetables.

One set of reasons for this increasingly centralized—sometimes called "Europeanized"—leadership over the last two decades relates to the institutional contexts of policy making (on "Europeanization" see Andonova and VanDeveer, chapter 11, this volume). EU-level actors used climate change to advance the project of European integration, building more authoritative policies around a host of energy and climate issues and seeking to legitimize integration and regional institution building. EU organizational incentives often align in efforts to advance pan-European integration and policy development while attempting to establish global leadership for the EU. Other factors driving climate change policy making include the relative lack of vocal private sector or citizen opposition to climate change policies. Private sector actors lobby, of course, to avoid unwanted costs or for details that may offer them competitive advantage, but only rarely do they state categorical opposition to new or proposed regulations. Furthermore, the European Parliament has not been a place where private sector actors have been able to weaken new regulation; instead, the European Parliament has acted to strengthen many environmental and energy standards.

By the 2007–2009 period, in the run-up to the 2009 Copenhagen Summit, the EU's "climate and energy package" of policies included a substantial revision of the ETS directive, a new renewable energy directive, and other directives designed to promote carbon capture and storage and to help to reduce GHG emissions from economic sectors not covered by the ETS. Added to this package in 2009 were additional policies aimed at increasing vehicle efficiency and lowering carbon and other pollutants from vehicle fuels. This suite of policies enacted the 20–20–20 goals into law across the EU's economy and its member states, renegotiating (and renaming) the earlier burden-sharing agreements of the 1990s into "effort-sharing" targets. These targets afford member states substantial implementation discretion, allowing them to prioritize sectoral policies and trade and borrow emissions credits to achieve targets across sectors, years, and so on (Oberthur and Pallemaerts 2010). By late 2010, some environmental activists and leading member states were calling for more ambitious goals for 2020 and beyond.

An oft-cited strength of federalist systems—the tendency to induce actors to innovate at multiple levels of policy making—has also been on display in the EU. The ability of member states to meet collective targets by designing their own domestic implementation measures has resulted in a plethora of domestic policy approaches. Environmental leader states have long focused on both supply and demand aspects of energy issues, as they use different mixes of energy sources based on domestic conditions and public opinion. For example, Sweden has introduced CO_2 taxes on fossil fuels, subsidized the expansion of domestically produced biofuels and wind power, and given consumers rebates for buying biogas and electric vehicles or vehicles that emit less than 120 grams of CO_2 per kilometer. Swedish authorities, like those in other leader states, have also focused on improving energy efficiency in buildings and expanding public transportation systems, while introducing congestion fees for driving in urban areas.

In multilevel and federal governance systems, the ability to meet collective GHG reduction goals is determined by the capacity of most (if not all) jurisdictions to find ways to bring down their emissions. Of course, the enactment of a multitude of different policies neither guarantees their implementation nor ensures the promised emissions reductions. There are many implementation challenges for the EU, as there is significant variation in domestic implementation and some member states have been decidedly more successful than others in reducing emissions. Between 1990 and 2006, member states' trends in GHG emissions ranged from –18 percent (Germany) to +51 percent (Spain). A 2010 report by the European Environment Agency (EEA) judged both the EU-15 and the EU-27 to be on track to meet their Kyoto commitments (EEA 2010). The EEA estimates that 2009 EU-15 emissions came in under the –8 percent Kyoto commitment and that EU-27 emissions were 17.3 percent below 1990 levels. Though 2008 and 2009 emissions declines are attributed largely to the economic recession and slow growth, EEA's analysis suggests that EU policies will keep emissions levels in compliance with set goals even as economic recovery and growth accelerate.

US Climate Change Politics: Washington as the Last to Know (and Act)

Since its inception, the United States has been home to contentious debates and relations between the federal government and state governments competing for legal authority and resources (Rabe 2010). US climate politics has been characterized by a lack of federal leadership, as many leading politicians have either ignored the issue or downplayed its importance and rejected the need for government interventions. The US federal government enacted no significant climate change or energy efficiency policies in the run-up to the 1997 Kyoto Protocol, which was signed by the Clinton administration. There was also strong Senate opposition to the Kyoto Protocol. In nearly every international forum, and in a host of congressional debates, US national policy makers generally remained unwilling to commit to GHG emissions reductions comparable to those adopted by the EU, and often argued that other industrialized countries should follow the United States on this issue.

In the early 2000s, the few congressional attempts to regulate GHG emissions all failed. Instead, Congress added amendments to appropriation bills prohibiting the use of funds "to propose or issue rules, regulations, decrees, or orders for implementation, or in preparation for implementation, of the Kyoto Protocol."[3] The number of officials in the EPA working on climate change was also dramatically cut, and many left their posts in response to the federal government's unwillingness to take any serious action (Schreurs, Selin, and VanDeveer 2009). The George W. Bush administration announced voluntary programs claiming to support energy efficiency and some emissions reduction efforts, but these initiatives yielded little or nothing in the way of demonstrable emissions reductions. Through Bush's two terms as president (2001–2009), the Environmental Protection Agency consistently opposed all efforts to regulate carbon dioxide emissions under the existing Clean Air Act.

In the absence of any meaningful leadership by the federal government, US subnational jurisdictions have stepped in (Selin and VanDeveer 2007, 2009a; Rabe 2004, 2010). These developments follow a longer historical trend of "environmental federalism," whereby states have taken the lead on issues such as air pollution and hazardous substance abatement in the face of federal inaction. Under the US federal system, states also have substantial authority and discretion as they implement many federal environmental laws. For example, they issue more than 90 percent of all environmental permits and conduct more than 75 percent of all environmental enforcement actions (Rabe 2004). With respect to climate change, states can control GHG emissions through the many policy areas in which they have regulatory competence, including the generation and distribution of electricity, transportation infrastructure, land use and planning, agriculture and forestry, and waste management.

Although many US states have taken policy actions to reduce GHG emissions, California has emerged as a leading force on policy development and GHG mitigation—sometimes ahead of EU policy goals (Farrell and Hanemann 2009). Many states in the northeastern United States were also early in formulating state-level policy (Selin and VanDeveer 2005, 2009b). By 2007, more than half of all the states had formulated individual climate change action plans. States are also setting GHG emission reduction goals. As in Europe, there are large differences in state GHG emission trends; since 1990, states have ranged from a 5 percent decrease to a 43 percent increase (Rabe 2008). These differences stem from many factors, including disparities in economic and population growth rates, in energy and environmental policies, and in the sources of energy used. US states also vary considerably in their emission profiles due to geographic differences in major economic sectors such as energy production and transportation.

Nevertheless, states are taking a host of energy-related actions including establishing renewable portfolio standards (RPS) that require electricity providers to obtain a minimum percentage of their power from renewable sources. By 2010, 29 states had enacted such standards; some of these are fairly ambitious, and others are much more modest. Many states are also formulating ethanol mandates and incentives, and at least ten will adopt California's CO_2 vehicle emission standards as these come into force. Furthermore, many states are updating energy codes, adopting green building standards, and mandating the sale of more efficient appliances and electronic equipment. A few states, including California, Oregon, and Colorado, have established climate change and renewable energy initiatives as a result of supportive referendums, in an example of how local elections can play a direct role in federal systems (Rabe 2008). Also, a 2010 referendum question on the California ballot to roll back the state's climate change standards was rejected by voters. This suggests public support for ambitious climate change policies in some states.

In addition, US states enact collaborative GHG policies. In 2000, the Conference of New England Governors (which includes Maine, New Hampshire, Vermont, Massachusetts, Rhode Island, and Connecticut) joined the Eastern Canadian Premiers (Nova Scotia, Newfoundland and Labrador, Prince Edward Island, New Brunswick, and Quebec) in adopting a resolution recognizing climate change as a joint environmental and economic concern. Out of this emerged a 2001 Climate Change Action Plan, under which states and provinces pledged to reduce their GHGs to 1990 levels by 2010 and 10 percent below 1990 levels by 2020. They also agreed to ultimately decrease emissions to levels that do not pose a threat to the climate, which according to an official estimate would require a 75–85 percent reduction from 2001 emission levels (Selin and VanDeveer 2005).

The Regional Greenhouse Gas Initiative (RGGI) is another multistate initiative setting important domestic policy precedents (Selin and VanDeveer 2009b). First proposed in 2003, by 2009 RGGI had created a cap-and-trade scheme for CO_2 emissions from major power plants in the participating ten states: Maine, Vermont, New Hampshire, Massachusetts, Rhode Island, Connecticut, New York, New Jersey, Maryland, and Delaware. There is nothing in the RGGI statutes preventing other states in the same region or from other parts of the country from joining the trading scheme in the future. RGGI is designed to stabilize CO_2 emissions from the region's power sector between 2009 and 2015. Between 2015 and 2018, each state's annual CO_2 emissions budget is expected to decline by 2.5 percent per year, achieving a total 10 percent reduction by 2019. Although the goals of both the regional initiatives in the northeast are relatively modest, they are ahead of federal policy.

In 2007, the largest group of states to date to join a collaborative climate change policy initiative was announced: thirty-one states signed on as charter members of the Climate Registry. This registry is a collaborative effort to develop a common system for private and public entities to report their GHG emissions, allowing officials to measure, track, verify, and publicly report emissions in a consistent manner across states. By 2010, forty-three states, three native tribes, and the District of Columbia were members, together with ten Canadian provinces and six Mexican states. Working together, these subnational levels of government in all three federal systems are standardizing GHG reporting procedures for public and private sector emitters, laying an important technical basis for possible expansions of political cooperation.

In addition, the Western Climate Initiative (WCI), set in motion with leadership from California, involves technical and political collaboration among seven US states and four Canadian provinces and is working to launch a cap-and-trade emissions reduction system and other joint measures in 2012. Furthermore, several states and provinces around the North American Great Lakes have begun discussions about how to enhance climate change cooperation, issuing a joint accord of recommended actions. These subnational actors may establish a cap-and-trade system of their own or may find ways to connect with RGGI or the WCI. In 2010, these three regional cooperation initiatives issued a joint white paper about ensuring the quality of GHG offsets as part of a joint "three regions" initiative, and officials from all three regions were studying the prospect of strengthening linkages among the initiatives. If developed further, these initiatives could have a notable impact on federal (and potentially continental) politics and policy making.

Cities often play important agenda setting and policy-making roles in federal systems, and there is also considerable US action at the municipal level. More than 830 mayors from all 50 states, representing approximately 80 million Americans, signed a declaration of meeting or exceeding the reductions negotiated in the Kyoto Protocol for the United States (a 7 percent reduction from 1990 levels by 2012). More than 260 North American municipalities are members of the International Council for Local Environmental Initiatives and its Cities for Climate Protection program. Though many municipal climate change programs are modest, some have achieved impressive results (Gore and Robinson 2009). American municipalities are increasingly developing new GHG reduction and energy efficiency programs that rely in part on innovative private financing. The most successful municipalities often link climate change issues, including efforts to cut CO_2 emissions, to broader goals associated with promoting smarter growth and sustainable urban development and transportation systems.

US federal climate change politics are also shaped by the judicial branch (Engel 2010; Selin and VanDeveer 2009b). In 1999, environmental groups petitioned the EPA to set CO_2 emissions standards for vehicles. This request was rejected on the grounds that during the Clinton era the agency did not believe that the Clean Air Act provided authority for regulating CO_2. Frustrated by federal inaction, in 2003 attorneys general from California, Connecticut, Illinois, Maine, Massachusetts, New Jersey, New Mexico, New York, Oregon, Rhode Island, Vermont, and Washington filed suit in federal court challenging the earlier agency decision. Following a long legal process—with the George W. Bush administration, several states, and the auto industry in opposition—in April 2007 the US Supreme Court determined in a 5 to 4 ruling that CO_2 can be classified as a pollutant under the Clean Air Act. The ruling has served as a basis for extensive EPA activity in preparing to regulate carbon emissions. Advocates of federal climate change policy regularly hold up EPA carbon regulation as a threat should Congress fail to act.

By early 2011, the US Congress had not passed climate change legislation, and the EPA continued to move ahead with rule making based on the Supreme Court decision. In 2009, the EPA issued an "endangerment finding" stating that the current and projected concentrations of the six GHGs—CO_2, methane, nitrous oxide, hydrofluorocarbons, perfluorocarbons, and sulfur hexafluoride—in the atmosphere threaten the public health and welfare of current and future generations. However, although almost thirty US states constituting more than 80 percent of the US population had enacted renewable portfolio standards, the federal government remained unwilling to mandate any stringent renewable energy or GHG standards. Throughout the 2000s, the ability of opponents of climate change policy to stop or significantly weaken policy initiatives was stronger at the federal level than elsewhere in the federal system. Environmental leader states and municipalities continued to advocate for stronger federal action, while significant public and private sector opposition remained focused on the US Congress. Particularly challenging for advocates of climate change action has been the need, according to Senate rules, to obtain sixty (out of one hundred) votes to advance a piece of legislation to the Senate floor for voting (where it then needs only a majority vote to pass). Any bill that passed the Senate would also need to be reconciled with legislation that passed in the House of Representatives. The substantial Republican gains in the 2010 Congressional elections appeared to make the passage of climate change legislation less likely in 2011–2012 because the vast majority of the new members stated their opposition to capping or taxing GHG emissions.

The 2009 arrival of the Obama administration produced some federal action, most of it based in the executive branch. Automobile efficiency standards (Corporate Average Fuel Economy, or "CAFE" standards) were raised and the EPA's preparations to issue carbon emissions regulations accelerated, as were agency efforts to further raise efficiency standards for automobiles, trucks, vehicle fleets, and other products. Nevertheless, the early years of the Obama administration demonstrated that opponents of climate change and clean energy policies remained strongest at the federal level, though advocates in government and in civil society vowed to continue to push for significant GHG mitigation and renewable energy legislation. Challenges to climate change policy making and implementation also exist at the state and local levels. The 2010 electoral outcomes in governors' offices and state legislatures seemed likely to reduce some states' commitment to emissions reductions goals. Meanwhile, the extremely low price for emissions permits in the RGGI trading scheme resulting from an oversupply of permits, and the fading hope of a federal GHG trading scheme, threatened to undermine RGGI's effectiveness. US national

GHG emissions were 14 percent higher in 2008 than they were in 1990 (EPA 2010). Although emissions declined in 2008 as a result of economic recession, they are expected to increase, as most GHGs remain unregulated nationally. If federal, state, and local emissions reduction are implemented, however, US emissions could be curbed.

Transatlantic Interaction and Hybridization

As these brief case descriptions demonstrate, patterns of climate policy making and politics across the Atlantic have both similarities and differences. Many similar policies have been enacted on each side, but the EU has seen substantially more federal-level policy making. The more stringent subnational policies on the US side are found in a minority of leading states and cities. But climate change politics across the Atlantic cannot be characterized as two totally separate processes or isolated and controlled experiments. Many public officials, advocacy groups, and firms are connected across the Atlantic. Officials from Washington, Brussels, and the capitals of EU member states meet regularly at the Conferences of the Parties to the UNFCCC as well as in other multilateral forums. Many of the policy proposals debated at the federal level in the United States since the mid-2000s have already been enacted in some US states and in the EU. Details of these policies differ, of course, and the differences can be quite significant, but climate policy debates are increasingly transatlantic in content, as are the networks of the participants in these debates (Schreurs, Selin, and VanDeveer 2009).

At the same time, Wiener (2004) cautions against thinking in exclusively binary terms about convergence and divergence in policy outcomes. He suggests that transatlantic politics more often produces a kind of "hybridization" through which political systems borrow from one another. Because of institutional differences, this borrowing does not necessary produce convergence or divergence in a strict sense. Rather, policy making on each side of the Atlantic influences the other side. For example, bills debated in the US Congress that include emission trading mechanisms draw lessons from the ETS experience in Europe, and EU action on low-carbon fuels is influenced by California's activity on this issue. The frequent claim that globalization is producing convergence does not mean that "everything becomes the same." Instead, hybridization means that comparative politics researchers must explore how states moving in the same direction—toward more GHG emissions regulations, for example—do not necessary become identical or converge in their policies and practices.

Transatlantic comparisons tend to focus on national-level outcomes. However, such top-level interaction is only part of the story. In the case of climate change, the most interesting and significant policy activity in the United States since early 2000s has occurred at state and municipal levels and in the private sector (Selin and

VanDeveer 2007, 2009a). Reactions to Washington's dismissal of the Kyoto Protocol and its opposition to mandatory GHG regulations were not only strong in Europe, but also in many environmentally progressive states and cities across the United States. Despite their differences, as US federal, state, and municipal policies expand alongside European climate change policies, there are increasing opportunities for transatlantic cooperation and lesson learning, as North American and European states share many multilevel governance opportunities and challenges.

The developing transatlantic networks often bypass formal channels between Washington and European capitals, creating new channels of communication and political influence. Members use these networks and associated organizations to share knowledge and policy ideas beneficial to both the United States and the EU. For example, the International Carbon Action Partnership held its first meeting in 2007 to share best practices in designing and implementing GHG cap-and-trade systems. Founding members include the European Commission, several EU member states, and a multitude of US states working on emissions trading issues under RGGI and the Western Climate Initiative. Other jurisdictions and organizations may join in the future. Such collaboration not only supports the diffusion of policy ideas and lesson learning across different trading schemes, but also influences transatlantic and federal politics (Selin and VanDeveer 2010). These kinds of collaborative networks and forums may be important for stimulating transatlantic policy hybridization.

A growing number of US and European cities are expanding collaboration in both old and new forums. In addition to the Cities for Climate Protection program operated by the International Council for Local Environmental Initiatives, the Clinton Foundation launched its Clinton Climate Initiative, which works with twelve large European and twelve large American cities. This initiative is linked with the C40 Cities program, an association of large cities around the world seeking to accelerate efforts to reduce GHG emissions. Several municipal networks connect efforts in the United States and Europe, diffusing information about mitigation and adaptation efforts and building local capacity in important policy areas such as building codes, transportation, and waste management. These networks and initiatives are part of the complex web of interactions that characterize multilevel governance. Comparative politics research must pay increasing attention to these dynamics if its explanations are to capture the changing contours of politics.

Comparative Climate Change Politics around the Globe

Differences between Washington and Brussels on climate change policy since the 1990s have been stark, often described as symbolic of a deep "climate divide" across the Atlantic (Schreurs 2002, 2004, 2005; Busby and Ochs 2004; Cass 2006). Yet when viewed at a subnational level, the divide becomes less visible and the similarities among a host of public and private sector actors are more apparent. For example, the climate change policies and actions of Germany and California are more similar to each other than are those of Germany and Greece or California and Mississippi. Just as EU member states have different levels of commitment to climate change action, so too do states and municipalities within the United States (Selin and VanDeveer 2007). There are climate change policy leaders and laggards on both sides of the Atlantic. To explain their influence on US and European politics, we must attend to the similarities and differences in the federal systems on each side.

Looking beyond the cases discussed in this chapter, what global lessons can be drawn from these transatlantic comparisons? One lesson certainly is that researchers and observers should avoid overstating the causal role of either economic development levels or public opinion in explaining the cross-national differences in environmental politics. It is common in global climate debates to speak primarily of economic development levels when debating mitigation and adaptation issues. While some focus on the industrialized North versus the global South, others focus on variations within the South, contrasting the situation of China and other high-growth, large GHG emitters with that of poorer, low-growth low emitters (Axelrod, VanDeveer, and Downie 2010). Levels of economic development are significant explanatory variables, of course, but they do not tell us why the United States and the EU have taken such different policy paths at the federal level. Nor do they explain US, Canadian, and Mexican climate policy outcomes (Selin and VanDeveer 2009a).

Comparative research on environmental federalism calls attention to the importance of governance structures of all kinds, as well as the formal and informal roles of public and private sector actors operating within and across these structures. This chapter compares two federalist systems with similar levels of economic development and some similarities in their approaches to climate change policymaking, but a collective understanding of climate change politics would be advanced by comparing other, more diverse federal cases such as Canada and Mexico or the United States and Brazil, to name just two examples. A related question is whether China and India should be so casually tossed together, as they sometimes are in policy debates and scholarly analyses of international climate politics, given that one is governed via one-party authoritarian rule and the other is a federalist democracy.

In addition to the United States and EU, high-income federalist systems include Australia, Canada, and Switzerland, as well as a number of individual EU member states. Climate change policies at national and subnational levels vary substantially across these states and societies. Might an examination of the structure of each country's federalist system help us to understand why? Australian climate politics suggest patterns that are similar to those of the United States: federal-level hostility and inaction on GHG emissions, active state-level policy making and interstate collaboration, and a similar set of climate policy opponents. Similarly, Canadian climate change politics is characterized by contentious debates between the federal government and provinces over issues of policy-making jurisdiction and responsibilities to take action. Comparative political research can help us understand the Australian and Canadian cases in light of the politics of climate change in other federal systems.

Other comparative opportunities stem from the fact that all three large North American countries have a federal structure. Climate change policies are being debated, adopted, and implemented at the federal level, in states and provinces, in municipalities, and in many private-sector initiatives across the North American continent. However, decision-making authority is divided differently in each of the three federal systems, and many federal divisions of authority remain unsettled. For example, the emergence of the province of British Columbia as a policy leader with its use of carbon taxes may have implications for politics in Canada and in other countries, but the nature and form of this influence may vary across political systems. Unlike in Europe, North American citizens and public officials show little interest in transnational federalist structures. However, there are likely to be many benefits from greater cooperation on climate change and energy policy among the continent's three large federal systems (Selin and VanDeveer 2009c).

There is no need to confine comparative analysis of multilevel governance to federalist states, of course. Drawing from the work on environmental federalism, one can compare federalist states to other types of governing systems, such as more centralized states operating under parliamentary or presidential systems. Our understanding of industrial democracies can be expanded by comparing the influence of federalist versus nonfederalist democratic structures on environmental politics and policy outcomes. As Sowers (chapter 9, this volume) demonstrates, multilevel governance matters in authoritarian states as well, and the institutions mediating interactions between central and local authorities differ across parts of the state and change over time. Moreover, governance institutions vary across systems with "the same" type of government. When examined through the analytic lenses of comparative politics, variance in governance institutions and in the interaction of domestic and transnational actors can help to explain political and physical outcomes in a host of countries around the world.

Notes

1. According to Bednar (2009, 2), approximately half of the world population lives in federalist or quasi-federalist systems.

2. A partial exception is the reduction of GHG emissions that accompanied US federal efforts to reduce emissions of ozone-depleting gases and methane emissions under the Clean Air Act.

3. Title V, Sec. 577 of H.R. 4811: Foreign Operations, Export Financing, and Related Programs Appropriations Act of 2001.

References

Anderson, Terry Lee, and Peter Jensen Hill, eds. 1997. *Environmental Federalism*. Lanham, Md.: Rowman and Littlefield.

Andonova, Liliana B., and Ronald B. Mitchell. 2010. The Rescaling of Global Environmental Politics. *Annual Review of Environment and Resources* 35:255–282.

Axelrod, Regina S., Stacy D. VanDeveer, and David Downie, eds. 2010. *The Global Environment: Institutions, Law and Policy*. 3rd ed. Washington, D.C.: CQ Press.

Bache, Ian, and Matthew Flinders, eds. 2004. *Multi-level Governance*. Oxford, UK: Oxford University Press.

Baker, Susan. 2006. *Sustainable Development*. London: Routledge.

Baker, Susan, Maria Kousis, Dick Richardson, and Stephen Young, eds. 1997. *The Politics of Sustainable Development: Theory, Policy, and Practice within the European Union*. London: Routledge.

Bednar, Jenna. 2009. *The Robust Federation: Principles of Design*. Cambridge, UK: Cambridge University Press.

Betsill, Michele M., and Harriet Bulkeley. 2006. Cities and the Multilevel Governance of Global Climate Change. *Global Governance* 12 (2): 141–159.

Bomberg, Elizabeth. 1998. *Green Parties and Politics in the European Union*. London: Routledge.

Breitmeier, Helmut, Oran R. Young, and Michael Zürn. 2006. *Analyzing International Environmental Regimes: From Case Studies to Database*. Cambridge, Mass.: MIT Press.

Breton, Albert, Giorgio Brosio, Silvana Dalmazzone, and Giovanna Garrone, eds. 2009. *Governing the Environment: Salient Institutional Issues*. Northampton, Mass: Edward Elgar.

Burchell, Jon. 2002. *The Evolution of Green Politics: Development and Change within European Green Parties*. London: Earthscan.

Burgess, Michael. 2006. *Comparative Federalism: Theory and Practice*. London: Routledge.

Busby, Joshua, and Alexander Ochs. 2004. From Mars and Venus Down to Earth: Understanding the Transatlantic Climate Divide. In *Climate Policy for the 21st Century: Meeting the Long-Term Challenge of Global Warming*, ed. David Michel, 35–76. Washington, D.C.: Center for Transatlantic Relations, School of Advanced International Studies, Johns Hopkins University.

Cass, Loren R. 2006. *The Failures of American and European Climate Policy: International Norms, Domestic Politics, and Unachievable Commitments*. Albany: State University of New York Press.

Dunlap, Riley E., and Aaron M. McCright. 2008. A Widening Gap: Republican and Democratic Views on Climate Change. *Environment* 50 (5): 26–35.

Engel, Kirsten H. 2010. Courts and Climate Policy: Now and in the Future. In *Greenhouse Governance: Addressing Climate Change in America*, ed. Barry G. Rabe, 229–259. Washington, D.C.: Brookings Institution Press.

EPA (Environmental Protection Agency). 2010. *Inventory of US Greenhouse Gas Emissions and Sinks: 1990–2008. Executive Summary*. Washington, D.C.: Environmental Protection Agency.

Erk, Jan, and Wilfried Swenden, eds. 2010. *New Directions in Federalism Studies*. London: Routledge.

EEA (European Environment Agency). 2010. *Tracking Progress toward Kyoto and 2020 Targets in Europe*. Copenhagen: EEA.

Farrell, Alexander E., and W. Michael Hanemann. 2009. Field Notes on the Political Economy of California Climate Policy. In *Changing Climates in North American Politics*, ed. Henrik Selin and Stacy D. VanDeveer, 87–110. Cambridge, Mass.: MIT Press.

Finger, Matthias, Ludivine Tamiotti, and Jeremy Allouche, eds. 2006. *The Multi-governance of Water: Four Case Studies*. Albany: SUNY Press.

Gore, Christopher, and Pamela Robinson. 2009. Local Government Responses to Climate Change: Our Last, Best Hope? In *Changing Climates in North American Politics*, ed. Henrik Selin and Stacy D. VanDeveer, 137–158. Cambridge, Mass.: MIT Press.

Grant, Wyn, Duncan Matthews, and Peter Newell. 2000. *The Effectiveness of European Union Environmental Policy*. New York: St. Martin's Press.

Guehlstorf, Nicholas, and Lars Hallstrom. 2002. Culture Wars over the Risks, Regulations, and Responsibilities in Genetic Agriculture: A Comparison of Food Biotechnology Policy in the United States and the European Union. Paper presented at the annual meeting of the American Political Science Association, Boston, August 28.

Haas, Peter M., Robert O. Keohane, and Marc A. Levy. 1993. *Institutions for the Earth: Sources of Effective International Environmental Protection*. Cambridge, Mass.: MIT Press.

Harrington, Winston, Richard Morgenstern, and Thomas Sterner, eds. 2004. *Choosing Environmental Policy: Comparing Instruments and Outcomes in the United States and Europe*. London: RFF Press.

Harrison, Kathryn, and Lisa Sundstrom eds. 2007. Comparative Politics of Climate Change. Special issue of *Global Environmental Politics* 7 (4): 1–153.

Harrison, Kathryn, and Lisa Sundstrom, eds. 2010. *Global Commons, Domestic Decisions: The Comparative Politics of Climate Change*. Cambridge, Mass.: MIT Press.

Hasenclever, Andreas, Peter Mayer, and Volker Rittberger. 1997. *Theories of International Regimes*. Cambridge, UK: Cambridge University Press.

Hooghe, Liesbet, and Gary Marks. 2001. *Multi-level Governance and European Integration*. Lanham, Md.: Rowman and Littlefield.

Hueglin, Thomas, and Alan Fenna. 2005. *Comparative Federalism: A Systemic Inquiry*. Toronto: University of Toronto Press.

Hunter, Janet R., and Zachary A. Smith. 2005. *Protecting Our Environment: Lessons from the European Union*. Albany: SUNY Press.

Jänicke, Martin, and Helmut Weidner, eds. 1997. *National Environmental Policies: A Comparative Study of Capacity-Building*. Berlin: Springer.

Jasanoff, Sheila. 2005. *Designs on Nature: Science and Democracy in Europe and the United States*. Cambridge, Mass.: Harvard University Press.

Jordan, Andrew, Dave Huitema, Harro van Asselt, Tim Rayner, and Frans Berkout, eds. 2010. *Climate Change Policy in the European Union*. Cambridge, UK: Cambridge University Press.

Kelemen, Daniel R. 2000. Regulatory Federalism: EU Environmental Policy in Comparative Perspective. *Journal of Public Policy* 20 (2): 133–167.

Kelemen, Daniel R. 2004. Environmental Federalism in the United States and the European Union. In *Green Giants? Environmental Policies of the United States and the European Union*, ed. Norman J. Vig and Michael G. Faure, 113–134. Cambridge, Mass.: MIT Press.

Keohane, Robert O. 1989. *International Institutions and State Power: Essays in International Relations Theory*. Boulder: Westview Press.

Koehn, Peter. 2010. Climate Policy and Climate Action underneath Kyoto: China and the United States. *Wiley Interdisciplinary Reviews: Climate Change* 1:405–417.

Kraft, Michael E., and Sheldon Kamieniecki, eds. 2007. *Business and Environmental Policy: Corporate Interests in the American Political System*. Cambridge, Mass.: MIT Press.

Krasner, Stephen D. 1983. Structural Causes and Regime Consequences: Regimes as Intervening Variables. In *International Regimes*, ed. Stephen D. Krasner, 1–21. Ithaca: Cornell University Press.

Klyza, Christopher McGrory, and David Sousa. 2008. *American Environmental Policy, 1990–2006*. Cambridge, Mass.: MIT Press.

Lafferty, William M., and J. Meadowcroft, eds. 2000. *Implementing Sustainable Development: Strategies and Initiatives in High Consumption Societies*. Oxford, UK: Oxford University Press.

Levy, Marc A., Oran R. Young, and Michael Zürn. 1995. The Study of International Regimes. *European Journal of International Relations* 1 (3): 267–331.

Martinelli, Alberto, ed. 2007. *Transatlantic Divide: Comparing American and European Society*. Oxford, UK: Oxford University Press.

Morgenstern, Richard D., and William Aaron Pizer, eds. 2007. *Reality Check: The Nature and Performance of Voluntary Environmental Programs in the United States, Europe, and Japan*. London: RFF Press.

Müller-Rommel, Ferdinand, and Thomas Poguntke, eds. 2002. *Green Parties in National Governments*. London: Frank Cass.

Netherlands Environmental Assessment Agency. 2009. Global CO_2 Emissions: Annual Increase Halves in 2008. June 25. http://www.pbl.nl/en/publications/2009/Global-CO2-emissions-annual-increase-halves-in-2008.html, accessed June 5, 2011.

Oberthur, Sebastian, and Marc Pallemaerts, eds. 2010. *The New Climate Policies of the European Union*. Brussels: University of Brussels Press.

Rabe, Barry G. 2004. *Statehouse and Greenhouse: The Emerging Politics of American Climate Change Policy*. Washington, D.C.: Brookings Institution Press.

Rabe, Barry G. 2008. States on Steroids: The Intergovernmental Odyssey of American Climate Policy. *Review of Policy Research* 25 (2): 105–128.

Rabe, Barry G., ed. 2010. *Greenhouse Governance: Addressing Climate Change in America*. Washington, D.C.: Brookings Institution Press.

Rabe, Barry G., and Christopher Borick. 2010. The Climate of Belief: American Public Opinion on Climate Change. *Issues in Governance Studies* 31:1–12.

Sadeleer, Nicolas de, ed. 2007. *Implementing the Precautionary Principle: Approaches from the Nordic Countries, EU, and USA*. Washington, D.C.: Earthscan.

Scheberle, Denise. 2004. *Federalism and Environmental Policy*. Washington, D.C.: Georgetown University Press.

Schreurs, Miranda A. 2002. *Environmental Politics in Japan, Germany, and the United States*. Cambridge, UK: Cambridge University Press.

Schreurs, Miranda. 2004. The Climate Change Divide: The European Union, the United States, and the Future of the Kyoto Protocol. In *Green Giants? Environmental Policy of the United States and the European Union*, ed. Norman J. Vig and Michael G. Faure, 207–230. Cambridge, Mass.: MIT Press.

Schreurs, Miranda A. 2005. Global Environment Threats and a Divided Northern Community. *International Environmental Agreement: Politics, Law and Economics* 5 (3): 349–376.

Schreurs, Miranda A. 2010. Multi-level Governance and Global Climate Change in East Asia. *Asian Economic Policy Review* 5:88–105.

Schreurs, Miranda A., Henrik Selin, and Stacy D. VanDeveer, eds. 2009. *Transatlantic Environmental and Energy Politics: Comparative and International Perspectives*. Aldershot, UK: Ashgate.

Selin, Henrik. 2010. *Global Governance of Hazardous Chemicals: Challenges of Multilevel Management*. Cambridge, Mass.: MIT Press.

Selin, Henrik, and Stacy D. VanDeveer. 2005. Canadian-US Environmental Cooperation: Climate Change Networks and Regional Action. *American Review of Canadian Studies* 35 (2): 353–378.

Selin, Henrik, and Stacy D. VanDeveer. 2006. Canadian-US Cooperation: Regional Climate Change Action in the Northeast. In *Bilateral Ecopolitics: Continuity and Change in Canadian-American Environmental Relations*, ed. Philippe G. Le Prestre and Peter John Stoett, 93–114. Aldershot, UK: Ashgate.

Selin, Henrik, and Stacy D. VanDeveer. 2007. Political Science and Prediction: What's Next for US Climate Change Policy? *Review of Policy Research* 24 (1): 1–27.

Selin, Henrik, and Stacy D. VanDeveer, eds. 2009a. *Changing Climates in North American Politics: Institutions, Policymaking and Multilevel Governance*. Cambridge, Mass.: MIT Press.

Selin, Henrik, and Stacy D. VanDeveer. 2009b. Climate Leadership in Northeast North America. In *Changing Climates in North American Politics: Institutions, Policymaking and Multilevel Governance*, ed. Henrik Selin and Stacy D. VanDeveer, 111–136. Cambridge, Mass.: MIT Press.

Selin, Henrik, and Stacy D. VanDeveer. 2009c. Continental Climate Governance in North America. *Issues in Governance Studies* 30: 1–14.

Selin, Henrik, and Stacy D. VanDeveer. 2010. Multilevel Governance and Transatlantic Climate Change Politics. In *Greenhouse Governance: Addressing Climate Change in America*, ed. Barry G. Rabe, 336–352. Washington, D.C.: Brookings Institution Press.

Vig, Norman J., and Michael G. Faure, eds. 2004. *Green Giants? Environmental Policies of the United States and the European Union*. Cambridge, Mass.: MIT Press.

Vogel, David. 1995. *Trading Up: Consumer and Environmental Regulation in a Global Economy*. Cambridge, Mass.: Harvard University Press.

Vogel, David. 2003. The Hare and the Tortoise Revisited: The New Politics of Consumer and Environmental Protection in Europe. *British Journal of Political Science* 33 (4): 557–580.

Ward, Ann, and Lee Ward. 2009. *The Ashgate Research Companion to Federalism*. Aldershot, UK: Ashgate.

Watts, Ronald L. 2008. *Comparing Federalist Systems*. 3rd ed. Kingston, Ontario: McGill-Queen's University Press.

Weibust, Inger. 2009. *Green Leviathan: The Case for a Federal Role in Environmental Policy*. Aldershot, UK: Ashgate.

Wiener, Jonathan B. 2004. Convergence, Divergence and Complexity in US and European Risk Regulation. In *Green Giants? Environmental Policies of the United States and the European Union*, ed. Norman J. Vig and Michael G. Faure, 73–110. Cambridge, Mass.: MIT Press.

Young, Oran R. 1989. *International Cooperation: Building Regimes for Natural Resources and the Environment*. Ithaca: Cornell University Press.

Young, Oran R. 2002. *The Institutional Dimensions of Environmental Change: Fit, Interplay, and Scale*. Cambridge, Mass.: MIT Press.

Young, Oran R., Leslie A. King, and Heike Schroeder, eds. 2008. *Institutions and Environmental Challenges: Principal Findings, Applications, and Research Frontiers*. Cambridge, Mass.: MIT Press.

VI

Future Directions

14

Comparative Theory and Environmental Practice: Toward Doubly Engaged Social Science

Paul F. Steinberg and Stacy D. VanDeveer

Participants in environmental studies programs typically approach research with a set of pressing real-world concerns that they hope will be illuminated with further study. What will it take to reverse trends toward the extinction of fish populations worldwide? How can we protect biodiversity while promoting rural livelihoods? Can business be greened to help reduce carbon emissions?

Students of comparative politics, on the other hand, approach the world with very different kinds of questions: why does democracy thrive in some parts of the world and not in others? Under what conditions do social movements have an influence on government policy? Where do political values come from and how do they differ across borders?

The central argument of this book is that both categories of questions would be well served by building bridges between these separate lines of inquiry. And each of the contributors illustrates the value of doing so, pairing practical concerns of environmental well-being with insights from specific research literatures in comparative politics and related fields of comparative social science. To conclude this exercise in bridge building, let us return to a puzzle first raised in chapter 2: why has there been so little interaction between the fields of comparative politics and environmental politics?

Environmental researchers with a keen interest in political outcomes around the world have generally not availed themselves of the very field (comparative politics) that studies precisely that. Research on questions such as why the United States and the European Union have such different political reactions to climate change, why the performance of environmental bureaucracies varies from one country to the next, and why citizens embrace or ignore environmental concerns only rarely (and recently) takes advantage of insights from relevant literatures in comparative politics. Students eager to explore these and similar questions too often write case studies that document cross-national disparities without attempting to explain them. Convincing explanations in comparative social science require theory, which offers a medium of exchange, a conceptual currency that allows the analyst to "purchase" understanding of one political setting with insights accumulated in another. Comparative politics researchers, meanwhile, have paid little attention to the environment despite the fact that ecological concerns figure prominently—in physical terms, in citizen demands, and in policy circles—in practically every country they study, be it Hungary, Honduras, China, or Chad. The following section offers a provisional diagnosis of the causes of these fields' mutual disengagement, with an emphasis on the tension between theoretical rigor and practical application. The remainder of the chapter prescribes a remedy, highlighting the benefits of what Theda Skocpol has termed "doubly engaged social science"—the pursuit of theoretically informed research that stays in close conversation with real-world problems.

Measuring the Distance

To put a finer point on the matter, we conducted an empirical analysis of the substantive focus of research articles and book reviews published in major comparative politics journals, focusing on *Comparative Political Studies* and *Comparative Politics*.[1] We are especially interested in exploring two questions. First, is it true that environmental issues have been largely ignored by the field of comparative politics? Second, if this is indeed the case, what might explain this pattern?

We hypothesize that (1) environmental issues have a low profile in the field of comparative politics (as asserted throughout this book) and (2) this situation results from the lower status accorded applied policy concerns within the field relative to research on broader political structures and processes. If this second hypothesis is true, we would expect to find that other policy issues such as health care and education likewise receive little attention from scholars of comparative politics. If coverage of these issues is comparable to that of the environment, this would suggest that disinterest in environmental issues is not the result of a perception on the part of researchers and journal editors that environmental issues are less important than other social concerns. Rather, the problem is that they belong to a category of research—scholarship aimed in large part at solving social problems—that has no place in the field.

Covering all even years from 1990 to 2010, we coded articles for the presence of applied social issues mentioned in their title or abstract.[2] The starting date was chosen to correspond with a point in history when environmental concerns had received a high level of attention in societies throughout the world. If the field is paying attention to the environment, it would show up in this time span. The issue areas included health care, education, the environment, human rights, social welfare (pensions, social security, and the welfare state), and the economy.[3] The categories are not mutually exclusive by design, though only twenty-eight articles (less than 5 percent of the total) mentioned more than one social issue. Any mention of an issue

Table 14.1
Attention given issue areas in leading comparative politics journals, 1990–2010
(Number of articles that mention a given topic in title or abstract. Data cover even years only.)

Journal	Environment	Health	Human rights	Economic policy and growth	Education	Social welfare
Comparative Politics (N = 217 articles)	2	0	1	79	1	14
Comparative Political Studies (N = 397 articles)	7	2	5	134	5	21

area was sufficient for its coding as present in that article, on the assumption that even brief mention in the title or abstract (where concision is paramount and thus every word counts) is evidence of its significance in the analysis. This collection procedure produced a dataset with a total of 614 articles.

The findings are summarized in table 14.1. We find these results telling. On the first question, regarding the profile of environmental issues within comparative politics, the analysis shows, as expected, that the environment is rarely a focus of attention. In fact, the subject figures in 1 percent of all articles. Health care, education, and human rights fared no better, supporting the hypothesis that the lack of attention accorded environmental issues is a function of a broader distaste for applied policy concerns. Social welfare policy fared slightly better at 6 percent.

These findings are consistent with those of Munck and Snyder (2007), who analyzed 319 comparative politics articles as part of their assessment of major trends within the field.[4] They report that "virtually none addressed policy questions in a way that could be construed as talking to public policy makers or offering results relevant to debates in policy circles" (27). It is important to note that the measure of policy engagement used in the present analysis is more inclusive; we include articles that use a policy issue as background for exploring political questions even if they do not speak to policy debates. Even measured by this more forgiving criterion, efforts to address pressing problems of health, education, human rights, social welfare, and the environment—efforts spanning decades, sometimes centuries, and involving countless grassroots mobilizations, nonprofit organizations, international institutions, donor agencies, state regulatory bodies, corporate boardrooms, and politicians of every stripe—have not managed to attract significant attention from the major publishing venues in the field of comparative politics.

The most striking result, however, is the relative emphasis given to economic issues. Fully 35 percent of the articles feature economic growth or development—almost four times the number of articles discussing all other social issues combined. What could explain such an outcome?[5] It is highly doubtful that this degree of skew reflects a corresponding sense of priorities in the various societies studied by comparative politics scholars, in terms of what people care about, mobilize for, read about in domestic newspapers, and emphasize in policy debates and agency budgets. More likely, this bias reflects a notion shared by comparative politics scholars that economic growth is, for whatever reason, a more important subject for inquiry. It may also reflect the central role of the economy in the major intellectual traditions of comparative politics. Researchers who deploy the methodologies of rational choice may find it convenient to apply this economic model of individual decision making to economic topics. Those emphasizing macrosocial analysis (such as the rise of capitalism, urbanization, state formation, and revolution) often draw on older traditions of political economy whose foundational thinkers (such as Marx, Weber, Locke, Durkheim, and Moore) paid little attention to sustainable growth and environmental quality. Comparative politics scholarship seems to ignore what every environmental studies student knows—that environmental challenges are deeply related to every facet of the economy.

It is difficult to resist making a comparison to the challenge of "greening" the state described by James Meadowcroft (chapter 3, this volume). States have been moving unevenly from early emphases on security and economic growth to social welfare and, most recently and tentatively, toward embracing environmental concerns as a core state function. This greening is taking place in society as well, in rich and poor nations alike, as is clear from the analysis of public opinion data provided by Riley Dunlap and Herbert York (chapter 4), and Kate O'Neill's discussion of environmental movements (chapter 5). It would appear that the field of comparative politics has a lot of catching up to do.

What about researchers in environmental politics and policy—why are they paying so little attention to insights from comparative politics? Although we have not conducted a corresponding journal analysis, we can offer some speculation informed by our long involvement in this field. We believe that an emphasis on solving pressing problems leads many investigators to shun the more theoretical and macro-orientation of comparative politics researchers, whose broad brush strokes may seem ill equipped to address concrete challenges of improving environmental and social outcomes. Ironically, while we were conducting the journal content analysis described earlier, one of these comparative politics journals asked one of the authors of this chapter to review a manuscript focusing on the environment; with much chagrin, he had to recommend against publication because the article's authors made no effort to relate their applied analysis to an identifiable literature in the field of comparative politics.

This rupture between theory and practice is troublesome for both undertakings. This point is made forcefully by Theda Skocpol in advocating for "doubly engaged" comparative social science. Against "atemporal and overly abstracted approaches," she advocates an intellectual agenda that simultaneously seeks "to understand real-world transformations" while remaining "enmeshed in scholarly debates about causal hypotheses, theoretical frameworks, and optimal methods of empirical investigation" (Skocpol 2003, 407, 409). In an essay published in 1978 titled "The Comparative Study of Environmental Politics: From Garbage to Gold?" L. J. Lundqvist reflected on the challenge facing political scientists in the 1970s who were struggling to define their professional roles in light of the environmental crises then coming to light:

> I keep thinking that the present drive for policy evaluation could involve political scientists in a "clientele" situation, where they would be acting mainly on the premises and problem formulations of political practitioners. But research results based on such extra-disciplinary criteria may well turn out to be mere glitter, of little use to either fellow scholars or the men of practical action. . . . [I]t is by bringing our disciplinary heritage into the description, explanation, forecast and criticism of environmental politics and policy that our claims of striking gold can be upheld, both before fellow scientists interested in the cumulative growth of knowledge on politics, and before practitioners faced with the tough choices that must be made in an affluent, but unfortunately also effluent, society. (1978, 95–96)

As is demonstrated in figure 14.1, the payoff from bringing together substantive concerns of environmental problem solving with theoretically sophisticated approaches to comparative politics is substantial. This figure highlights only a few of the many possibilities for doubly engaged research and points to exemplary publications in these areas. The remainder of the chapter addresses the relationship between practice and theory more systematically. This discussion neither assumes nor advocates that readers position themselves at any particular point along a spectrum from theoretical to applied research. Authors in this volume vary considerably in this regard, and many researchers adjust the mix across research projects and publication venues and over the course of their careers. Moreover, this volume is geared toward researchers as well as those who will use training in political science as a foundation for other professional pursuits. With these provisos in mind, we outline the benefits of greening the field of comparative politics and of more serious engagement with comparative political theory by those interested in the study and practice of environmental politics.

The following section considers the benefits that theory offers to those grappling with difficult questions about what it will take to move human societies onto a more sustainable path. The subsequent section takes up the mirror image of this question, considering how research on applied environmental concerns can enrich theory in comparative politics, offering a panoply of new empirical puzzles, challenging theoretical assumptions, and expanding the idea of macrosocial analysis to

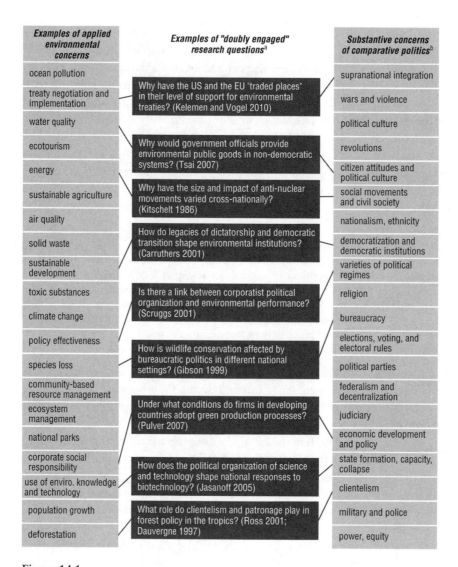

Figure 14.1

Pairing theory and practice

[a]Questions are cast here at the broadest level to emphasize connections among fields; empirically testable propositions must often be crafted in narrower terms. See the studies cited here for examples.

[b]Drawing on Table 1 of Munck and Snyder 2007.

include not only state, society, and economy, but also the environmental foundations of the whole. The final sections offer practical advice on research methods for assessing complex social outcomes and identify promising avenues for future research.

What Can Theory Offer Practice?

Understanding Context

In recent decades, economists have made important contributions to environmental policy practices by laying the theoretical foundations for specific regulatory tools—carbon taxes, deposit-refund schemes, bonds for environmentally damaging industries, and, most famously, tradable pollution permits (Stavins 2003; Tietenberg 1990). One of the major contributions of comparative political analysis is to provide insight into the social contexts in which these and other practical tools are employed. It is well-known among historically oriented scholars that the impact of a causal variable can vary widely depending on the social context into which it is introduced (see Tilly and Goodin 2006)—so too with the impact of policy tools.

Consider, for example, environmental impact assessment—the process of evaluating ex ante the potential impacts from a proposed development project. First introduced in the United States under the National Environmental Policy Act of 1969, environmental impact assessment is now a routine part of governmental decision making in dozens of countries around the world. Yet this tool is employed for strikingly different purposes in different national settings. In the United States, it is seen as a mechanism for transparency and public input in a political system with comparatively high levels of public access to information and in which citizens can use the courts to sue agencies that fail to meet their responsibilities. In contrast, in less open political systems these assessments are planning processes pure and simple, dominated by government planners and technical experts and providing few opportunities for public participation (see, e.g., Tang, Tang, and Lo 2005).

Another example is found in cap-and-trade programs for regulating greenhouse gas emissions and other pollutants. Economic models of these policies rarely pay attention to institutional contexts, but in practice, variance in institutional settings matters a great deal. The European Trading Scheme for carbon emissions operates within EU institutions and the political compromises they embody; others operate under the United Nations Framework Convention on Climate Change, within and among individual US states, within a single corporation, or in distinct commodities exchange markets. These programs, drawing on the same economic theories and inspired by the same set of early experiences (like the trading of sulfur emissions permits in the eastern United States), are shaped by varied and sometimes overlapping sets of national laws and regulatory institutions. Each program reflects the priorities of unique constellations of organized interests that jockeyed for influence during the design phase. Comparative political analysis allows us to tease out and explain variance in these programs' goals, regulatory approaches, and effectiveness and how all of these are shaped by politics.

The influence of political context on policy tools is clearly shown by Gallagher and Weinthal (chapter 6, this volume), who argue that corporate social responsibility programs have assumed quite distinct forms in different political settings depending on whether a state already has in place a well-developed regulatory apparatus. In industrialized countries with comparatively strong environmental bureaucracies, voluntary corporate initiatives initially arose as a defensive posture to forestall regulation. In contrast, these voluntary programs are promoted by government officials in countries such as Mexico, where they are seen as one solution to widespread noncompliance with state regulations.

The contextual political factors shaping the purpose and effects of policy tools are numerous. Cultural norms affect the receptiveness of a society to particular policy approaches, such as market-based regulatory tools, individual or community property rights regimes, and restrictions on the use of genetically modified organisms (Jordan, Wurzel, and Zito 2003; Jasanoff 2005). Expectations that educated consumers will "buy green" after they receive certain information are often disappointed because they ignore the institutional impediments to being a socially responsible consumer or to changing a larger market (VanDeveer 2010). Additionally, in many political settings, the reach of the state is relatively limited and must compete with alternative regulatory regimes dominated by religious organizations, community norms, ties of kinship and clan, and criminal networks (McAllister 2008; Tsai 2007; Helmke and Levitsky 2004). In these settings, the passage of environmental laws might score well in an analysis of treaty ratification but is meaningless for environmental outcomes unless these become embedded in effective domestic institutions.

The broader implications of this context-driven conception of environmental problem solving may be inconvenient for certain worldviews held by researchers and practitioners working on these issues, but comparative scholarship often complicates and deepens understanding rather than simplifying or reifying it. For example, there is little evidence in this volume, or in comparative environmental inquiry generally, to justify the view—common in some quarters—that social-ecological systems should be managed according to a relatively invariant set of science-based management prescriptions and technologically superior tools. These universalistic approaches simply do not accord with the institutionalized differences common across and within human societies.[6] Examples of the resulting disappointments include the role of science-based sustainable forestry in accelerating deforestation in parts of Southeast Asia (Dauvergne 2001), as well as the unfounded faith that stakeholder-based ecosystem management will necessarily produce outcomes superior to top-down regulatory approaches (Layzer 2008). Environmental politics is neither a globally homogenizing set of social processes nor a standard collection of technical solutions for a set of common problems. A careful read of the relevant research endows the critical practitioner with a deeper appreciation for the context in which new regulatory approaches play out against broader sets of social forces.

Making Sense

Anyone who wishes to make a constructive contribution to social and environmental outcomes around the world—be it the citizen activist, water quality professional, or "doubly engaged" scholar—is confronted with a bewildering and often unintelligible collection of social relationships. As the geographic range of concern spreads in response to new global problems and novel transnational relationships, myriad constellations of peoples and politics can at times seem overwhelming. Theory offers the practitioner conceptual lenses with which to make sense of this world. The human mind inevitably resorts to conceptual constructs as we go about our daily activities, and these concepts, socially constructed and learned, allow us to make sense of the particulars by placing them in recognizable categories ("property," "progress," "pollution," and the like) that we can measure (by qualitative and/or quantitative means), evaluate, and act upon. Theories of comparative politics broaden and deepen the pool of conceptual approaches we instinctively draw upon when confronted with empirical realities, whether familiar or exotic. As such, theory offers a valuable tonic against the more ad hoc and stereotypical conceptual shortcuts that cloud so much cross-cultural interaction.

Consider, for example, the concept of common property regimes reviewed here by Arun Agrawal (chapter 12). It is impossible to read such an account without taking away a new understanding of the particular situations that one might encounter in a tropical forest. That raucous scene over there is no longer merely a collection of farmers haggling over the placement of a fence; at play are conflict resolution mechanisms (or the lack thereof) within an institution for the management of shared resources. Theory helps practitioners to recognize empirical phenomena and relate them to larger classes of events. But it also generates questions that can leverage greater insight into particular situations. When reality seems to be starkly at odds with what we have learned from the research literature, urgent questions arise that might not otherwise have attracted attention. For example, given Steinberg's depiction (chapter 10, this volume) of the chronic institutional turnover that plagues policy making in many developing and postcommunist countries, how have some of these countries managed to build reasonably effective conservation institutions? What are the causal mechanisms at play? Similarly, if a green party enjoys electoral success, Michael O'Neill's analysis (chapter 7, this volume) leads us to ask how they walked the tightrope of strategic and ideological trade-offs that inevitably confront "new politics" parties. Sense-making through comparative social analysis helps us know what to look for.

Revisiting Causal Models

Political economist Richard Zeckhauser has observed that behind any good policy prescription is a good description of the world. Public policies and other targeted social interventions (including those of public interest groups) carry hard-wired causal assumptions regarding the nature of a social problem and the anticipated impact of proposed interventions (Pressman and Wildavsky 1973, xxi). By providing insights into causal processes, better social theories make for more effective and appropriate policies.

Bringing together theory with empirical analysis, the chapters in this volume upend some of the most cherished causal notions guiding environmental practices today. Dunlap and York's analysis of environmental public opinion, together with Kate O'Neill's overview of green social movements, provides a startling rebuke to the idea that poorer countries are unconcerned with environmental protection. These findings challenge basic precepts on which causal theories of the left and right are based. Proponents of neoliberal approaches argue that wealth creation is the surest path to environmental protection because (they claim) environmental attitudes arise with increases in consumption (see, e.g., Tierney 2009). A second variant of the argument that environmentalism is a concern for wealthy countries comes from those theorists and commentators on the left who assert that international environmental policy amounts to little more than Western imperialism in disguise (Driessen 2006). Neither account allows for the possibility of agency and the pursuit of enlightened self-interest in non-Western societies, and neither can accommodate the inconvenient facts on display throughout this volume, which show that environmental concern, advocacy, and efforts at institutional reform are widespread in developing countries (see also Pulver 2007; Steinberg 2001).

When practitioners observe poor environmental outcomes in a developing country, such as a flailing national park system or poor urban air quality, a causal model that assumes ignorance or apathy is likely to produce recommendations for "education" and financial inducements. If this mental map of the problem prevents outside observers from noticing that a country's citizens and policy reformers have been trying for years to address a problem, they are likely to promote the transfer of lessons and expertise rather than support ongoing efforts. Once the causal model is changed—recognizing that substandard conditions persist alongside substantial public interest and advocacy—this shifts the burden of explanation (and the focus of action) to explore the political and institutional factors that mediate the relationship between public concern, social mobilization, policy change, and environmental outcomes.

Another set of causal assumptions challenged by this volume concerns the causes of variance in environmental policy responses among industrialized countries. Many analysts and commentators overlook transatlantic similarities and explain differences with sweeping claims that focus on the symptoms of variance (such as divergent climate change policies in the United States and the European Union) rather than the causes. Comparative politics research offers models for understanding this variance, demonstrating how the institutions of governance shape political action and outcomes. Drawing on literatures in comparative federalism and multilevel governance, Selin and VanDeveer (chapter 13, this volume) use institutional analysis to explain why "California's climate change and energy policies more closely approximate those of the EU than those of the US federal government, and Germany's responses are closer to California's than those in Italy, Greece, and Romania."

Expanding Time Horizons

By focusing attention on long-term processes of social change, research in comparative environmental politics differs substantially from applied policy analysis. When policy analysts are called upon to research a specific problem—conducting a quantitative analysis for a government agency or distilling lessons from case studies for a nonprofit organization—they are typically asked to focus on problem solving in the here and now. The same is true of environmental advocacy organizations, which, in the rush to head off the latest ecological disaster, rarely have the luxury of thinking about social processes that unfold over decades. The work of environment and development professionals is often organized into discrete "projects" that are by definition limited in duration, lasting perhaps two to five years. Making the world a better place, in this organizational framework, consists of effective management of projects that fulfill concrete near-term objectives, measured in a currency of tourist guides trained, community meetings convened, laws passed, school gardens established, and so on.

In contrast, the chapters in this volume explore the longer-term social processes that promote or impede progress toward sustainability. The study of comparative environmental politics can help practitioners appreciate how their day-to-day efforts fit within these historical processes of social change and institutional transformation. This historical perspective matters not only because it enables one to attach deeper meaning to the blur of proper nouns that fill a busy workday. It is also the case that short-term projects can be designed in ways that contribute to the longer-term processes—spanning time horizons of ten to a hundred years—that will ultimately determine whether societies move onto a more sustainable track (see Sprinz 2009).

A number of possibilities for "historical spillover" from short-term projects can be found in the chapters presented here. Meadowcroft and Steinberg both emphasize that for state regulatory capacity to grow, environmental concerns must become mainstreamed—embedded in the missions and standard operating procedures of diverse bureaucracies and political constituencies inside and outside of the state. This is a long-term process, to be sure, but one that can be catalyzed by project designs and advocacy campaigns that make a point of involving diverse actors (ministries of finance, farmers unions, and many others) outside the boundaries of specialized environmental agencies. Several chapters explore how environmental problem solving takes place within long-term processes of evolving state-society relations. Hochstetler (chapter 8, this volume) positions environmental policy reform within broader processes of democratization and economic change in Central and Eastern Europe and Latin America. Jeannie Sowers's analysis of water management institutions in Egypt (chapter 9), as well as Arun Agrawal's discussion of decentralization and community forestry, suggest that practitioners should consider how a given project affects the broader historical trajectory of opportunities for political participation. Kate O'Neill shows that state restrictions on civil liberties pose a major challenge for environmental advocates in Burma and Iran, and a tax code more favorable to nonprofit organizations might have prevented the dissipation of Japan's grassroots environmental movement in the 1970s. Short-term projects that strengthen opportunities for constructive state-society relations—for example, inserting provisions for transparency in a program design or creating a formal role for community organizations in a particular law—can have long-lasting effects. Indeed, Rochon and Mazmanian (1993) conclude that one of the most enduring impacts of the US environmental movement is the way it changed broader policy-making processes, establishing new opportunities for citizens to scrutinize and influence government decisions.

Viewing International Policy Impacts from the Inside Out

A final example of what comparative theory can offer practice comes in evaluating the impact of international environmental institutions (such as treaties) and transnational advocacy campaigns. International relations scholars have long recognized the need for research on domestic politics and institutions and their interactions with international policy processes (Krasner 1976; Putnam 1988; Moravcsik 1997). Within the field of global environmental politics, the literature on domestic-international linkages has grown steadily over the past two decades (e.g., Schreurs and Economy 1997; Weinthal 2002; Harrison and Sundstrom 2010), but has yet to affect many of the basic premises of the field. This volume demonstrates the need to embrace an "inside-out" perspective on the causal influence of international regimes and non-state actors (see Steinberg 2001, 193–210). In the literature on treaty effectiveness, for example, an unstated but widely shared conceptual orientation privileges the causal importance of design elements within international institutions, emphasizing factors such as the need for specific regulatory commitments and the influence of voting rules. How might we reconcile this conceptual world with the perspective provided by James Meadowcroft's chapter, which describes the greening of state institutions as a process unfolding over many decades and across numerous social sectors?

From a comparative perspective, the essential question for the design of international institutions can be stated as follows: Given a *domestic context*, what can and should international organizations do to promote the *domestic institutionalization* of environmental practices? Andonova and VanDeveer (chapter 11, this volume) confirm that the domestic institutionalization of international ideas and practices varies widely across EU member states, both in its extent and causal pathways. Other domestic contexts discussed in this volume include shifting public preferences, the rise of new social movements, decentralization, democratization and authoritarian rule, chronic political instability, and the evolution of political party systems and state institutions. An inside-out perspective on international environmental treaties and advocacy campaigns does not deny the importance of international and transnational relations. To the contrary, viewed from the inside-out and in the aggregate, international influences are often more pronounced than is apparent from the study of isolated projects and treaties (Steinberg 2001, 203–206). Andonova and VanDeveer find that international institutions have had a profound impact on domestic environmental practices in the EU. Selin and VanDeveer argue that climate change policymaking in the United States and the European Union frequently manifests hybridization, as the regions influence each other through international and transnational channels. Many of the literatures described here highlight the growing importance of transnational relations, from the scientific networks influencing Egyptian water management to growing cross-border activism and the spread of ideas like corporate social responsibility. It is a matter of placing these international influences in concrete political and historical circumstances.

An inside-out perspective on global environmentalism carries direct implications for practice. The literature on international environmental relations has appropriated the language of agenda setting and implementation from the policy sciences, yet a deeper reading of the policy literature reveals that effective policies must be designed in light of the problem context they hope to affect. The idea that one can design policies in the political center, absent knowledge of the local conditions where those policies are to be implemented, has long been discredited. As Richard Elmore put the matter more than thirty years ago, "The notion that policymakers exercise— or ought to exercise—some kind of direct and determinant control over policy implementation might be called the 'noble lie' of conventional public administration and policy analysis" (1979, 603). Practitioners of international environmental policy and those researchers who hope to inform their efforts would do well to borrow a page from Elmore's work on "backward mapping," which begins with a careful assessment of the incentives, relationships, resources, and constraints shaping outcomes in the field, and on this basis identifies higher-level policy interventions that can facilitate meaningful change.

What Does the Study of Environmental Practice Offer Theory?

Major advances in social science theory are often motivated by concerns over concrete social problems. Historically, we see this in the genesis of game theory, initially developed in a context of strategic posturing by nuclear powers, as well as in research on the political economy of development that followed on the heels of decolonization (Schelling 1960; Bates 1981). More recent examples include literatures tracking democratization and EU expansion (Rueschemeyer and Evans 1985; O'Donnell 1996; Knill 2001). It should therefore come as little surprise that research on how diverse societies come to grips with pressing environmental problems offers fresh insights into many of the central concerns of comparative social science.

Indeed, the chapters in this volume challenge many established orthodoxies within comparative politics. Dunlap and York's analysis debunks the most widely cited model of attitude formation, showing that Inglehart's (1990) work on postmaterialism offers only limited explanatory power for the rise of environmental concern. In her study of Egyptian water politics, Sowers concludes that conventional models of hierarchical state control in "hydraulic societies" is oversimplified. Water policy is dominated by "multilevel governance shaped by institutions and networks within the state itself, between the state and various social groups, and across international institutions and transnational networks." She concludes, "The picture of monolithic, authoritarian states with strong capacities to regulate society or even control the state apparatus is thus a poor starting point for understanding the dynamics of environmental politics in the Middle East." Steinberg finds that predominant theories of policy change are out of touch with the social conditions pertaining in developing and postcommunist countries, and Gallagher and Weinthal demonstrate that corporations may enhance, rather than undercut, the development of state regulatory structures. Instead of recapitulating the theoretical implications of each chapter, here we focus on three major themes that demonstrate how comparative environmental politics contributes to long-standing theoretical debates in comparative social science and opens up exciting new lines of inquiry.

New Perspectives on Globalization and Convergence
The fields of international relations and comparative politics share a keen interest in understanding whether the growing connectedness that is the hallmark of globalization is precipitating convergence in the ways that societies define and respond

to public problems. To the question of whether countries are becoming more similar or more different, this book responds with a resounding "yes." To be sure, there is ample evidence of convergent processes associated with the intensifying worldwide exchange of information, materials, and people (see Keohane and Nye 2000). If convergence denotes a tendency "to develop similarities in structures, processes and performances" (Kerr 1983, 3; cited in Bennett 1991, 215), then examples are easy to find. States often adopt similar policy tools (such as cap-and-trade schemes for reducing carbon emissions), create analogous administrative structures (park systems, environmental agencies), and emulate procedural norms such as requirements for public input. Political and economic integration often drives environmental standards up and closer together (Vogel 1995; Selin and VanDeveer 2006). Social movements adopt problem definitions and borrow protest techniques from their counterparts abroad (McAdam and Rucht 1993). The contributors to this book also reveal many areas of convergence among states and societies. Dunlap and York show that environmental concerns have grown substantially and somewhat simultaneously across different polities. Meadowcroft traces a similar phenomenon at play within government, as states adopt a widening array of environmental responsibilities. Gallagher and Weinthal argue that the corporate social responsibility movement has globalized rapidly in the wake of expanding markets and the transnationalization of corporate structures. Kate O'Neill finds that "It is very hard these days to study movements in isolation from their transnational networks or from the influence of ideas originating elsewhere."

The essays in this book demonstrate, however, that the political consequences of globalization are much more complex than a simple convergence narrative would suggest. Even in cases in which we might expect high levels of convergence in policy outcomes, we often find persistent (even growing) divergence. Few countries have more in common than the United States and Canada, yet substantial differences in environmental politics and policy remain among these increasingly integrated states (Le Prestre and Stoett 2006). Within the European Union—a setting in which centralized rule-making bodies and innumerable transnational linkages lend themselves to the rapid diffusion of ideas and practices—research reveals a complex mixture of convergence and divergence among member states and societies. Andonova and VanDeveer conclude that international cooperation has produced "diverging convergence" in the environmental politics of Central and Eastern European states. EU membership has fostered considerable convergence in the norms and substantive requirements of these states' environmental policies, alongside "a persistent divergence in domestic environmental institutions, particularly with respect to the implementation of international and national policies" (see also Carmin and VanDeveer 2005; Knill 2005; Schreurs, Selin and VanDeveer 2009; Vig and Faure 2004).

In other instances, a process of hybridization unfolds as political systems borrow ideas and practices from abroad and combine these in unique ways in their new political settings, where they encounter and interact with existing institutions (Weiner 2004; Steinberg 2001, 183–190). This dynamic view of globalization paints a picture quite different from that of a globalizing juggernaut of sameness sweeping away national peculiarities. Instead, we expect to find complex mixtures of convergence, divergence, and hybridization. We see this dynamic in Meadowcroft's account of the historical evolution of state responsibilities. Even as he identifies a general trend toward greening, Meadowcroft notes that modern states are enmeshed in a web of contradictions within their multiple roles as promoters of national security, economic development, and social welfare. Greening entails a competition of ideas within state and societal structures when, for example, ideas associated with neoliberal economics compete with those focused more centrally on human and ecological sustainability. These contradictions make the process of environmental reform infinitely more complex, but also give rise to ideational and institutional dynamism. This dynamism is apparent in Selin and VanDeveer's exploration of transatlantic climate change politics. They find that actors and institutions on both sides of the Atlantic influence each other across various levels of governance and across public, private, and civil society sectors.

Convergence may also result from causal processes that do not entail crossnational exchanges per se but lead diverse countries to respond similarly to widespread phenomena, such as worsening environmental conditions or shifts in economic conditions. Yet the findings in this book reveal that here too the process is much more nuanced (and more interesting from an analytic standpoint) than a simple dose-response model might suggest. We discover a multifaceted story at every link in the chains of relationships connecting environmental problems to political responses. Dunlap and York's finding that environmental attitudes are not correlated with levels of economic development challenges the assumption that convergence in values will proceed apace with economic growth; the sheer breadth of public environmental concern shows that significant levels of environmentalism exist in countries with widely divergent physical conditions. Kate O'Neill demonstrates, in turn, that the relation between public concern and social mobilization is mediated by institutionalized state practices that promote or inhibit social movement activity. Continuing along our deliberately simplified causal chain, Gallagher and Weinthal document how corporate actors respond in diverse ways to the pressure applied by these environmental movements. And Michael O'Neill shows that the link between social movements and political change is shaped by the contours of the existing party system, which affects the viability of green parties and their prospects for electoral success. He observes, moreover, that the rise of green parties in Western Europe was as much a reaction of new left egalitarians to the authoritarian style of old left politics as it was a response to concerns regarding nuclear power or environmental degradation.

By transcending a simple convergence story and studying the ways in which social reformers pursue environmental agendas in diverse national settings, we can appreciate two important dimensions of environmental politics. First, institutional change occurs in a broader context of enduring social structures. However much environmental visionaries exhort us to "completely rethink" the organization of society in light of new environmental concerns, activists do not work with a tabula rasa. Indeed, the content of activist demands is strongly shaped by long-standing domestic political concerns, as can be seen in the pairing of environmentalism with nationalism, development, feminism, democracy, and indigenous rights (Dawson 1996; O'Neill and VanDeveer 2005; Hsiao et al. 1999; Steinberg 2001). New entrants in a given policy-making arena, be they green parties or newly established environmental agencies, operate within deeply entrenched patterns of bargaining and power appropriation (Kitschelt 1986). Environmental NGOs navigating processes of democratization are part of larger social and historical process whose contours and outcomes they influence but do not control. Efforts to decentralize environmental management or to enhance local participation unfold in institutional settings shaped by long histories of authoritarian and exclusionary decision making. The enduring aspects of social structures are, of course, only half the story. To understand convergence and divergence also requires an appreciation for the strategies that agents use to engender change in varied and evolving national contexts (O'Neill, Balsiger, and VanDeveer 2004).

A Renewed Focus on Policy and Governance

Although the field of comparative politics prides itself on having relevance to real-world issues (Lichbach and Zuckerman 1997, 4), in practice, policy-relevant research is often a subject of disdain among comparativists (see, e.g., Katznelson 1997, 85). This orientation may stem from a lack of appreciation for the diverse traditions within policy studies, which include not only applied policy analysis (concerned with near-term solutions for highly specific policy problems) but also historically situated research on policy processes. (For an excellent discussion of this distinction, see Scharpf 2000.) As the question for many new democracies moves from regime change to the business of governance, and as the once inscrutable decision-making processes of authoritarian regimes give way to more open processes amenable to empirical investigation, the field of comparative politics would benefit from more systematic attention to policy processes, building on existing lines of inquiry into topics such as political development and state regulatory capacity. Public policy is not a mere detail, a mundane distraction from the grand questions of political research. It is the very stuff of politics, the focus of power struggles and collective action by people whose lives and well-being depend on the outcome. Public policies selectively institutionalize ideas and practices shaping the experiences of people everywhere—from the urban family seeking access to clean water to the farmer hoping to reconcile her need to make a living with her desire to live in a healthy forest.

There is a certain irony in an intellectual position that considers the earth to be a parochial policy concern, insufficiently broad to satisfy the wide-ranging interests of political scientists. One need only consider the role of land in economic development and political mobilization—and its role in foundational theories of classical political economy—to appreciate the barrenness of this point of view. Today, issues such as air pollution, coastal resource management, and toxic waste are equally wide-ranging in their connections with the institutions of states and societies. Environmental processes are long-lasting and often large-scale, providing an opportunity to explore long-term social processes. Examples of processes explored in this volume include the transformation of party systems, shifts in power among levels of government, value change, evolving forms of social mobilization, institutional stability and reform, and expanding conceptions of state identity.

"Policy" is indeed too narrow a term to fully describe this new canvas for comparative politics, as it implies action by governments alone. It is telling that in a book with many policy-oriented contributors, nonstate actors figure prominently in every chapter. Understanding environmental politics requires a broader understanding of the concept of governance (Kohler-Koch and Rittberger 2006). This is an exciting area for theory development, as there is a need for empirically grounded explanations of efforts to improve social well-being at the place where states, civil society, and the private sector come together—sometimes in collaboration, sometimes in a context of bitter power struggles, often both.

Research on governance should not consist of a breathless chronicling of the latest legal developments in the European Union or of the newest twist on conservation project design. This is a sure recipe for obsolescence and provides little of value to social science. Given the change-oriented nature of this subject and the pervasiveness of institutional experimentation, empirical studies of environmental politics can at times be likened to taking a close-up photo of a fast-moving train. Here again the use of theory is indispensable, allowing the cumulative growth of knowledge across cases and countries. One discovers in Michael O'Neill's chapter on the evolution of party systems in Western Europe, or in Arun Agrawal's insights into the operation of local forestry institutions, that theoretically situated studies of governance can leverage insights into culture, institutions, history, and the evolving organization of political life. This wider lens not only enables environmental research to contribute to broader scholarly debates, but also offers insights that knowledgeable practitioners on the front lines of these struggles are unlikely to figure out on their own.

Comparative Local Politics

In a review of political science research on local institutions, Gerry Stoker finds that "the study of local governance is regarded by many as a rather disappointing backwater, outshone and left behind by the more dynamic areas of investigation" (2006, 495). The most significant problem, according to Stoker, is the lack of comparative work. Promising theoretical strands such as urban regime theory have been limited to studies of the United States and, to a lesser extent, Europe. "What the field lacks and has yet to deliver is a genuine global take on comparative local governance"—a task made more urgent by the democratization and political decentralization of recent decades. A renewed emphasis on local politics is surely one of the greatest gifts that research with an empirical focus on the environment can offer the field of comparative politics.

What is it about environmental issues that brings local politics into such sharp focus? Part of the answer resides in the physical characteristics of pollution and natural resource management, which resist the centralizing tendencies of capitalism and state development. Markets work best when assets can be turned into fluid, abstract representations of value to be combined, divided, and traded across space (de Soto 2000). State building entails the aggregation of resources, interests, and identities, the standardization of laws and the creation of centralized bureaucracies for the collection of data and taxes and the mass mobilization of resources (through central banks, armies, and pension funds). In both projects, there is a struggle against the gravitational pull of particular places.[7] Political scientists interested in sources of power and dynamism in modern societies perhaps understandably look to centralized institutions as the site for empirical investigation. There are also disciplinary identities at stake—studies of "local" social relations are often considered the turf of anthropology and sociology.

Environmental issues challenge these disciplinary biases. Against the centralizing tendencies of states and markets, environmental resources are often "sticky"—they reside in particular places and affect and are influenced by local actions. Uniformly distributed resources (such as carbon dioxide in the atmosphere) are the exception, rather than the rule—and even here the emissions sources and the impacts of climate change vary substantially across time and space. Notwithstanding the importance of global environmental impacts, when a factory releases pollution, more often than not it is local communities and workers who bear the brunt (and often raise the alarm). The vast majority of species have quite limited ranges (Press, Doak, and Steinberg 1996), placing it within the power of individual communities to permanently reduce the global stock of biological diversity. Conca notes that many "global" environmental problems, such as water shortages, are actually "globally accumulating 'local' problems" that manage to attract international attention (2006, 16). Combined with the shift in power and authority accompanying democratization and decentralization, local politics clearly offers a compelling focus for research that can contribute to both theory and practice.

To date, the gap created by this blind spot within comparative political science has been filled by sociologists, anthropologists, and geographers with a focus on agrarian studies, particularly within the field of political ecology (see, e.g., Peet and Watts 1996). This large literature has produced impressive results, reflecting cultures of research within the parent disciplines that emphasize the pairing of theory with rigorous and methodical fieldwork. However, by hewing closely to Marxist-inspired models of social relations—emphasizing irreconcilable conflicts and mechanisms of exploitation and control—research in political ecology has served up a full plate of research drawn from a narrow portion of the menu. The gap left by political science has also been filled to some extent by the work of economists studying "informal regulation," which tracks the ways in which the polluting behavior of factories is shaped by local community pressure, as firms seek to protect reputational assets and navigate patterns of obligation within local social networks (Dasgupta, Hettige, and Wheeler 2000; Hettige et al. 1996; see also Tsai 2007).

It remains to be seen whether Elinor Ostrom's influential work on common-pool resources will catalyze a renewed focus on the local within comparative political science. The contributions to this book suggest that Ostrom's impressive corpus of research has revealed merely the tip of the iceberg. Arun Agrawal, who has been a leading figure in this research tradition, demonstrates in his chapter that local politics must be situated within a broader understanding of interactions among levels of authority. The number and forms of local forestry institutions have expanded largely in response to international and national policy initiatives. Local institutions do not, in other words, spring from the ground like mushrooms, but emerge as a response to the broader political and economic forces that promote or impede the ability of local actors to make authoritative decisions on public problems. Selin and VanDeveer's contribution illustrates that local public and private sector organizations are grappling with climate change around the world. This "global" challenge is prompting multilevel governance in federal and nonfederal systems alike, in cities and towns in Europe, North America and well beyond. Sowers's insights into the internal workings of the state in authoritarian Egypt build on a theoretical tradition examining the "local state." Despite high-level political support for the creation of local water user associations, in practice the influence of farmers and other participants has been circumscribed by local officials wary of challenges to their authority. Similar findings are likely to emerge when comparativists turn their attention from the study of national regime change to questions of governance. The institutionalized values and practices that predominate in particular sites within a state affect how officials define and respond to public problems. Research on the local state reveals internal contradictions within state institutions that often appear (and certainly present themselves) as internally coherent political entities.

Methods for Doubly Engaged Research

How does one go about producing socially relevant, theoretically grounded research in comparative environmental politics? Clearly, given the impressive diversity of the scholarship discussed throughout this book, many different research designs lend themselves to this task. Fortuitously, in recent years there has been an unprecedented amount of work on research methods within comparative social science, including many path-breaking publications that can serve as useful guides for key elements of research practice: How does one construct social science concepts that are useful for theory building and lend themselves to empirical testing (Goertz 2006)? What are the relative merits of quantitative and qualitative research designs in efforts to uncover causal relationships (Mahoney 2010; Brady and Collier 2004)? What exactly is a case study, and how does one go about designing and conducting the relevant research to maximize its explanatory power (Gerring 2007)?

Here we limit our attention to a particular dimension of research practice that carries special relevance for comparative environmental politics: strategies for dealing with complexity. As we argue in chapter 1, a central challenge for those adopting a comparative perspective on global environmental problems is to embrace complexity without becoming overwhelmed by it. We must move beyond the simplistic holism of "spaceship Earth" and study the diverse ways in which societies around the globe generate and respond to environmental problems. But it is not enough to simply reveal the incredible complexity of the human dimensions of environmental problems—the interests, ideas, and institutions that interact, evolve, and assume distinctive forms in different places at different historical junctures. We must also make sense of the stories.

It is noteworthy that this challenge manifests itself most clearly in three of the chapters that cover the most mature fields, measured in terms of the size and breadth of their research literatures: Kate O'Neill's coverage of environmental movements, Michael O'Neill's analysis of green parties, and Arun Agrawal's chapter on local common property regimes. Having attracted the sustained attention of hundreds of researchers over a period of decades, it is in these literatures that numerous causal explanations emerge and the complexity of the underlying social relationships is most apparent. Agrawal, for example, demonstrates how the causal impact of a variable is contingent on context, noting that roads are associated with tropical deforestation in the absence of effective institutions but are associated with forest protection when these institutions are present. Michael O'Neill observes that the rise of green parties has been shaped by catalysts and contingent events (such as the

1986 Chernobyl disaster) as much as by more systemic changes in values and social conditions. Kate O'Neill shows that causal analysis of the origins and impacts of environmental movements is complicated by the diversity of forms these assume, with distinctive environmental concerns, movement types, strategies, and impacts playing out against a backdrop of diverse political systems and growing transnational connections.

A similar phenomenon can be seen in intensively studied topics within the broader field of comparative politics, such as democratization or war (see, e.g., Geddes 1999; Levy 1989). In his influential book *The Third Wave*, Huntington concludes the following:

(1) No single factor is sufficient to explain the development of democracy in all countries or in a single country. (2) No single factor is necessary to the development of democracy in all countries. (3) Democratization in each country is the result of a combination of causes. (4) The combination of causes producing democracy varies from country to country. (5) The combination of causes generally responsible for one wave of democratization differs from that responsible for other waves. (6) The causes responsible for the initial regime changes in a democratization wave are likely to differ from those responsible for later regime changes in that wave. (1991, 38)

The complexity on display in these fields suggests that research questions at an earlier stage of development, such as whether democratic systems produce better environmental outcomes (reviewed here by Hochstetler) or what explains the origins of environmental concern (discussed in the chapter by Dunlap and York), might have similar challenges waiting around the corner.

Precise Answers to General Questions

What are some practical strategies for making sense of complex causal settings?[8] For those interested in doubly engaged research, it is important to keep in mind that there is an inherent tension between the specificity that practitioners demand and the generalizability that theorists pursue (Steinberg 2005). The practitioner needs to know how to fix this problem, here, and soon. The theorist prizes insights that encompass many experiences, across space and time, even if this comes at the expense of specificity. These competing projects can be reconciled by crafting productive questions of wide relevance that give rise to different answers in different settings. We argue in chapter 1 that good questions transcend borders. Yet the answers to these social questions emerge from multifaceted and interacting assemblages of social forces that inevitably assume unique forms in particular places and times. Reflecting on the challenge of producing socially relevant, theoretically informed knowledge in development studies, Christian Lund offers the following perspective:

To understand the politics of decentralisation in, say, Indonesia, it may be very productive to look to Weber for the questions he asks about legitimacy, and rather less rewarding to look at the (ultimately historically contingent) answers he provides. Likewise, to understand the political economy of rural Africa, it may be very productive to look to Marx for the questions he asks about power, property and control, and a lot less so to subscribe to his class analysis of nineteenth century Europe. (2010, 27)

Arun Agrawal's analysis of local forestry institutions is instructive. He notes that there are no simple and universally applicable guidelines for designing effective local institutions for environmental governance. Translating general prescriptions from the research literature, such as "rules should be locally created and enforced," requires "clarification about types of rules, meanings of 'local,' and forms of enforcement." He notes that Ostrom "suggests that there may be literally hundreds of thousands of different rule combinations from which decision makers can choose. The interpretation of seemingly clear and concrete recommendations runs headlong into this plethora of possibilities." Yet the analyst who wishes to evaluate and improve conditions in a given setting would be well served by a list of questions common to these studies. Are the rules governing resource use easy to understand and enforce? Are they locally designed and accepted? Do they, in Agrawal's terms, "take into account differences in types of violations, help manage conflicts, and hold users and officials accountable"? The use of general questions to produce context-specific answers is possible only when research results are cast in a form that travels well across borders, thereby allowing the accumulation of knowledge that points to certain questions deserving special attention. As we have argued throughout this volume, this sort of cumulative, cross-national conversation is possible only through the use of theory.

Causal Mechanisms as Modular Explanations

Research strategies emphasizing causal mechanisms offer another promising approach for dealing with complex causation. A causal mechanism describes the precise processes through which a posited explanatory variable (such as electoral democracy) influences a given outcome (such as the propensity of countries to participate in environmental treaties). In this example, one mechanism is the recurrent tendency for NGOs in democratic polities to reach out to their civil society counterparts in other democracies, diffusing ideas and resources that promote pro-environment actions on the part of states. In common with all forms of process tracing, research on causal mechanisms moves us beyond observed correlations among variables to explore the *logic* of association between antecedents and outcomes (see Roberts 1996; George and Bennett 2005). It pushes researchers to specify exactly how and why a given set of conditions produce a particular social outcome. Charles Tilly contrasts research on causal mechanisms with epistemological approaches favoring grand theory and covering laws, noting that mechanism-oriented scholars embrace theoretical explanation but "question the utility of seeking law-like empirical generalizations—at any level of abstraction—by comparing big chunks of history . . . although mechanisms by definition have uniform immediate effects, their aggregate, cumulative, and longer-term effects vary considerably depending on initial conditions and on combinations with other mechanisms" (2001, 25). The impact of a causal mechanism varies depending on the political context in which it plays out, and this context commonly varies from one geographical and historical setting to the next (Goodin and Tilly 2006; see also Falleti and Lynch 2009).

The agility of this approach stems from the modular nature of causal mechanisms, which can be moved across cases and countries and combined with other causal mechanisms as needed to create testable propositions about the causes of particular historical outcomes. This approach allows researchers to advance the theoretical goal of generalizability—speaking to and drawing on a larger literature and associated set of empirical experiences—without having to sacrifice realism or downplay the role of historical contingency. Returning to the example of transnational relations and state participation in environmental treaties, there are strong transnational exchanges among environmental NGOs and related constituencies in the United States and Europe (documented in this volume by Selin and VanDeveer), but the attempts of United States–based NGOs to promote a federal climate policy are hindered by another causal mechanism (discussed in Michael O'Neill's chapter)—the tendency of winner-take-all electoral systems to discourage the emergence of minor parties (such as green parties) that amplify the political profile of environmental concerns. Thus, an emphasis on recurrent causal mechanisms—cause-and-effect relationships that appear with frequency in diverse political settings—promotes the growth of a cumulative research program without resorting to simplistic, one-size-fits-all explanations.[9]

Mixed Methods

Investigators in comparative environmental politics often grapple with two types of complexity. The first consists of scenarios in which multiple and interacting causal factors account for a given outcome, such as a community's success in establishing institutions for the sustainable management of a resource. The second type concerns differences in the causal forces at play across cases and countries (the success of community X stems from factors quite different from those at play in community Y). Comparativists are often interested in both types of questions, yet these present a stark trade-off for research designs. To ferret out the first type of complexity requires process tracing—an in-depth and context-rich investigation into the streams of events that connect explanatory variables and outcomes (Roberts 1996). The second question, regarding variance across a larger number of countries and cases, typically requires the use of quantitative analysis.

Mixed methods offer one approach for dealing with this challenge (Clark and Creswell 2008). In some instances, researchers combine quantitative and qualitative methods within the same research project. In Lily Tsai's (2007) study of the provision of local public goods in China, she combines original ethnographic research within a select number of sites together with a quantitative survey of more than three hundred villages. Although this is among the most logistically challenging research designs (difficult to achieve even within the time frame of a doctoral dissertation), the results provide a compelling explanation both within and across cases. A second approach, represented by Elinor Ostrom's book *Governing the Commons* (1990), applies quantitative modeling to evaluate case studies written by other researchers. A third strategy is one in which a researcher spends a number of years investigating specific cases and on this basis eventually derives categories that are explored on a larger scale through statistical and other quantitative approaches. A representative work along these lines is Chhatre and Agrawal's (2009) assessment of the factors associated with successful outcomes in the governance of forest commons. The difference between the second and third approaches is that when drawing primarily on materials written by others, researchers face the disadvantage of not having influenced the strategy for data collection (for a critique, see Lustick 1996), alongside the advantage of marshaling empirical evidence far beyond what any one research team could accomplish alone (for a discussion, see Skocpol 1984).

Future Directions

Where are the most significant gaps in comparative environmental politics research? Perhaps the most glaring gap is geographic. As in many areas of social science, there remains a transatlantic dominance in comparative environmental research. The literature is slowly expanding to include Latin America and some of the largest Asian states and societies (notably China, India, and Japan), but little attention has been directed beyond these areas. Why is there so little work on environmental mobilization and policy reform in sub-Saharan Africa? Is it that problems of governance (such as wars, political instability, and corruption) are so profound that there are few government initiatives worthy of study? Clark Gibson's (1999) important work on the politics of wildlife conservation policy suggests that even in the tragically trying circumstances facing sub-Saharan Africa, there are important policy lessons to be learned and theoretical insights to be gained. Or is it that there are simply no significant environmental mobilizations outside of South Africa and well-publicized cases like Kenya's Greenbelt movement and protests in the Nigerian oil fields? How then are problems like water shortages and deforestation articulated through national political processes, and to what extent have advocates for change adopted (and adapted) the discourse of environmental protection and sustainable development?

At a time when environmentalism is having an impact on nearly every polity on the planet, and when the number of democratic and democratizing states is larger than ever, remarkably little is known about the relation between environmentalism and political parties in the developing world. Analyses of European politics suggest that the activities of environmental movements are often most influential when combined with the organization of green parties, yet many political systems do not afford opportunities for such parties. How then do environmental movements in these settings influence party platforms, electoral processes, and legislative outcomes at local and national levels? Research on environmental policy making in the developing world rarely refers to theories of the state, missing an opportunity to contribute to the literature on state "greening" reviewed by Meadowcroft. Moreover, we lack convincing metrics of greening to facilitate comparison across diverse types of states. Dunlap and York demonstrate that postmaterialism cannot account for the rise environmental concern in poor countries. But we still lack an alternative set of explanatory hypotheses that might account for cross-national variation. Gallagher and Weinthal conclude that there is a dearth of studies on corporate social responsibility beyond North America and Europe. And Sowers finds that political scientists have paid little attention to the environmental challenges facing the Middle East. We would extend her argument to highlight the relative paucity of research on environmental governance in authoritarian regimes generally, with China as a notable exception.

Even the more closely studied regions of the developing world are too unevenly covered to facilitate systematic comparison. Agrawal reports that common property research in Asia and elsewhere is only beginning to grapple with the large variety of ownership patterns governing natural resources and that basic data on forest ownership remain scarce. As Hochstetler's contribution makes clear, the paucity of empirical research on the relation between democratization and ecological outcomes in Latin America makes any systematic comparison challenging. And the large body of research on local environmental institutions in developing countries remains almost completely divorced from the concepts and methods of comparative politics.

A number of critical areas of inquiry not covered in this book deserve attention as part of a future research agenda in comparative environmental politics. Important dimensions of environmental politics such as power, justice, feminism, political theory, ethnic and class conflict, and rural-urban relations are among the themes that have been explored by environmental social scientists but receive inadequate coverage here. Considering the right-hand column of figure 14.1, major concerns within comparative politics that are given less attention than they deserve in this book include nationalism, identity, religion, comparative judicial systems, and voting behavior. Moreover, our understanding of the relation between domestic political processes and broader trends within global environmental politics is in its infancy. Do some societies participate more frequently than others in transnational environmental relations—and if so, why? How is democratization affecting the process of interest aggregation that leads to foreign policy positions on global environmental issues? How do decision makers in diverse political systems arrive at conceptions of national interests vis-à-vis global problems? Do international actors and institutions serve as a source of policy continuity in nations that experience chronic institutional turnover? How do competing sectors within states strategically avail themselves of international support? What are the implications of decentralization for the practice of international environmental policy?

Of course, no single volume can cover the entire nexus (both actual and potential) of research in comparative politics and environmental studies, nor is this our intention. Rather, we hope the success of this volume is measured by its ability to articulate a distinctive research agenda, to identify and illustrate some of its leading edges, to convey excitement about the promise of this field, and to inspire and facilitate more research in comparative environmental politics. We expect that others will find that we have drawn boundaries too narrowly or in the wrong places, attesting to the expansive potential of this field and to the truism that great insights are the product of many minds.

Notes

1. According to Munck and Snyder, these two journals, along with *World Politics*, "are widely seen as the leading ones in the field, where much of the best research in comparative politics appears and where collective standards get set" (2007, 7). *World Politics* includes many articles emphasizing international relations, rather than comparative themes, so for simplicity we focused on the other two journals.

2. Coding was conducted by a research assistant under supervision by Steinberg.

3. Coding sheets and further details on coding criteria are available from the authors upon request.

4. The analysis by Munck and Snyder covers every third year from 1989 to 2004.

5. It is difficult to discern how much of this is a function of editorial policy versus the pool of submitted manuscripts; we would expect these to be mutually reinforcing trends, as editorial emphases send signals to prospective authors about whether to submit a manuscript, and a large pool of high-quality manuscripts on a topic might cause editors to revisit their assumptions regarding appropriate topics. Whereas journals offer a glimpse of the leading edges of a field, a review of various handbooks of comparative politics (Boix and Stokes 2009; Landman and Robinson 2009) readily supports the conclusion that environmental issues have not entered the mainstream of comparative politics. Environmental issues are beginning to receive some attention in selected introductory comparative politics texts (such as Kesselman,

Krieger, and Joseph 2009) with greater coverage in the minority of such texts that include sustained attention to public policy (Adolino and Blake 2001; Orvis and Drogus 2009).

6. Nor do they reflect the inherent diversity and contingency of complex ecological systems (see Schön 1983).

7. There is a substantial literature on regional economic development that emphasizes the "pull" of particular places. For example, dense regional networks give rise to increasing returns to scale in particular industries (North 1981), such as software development in Silicon Valley or customer service centers in Bangalore. But these depend crucially on the benefits of the movement of capital unconstrained by geography.

8. For an elaboration of techniques for adjudicating the relative importance of contributing causes in qualitative research, see Steinberg 2007.

9. Ragin (2008) has developed quantitative methods that allow a modular approach to causal assessment, using Boolean algebra to explore how diverse collections of causal factors produce different outcomes in different combinations.

References

Adolino, Jessica Rose, and Charles H. Blake. 2001. *Comparing Public Policies: Issues and Choices in Six Industrialized Countries*. Washington, D.C.: CQ Press.

Bates, Robert H. 1981. *Markets and States in Tropical Africa: The Political Basis of Agricultural Policies*. Berkeley: University of California Press.

Bennett, Colin J. 1991. What Is Policy Convergence and What Causes It? *British Journal of Political Science* 21:215–233.

Boix, Carles, and Susan C. Stokes. 2009. *The Oxford Handbook of Comparative Politics*. New York: Oxford University Press.

Brady, Henry E., and David Collier, eds. 2004. *Rethinking Social Inquiry: Diverse Tools, Shared Standards*. Lanham, Md.: Rowman and Littlefield.

Carmin, JoAnn, and Stacy D. VanDeveer. 2005. *EU Enlargement and the Environment: Institutional Change and Environmental Policy in Central and Eastern Europe*. London: Routledge.

Carruthers, David. 2001. Environmental Politics in Chile: Legacies of Dictatorship and Democracy. *Third World Quarterly* 22 (3): 343–358.

Chhatre, Ashwini, and Arun Agrawal. 2009. Trade-Offs and Synergies between Carbon Storage and Livelihood Benefits from Forest Commons. *Proceedings of the National Academy of Sciences of the United States of America* 106 (42): 17667–17670.

Clark, Vicki L. Plano, and John W. Creswell, eds. 2008. *The Mixed Methods Reader*. Thousand Oaks, Calif.: Sage Publications.

Conca, Ken. 2006. *Governing Water: Contentious Transnational Politics and Global Institution Building*. Cambridge, Mass.: MIT Press.

Dasgupta, Susmita, Hemamala Hettige, and David Wheeler. 2000. What Improves Environmental Compliance? Evidence from Mexican Industry. *Journal of Environmental Economics and Management* 39 (1): 39–66.

Dauvergne, Peter. 2001. *Loggers and Degradation in the Asia-Pacific: Corporations and Environmental Management.* Cambridge, UK: Cambridge University Press.

Dawson, Jane I. 1996. *Eco-Nationalism: Anti-Nuclear Activism and National Identity in Russia, Lithuania and Ukraine.* Durham: Duke University Press.

de Soto, Hernando. 2000. *The Mystery of Capital: Why Capitalism Triumphs in the West and Fails Everywhere Else.* New York: Basic Books.

Driessen, Paul. 2006. *Eco-Imperialism: Green Power, Black Death.* New Delhi: Academic Foundation.

Elmore, Richard F. 1979. Backward Mapping: Implementation Research and Policy Decisions. *Political Science Quarterly* 94 (4): 601–616.

Falleti, Tulia G., and Julia F. Lynch. 2009. Context and Causal Mechanisms in Political Analysis. *Comparative Political Studies* 42 (9): 1143–1166.

Geddes, Barbara. 1999. What Do We Know about Democratization after 20 Years? *Annual Review of Political Science* 2:115–144.

George, Alexander L., and Andrew Bennett. 2005. *Case Studies and Theory Development in the Social Sciences.* Cambridge, Mass.: MIT Press.

Gerring, John. 2007. *Case Study Research: Principles and Practices.* Cambridge, UK: Cambridge University Press.

Gibson, Clark C. 1999. Bureaucrats and the Environment in Africa: The Politics of Structural Choice in a One Party State. *Comparative Politics* 31 (3): 273–293.

Goertz, Gary. 2006. *Social Science Concepts: A User's Guide.* Princeton: Princeton University Press.

Goodin, Robert E., and Charles Tilly, eds. 2006. *The Oxford Handbook of Contextual Political Analysis.* New York: Oxford University Press.

Harrison, Kathryn, and Lisa McIntosh Sundstrom. 2010. *Global Commons, Domestic Decisions: The Comparative Politics of Climate Change.* Cambridge, Mass.: MIT Press.

Helmke, Gretchen, and Steven Levitsky. 2004. Informal Institutions and Comparative Politics: A Research Agenda. *Perspectives on Politics* 2 (4): 725–740.

Hettige, Hemamala, Mainul Huq, Sheoli Pargal, and David Wheeler. 1996. Determinants of Pollution Abatement in Developing Countries: Evidence from South and Southeast Asia. *World Development* 24 (12): 1891–1904.

Hsiao, Hsin-Huang Michael, On-Kwok Lai, Hwa-Jen Liu, Francisco Magno, Laura Edles, and Alvin Y. So. 1999. Culture and Asian Styles of Environmental Movements. In *Asia's Environmental Movements: Comparative Perspectives*, ed. Yok-shiu F. Lee and Alvin Y. So, 210–229. Armonk, N.Y.: M. E. Sharpe.

Huntington, Samuel P. 1991. *The Third Wave: Democratization in the Late Twentieth Century.* Norman, Okla.: University of Oklahoma Press.

Inglehart, Ronald. 1990. *Culture Shift in Advanced Industrial Society.* Princeton: Princeton University Press.

Jasanoff, Sheila. 2005. *Designs on Nature: Science and Democracy in Europe and the United States.* Princeton: Princeton University Press.

Jordan, Andrew, Rüdiger K. W. Wurzel, and Anthony R. Zito. 2003. "New" Instruments of Environmental Governance: Patterns and Pathways of Change. *Environmental Politics* 12 (1): 1–24.

Katznelson, Ira. 1997. Structure and Configuration in Comparative Politics. In Comparative Politics: Rationality, Culture, and Structure, ed. Mark I. Lichbach and Alan S. Zuckerman, 81–114. New York: Cambridge University Press.

Kelemen, R. Daniel, and David Vogel. 2010. Trading Places: The Role of the United States and the European Union in International Environmental Politics. *Comparative Political Studies* 43 (4): 427–456.

Keohane, Robert O., and Joseph S. Nye Jr. 2000. Globalization: What's New? What's Not? (And So What?). *Foreign Policy* 118:104–119.

Kerr, Clark. 1983. *The Future of Industrial Societies: Convergence or Continuing Diversity?* Cambridge, Mass.: Harvard University Press.

Kesselman, Mark, Joel Krieger, and William A. Joseph. 2009. *Introduction to Comparative Politics.* Boston: Wadsworth.

Kitschelt, Herbert P. 1986. Political Opportunity Structures and Political Protest: Anti-Nuclear Movements in Four Democracies. *British Journal of Political Science* 16 (1): 57–85.

Knill, Christoph. 2001. *The Europeanization of National Administrations: Patterns of Institutional Change and Persistence.* Cambridge, UK: Cambridge University Press.

Knill, Christopher. 2005. Introduction: Cross-National Policy Convergence: Concepts, Approaches and Explanatory Factors. *Journal of European Public Policy* 12 (5): 764–774.

Kohler-Koch, Beate, and Berthold Rittberger. 2006. Review Article: The "Governance Turn" in EU Studies. *Journal of Common Market Studies* 44 (Supplement 1): 27–49.

Krasner, Stephen D. 1976. State Power and the Structure of International Trade. *World Politics* 2 (3): 317–347.

Landman, Todd, and Neil Robinson. 2009. *The SAGE Handbook of Comparative Politics.* Thousand Oaks, Calif.: Sage Publications.

Layzer, Judith A. 2008. *Natural Experiments: Ecosystem-based Management and the Environment.* Cambridge, Mass.: MIT Press.

Le Prestre, Phillipe, and Peter Stoett, eds. 2006. *Bilateral Ecopolitics: Continuity and Change in Canadian-American Environmental Relations.* Aldershot, UK: Ashgate.

Levy, Jack S. 1989. The Causes of War: A Review of Theories and Evidence. In *Behavior, Society, and Nuclear War*, ed. Philip E. Tetlock, Jo L. Husbands, and Charles Tilly, 210–333. New York: Oxford University Press.

Lichbach, Mark Irving, and Alan S. Zuckerman. 1997. Research Traditions and Theory in Comparative Politics: An Introduction. In *Comparative Politics: Rationality, Culture, and Structure*, ed. Mark Irving Lichbach and Alan S. Zuckerman, 3–16. New York: Cambridge University Press.

Lund, Christian. 2010. Approaching Development: An Opinionated Review. *Progress in Development Studies* 10 (1): 19–34.

Lundqvist, L. J. 1978. The Comparative Study of Environmental Politics: From Garbage to Gold? *International Journal of Environmental Studies* 12 (2): 89–97.

Lustick, Ian S. 1996. History, Historiography, and Political Science: Multiple Historical Records and the Problem of Selection Bias. *American Political Science Review* 90 (3): 605–618.

Mahoney, James. 2010. After KKV: The New Methodology of Qualitative Research. *World Politics* 62 (1): 120–147.

McAdam, Doug, and Dieter Rucht. 1993. The Cross-National Diffusion of Movement Ideas. *Annals of the American Academy of Political and Social Science* 528:56–74.

McAllister, Lesley K. 2008. *Making Law Matter: Environmental Protection and Legal Institutions in Brazil*. Stanford: Stanford Law Books.

Moravcsik, Andrew. 1997. Taking Preferences Seriously: A Liberal Theory of International Politics. *International Organization* 51:513–553.

Munck, Gerardo L., and Richard Snyder. 2007. Debating the Direction of Comparative Politics: An Analysis of Leading Journals. *Comparative Political Studies* 40 (1): 5–31.

North, Douglass C. 1981. *Structure and Change in Economic History*. New York: W.W. Norton.

O'Donnell, Guillermo. 1996. Illusions about Consolidation. *Journal of Democracy* 7 (2): 34–51.

O'Neill, Kate, Joerg Balsiger, and Stacy D. VanDeveer. 2004. Actors, Norms and Impact: Recent International Cooperation Theory and the Influence of the Agent-Structure Debate. *Annual Review of Political Science* 7 (1): 149–175.

O'Neill, Kate, and Stacy D. VanDeveer. 2005. Transnational Environmental Activism after Seattle: Between Emancipation and Arrogance. In *Charting Transnational Democracy: Beyond Global Arrogance*, ed. Janie Leatherman and Julie Webber, 195–220. New York: Palgrave MacMillan.

Orvis, Steven, and Carol Ann Drogus. 2009. *Introducing Comparative Politics: Concepts and Cases in Context*. Washington, D.C.: CQ Press.

Ostrom, Elinor. 1990. *Governing the Commons: The Evolution of Institutions for Collective Action*. New York: Cambridge University Press.

Peet, Richard, and Michael Watts. 1996. *Liberation Ecologies: Environment, Development, Social Movements*. New York: Routledge.

Press, Daniel, Daniel F. Doak and Paul Steinberg. 1996. The Role of Local Government in the Conservation of Rare Species. *Conservation Biology* 10 (6): 1538–1548.

Pressman, Jeffrey L., and Aaron Wildavsky. 1973. *Implementation*. 2nd ed. Berkeley: University of California Press.

Pulver, Simone. 2007. Introduction: Developing-Country Firms as Agents of Environmental Sustainability? *Studies in Comparative International Development* 42 (3–4): 191–207.

Putnam, Robert D. 1988. Diplomacy and Domestic Politics: The Logic of Two-Level Games. *International Organization* 42 (3): 427–460.

Ragin, Charles. 2008. *Redesigning Social Inquiry: Fuzzy Sets and Beyond*. Chicago: University of Chicago Press.

Roberts, Clayton. 1996. *The Logic of Historical Explanation*. University Park: Penn State University Press.

Rochon, Thomas R., and Daniel A. Mazmanian. 1993. Social Movements and the Policy Process. *Annals of the American Academy of Political and Social Science* 528:75–87.

Ross, Michael L. 2001. *Timber Booms and Institutional Breakdown in Southeast Asia*. New York: Cambridge University Press.

Rueschemeyer, Dietrich, and Peter B. Evans. 1985. The State and Economic Transformation: Toward an Analysis of the Conditions Underlying Effective Intervention. In *Bringing the State Back In*, ed. Peter B. Evans, Dietrich Rueschemeyer, and Theda Skocpol, 44–76. New York: Cambridge University Press.

Scharpf, Fritz W. 2000. Institutions in Comparative Policy Research. *Comparative Political Studies* 33 (6/7): 762–790.

Schelling, Thomas C. 1960. *The Strategy of Conflict*. Cambridge, Mass.: Harvard University Press.

Schön, Donald A. 1983. *The Reflective Practitioner: How Professionals Think in Action*. New York: Basic Books.

Schreurs, Miranda A., and Elizabeth Economy, eds. 1997. *The Internationalization of Environmental Protection*. Cambridge, UK: Cambridge University Press.

Schreurs, Miranda, Henrik Selin, and Stacy D. VanDeveer. 2009. *Transatlantic Environmental and Energy Politics*. Burlington, Vt.: Ashgate Press.

Scruggs, Lyle. 2001. Is There Really a Link Between Neo-corporatism and Environmental Performance? Updated Evidence and New Data for the 1980s and 1990s. *British Journal of Political Science* 31 (4): 686–692.

Selin, Henrik, and Stacy D. VanDeveer. 2006. Raising Global Standards: Hazardous Substances and E-Waste Management in the European Union. *Environment* 28 (10): 6–17.

Skocpol, Theda. 1984. Emerging Agendas and Recurrent Strategies in Historical Sociology. In *Vision and Method in Historical Sociology*, ed. Theda Skocpol, 356–391. Cambridge, UK: Cambridge University Press.

Skocpol, Theda. 2003. Doubly Engaged Social Science: The Promise of Comparative Historical Analysis. In *Comparative Historical Analysis in the Social Sciences*, ed. James Mahoney and Dietrich Rueschemeyer, 407–429. New York: Cambridge University Press.

Sprinz, Detlef F., ed. 2009. Special Issue on Long-Term Policy Problems. *Global Environmental Politics* 9 (3): 1–133.

Stavins, Robert N. 2003. Experience with Market-Based Environmental Policy Instruments. In *Handbook of Environmental Economics*, ed. Karl-Göran Mäler and Jeffrey R. Vincent, 355–435. Boston: Elsevier.

Steinberg, Paul F. 2001. *Environmental Leadership in Developing Countries: Transnational Relations and Biodiversity Policy in Costa Rica and Bolivia*. Cambridge, Mass.: MIT Press.

Steinberg, Paul F. 2005. Bringing Political Science to Bear on Tropical Conservation. *International Environmental Agreement: Politics, Law and Economics* 5 (4): 395–404.

Steinberg, Paul F. 2007. Causal Assessment in Small-N Policy Studies. *Policy Studies Journal* 35 (2): 181–204.

Stoker, Gerry. 2006. Comparative Local Governance. In *The Oxford Handbook of Political Institutions*, ed. R. A. W. Rhodes, Sarah A. Binder, and Bert A. Rockman, 495–513. New York: Oxford University Press.

Tang, Shui-Yan, Ching-Ping Tang, and Carlos Wing-Hung Lo. 2005. Public Participation and Environmental Impact Assessment in Mainland China and Taiwan: Political Foundations of Environmental Management. *Journal of Development Studies* 41 (1): 1–32.

Tierney, John. 2009. Use Energy, Get Rich and Save the Planet. *New York Times* (Science Times), April 21, p. D1.

Tietenberg, Thomas H. 1990. Economic Instruments for Environmental Regulation. *Oxford Review of Economic Policy* 6 (1): 17–33.

Tilly, Charles. 2001. Mechanisms in Political Processes. *Annual Review of Political Science* 4:21–41.

Tilly, Charles, and Robert E. Goodin. 2006. It Depends. In *The Oxford Handbook of Contextual Political Analysis*, ed. Robert E. Goodin and Charles Tilly, 3–32. New York: Oxford University Press.

Tsai, Lily L. 2007. Solidarity Groups, Informal Accountability, and Local Public Goods Provision in Rural China. *American Political Science Review* 101 (2): 355–372.

VanDeveer, Stacy D. 2010. Consumption, Commodity Chains and the Global Environment. In *The Global Environment: Institutions: Law and Policy*, 3rd ed., ed. Regina Axelrod, Stacy D. VanDeveer, and David Leonard Downie, 311–332. Washington, D.C.: CQ Press.

Vig, Norman J., and Michael G. Faure. 2004. *Green Giants: Environmental Policies of the United States and the European Union*. Cambridge, Mass.: MIT Press.

Vogel, David. 1995. *Trading Up: Consumer and Environmental Regulation in the Global Economy*. Cambridge, Mass.: Harvard University Press.

Weiner, Jonathan B. 2004. Convergence, Divergence, and Complexity in US and European Risk Regulation. In *Green Giants: Environmental Policies of the United States and the European Union*, ed. Norman J. Vig and Michael G. Faure, 73–109. Cambridge, Mass.: MIT Press.

Weinthal, Erika. 2002. *State Making and Environmental Cooperation: Linking Domestic and International Politics in Central Asia*. Cambridge, Mass.: MIT Press.

Index

American and Comparative Environmental Policy

Sheldon Kamieniecki and Michael E. Kraft, series editors

Russell J. Dalton, Paula Garb, Nicholas P. Lovrich, John C. Pierce, and John M. Whiteley, *Critical Masses: Citizens, Nuclear Weapons Production, and Environmental Destruction in the United States and Russia*

Daniel A. Mazmanian and Michael E. Kraft, editors, *Toward Sustainable Communities: Transition and Transformations in Environmental Policy*

Elizabeth R. DeSombre, *Domestic Sources of International Environmental Policy: Industry, Environmentalists, and U.S. Power*

Kate O'Neill, *Waste Trading among Rich Nations: Building a New Theory of Environmental Regulation*

Joachim Blatter and Helen Ingram, editors, *Reflections on Water: New Approaches to Transboundary Conflicts and Cooperation*

Paul F. Steinberg, *Environmental Leadership in Developing Countries: Transnational Relations and Biodiversity Policy in Costa Rica and Bolivia*

Uday Desai, editor, *Environmental Politics and Policy in Industrialized Countries*

Kent Portney, *Taking Sustainable Cities Seriously: Economic Development, the Environment, and Quality of Life in American Cities*

Edward P. Weber, *Bringing Society Back In: Grassroots Ecosystem Management, Accountability, and Sustainable Communities*

Norman J. Vig and Michael G. Faure, editors, *Green Giants? Environmental Policies of the United States and the European Union*

Robert F. Durant, Daniel J. Fiorino, and Rosemary O'Leary, editors, *Environmental Governance Reconsidered: Challenges, Choices, and Opportunities*

Paul A. Sabatier, Will Focht, Mark Lubell, Zev Trachtenberg, Arnold Vedlitz, and Marty Matlock, editors, *Swimming Upstream: Collaborative Approaches to Watershed Management*

Sally K. Fairfax, Lauren Gwin, Mary Ann King, Leigh S. Raymond, and Laura Watt, *Buying Nature: The Limits of Land Acquisition as a Conservation Strategy, 1780–2004*

Steven Cohen, Sheldon Kamieniecki, and Matthew A. Cahn, *Strategic Planning in Environmental Regulation: A Policy Approach that Works*

Michael E. Kraft and Sheldon Kamieniecki, editors, *Business and Environmental Policy: Corporate Interests in the American Political System*

Joseph F. C. DiMento and Pamela Doughman, editors, *Climate Change: What It Means for Us, Our Children, and Our Grandchildren*

Christopher McGrory Klyza and David J. Sousa, *American Environmental Policy, 1990–2006: Beyond Gridlock*

John M. Whiteley, Helen Ingram, and Richard Perry, editors, *Water, Place, and Equity*

Judith A. Layzer, *Natural Experiments: Ecosystem-Based Management and the Environment*

Daniel A. Mazmanian and Michael E. Kraft, editors, *Toward Sustainable Communities: Transition and Transformations in Environmental Policy, second edition*

Henrik Selin and Stacy D. VanDeveer, editors, *Changing Climates in North American Politics: Institutions, Policymaking, and Multilevel Governance*

Megan Mullin, *Governing the Tap: Special District Governance and the New Local Politics of Water*

David M. Driesen, editor, *Economic Thought and US Climate Change Policy*

Kathryn Harrison and Lisa McIntosh Sundstrom, editors, *Global Commons, Domestic Decisions: The Comparative Politics of Climate Change*

William Ascher, Toddi Steelman, and Robert Healy, *Knowledge in the Environmental Policy Process: Re-Imagining the Boundaries of Science and Politics*

Michael E. Kraft, Mark Stephan, and Troy D. Abel, *Coming Clean: Information Disclosure and Environmental Performance*

Paul F. Steinberg and Stacy D. VanDeveer, editors, *Comparative Environmental Politics: Theory, Practice, and Prospects*